P9-CEX-007

Industrial Arts WOODWORKING

Second Edition

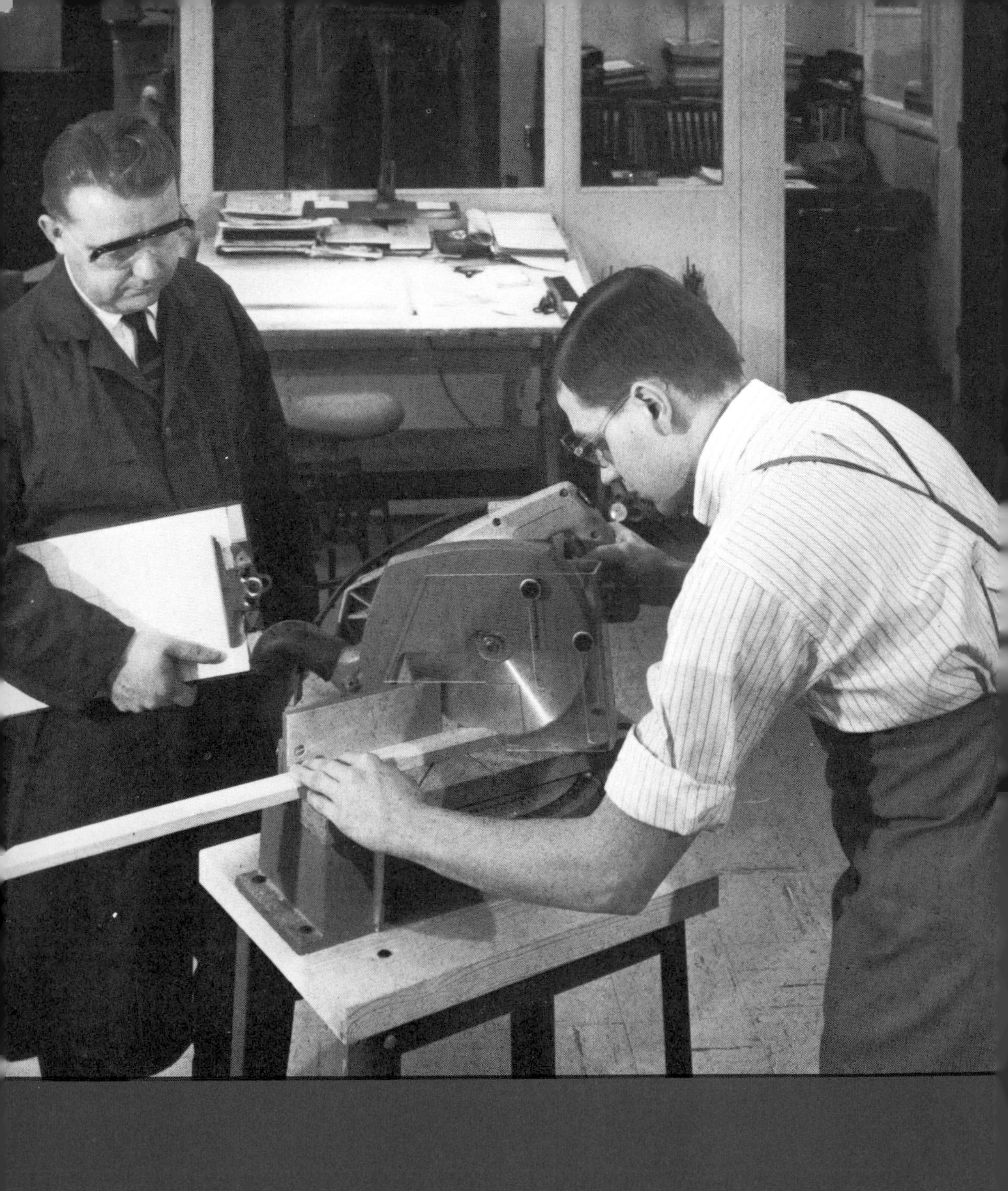

Industrial Arts WOODWORKING

Second Edition

JOHN L. FEIRER

Head, Industrial Education Department
Western Michigan University
Kalamazoo, Michigan

CHAS. A. BENNETT CO., INC.
Peoria, Illinois 61614

By JOHN L. FEIRER

Printed in the United States of America
LIBRARY OF CONG. CAT. NO. 65–7002
27 7VH3 15

72SBN 87002–111–7

COLOR ILLUSTRATION LIST

PREFACE

Woodworking has always been the most popular industrial arts activity. In spite of the many new courses that have been added to the industrial arts curriculum in recent years, woodworking has increased rather than decreased in popular favor. The reasons are plain, for wood is one of man's most abundant materials and is one of the easiest materials for students to work with. Articles made of wood have general usefulness, and tools and machines especially suited to school workshops are readily available.

It is with this in mind that INDUSTRIAL ARTS WOODWORKING has been written. The content has been organized to meet the needs of students at all levels of the junior and senior high school. The book has been divided into five major parts:

SECTIONS I–X give instruction on how to do the fundamental processes in hand woodworking, with particular stress on student participation in shop activities. The units have been written in the informal style and have been well illustrated to utilize the visual approach. They are complete as to information about tools, materials, and the ways to use them. They have been organized in the approximate order in which they would be needed to make larger projects. Tools, materials, and processes have been carefully evaluated to include only those which are considered important and significant as based upon recent research. The student is given an opportunity to preview the content in each section and to check his understanding at the end of each unit.

SECTION XI describes the use of the fundamental machine tools in woodworking. Each tool has been completely treated but without an unnecessary quantity of detail, since the book is intended for beginning students. This is done so that the instructor may conveniently determine which machines are desirable and in what order the students will be allowed to use them. The smaller types of woodworking machines have been used to illustrate the instruction, since these are most desirable for both school and home workshops.

SECTION XII introduces the reader to the simple upholstery processes.

SECTION XIII deals with the related information about woods, wood products, and opportunities in woodworking. Only the most significant information has been included, since there is a wealth of reference material available on these subjects and since any industrial arts course should be limited in the amount of related information presented to make sure that the program will remain an activity one.

SECTION XIV discusses design and provides a group of carefully selected wood projects. An effort has been made to display a variety of well-designed projects and to show how woods can be combined with other materials. Also, they have been constructed in a good range of difficulty and with emphasis on student motivation based on likes and interests. No specific directions on making each project have been included, but rather an opportunity for student selection and planning under carefully guided conditions has been given.

As in any other book, many individuals and concerns have cooperated generously.

SECOND EDITION

Since its publication, Industrial Arts Woodworking has been a very popular textbook. Its success has undoubtedly been due to the fact that it meets the needs of both teachers and students for a book that covers hand and machine processes in woodworking as well as extensive related technical instruction. In the intervening years there have been changes in materials, tools, and processes. This second edition reflects these changes. While the book maintains the good features and organization of the first edition, it has been enlarged and improved in many ways. The *second color* which appears throughout was used to emphasize important features both in the text and in the illustrations. A series of *full-color* pictures has been added to allow the student to study good design, woods, and finishes in their natural beauty. *Several new units* have been added to include the more modern applications of wood such as wood lamination, plastic laminates, and finishes. The *machine-tool section* has been greatly enlarged, and *many new projects* have been added, as well as new information on *machine safety*.

ACKNOWLEDGMENT LIST

Adjustable Clamp Company
American Forest Products Industries
American Hardboard Association
American Hardwood Company
American Plywood Association
American Screw Company
Andersen Corporation
E. C. Atkins Manufacturing Company
Atlas Press Company
Baker Furniture Company
Behr-Manning Company
Berry Brothers, Incorporated
Brandt Cabinet Works, Incorporated
British Columbia Industrial Design Committee
Buck Brothers Company
Buss Machine Works, Incorporated
California Redwood Association
Carborundum Company
Cincinnati Tool Company, The
Dansk Designs, Incorporated
DeVilbiss Company, The
De Walt Power Tools
Henry Disston & Sons, Incorporated
Drexel Furniture Company
Dunbar Furniture Corporation of Indiana
Ford Motor Company
Forest Products Laboratory
Formica Corporation
Allan Gould Designs
Imperial Furniture Company
Arvids Iraids Multi-Purpose Spring Clamp
Jam Handy Organization, The
Madison Glass Specialties Company
Masonite Corporation
Herman Miller Furniture Company
Millers Falls Company
North Brothers Manufacturing Company
No-Sag Spring Company
Panelyte Division, St. Regis Paper Company
Philippine Mahogany Association
Porter Cable Machine Company
Powermatic Machine Company
Reynolds Metals Company
Rockwell Manufacturing Company
Rubber Manufacturer's Association, The
Russell Electric Company
Sherwin-Williams Company
Skil Corporation
Sprague and Carleton Furniture Company
Stanley Tools Division, The Stanley Works
Sunbeam Corporation
Tempo Products Company
U. S. Forest Service
United States Plywood Corporation
Western Pine Association
Consider H. Willett, Incorporated
Woman's Day
X-Acto Crescent Products Incorporated

CONTENTS

FROM WOOD TO PRODUCT THROUGH PROCESSES

When you see a wood project such as the table shown in Figure *A*, you may feel an immense appreciation for the fine workmanship, the finish, and the beautiful lines of the piece. However, you may say to yourself, "But that is too complicated for me to build." Yet *the essential elements of this table are as fundamental as the little trays in Figure B*. Each resulted from choosing a piece of wood and applying to it certain basic processes to shape, form, assemble, and finish it. Naturally, the table contains many more pieces of wood and involves much more time and effort, but fundamentally it has only a few more applications of basic processes.

If you want to build attractive projects, you must first start with good raw material. A fine piece of furniture or a good project cannot be made from poor wood. Wood is the most fundamental of all materials used by man. This raw material, used to make the finished product, is supplied in its natural form. Also, many other manufactured articles, whether they are of metal, plastic, or other substances, are first made of wood in the factory. For example, automobiles, refrigerators, aircraft, and even the telephone were first made from wood in the designing rooms of factories.

A. An example of what an advanced high school student can make in woodworking. The rails and finesse of the legs are beautiful. The choice of woods and the design are excellent, not only for the building of the project, but for final appearance as well.

B. In contrast to the table, these simple serving trays are typical of what you might attempt as a first project. They involve many of the same processes needed to do all kinds of woodworking.

WHAT YOU CAN DO WITH WOOD

Wood is a very interesting material. It is made up of fibers (grain) that cut more easily *with* the grain than across it. Wood itself is only the raw material. From the same piece of wood you could build a beautiful tray with a very fine finish or a platform for your garbage can! The only difference in the products is the difference in the basic processes applied to the wood. These fundamentals are described in the 70 units in this book. Here is described how to do these processes with hand tools and simple machines. Figure C. By these same methods you can construct such different projects as the tray or the table.

THREE BASIC ELEMENTS IN CONSTRUCTION

Building an attractive project depends on the following three elements: the kind of wood you select, the design of the project, and how well you do the basic processes. If you learn to do these basic processes correctly, you can apply them to any product with good results. In the latter section of this book, you will find many projects, some very simple and others that take much more time. Regardless of size, however, each one includes these same three elements.

If you are a beginner in wood, you must select your project wisely and learn to do the processes accurately and correctly. Once the skills are learned, greater enjoyment will be yours. Also, much greater success will be attained in the projects you will be able to make.

WHY TAKE WOODWORKING?

Woodworking is much more than making a few small pieces of furniture that you can take home. Here are some of the other things that you should accomplish in your course:

1. *Develop an interest in the wood industry.* No industry has a more important role in the growth of our country than the wood industry. It

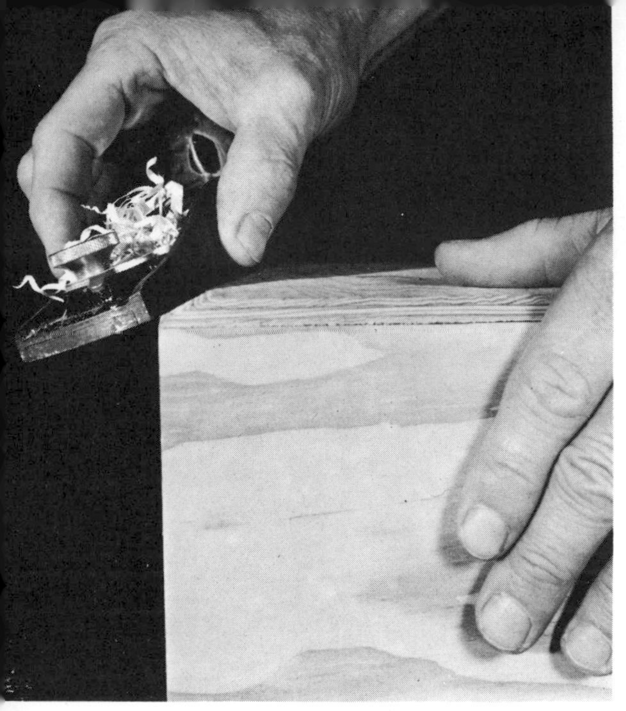

Bench or hand.

Machine.

C. Four areas of woodwork you'll find described in this book.

Upholstery.

Finishing.

D. An apprentice patternmaker in a foundry has the opportunity to learn a highly skilled and well-paid woodworking occupation.

has made possible the record-breaking building boom of homes, offices, and other commercial buildings. The whole furniture industry is dependent on wood as a raw material. Well over two million people work at woodworking occupations, the forester, the carpenter, and the cabinetmaker to name only a few. Figure *D*. Wood is and always will be essential to everyday living. You are probably sitting in a wood chair and using a wood pencil to write with. You wouldn't have this book if it weren't for the wood used to make the paper. In this course you will study the sources of wood, the changes that take place in it from raw material to finished product, and how wood products such as homes, furniture, sports equipment, and other items are produced.

2. *Develop basic hand and machine skills*. Learning to work with tools and machines can be very valuable to you if you should decide on an occupation in woodworking. Figure *E*. However, even if you don't earn a living in some area of woodworking, you will still find the skills very useful as a "do-it-yourselfer." You may find making things of wood so fascinating that you will choose it as your hobby.

3. *Develop good safety habits*. Being able to use hand and machine tools safely and skillfully is a most important part of your work. More accidents happen in the wood shop than in any other area of industrial arts. Learn to perform each task carefully so that you will not contribute to the number of accidents.

4. *Learn about good design*. You should learn to recognize good design in wood products. Figure *F*. After you learn the difference between good and bad design, you will never

E. A drafting teacher must have knowledge and skills in woodworking. His students will learn much about house plans as he guides them in making a detailed model house.

F. **This beautiful mahogany table illustrates good design in furniture making. Even the small projects that you make should be attractive.**

H. **It's fun to work with wood. A feeling of real satisfaction comes to you when you have built something yourself.**

again find poor design attractive. You may also want to try your hand at designing a wood product, using your own ideas.

5. *Learn to judge the quality of wood products.* A home and furniture are two of the largest purchases you will ever make. Figure *G*. Before you buy wood products, you should understand good design and construction and be able to judge if the product is a good value.

6. *Enjoy the satisfaction of planning and building a product with your own hands.* Figure *H*. There is real pride of accomplishment in doing a good job of making an attractive wood product. In completing the product you will learn to solve problems about materials and processes.

G. **When you visit a furniture store, you should be able to recognize good woods, fine design, and excellent finish. This knowledge will help you to obtain proper value for your money.**

Section I
Getting Started in Woodworking

The first 5 steps in hand woodworking—what you must know and be able to do.

1. How to select a project: the size, difficulty, kind of wood; design and finish.
2. The difference between pictorial and working drawings: what they mean and how to read, use, and understand working drawings.
3. The importance of a bill of materials: size and number of pieces, description, amount of lumber; the grade, quality, finish, and how it is dried.
4. Being efficient: first plan, then carry out the steps needed for building with wood.
5. Taking care of the shop: how to keep the shop running well, how to keep oneself neat, orderly, and free from accident; and how to treat an accident if it occurs.

During your first few days in the woodshop, you won't be able to get right to the work of building a project. As in everything worth while, there are things to be learned first. A man who decides to build a house can't start putting up the frame immediately. He has a lot of planning to do first on what kind of house he wants, what materials to use and how much of them, how to go about using these materials, and a great many other questions to decide. In the school shop, we also need to become acquainted with the working conditions before we can begin. These are listed in the "box" above. Further steps are on pp. 43, 60, 94, 108, 132, 143, 170, 219, 244.

Section I

UNIT 1. SELECTING THE PROJECT

Since the project is the end result of all of your efforts, it is very important that you spend some time choosing a good one. There are many things to consider: what you need, the size of the project, the kind and cost of the wood, the finish, and the design.

DO YOU HAVE A NEED AND USE FOR THE PROJECT?

The most important thing to decide is whether you have a use for the article. Too many of the things made in school and home workshops find their way into storage rooms, attics, or basements. There are so many practical and useful things that can be made of wood that it is foolish to waste your time and effort on something useless.

Before deciding, ask yourself what you need for your house, yard, for sports, or for some other activity in which you are interested. Figure 1–1. This should give you a good clue to the type of project you will find most satisfying.

You will notice that the project section in this book has been organized around different areas of interest.

CAN YOU BUILD IT?

The next thing to think about is the size of the project and how difficult it is to build. Beginners usually want to make something too big, too fancy, or too difficult. While you need not "fear" any project, you must have the time and experience for it. Figure 1–2. If you choose too big a project at first, you face so many problems that you may lose interest, become discouraged, and never finish the project. So begin by

1–1. This outdoor chair would be a rather ambitious project for your first experience in woodworking.

1. Traditional. This traditional design combines the best features of European styling from the Eighteenth and early Nineteenth centuries. The furniture is made from handsome cherry veneers and solids, with a warm fruitwood finish. Handsome bookcases give an architectural look to the room. This furniture illustrates the great beauty of traditional designs, yet it is well adapted to the practical needs of the Twentieth century. (See the Design Section, especially pages 376 and following.)

2. Early American or Colonial. This living-room group illustrates the best features of Early American or Colonial design. Notice the beautifully turned parts on the chairs and davenport, including the ladderback dining-room chairs. The structural parts of the furniture, including legs, rails, and turned spindles, are of cherry, while knotty pine veneers were used on the drawer fronts of the large chests and buffet. The federal eagle on the chest section is a popular accent in this particular furniture design. The wall-storage unit includes a book shelf, a drop-down shelf to be used as a writing desk, drawer storage, and other storage for dishes, glassware, and decorative objects. Compare the finished woods with the samples shown in Figure *68–6*—black cherry—and examples of pine shown in Figures *68–17* and *68–18*.

3. French Provincial. The handsome, functional storage cases and desks are the keynote of this French Provincial living room. The highbacked chairs slope gracefully to form a scroll motif. The table legs show the graceful curve typical of the style. Made of beautiful walnut, the furniture has been given a soft natural finish. Compare the finished wood with the sample shown in Figure *68–14*.

4. Modern or Contemporary. Modern or Contemporary is planned primarily to fill the practical needs of today. The design concept of these pieces is straightforward Contemporary, but there is an ingenious addition of Early American shown in the sturdy rim locks, butterfly hinges, and plank-top tables. Walnut is the basic wood and has been finished in a luxurious tone of high-figured veneers. Oak makes up the door panels, drawer fronts, and table bases. The oak has been heavily "distressed" and antiqued, and has been given a lighter finish to provide a keen contrast to the medium-toned walnut. An interesting piece is the arched-top cupboard. Notice that Modern or Contemporary design does not feature the harsh, sharp lines that we used to think of as "Modern." Compare the oak with that shown in Figure *68–12*.

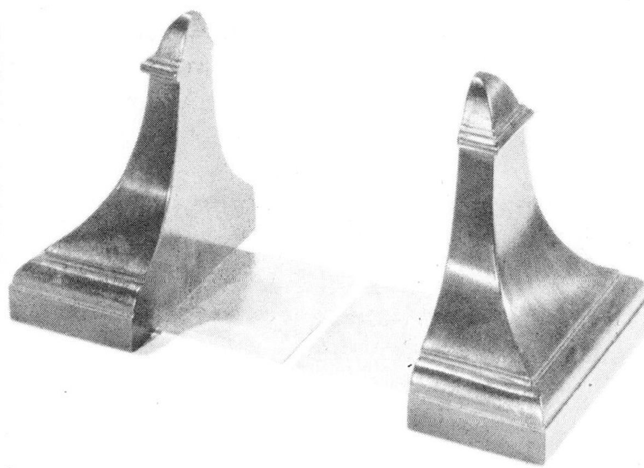

1–2. Even though these book ends are an elementary project, they will test your skill. They require accurate cutting on the jig saw.

making small articles that take only a few tools and processes until you have some experience and know how long it takes. The size of the project shouldn't be the measure of its appeal.

IS THE KIND AND COST OF THE WOOD SATISFACTORY?

The kind of wood to use and how much you want to spend are both important to decide. Figure 1–3. The wood you choose will affect the cost of the project. One made of oak or walnut will cost twice as much as the same one of fir, spruce, poplar, or red gum.

Difference in the working qualities of woods makes the right choice important also. For the beginner, especially, it is much easier to work with soft woods like poplar, pine, or bass. It takes a good deal more skill to work on a hardwood like birch, for example, than on a soft wood, because hardwoods tend to resist tools.

WHAT KIND OF FINISH WILL YOU APPLY?

The color or kind of finish you want to apply must be decided. If you use an opaque finish such as lacquer or paint, it is just as well to choose an inexpensive wood like pine, basswood, or poplar. Figure 1–4. If you plan to have a transparent finish, it will be important to decide on the color and kind of finish before you begin. All woods can be bleached to give them a light appearance, but, generally speaking, we think of oak or maple as being lighter than walnut, mahogany, or cherry. The kind of finish you apply should bring out the best qualities in the wood.

1–3. This Early American shaving stand is a fine example of clean simple lines, natural lacquer finish, and top craftsmanship. It is made of cherry.

1–4. This large project is relatively simple to make. Since it was made of pine, an enamel finish was applied. Would you use enamel over walnut veneer? Why not?

HAVE YOU CONSIDERED THE DESIGN OF THE PROJECT?

Regardless of the size or the kind of article you choose, the style or design should fit your needs and the kind of home in which you live. Too frequently small projects such as book ends, tables, and similar pieces are made with no regard to the kind of room in which they will be used. Even such a project as a small watch stand can be varied between traditional and modern styles to fit your tastes.

WHERE CAN YOU FIND GOOD PROJECT DESIGNS?

After you have decided on what you want to make, you come to the question of size, shape, and design. Now you need a working drawing or sketch. There are many places to look for ideas. In the last section of this book are groups of projects for your room, your home, for sports, and for other activities. If none of these satisfy, you can turn to magazines. You may have seen an article you like in a store, or you may want to design and make a finished drawing of one of your own ideas. This last ought not be attempted until you have had a little experience with drawings already available.

When all of these questions have been answered and exactly the right project selected, you are ready for the fascinating job of building it. From now on you will need lots of patience and attention to detail, but the results will be well worth it.

CAN YOU ANSWER THESE QUESTIONS ON SELECTING THE PROJECT?

1. Name the most important thing to consider when selecting a project.
2. Why isn't it a good idea to start with a large project?
3. Do all woods work about the same? Explain your answer.
4. If oak is chosen for the project, a paste filler may be selected for finishing. Give several other examples of how the wood chosen determines the kind of finish that is to be applied.
5. Give several sources for good projects.

Section I

UNIT 2. READING THE WORKING DRAWING OR SKETCH

A working drawing or sketch is the map you follow in making the project. It will tell you the exact size of the article, the number and sizes of the pieces, the design of each part, the way in which the project fits together, and every other detail of construction and finish. Without it you would be lost, especially if you are just beginning to learn woodworking.

It is extremely important to understand your working drawing *before beginning to build the project.* In industry, everything to be produced is first drawn in the drafting room. You should study the working drawing carefully to keep from making mistakes.

PICTORIAL DRAWINGS

A pictorial or picture drawing is the kind you know best. It shows the project the way it looks in use. Figure 2–1. The most common kinds of pictorial drawings are isometric (equal angle), cabinet, and perspective. Figure 2–2. Drawings for woodwork do not follow the rigid rules you may have learned for machine drawings. A

2–1. This pictorial drawing of a patio end table can be used to construct the project.

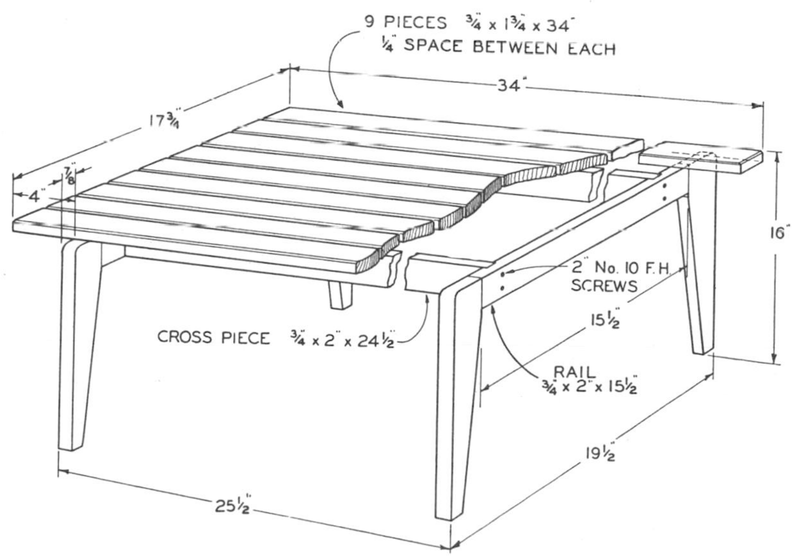

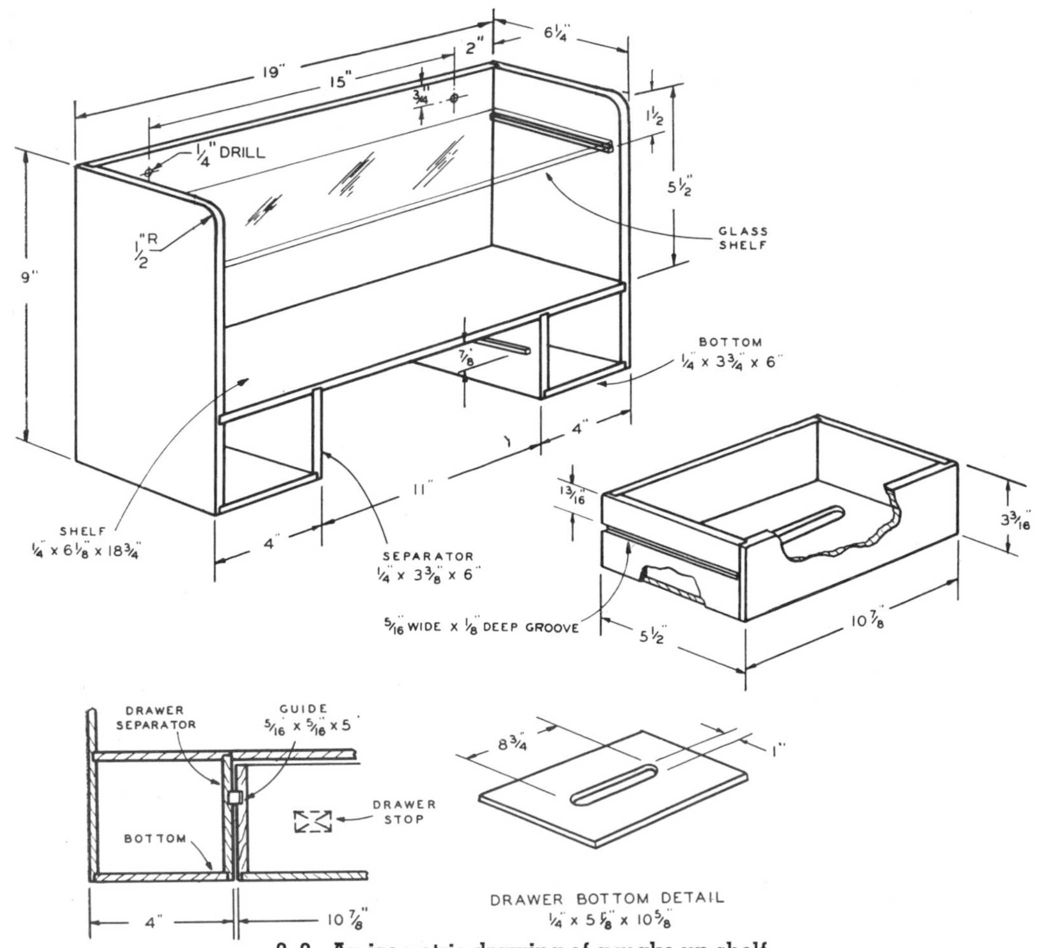

2–2. An isometric drawing of a make-up shelf.

drawing for a project will often be partly a "view" drawing and partly a pictorial drawing. Sometimes, when view drawings are used, the views are not placed correctly; that is, the right side or end view isn't always to the right of the front view. You will also find that many isometric or perspective drawings are made as exploded (taken apart) drawings. Figure 2–3. The exploded view clearly shows the dimension of each part and how the parts go together.

WORKING OR VIEW DRAWINGS

Drawings used for construction, called working drawings, have one, two, three, or more *views* showing the article many different ways. Most projects require two or three views. In the three-view drawing, the lower lefthand view shows the way the project looks from the *front*, the view above that shows how the project looks from the *top*, and the view to the right is the *right side or end view* of the project. Figure 2–4. These

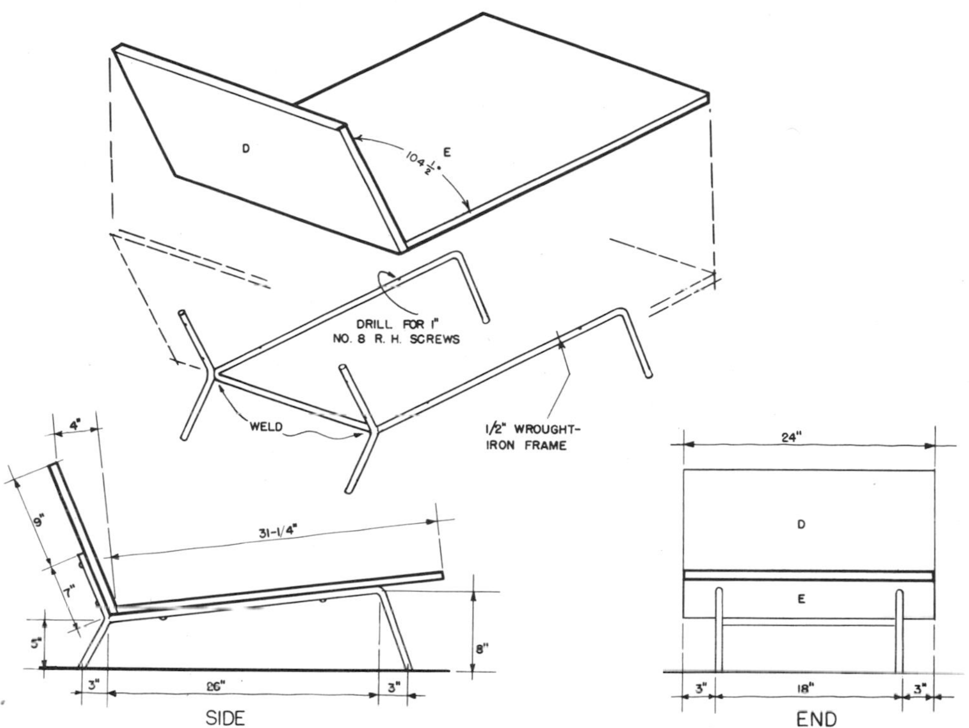

2–3. A fireplace log holder which shows how a combination of drawings can be used. The top drawing is an exploded isometric. The lower two are view drawings.

2–4. A typical three-view drawing of a box. This is the type of drawing most commonly used for construction.

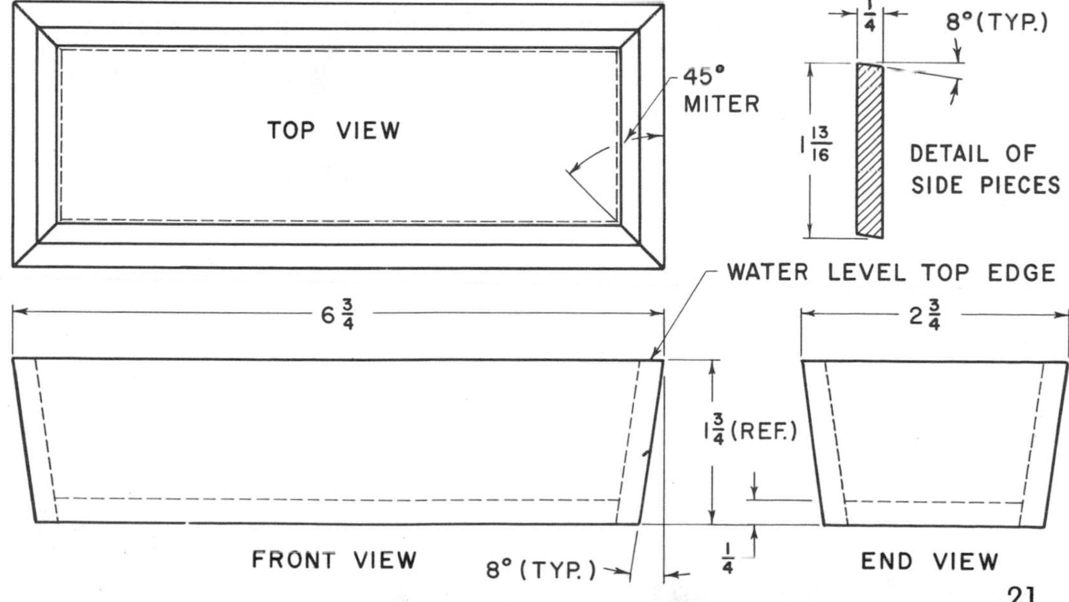

views give the correct dimensions of each piece. The dimensions are placed on the views to be read from the bottom or right side. If only two views are included, either the front and top or front and side views are shown. Figure 2–5.

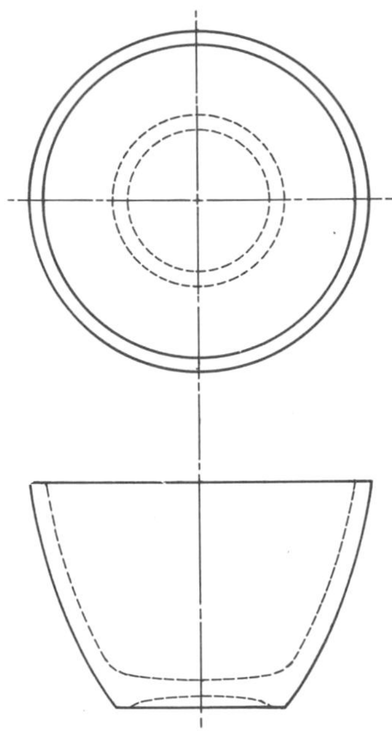

2–5. Many projects such as this turned bowl require only two views.

MEANING OF LINES

In a working drawing or sketch, different kinds of lines are drawn, each showing a certain thing. A wrong line on a working drawing is a much worse mistake than a wrong direction for its construction; however, any mistake on the drawing can give you a great deal of trouble in construction. Figure 2–6 shows the drawing of a planter. These lines indicate the following:

Outline ————————

Invisible Outline — — — — — — —

Center line ——— - ———

Extension Line ————————

Dimension Line ←— 4" —→

Visible outline. The major outline of the article.

Invisible outline. Indicates invisible outline that cannot be seen from the surface.

Center line. Shows the center or divides the drawing into equal or symmetrical parts.

Extension line. Extends out from the outline; provides two lines between which measurements or dimensions can be shown.

Dimension line. Usually has arrowheads at either end and is broken in the center. These lines run between the extension lines and give the measurements or dimensions.

SCALE OF THE DRAWING

When large projects must be drawn, it is necessary to reduce the size of the drawing so that all of it can be put on one page. In this case, the drawing is made to scale. Frequently, for example, a drawing is made half size (6″ = 1′) and the scale is so stated. If even larger projects must be drawn, a scale such as ¼″ to the foot (¼″ = 1′ 0″) may be followed, as in house plans.

READING THE WORKING DRAWING

In reading a working drawing, it is important to read all dimensions.

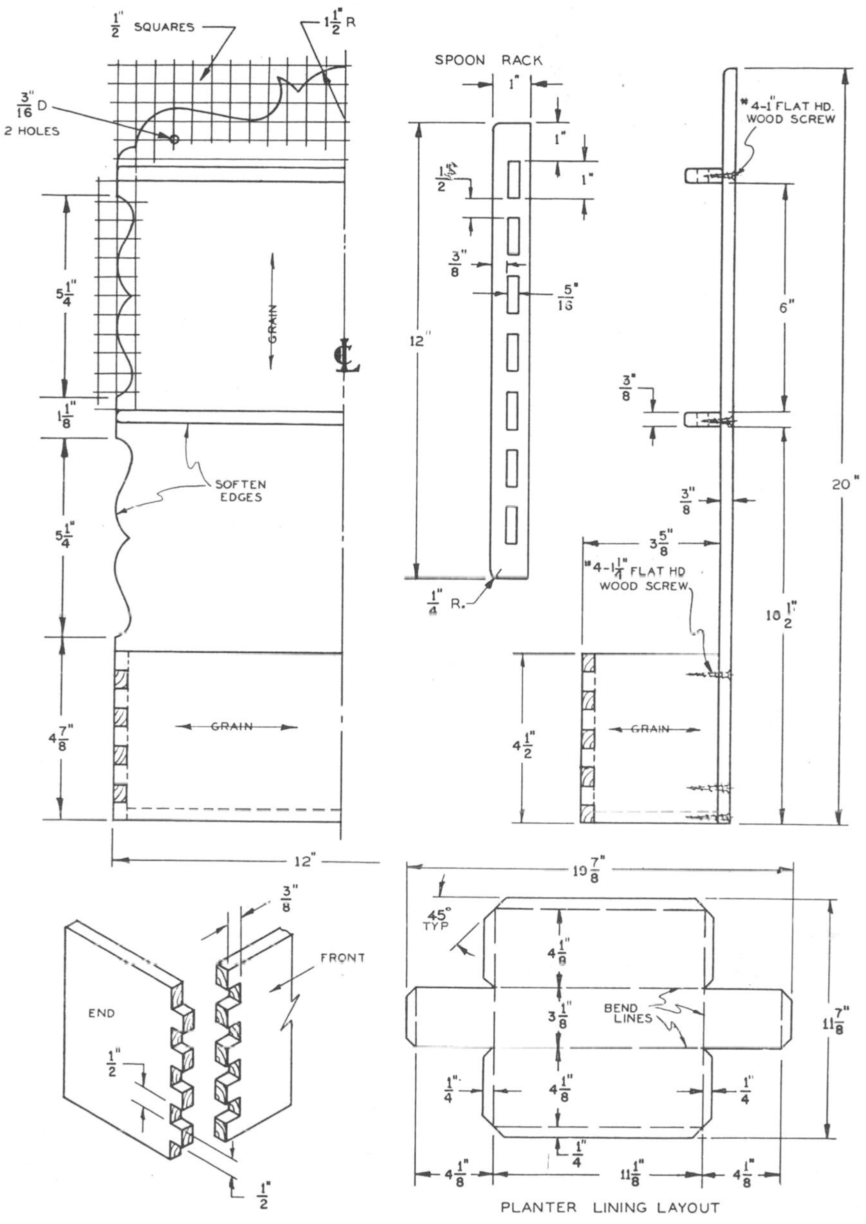

2–6. Two-view drawing of a planter. Note the different lines in this drawing and then refer to the meaning of these lines as described on page 22.

When you make out the bill of materials, you must be sure to read these dimensions correctly. Then, after the materials are purchased and you are ready to begin, equal care must be taken in transferring these measurements to the pieces of wood. Even if the drawing is made full size, never attempt to measure the drawing itself. Always use the dimensions stated, since the paper on which the drawing is printed may have shrunk. More mistakes are made through carelessness in reading the drawings and in transferring these measurements to the wood than in any other point in construction.

CAN YOU ANSWER THESE QUESTIONS ON READING THE WORKING DRAWING OR SKETCH?

1. Why must you be able to understand your working drawing?
2. Name the kind of drawing that is similar to a photograph.
3. Does a working drawing always have three views?
4. How are invisible parts shown on a working drawing?
5. If the working drawing is full size, can you trace it to make the layout?

Section I

UNIT 3. BILL OF MATERIALS

After choosing your project, you will list what materials you need in the way of lumber, hardware, and finishing supplies. Write down in an organized form just what and how much you need.

FINISHED BILL OF MATERIALS

Use a form similar to the one in Figure 3–1. From information on the working drawing, write out a complete description of each different item. For lumber, include the number of each piece needed, the size of the piece, a description of the item, and the kind of lumber. Figure 3–1 shows a bill of materials for the beverage cart in Figure 3–2.

Information about the size of each piece is given, with thickness, width, and length indicated in that order. Thickness and width are always shown in inches (″); length is indicated either in inches (″) or feet (′). For small pieces, the length is shown in inches. In listing these items, the width is always measured *across* the grain and the length *with* the grain. Therefore you may have some pieces that are wider than they are long. If you need different kinds of wood, organize the list with pieces to be made of one kind of wood listed together. In some cases, the dimensions given on the drawing will not include enough material for the joints; then you must add the length as needed.

MAKING A ROUGH BILL OF MATERIALS OR STOCK-CUTTING LIST

The finished bill of materials must now be changed into what may be called a rough bill of materials or

BILL OF MATERIALS

Name____________________________________Date Started____________
Last First Middle

Project Beverage Cart Date Completed____________

FINISHED BILL OF MATERIALS

No. of Pieces	SIZE			Description	Kind of Wood
	T	W	L		
2	1⅝	3⅝	32	Frame Sides	Pine
2	1⅝	3⅝	18¼	Frame Ends	Pine
2	¾	6	24	Front Legs	Pine
2	¾	3	24	Back Legs	Pine
2	¾	6	36	Exterior Sides	Pine
2	¾	6	24	Exterior Ends	Pine
2	¾	2	17	Handles	Pine
1	¾	22½	34½	Top	Fir Plywood
4	¾	8	8	Wheels	Fir Plywood
(Two thicknesses must be nailed together for wheels)					
1	1¼ dia.		30½	Axle	Birch dowel
2	¼ dia.		3¼	Axle Pin	Birch dowel

STOCK CUTTING LIST

No. of Pieces	SIZE			Description	Bd. Ft. or Sq. Ft.	Cost per Bd. Ft. or Sq. Ft.	Total Cost
	T	W	L				
2	1¾	3¾	32½	Frame Sides }	6*		
2	1¾	3¾	18¾	Frame Ends }			
2	⅞	6¼	24½	Front Legs }	9¼*		
2	⅞	3¼	24½	Back Legs }			
2	⅞	6¼	36½	Exterior Sides }			
2	⅞	6¼	24½	Exterior Ends }			
2	⅞	2¼	17½	Handles }			
1	¾	22¾	35	Top }	7½*		
4	¾	8¼	8¼	Wheels }			
1	1¼ dia.		31	Axle			
2	¼ dia.		3½	Axle Pins			

Other items: nails, paint..
* Approximately.

3–1. The bill of materials and stock-cutting list for the beverage cart. This project was selected as a sample because it illustrates a variety of materials and shows the need for planning both the finished bill of materials and the rough cutting list before beginning to work.

stock-cutting list. Figure 3–1. In this list you must add to the thickness, width, and length of the stock to allow for cutting, planing, chiseling, and other operations. Usually $\frac{1}{16}$ to ⅛ inch is added to the thickness, ⅛ to ¼ inch to the width, and about ½ inch to the length.

DETERMINING BOARD FEET OF LUMBER

After you have made a rough bill of

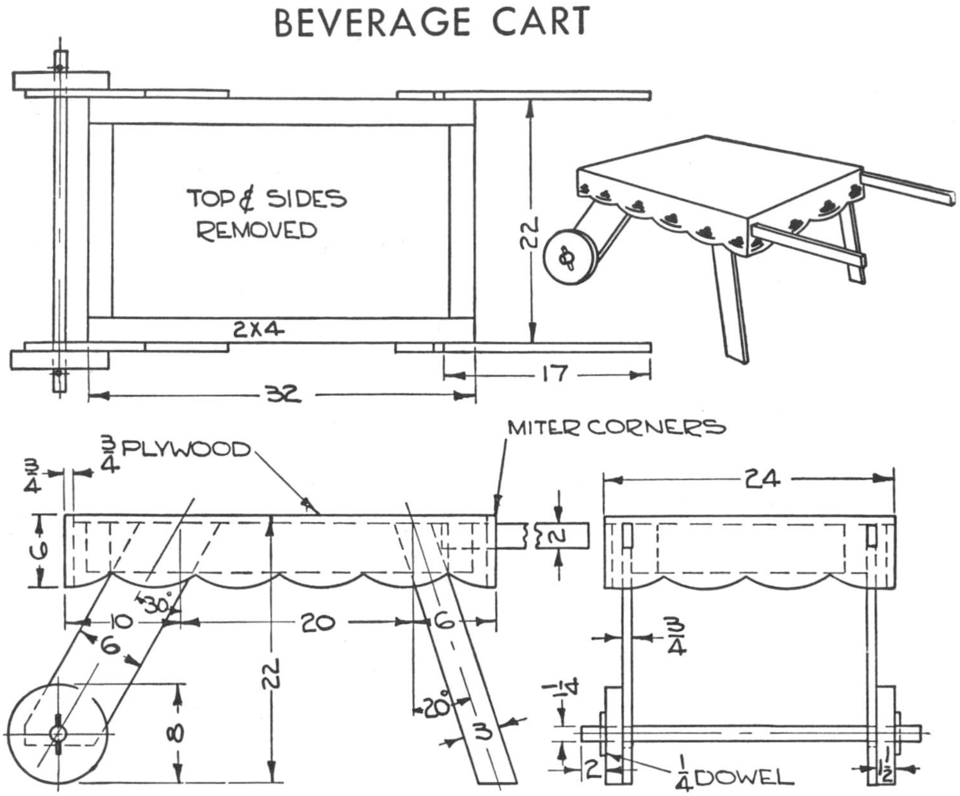

BEVERAGE CART

3–2. **Beverage cart. The working drawing from which the sample bill of materials was made. Notice how the dimensions of each piece are clearly indicated.**

material or stock-cutting list, then figure the number of board feet in each piece or group of identical pieces. A board foot of lumber is a piece 1 inch thick, 12 inches wide, and 12 inches long. Figure 3–3. Stock less than 1 inch thick is figured as 1 inch. Stock more than 1 inch is figured by actual measurement. For example, a piece of stock ¼″ by 6″ by 4′ would have 2 board feet of lumber.

The formula to use for board feet is:

$$\text{Bd. Ft.} = \frac{T \times W \times L \text{ (all in inches)}}{144}$$

Board feet equals thickness in inches times width in inches times length in inches divided by 144.

3–3. **Note the terms included in these drawings. Each piece is one board foot of lumber. The length of the board is always given *with* the grain and the width of the board is given *across* the grain.**

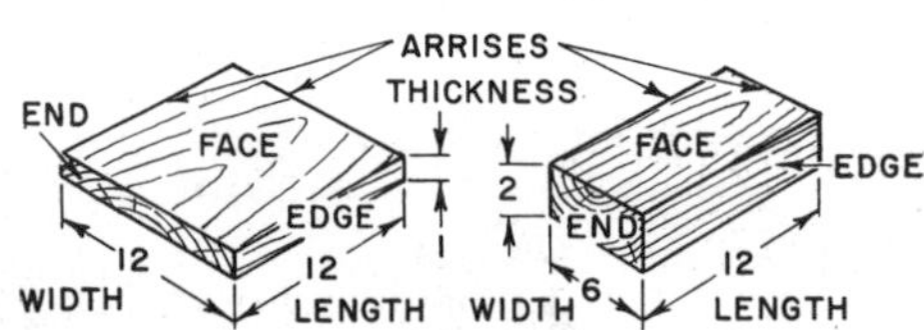

Another formula that can be used is:

$$\text{Bd. Ft.} = \frac{\text{T (inches)} \times \text{W (inches)} \times \text{L (feet)}}{12}$$

DETERMINING COST OF LUMBER

When you buy lumber, the price is quoted as so much per board foot, per hundred board feet, or per thousand board feet (M). Figure 3–4. To find the cost of each item on the rough bill of materials, multiply the number of board feet in each piece or group of identical pieces by the cost per board foot. When the cost of hardware items and finishing materials is listed, all items can be added up to find the total cost of materials. *Plywood* and *hardboard* are sold as so much per square foot and molding and special pieces as so much per linear foot. Prices vary according to quality.

LUMBER DEFECTS

In selecting lumber, check for these common defects:

3–5. A check in a piece of lumber.

1. A *knot* is the base of a branch that forms a mass of woody fiber running at an angle to the grain.
2. A *check* is a lengthwise separation of the wood, like a small crack or split. Figure 3–5. It often appears at the end of a board. *Honeycombing* is an area of checks that is not visible at the surface.
3. A *split* is a lengthwise break or a big crack in the board.
4. *Decay* is rotting of wood.
5. A *stain* is a discoloration of the wood surface.

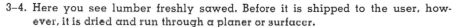

3–4. Here you see lumber freshly sawed. Before it is shipped to the user, however, it is dried and run through a planer or surfacer.

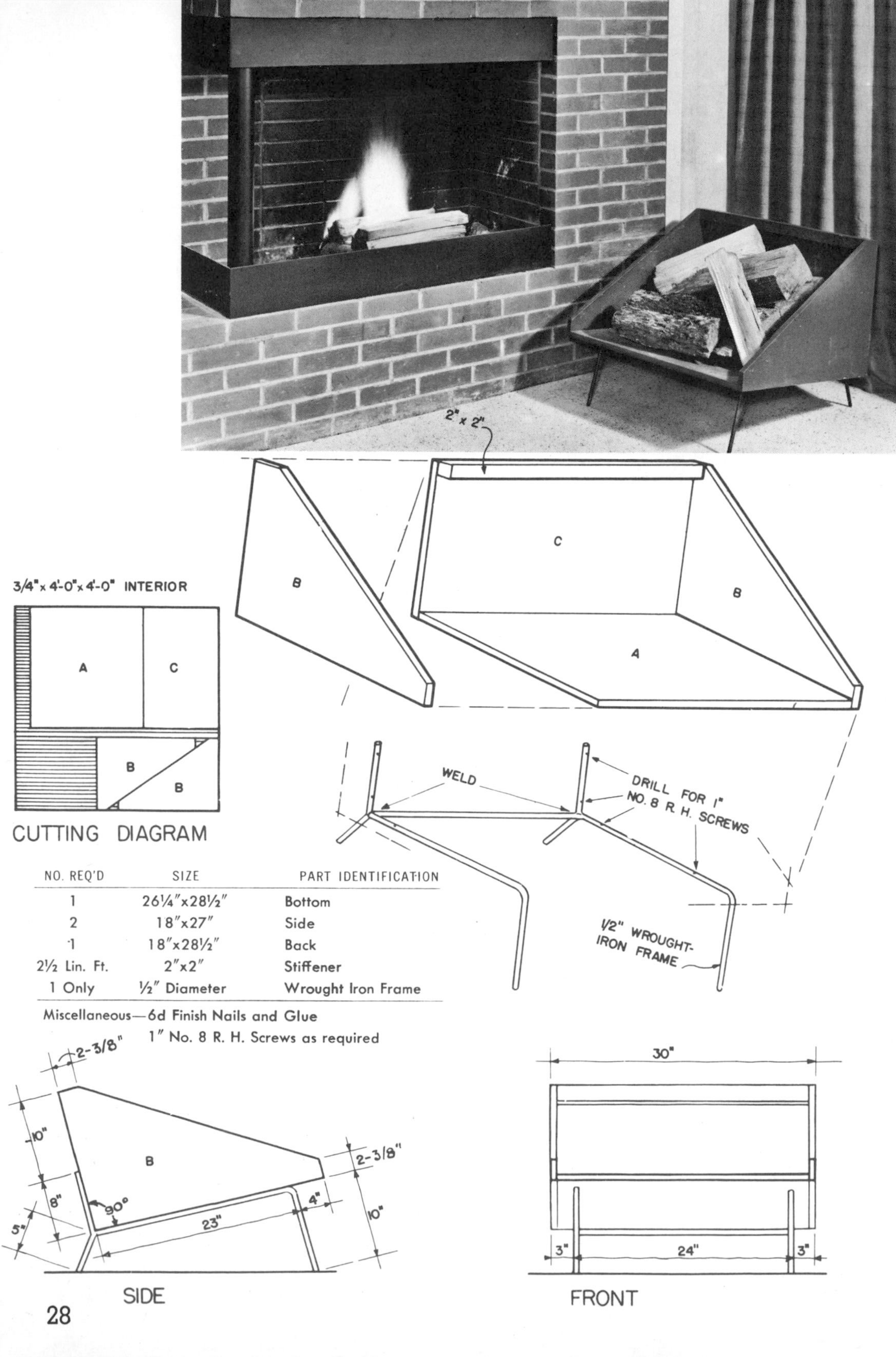

NO. REQ'D	SIZE	PART IDENTIFICATION
1	26¼"x28½"	Bottom
2	18"x27"	Side
1	18"x28½"	Back
2½ Lin. Ft.	2"x2"	Stiffener
1 Only	½" Diameter	Wrought Iron Frame

Miscellaneous—6d Finish Nails and Glue
1" No. 8 R. H. Screws as required

(At Left)

3–6. Photograph and drawing of a wood bin for a fireplace. The cutting diagram shows how, by efficient layout, you can use a minimum of materials. Remember that wood products are expensive and waste adds to the cost of the project without adding to its value.

Sometimes defects such as knots add interest. For example, knotty pine is used for interior paneling.

FIGURING THE STANDARD PIECES OF LUMBER NEEDED

After making out the rough bill of materials and figuring the board feet you need, it is a good idea to decide on the number of pieces of standard size lumber required. Group together all of the pieces made from the same thickness of lumber. Then make an imaginary layout of these pieces on larger standard pieces of stock, as in Figure 3–6.

Softwood lumber comes in standard widths from 2 to 12 inches, increasing by 2-inch intervals, and in standard lengths from 8 to 20 feet, increasing at intervals of 2 feet. Hardwood lumber comes in standard thicknesses, but because of its high cost, it is cut in whatever widths and lengths are most economical and convenient. If you are selecting lumber from a rack, use shorter pieces first and cut the lumber as economically as possible. Never waste lumber.

POINTS TO CONSIDER WHEN BUYING LUMBER AND PLYWOOD

Remember the following when you are ready to select lumber or plywood:

LUMBER

1. Rough or finished. You can purchase lumber *rough* (specified "Rough") or *finished* (specified S2S or S4S, surfaced on two sides or surfaced on four sides). Rough lumber comes just as it was cut at the sawmill. Finished or dressed lumber has been put through a planer. Of course, finished or dressed lumber costs a little more than rough lumber, but is worth the extra cost if you don't have a planer in the shop. When you buy finished or surfaced lumber, the actual dimensions will be less than the size indicated. For example, one-inch hardwood will be about 13/16 inch thick and standard construction 2″ × 4″ will actually measure 1⅝″ × 3⅝″. Figure 3–7.

2a. Grade of Lumber—Softwoods. It is important to specify the grade of lumber you want. The grading of softwoods (pine, fir, redwood, etc.) is a little different from the grading of hardwood. Softwood is classified first according to use: yard lumber, factory or shop lumber, and structural lumber.

Yard lumber is cut for a wide variety of uses, is handled by all lumber yards and is divided into two main classes: select and common. The select grade is lumber of good appearance that will take various kinds of finishes (stain, paint, enamel, etc.). It is the kind that you would choose for projects.

Select lumber is available in four grades as follows:

Grade A: Practically clear and suitable for natural finishes.

Grade B: High quality, generally

YOUR GUIDE IN SELECTING LUMBER AND PLYWOOD

LUMBER

Surface	Grade: Softwood	Grade: Hardwood	Method of Drying	Method of Cutting
Rgh. or Rough—as it comes from the saw mill. S2S—surfaced on two sides. S4S—surfaced all four sides.	1. Yard Lumber *Select*—Good appearance and finishing quality. Grade A—Clear. Grade B—High Quality. Grade C—For best paint finishes. Grade D—Lowest select.	FAS—Firsts and seconds. Highest Grade. No. 1 Common and Select. Some Defects. No. 2 Common. For small cuttings.	A.D.—Air dried. K.D.—Kiln dried.	Plain Sawed or Flat Grain Quarter Sawed or Edge Grained

Common—General utility. Not of finishing quality.
Construction or No. 1—Best Grade.
Standard or No. 2—Good Grade.
Utility or No. 3—Fair Grade.
Economy or No. 4—Poor.
No. 5—Lowest.

2. Shop Lumber—For manufacturing purposes. Equal to Grade B Select or better of Yard Lumber.
No. 1—Average 8″ wide.
No. 2—Average 7″ wide.

3. Structural Lumber.

Standard Sizes of Softwoods: Stock Size	Standard Sizes of Softwoods: Actual Size	Standard Thickness of Hardwoods: Rough	Standard Thickness of Hardwoods: S2S
1″ x 2″	3/4″ x 1 5/8″	3/8″	3/16″
1″ x 3″	3/4″ x 2 5/8″	1/2″	5/16″
1″ x 4″	3/4″ x 3 5/8″	5/8″	7/16″
1″ x 8″	3/4″ x 7 1/2″	3/4″	9/16″
1″ x 10″	3/4″ x 9 1/2″	1″	13/16″
2″ x 2″	1 5/8″ x 1 5/8″	1 1/4″	1 1/16″
2″ x 4″*	1 5/8″ x 3 5/8″		
2″ x 6″	1 5/8″ x 5 5/8″		
2″ x 10″	1 5/8″ x 9 1/2″		
4″ x 4″	3 5/8″ x 3 5/8″		

*Recommended new standard 2″ x 4″ would be 1 1/2″ x 3 5/8″.

PLYWOODS

Hardwoods

Grade	Uses
Premium Grade	Best quality for very high-grade natural finish. Too expensive except for best cabinet work or paneling.
Good Grade (1)	For good natural finish. Excellent for cabinets, built-ins, paneling and furniture.
Sound Grade (2)	For simple natural finishes and high-grade painted surfaces.
Utility Grade (3)	Not used for project work.
Reject Grade (4)	Not used for project work.

Widths from 24″ to 48″ in 6″ multiples.
Lengths from 36″ to 96″.
Veneer-core panels in plies of 3, 5, 7 and 9 are available as follows:
3 ply—1/8″, 3/16″, 1/4″; 5 ply—5/16″, 3/8″, 1/2″;
5 and 7 ply—5/8″; 7 and 9 ply—3/4″.
There are three types: Type I is fully waterproof, Type II is water resistant, and Type III is dry bond.

Fir (Softwood)

Grade	Uses
A-A	Best grade for all uses where both sides will show. Exterior or interior.
A-B	An alternate for A-A grade for high-quality uses where only one side will show. Exterior or interior. The back side is less important.
Plypanel	A good all-purpose "good-one-side" panel for lesser quality interior work.
Plyshield	A "good-one-side" grade for exterior uses where the back won't show. Used for such things as fences and siding.

Many other grades for special uses in home construction are available in thicknesses of 1/2″, 3/8″, 5/8″ and 3/4″; both exterior and interior; 1″ is also available in exterior grades. Common widths 3′4″, or 4′; common length is 8′. Be sure to specify exterior grade for outside work (including boats) and interior grade for interior construction.

3–7. Lumber and plywood chart.

clear, and also suitable for natural finishes.

Grade C: Quality suitable for a good paint finish.

Grade D: Lowest select grade; can be painted.

Common lumber is the type suitable for rough carpentry. It is not of finishing quality. It is graded Nos. 1, 2, 3, 4, and 5. Only Nos. 1, 2, and 3 are suitable for good, rough construction.

Factory or *shop lumber* is lumber that is to be cut up for manufacturing purposes. It is usually handled only by lumber yards that do millwork or sell to manufacturing concerns and school shops. It is the grade that you would order for projects in place of one of the select grades listed above. There are two grades of shop lumber, Nos. 1 and 2 as said above. Both compare in quality to B select or better of yard lumber and differ only in the average width of the pieces. No. 1 averages 8 inches wide and No. 2 averages 7 inches wide.

Structural lumber grading is based upon the strength of the pieces and is not of particular concern to the average woodworker.

2b. Grade of Lumber—Hardwoods.

The *top grade* is indicated by FAS, meaning firsts and seconds. This is not perfect lumber, but it will produce about 90 per cent clear stand cuttings. The *next grade* is called No. 1 common and select. It contains more knots and defects. The *poorest grade* is No. 2 common, which contains many defects and is suitable for small cuttings.

3. Methods of drying. Another thing to know about the lumber you buy is whether it is air dried (AD) or kiln dried (KD). Air-dried lumber has been dried over a long period of time by exposure to the weather. It has a moisture content of from 12 to 15 per cent. Kiln-dried, on the other hand, has been scientifically dried to a moisture content of about 6 to 12 per cent or less in a controlled-temperature building. Projects to be glued must have a moisture content of not more than 9 per cent. Therefore, specify kiln-dried lumber.

4. Method of cutting. Most lumber is cut in such a way that the annular rings form an angle of less than 45 degrees with the surfaces of the piece. This is called *plain-sawed* (when it is hardwood) or *flat-grained* (when it is softwood).

When lumber is cut with the annular rings making an angle of more than 45 degrees with the surface of the piece, it is called *quarter sawed* or edge grained or vertical grained. Quarter-sawed lumber usually costs more. It is more expensive to cut it this way and it is considered more beautiful.

PLYWOOD AND HARDBOARD

The use of *plywood* is so common that you should become acquainted with typical differences. Plywood is either veneer core or lumber core. In *veneer-core* plywood, from three to nine layers of thin veneer make up the "panel." *Lumber-core* plywood has a thick middle layer of solid wood. This is commonly chosen for fine furniture. Figure 3–8.

The grade of plywood depends on the quality of its two faces. The exact grading of soft and hard plywoods is shown on page 30. When you go to the lumber yard, you can

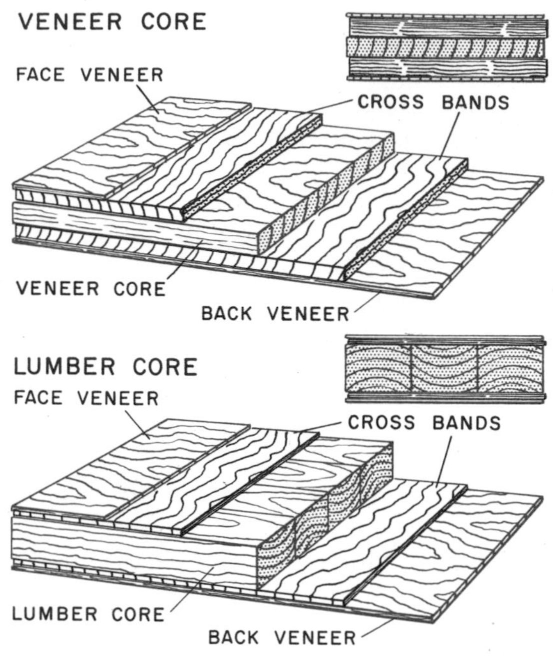

3–8. Here you see the difference between veneer-core plywood and lumber-core plywood. Most plywood used for interior and exterior buildings is veneer-core.

usually get the grade of plywood you want by indicating "good two sides" (G2S) for the most expensive grade or "good one side" (G1S), which is only good on one side. Specify whether it is for interior or exterior use. Figure 3–9.

Hardboard is a man-made wood board produced by "exploding" wood chips into wood fibers and then forming them into panels under heat and pressure. There are two types: standard, or untreated, and tempered, or treated. In the tempering, the board is dipped in drying oils and baked. On some hardboard one face is smooth while the other is rough and looks like screening. Other hardboard has two smooth surfaces. Tempered hardboard can be purchased with evenly spaced holes drilled all over the surface. Figure 3–10. This is used for hanger boards for tools, displays, and many other purposes. The standard sizes of hardboard are 1/8″ thick by 4′ by 6′ and 1/4″ thick by 2′ by 12′.

3–9. Plywood is an excellent material for many kinds of projects. The wide widths and smooth surfaces make rapid construction possible.

3–10. Perforated hardboard. This is an excellent material for sliding doors, display boards, and other similar uses.

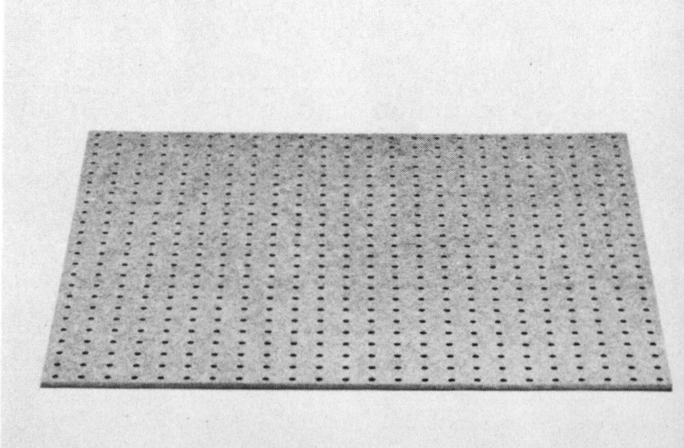

CAN YOU ANSWER THESE QUESTIONS ON A BILL OF MATERIALS?

1. Describe a bill of materials.
2. How is the width of stock measured?
3. Is the longest measurement of a piece of stock always the length? Explain.
4. How many board feet of lumber are there in a piece 1½″ thick, 8″ wide, and 10′ (feet) long?
5. Suppose one kind of lumber cost $200.00 per M. What would be the cost of five board feet?
6. How is plywood sold?
7. How is hardwood lumber cut?
8. What does "S2S" mean?
9. How would you describe the best grade of walnut? of pine?
10. Describe the two methods of drying lumber.

Section I

UNIT 4. PLANNING YOUR WORK

Before you begin to work with tools, it is wise to plan carefully the steps you will follow in making the project. This is just good sense and protects you from making unnecessary mistakes. This is done in industry. Like good business, you should "Plan your work; then work your plan."

PLANNING A PROJECT

The idea in planning a project is to think through exactly (1) what materials you need, (2) what tools and equipment are necessary, (3) what steps you will follow, and in what order they will be done to complete the project in the best way possible.

If you fail to plan your work, you may, for example, begin to sand parts of the project before all of the cutting tool operations are completed, with the result that you will dull some of your tools. Or you may forget to make the proper allowance for the joints needed and waste lumber. Many such mistakes can creep into your work.

4–1. This attractive sewing box might be a good beginning project. Note the various parts of the project as you read through the plan of procedure.

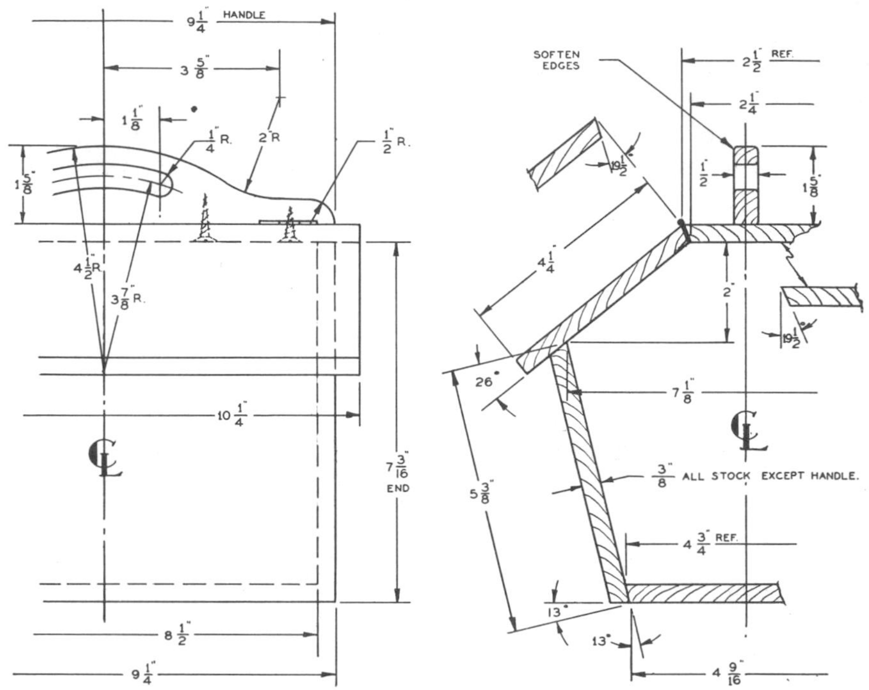

4–2. Drawing for the sewing box.

METHOD OF PROCEDURE

In planning your job, you should first decide on the order in which the parts are to be made; then list all of the things you will need to do to complete each particular part.

For example, suppose you are making a sewing box as shown in Figure 4–1 and 4–2. You first decide on all of the materials needed. Then you think through all of the steps in cutting, shaping, fitting, and finishing the project. In written form, this might be as follows:

Sewing Box

TOOLS AND EQUIPMENT:

Crosscut saw, ripsaw, backsaw, plane, chisel, coping saw, twist drill, hand drill, jig saw, rasp, sandpaper, try square, sliding T bevel, ruler, pencil.

PROCEDURE:

1. Cut all pieces to size.
2. Cut angle on both edges of bottom piece. Cut the same angle on bottom edge of side pieces.
3. Cut angle on one edge of each lid and both edges of top piece.
4. Cut angle on top edge of each side piece.
5. Cut side angles on end pieces. Cut top angles on end pieces.

BILL OF MATERIALS:

Important: All dimensions listed below are *finished* size.

No. of Pieces	Thickness	Width	Length	Description	Kind of Wood
1	1/2″	1 5/8″	9 1/4″	Handle	Pine
2	3/8″	5 3/8″	9 1/4″	Sides	Pine
2	3/8″	7 1/8″	7 3/16″	Ends	Pine
1	3/8″	2 1/2″	10 1/4″	Top	Pine
2	3/8″	4 1/4″	10 1/4″	Lids	Pine
1	3/8″	4 3/4″	8 1/2″	Bottom	Pine
4				1″ Brass Butt Hinges	
2				No. 6 x 3/4″ F.H.Wood Screws	
2				No. 6 x 1 1/4″ F.H.Wood Screws	
2				No. 18 x 1″Wire Brads	

PROCEDURE CONTD:

6. Lay out handle. Cut outside contour. Bore 1/2″ hole in each end of handle opening and cut out interior on jig saw. File and sand smooth all curved surfaces. Soften all edges.

7. Drill and countersink screw shank holes in top. Drill anchor holes in handle.

8. Cut gains in top piece and lids for hinges. Drill screw holes.

9. Sand all pieces.

10. Assemble ends, bottom and sides with glue and wire brads.

11. Install hinges and attach handle to top with No. 6 flat head wood screws.

12. Attach top assembly to box with glue and wire brads.

13. Fill all nail holes and finish sand entire project.

14. Apply antique pine finish.

This written plan, though not always absolutely necessary, is an excellent idea. You should at least think carefully through each step you will take before you begin to work. In this way you avoid a great deal of trouble. Remember again, "Plan your work; then work your plan."

CAN YOU ANSWER THESE QUESTIONS ON PLANNING YOUR WORK?

1. What is a good motto to adopt in starting a project?
2. List the important parts of a plan sheet.
3. Answer these questions about the sewing box:
   a. What kind of wood is used?
   b. How many different thicknesses of wood are needed?
   c. How many parts make up the box?
4. What kind of a drawing is Fig. 4–2?

Section I

UNIT 5. YOU, YOUR FELLOW STUDENT, AND YOUR SHOP

There are many wonderful things that can be made of wood. We can see these things everywhere—in people's homes, in store windows, in magazines, and in exhibitions. Although we all want to do things that will make us proud and happy, sometimes we are not willing to put forth the effort necessary for good and satisfying work. As a result, we are miserable and discontent. All that is required to make very fine things of wood is a willingness to start right and to keep that way.

The woodshop has the tools and machines that make it possible to have these wood projects. You will get a great deal of satisfaction and pleasure from woodworking and will find it a source of great interest and enjoyment. However, it is important first to take good care of the shop and to be man enough to persevere in good working habits, the kind described in this book.

Tools are designed to help us with our work, and the machines are built for certain jobs. Figure 5–1. When we treat the tools and machines with the proper respect and use them and care for them as they deserve to be, they will give us better service and will add greatly to our enjoyment of shopwork. Use the tools exactly as they should be used, keep them sharp and in their proper places, and they will reward you with the ease with which they can be handled. Figure 5–2. When you are qualified, use the machines as they are meant to be used, keep them in good shape, and they too will increase your ability to do woodworking.

Horseplay, running, or playing practical jokes is not only bad, but downright dangerous. After you have begun your work in the workshop, you will find that you resent anyone's mistreating the shop, the tools, or the machines.

5–1. Every tool is designed to do a specific job. Make sure you learn to use the tools correctly and safely.

START RIGHT, WORK RIGHT, BE RIGHT

First, think of the place in which you work as *your* shop. Each one of you has an equal responsibility to care for it and to see that the tools and machines are used correctly. If *you* don't, the others won't either and the shop will become anything but a place for work. The things you learn in the shop should be done accurately and correctly. The best way to get your project done and to develop the ability to do things well in woodworking is to try to do everything the correct way. When you come into the shop, treat it as your own.

When you are taught to do a mechanical job properly, don't try to do it differently *just this once*. It's learning the hard way if you have to let a piece of wood kick back from a circular saw and strike you in the stomach with the force of a baseball bat swung by a major leaguer. It's no joke to see a fellow student lose several fingers because he has tried to plane too small a piece on the jointer. In the shop we learn by doing, but that means by doing correctly.

ACT THE PART

If you are getting ready to play in a football game, you don't dress in a basketball outfit. For everything that you do, whether it's ice skating, playing football, or working, there are correct clothes that should be worn. In the shop, all outer clothing, such as coats, sweaters, and jackets, should be removed. Make sure your tie is tucked into your shirt. Roll up your sleeves and put on a shop apron. Figure 5–3. This kind of clothing will protect your other clothes from dust, paint, and shop dirt. It will also help to prevent accidents, since nothing is more likely to cause trouble than a loose tie or sleeves hanging over a machine. Also, if your hair is long, make sure that it doesn't fall loosely over your forehead to be caught in

5–2. Here is the correct way to keep your tools. Never pile them one on top of the other. The results you achieve in woodworking depend largely on the way in which you take care of your tools. An additional reward will be found in your health and safety. Courtesy the Jam Handy Organization.

5–3. Here is a boy dressed properly for work in the woodshop. He is wearing a shop apron, his sleeves are rolled up, his tie is tucked in, his hair is not too long, and he has no loose articles dangling from his clothing. Courtesy the Jam Handy Organization.

some revolving machine. That could scalp you faster than an Indian of 1849.

DOING YOUR SHARE

Keeping up a shop requires cooperative effort, and everyone must do his part in maintaining a safe and well kept shop. Here are some of the things you can do:

1. Pick up small pieces of wood on the floor and throw them in the waste box. Some student may turn his ankle on them.
2. Keep the aisles clear by placing projects in their proper places.
3. Keep your tools properly arranged on your bench. Don't allow sharp-pointed tools to stick out.
4. Keep oil wiped up from the floor. Oil may cause a bad fall.
5. Don't come up behind a student when he is working on a machine. He may be startled and make a false move. If someone is using a machine, wait until he is finished. Accidents usually happen at this time.
6. Be ready and willing to sign a safety pledge card. Your instructor is having you do this to protect you, himself, and your fellow students.
7. Know the fire regulations in your shop. The shop is one of the places most likely to have a blaze. Figure 5–4. This is because there is a great fire hazard due to wood dust and finishing materials. Dust in the air can cause an explosion, especially if it is ignited by a spark from a loose wire on a piece of electrical equipment. The finishing room is a particularly dangerous place. The solvents used in applying finishes form a vapor in the air that ignites easily and can cause an explosion.

IT CAN HAPPEN HERE

This is a true story. Two boys were working on the project of turning a large table top on a lathe. They came down to the shop to work extra time. One boy stood by the lathe and the other turned on the master

5–4. Keep finishing rags in a metal container. One of the most common causes of fire is the combustion of rags that have been soaked in oil or paint and allowed to lie piled together in an open place. Courtesy the Jam Handy Organization.

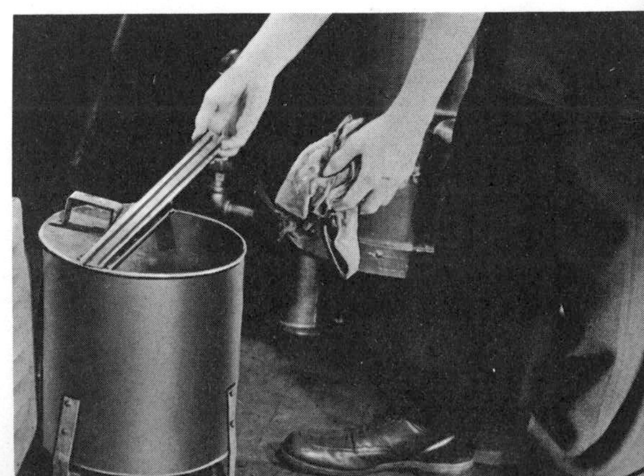

5–5. Watch carefully as your instructor demonstrates the use of tools and machines. He will show you the correct safety practices to follow.

switch. By mistake the lathe was set at high speed. The lathe started with terrific force, the table top flew off, struck and killed the boy standing there. This actually happened and it can happen in your shop. Not many accidents occur in school shops, but each year some students are victims. *Every one of these accidents could have been prevented.* They all occur because someone does something he is not supposed to do.

Do you plan to play baseball or to play some musical instrument? If so, you will need all of your fingers! More often than you realize, someone cuts one or more fingers off on the circular saw or the jointer. You can do your part to prevent this by:

1. Carefully watching your teacher's demonstrations on how to use each tool and machine. Figure 5–5.

2. Getting your teacher's permission before using a power machine. You may not be ready to use power machinery, so don't try it until you are. The machines may look harmless, but they are far from it.

AN OUNCE OF PREVENTION

Even when you are working correctly with tools and machines, small accidents happen. The most common are slight cuts and bruises, a sliver in your finger, minor burns, or getting something in your eye. None of these may be serious, but they all *can* be. A sliver, for example, can cause blood poisoning. Figure 5–6. Your eyes can be permanently damaged if they are not treated immediately. Give immediate first aid.

5–6. Use a tweezers to lift out a sliver carefully. Be sure the wound bleeds and then dress it properly. Courtesy the Jam Handy Organization.

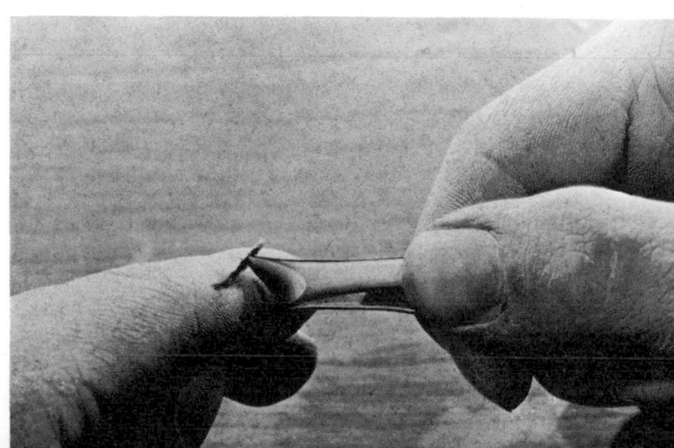

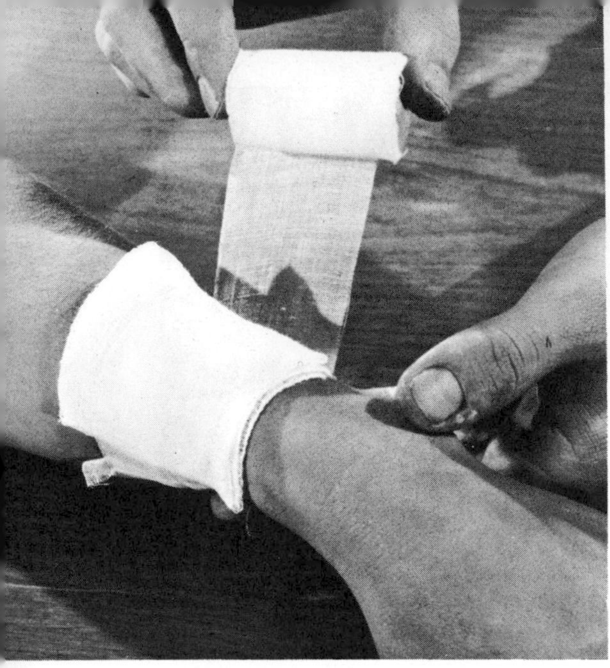

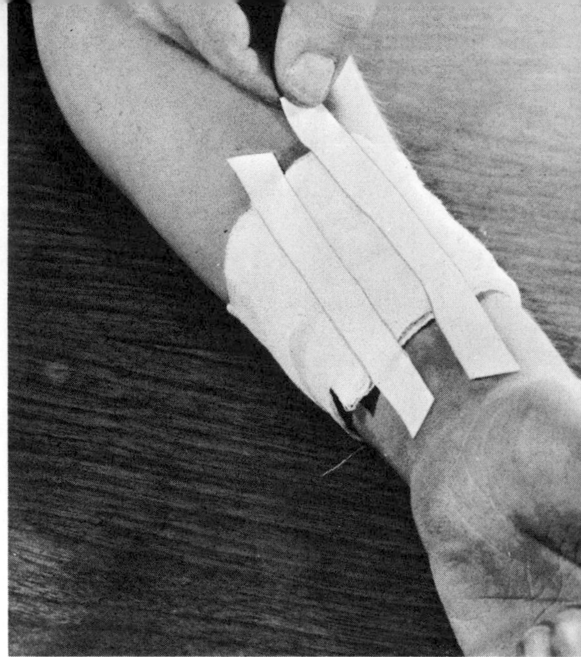

5–7. The proper way of dressing a burn, cut, or wound. Wrap a gauze bandage around the dressing to hold it in place. Put adhesive tape across to secure the bandage. Courtesy the Jam Handy Organization.

If it is a slight cut, allow it to bleed freely for a short time and then bandage it properly. Figure 5–7. Remove slivers immediately with a clean knife or tweezers and then sterilize the wound. If it is a slight burn, apply baking soda and water or carbolated petroleum jelly. If a more serious burn, it should be treated by a doctor. If you get something in your eye, hold your handkerchief over it lightly without rubbing, to let your eye water. If this doesn't remove the trouble, have a doctor or nurse take it out. Figure 5–8. Don't let another student remove a particle from your eye.

5–8. Eye injuries are a serious matter. See a doctor or nurse immediately to take care of this type of injury. Courtesy the Jam Handy Organization.

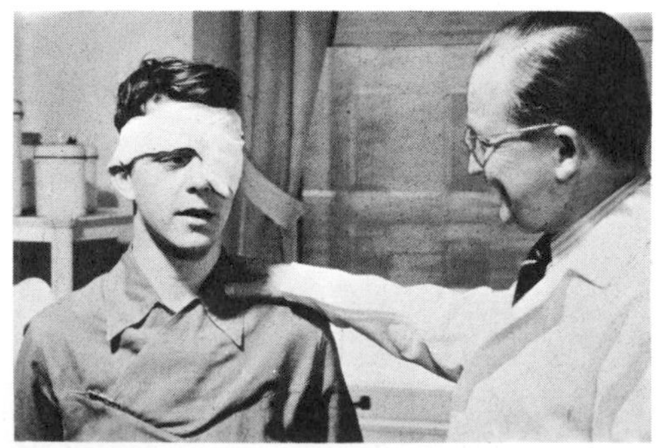

IS IT WORTH IT?

In the shop, you will be handling many different kinds of materials including lumber, nails, screws, and unfinished projects. You should learn to handle them correctly. Figure 5–9 shows the right way to carry lumber when you are taking it off a storage rack. Be careful not to squeeze your fingers. Always make sure that the lumber is kept in a neat pile; poorly stacked lumber is dangerous.

Screws and nails are fine for fastening work together, but they don't digest; so don't carry them around in your mouth! There is also danger of infection when you do this. When

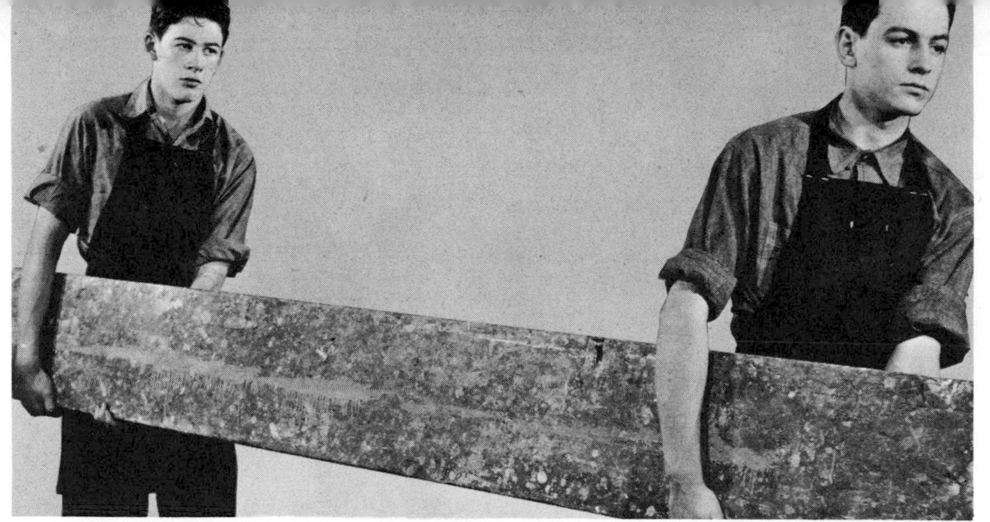

5–9. When lumber must be carried, ask someone to give you a hand. Make sure that the way is clear, and then carry it as this paint board is carried here. Courtesy the Jam Handy Organization.

storing your project, do it neatly and never place it high on a locker or window ledge where it can fall off on someone. If you have a large finished project or a machine that should be moved, lift it correctly. There is danger of rupture from improper lifting.

IT'S THE LITTLE THINGS THAT COUNT

Many of the tools in the woodshop have sharp cutting edges that are used for marking, shaping, and cutting stock. These tools can cause small accidents. Some rules to follow are: (1) never carry pointed tools in your pockets (Figure 5–10); (2) always grind off a mushroom head; (3) always cut and chisel *away from* yourself; (4) never use tools with loose handles (Figure 5–11); (5) always carry cutting tools with the sharp edge down; and (6) use tools for the proper purpose. Figure 5–12.

The best way of working with hand tools is to follow the instructions given in the units that follow. Always remember that the correct way is the safe way.

CAN YOU QUALIFY?

Before you are allowed to drive a car you must be a certain age, have instructions, and be able to pass certain tests. This is to protect you and others. The same things apply to your shop. You can't expect to use power machinery until you are old enough to use it safely, until you have been given proper instructions, and until you have shown ability to do so by passing a performance test. In this book you will find suggestions for using each machine.

5–10. Here is everything that should NOT be done. This careless woodworker is not looking where he is going. He's carrying sharp-pointed tools incorrectly, and has his arms too full. Courtesy the Jam Handy Organization.

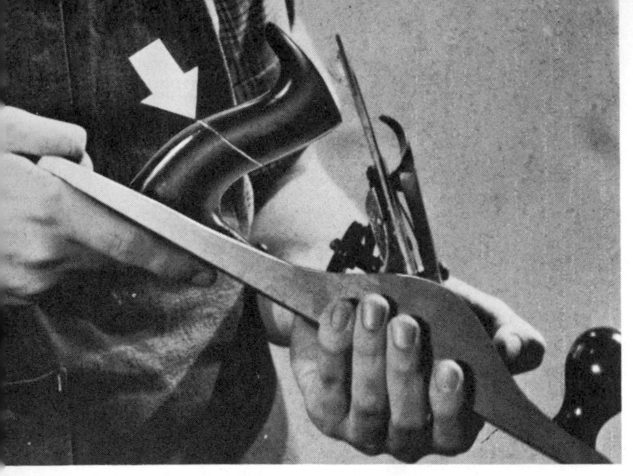

5–11. **Check your tools to see if the handles are in good condition. Cracked or rough handles on saws, chisels, planes, and gouges can cause blisters which may become infected. Then, too, it is irritating to work with a tool that has a rough handle and you can't do a good job with it.** Courtesy the Jam Handy Organization.

CAN YOU ANSWER THESE QUESTIONS ON YOU, YOUR FELLOW STUDENT, AND YOUR SHOP?

1. Who is responsible for taking care of the tools and machines?
2. Why is the right attitude important before beginning to work?
3. Describe the proper clothes for the woodshop.
4. Why is long hair dangerous?
5. List five things you can do to keep the shop in order.
6. Can you tell what causes most accidents?
7. How would you treat a slight burn?
8. If you get something in your eye in the shop, should you ask a fellow student to remove it? Explain your answer.
9. There is a correct way of carrying lumber in the shop. Can you tell how it should be done?
10. List three good ways for taking care of sharp cutting tools.

5–12. **Here is a picture you should study, for it shows every good practice, especially protection of the eyes. You have only two eyes and money can't buy a new pair.** Courtesy the Jam Handy Organization.

Section II
Getting Out the Rough Stock

The second 2 steps in hand woodworking—what you must know and be able to do.

6. Getting acquainted with measuring and marking tools: kinds of rules, other layout and measuring tools and how to use them, marking tools, holding devices, how to measure and mark for cutting.

7. Learning about the saws: set, point, and size. The difference between ripsaw and crosscut saw and what they are used for, how to saw and do it right.

You are ready to get out the rough stock for your project after you have made your plans according to the suggestions in the first five units. Now comes the actual work with the wood and with the tools in the shop. You may be asked to take the wood directly from the lumber pile. However, if this is your first project, your instructor may have already rough-cut the lumber to size to help the class in getting started and to provide time for other things.

Measuring, marking, and cutting are important things to learn and to do now. They will be done over and over again in any kind of woodworking, so it is wise to learn them well. Learn these skills well enough to make them almost automatic. See the "box" above. Further steps are on pp. 15, 60, 94, 108, 132, 143, 170, 219, 244.

UNIT 6. MEASURING AND MARKING OUT THE ROUGH STOCK

After you have the lumber for your project, you will measure and mark out the amount of stock needed for each piece shown in the rough bill of materials or the drawing. You need several measuring tools. These may seem very simple but accuracy is impossible unless you take enough time and care to use them properly.

RULES FOR MEASURING SHORT LENGTHS

There are several kinds of rules in common use for woodworking. The best one for measuring small pieces and marking short distances is the bench rule. Figure 6–1a and 6–1b.

6–1a. The bench rule is 12″, 24″, or 36″ long. Sometimes a 3-foot (36″) rule is called a yardstick. The rule is graduated in sixteenths of an inch on one side and eighths of an inch on the other. The illustration below shows these graduations, and larger ones for comparison.

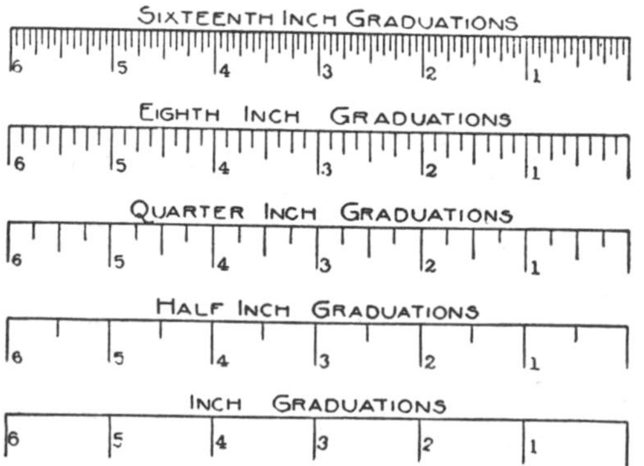

This is a wooden rule 1 to 3 feet long with a brass cap at either end to protect it. Figure 6–2. One side of the rule is divided into halves, quarters, and sixteenths of an inch. The *folding rule* is simply a 2-foot rule that can be folded.

RULES FOR MEASURING LONGER PIECES

The zigzag rule for long measurements (Figure 6–3) is about 8 inches

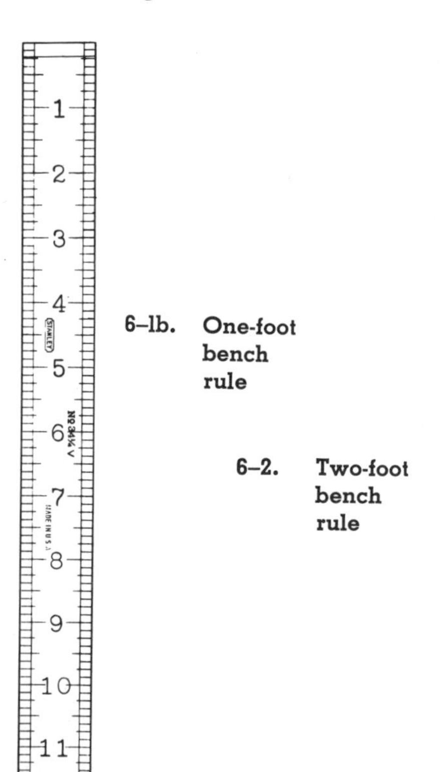

6–1b. One-foot bench rule

6–2. Two-foot bench rule

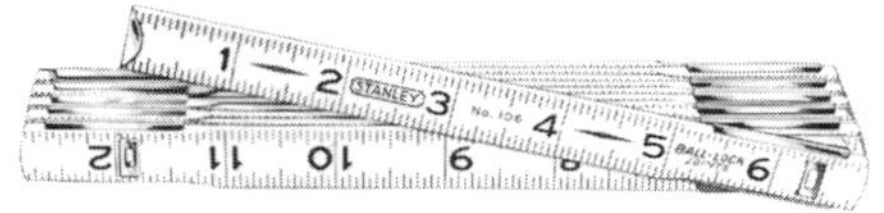

6–3. Six-foot zigzag extension rule. It is useful, mostly to carpenters, in measuring longer lengths.

long when folded and can be extended to its full length of 6 to 8 feet. This rule is the standby of most carpenters. Another rule for measuring long dimensions is the steel tape. Figure 6–4. A small catch at its end slips over the end of a board, making it easier to pull out the tape. The steel tape has a standard length of 6 feet.

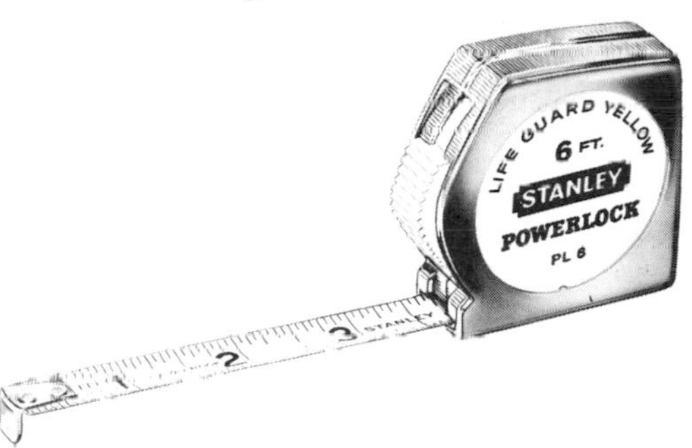

6–4a. A push-pull steel tape rule. It is particularly adaptable as a shop rule since it will accurately take inside and outside measurements.

6–4b. Using a steel tape to locate a point.

SQUARES

The *try square* has a metal blade marked in eighths of an inch along its top and a handle usually of metal. Figure 6–5. The try square is used for many things; the most common are laying out a line square with an edge, checking the squareness of two surfaces, and testing 90-degree angles. Figure 6–6. *Never use this tool for hammering or pounding* because this would make it inaccurate.

The *carpenter's square* (framing square) is used in general building work. Figure 6–7.

The *combination square* is very useful for measuring and marking. Figure 6–8. It is called a combination tool because it is a try square, a miter square, a level, a plumb, a depth gauge, and a scriber. The combination blade has a groove cut along its length. The head slides along and can be tightened at any position.

The *sliding T bevel* is for laying out all angles other than 90 degrees. Figure 6–9. It has an adjustable blade in a handle. To lay out a 45-degree angle, for instance, the adjustable T bevel can be set with the framing square as shown in Figure 6–10. To set the tool to such angles as 30 and 60 degrees, the bevel can be checked

6–5. Try square.

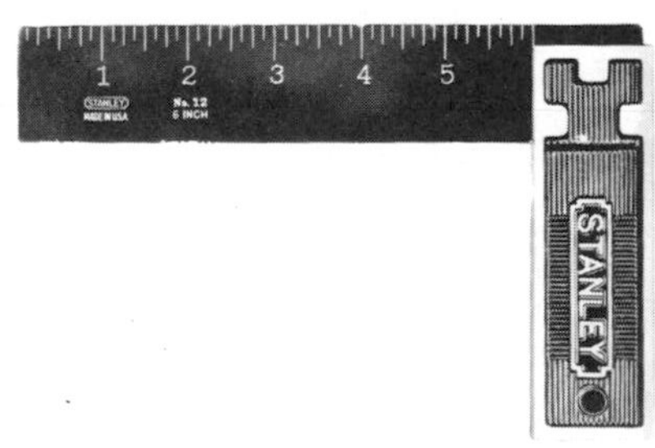

with the triangles used in drawing. It can also be set by laying out a right triangle with the hypotenuse two units long and one side one unit long. Figure 6–11. For other angles, the sliding T bevel can best be set with a protractor as shown in Figure 6–12.

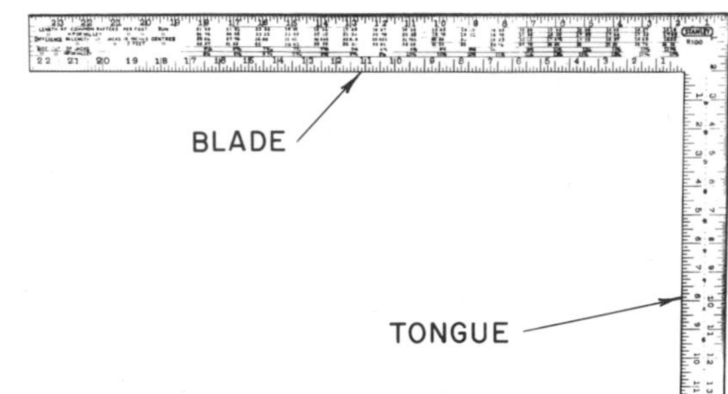

6–7. Carpenter's framing square. Of all the carpenter's tools, none is more nearly indispensable than this steel square. It has a table stamped on the body for figuring rafters. Other squares also contain tables for figuring board measurements.

6–6. A six-inch try square with a metal blade and handle. This tool is accurately machined so that the handle and the blade will be at right angles to each other. Therefore never use the tool as a pounding device. The lower picture shows a try and miter square with one edge of the handle shaped at an angle of 45 degrees. For many layout jobs this kind of try square is better and more convenient to use.

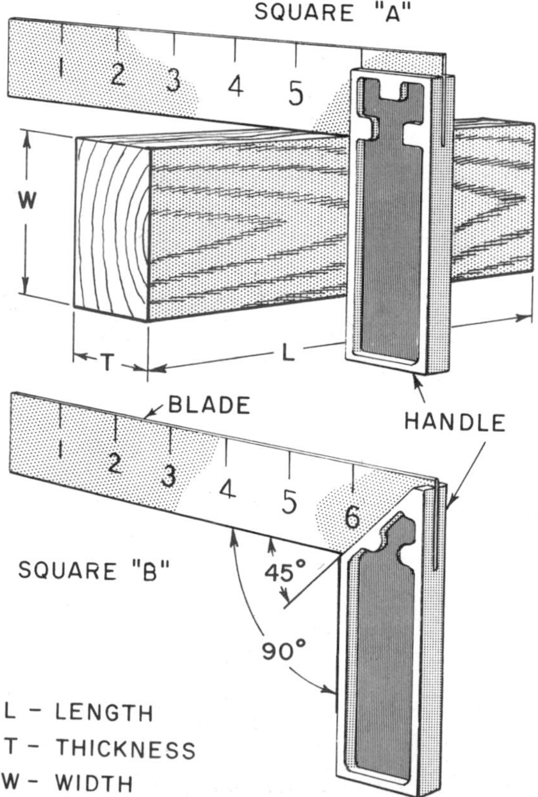

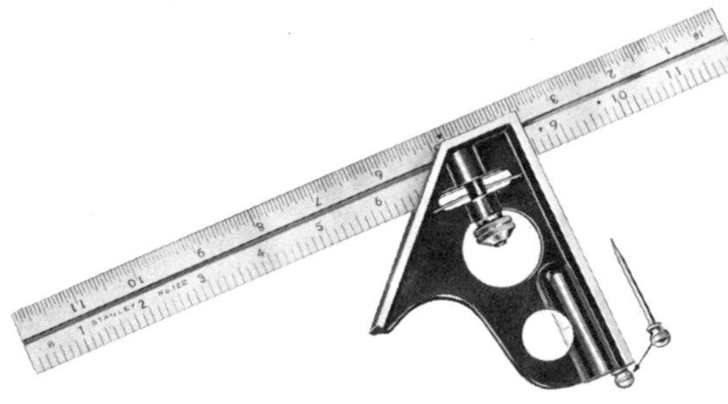

6–8. A combination square is a valuable tool for various uses in measuring and marking.

6–9. This tool is called a sliding T bevel. It gets its name from the fact that it can be adjusted at any angle desired. The blade slides back and forth in the handle and can be locked in position with a little thumb screw.

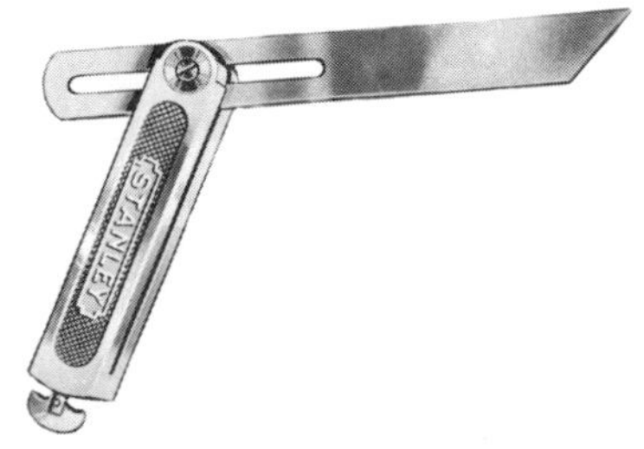

MARKING TOOLS

An ordinary *lead pencil* is the most common marking tool because its mark can be easily seen on both rough and finished lumber, is easy to remove, and does not scratch or mar the wood surface. Use a pencil with a rather hard lead for laying out fine, accurate lines. Keep the pencil sharpened in the shape of a chisel so the point can be held directly against the edge of the rule or square.

6–10. A method of setting the sliding T bevel by using a steel square. This shows the bevel being set at an angle of 45 degrees.

6–11. Using a triangle to set a sliding T bevel. By drawing a triangle with the hypotenuse two units long and one leg one unit long, you have a right triangle with 30- and 60-degree angles.

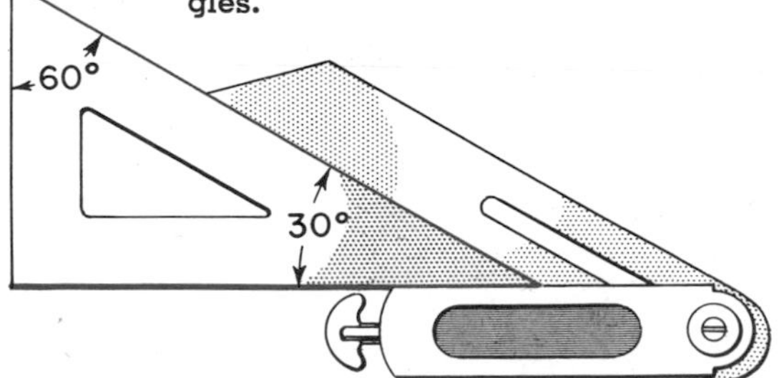

A *knife* is a good tool for very accurate marking. Figure 6–13. Be careful, however, not to use it except when you know that the mark will disappear as the wood is cut, formed, or shaped. A *sloyd knife* (Figure 6–14) is used for marking and is a very handy tool since it can be used for such jobs as trimming a fine edge, slicing a piece of thin veneer, and whittling a small peg.

A *scratch awl*—a thin metal-pointed tool with a wooden handle—is good for marking and for punching the

6–12. Setting a sliding T bevel by using a protractor. Any angle can be quickly and accurately established.

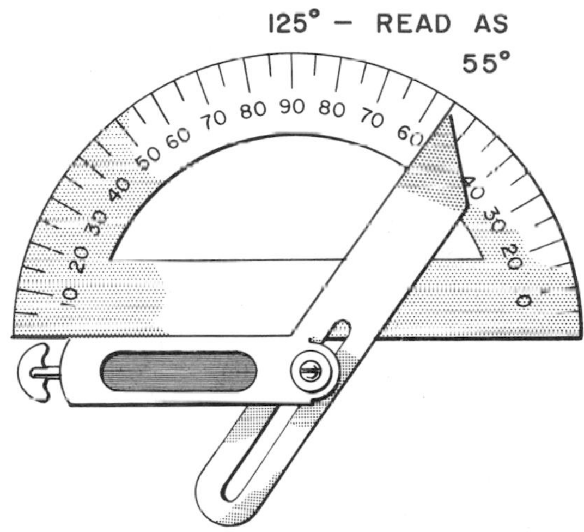

6–13. The layout and cutting knife. This type has a blade that slides into the handle.

6–14. The sloyd knife is excellent for layout work and also for many odd jobs such as cutting, trimming, and whittling. This tool was so named because it was used in the old "sloyd" or Swedish system of teaching.

6–15. The scratch awl is another layout tool that is very handy. It is used to lay out the position for drilling and boring holes.

locations of holes to be drilled or bored. Figure 6–15.

HOLDING DEVICES

For good work you must have a solid workbench with a sturdy bench vise. Figure 6–16. The *bench vise* holds work to be cut, formed, or shaped. Figure 6–17. Line the metal jaws with wood inserts to protect the pieces to be clamped. The movable jaw of the vise has a small, sliding section called a vise dog. This, with a metal stop, can be placed in various holes across the top of the bench for holding long, flat pieces of stock when planing, cutting, forming, or shaping. Figure 6–18.

When handling larger pieces for layout, sawing, and assembling, one or two wood sawhorses are needed.

6–16. A sturdy woodworking bench is a prime requirement for doing good work.

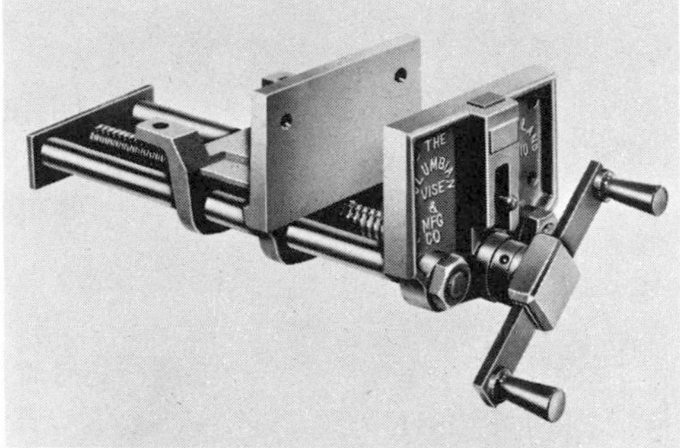

6–17. A woodworking vise in which the jaws are lined with wood should be attached to the left front side of the bench.

They should be about 20 inches high; the best kind to have is one like that shown in Figure 6–19, which is open down the center.

MEASURING STOCK

1. Measuring thickness. The lumber should be checked for thickness, width, and length. Measure the thickness of the lumber by holding the rule over the edge. The thickness is found by reading the two lines on

6–18. The proper method of locking stock on a bench top for doing planing, cutting, forming, and shaping. As you can see, the vise dog is in a raised position so that the wood can be clamped between it and the metal stop at the other end which cannot be seen in this picture. The metal stop fits into one of the holes drilled along the top of the bench.

6–19. This kind of sawhorse is most practical for layout and cutting. Because it is open down the center, the sawing can be done with the blade free to move down the center of the opening.

the rule that just enclose the stock. Figure 6–20.

2. Measuring width. Measure the width by holding the left end of the rule (or the inch mark) on one edge of the stock. Slide your thumb from

6–20. Measuring the thickness of stock with a bench rule. One end of the rule is held directly over one arris of the wood and the thumb is slid along until the thickness of the stock is indicated.

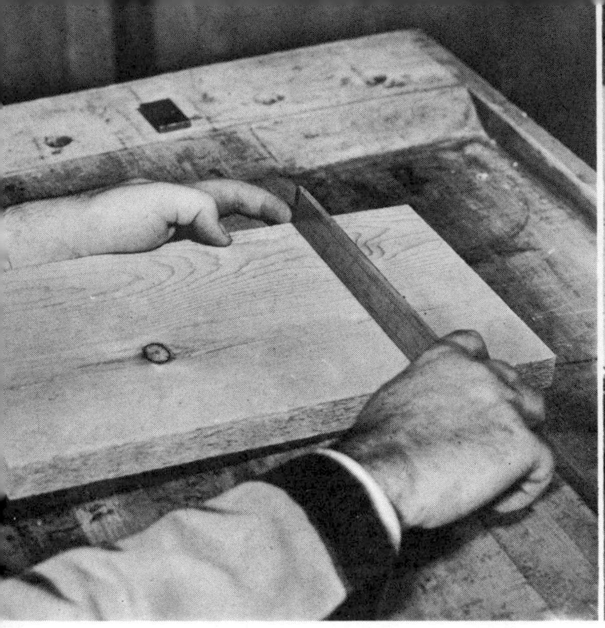

6–21. Measuring the width of stock. The rule is held on edge for more accurate measurement. The left end of the rule is held even with the left side of the board with the forefinger of the left hand. The thumb is slid along the rule until the correct width is indicated.

6–23. Using a steel tape to measure longer lengths. This procedure is more accurate. With a short rule there is always a possibility of mistakes. A steel tape is especially convenient because the metal hook on the end can be dropped over the end of the stock and the tape drawn out to length.

right to left along the rule until the width is shown. Figure 6–21.

3. Measuring short lengths. Select the end of the stock from which the measurement is to be taken. Check its squareness by holding a try square against the truest edge. Make sure that the end is not split or checked.

6–22. For measuring short lengths the end of the rule is placed directly over the end of the stock, with the rule on edge. Then the correct length of stock needed is marked with a pencil.

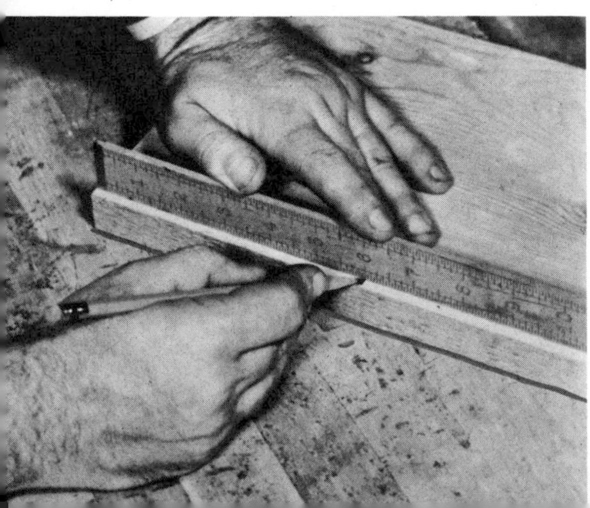

6–24. Using a pencil to mark across the face of stock. Make sure it is sharpened to a point so it will make a thin, accurate line on the wood surface.

6–25. Marking across the face of stock with a knife. Notice that the try square is held firmly against one edge of the stock and then the knife drawn toward you. Always *turn the knife in slightly* toward the blade of the try square. Courtesy the Jam Handy Organization.

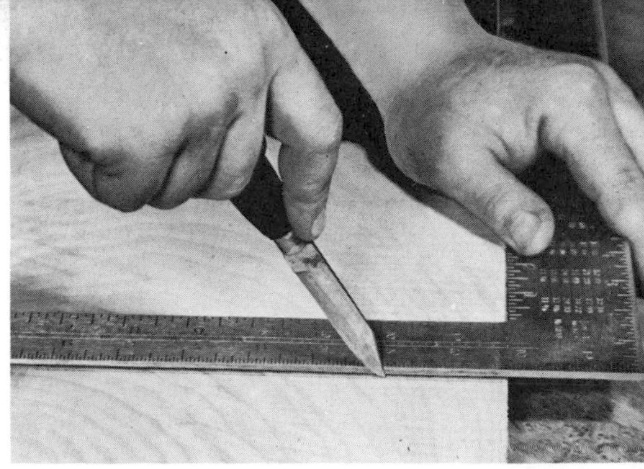

6–26. On wide stock the framing square is used to mark the line. The blade is tipped slightly and is held firmly against the edge of the stock as the knife marks across the face of the work.

If it is, the end of the wood should be squared off and cut and the measurement taken from the sawed end. If a short length of stock is needed, hold the rule on edge and mark the length with a pencil or knife. Figure 6–22.

4. Measuring longer lengths. For measuring longer distances use a zigzag rule or a steel tape. This will eliminate measuring errors that come from moving a short rule several times. Figure 6–23. Make a small mark at the point to be squared.

MARKING STOCK FOR CUTTING TO LENGTH

1. Marking lengths on narrow lumber. If rather narrow lumber is being marked for cutting, hold the handle of the try square firmly against the truest edge of the stock. Square off a line. Figures 6–24 and 6–25.

2. Marking lengths on wider lumber. Use a framing square on wider stock. The framing square is uniform in thickness. Therefore the blade should be tipped slightly and then held firmly against the truest edge while the mark is made across the stock. Figure 6–26. To be sure of trueness, square a line across the edges with the face line. This can be done with a try square as shown in Figure 6–27.

3. Marking duplicate parts. If a group of pieces must be measured and marked out to equal lengths, place them side by side. Make sure that the ends are lined up by holding a try square over the ends; then move the try square to correct length to mark the pieces. Figure 6–28.

6–27. Squaring the lines across the edge of stock. It is a good idea to mark a line on the edge as shown. This will help you make the saw cut more accurate.

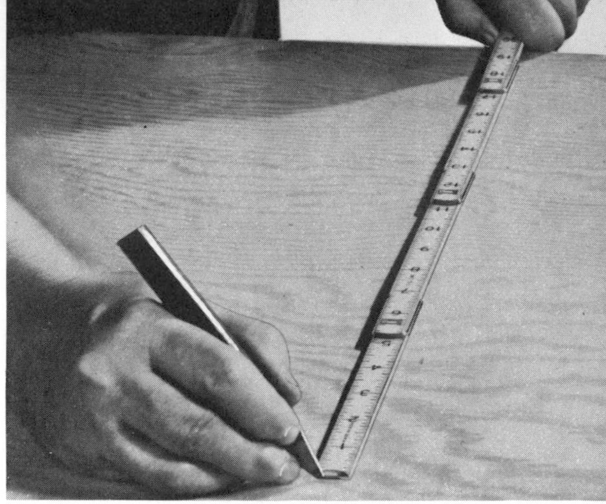

6–28. Frequently, several pieces of the same length are needed. It is easier and more convenient to mark them at the same time as shown here. Hold the try square over the ends to align them before marking the correct length.

6–29. Measuring the correct width of stock with a zigzag rule. On narrow widths, a try square is the marking tool. Place your left thumb on the correct width and hold this firmly against one edge of the stock while you mark the width with a sharp pencil.

MEASURING AND MARKING STOCK FOR CUTTING TO WIDTH

Decide on the width of stock you need. Hold the rule at right angles to the truest edge of the stock and measure the correct width. Figure 6–29. This can also be done with a try square. Do this at several points along the stock; then hold a straightedge over these points and connect them. Figure 6–30.

A framing square may be used to measure the width of stock needed. Another method of marking the width of rough stock is to hold a rule to the correct width between the thumb and forefinger. Then guide it along the truest edge of the stock with a pencil held against the end of the rule. Figure 6–31.

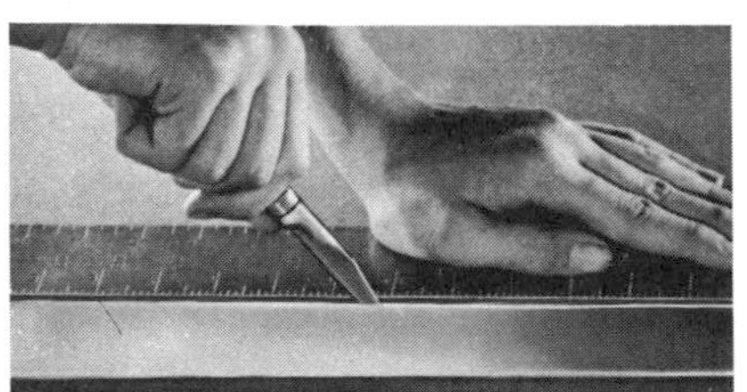

6–30. After several points have been indicated, a straightedge is held over these points and a knife or pencil used to mark the correct width. In doing this be careful that the straightedge doesn't slip. Courtesy the Jam Handy Organization.

6–31. Laying out the width of stock. Hold the rule in one hand. Hold the pencil in your other hand against the end of the rule and slide both along at the same time.

DIVIDING A BOARD INTO EQUAL PARTS

To divide a board into two or more equal parts, hold a rule at an angle

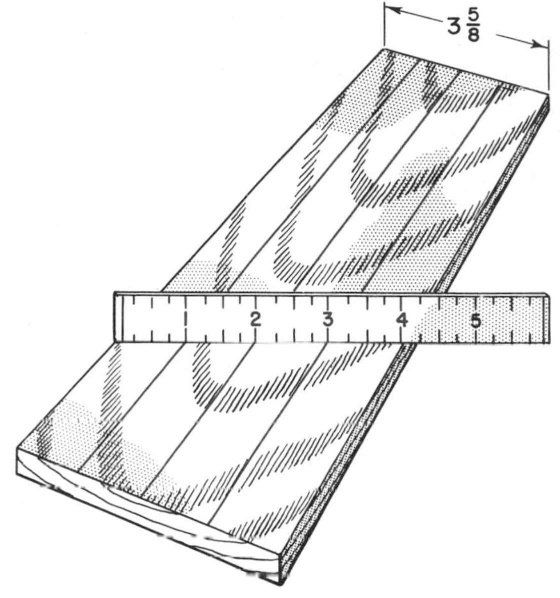

6–32. The proper method of dividing a board into several equal parts. This piece is 3 inches wide and is divided into four parts. The end of the rule is held over one edge of the board and the rule shifted at an angle until the 4-inch mark is over the other edge. Then by placing a mark at the 1-, 2-, and 3-inch marks, the board is divided equally into four parts.

across the face of the stock until the inch marks evenly divide the space. Figure 6–32. The board must be true along both sides for this to work.

CAN YOU ANSWER THESE QUESTIONS ON MEASURING AND MARKING OUT THE ROUGH STOCK?

1. Name two rules used for measuring short distances.
2. The carpenter usually employs what square?
3. Give the parts of a try square. List three uses.
4. When is a framing square used in the woodshop?
5. The sliding T bevel can be used in a way that no other layout tool can. What is this use?
6. Why is the lead pencil the most commonly used tool for marking on wood?
7. What kind of knife is best for marking wood before making a fine cut?
8. The scratch awl is a marking tool but is also used for what other job?
9. How many sixteenths in 1¼ inches?
10. Why is the bench vise frequently lined with wood inserts?
11. To secure the most accurate measurement, should the rule be held flat or on edge?
12. For measuring longer lengths, why is it better practice to measure with a zigzag rule or steel tape than with a bench rule?
13. Why do you square a line across a board with a try square or framing square rather than with a rule?
14. Describe the method of dividing a board into equal parts.

Section II

UNIT 7. CUTTING OUT ROUGH STOCK

For cutting stock into unfinished pieces you will need either a ripsaw or crosscut saw and sometimes both. Figure 7–1. If a circular saw is available, much time can be saved.

SAWS

The saw used for cutting across grain is the crosscut and the one for cutting with the grain is the ripsaw.

The *crosscut saw*. The teeth of the crosscut saw are shaped like little knife blades. Figure 7–2. They are bent alternately to right and left. This is called the "set" of the saw. When you use a crosscut saw with the proper set, the outside edges of the teeth cut the small fibers on either side and the center of the saw removes these fibers to form the saw *kerf*. Figure 7–3. The teeth are bent in this way to make them wider than the saw itself;

7–1. A high-quality handsaw. It is always wise practice to buy a good grade. With proper maintenance, it will give years of service.

7–2. An enlarged view of a crosscut saw blade section, showing the knifelike shape of the teeth. Looking at the blade from the top, the teeth are bent alternately to the left and right.

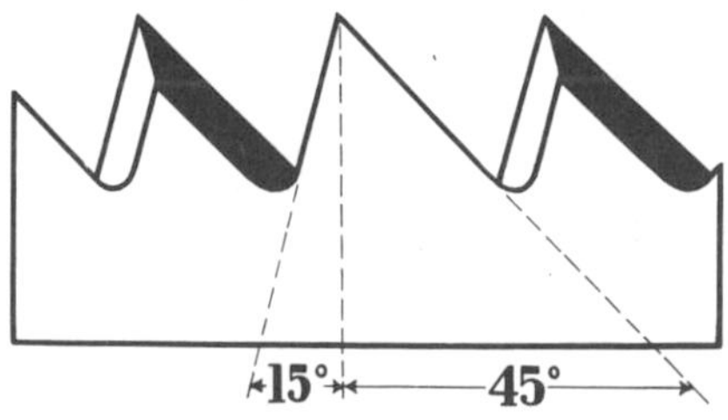

7–3. Here you see how the teeth of the saw blade form a kerf that is wider than the blade.

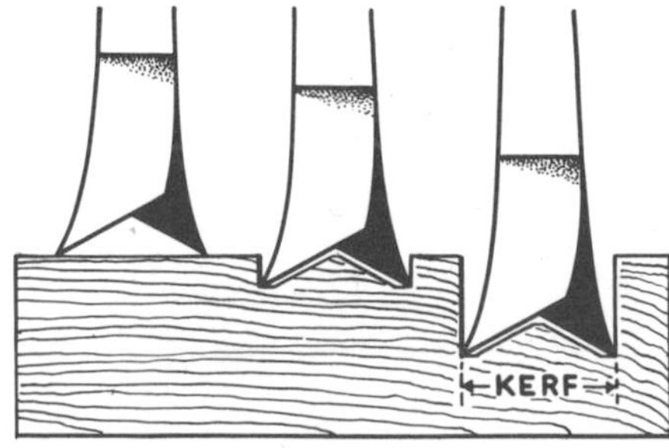

7–4. "Blown-up" example of how a crosscut saw performs its cutting operation. The beginning cut makes two grooves if drawn lightly over the surface.

7–5. There is always one more point to the inch than there are teeth. The fewer the number of points *to the inch*, the rougher the cut.

7–6. Ripsaw teeth cut like vertical chisels. First, on one side of the set, small pieces of the wood are cut loose across the grain and pushed out. Then, on the other side, the tooth following plows out a similar bit of material.

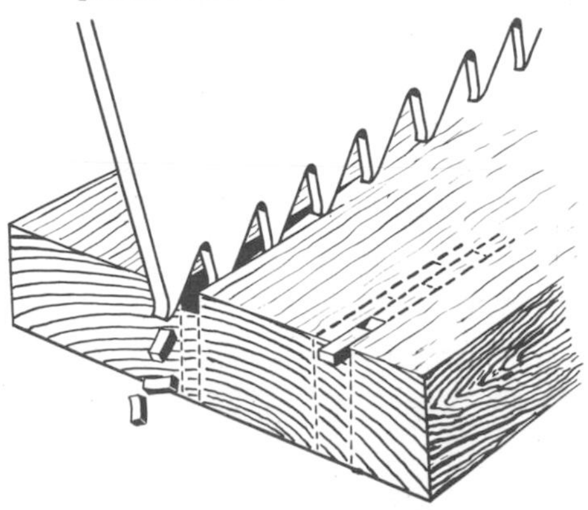

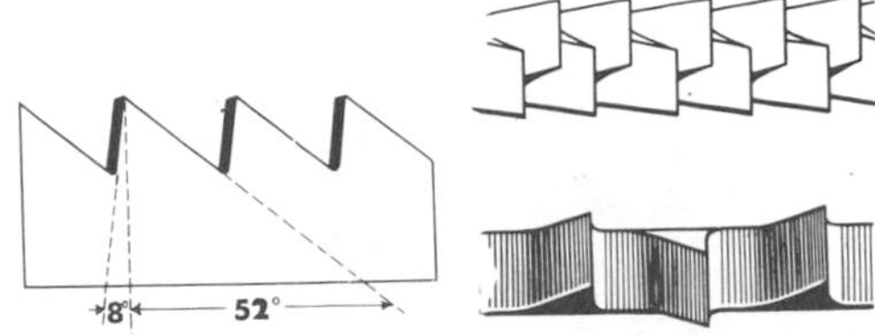

7–7. Ripsaw teeth are designed to cut with the grain. The teeth appear as a series of chisel edges, when you look at the edge of a ripsaw. Note that the teeth are filed straight across.

this keeps the saw from buckling or scraping. Figure 7–4.

Crosscut saws come in many different lengths, but the easiest size to handle is one about 20 to 26 inches long. If you are cutting rather wet, green wood, use a saw with about five or six points to the inch. There is always one more point to the inch than there are teeth, as you can see in Figure 7–5. For hard, dry wood, a finer saw with perhaps seven, eight, or nine points to the inch is best.

The *ripsaw*. The ripsaw is used to cut with the grain. Figure 7–6. It has chisel like teeth that form the saw kerf by cutting the ends of the fibers. Figures 7–7 and 7–8. A ripsaw used for ordinary woodworking ought to

7–8. This shows the chisel-like action of ripsaw teeth.

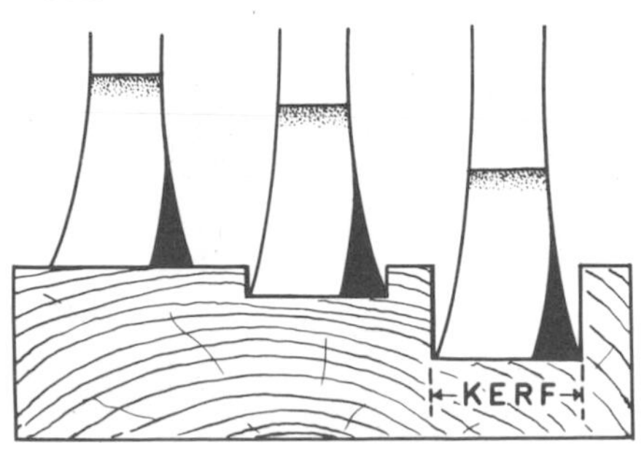

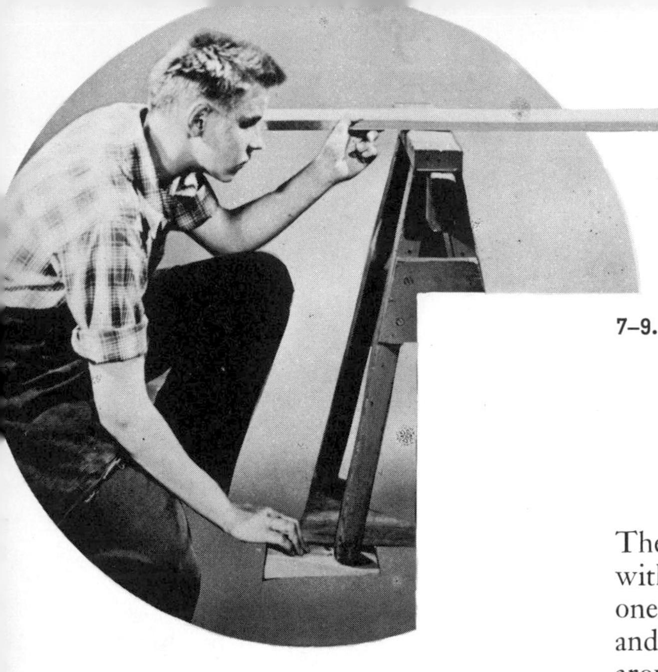

7–9. If long stock is being cut, place it over two sawhorses with the cutting line extending just beyond one of the horses. Never try to make a cut in between the supports. Courtesy the Jam Handy Organization.

be 24 to 26 inches long with 5½ points per inch.

SAWING LONG STOCK TO LENGTH

1. Laying out the cutting line. If the stock must be cut from stock 8 to 16 feet long, the board should be laid across two sawhorses. Mark the cutting line and place this point beyond the top of one of the sawhorses. Figure 7–9.

2. Beginning the cut. Place your left knee over the board to hold it. Then grasp the handle of the saw with the forefinger straight out on one side of the handle and the thumb and other fingers clamped tightly around the handle opening. Put your left thumb against the smooth surface of the blade to guide the saw in starting. Figure 7–10. Start the saw near the handle and draw up on it to begin the kerf. Hold the saw at an angle of about 45 degrees to the stock. Figure 7–11. Make sure the cut is started just outside the measuring line, to keep the kerf in the waste stock.

3. Precautions to take in beginning the cut. If you try to begin the cut on the downward stroke immediately, you may find that the saw

7–10. Starting a cut. The thumb of one hand is held against the smooth surface of the blade to guide the saw as it is being drawn toward you. Courtesy the Jam Handy Organization.

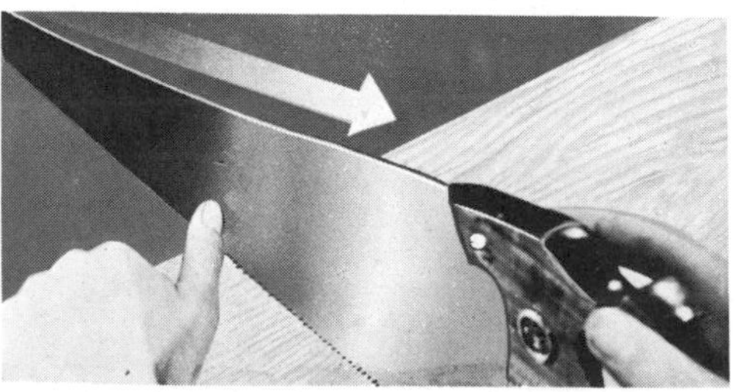

7–11. Hold the crosscut saw at an angle of about 45 degrees to the stock.

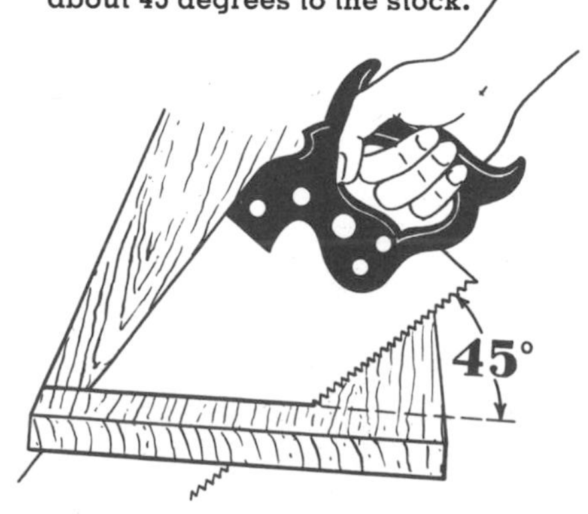

7–12. A way to keep the saw cut square with the face of the board. The operator places the handle of the try square firmly on the face of the wood and then slides it along until the blade of the try square comes in contact with the blade of the saw, to check it for squareness.

jumps out of place to cut your hand or nick the wood. Therefore, draw up on the saw once or twice before you begin the cutting. When cutting, establish a steady, even movement. Do not force the saw. If it is sharpened properly, its own weight is enough to make it cut correctly.

4. Making the cut. Make sure that you are cutting square with the surface of the board. If you are a beginner, you should hold a try square against the side of the saw blade to check it. Figure 7–12. As you saw, watch the line and not the saw itself. Blow the sawdust away from the line so you can see it. If the saw starts to go wrong, twist the handle slightly to get it back on the line. When you have cut almost through the board, hold the end of the board to be cut off while you make the last few cuts. This will keep the board from splitting off before the saw kerf is complete. Figure 7–13.

CUTTING SHORT PIECES OF STOCK TO LENGTH

If you are working with short lengths of stock, you will be cutting them to length with the work held in a vise. Figure 7–14. Place the stock in the vise in a flat position with the cutting line sticking out just a little bit from the left side of the vise. Hold and start the saw in the same way as before. You will do a good job if you follow the same directions given above.

CUTTING LONG PIECES OF STOCK TO WIDTH

Sometimes lumber is too wide and must be cut to width. For cutting

7–13. Taking the last few cuts in sawing off a board. Notice that you should hold the stock to be cut off in one hand while sawing with the other. In this way, the wood will not crack off before the saw kerf is completed. Courtesy the Jam Handy Organization.

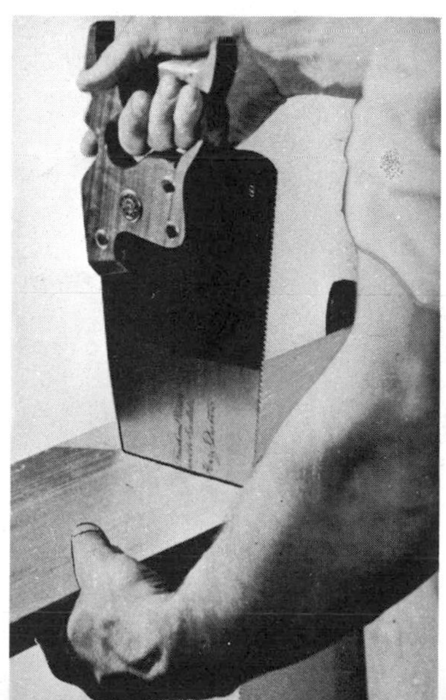

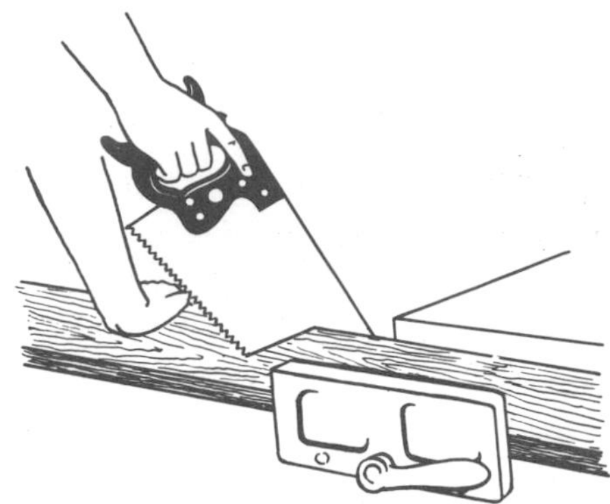

7–14. **Cutting stock to length with the work clamped in a vise.**

along the grain of the wood you will use a ripsaw. Short stock is easily handled, but if the stock is long, place it over two sawhorses. Because the teeth are different from the crosscut, the saw should be held at an angle of about 60 degrees. Figure 7–15. As you cut a long piece of stock to width, the saw kerf may close in behind the saw and cause binding. Figure 7–16. Placing a little wedge at the beginning of the saw kerf will help keep it open. Move the wedge along as you proceed.

7–15. **Hold a ripsaw at an angle of about 60 degrees when cutting to width.**

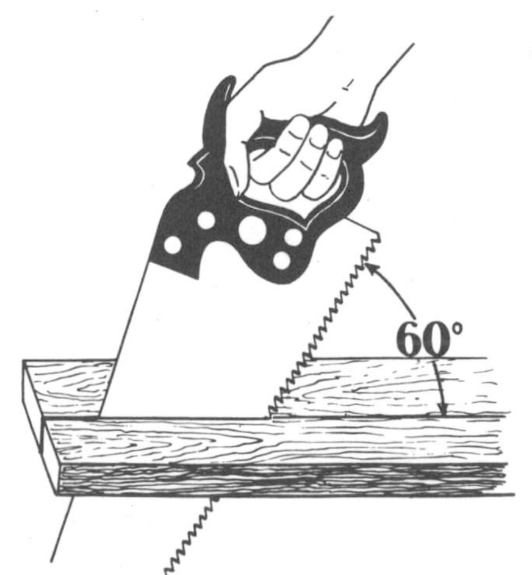

CUTTING SHORT LENGTHS TO WIDTH

If a short length is to be ripped, place it in the vise as in Figure 7–17. The sawing should not be done too far above the surface of the vise, because this causes too much vibration. Begin with the board near the top of the vise and move it up a little at a time as you continue your work.

CUTTING PLYWOOD

Place the plywood with the finished face up. Use a saw having about ten points per inch. Support the panel firmly so that it won't sag. You can reduce splitting out of the underside by putting a length of scrap lumber under the saw line. Use a sharp saw and hold it at a low angle to do the cutting. Figure 7–18.

7–16. **Ripping a board with the work held over sawhorses. As the saw progresses, place a little wedge at the beginning of the saw kerf to hold it open. You may have to move it along as you work.** Courtesy the Jam Handy Organization.

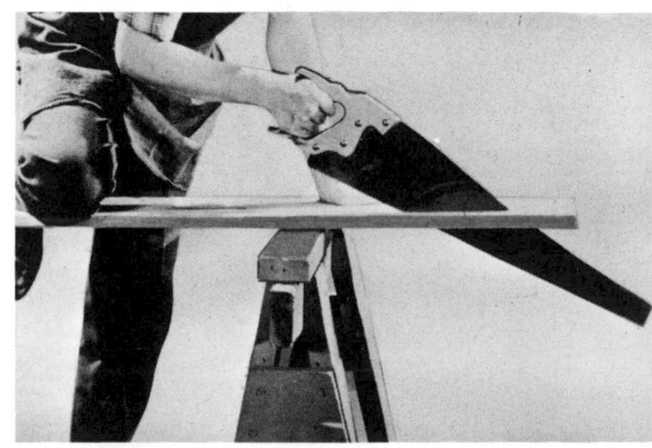

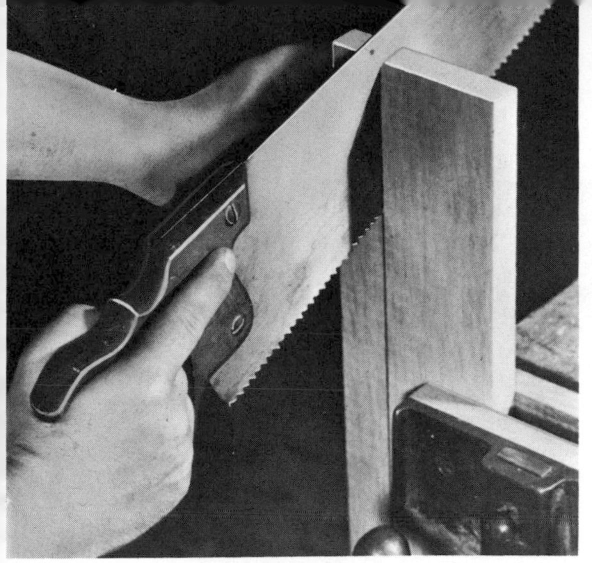

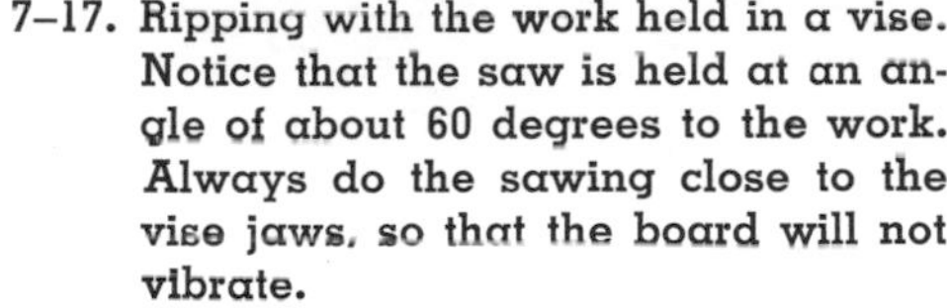

7–17. Ripping with the work held in a vise. Notice that the saw is held at an angle of about 60 degrees to the work. Always do the sawing close to the vise jaws, so that the board will not vibrate.

7–18. When hand sawing, place plywood with the finished face up, using a sharp saw having ten to fifteen points to the inch. Make sure the panel does not sag during the cutting. Hold the saw at a low angle.

CAN YOU ANSWER THESE QUESTIONS ON CUTTING OUT ROUGH STOCK?

1. There are two kinds of handsaws. Name them and tell what the parts of a handsaw are.
2. Why must a saw have the proper set in order to cut correctly?
3. A saw with five points to the inch would be best for cutting wet, green wood. Why?
4. What does a ripsaw tooth resemble?
5. If you could have only one saw for your shop, which one would you choose?
6. Why shouldn't the cutting line on a long board be placed between the sawhorses?
7. At what angle to the stock should you hold the crosscut saw?
8. To start a cut, should you push down or draw up on the saw? Why?
9. Which should you watch, the action of the saw or the cutting line?
10. What is a saw kerf?
11. Why does the crosscut saw have knifelike teeth?
12. When a saw binds or sticks, what is the most likely cause? How do you prevent it?
13. Tell how you can prevent the board from splitting off just before the saw cut is completed.
14. How is plywood handled in sawing? What support may be required under the saw line? Why?

Section III
Completing the Squaring Operations

The third 7 steps in hand woodworking—what you must know and be able to do.

8. Everything about a plane: its parts, the many kinds and how they differ, why we keep the iron sharp, how to put a plane together so it is ready to work.

9. The first surface: how to tell if it has warp or wind and how to remove it, locking the board in place, how to plane the surface true and smooth, and how to check it.

10. Working to width and thickness: which edge to choose first, what plane to choose, holding the stock, using a marking gauge, how to hold the plane correctly, how to do planing, and planing the stock to thickness and width.

11. Learning to cut end grain: why it is more difficult to cut, cutting with the block plane, how to plane end grain, how to check.

12. Making a very fine saw cut: how to use the backsaw, the dovetail saw, the handy bench hook; how to do crosscutting and ripping with a backsaw.

13. Gluing up stock: how wood is prepared for gluing, how to know what glue to select, clamps, different ways of joining wood with glue, and how to do the gluing.

14. Correct procedure for squaring up stock: the three different methods that can be followed.

Every piece of wood you use must be true, smooth, and square on two or more surfaces.

Lumber sometimes comes to the shop exactly as it is cut in the sawmill, with all surfaces rough; but more often it has been run through a planer and the sides are surfaced or dressed. Even these surfaces must be planed a little by hand to make sure that they are true and smooth.

When stock is not large enough in either thickness or width, you will need to glue up to form larger pieces before doing any squaring. See the "box" above. Further woodworking steps are on pp. 15, 43, 94, 108, 132, 143, 170, 219, 244.

Section III

UNIT 8. ASSEMBLING AND ADJUSTING A PLANE

After the pieces are sawed, they are rough and need to be planed smooth. For most of your work you will begin with stock that has been surfaced on two sides (S2S) at the mill. However, if you look closely at this surface you will see small mill or knife marks (waves) made by the rotating cutter of the planer or surfacer. Figure 8–1. These must be removed before using the stock in any project. Enough hand planing must be done to remove these mill marks completely. If you do not hand plane the surface, these marks will show up after you have applied a finish.

PARTS OF A PLANE

The plane is perhaps the most complicated hand woodworking tool you will use. It takes more care, attention, and adjustment than any other tool. Figure 8–2 is an illustration of the major parts.

The body of the plane is made of cast steel. The *base* or *bottom*, as it is sometimes called, is either smooth or ribbed. There is no difference between these two planes, except that some woodworkers feel that the plane with the ribbed base works a little better.

Right behind the opening in the plane is a *frog* that provides the support for the plane iron. This frog contains two adjustments. A *brass knurled nut* adjusts the depth of cut or regulates the thickness of the shavings. A long slender lever, called the *lateral adjusting lever*, provides for the sidewise adjustment of the cutter.

8–1. Exaggerated mill or knife marks that are made by the planer or surfacer. These must be removed by hand planing.

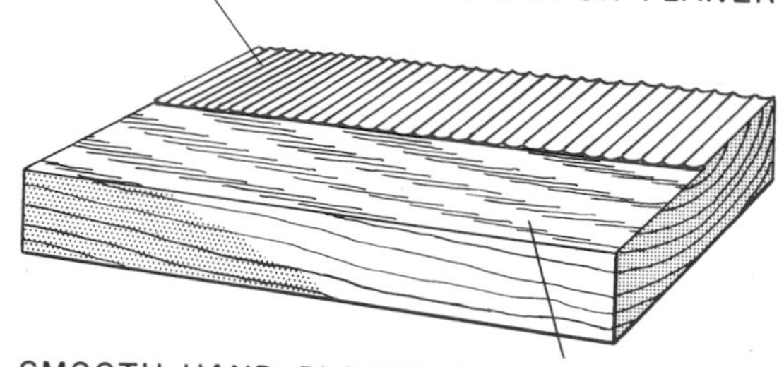

8–2. Study the parts of this plane, as you will need to know them when learning to use it.

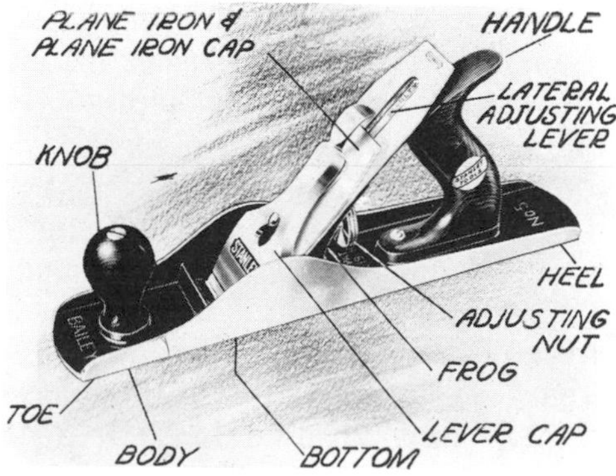

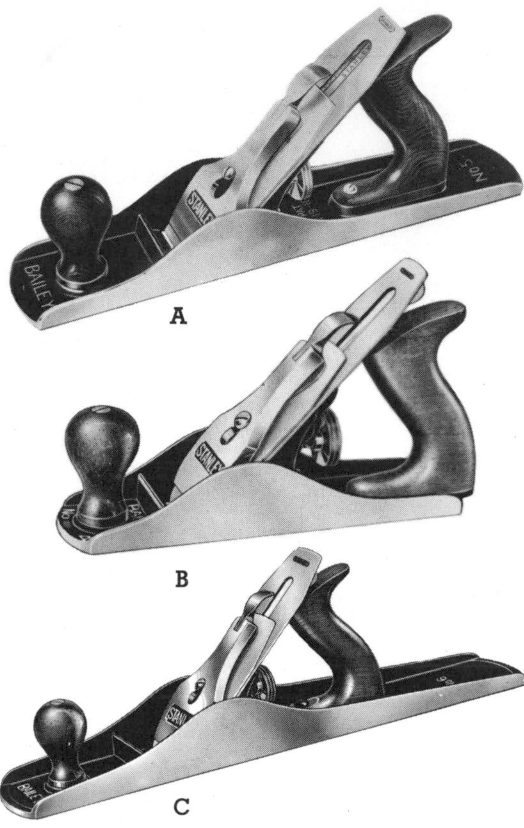

8–3. Three types of hand planes. A. This is a jack plane, which has a bed 14 or 15 inches long. It can be used to true the edges of boards and for general planing. B. This is a smooth plane which can be purchased in lengths from 7 to 9 inches. It is good for smoothing and finishing work for which a light plane is preferred. C. This is the fore or jointer plane. It is the type used to obtain a true surface on long edges in preparation for gluing up stock.

The *double plane* iron consists of the plane iron itself, sometimes called the cutter, and the plane iron cap. The plane iron fits over the frog and is held firmly with a *lever cap.*

KINDS OF BENCH PLANES

There are three common types of bench planes, all very similar. The big difference is in their lengths. Figures 8–3a, b, and c. The *jack plane* is from 11½ to 15 inches long. This tool is for all types of general planing. The *smooth plane* is the same, except that it ranges from 7 to 9 inches in length. The *fore* and *jointer* planes are much longer, from 18 to 24 inches. These are especially useful for planing long edges straight, as in fitting large doors. They are used frequently for jointing long pieces of stock before gluing them up.

TESTING A PLANE IRON FOR SHARPNESS

Check the plane iron or cutter to be sure it is sharp. One way to do this is to sight along the edge. A sharp blade will not reflect any light. Another method is to cut a piece of paper with it. Figure 8–4. It can also be tested on your thumbnail. Let the cutting edge rest on your nail and then push it lightly. If the blade tends to cling to the nail, it is sharp; but if it slides easily it needs sharpening or whetting. You should never use a dull plane iron. Sharpen it before you assemble the plane. (See the unit on sharpening hand tools.)

8–4. One method of checking a plane for sharpness. The blade will cut paper when it is sharp. Courtesy the Jam Handy Organization.

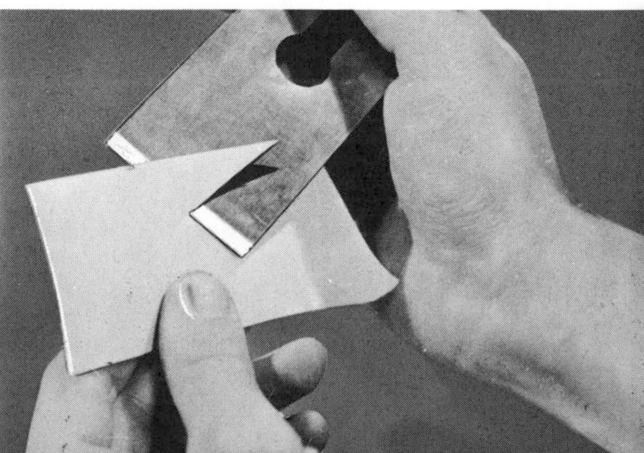

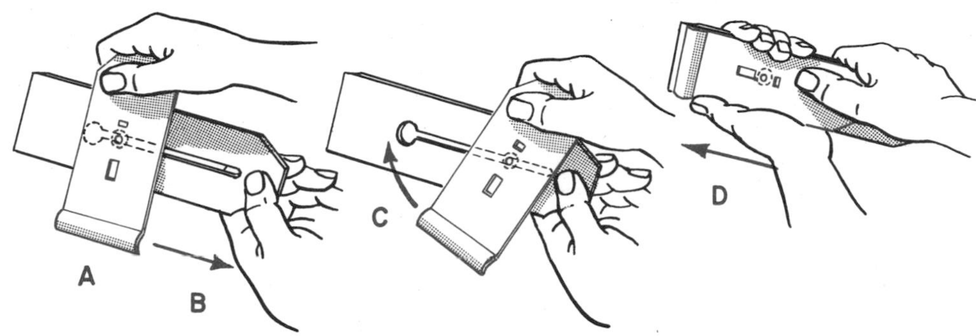

8–5. The correct method of assembling a double plane iron. A. Hold the plane iron in one hand, with the bevel side down. Place the plane iron cap at right angles to it and drop the set screw through the large opening. B. Slide the plane iron cap back as far as it will go and then, C, turn it so it is parallel to the plane iron. D. Move the plane iron cap to within about 1/16 inch of the cutting edge. Then tighten the set screw with a screw driver or the lever cap.

ASSEMBLING THE DOUBLE PLANE IRON

Hold the iron in your left hand in a vertical position with the bevel away from you. Place the plane iron cap at right angles to the plane iron and drop the setscrew into the plane iron through the large opening. With the plane iron cap still at right angles, slide it back and away from the cutting edge. Turn the plane iron cap parallel to the plane iron. Slip it forward until it is about 1/16 inch away from the cutting edge for finished work. Figure 8–5. Make sure that you do not injure the cutting edge of the plane iron by shoving the cap too far forward. Tighten the setscrew firmly.

The plane iron cap serves two purposes. It helps to stiffen or strengthen the plane iron and serves as a chip breaker. Figure 8–6.

8–6. The plane iron cap must be properly fitted to the plane iron so that chips of wood do not get between the two parts.

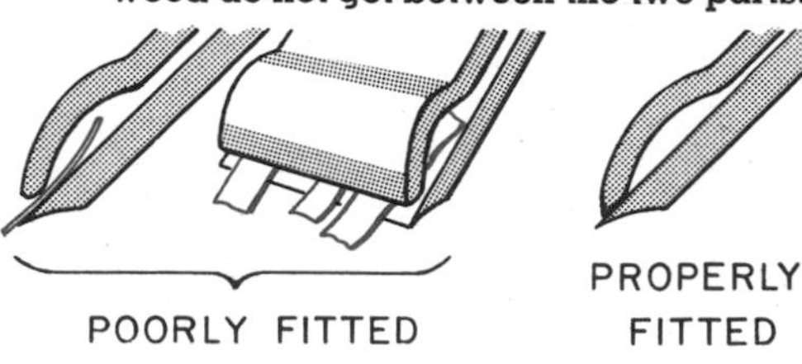

INSERTING THE PLANE IRON IN THE PLANE

Insert the double plane iron in the plane with the bevel side down. There are several things that you must watch when doing this. Figure 8–7.

8–7. Inserting the plane iron in the plane. Be extremely careful in doing this to keep the cutting edge from becoming nicked.

8–8. **Steps in installing a double plane iron in the plane. A. The iron is assembled and placed over the frog. B. The iron is in place and the cap is inserted. C. The plane iron cap holds the other plane iron in place.**

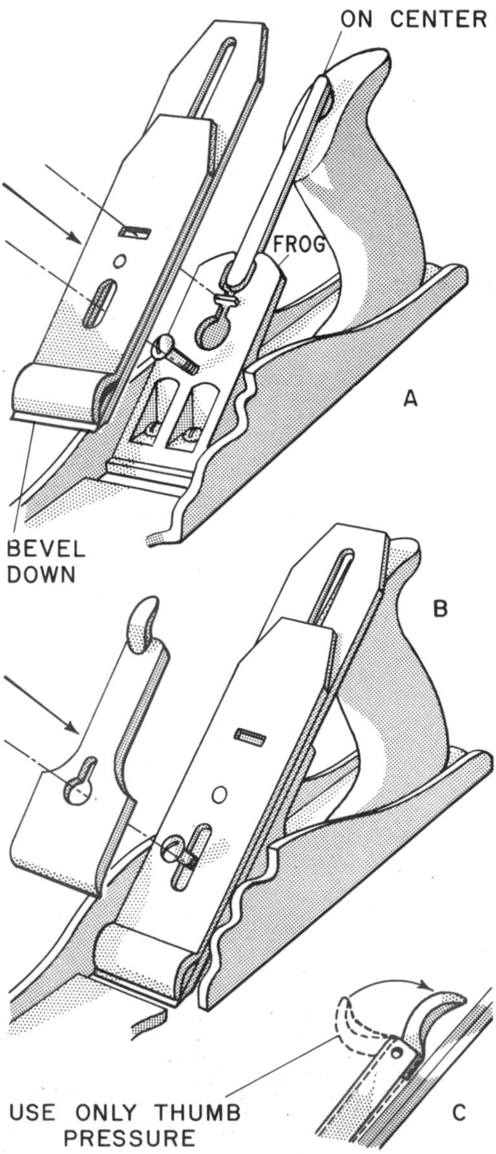

First, don't hit the cutting edge on the body of the plane as you insert it over the frog; second, make sure that the slot in the plane iron cap fits over the little Y adjustment; and third, check to see that the roller on the lateral adjustment slips into the slot of the plane iron.

Next, pull the little thumb-adjusting cam on the lever cap up at right angles (Figure 8–8); then slip the lever cap over the lever cap screw on the frog. Push the thumb-adjusting cam down to fasten the plane iron securely in the plane. If you find it must be forced, you probably need to unscrew the lever cap screw just a little bit or, if it is too loose, to tighten it a little.

ADJUSTING THE PLANE

The plane should be adjusted before beginning the cutting and again several times while the planing is being done. To make the first adjustment, turn the plane upside down with the bottom about eye level. Turn the brass knurled nut until the plane iron appears just beyond the bottom of the plane. Then, with the lateral

8–9. **Adjusting the plane. Hold it with the bed or bottom at eye level. Turn the knurled brass screw until the plane iron just appears.** Courtesy the Jam Handy Organization.

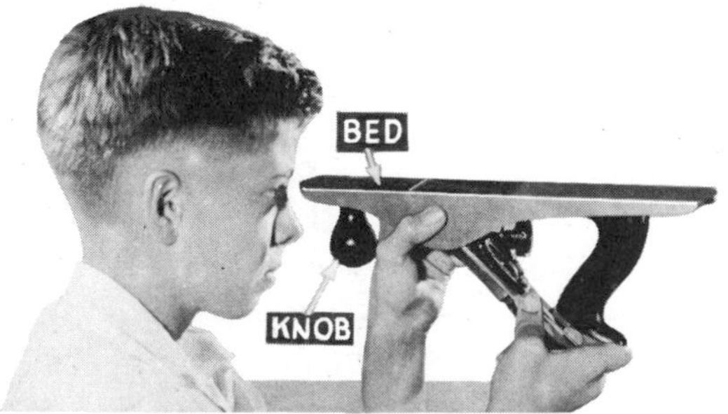

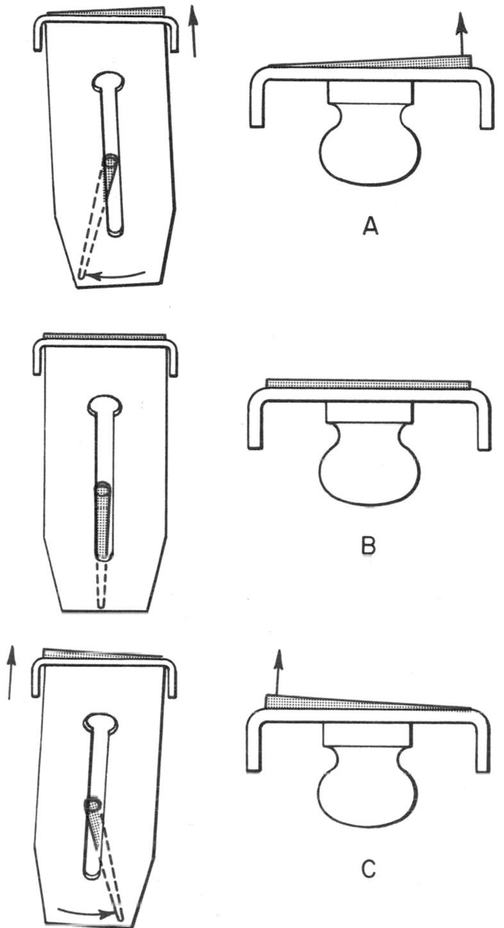

adjustment lever, move the blade to one side or the other until it is parallel to the bottom. Figures 8–9 and 8–10.

The experienced woodworker then tries the plane on a piece of scrap stock to see how it cuts, adjusting it to the chip he wants. For rough planing and when much stock is to be removed, set the plane deeper. When you are truing up a surface and making it smooth, a light cut that forms a feathery shaving is best.

8–10. Move the lateral adjustmont from left to right until the plane iron is parallel to the bed. A. Moving the lateral adjustment to the left raises the right side of the plane iron. B. The plane iron is parallel to the bottom. C. Moving the lateral adjustment lever to the right raises the left side of the plane higher.

CAN YOU ANSWER THESE QUESTIONS ON ASSEMBLING AND ADJUSTING A PLANE?

1. Name the important parts of a plane. Why is it necessary to know these parts?
2. Name the three common types of bench planes. What is the major use of each?
3. Why do you suppose the jack plane is best for the school shop?
4. Tell three ways of testing the sharpness of the plane iron.
5. To do finished planing, how far should the cap be set from the cutting edge? How far for rough work?
6. What is the purpose of the plane iron cap?
7. Describe in detail the steps to follow in fastening a plane iron in a plane.
8. Tell how to make the depth adjustment on a plane.

Section III

UNIT 9. PLANING A SURFACE

The first surface you choose to plane should be the best flat surface of the piece. It should be free of flaws and should be the side with the most interesting grain, because it will show.

INSPECTING A SURFACE FOR WARP

Warp is any variation from a true or plane surface. It includes crook, cup, bow, wind or twist or any combination of these. *Crook* is a deviation edgewise from a straight line drawn from end to end. *Bow* is a deviation flatwise from a straight line drawn from end to end of a piece. *Cup* is a curve across the grain or width of a piece. A beginner can check if the board is cupped with a straightedge or the blade of a try or framing square. Figure 9–1.

Wind or *twist* in a board indicates that the board is twisted throughout its length. One way to check this is to lay the board on a level surface to see if it rocks on two corners. Another method is to place two parallel pieces of wood across the grain, one on either end of the board. Then sight along the top of the first parallel. If you can see one end of the second parallel, you know that the board has a wind. Figure 9–2. With a pencil, mark the high points of the board if it is warped or has a wind; more stock must be removed at these points.

FASTENING A BOARD IN THE VISE

If the wood is rough, you may need to take a few cuts with the plane

9–1. Checking the material to see if it is cupped.

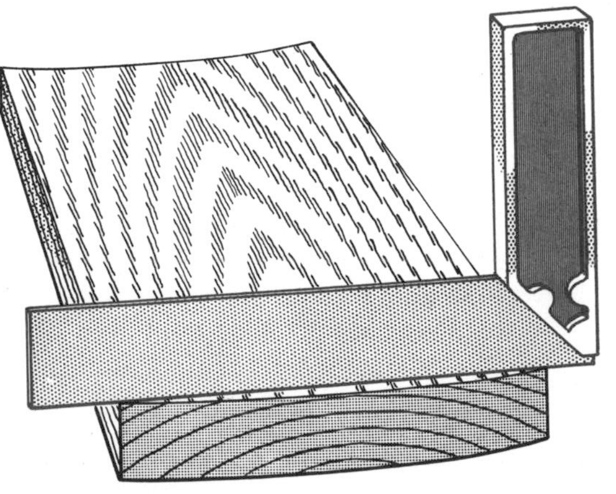

9–2. Sticks placed across either end of the board will show wind or twist.

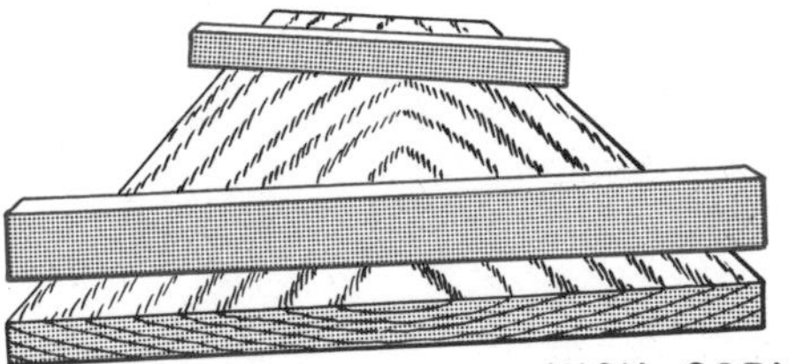

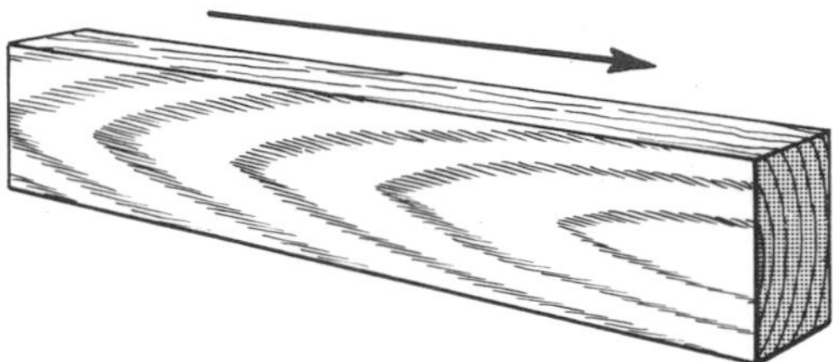

9–3. The arrow indicates the direction in which the stock should be planed.

before the direction of the grain shows. Planing against grain roughens the surface. Figure 9–3. Lock the board between the dog of the vise and the bench stop, or lay the board on top of the bench with one end supported against the bench stop. Never lock a board cross-grain, as this tends to warp it.

PLANING THE SURFACE TRUE AND SMOOTH

Grasp the knob of the plane in your left hand and the handle in your right hand. Figure 9–4. Stand just back of the work with your left foot forward. In this way you can swing your body back and forth as you plane and at the same time use a forward motion with your arms.

Place the toe or front of the plane on the board. Apply pressure to the knob at the start of the stroke. As the whole base comes in contact with the wood, apply even pressure to the knob and handle. Then, as the plane begins to leave the surface, apply more pressure to the handle. Figure 9–5. In this way you won't cut a convex curve in the board.

Lift the plane off the board on the return stroke. Don't drag the plane back to the starting position. This would dull the blade. Sometimes the plane will cut more easily if you take a shearing cut rather than a straight cut.

Work across the board gradually. If you have marked any high points,

9–4. Planing the face of a board. Note that the work is locked securely between the bench top and the top of the vise. You can tell when the plane is cutting properly by the kind of shaving being formed. The shaving should be uniform in thickness and width. The thickness of the shaving depends on the setting of the plane. For rough cutting a heavy shaving should be taken. For finished work, shavings should be light and silky. Always plane with the grain of the wood.

9–5. Proper method of applying pressure when planing. More pressure is applied to the knob at the start of the stroke and to the handle at the end of the stroke so that you don't cut a convex surface.

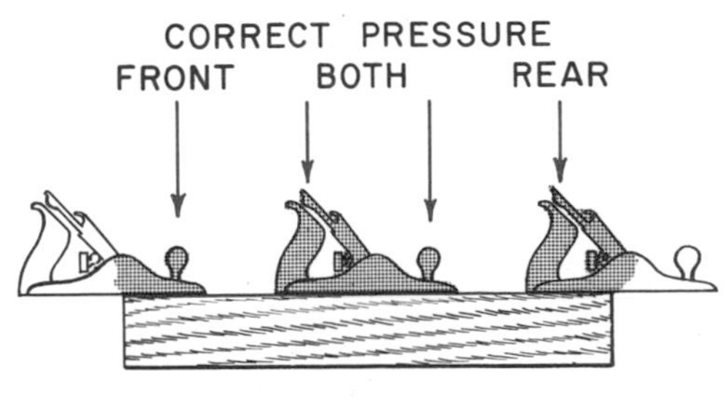

STRAIGHTEDGE

NO LIGHT SHOWS UNDER STRAIGHTEDGE

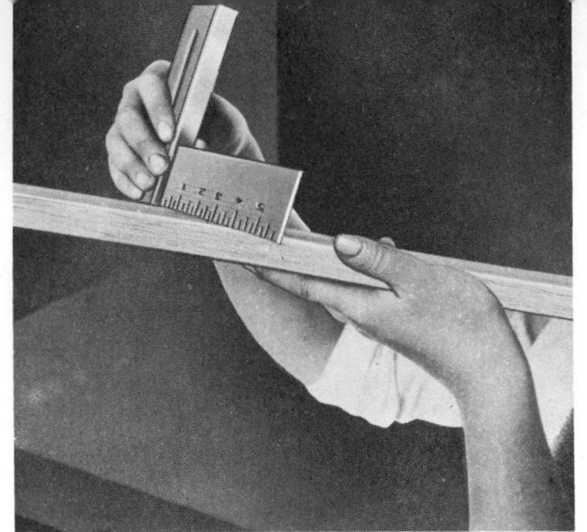

9–6a. Checking a board. Hold the board at about eye level and place a straightedge across it. If any light shows through, you know that it is a low spot. Mark the *high spot* on a board with a pencil and then plane lightly over these areas.

these will take more planing than other areas.

REMOVING WIND OR TWIST FROM A BOARD

Wind in a board requires taking a partial cut at either the beginning or end of the board.

To take a partial cut at the begin-

9–6b. Check several places across the width of the board for high and low spots.

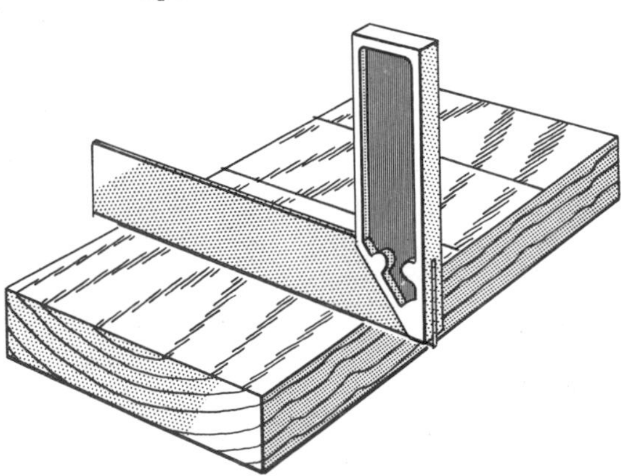

A – ACROSS

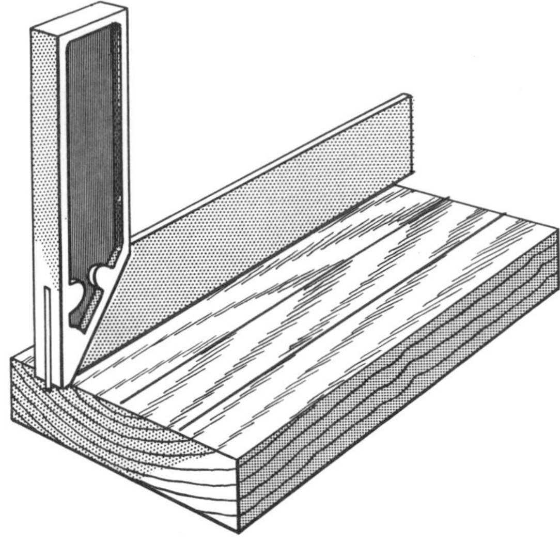

B – LENGTHWISE

9–7. Check with a straightedge from one end to the other. Make sure that the surface is straight and true.

9–8. Checking across the corners.

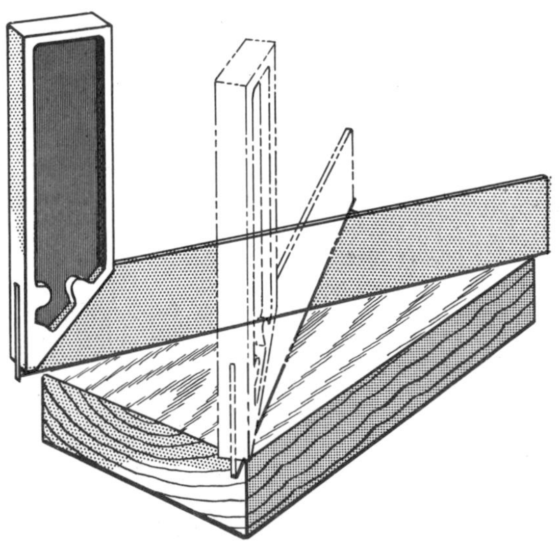

C – ACROSS CORNERS

ning of the board, begin the stroke as before. Then, as you plane along the board as far as you think necessary, slowly lift the handle to finish the cut.

To take the wind out of the end of the board, start the partial cut at some point in the center of the board. Begin with the handle held away from the surface and gradually lower it as you begin the forward motion.

CHECKING THE SURFACE

After the surface begins to get smooth, check it with a straightedge to see if it is true. Light will show through where there are low spots on the board or the straightedge will touch the high points. Figures 9–6a and 9–6b. It is well to check the total width and length every few inches and diagonally across the corners, using a pencil to mark the high points. Figure 9–7 and 9–8. Sometimes one plane stroke will remove these. Figure 9–9.

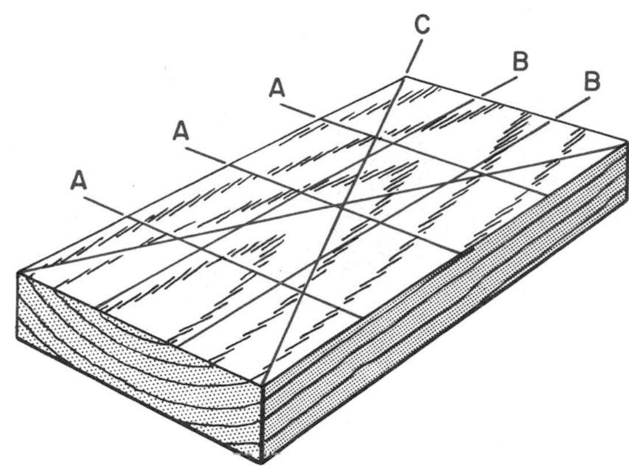

9–9. Checking the surface for flatness. Check from edge to edge, end to end, and finally across the corners.

The first surface which has been planed true and smooth is called the *face surface* or *face side*. This is the side you use as a start in squaring up stock.

CAN YOU ANSWER THESE QUESTIONS ON PLANING A SURFACE?

1. Which surface of the board is the first to be planed?
2. Can you see if a board is warped? How is this checked?
3. What are the two ways of checking wind in a board?
4. Planing against grain will roughen the board. Why?
5. What is likely to happen if the plane is dragged rather than lifted back to the starting position?
6. Tell how you would go about removing wind from a board.
7. What is the surface called that is planed first?

Section III

UNIT 10. PLANING STOCK TO WIDTH AND THICKNESS

Most project pieces must be planed to width and thickness to make the surfaces smooth and true and to bring the stock down to the finished size. In doing this, you will have constant use for a marking gauge. Figure 10–1. This tool is used for marking thickness and width on small pieces of stock. In planing to thickness and width, all measurements should be taken from the face surface or side. This surface should be marked with the number "1" or some small mark near the first edge that you are going to plane.

10–1. A marking gauge. This tool is necessary in laying out and marking the thickness and width of stock. Note: GAUGE is the preferred spelling, but some handbooks and technical magazines spell it GAGE.

10–3. Locking stock in a vise. Make sure that the stock is held firmly in the vise jaws so that there will be no movement when using the plane. Courtesy the Jam Handy Organization.

10–2. This shows the reason for using a plane with a longer bed to plane the edge of long stock. The longer plane tends to straighten out any irregularities, while the shorter plane tends to follow curves.

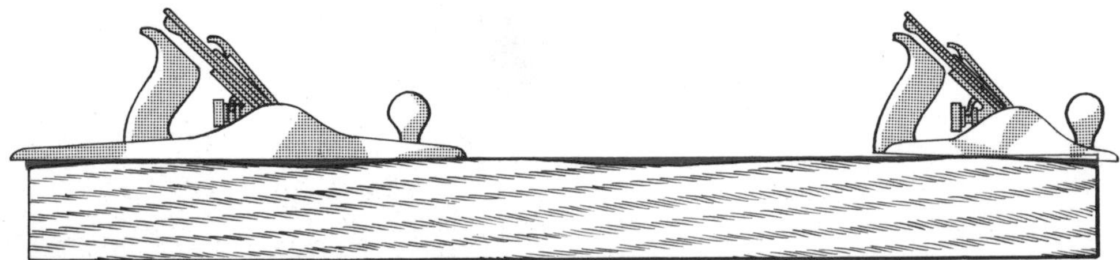

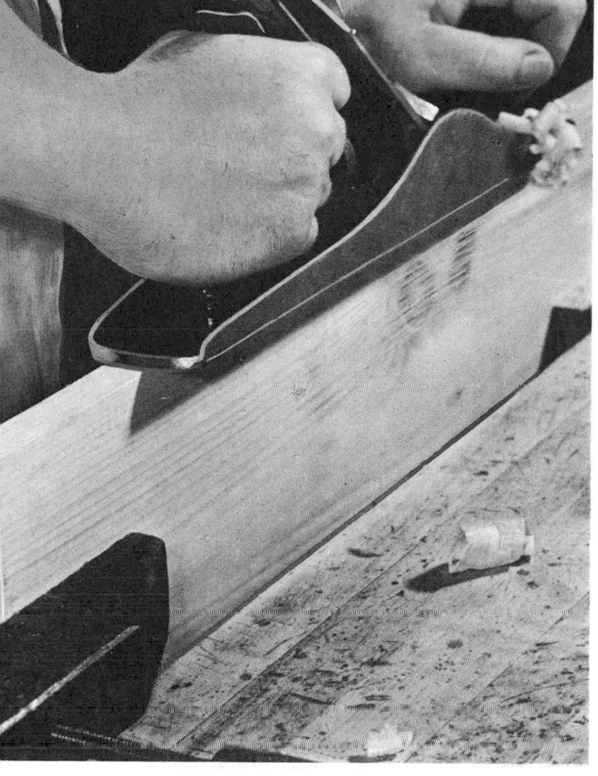

10–4. Supporting long pieces of stock when planing an edge. The hand screw is fastened to support the end of the stock while the front is locked in the vise.

SELECTING AND CHECKING THE FACE OR JOINT EDGE

Select the edge that is truest and best. With the try square held against the face surface, test the edge at several points along the stock for squareness. Also check with a straightedge along the length. Mark with a pencil the high points where you must do most of the planing.

SELECTING THE PROPER PLANE

For shorter pieces, the jack plane will be very satisfactory. In planing an edge, however, especially a long one, it is better to use a plane with a longer base such as the fore or jointer plane. As you see in Figure 10–2, the jointer plane tends to straighten the edge while the shorter plane will follow any curve that may be in the edge.

FASTENING THE WORK IN THE VISE

Lock the stock in the vise with the edge above the surface. Figure 10–3. If the stock is long, the front end should be supported by the vise and the back held in place with a hand screw as shown in Figure 10–4. Sometimes the work is held against a V block on the top of the bench. Figure 10–5.

10–5. Holding stock against a V block to do edge planing. This is especially satisfactory for planing long stock or when a vise is not available. Note how the thumb is held around the back of the knob and the fingers curled under the bottom of the plane to guide it.

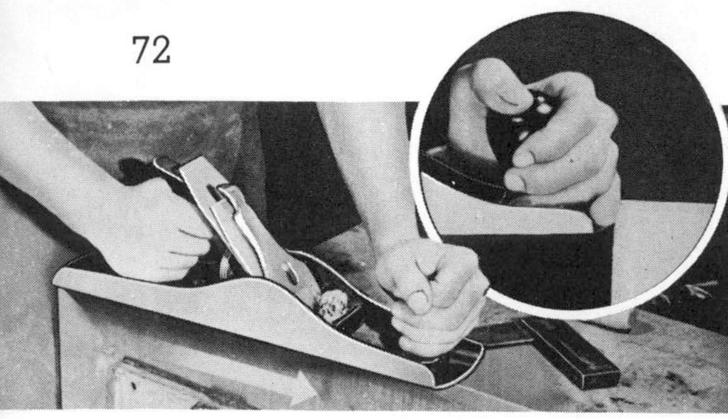

10–6. Planing the edge of a board by holding the knob firmly in one hand. When using this method, you must be extremely careful not to rock the plane. Courtesy the Jam Handy Organization.

HOLDING THE PLANE

Adjust the plane to take a very fine cut. In planing an edge you may hold the handle of the plane the same way as for surface planing. Figure 10–6. To use the second method, you can place the thumb around the back of the knob with the other fingers curled under the bottom of the plane. In this way you can use your fingers to guide the plane along the face side in keeping the plane at right angles. Figure 10–5.

10–7. Starting the cutting stroke in planing an edge. Pressure is applied to the knob. Courtesy the Jam Handy Organization.

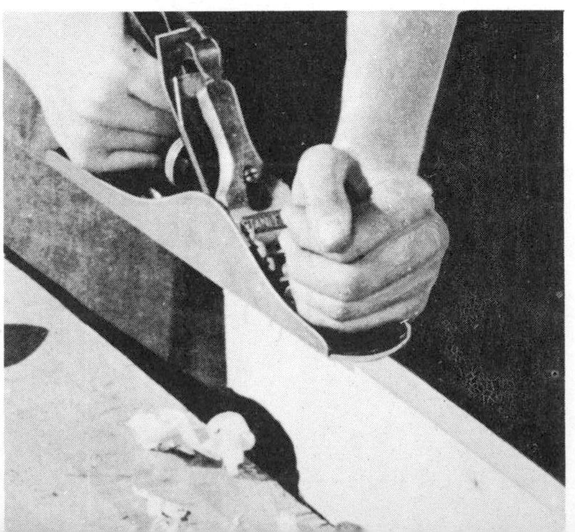

PLANING THE EDGE

Plane with the grain. First remove any high spots that you have marked. Then take long, continuous strokes to remove a thin chip all along the edge. Be sure to apply pressure on the knob in starting the stroke and on the handle when finishing it. Figure 10–7. The idea in planing this first edge is not to remove stock, but to get this edge square with the face surface and straight along its entire length. Check with the try square and straightedge as shown in Figures 10–8 and 10–9. Mark this edge with two light pencil lines to show that it is the face or joint edge.

SETTING THE MARKING GAUGE

Check the drawing for the width of stock needed and then set the marking gauge to this width. To mark stock too wide for the marking

10–8. Checking the joint edge by holding the handle of a try square against the face side or surface. Move the try square to make certain that the edge is square along its total length.

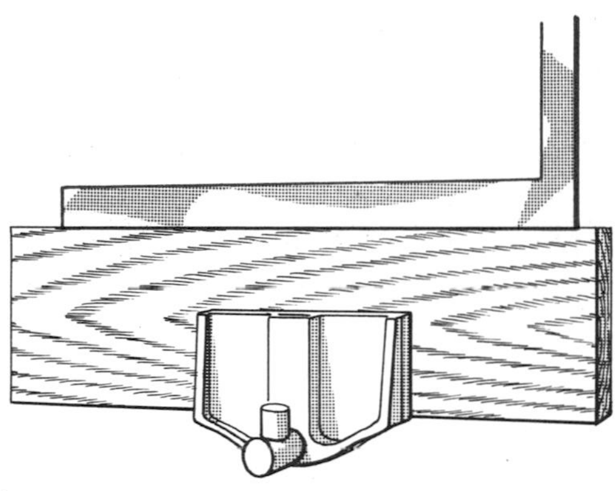

10–9. Checking an edge for straightness. This is especially important on long stock. The edge must be square with the face surface and not form a convex or concave curve. Hold the straightedge against the planed edge and sight at eye level to see if any light shows through.

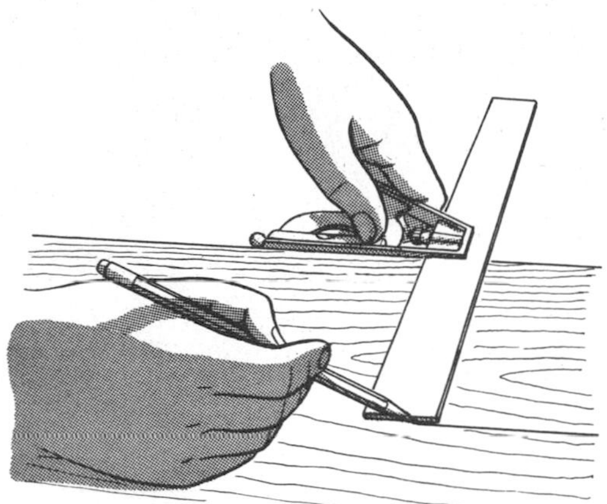

10–10. Using a combination square and pencil to mark for correct width. The carpenter uses this method.

gauge, use a pencil and a combination square. Figure 10–10. As you have noticed, the marking gauge has a scale along one surface. This scale is usually not correct. In sharpening the small spur to wedge shape by filing, the starting point of the scale becomes inaccurate. Set the head of the scale to the correct distance as shown on the beam and then lightly turn the thumbscrew. Then hold the marking gauge upside down in one hand and use the rule to check the distance from the head to the point of the spur. Figure 10–11. If the measurement is wrong, tap the head a bit one way or the other to correct it and then tighten the thumbscrew. Always recheck the measurement before using the marking gauge.

MARKING THE STOCK TO WIDTH

Hold the stock to be marked with the face surface up and the face or joint edge to your right. Place the head of the marking gauge firmly against this joint edge. Then tip the marking gauge forward with a slight twist of your wrist until the spur just touches the surface of the wood. Beginning at the end toward you, push the marking gauge forward, applying pressure as shown in Figure 10–12.

Sometimes, when widths too wide for the gauge must be marked, it will be necessary to mark the width at several points. Then hold a straight-

10–11. Setting a marking gauge. Note that the gauge is held upside down in one hand and a rule held in the other hand to check the distance from the point or spur to the head of the marking gauge.

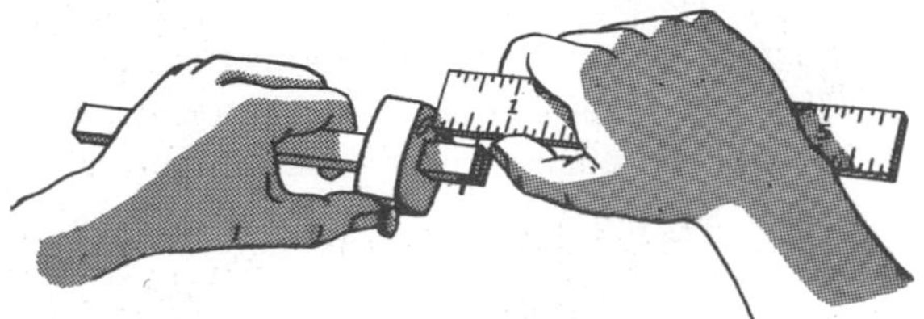

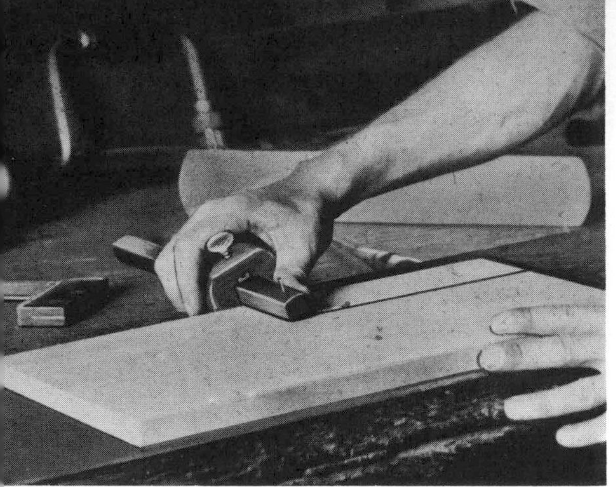

10–12. Using a marking gauge. Notice that the marking gauge is tilted slightly and that the worker is pushing it away from himself. In doing the marking, pressure should be applied to hold the head of the gauge firmly against the edge while forward pressure is applied.

edge along these points, marking a fine line with a knife.

PLANING THE SECOND EDGE

If there is much stock to be removed, the board should be ripped to within 1/8 to 3/16 inch of the finished line.

Lock the stock in the vise as described above and begin to plane the second edge. As the plane approaches the layout line, use the try square frequently to check the edge for squareness with the face surface and a straightedge to check the length. Take special care at the finished line to take light, even shavings that are the total width and length of the edge. The last cut you take should just split the dent made by the marking gauge.

MARKING THE STOCK TO THICKNESS

Check the thickness of the stock and then set the marking gauge to this measurement. Hold the head of the marking gauge against the face surface. Mark a line on both edges to indicate the proper thickness.

PLANING TO THICKNESS

Check the lines that show thickness to see if there are any spots that are higher than the rest of the board. These need extra planing. Lock the stock between the dog of the vise and the bench stop and plane these areas first. Then begin to plane the total length of the stock, working from one side to the other to bring it down to proper thickness. Planing to thickness is the same as planing the first surface, except that you must constantly check the two lines showing thickness. You should be able to hold the handle of the try square against this second surface and find that the edges are square, as they were with the face surface.

CAN YOU ANSWER THESE QUESTIONS ON PLANING STOCK TO WIDTH AND THICKNESS?

1. When is a fore or jointer plane used?
2. The first planing should be done on which edge?
3. How can a piece of long stock be supported for planing along one edge?
4. Describe the two ways of holding the knob of the plane in planing an edge.
5. What should be accomplished by planing this first edge? Should a large amount of stock be removed? Explain.

6. Describe a marking gauge and name its parts.
7. Should you depend on the marking gauge scale for setting the tool to width? Why?
8. Should the mark made by the marking gauge be heavy and deep?
9. Suppose that considerable stock must be removed to bring the stock to width. Can you tell how this should be done?
10. Would you completely remove the marking gauge line when you planed the second edge?
11. A piece of stock that has been squared to thickness and width has certain characteristics. What are these?

Section III

UNIT 11. PLANING END GRAIN

Planing end grain is harder than planing the face or edge with the grain. In planing the end, you actually cut off the tips of the wood fibers. This takes a very sharp plane iron.

When the stock to be planed can be locked in a vise, a jack plane is used. For other jobs, use the block plane.

11–1a. Here is a block plane that can be used for planing end grain and for doing small forming and shaping work. The cutter rests at a much lower angle than on other types of planes, which makes it ideal for planing across grain.

THE BLOCK PLANE

The block plane (Figure 11–1a and 11–1b) is much smaller than the others you have used so far. It has a single plane iron which is placed in the plane with the *beveled side up*. The plane iron also rests in the plane at a much lower angle than the iron in a regular plane. This makes it easier to cut end grain. As you can see, this one has no lateral adjustment, but only an adjusting screw to regulate the depth of cut. These are block planes that do have a lateral adjustment.

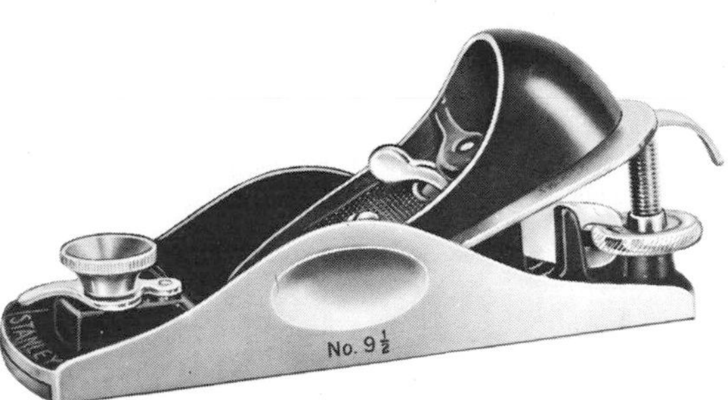

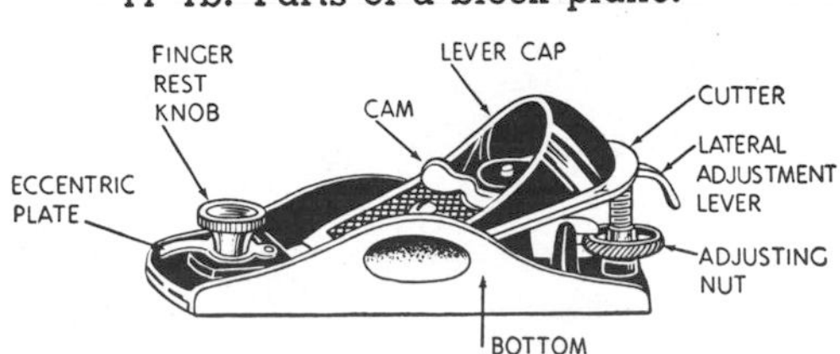

11–1b. Parts of a block plane.

11–2. **Planing end grain with a block plane. Note how the plane is held. Because of its size, the block plane is most convenient when work cannot be locked in the vise.**

A

11–3. **A. Planing end grain with a hand plane by planing halfway across and then reversing the plane to finish the cut. B. The block plane is excellent for end grain because of the low angle of the blade.**

B

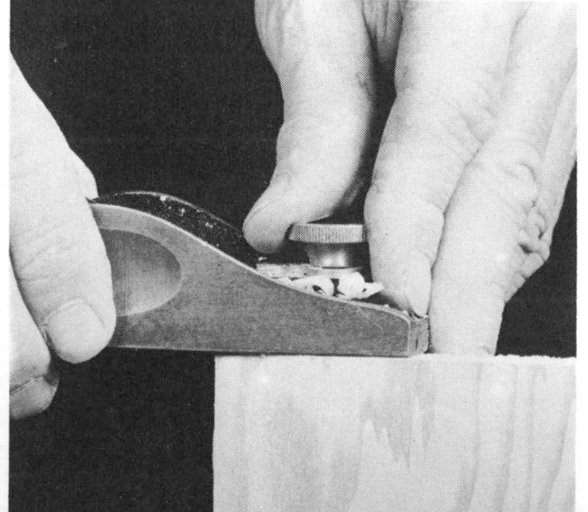

ADJUSTING THE BLOCK PLANE

The block plane is adjusted the same way as other planes, except when there is no lateral adjusting lever. To make this adjustment, loosen the plane iron cap and sight along the bottom of the plane. Then, with your fingers, press the plane iron to the right or left until it is parallel to the bottom of the plane. Tighten the lever cap screw. The depth adjustment is made the same way as on other types of planes.

USING THE BLOCK PLANE

Hold the block plane in one hand with the thumb on one side, the forefinger over the finger rest, and the other fingers on the other side. Begin from one edge to work toward the center. Figure 11–2. Begin from the other edge, doing the same. Take pains to hold the block plane square with the work. You will find that it takes effort and experience to cut end grain properly. It is best to take a shallow cut to keep the plane from jumping.

The block plane is also used for planing with the grain, especially in model work.

11–4. **Planing end grain halfway across the stock.**

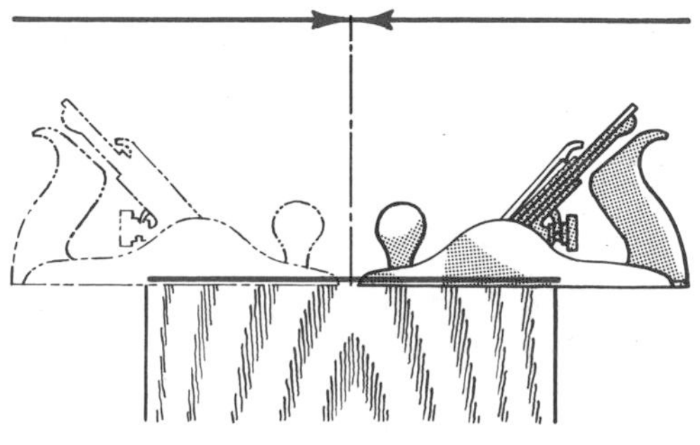

11–5a. Testing the end from the face surface. Move the try square back and forth.

PLANING END GRAIN

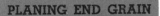

Make sure that the plane iron is very sharp. The iron cap should be set very close to the cutting edge, not over 1/32 inch. Lock the stock firmly in the vise with the end showing a little. In planing end grain, it is not possible to go completely across the end; this will split out the wood. Therefore one of the following methods should be followed:

1. Plane about halfway across the stock; then lift the handle of the plane slowly. Figure 11–3. Begin at the other end to do the same thing. Figure 11–4. Check the end for squareness with the working face and working edge. Figure 11–5a and 11–5b.

2. Plane a short bevel on the waste edge of the stock and then begin from the other side to plane all the way across. Figure 11–6.

3. Get a piece of scrap stock exactly the same thickness as the piece you are working. Lock it in the vise just ahead of the finished piece. In this way you have actually extended the end grain. Then you can plane all of the way across the end grain without fear of splitting out the piece. Figure 11–7.

Whichever method is used, frequently check the end grain from both the working face and working edge to make sure that it is square.

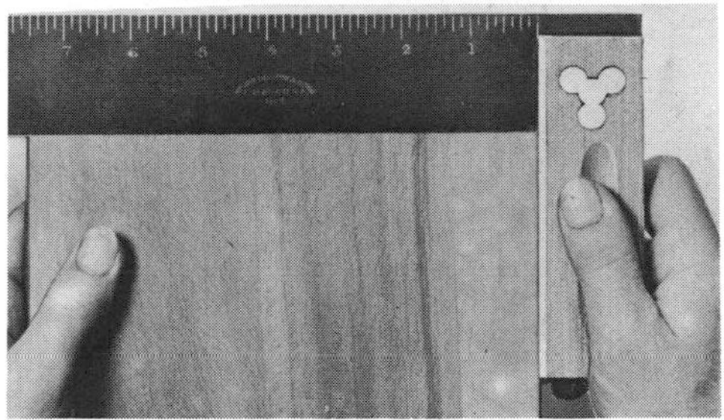

11–5b. Checking the end from the edge. Hold the try square against the joint edge to make sure that the end is square both ways.

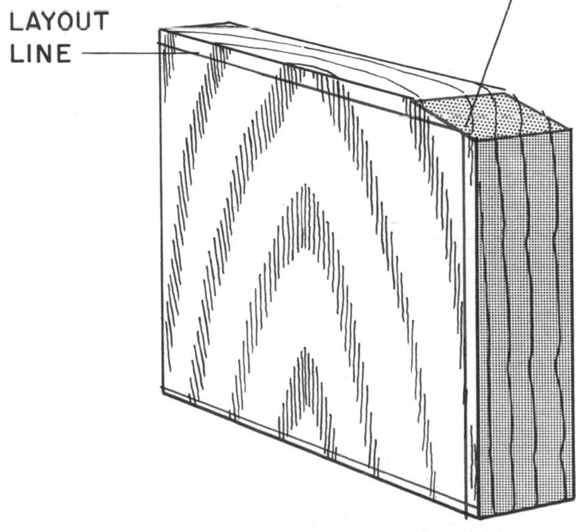

11–6. A second method of planing end grain. Note that a bevel is cut. This tends to prevent the wood from splitting out, and you can, therefore, plane completely across the end.

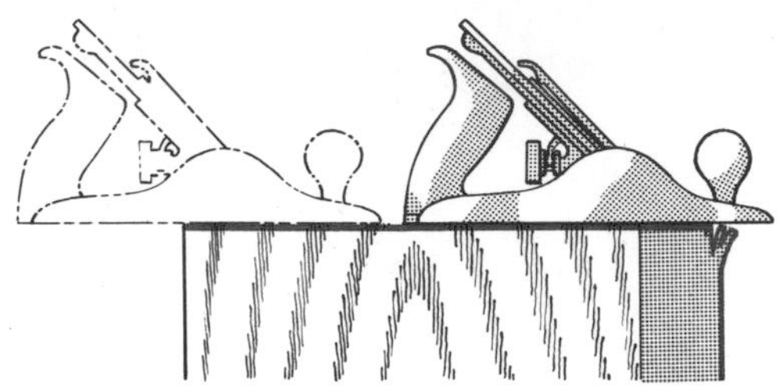

11–7. A third method of planing end grain. A scrap piece of the same thickness is placed against the edge of the piece to be planed. With this method you are actually extending the end grain.

CAN YOU ANSWER THESE QUESTIONS ON PLANING END GRAIN?

1. What is there about end grain that makes it difficult to plane?
2. How is a block plane different from other planes?
3. When would you choose a block plane to plane with the grain?
4. Describe the three ways of planing end grain.

Section III

UNIT 12. CUTTING STOCK WITH A BACKSAW

To make a very fine saw cut, as in squaring up stock or in making joints, you will use a backsaw or a dovetail saw.

THE BACKSAW AND DOVETAIL SAWS

The *backsaw* (Figure 12–1) has a very thin blade with fine teeth. It can make a very accurate cut. This saw is used to cut both across grain and with the grain. It gets its name from the fact that an extra band of metal must be put across the back to make it stiff. The *dovetail* saw is very similar to the backsaw except that it has a narrower blade and finer teeth. Figure 12–2.

THE BENCH HOOK

A "helper" that you will need with the backsaw is the bench hook. Figure 12–3. This is a piece of wood with a hook or stop on either end, one of which is shorter than the width of the board itself. When in use, the wide stop goes over the edge of the bench and the piece to be sawed is held against the shorter stop. This hook protects the top of the bench from damage by the backsaw.

LAYING OUT THE CUT-OFF LINE

Accurately lay out the location of the cut to be made, using a try square and pencil. Or, for very accurate lay-

Section III. Unit 12. Cutting Stock with a Backsaw

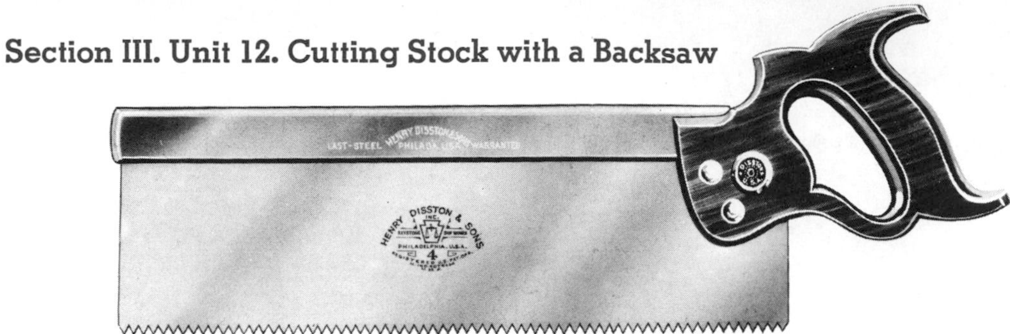

12–1. **A backsaw. In hand woodworking, this is one of the most frequently used tools whenever an accurate cut is required. Because the blade is relatively thin, it is strengthened on the back with a metal strip, from which it gets its name.**

12–2. **A dovetail saw. This is very similar to the backsaw except that it is smaller and has a thinner blade. It is used for extremely accurate work.**

out, mark a line with a knife. If the stock is to be cut to length, lay out a line across the face side of the board and across both edges. If no planing is to be done, the cut should be taken just inside or outside the layout line, *with the saw kerf in the waste stock.*

12–3. **The bench hook, which is simply a piece of wood with a wood cleat on either end, is used to protect the top of the bench when sawing, cutting, and doing other forming operations.**

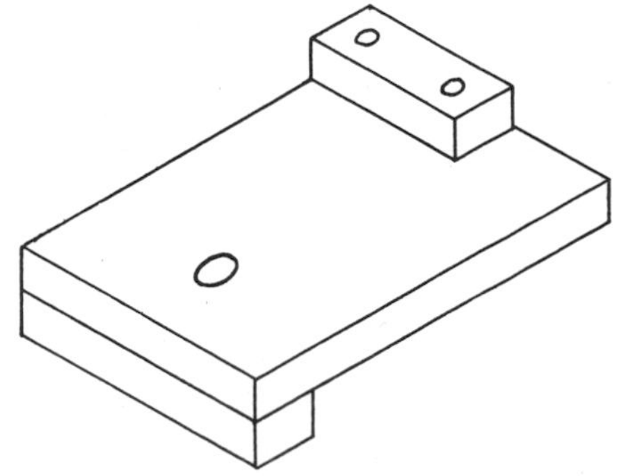

Figure 12–4. However, if the edge is to be planed or chiseled, allow about 1/16 inch.

CROSSCUTTING

Place the bench hook over the edge of the bench. Hold your work with one hand firmly against the stop as shown in Figure 12–5. Use the thumb of your left hand to guide the blade of the saw. Hold the saw in a slanting position across the work and draw it back once or twice to start the saw

12–4. **Always make sure that the saw kerf is in the waste part of the stock.**

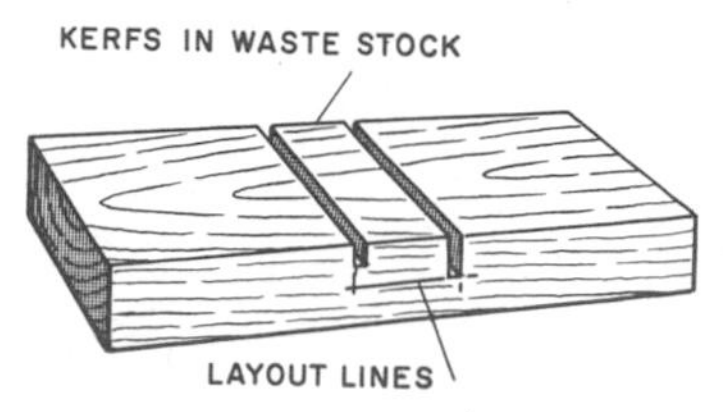

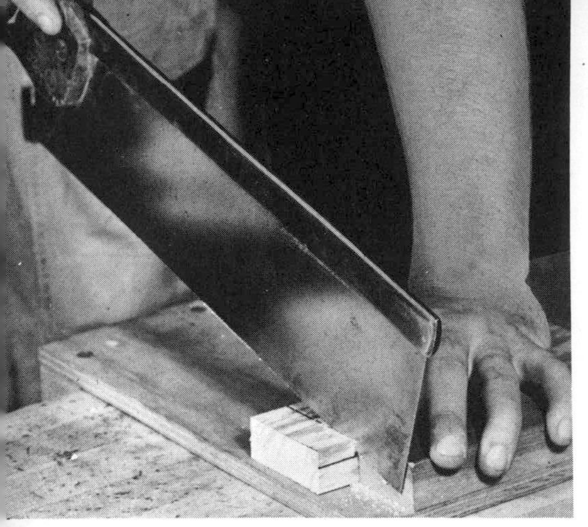

12–5. Starting a cut with a backsaw. The stock is held firmly against the bench hook and the handle of the saw is held high until the first two or three strokes are taken.

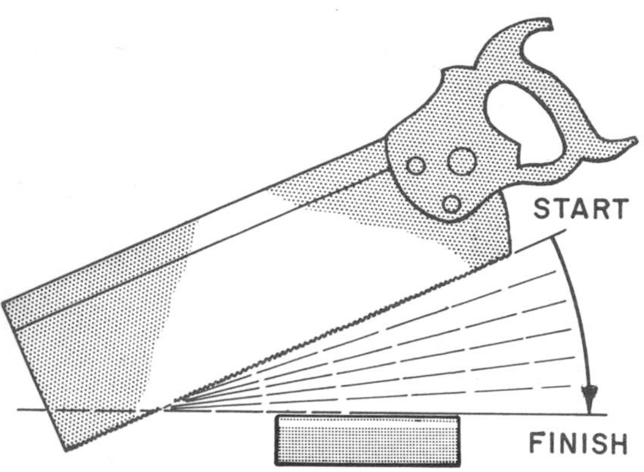

12–6. After the saw kerf is started, the handle is lowered slowly until it is parallel with the top of the bench.

12–7. Continuing the cut with the backsaw.

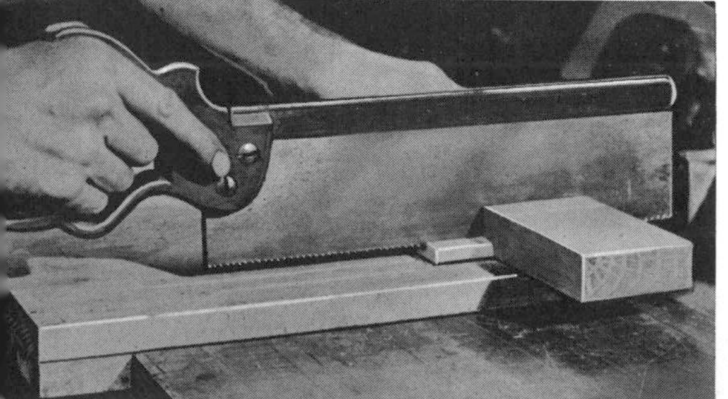

kerf. As the cut begins, gradually lower the saw until it is parallel to the wood. Figure 12–6.

Make sure that you are holding the saw at right angles to the face of the work. Be careful to take light, easy cuts as the saw goes through the opposite side of the wood. Figure 12–7. If you aren't careful, the wood will splinter.

RIPPING

The backsaw is also used for cutting with the grain of stock, especially in

12–8. Ripping with the backsaw. The proper method of cutting with the grain to form a tenon for a mortise-and-tenon joint.

making joints and in doing other fine cabinetwork. Lock the stock in a vise, with the end to be cut showing slightly above the vise jaws. Begin the cut the same way you did in crosscutting; continue to lower the handle until it is cutting the total width of the wood. Figure 12–8. In cutting with the grain, be very careful not to allow the saw to creep in at an angle, as this will make a crooked cut.

There are many uses for the backsaw in making all types of joints, as you will see later.

CAN YOU ANSWER THESE QUESTIONS ON CUTTING STOCK WITH A BACKSAW?

1. How did the backsaw get its name?
2. In what ways does the dovetail saw differ from the backsaw?
3. What is a bench hook and how is it used?
4. Can the backsaw crosscut and rip?
5. When using the backsaw, some stock must remain for planing. How much?
6. Which saw resembles the backsaw the most—the crosscut or the ripsaw?
7. Why must care be taken when sawing with the grain?

Section III

UNIT 13. GLUING UP STOCK TO FORM LARGER SURFACES

When you begin to make larger projects, one of the first problems is gluing up several pieces of stock to form a larger piece. Sometimes this means gluing stock edge to edge for making anything from a cutting board to a table top. At other times, you will need to glue stock face to face to form a thicker piece for making a turned bowl or perhaps the legs of a table or stool. Later you will need to clamp and glue up stock when you assemble your project.

Glues are an adhesive used to bond or hold materials together. Figure 13–1. The fact that two pieces of wood can be held together with an adhesive is due to *adhesion*. This is the force that causes certain molecules of different materials to attract each other. This force, for example, makes it possible to glue wood together or for paint or enamel to stick to wood. Glue holds pieces of wood together because the molecules of glue adhere to the wood and also to other molecules of glue.

13–1. Good wood gluing means that the joint will last almost forever and is stronger than the wood itself.

13–2. Chart of wood glues.

Type	Description	Recommended Use	Care in Using	Correct Use
Hide Glue	Comes in flakes to be heated in water, or in prepared form as liquid hide glue. Very strong, tough, light color.	Excellent for furniture and cabinetwork. Gives strength even to joints that do not fit very well.	Not waterproof; do not use for outdoor furniture or anything exposed to weather or dampness.	Apply glue in warm room to both surfaces and let it become tacky before joining. Clamp 3 hours.
Casein	From milk curd. Comes in powdered form. Must be mixed with water.	For inside and woodwork. Almost waterproof. Good for oily woods. Inexpensive. Good for heavy wood gluing.	Some types require bleaching. Will deteriorate when exposed to mold.	Mix with water to creamy consistency. For oily woods, sponge surfaces with dilute caustic soda one hour before gluing. Apply with brush. Clamp and allow to dry for three hours at 70 degrees.
Plastic Resin Glue	Comes as powder to be mixed with water and used within 4 hours. Light colored. Very strong if joint fits well.	Good for general wood gluing. First choice for work that must stand some exposure to dampness, since it is almost waterproof.	Needs well-fitted joints, tight clamping, and room temperature 70° or warmer.	Make sure joint fits tightly. Mix glue and apply thin coat. Allow 16 hours drying time.
Resorcinol (waterproof) Glue	Comes as powder plus liquid, must be mixed each time used. Dark colored, very strong, completely waterproof.	This is the glue to use with exterior type plywood for work to be exposed to extreme dampness.	Expense, trouble to mix and dark color make it unsuitable to jobs where waterproof glue is not required.	Use within 8 hours after mixing. Work at temperature above 70°. Apply thin coat to both surfaces. Allow 16 hours drying time.
Liquid Resin (white) Glue	Comes ready to use at any temperature. Clean working, quick setting. Strong enough for most work, though not quite as tough as hide glue.	Good for indoor furniture and cabinetwork. First choice for small jobs where tight clamping or good fit may be difficult.	Not sufficiently resistant to moisture for outdoor furniture or outdoor storage units.	Use at any temperature but preferably above 60°. Spread on both surfaces, clamp at once. Sets in 1½ hours.
Contact Cement	Comes in a can as a light tan liquid.	Excellent for bonding veneer plastic laminates, leather, plastics, metal foil, or canvas to wood.	Adheres immediately on contact. Parts can't be shifted once contact is made. Position accurately. Temperature for working must be 70° F. or above.	Stir cement. Apply two coats to both surfaces. Brush on a liberal coat. Let dry for 30 minutes. Apply second coat. Allow to dry for not less than 30 minutes. Test for dryness by pressing wrapping paper to surface. If paper doesn't stick, the surfaces are dry and ready for bonding.
Epoxy Glue	Comes in two tubes, or cans, that must be mixed in exact proportions.	Excellent for attaching hardware and metal fittings to wood. Good for extremely difficult gluing jobs. Will fill large holes.	Epoxies harden quickly. Mix only what can be used in half hour. Use at temperatures above 60 degrees. Keep epoxy compounds separate. Don't reverse caps.	Mix small amounts. Clean and roughen the surfaces. Remove oil, dirt, and other loose matter. Apply to surfaces with putty knife. Clean tools immediately. Press parts together.

KINDS OF GLUE

There are seven common kinds of glue that may be used in the school shop. Figure 13–2. These come under many trade names. A description of the glue will tell you which type it is. Learn about these basic glues so you can use them properly.

1. Animal or hide glue is made from hoofs, hides, bones, and other animal refuse. It is refined, purified, and then made into sticks or ground into powder. There are many grades, depending on the quality and kind of wood for which it is meant. Animal glue makes a stronger-than-wood joint, but is not waterproof. If it is used dry, you need a glue pot or double boiler to prepare it. It has long been used as an all-purpose furniture glue. It also comes in liquid form which doesn't need to be heated or mixed. Stick or powder glue must first be soaked in cold water from 6 to 12 hours. While there are strict manufacturer's specifications as to the amounts of glue and water, a satisfactory mixture can be made by soaking the glue in just enough water to cover. The glue will absorb this water and then, when the heating is done, a small amount of water can be added as needed. After animal glue is soaked, place it in the top of a double boiler, or a regular glue pot, and heat it to steam temperature. The glue will dry out too much if heated directly over a flame. Animal glue is ready to use when it runs off the brush in a light stream.

Before applying hot animal glue, the wood must be brought to a temperature of about 80 to 90 degrees. This type of glue must be applied rapidly, as it sets very quickly after cooling. Cold liquid animal glue eliminates tedious preparation and the necessity for speed and critical temperature control.

2. Casein glue, made from milk curd, is available in powdered form. It is mixed with cold water to the consistency of cream and applied cold to the wood. It is easy to mix and makes a stronger-than-wood joint. It is not completely waterproof. Some types stain oak, mahogany, and other acid woods and must be bleached off. It is excellent for all indoor and outdoor gluing with the exception of articles which require complete waterproofing.

Do not mix more than you need at one time, as it loses its strength in a few hours after mixing. To mix, pour the powder in a container and add a small amount of water, stirring until it becomes a heavy paste. Add more water until the mixture is about the consistency of thick cream. Allow the glue to set about fifteen minutes before applying it with a stick or brush.

3. Plastic resin glue is made from urea resin and formaldehyde. It comes in powder form and is mixed with water to the thickness of cream. It does not stain woods, is waterproof, and dries to a light color. It is used the same way as casein glue, but the manufacturer's directions must always be followed for mixing and drying. It is very good for cabinetwork and for bonding plywood.

4. Resorcinol resin glue is made by mixing liquid resin with a powder catalyst. It comes in a can divided into two compartments and should be mixed only as needed, according to the manufacturer's directions. It does

13–3. White liquid resin glue from a squeeze bottle provides a good way to apply an adhesive.

not require much pressure. It will fill gaps and can be used for gluing poorly fitted joints. It provides complete protection from both fresh and salt water and is therefore ideal for outdoor sports equipment.

5. Liquid resin (polyvinyl) glue, white in color, is excellent for furniture making and repair. It is always ready for use, is nonstaining, economical, and odorless. It cannot be exposed to weather and is not as strong or lasting as liquid hide glue, which is best for fine furniture. Figure 13–3.

6. Contact cement is a ready-mixed rubber type bonding agent. It bonds practically all materials to themselves or in combination without need for clamps, nails, or pressure. It is an ideal material for bonding veneer or plastic laminates to plywood.

7. Epoxy glue and compound is a two-part adhesive that sticks practically anything. It can be used on wood, plastics, leather, metal, ceramics, and any material to produce a strong waterproof joint. Epoxy glues come in two containers because, unlike ordinary glues, they do not contain an evaporative solvent. They consist of a special resin and a chemical hardener that are mixed together at time of use. This glue produces super-strength joints without clamping.

TEN HINTS FOR SUCCESSFUL GLUING

1. Make sure the surfaces are clean and dry.
2. Make well fitting joints. Figure 13–4.
3. Choose the correct glue.
4. Mix the glue to proper thickness.
5. Mark the pieces to be glued for correct assembly.
6. Have the proper clamps ready.
7. Apply the glue to both surfaces of the joint. Figure 13–5.
8. Clamp parts together properly.
9. Remove extra glue from joints before it dries.
10. Allow the assembly to dry completely.

KINDS OF CLAMPS

1. The cabinet and bar clamp. Figure 13–6. This clamp is used for gluing up larger surfaces edge to edge and for clamping parts together when assembling projects. It is made in various lengths from 2 to 8 feet and in several styles. One end is adjusted to length by friction or by catches, while the other is moved in and out by a screw. Figure 13–7. When using a cabinet clamp, the screw is turned out completely; then the catch or friction end is moved in until the

13–4. Make sure that the parts fit properly. Test the fit of the joint before applying glue.

clamp is slightly wider than the total width of the stock to be clamped. When using cabinet clamps on finished stock, the surface of the wood should be protected. Place small pieces of scrap stock between the clamp jaws and the wood.

2. Hand screws. Figure 13–8. These are wooden parallel clamps about 6 to 20 inches long which open from 4 to 20 inches. When using hand screws, the center screw is held in the left hand and the outside screw in the right hand. The clamp can then be

13–5. Chair rungs and similar joints can be reglued even when it is not possible to pull them apart. Drill a small hole into the joint and inject glue with an oil can. A hypodermic needle is also excellent for this.

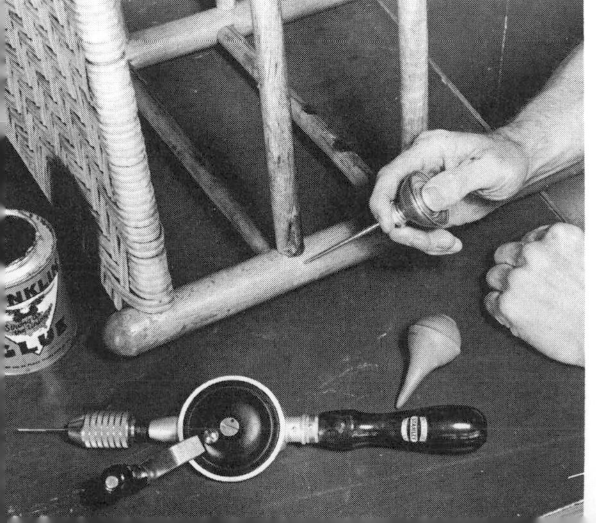

13–6. Cabinet clamps can be used for general-purpose work. They are particularly useful in all wide clamping for furniture construction.

13–7. Bar clamps are made with a single pipe, or double pipes, as shown here.

opened and closed by twisting the handles in opposite directions. Figure 13–9. The hand screw is for gluing stock face to face or for clamping together any work that is within the range of the clamp jaws.

3. The C clamp comes in many sizes. It is used to assemble and clamp parts. Figure 13–10.

4. Speed (instant-acting) clamps are very convenient because they can be instantly adjusted for quick assembly. Figure 13–11.

5. Spring clamps are quick and easy to use. Some types have pivoting jaws made of stainless steel with double rows of serrated teeth along the pressure edge. These toothed jaws take hold of the surface of parts so that miter joints and other odd shapes can be held together. Figure 13–12.

13–8. Correct and incorrect way of clamping with hand screws. On the left the clamps are not parallel and, therefore, will not apply pressure correctly.

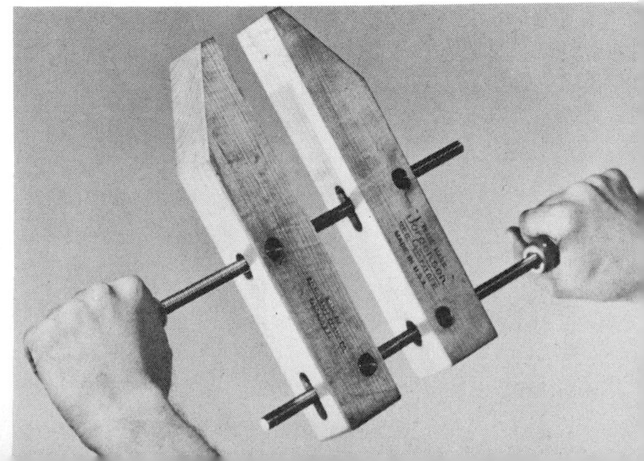

13–9. Hold the middle spindle and revolve the end spindle to open or close a hand screw.

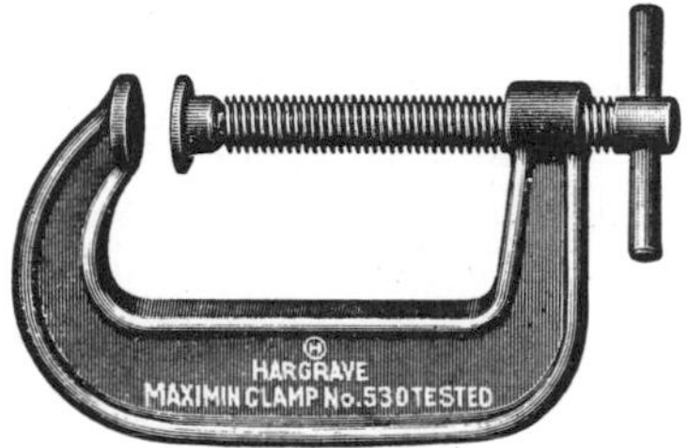

13–10. C clamp is used for clamping irregular or odd-shaped pieces and for many special jobs in the workshop.

13–12. Spring clamps with special jaws make it possible to clamp odd-shaped pieces.

MAKING AND GLUING UP AN EDGE JOINT

1. Choose and cut the stock. Select rough stock that will form the larger surface. If it is wider than 8 to 10 inches, it is usually ripped into narrower strips. In this way the total surface will not warp so much when the pieces are glued together. After the pieces have been cut, arrange them in their correct order, remembering the following:

a. Make sure that the grain of all pieces runs in the same direction so that, after you have glued up the pieces, it will not be difficult to plane.

b. Alternate the pieces so the annular rings face in opposite directions. Figure 13–13. This will help to prevent the surface from warping.

c. Try to match the pieces to form the most interesting grain arrangement.

Now mark the adjoining face of each matching joint with matching numbers, "X's" or lines, in a place where the marks can be easily seen.

2. First planing. Plane one surface of each piece to remove wind or warpage. This will also help you to see the direction the grain runs. If you have any pieces running in opposite directions, reverse them and re-mark the ends. It will not be necessary to

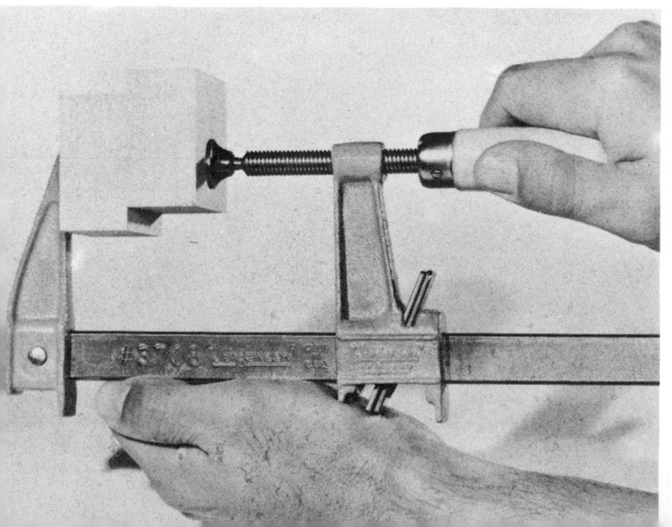

13–11. Speed bar clamps such as this one are easily adjustable. This makes gluing a great deal easier.

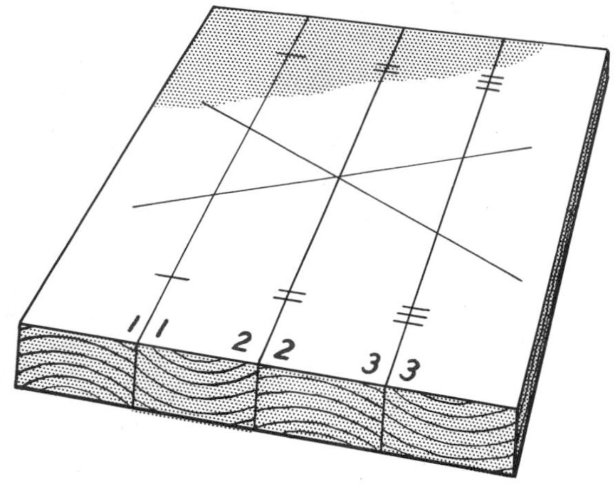

13–13. Note the proper method of arranging stock before it is glued together. Also mark the adjoining boards so that they will be easy to assemble.

plane this surface accurately now because the assembled stock will have to be planed again.

3. Plane both edges until they are square with the face surface. In planing an edge, the center should be slightly lower than the ends. When the two matching edges are planed,

13–14. Spring-joint construction. Note that the ends are tight and that there is a small amount of light showing through the center.

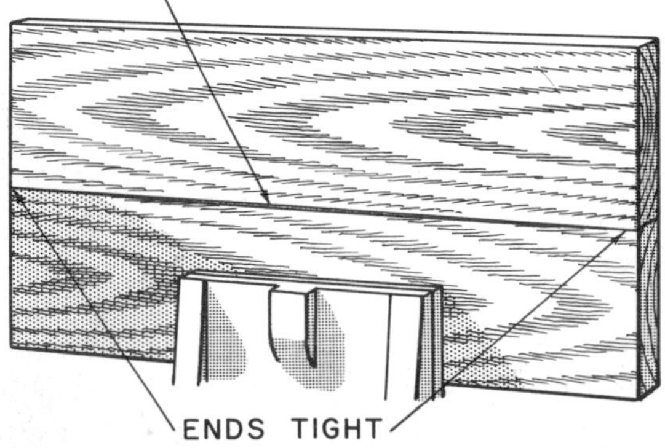

clamp one piece in a vise and set the other piece over it edge to edge. Look to see if a little light is coming through the crack toward the center of the joint. The ends should be tight. Figure 13–14. This is called spring-joint construction. If this is not done, the ends tend to separate after the pieces have been glued together. Also, hold a straightedge against the face surfaces of all the pieces to make sure they do not bow. Figure 13–15. Tap the top piece with your finger to see that it does not rock. Finally, slide the top piece along the bottom one to see if it tends to have a suction action. Continue to plane one surface and the two edges of each piece and match each of the joints.

13–15. Holding a straightedge against the face surfaces of stock to see if the surfaces are straight and do not bow.

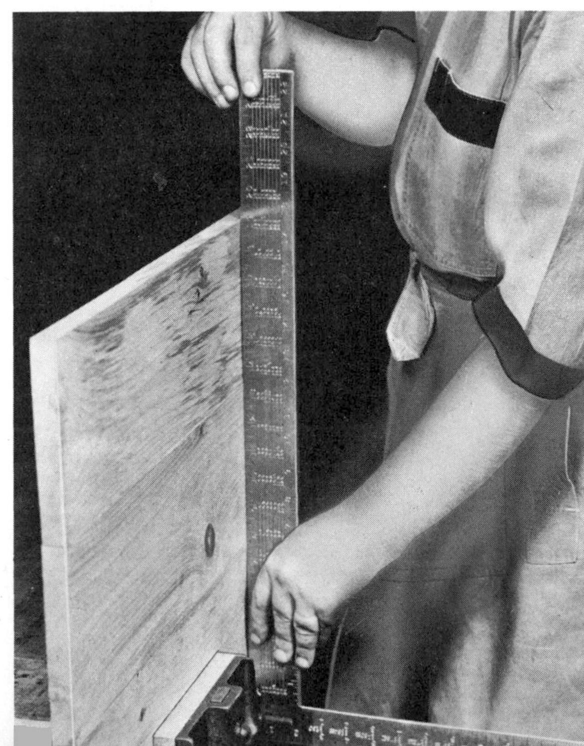

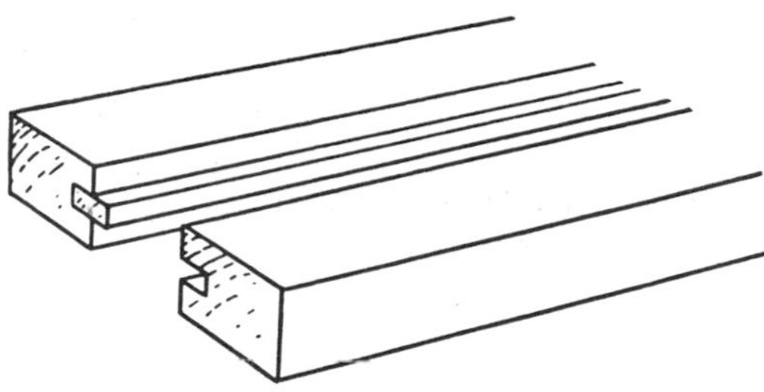

13–16. Enlarged view of spline-joint construction. This type strengthens the two adjoining pieces.

ADDING DOWELS OR SPLINES

When joints with additional strength are needed, dowels or splines can be added to each joint. Unit 25 (making a dowel joint) gives detailed instructions for making an edge dowel joint. To make a spline joint (Figure 13–16), cut a groove on the circular saw that is about one third as wide and deep as the thickness of the stock. Then cut and fit splines into these grooves. Allow a small clearance at the bottom of each spline for glue.

MAKING A TRIAL ASSEMBLY OF THE STOCK

After all joints have been constructed, place the pieces in position again on the top of a bench. If the pieces are very long, place them over two sawhorses. If they are placed on top of a bench, use a jig (Figure 13–17) to hold the bar clamps. Select three or more cabinet or bar clamps, depending on the length of the stock. There should be a clamp for about every 15 inches of stock. Carefully set all cabinet clamps to the proper openings, so they will be ready to clamp the stock as soon as the edges are glued. When gluing on a wood-top bench, cover the surface with wrapping paper to protect the surface.

GLUING UP THE STOCK

Hold the two matching edges together so they are flush. Apply (spread) the glue with a brush, stick, or roller. Figure 13–18. Make sure that both edges are completely covered. This is called *double spread.* When glue is applied to only one surface and the surfaces rubbed together, it is called *single spread*. However, do not apply too much glue. It will squeeze out of the joint when it is put together and give you extra trouble in removing it later.

When all edges have been glued, rapidly lay the pieces on the lower clamps till all are in place. If possible, rub the two pieces together to work the glue into the pores. Tighten the outside clamps lightly; then place another clamp upside down on the stock at the mid-point and clamp this lightly. Use a rubber mallet to tap the ends or the face surfaces to line them up. Check all the joints to make sure that the face surfaces are flush and the ends are in line. Strike the

13–17. A jig to hold the bar clamps. With a jig of this sort, the clamps will be held in correct position, making it a simple job to apply glue to the edges and to place the stock in between the clamps.

A

B

13–18. Two methods of spreading glue: A. Spreading cold glue with a roller after it is applied with a brush. B. Applying hot glue with a brush.

pieces with a mallet to bring them in place. Then tighten each clamp until it applies firm pressure. Don't squeeze the wood too tightly. If the joint is constructed badly, it will never draw into place. Place a wood cleat above and below the surface at either end and clamp these in place with hand screws or clamps. Figure 13–19. This will tend to keep the surface true and free from warpage. A piece of paper under the cleats will keep them from sticking. Before the glue begins to harden, wipe off the excess from the outside of the joint.

MAKING AND GLUING UP STOCK FACE TO FACE

Select and cut out several pieces of stock that will make up the correct size when glued together. Arrange the pieces with the annular rings alternating in direction. Also make sure that the grain of the pieces runs in the same direction. Mark the ends and face surface so that you will know how the pieces should be arranged for gluing. Plane the face surface of the two outside pieces true and smooth. If more than two pieces are glued together, the center pieces must be planed to thickness. Select several hand screws or C clamps and open them slightly wider than the stock to be clamped. Apply glue evenly and then clamp as shown in Figure 13–20. When you tighten the hand screw, you must take care that the jaws are parallel. In this way pressure will be even.

13–19. Stock glued up and bar clamps holding the stock together. Note the cleat that has been fastened to one end of the stock.

13–20. Gluing up stock face-to-face. Several different types of clamps are holding two pieces of work together. Cleats are fastened underneath the clamps to protect the surfaces of the wood.

DRYING AND REMOVING THE EXCESS GLUE

The time required for glue to dry varies with the kind of glue, the kind of wood, and the temperature. For white resin glue, the time required for an initial set is about one half hour. In most cases glues should be allowed to dry overnight. Any excess glue can be removed with a scraper or sharp chisel.

CAN YOU ANSWER THESE QUESTIONS ON GLUING UP STOCK TO FORM LARGER SURFACES?

1. Name seven kinds of glue and tell of what they are made.
2. Which glues are waterproof?
3. Which is best for a small repair job?
4. Tell what cabinet or bar clamps are needed for and how they are used.
5. Of what material are the clamps of hand screws made?
6. For what special kinds of gluing jobs can C clamps be helpful?
7. To glue up a large board, wider stock is ripped into narrow strips. Explain the reason for this and how it is done.
8. What three things must you consider when gluing up stock?
9. Describe a spring joint.
10. To make this type of joint, what checks should be made?
11. A trial assembly is always made before gluing. What is accomplished by it?
12. About how much glue should be applied to the edges?
13. With what kind of mallet should wood surfaces be pounded?
14. How can you keep the surface true and free from warpage?
15. Why must the jaws of hand screws be parallel?

Section III

UNIT 14. SQUARING UP STOCK

It is usually necessary to plane several or all of the surfaces of the pieces for your project. Figure 14–1. In some cases, you will be planing only the edges of the stock and sawing the ends. In other cases, such as in making a cutout design, you may plane the face surface, one edge, and the other surface. In many instances in which parts are to be assembled, you will be planing the stock to thickness and width and perhaps finishing the ends by sawing with the backsaw and then sanding.

There are many times, however, when you will need to plane all six surfaces of the board. This is called squaring up the stock. If you apply the instructions given in the last six units, you should be able to do a good job. It should be remembered, though, that this job is very difficult when done with a hand plane and you should not attempt to plane any more surfaces than are necessary to do the job properly. If machine tools are available, a planer and jointer can be used, following the same procedure as with a hand plane. There are several methods of squaring up stock.

METHOD A

1. Plane the face surface or side (working face).
2. Plane the working edge.
3. Plane the stock to width (second edge).
4. Plane the stock to thickness (second surface or side).
5. Plane one end (working end).
6. Cut stock to length.
7. Plane other end (second end).

METHOD B

1. Plane the face surface (working surface).

14–1. The base of this lamp is a good example of stock that must be planed on all sides.

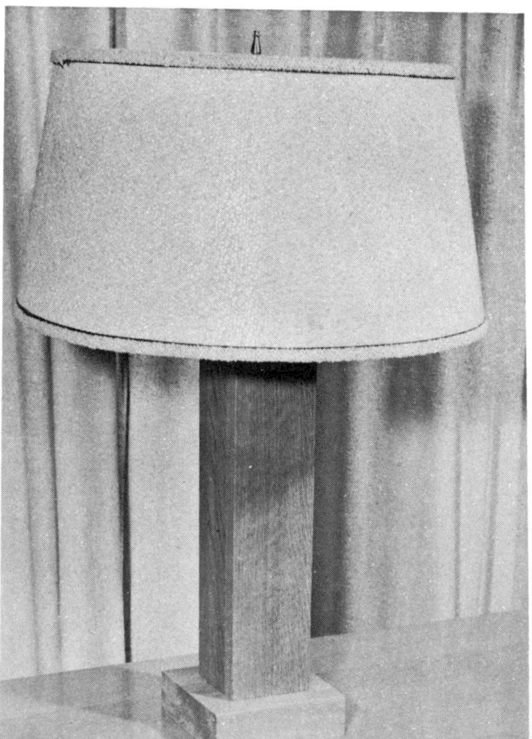

2. Plane the working edge.
3. Plane one end square with the face surface and joint edge.
4. Plane stock to width.
5. Plane stock to thickness.
6. Cut off stock to length.
7. Plane other end.

METHOD C (Recommended)

1. Plane the face surface. Figure 14–2.
2. Plane the working edge.
3. Plane one end square with the face surface and joint edge.
4. Cut off stock to length and plane other end.

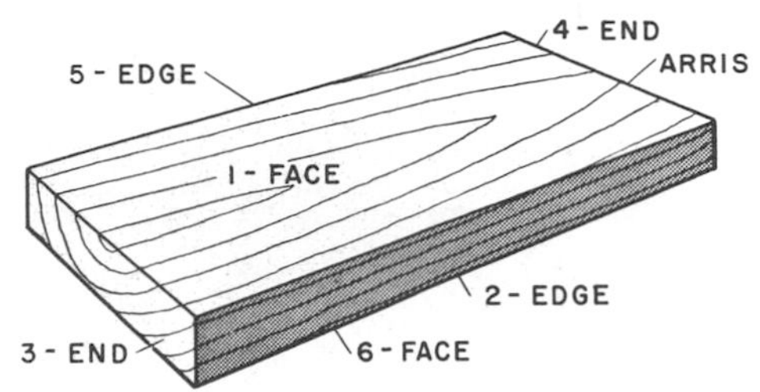

14–2. This is the recommended method of squaring up stock.

5. Plane stock to width.
6. Plane stock to thickness.

CAN YOU ANSWER THESE QUESTIONS ON SQUARING UP STOCK?

1. Must all six surfaces of the board be planed?
2. Name the machine tools that are useful in squaring up stock.
3. There are three methods of squaring up stock. Describe them.

Section IV
Making Pieces of Curved or Irregular Designs

The fourth 3 steps in hand woodworking—what you must know and be able to do.

15. How to transfer curves and irregular lines: using dividers, drawing circles, working with some geometric patterns like the octagon and hexagon, and drawing an ellipse.

16. Cutting many and varied curved patterns with the coping saw and the compass saw, and the proper way to cut with these saws.

17. Forming and trimming these various shapes to make them smooth and ready for assembly, using the spokeshave, drawknife, homemade scraper, and file or rasp.

You would find woodworking rather dull if everything were made in flat, straight planes. Curves, geometric designs, and shapes in the form of animals and other forms of Nature are added. These lend beauty to your projects and interest to the building of them. There are many things which must have a curved or molded shape, such as archery bows, canoe paddles, or boat hulls.

In this section you will begin your work with saws and other cutting tools especially suited to the making of irregular, molded, curved, and formed designs.

The new ideas and skills you will study and learn, to create some of these projects and designs, are listed in the "box" above. Further woodworking steps are on pp. 15, 43, 60, 108, 132, 143, 170, 219, 244.

Section IV

UNIT 15. LAYING OUT AND TRANSFERRING CURVES AND DESIGNS

Many projects contain pieces with irregular designs or geometric shapes. These must be transferred to the wood from a drawing before further work can be done. Figure 15–1. If it is a geometric design, the layout can usually be made directly on the wood. However, if the design is irregular, you must first draw a full-size pattern on paper and then transfer it to the wood.

DIVIDERS

A dividers or an ordinary pencil compass is used for laying out small circles. Figure 15–2. The dividers is more accurate and has other uses in layout work, such as dividing space equally, transferring measurements, and scribing arcs. Figure 15–3. To set the dividers, place one leg over the inch mark on the rule and then open the other leg to the width you want. Lock the thumbscrew. Some dividers have an additional spring nut that is used to make fine corrections in settings.

DRAWING CIRCLES

Set the dividers to equal half the diameter of the circle. Place one leg over the center of the circle, tip the dividers at a slight angle, and, working from left to right, scribe the circle. Figure 15–4. When drawing circles on finished wood, place an eraser from the end of a pencil over the point that is to act as the center.

15–1. The end designs of this Early American tray must be enlarged to full size and transferred to the wood before they can be cut out and finished.

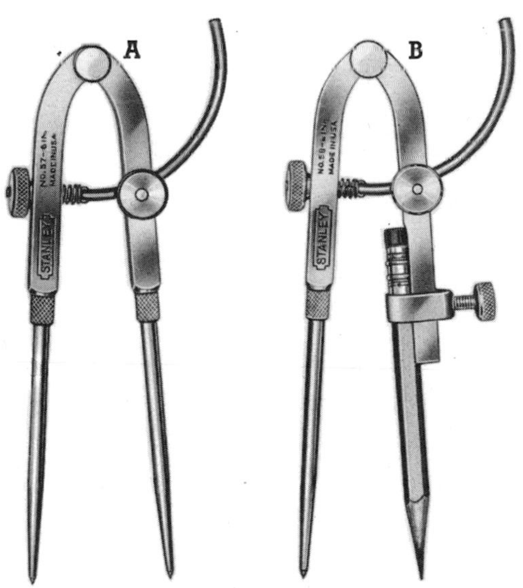

15–2. Two tools for drawing circles and arcs: A. Dividers. B. Pencil compass.

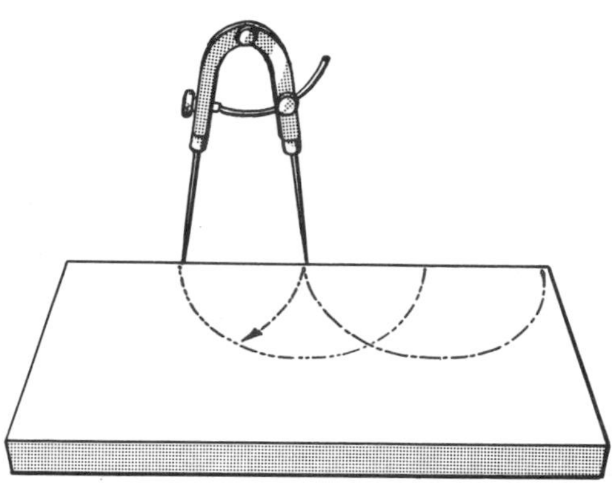

15–3. Using a dividers.

15–5. Trammel points are used when laying out large circles. These points fit on a long, thin piece of metal or wood, and can be adjusted to any length.

To lay out larger circles, use a set of trammel points (Figure 15–5) or tie a piece of string to a pencil and use this as a compass.

LAYING OUT A ROUNDED CORNER

The corners on many projects are rounded. To lay out these corners, first check the drawing to get the radius of the arc. Then mark this distance from the corner on the next side and end. Figure 15–6. With a try square held against edge and end, draw two lines that intersect (cross) the center of the arc. Set the dividers to the proper radius and draw the arc.

15–4. Laying out a circle with a dividers. The dividers is tipped slightly as it is swung around.

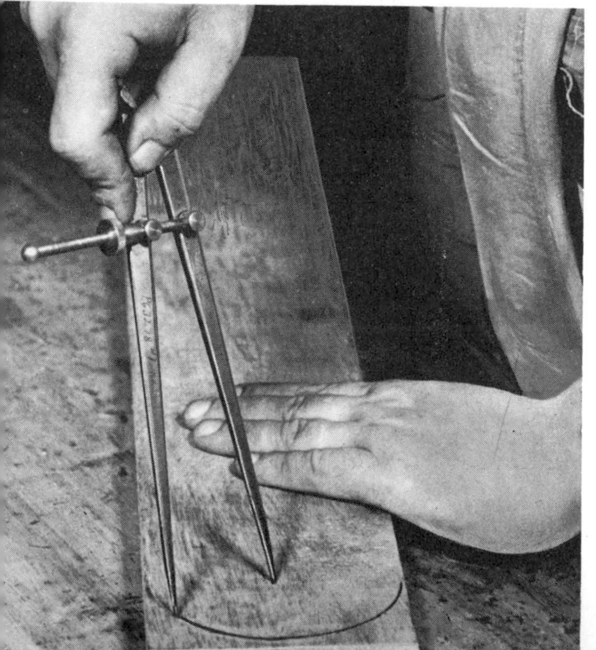

15–6. Locating the center for laying out a rounded corner.

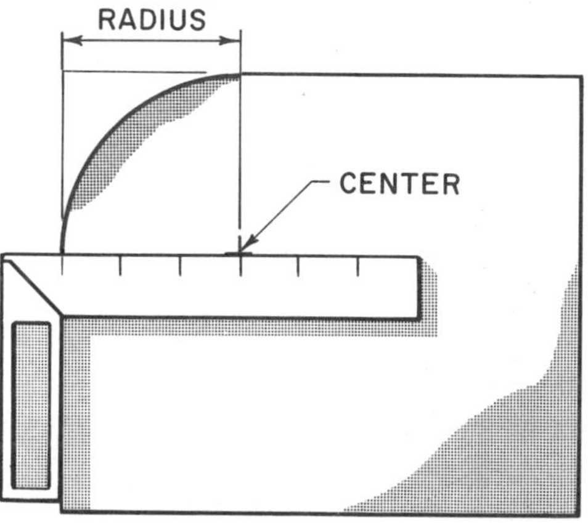

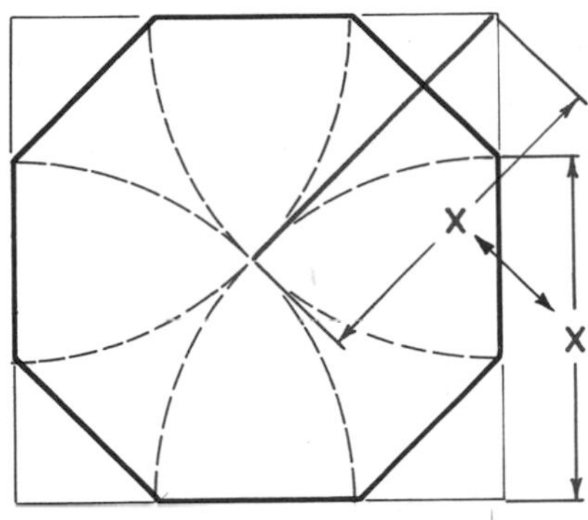

15–7. Layout of an octagon.

LAYING OUT AN OCTAGON

An octagon has eight equal sides with all angles equal. Find the distance across the octagon from one side to the other and lay out a square this size. Next, set a dividers or compass to half the diagonal length across the square. Set the point of the compass at each corner of the square and strike an arc from one side of the square to the other. Do this from each of the four corners. Join the points where the arcs meet the sides of the square. Figure 15–7.

LAYING OUT A HEXAGON

A hexagon has six equal sides with all angles equal. Find the length of one side. Set a compass or dividers to equal this measurement and draw a circle with this radius. Begin at any point on the circle; without changing the setting, draw a series of arcs, moving the point to the place where the preceding arc has intersected the circle. Figure 15–8. The last arc should intersect the circle at the first point made by the compass. Join these points with a straightedge.

DRAWING AN ELLIPSE

An ellipse is a regular curve that has two different diameters. Lay out the two diameters at right angles to each other—namely, AB and CD as shown in Figure 15–9a. Set a dividers equal to half the longest diameter. Place the point of the dividers on point D and strike an arc to intersect the longest diameter at points X and Y. Figure 15–9b. Place a thumbtack at these two points and another at one end of the shortest diameter. Tie a string around the two outside thumbtacks. Remove the outside thumbtack and place a pencil inside the string. Figure 15–9c. Hold the pencil at right angles to the paper and carefully draw the ellipse.

ENLARGING IRREGULAR DESIGNS

Projects found in a book or magazine are seldom drawn to full size. If the project contains irregular parts, it will be necessary to make an enlarged drawing. This is used as a pattern in making the layout on wood. Do this as follows:

1. Find out how much smaller the original drawing is than full size. Usually drawings in books or magazines

15–8. Layout of a hexagon.

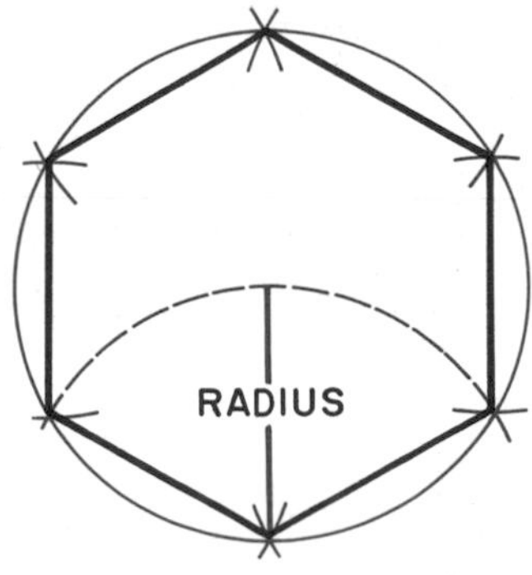

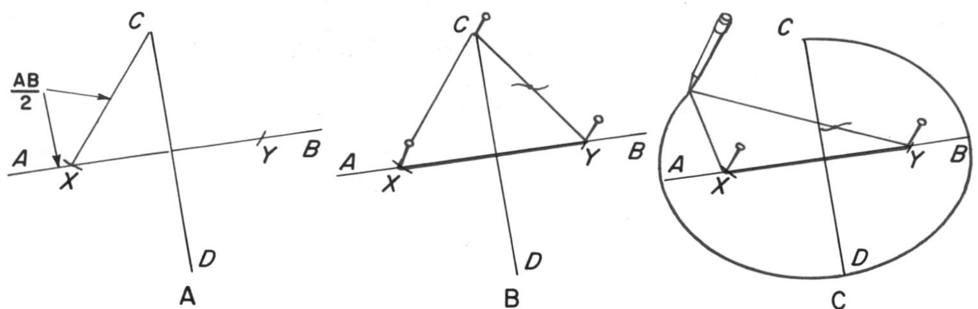

15–9. **How to make an ellipse: A. Laying out the two diameters at right angles to each other. B. Striking an arc to intersect two points X and Y on the long diameter. C. Drawing the ellipse. Note that the outside thumbtack has been removed and a pencil put in its place. Be sure the pencil is held at right angles to the wood in forming the ellipse.**

are one-half or one-fourth full size. If the original drawing is not already on squared paper, lay out squares over the print. *For example, if the pattern is one-fourth of full size, draw ¼″ squares.*

2. On a large piece of wrapping paper, carefully lay out 1″ squares.

15–10. **Enlarging an irregular design. Crosshatch paper is numbered the same, both in the original and the enlargement. This helps to locate the points needed to make an enlargement.**

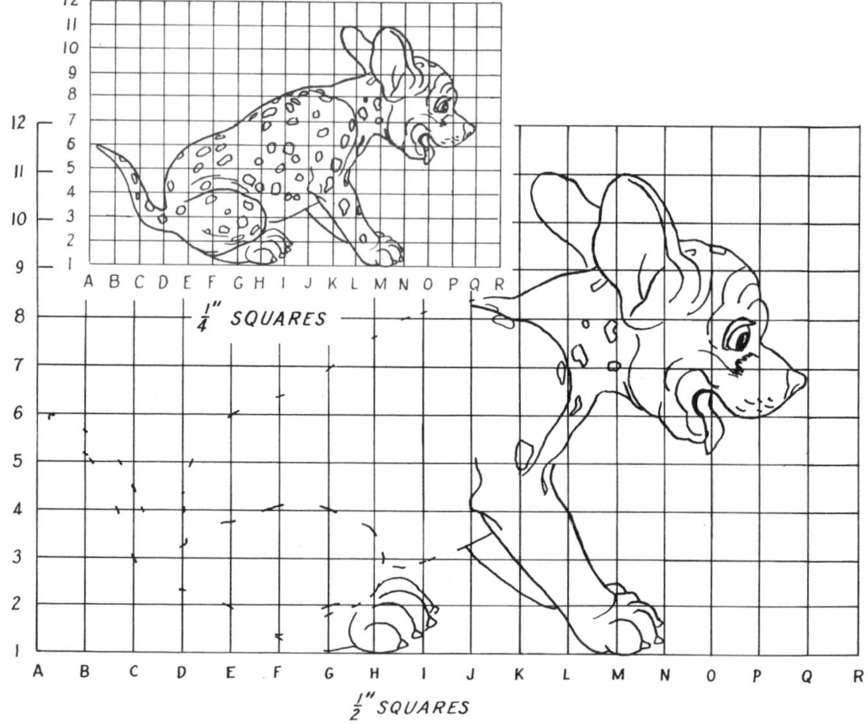

From the lower lefthand corner of both the original drawing and the layout paper, letter all horizontal lines A, B, C, etc., and all vertical lines 1, 2, 3, etc. Using these letters and numbers, locate a position on the original drawing, then transfer this point to the full-size pattern. Figure 15–10. Continue to locate and transfer positions until enough points are marked for the full-size pattern.

3. With these points located, sketch the full-size pattern. Use a ruler for straight lines. On curved sections, a piece of wire solder can be bent to serve as a guide in drawing these lines. Now examine your design. A little change here and there may smooth out the curves and make it look the way you want it to.

4. If the piece is symmetrical (the same on both sides), you need to lay out only half the design. Then fold the sheet of paper down the center and cut the full pattern.

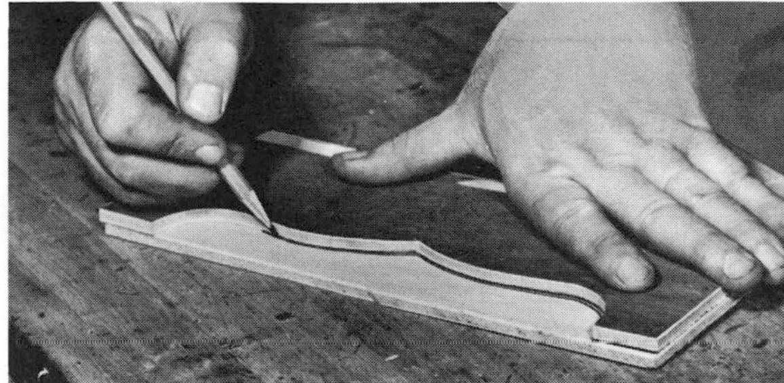

15–11. Using a templet to make a layout. When several pieces of the same design are to be cut, it is much simpler to use a templet of thin wood or metal.

5. Place this paper pattern on your piece of stock and trace around it. You may need a little tape to hold it in place. Care is needed to do this.

6. If you are making many parts of the same design, make a templet (pattern) of thin wood, or sheet metal, from the paper design. Use this templet to make the layout. Figure 15–11.

CAN YOU ANSWER THESE QUESTIONS ON LAYING OUT AND TRANSFERRING CURVES AND DESIGNS?

1. Name three uses for a dividers.
2. How should a dividers be set to measurement?
3. What precautions should be taken when drawing a circle on a finished piece?
4. What are trammel points?
5. Why is it customary to round the corners of projects?
6. How many sides has an octagon? A hexagon?
7. How is an octagon drawn?
8. Define an ellipse. Describe the method of drawing one.
9. When is it necessary to enlarge an irregular design?
10. Why are most of the designs in books drawn on squared paper?
11. Is it always necessary to lay out the whole design? Why?
12. Describe a templet and how it is used.

Section IV

UNIT 16. CUTTING OUT CURVES

Many projects have curves or irregular shapes that must be cut to form the design. To cut curves, the saw must have a thin blade. The two saws most commonly used are the coping and compass. This work can also be done on the jig or band saw. (See Machine Woodworking.)

THE COPING SAW

The *coping saw* has a handle and a U-shaped frame into which a removable blade is fastened. One inexpensive type has a wire frame in which the blade is held tight by the spring of the frame itself. The one shown in Figure 16–1 is more practical for general woodworking because the blade is tightened by a screw in the handle. It is also better because the blade can be turned at any angle to the frame. Blades for the coping saw have ripsaw-like teeth and are made with several different numbers of points to the inch. For most work, choose a blade with sixteen points (fifteen teeth) to the inch.

1. Cutting with the work supported on a saw bracket. Mount the blade in the frame with the teeth pointing toward the handle. If the opening to be cut is internal, drill a small hole in the waste material just large enough for the blade to pass through. Slip the blade through the hole and fasten it into the frame. Hold the work to the bracket with your left hand. Figure 16–2. Grasp the handle of the coping saw in your right hand and move the saw up and down. The cutting action takes place on the downward stroke, with the pressure released as the saw is pushed upward. The saw must be worked freely so there should be very little pressure. Hold the work firmly. As you cut, it is better to move the work, keeping the saw blade inside the V cut of the bracket. If the cutting is hard, apply a little soap or wax to the blade. Keep the blade moving at a steady pace of about twenty to thirty strokes per minute. At sharp corners turn the handle

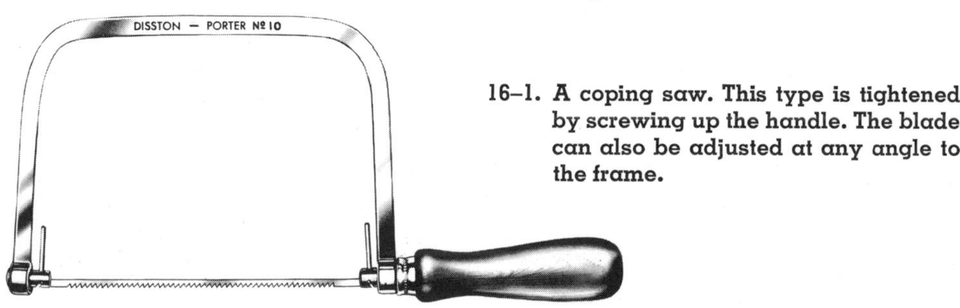

16–1. A coping saw. This type is tightened by screwing up the handle. The blade can also be adjusted at any angle to the frame.

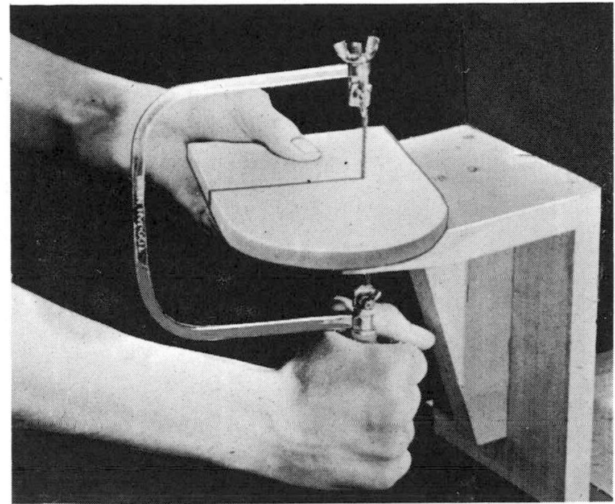

16–2. Cutting work with the stock held over a saw bracket. When doing this type of sawing, the blade is put in the frame with the teeth pointing toward the handle. This method is especially satisfactory for cutting intricate designs. Courtesy the Jam Handy Organization.

slowly in the direction of the line and keep moving the saw up and down without applying any pressure to the blade. Begin cutting again as the blade is turned. Twisting or bending the blade at the corners usually breaks it.

2. Cutting with the work held in a vise. Put the blade in the frame with the teeth pointing away from the handle. Lock the work in the vise with the place to be cut near the top of the vise jaws. Begin the cutting in the waste stock. Keep your strokes even as you bring the blade to the cutting line. Make sure that the saw kerf is in the waste stock and that the blade is held straight up and down on the work at all times. While cutting, the saw can be supported with both hands as shown in Figure 16–3. If the stock is very light, you can support the work itself with your left hand to prevent vibration.

THE COMPASS SAW

The *compass saw* looks like any other handsaw except that it is much smaller and has a thin, tapered blade. Usually a compass saw comes with several different-sized blades to fit into the handle. Figure 16–4. The narrow point at the end of the saw makes it possible to start the tool in a small opening and to cut small curves and circles. The saw is made in lengths from 10 to 18 inches with eight points to the inch. The average compass saw is 10 to 14 inches long.

A *keyhole saw* is very similar except that it is even smaller and is named for its most common use.

Cutting with the compass saw. Drill a hole in the waste stock large enough for the saw point to enter.

16–3. Cutting with a coping saw with the work held in a vise. In this type of work, the saw can be held in both hands, thus giving it more support for cutting heavy stock. The blade should be inserted with the teeth pointing away from the handle.

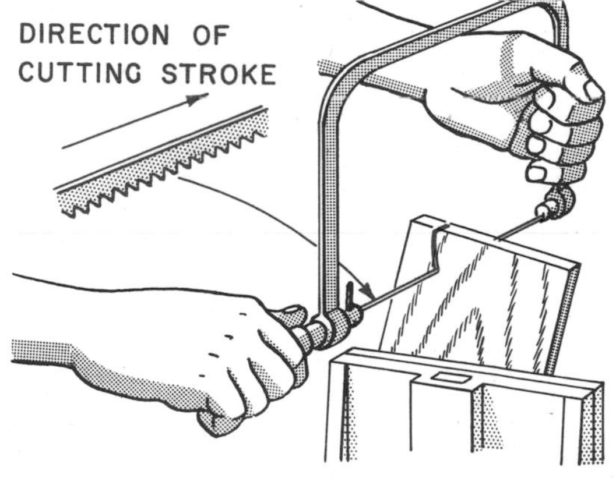

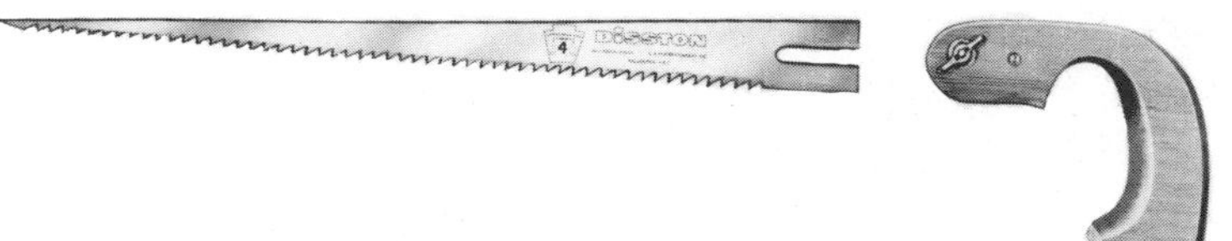

16–4. Compass saw. This one has several interchangeable blades for different types of jobs.

Figure 16–5. Insert the point of the saw in the first hole. Take several short, quick strokes to force more of the blade to pass through the stock. Figure 16–6. Cut a curve by slightly twisting the handle of the saw to follow the pattern. Figure 16–7.

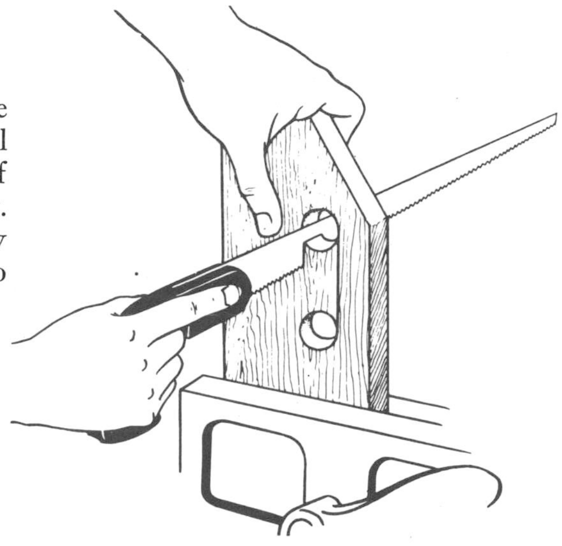

16–6. Cutting an internal opening in which two bored holes are part of the pattern.

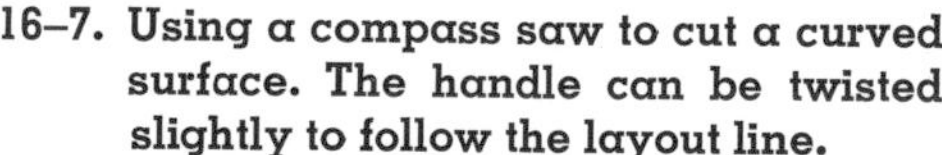

16–5. Using a compass saw for internal cutting. A hole is drilled in the stock to permit the saw blade to enter.

16–7. Using a compass saw to cut a curved surface. The handle can be twisted slightly to follow the layout line.

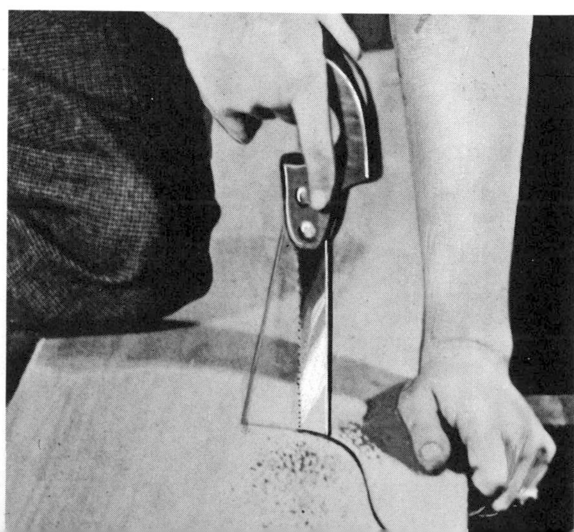

CAN YOU ANSWER THESE QUESTIONS ON CUTTING OUT CURVES?

1. What machine tools will cut curves in wood? What hand tools?
2. Blades of a coping saw resemble what type of handsaw?
3. When work is cut on a saw bracket, should the teeth be pointed toward or away from the handle?
4. How can you prevent the saw from sticking?
5. About how many strokes per minute should be taken with the coping saw?
6. What are the most common causes of saw blade breakage?
7. Exactly where should the saw kerf be in regard to the layout lines?
8. Describe a compass saw. Its use.

Section IV

UNIT 17. FORMING AND SMOOTHING CURVES

After the curve has been cut, the edge is rough. Some stock must be removed to smooth the edge and to bring it down to the finished line. Sometimes it is necessary to form or mold a curved surface. Figure 17–1. These jobs can be done with some kind of cutting tool such as a spokeshave or drawknife, or with a scraping tool such as a file or rasp.

THE SPOKESHAVE

A *spokeshave* has a frame with two handles which hold a small cutting blade. It is used to plane convex and concave edges. The depth of cut can be regulated with one or two small thumbscrews. The spokeshave was originally used for shaping the spokes of wheels but since has come to be a common tool for finishing the edges of curves and molding irregular shapes. Figure 17–2.

CUTTING WITH A SPOKESHAVE

Place the piece in the vise with the edge to be smoothed near the surface of the vise. Hold the tool with both

17–1. This coffee table made of oak and walnut has legs and rails that require forming.

17–2. A spokeshave is used to cut concave and convex edges and for molding and forming work. This type has two narrow nuts on the top for adjusting the depth of the cutter. The cutter is held in place with a cap, which is fastened by a thumb screw.

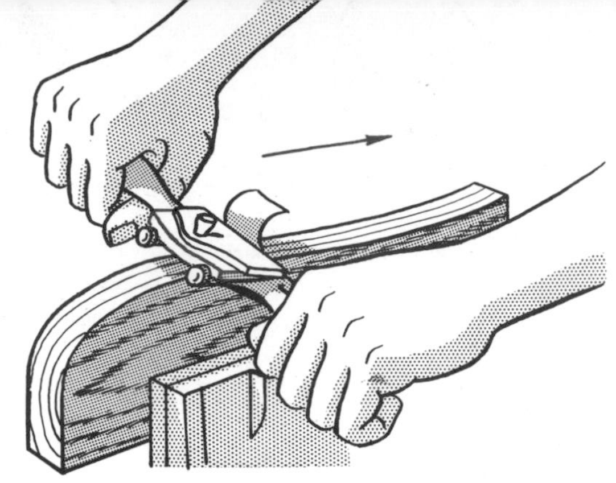

17–4. Cutting with a spokeshave by drawing it toward you. The blade should be set just deep enough to form a thin shaving. If set too deep, the tool will chatter.

hands. Figure 17–3. You can either draw the spokeshave toward you or put your thumbs behind the frame and push it as you would a small plane. Figure 17–4 and 17–5. Place the cutting edge on the wood and apply even pressure. Work *with* the grain of the wood. Your experience in using a plane will tell you if the proper chip is being formed. If the blade is set too deep, the tool will chatter.

When concave curves are being planed, the cutting is done from the top of a curve downward. Use the spokeshave as you would a small plane.

THE DRAWKNIFE

The *drawknife* is a U-shaped tool. It has a blade 8 or 10 inches long with a handle at either end. Figure 17–6. This tool is very good for removing

17–3. Correct method of holding a spokeshave.

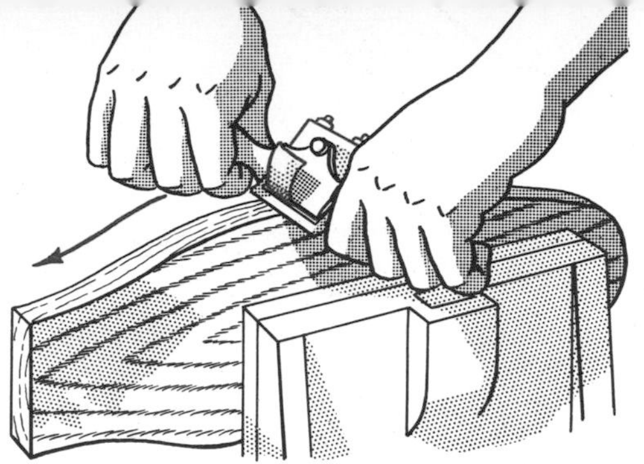

17–5. **Holding a spokeshave when pushing it away from you. Even pressure must be applied to do the cutting.**

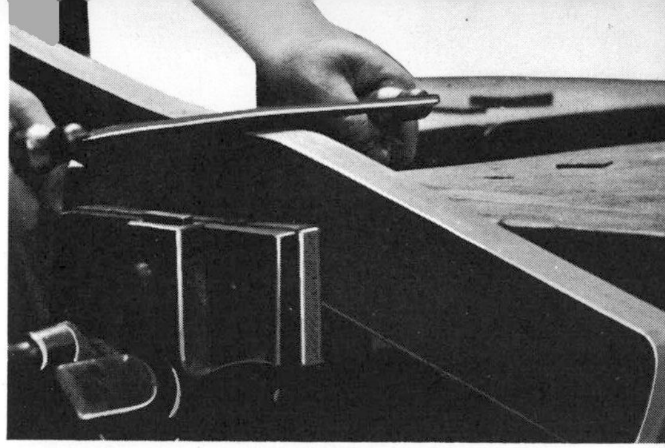

17–7. **Cutting with a drawknife. Tip the blade at a slight angle to the work to permit it to enter the stock. Be careful not to cut the stock too deeply.**

large amounts of stock rapidly and for doing molding work such as shaping a canoe paddle or building a model boat or airplane. Be very careful in using this tool, as the long, exposed blade can be dangerous.

CUTTING WITH THE DRAWKNIFE

Clamp the work in a vise in such a way that the cutting will take place *with* the grain of the wood. Hold the tool in both hands, with the blade firmly against the wood and the bevel side down. Figure 17–7. Turn the blade at a slight angle to the work. Carefully draw it into the wood until a thin chip forms; then draw the knife steadily toward you. Figure 17–8. Do not try to take too deep a cut at one time, as this will split the wood.

17–6. **A drawknife is especially useful when removing large amounts of stock rapidly.**

THE FILE OR RASP

A *file* or *rasp* is a scraping tool. It should be used only as a last resort. Too often the inexperienced woodworker prefers to use one of these tools when a cutting tool would do a much better job. There are a great many kinds of files, in many shapes and sizes. It would be impractical to describe even a few of them here. The two files used most often are half-round cabinet and flat files. Figure 17–9. A *rasp* looks a lot like a file, except that the face is cut with individually shaped teeth. Figure 17–10. The rasp removes large amounts of stock quickly and leaves a rough surface; the

17–8. **Using a drawknife to shape the hull of a model boat.**

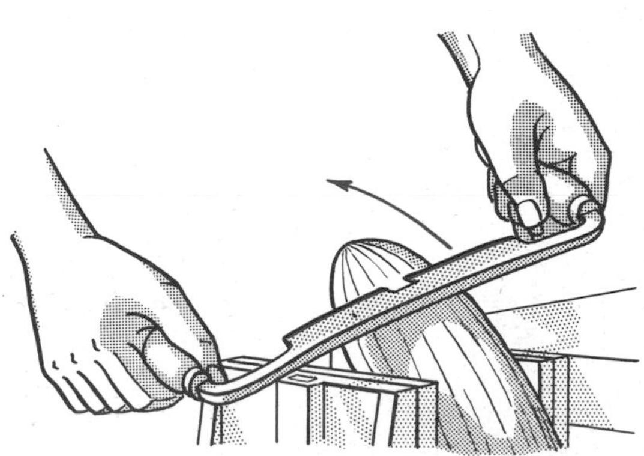

17–9. A cabinet file. Be sure that the handle is attached when using it for smoothing operations.

17–10. A rasp. Notice the individually shaped teeth. This tool is used when removing large amounts of stock, but it leaves quite a rough surface.

file leaves a smoother finish. Always put a handle on the rasp and file when using them because the tang can cause a bad injury.

SMOOTHING WITH A FILE OR RASP

Clamp the work tightly in the vise. Hold the handle in your right hand and the end of the tool in your left. Apply pressure on the forward stroke, making a slight shearing cut across the edge of the work. Figure 17–11. Release the pressure on the return stroke. When you are using a half-round, or rattail file, for finishing a convex curve, twist the tool slowly as the forward stroke is made. Don't rock a file or rasp as this would round off the edge of the work. These tools should be cleaned often with a file card.

17–11. Using a file to dress an internal curve. Make sure that you hold the file flat against the stock and that you do not rock it.

THE SURFORM TOOL

This is a forming tool with a hardened and tempered tool-steel cutting blade. Figure 17–12. The blade has 45-degree cutting edges with many small openings that make it easy to cut wood, plastics, or soft metals. The teeth never become clogged. The replaceable blade fits into either a file or plane type holder. This tool is used like a rasp. To obtain best results, apply light, even pressure against the material. Figure 17–13. This produces a smooth, flat surface. It is a good repair tool for smoothing an edge or end

17–12. A file type of surform tool.

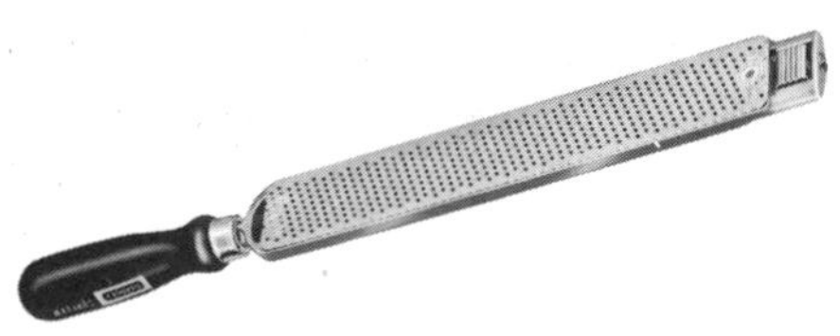

that is chipped or splintered. It is also good for shaping gun stocks, canoe paddles, wooden tool handles, and other odd-shaped projects.

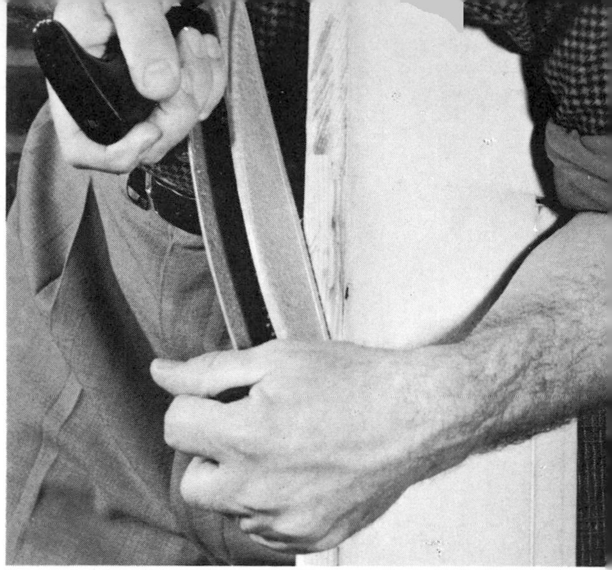

17–13. Using a plane type of surform tool for smoothing the edge of a door.

CAN YOU ANSWER THESE QUESTIONS ON FORMING AND SMOOTHING CURVES?

1. In what ways is a spokeshave like a plane?
2. Where did the spokeshave get its name?
3. Can a spokeshave be both drawn and pushed?
4. To what job is the drawknife best suited?
5. To make the cut, how should the drawknife be held against the wood?
6. What is the main use for a scraper?
7. Describe how you would make a homemade scraper.
8. How is a file different from a rasp?
9. Does a good woodworker use a file or rasp very often?
10. List the safety practices that should be observed when using a file or rasp.
11. Describe the way in which a file or rasp is handled; the surform tool.

Section V
Decorating, Shaping, and Bending Woods

The fifth 5 steps in hand woodworking—what you must know and be able to do.

18. Chamfer, bevel, or taper cutting: how it is done, what these are used for, and how they are different from other procedures.
19. Chiseling and gouging operations: kinds of chisels and gouges, chiseling with the grain, across grain, vertically and horizontally, and many other uses; how to use a gouge.
20. Carving: kinds of wood, woods to use, correct tools, methods of treating wood and techniques.
21. Wood bending: equipment needed and how to heat and bend the wood over forms.
22. Laminating: what it is, advantages, industrial application, uses in small projects.

In your work with woods, you will need many sharp-edged tools to cut or form the wood either in straight lines or curved designs. This cutting can be done with a plane, chisel, or gouge to decorate the pieces, to fit them, and to shape them. Study the chisel and gouge thoroughly, since these tools are used over and over in woodworking.

Sometimes you can get the shape you want by bending rather than by cutting. For example, you might make a boat model by cutting, shaping, and forming it from a single piece of stock. On the other hand, to build the boat to full size, you would probably use bent wood.

Not all of the operations in this section will be done on a single project, but eventually you will need all of them. See the "box" above. Further steps in woodworking are on pp. 15, 43, 60, 94, 132, 143, 170, 219, 244.

Section V

UNIT 18. CHAMFER, BEVEL, OR TAPER

Three angular cuts made in much the same way but used for different purposes are the chamfer, bevel, and taper.

The *chamfer* is an angular cut only part way across the corner or edge, used mostly as a decoration on an edge or end. Figure 18–1 and 2. The *bevel* is an angle cut completely across the edge or end of a piece. This is done when one piece is set at an angle to another, such as the sides of a book trough. Figure 18–3 and 4. A *taper* is cut on the legs of tables and stools to make them appear more lightweight and graceful. Figure 18–5 and 6. On some projects the taper is cut on all four sides; on others only the two inside surfaces are cut.

18–1. The base of this lamp illustrates the use of a chamfer.

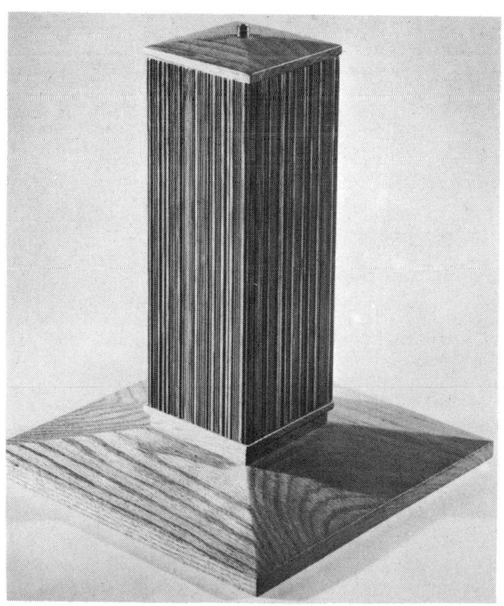

MAKING A THROUGH CHAMFER

1. Determine the amount of chamfer from the drawing. If this is not given, the usual practice is to cut a chamfer of about 3/16 inch on stock 1 inch thick. There are three methods for marking the chamfer. One is to hold a pencil between the fingers as a gauge and run it along the face surface and edge or end as shown in Figure 18–7. Another way is to insert a pencil point in a marking gauge and use the marking gauge to lay out the line. Do not use a regular marking gauge, however, as this would leave a rough edge on the chamfer. A third way is to use a combination square and pencil to mark the line.

18–2. A chamfer.

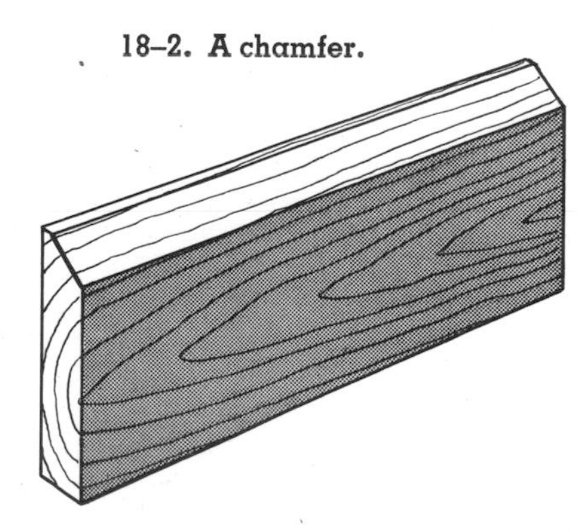

18–3. A bevel was cut on the two pieces to form the joint at the roof line of this bird house.

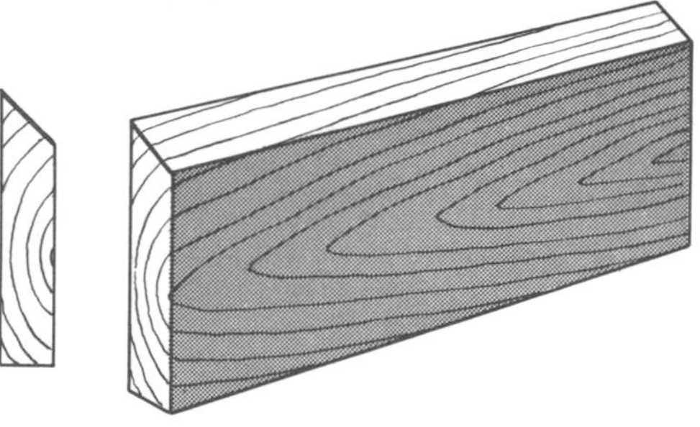

18–4. A bevel.

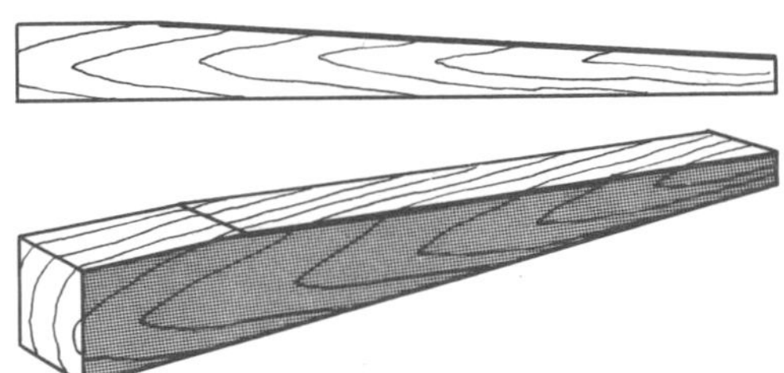

18–6. A taper.

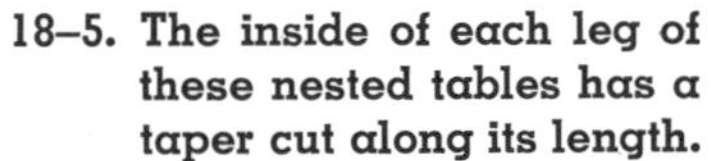

18–5. The inside of each leg of these nested tables has a taper cut along its length.

18–7. Marking a chamfer by using a pencil guided with your fingers held against the edge of the stock.

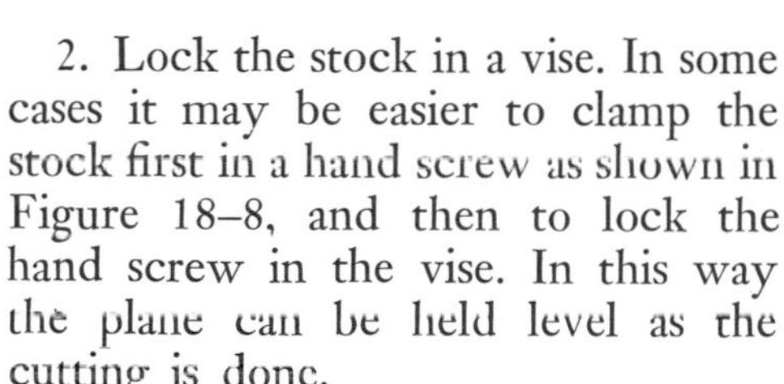

2. Lock the stock in a vise. In some cases it may be easier to clamp the stock first in a hand screw as shown in Figure 18–8, and then to lock the hand screw in the vise. In this way the plane can be held level as the cutting is done.

18–8. Planing a chamfer with the wood held in a hand screw. By this means you can cut the chamfer with the plane held in a level position.

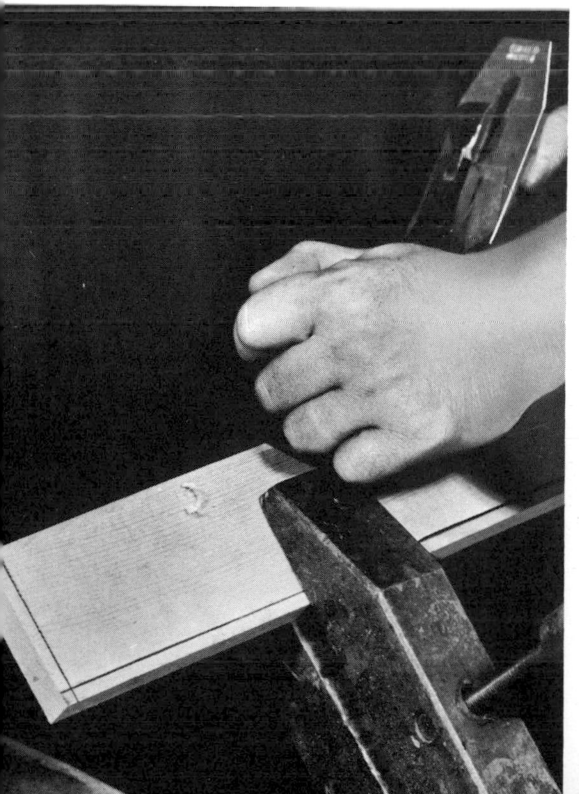

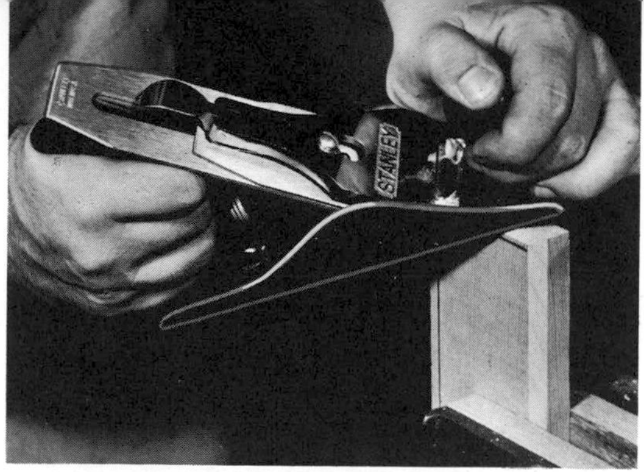

18–9. Cutting a chamfer on end grain. A shearing cut is taken to prevent the edge of the stock from splitting out.

3. Plane the corner with the grain along the total length of the stock. Remove the stock evenly so that the chamfer will come to the marked line on both sides at the same time. Use the fingers of your left hand to guide the plane and hold it at the proper angle. In taking the last cut, form a chip that is the full width of the chamfer across the total length of the stock.

When cutting a chamfer on end grain, hold the plane at an angle to the surface and take a shearing cut across the edge. Figure 18–9. If this is not done, there is danger of splitting out the chamfer on the edge. Figure 18–10. To check the chamfer, set a sliding T bevel at an angle of 45 degrees and hold it against the chamfer edge.

PLANING A BEVEL

Determine the angle at which the bevel is to be cut and, with a protractor, set a sliding T bevel to this angle. Hold the sliding T bevel against the face surface and mark the angle of the bevel on both ends of the stock. Figure 18–11. Begin to plane the bevel as you would plane an edge, except that the plane must be tipped at about the angle at which the bevel

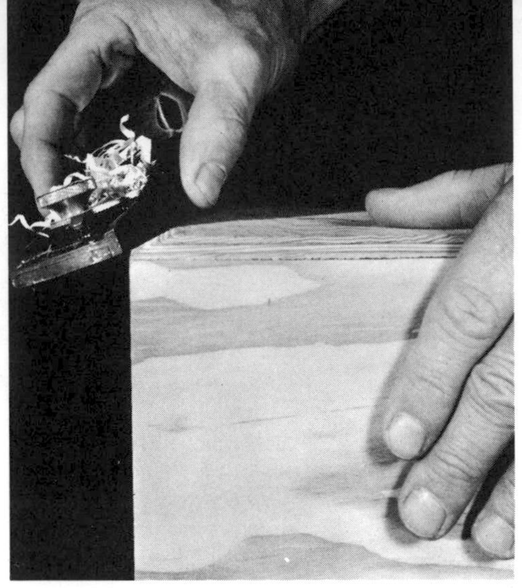

18–10. Using a block plane for cutting a chamfer on the edge of plywood.

is to be cut. Check this angle frequently with a sliding T bevel. Continue to plane the edge until the bevel is formed.

18–11. Using a sliding T bevel to lay out a bevel on one edge of a piece of stock. As the plane approaches the finish line, the sliding T bevel can be used in the same manner as a try square to check the bevel along the edge.

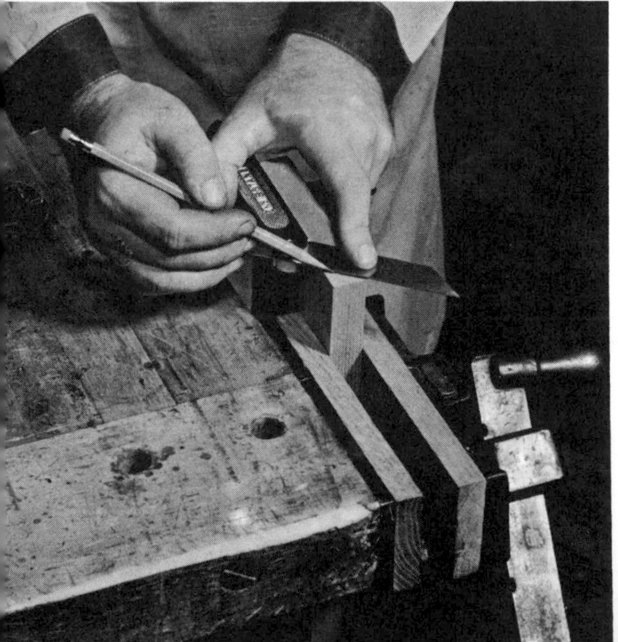

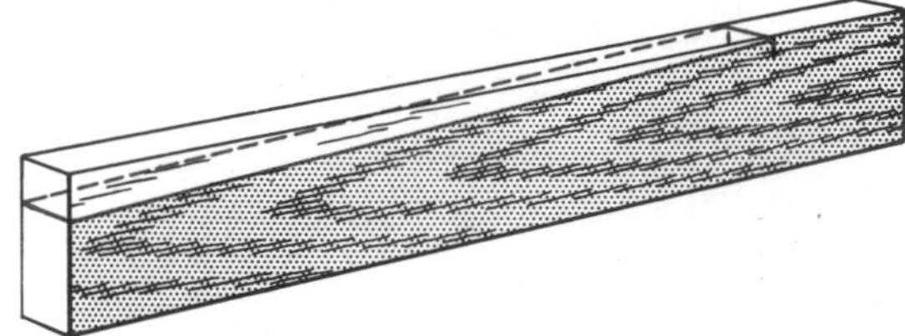

18–12a. Laying out a taper.

CUTTING A TAPER

Square up the legs on which the taper is to be cut. Lay the four legs side by side and mark the position at which the taper is to start. Figures 18–12a and b. Then square a line around all four sides of each leg. Next determine the amount of stock to be removed at the foot of the taper. Set a marking gauge to this amount and mark a line across the lower end of the leg on the two opposite sides, if all four sides are to be tapered, or on one side if only two sides are to be tapered. Draw a line along each side to show where the taper is to be cut.

18–12b. When the taper is to be cut on two adjoining surfaces, one side should be laid out and cut before the second layout is made.

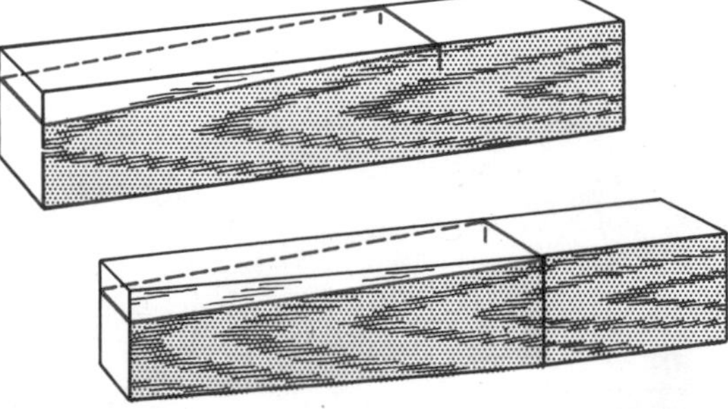

Cut the taper with a handsaw or, if one is available, a band or circular saw. Plane the tapered surface smooth and true. Figure 18–13.

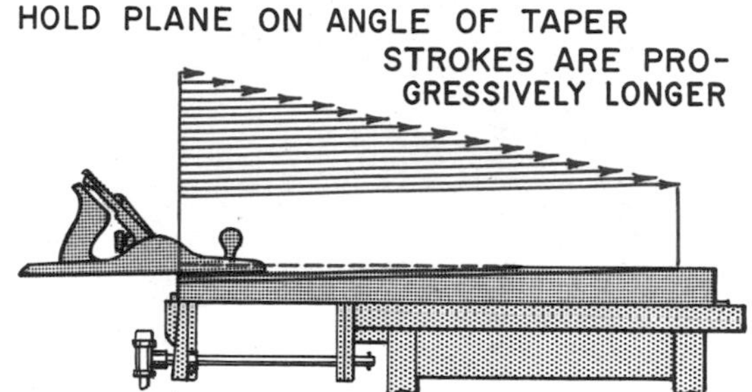
HOLD PLANE ON ANGLE OF TAPER
STROKES ARE PROGRESSIVELY LONGER

18–13. Planing a taper. Notice that longer and longer strokes are made until the total length of the taper is being planed.

CAN YOU ANSWER THESE QUESTIONS ON A CHAMFER, BEVEL, OR TAPER?

1. In what way is a chamfer different from a bevel?
2. Would you lay out a chamfer with a regular marking gauge? Discuss two methods of laying out an ordinary chamfer.
3. What precautions must be taken in cutting a chamfer on end grain?
4. How can you hold the plane level and still cut a chamfer?
5. Describe a stop chamfer.
6. Why is a sliding T bevel necessary when making a bevel?

Section V

UNIT 19. SHAPING STOCK WITH A CHISEL OR GOUGE

There are many cutting jobs that cannot be done with a saw or plane. These can be done with either a chisel or a gouge. You will find many uses for a set of good chisels.

CHISELS AND GOUGES

The chisels you buy can be either of two types, the *socket* or the *tang* chisel. The handle of the socket chisel fits into a funnel-shaped socket at the top of the blade. Socket chisels have heavier blades and will take pounding better than tang chisels. The tang chisel has a straight shank formed at the end of the blade. This tang is force-fitted into a plastic handle. The tang chisel is designed for paring, shaping, and similar light chiseling. It has a thin blade. Figure 19–1.

There are several kinds of chisels including:

a. *Paring* chisels which have a light, thin blade about 2½″ long.

b. *Butt* chisels which have standard weight blades but are about 3″ long. They are used on work where a longer chisel might be difficult to work.

c. *Pocket* chisels which have

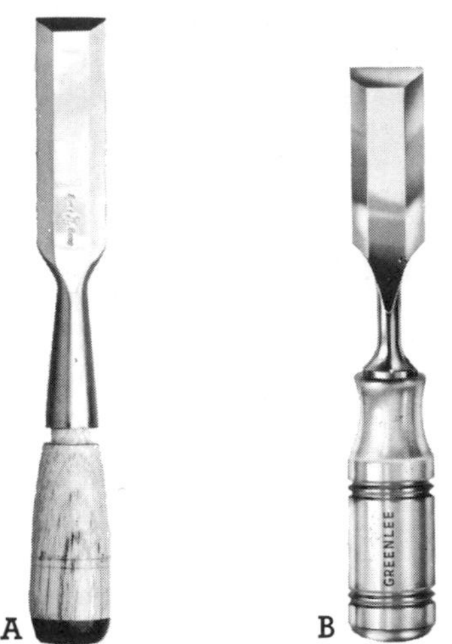

19–1. Types of chisels.
A. A socket-type chisel is made in such a way that the handle fits into a socket of the blade. B. Tang-type chisel has the tang of the chisel itself running into the handle.

heavier-weight blades about 4½″ long.

d. *Firmer* chisels that are all around chisels with heavier-weight blades about 6″ long. They are used for both heavy and light work.

When grinding a chisel, make sure the proper angle and shape are obtained. The harder and tougher the material, the greater the angle of the cutting edge. Figure 19–2.

19–2. This shows correct and incorrect grinding edges for chisels. The angle of the chisel will depend on the kind of work to be done.

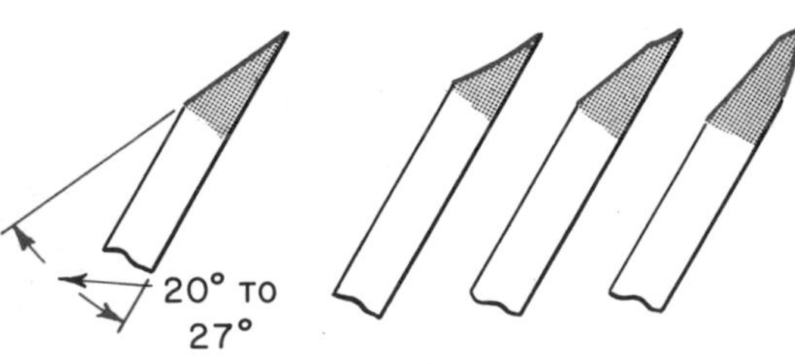

You will need at least six chisels with blades from ¼ to 1 inch wide, increasing at ⅛ inch intervals.

Gouges are chisels with curved blades. They are sharpened either with the bevel on the inside or the outside. Figure 19–3a and b. Gouges vary in size from ¼ inch to 2 inches.

To cut with a chisel or gouge, it is often necessary to pound the tool with a mallet that has a head of wood, hard rubber, or rawhide. Figure 19–4.

19–3. A. Gouge with a bevel on the outside. B. Gouge with a bevel on the inside.

A B

19–4. A mallet is used for pounding a chisel or gouge. The head should be wood, leather, or rubber.

CUTTING HORIZONTALLY WITH THE GRAIN

Lock the work in a vise so the cutting can be done with the grain of the wood. Figure 19–5. Never attempt to cut against the grain, as the wood will split out.

For rough cutting, hold the chisel with the bevel side against the stock. Grasp the chisel handle in your right hand and the blade in your left. Figure 19–6. Use your right hand to apply pressure to the tool and your left hand to guide the cutting action.

19–5. Cutting action of the chisel. Always cut with the grain, never against it.

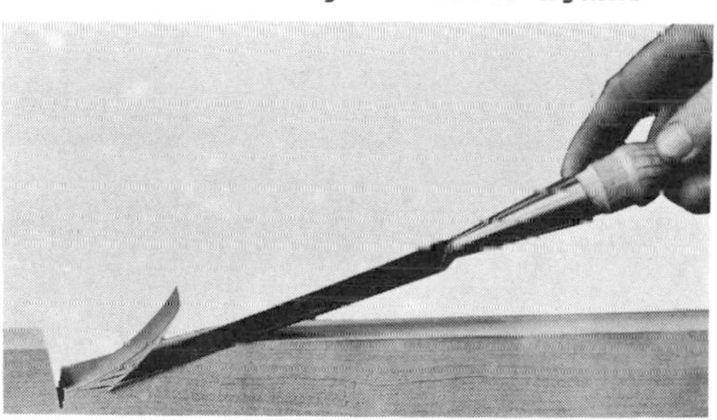

The cutting action may be taken in two ways. The blade may be forced into the stock parallel to the wood, or a shearing cut can be made with the blade moving from right to left as it cuts. You will find that the straight cutting takes more pressure. Also, it is more convenient to hold the tool in your left hand and pound with the mallet held in your right hand. When making light, paring cuts with the chisel, turn the tool around with the flat surface next to the wood. Hold the blade between your thumb and forefinger to guide it in taking these cuts.

HORIZONTAL CUTTING ACROSS THE GRAIN

Lock the work in a vise or clamp it to the top of the bench. Rough cutting can be done with the bevel down or by paring with the flat side down. In cutting across the grain to make a rabbet, dado, or lap joint, work from one side to about halfway across the stock. Figure 19–7. Never go completely across the stock, as

19–6. Holding a chisel for doing heavy horizontal cutting with the grain. The blade of the chisel is held firmly in the left hand. Courtesy the Jam Handy Organization.

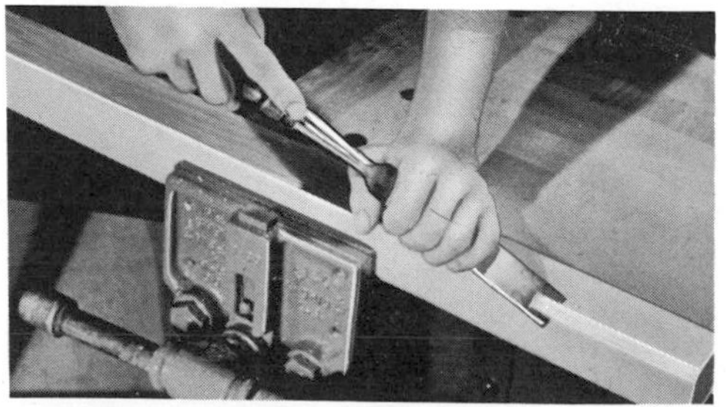

19–7. Roughing out a cut across grain. The chisel is held with the bevel side down and the mallet is used for driving. This illustrates cutting of a lap joint.

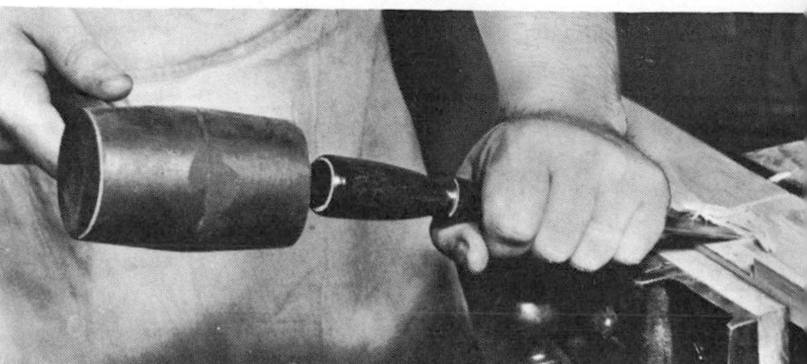

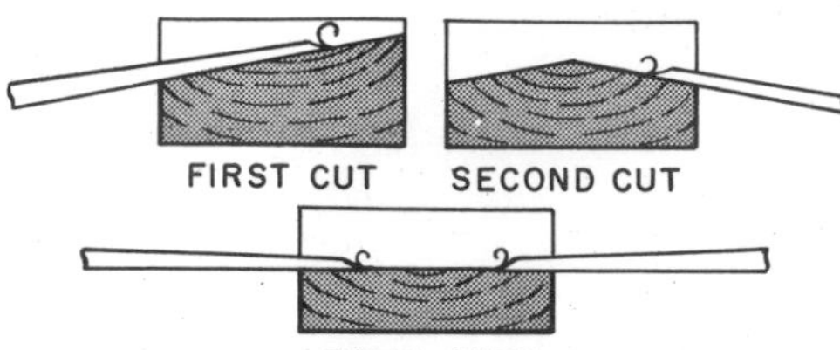

19–8. Proper method of cutting a lap joint from both sides, leaving the center high and then trimming the center down.

this will chip out the opposite side. Work from both sides to the finished line, leaving the center higher. Figure 19–8. Then with light paring cuts bring the center down to the line. Figure 19–9. To clean out the corners, hold the chisel in one hand with the flat side toward the shoulder and draw it across as you would a knife. Figure 19–10.

CUTTING CONVEX CURVES HORIZONTALLY

Remember when you lock the work in the vise that you will be cutting with the grain. Begin by taking straight cuts that tend to follow the curve. Figure 19–11. Remove most of

19–9. Making light paring cuts across the grain. The blade of the chisel is held between the thumb and forefinger for accurate control. The chisel is held with the flat side down.

19–10. Cleaning out the corners of a lap joint by pulling the chisel across with the flat side held against the shoulder of the joint.

the extra stock with these straight cuts until the curve is almost formed. Then hold the chisel with the flat side down and carefully cut the curve by applying forward pressure and raising the handle to follow the curve. Figure 19–12. Move the chisel sideways across the work, making a series of cuts close together.

CUTTING VERTICALLY ACROSS GRAIN

Hold the stock over a bench hook, clamp it over a scrap piece of wood, or place it over a bench stop. Never do vertical chiseling directly on the top of a bench, as this would damage it.

19–11. Cutting a convex curve. Note that several straight cuts can be taken to pre-form the curve to the approximate arc.

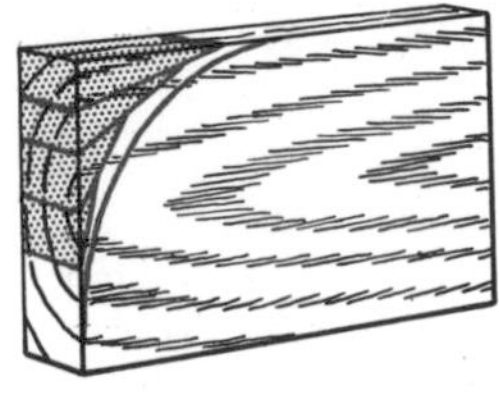

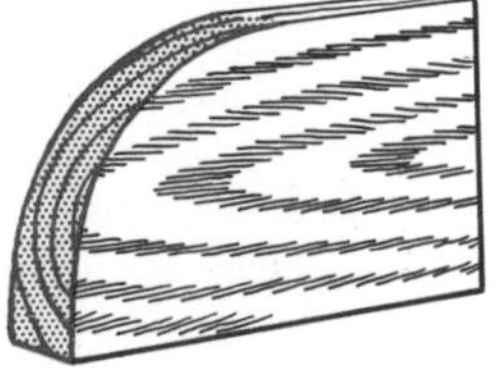

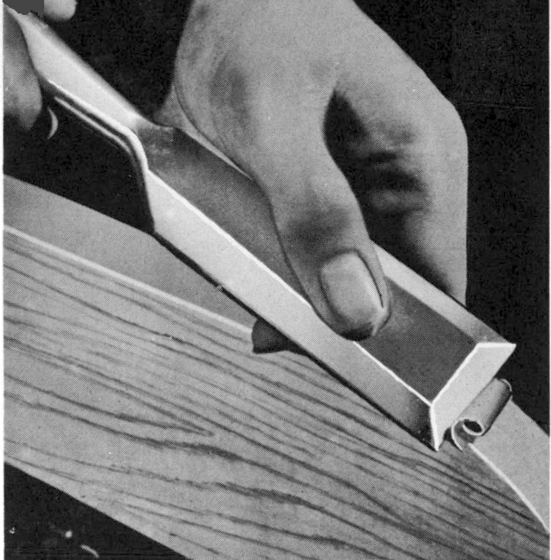

19–12. Finishing a convex curve. Forward pressure is applied and the handle is raised gradually to follow the proper curvature.

Hold the chisel in a vertical position with the handle in your right hand and the blade guided between your left thumb and forefinger. Take a shearing cut, working from right to left. On wide stock, you can regulate the depth of the cut by holding the flat side of the chisel against the surface that has already been cut. Figure 19–13a and b.

CUTTING END GRAIN VERTICALLY

Lay the work flat over a bench hook, or piece of scrap stock, and clamp it firmly in place. Begin at one corner of the stock to make the cut by tipping the handle to one side. Rotate the handle to get a shearing cut. Figure 19–14. Always start from the corner and work toward the center. Working the other way would split out the end grain.

CUTTING CONCAVE (HOLLOW OR CURVED INWARD) SURFACES VERTICALLY

Lock the work in a vise with the concave surface to be removed just above the end of the vise. Take straight cuts until most of the waste stock is removed. Work as always from the edge toward the end to

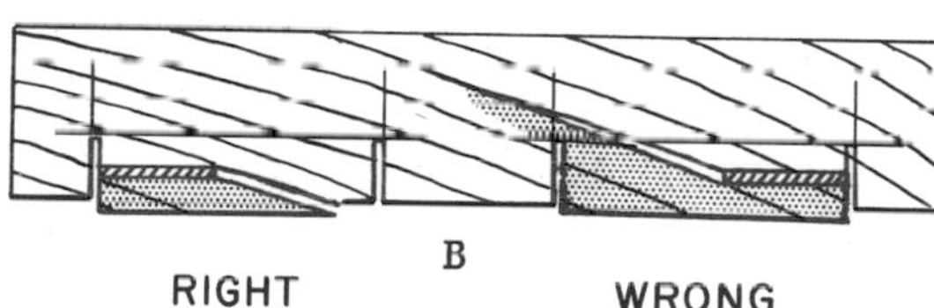

19–13. Cutting vertically across the grain. A. Notice how the left hand guides the chisel as the right hand applies pressure. The chisel should be tilted slightly to give a sliding action. B. Cut with the grain so that the waste wood will split away from the layout line.

19–14. Cutting end grain vertically. Note that the stock is held over a bench hook and pressure applied to the handle at the same time that it is rotated slightly to obtain a shearing cut.

19–15. Cutting a concave curve. The chisel is held with the bevel side down and the cut is being taken from the edge to the end grain. In this way the cut is made with the grain of the wood.

avoid splitting out the stock. To form the concave curve, hold the chisel with the bevel side toward the stock. Apply forward pressure, at the same time moving the handle in an arc (curve). Figure 19–15.

CUTTING WITH A GOUGE

Gouges are used in the same general way as chisels. Outside bevel gouges are handled in the same way as a chisel is handled when the bevel side is down. An inside bevel gouge is used as a chisel, with the bevel turned up.

To do heavy gouging with an outside bevel gouge, hold the handle in your right hand and the blade in your left hand. Push the gouge forward and rock it slightly from side to side to make a shearing cut. If very heavy work is being done, the gouge can be held in the left hand and the force

19–16. Doing heavy gouging to shape out the inside of a tray. The left hand holds the blade firmly, while the right hand applies the pressure.

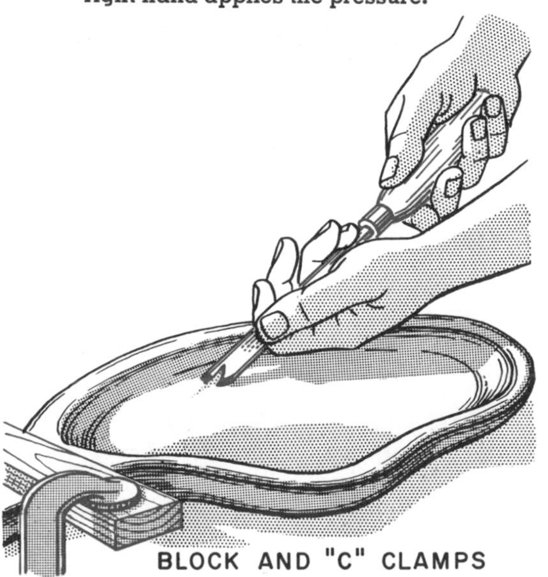

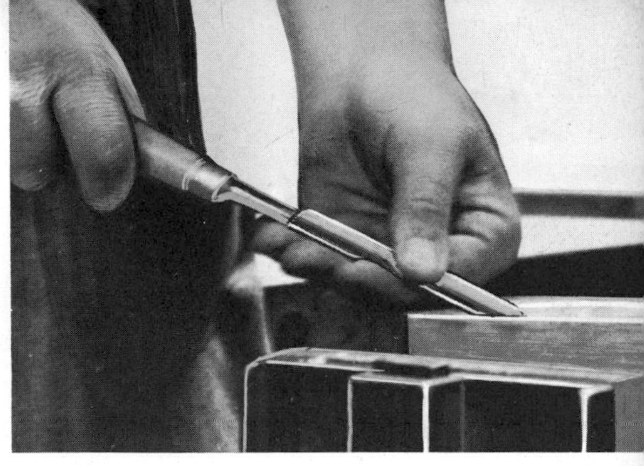

19–17. Doing light gouging with the gouge held between the thumb and other fingers for accurate, light work.

applied with a mallet. Figure 19–16. If a large surface is to be gouged out, it is better to work across the grain. The reason for this is that the gouge is less likely to dig in than when cutting in the direction of the grain.

To do light gouging, hold the blade in your left hand as shown in Figure 19–17, and take a long, thin shaving. Force the tool into the wood lightly and then push on the handle to finish it.

Gouging is done to form recesses, to do veining and decorating work on the surface of wood, to shape such articles as boat hulls, and to imitate the appearance of age as on the treasure chest.

CAN YOU ANSWER THESE QUESTIONS ON SHAPING STOCK WITH A CHISEL OR GOUGE?

1. Name the two types of chisels. What is a butt chisel?
2. How are gouges sharpened?
3. Do you cut with or against the grain of the wood?
4. How should a chisel be held for making heavy cuts?
5. What are the two ways to do the cutting?
6. When making light paring cuts, how should the blade be held?
7. Give the procedure for cutting a rabbet, dado, or lap joint.
8. How can the corners be chiseled out?
9. Should vertical chiseling be done directly on the top of a bench?
10. In cutting convex curves, why are straight cuts made first?
11. What kind of chisel action is best for cutting end grain vertically?
12. Can a concave surface be cut with a chisel?
13. How does a gouge differ from a chisel?
14. What kind of gouge is best for heavy gouge work?
15. To remove a great deal of stock, is it better to work with or across the grain?
16. What is the purpose of gouging?

Section V

UNIT 20. WOOD CARVING

Wood carving is a most ancient art, examples of which can be seen in museums, churches, and public buildings all over the world. Figure 20–1. It is also one of the most interesting woodworking hobbies. Many artistic and attractive objects can be made with very simple tools. Figure 20–2.

KINDS OF CARVING

There are several kinds of carving, which include the following: *Whittling* is a kind of freehand carving done with knives. Many interesting and useful projects can be made by using only the knife as a cutting tool. Figure 20–3. *Chip carving* is a method of forming a design by cutting shapes in the wood surface. It is used mostly for cutting geometric shapes such as triangles, squares, and curved variations of these. Chip carving can be done with carving tools or knives. In *chase carving*, a design is laid out and gouges used on the surface with long, sweeping cuts. Figure 20–4. Carved free-form bowls and a variety of other items can be made in this manner. In *relief carving*, the background is cut away to form the surface design. This is one of the most difficult kinds of carving. The design stands out in three-dimensional form. If the carving is fairly shallow, it is called *low* relief. If the design has greater depth it is known as *high* relief. In high relief the design is undercut so that it seems to stand away from the background. *Wood sculpture* or "carving in the round" is very interesting and perhaps the most difficult kind of wood carving. This method is used in forming a figure such as an animal, human replica, or caricature. The design is first traced on two sides of the wood. The

20–1. Wood carving is an ancient art.

20–2. High relief carving on domestic buckwood. Carving is a wood activity in which you can use your creative ability.

Jumbo

USE 1¼" THICK WOOD, PLACE ON BLOCK WITH GRAIN VERTICAL

BEGIN WHITTLING AT POINTS MARKED WITH ARROWS

BOTH SIDES WILL BE THE SAME.

NOTE. CURVE IN TAIL

¾" DEEP AT THIS POINT

1¼"

FINISH BY PAINTING WITH A MIXTURE OF BLACK & WHITE. DO NOT VARNISH.

THREE BLACK TOE-NAILS ON EACH FOOT

20–3. This kind of whittling can be done with simple knives.

outline can be jig-sawed on one face, then the block turned around a quarter turn and the side view cut out with the jig saw. From this point on, the work is completed with knives and gouges. Figure 20–5. Routing bits or carving burrs can be used on a drill press to do some of the rough shaping. Figure 20–6.

WOODS

Many kinds of woods can be used for carving, but among the most desirable are the following:

White pine is a good choice for the beginner. The fibers are close together yet are easily cut clean, both with and across grain. Pine is relatively straight-grained and has a rather even structure that makes for few hard and soft spots.

Both *genuine mahogany* and *Philippine mahogany* are excellent woods for carving. Genuine mahogany has a deep brown color that gives it a rich appearance. It also has an interesting grain pattern. Philippine mahogany is also easy to work, but has a less interesting grain.

Walnut is somewhat more difficult to work but is, nevertheless, an excellent wood for carving. It is especially good for such projects as handles for sports equipment.

TREATING WOOD FOR CARVING AND WOOD TURNING

One of the problems in making wood carvings and turning thin bowls on the lathe is that, after the project is completed, it often will split, check, or warp as the wood dries out. This is especially true if the moisture content of the wood is higher than that of the room in which it is used. However, with a relatively simple

20–4. Chase carving is illustrated in this hand-carved, leaf-shaped tray of walnut.

20–5. The delicate sculptured pieces at both sides illustrate fine craftsmanship and creative design ability.

20–6. To do freehand carving on the drill press, use a high speed of at least 5,000 r.p.m.

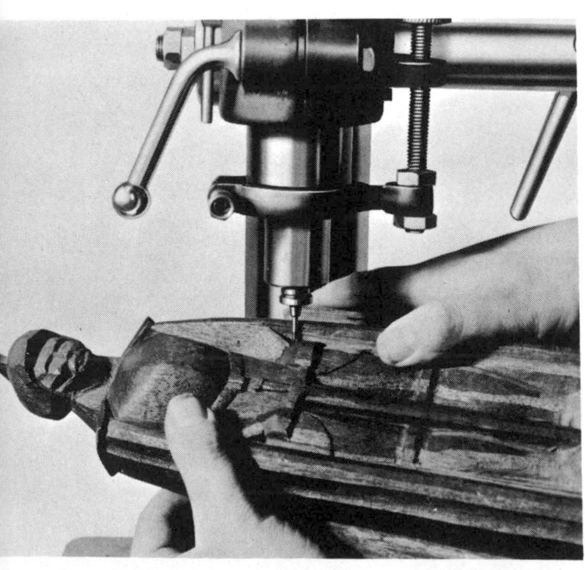

chemical treatment, these defects can be prevented even when starting with green or only partially dry wood. The first step is to rough shape the carving or rough turn the bowl to about ⅛″ oversize. Then make a watertight container of plywood or line a wood box with thin plastic sheet. Place a 30 per cent solution of polyethylene glycol-1000 in the tank. Soak the carvings or rough bowls in the solution at room temperature for about three weeks. The water-soluble, wax-like chemical is absorbed by the wood, thus preventing checking, splitting, and warping. Allow the rough carving or bowl to air dry on shelves in a heated shop for several weeks. Now complete the carving or bowl to final size. The only finish that works well

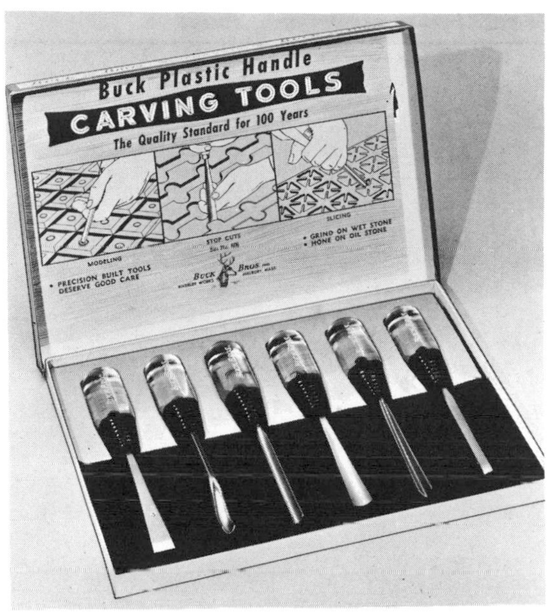

20–7. A matched set of carving tools.

20–9. A complete set of knives and other cutting tools for whittling.

on the treated wood contains polyurethane resin. Complete information on the use of this wood treatment can be obtained from the Forest Products Laboratory at Madison, Wisconsin.

KINDS OF CARVING TOOLS

Gouges, knives, and carving tools are needed for wood carving. There are many special carving tools that can be purchased but only a few are required for basic work. Figure 20–7. These include the following:

1. A *skew* or *flat chisel* that is ground on both sides to a sharp edge. Figure 20–8a.

20–8. Patterns of cutting edges of carving tools. A. Chisel. B. V parting tool. C. Veiner. D. Gouges and fluters.

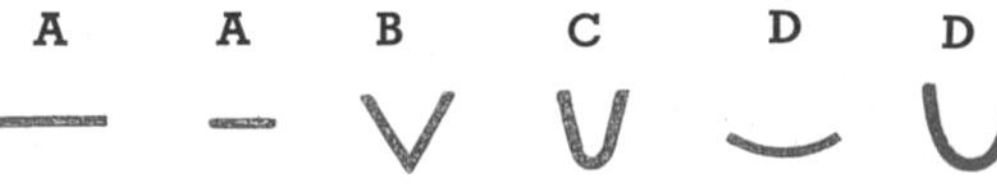

2. A *parting* tool, which is V-shaped, used to cut triangular shapes in the wood. Figure 20–8b.
3. A *veiner*, a very small gouge with a sharp V cutting edge. Figure 20–8c.
4. *Gouges* and *fluters* which are ground on the outside, in sizes from 3/8″ to 5/8″ and with cutting edges of different radii. Some are quite flat—almost chisel shaped—while others are shaped like half an ellipse. Figure 20–8d.
5. *Knives* for whittling. Figure 20–9.

A complete set of carving tools can be purchased as individual tools or as a set with a single handle into which various blades can be inserted.

GENERAL SUGGESTIONS FOR CARVING

1. Always work out a pattern before starting the carving. Enlarge the pattern to the size you want. Then

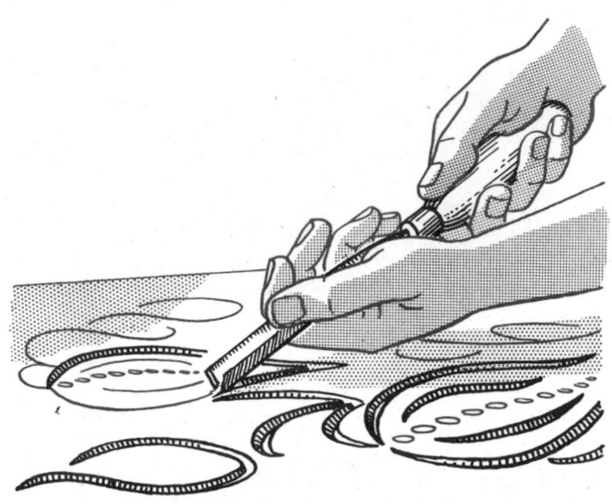

20–10. A parting tool used to outline the design.

carefully transfer the design to the wood.

2. Clamp the work securely. It is much better to work with the wood in a vise or clamped to the top of the bench. In this way both hands are free to do the carving. For some work, the tool is held in one hand and the end struck with a mallet. For other cutting, one hand applies the pressure while the other hand guides the tool.

3. Keep your fingers and body away from the front cutting edge as much as possible. There is always danger that the tool will slip and cut you severely. Sometimes, in whittling, it isn't always possible to keep your hands away from the front of the cutting edge. At these times, try to keep your fingers below so that if the knife slips it will not cut you.

4. The first cut should always sever or cut apart the grain. After the outline has been drawn (in chip carving, for example), the design is outlined with a sharp V parting tool. Figure 20–10. After this is done, you can then work up to the cut by removing clean-cut chips.

5. Try to cut with the grain as much as possible. Cutting with the grain is always easier and there is less chance that the tool will cut in and chip out a piece of your design. When cutting against the grain, roll the tool to the right and left to cut the fibers. This will help prevent tearing into the fibers and gouging out.

6. When cutting the raised portion (for example on relief carving), cut so that the base will be slightly wider than the upper part. Don't undercut until all of the carving is completed, as this will cause real trouble.

7. Start with a relatively simple design, to practice the art of tool control.

8. Remember that *sharp* cutting tools are best for all kinds of carving.

CAN YOU ANSWER THESE QUESTIONS ON WOOD CARVING?

1. Describe low relief carving.
2. What kind of carving is done to produce an animal or other free-standing object?
3. Tell what kinds of wood are best for carving.
4. List the common cutting tools needed for wood carving.
5. Is the procedure for all carving the same? Describe.
6. Tell how to treat wood to prevent warping and checking.

Section V

UNIT 21. BENDING SOLID WOOD

To make sports equipment such as toboggans, skis, and surfboards, stock must be bent. Figure 21–1. Sometimes stock is bent to form a furniture part that must be curved such as the front of a drawer. There are many kinds of wood suitable for building these projects, but ash, hickory, birch, and oak are the best.

Wood can be bent more easily when it is steamed or made soft by soaking in hot water. This makes the wood cells more plastic so they can be stretched or compressed. However, most of the bending is due to compression (squeezing the cells on the inside curve), and much less of the bending is due to the stretching of the cells (on the outside curve). As a matter of fact, the outside will stretch only 1 or 2 per cent, while the inside will compress as much as 25 per cent. When wood is properly moistened and heated, it will bend ten times more easily than dry wood.

EQUIPMENT

The most popular method of bending wood is to soften it by steaming or boiling in hot water. A necessary piece of equipment is the heating tube. It is closed on the lower end and has a cover on the upper end. Figure 21–2. The lower end of this tube is placed directly above a gas flame. Water is poured into the tube and the end closed. The heat and moisture soften the wood, as explained later.

Another piece needed is the form for bending the wood. A form like the one shown in Figure 21–3 can be used for the staves of a toboggan. Another form (Figure 21–4) is satisfactory for bending the tips of water skis.

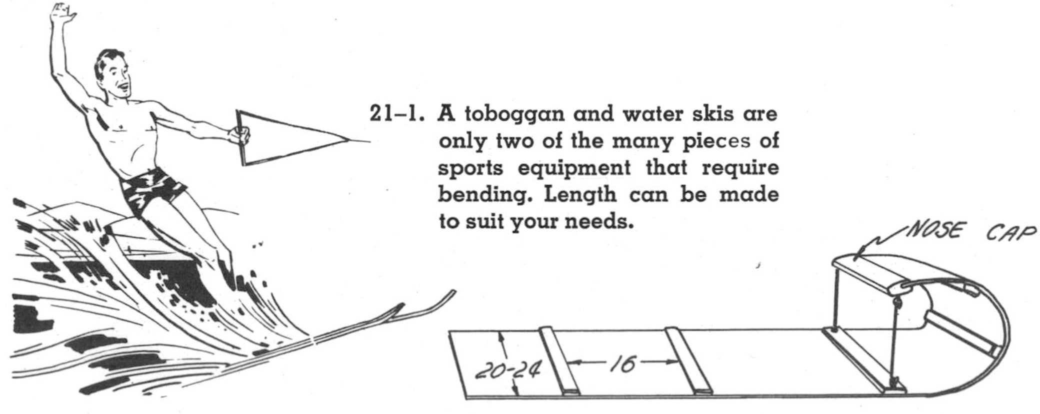

21–1. A toboggan and water skis are only two of the many pieces of sports equipment that require bending. Length can be made to suit your needs.

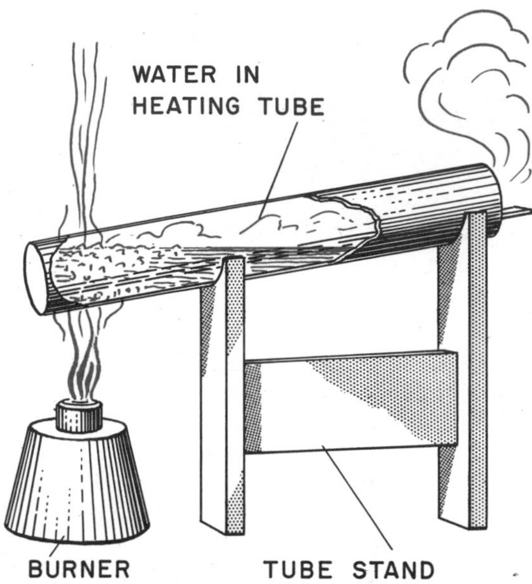

21–2. This is the type of heating tube you will need for bending wood. An old hot water heater can also serve this purpose. A tube is fastened to the wall at a slight angle and a burner placed under the lower end.

HEATING THE WOOD

Fill the heating tube about half full of water. Light the gas flame and close the end of the tube with a tight cover. There should be a tiny hole in the cover to keep it from blowing off. Prepare the staves at the same time. These should be cut to thickness and width and the edges chamfered or rounded off with a radius of ⅛ inch. When the water in the tube is boiling, put in the wood pieces. Don't add too many at one time, as the water should completely surround the end of each one. Leave the wood in the tube from two to three hours.

Prepare the bending equipment while the wood is being heated. You need the form for bending these pieces, several C clamps, and parallel hand screws. Also have ready a piece of thin sheet metal the same width as the staves and the length of the bend.

BENDING THE WOOD

When the pieces have been heated, remove them from the tube and insert the heated end under the protecting bar at the top of the form. Insert the thin sheet metal directly under it. Then begin to draw the stock around the form. Work slowly and clamp the staves at each cross support with a C clamp.

Do not try to pull the stave around

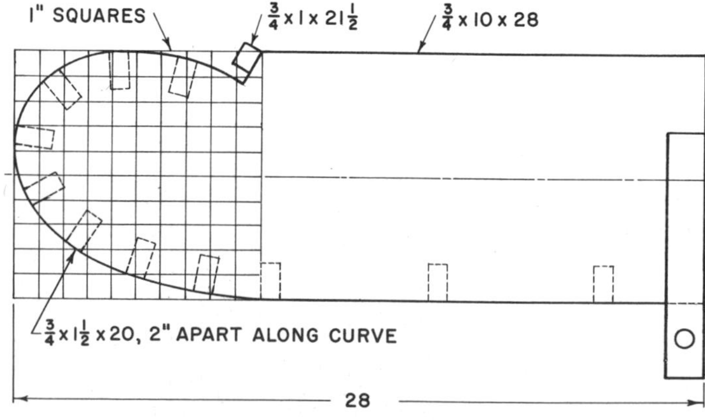

21–3. A form similar to this one is required to shape the front of toboggan staves or slats.

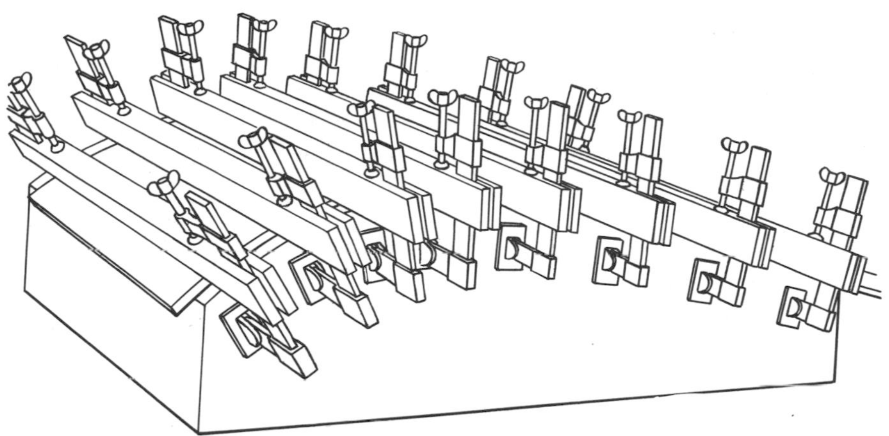

21–4. A form similar to this is needed to bend the tips of water skis. Each clamp must be tightened a little at a time.

the form too rapidly, as this will split out the wood. Continue to clamp the stave to the form, as shown in Figure 21–5. Allow each piece to dry for at least twenty-four hours before removing it from the form. You are now ready to sand, shape, and assemble the pieces.

BENDING WITHOUT HEAT AND MOISTURE

Water skis can be made by bending flat stock to shape without steam. Make the skis of mahogany, spruce, or ash. A bending form is needed. Cut the stock to size and square it up. Saw two or more kerfs, staggering the cut 13 to 15 inches in length from one end. Figure 21–6. Then cut veneer the thickness of the kerf,

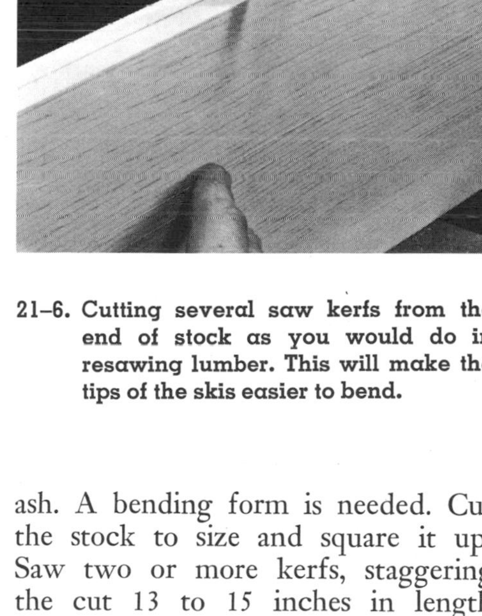

21–6. Cutting several saw kerfs from the end of stock as you would do in resawing lumber. This will make the tips of the skis easier to bend.

21–5. Clamping a stave or slat to the form with C clamps. A piece of sheet metal is placed directly over the wood to protect it.

21–7. Waterproof adhesive has been applied and the veneer has been slipped into the saw kerfs.

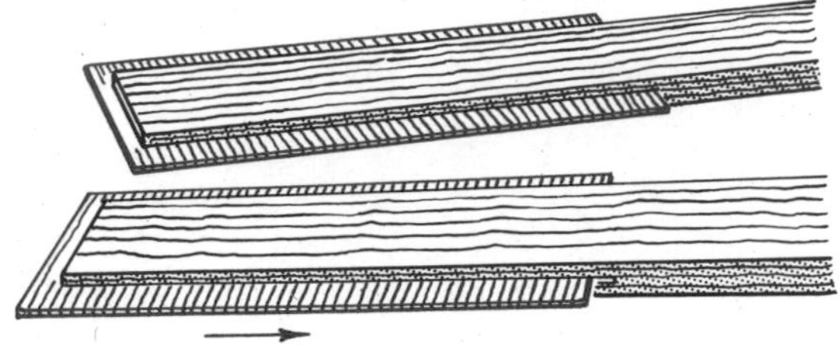

slightly wider than the stock and as long as the saw kerf. Apply waterproof glue to both sides of the veneer and slip it into the kerf. Figure 21–7. Clamp the stock in the form and allow it to dry at least twelve hours. Then shape and complete the skis as with pre-bent blanks.

CAN YOU ANSWER THESE QUESTIONS ON BENDING SOLID WOOD?

1. Toboggans, skis, and surfboards are most commonly made from what kinds of wood?
2. List the equipment needed for bending wood.
3. Wood is softened for bending in two ways. What are they and how is this done?
4. Can wood ever be bent rapidly?

Section V

UNIT 22. WOOD LAMINATION

Simple lamination is a process of building up the thickness or width of material by gluing several layers together, all with the grain running in approximately the same direction. Figure 22–1. However, in plywood lamination the layers of veneer are put together with the grain running at right angles to each other. Laminating is done commercially to produce a wide variety of structural pieces. Bent parts for furniture, plywood panels, arches and beams used in the construction of homes, schools, buildings, and churches are a few examples of lamination. Figures 22–2 and 22–3.

Wood laminations resist warpage, reduce the number of splits and checks, and produce a unit that is stronger than regular wood. A great advantage, also, is that shorter pieces of materials can be used to make the whole.

The laminating process can be applied very effectively in the school shop to make small, formed projects such as salad servers and bent bookends. Figure 22–4.

STEPS IN MAKING A LAMINATED WOOD PROJECT

1. First determine the kind of project or design you will use. For example, if you are going to make a

salad server, lay out the full-size pattern of the curve to which the server will be bent. Then decide on the number of thicknesses needed to make the server. Usually, the number is odd, such as three, five, or seven. However, some furniture manufacturers use four layers of veneer for curved laminations. This makes it possible to use two good quality veneers for face surfaces and two less expensive layers for the inside. Figure 22–5.

2. Make the form. Select a piece of hard maple or birch that is wide enough and long enough to enclose the veneer sandwich needed to make the project. The form must be thick enough to allow for at least 1 inch of material on either side of the curve. Lay out the full-size curve on the side of the block, following the grain direction.

3. Carefully cut the curve on the band saw. Be especially careful to eliminate as many irregularities as possible. The two halves of the form or die should fit perfectly. Figure 22-6. If necessary, very light sanding with fine paper can be done to remove saw marks.

4. Apply a thin coat of flexible material such as thin rubber to both sides of the form. This isn't absolutely necessary, but it helps in providing a better rough lamination. If rubber is used, it should be tacked onto the form and then the surface covered with wax.

5. Cut several pieces of veneer, $\frac{1}{28}$ inch thick and large enough to make the project. The number of pieces needed is usually three, five, or seven.

22–2. In industry, laminated parts for furniture are made in huge quantities on a hot press such as you see here.

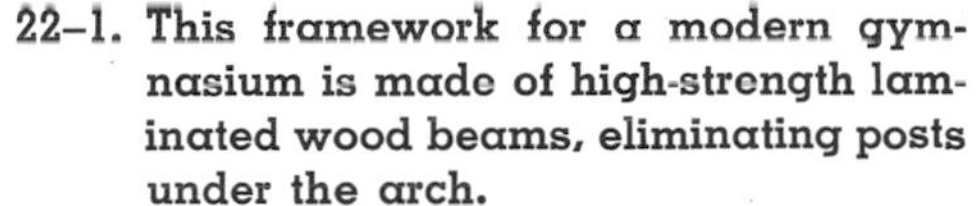

22–1. This framework for a modern gymnasium is made of high-strength laminated wood beams, eliminating posts under the arch.

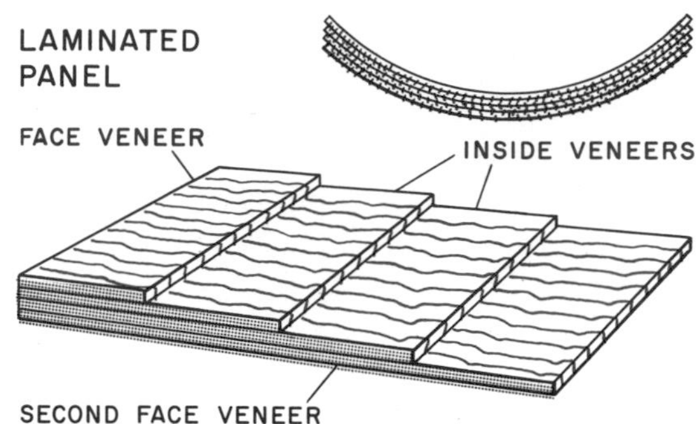

22–5. Four-ply laminated panel for curved furniture parts.

22–3. Parts of this wood chair are made by laminating stock together.

22–6. This is the kind of form needed to make the rough blank for a salad-server set.

22–4. These projects are typical of the laminated products that can be made in school shops.

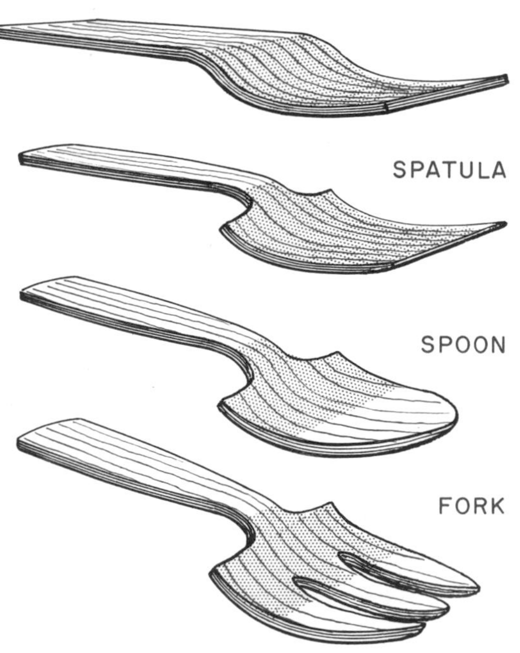

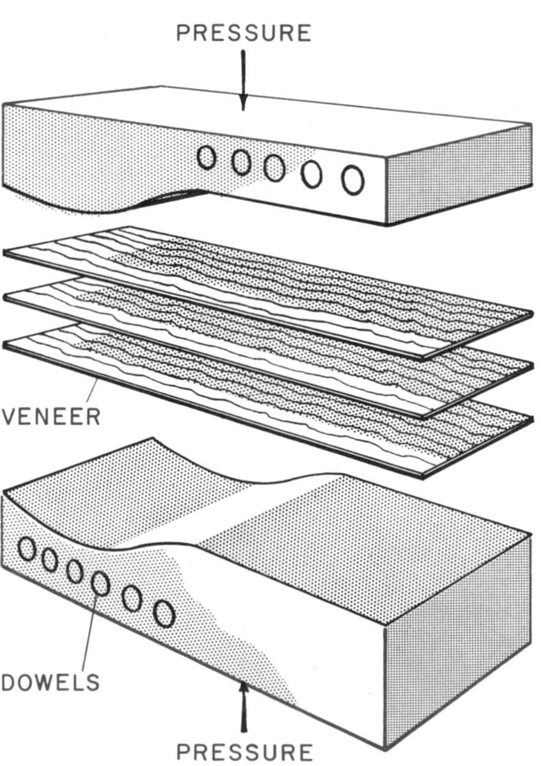

You may use only one kind of material such as mahogany or walnut or, for contrasting color, the layers can be alternated with a lighter wood such as birch or maple. Select a good quality casein glue or white resin glue. The glue must be spread evenly on both sides of each piece of veneer with, of course, the exception of the two outside pieces. The finished sides of these must be free of glue. Spread the glue on the veneer surfaces with a roller or notched glue spreader. Place a piece of wax paper over one side of the form. Stack the layers of veneer, and finally place another piece of wax paper over the last piece. Place the other half of the form over the pieces and clamp the two forms together with standard wood clamps. Allow the sandwich to remain under pressure for at least twenty-four hours.

6. Remove the rough lamination from the form and pull off the wax paper. Trace the outline of the project on the rough lamination and cut it out on a band or jig saw. Sand and smooth the edges. Apply penetrating finish to the object as soon as possible.

Caution: If the laminated project is to be used around food, use mineral oil as a sealer.

CAN YOU ANSWER THESE QUESTIONS ON WOOD LAMINATION?

1. What is the difference between a laminated wood product and plywood?
2. Describe some of the uses for wood lamination.
3. Tell the advantages of wood lamination.
4. Explain the method of making a form.
5. What kinds of glues can be used to make wood laminations?
6. Describe the steps in completing a project done by wood lamination.

Section VI
Cutting Holes

The sixth 2 steps in hand woodworking—what you must know and be able to do.

23. Boring holes with the auger, expansion, and Foerstner bits held in a bit brace, boring holes in both horizontal and vertical positions, through boring to prevent breaking out the opposite side of the hole, and using the depth gauge for regulating the depth of hole.

24. Drilling holes with a drill and small holes with a bit, using a hand drill for both vertical and horizontal drilling, and regulating the depth of the hole with a depth gauge.

Have you ever stopped to think why most holes made in woodworking are round? It is because making cutting tools that will cut a round hole and the whole process of assembly is based on the use of circular objects such as nails, screws, and dowels. Nevertheless, later on you will drill a square hole with a mortising attachment on the drill press.

Holes are cut in wood by boring or drilling. It is called *boring* if the hole is ¼ inch or larger in diameter and cut with some kind of bit. In *drilling* a small hole is cut with a drill. There are many different bits and drills and each is a very fine cutting tool that must be handled with care. There is usually only one set of bits or drills in the woodshop and you should be especially careful not to break one.

The tools and methods are listed in the "box" above. Further steps are on pp. 15, 43, 60, 94, 108, 143, 170, 219, 244.

Section VI

UNIT 23. BORING HOLES

The construction of many projects calls for boring holes such as cutting out a design, making a mortise-and-tenon joint, and fitting dowel rods.

BITS

For $\frac{1}{4}$ to $1\frac{1}{4}$ inch holes, an *auger bit* is used. Figure 23–1a and 23–1b. The size of the auger bit is stamped on the shank, always in a single number such as 4, 5, or 6, etc. This shows that it will bore a hole $\frac{4}{16}$, $\frac{5}{16}$, $\frac{6}{16}$, etc., inch in diameter. Figure 23–2. For holes larger than 1 inch, you need an *expansion* (expansive) *bit*. Figure 23–3. This tool can be adjusted with different cutters for diameters from $\frac{7}{8}$ to 3 inches. When you want to bore a hole partway into a thin board or when you want to enlarge an existing hole, a Foerstner bit is the tool to choose. Figure 23–4. Speed bits are also useful for boring holes, especially when using an electric drill. Figure 23–5.

INSTALLING A BIT IN A BRACE

The auger bit is held in a bit brace. Figure 23–6. To install the bit, hold the shell of the chuck in your left hand and turn the handle to the left

23–1a. A single twist auger bit with solid center.

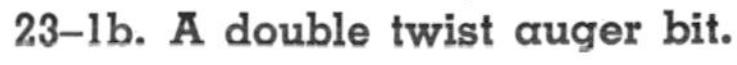

23–1b. A double twist auger bit.

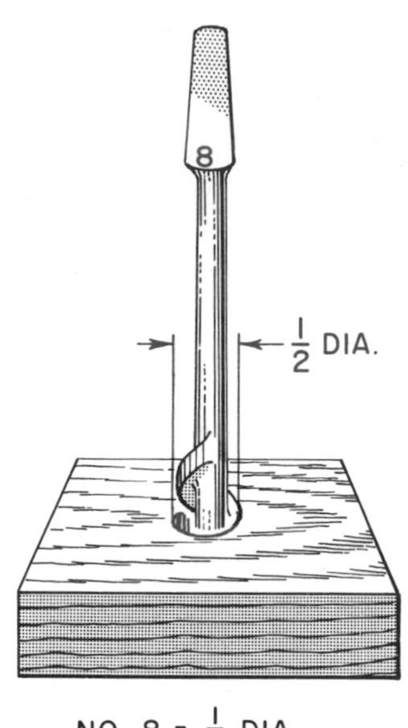

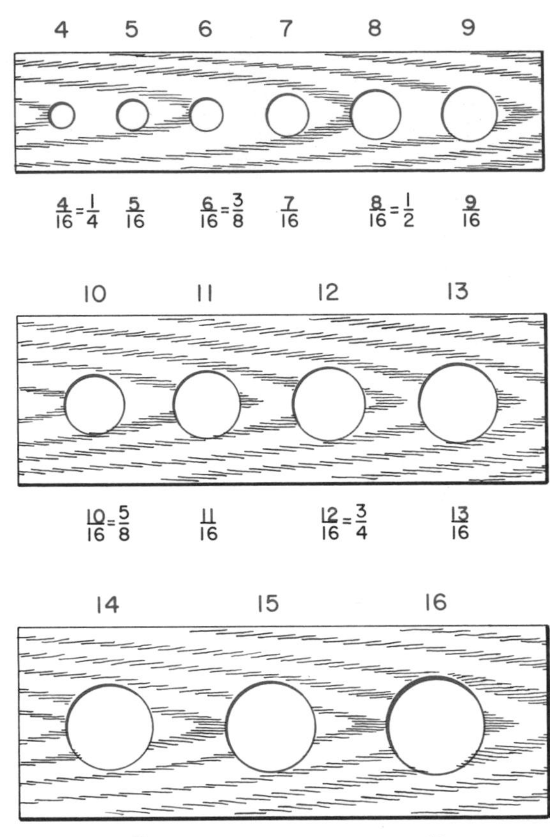

23–2. The number stamped on the tang shows the size of the auger bit. A. The number 8 on this auger bit indicates that it will bore a ½-inch hole. B. Study this chart to see what number auger bit you will need to bore the correct size of hole.

until the jaw is open slightly larger than the shank of the bit. Figure 23–7. Then insert the bit and turn the handle to the right to fasten it in the brace. Most bit braces have a ratchet attachment. This makes it possible to drill in corners or other tight places.

BORING HOLES IN A HORIZONTAL POSITION

Be sure that the center of the hole is properly located; punch the center with a scratch awl. Figure 23–8. Place the stock in a vise so that the brace

23–3. An expansion (expansive) bit. There are usually two cutters, a small one for holes of 1 to 2 inches in diameter and a larger one for holes 2 inches and more in diameter.

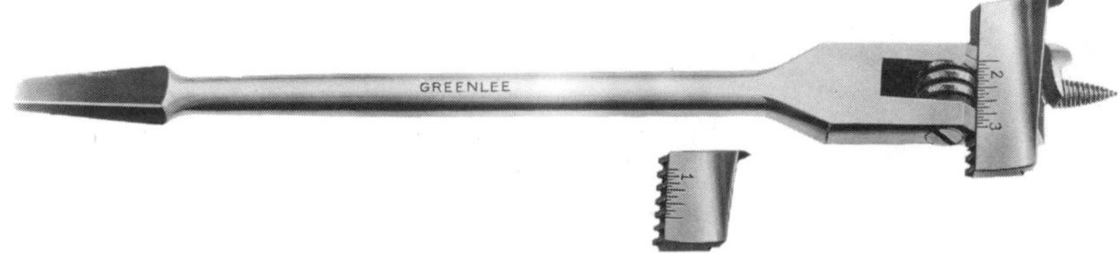

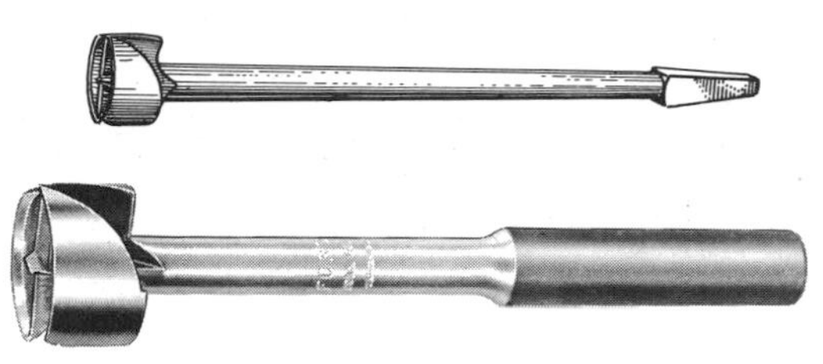

23–4. A Foerstner bit is used to enlarge existing holes or to cut a hole part-way through thin stock. Both hand and machine types are shown.

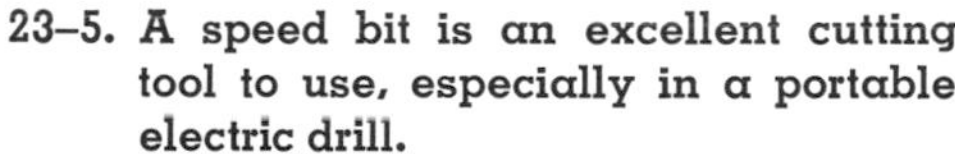

23–5. A speed bit is an excellent cutting tool to use, especially in a portable electric drill.

23–6. The bit brace is used for holding auger bits, Foerstner bits, and other tools with rectangular-shaped shanks. Most braces have a ratchet arrangement, making it possible to bore in corners and otherwise inaccessible places.

23–7. Inserting the shank into the two jaws. The corners should be in the V grooves of the jaws.

can be held in a horizontal position. Figure 23–9. Hold the head of the brace with your left hand cupped around it. Hold your body against the head for added pressure. Turn the handle with your right hand to start the hole. Figure 23–10. Be careful to keep the auger bit square to the work. It is easy to sight the top to see if it is square to right and to left. If another person is present, have him sight to make sure it is straight up and down.

Do not press too hard on the brace. The auger bit tends to feed itself into the wood. Continue to bore the

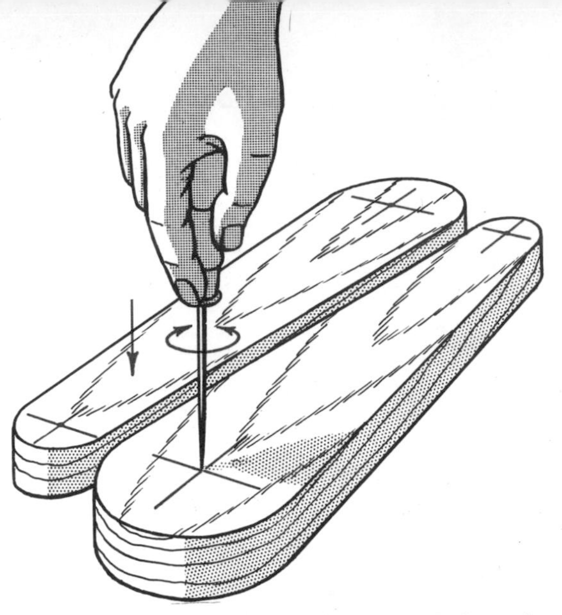

23–8. Marking the center of the hole with the scratch awl.

hole until the point of the bit just comes through the opposite side. Then turn over the wood to complete the hole. If this is not done, the hole will split out on the opposite side as the auger bit comes through. Figure 23–11. Another way to keep from splitting the wood is to put a piece of scrap wood back of the piece you are boring. Then you can go all the way through from one side.

23–9. The proper set up for a hole to be bored. The center has been accurately located. On thin stock a piece of scrap wood should be fastened to the back to support the wood while boring, as shown. Courtesy the Jam Handy Organization.

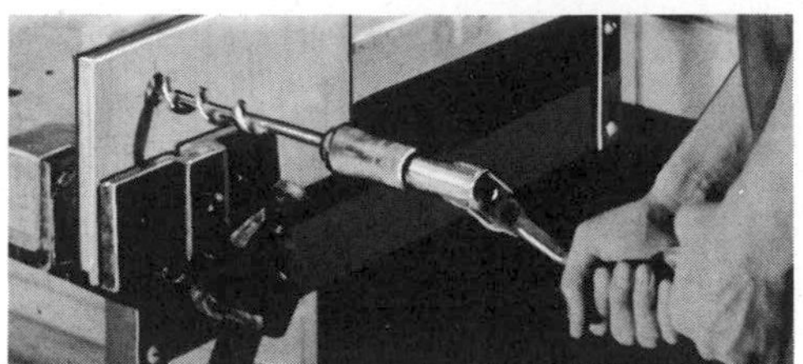

23–10. Horizontal boring with a bit and brace. Make sure that the auger bit is held at right angles to the stock. Courtesy the Jam Handy Organization.

23–11. The correct and incorrect method of boring a hole.

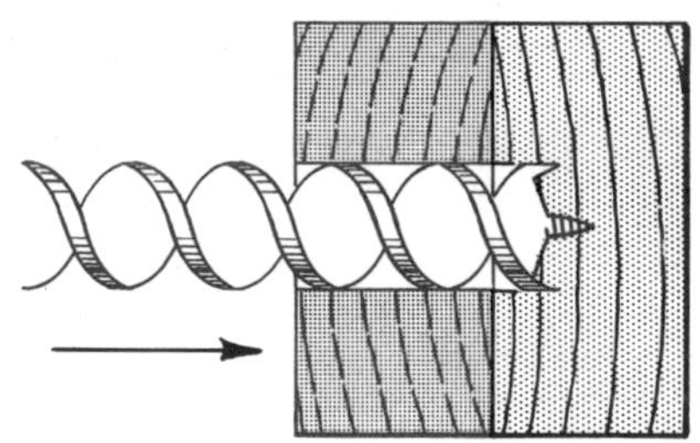
USE A PIECE OF SCRAP WOOD

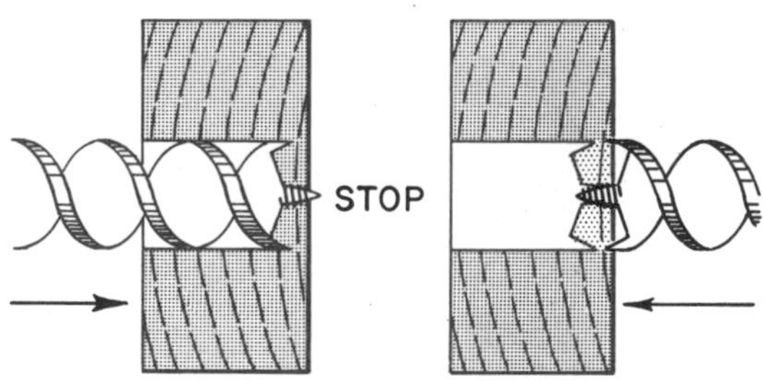
STOP
STOP - WHEN FEED SCREW PRICKS THROUGH
& BORE FROM OTHER SIDE
OR - BORE FROM BOTH SIDES

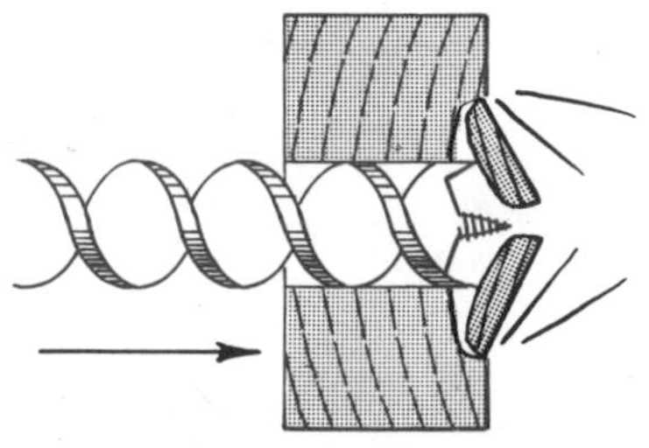
BUT - DON'T DO THIS

23–12. Boring holes with a bit and brace held in a vertical position. The hand is cupped over the head of the brace. Sometimes the chin is rested on the hand to steady the tool. Most boring in the shop will be done in a vertical position.

BORING HOLES IN A VERTICAL POSITION

Holes sometimes have to be bored with the auger bit held in a vertical position. Lay out and locate the position of the hole as before. Put one hand over the head of the brace and use the other hand to turn the handle. Figure 23–12. Sometimes you will find it natural to rest your chin on the handle to steady it. To make sure that you are boring square with the surface, you can sight along the board or use a try square. Figure 23–13.

In some kinds of construction you will need to bore only partway through the stock. You need a depth or bit gauge. There are two commercial types that can be clamped on the auger bit to the proper depth (Figure 23–14a and 23–14b). Another kind of depth gauge can be made by boring through a piece of wood or dowel rod, exposing the auger bit to the correct depth.

ANGLE BORING

To bore a hole at an angle, first adjust a sliding T-bevel to the required angle. This is used as a guide. Start the auger bit as you would for straight boring until the screw feeds

23–13. Checking to make sure the auger bit is square with the work.

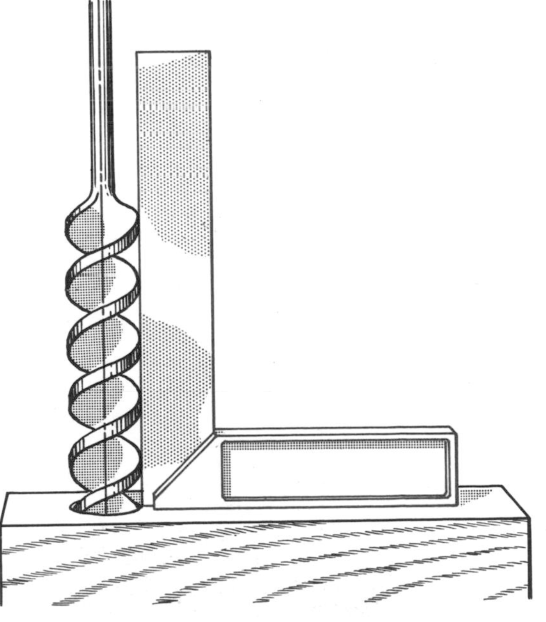

23–14a. Solid-type bit or depth gauge.

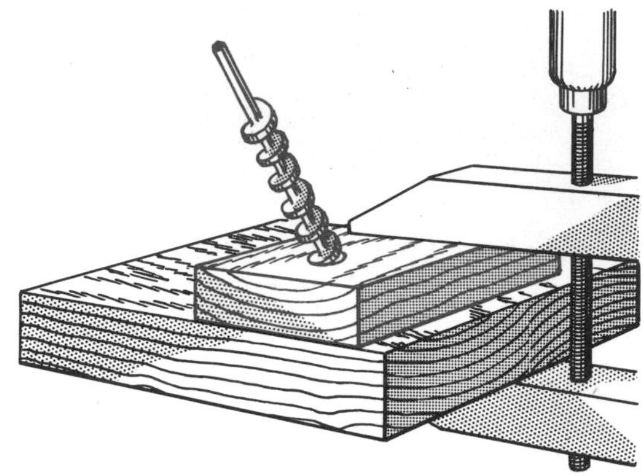

23–15. Using a small wood jig to bore a hole at an angle.

into the wood. Then tilt the bit so that it is parallel to the blade of the T-bevel. If several holes must be bored at an angle, it is a good idea to use a simple wood jig. First, bore a hole at the correct angle through a piece of scrap stock. Slip this jig over the auger bit. Place the feed screw of the auger bit on the center of the hole. Figure 23–15. Slip the jig against the wood and clamp it with a hand screw. This will guide the bit.

23–14b. Spring-type bit or depth gauge. This type will not mar the surface of the wood when the tool reaches the correct depth.

23–16. Notice that the expansion bit is set to 2½ inches in diameter.

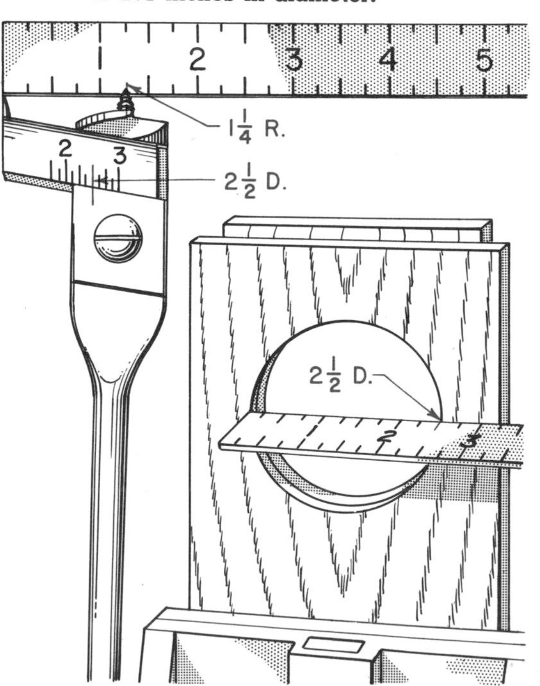

23–17. Using a expansion bit. Care should be taken as the bit begins to go through the opposite side to prevent it from splitting out. It's a good idea to cut a little over halfway through, reverse the stock, and cut through the other side.

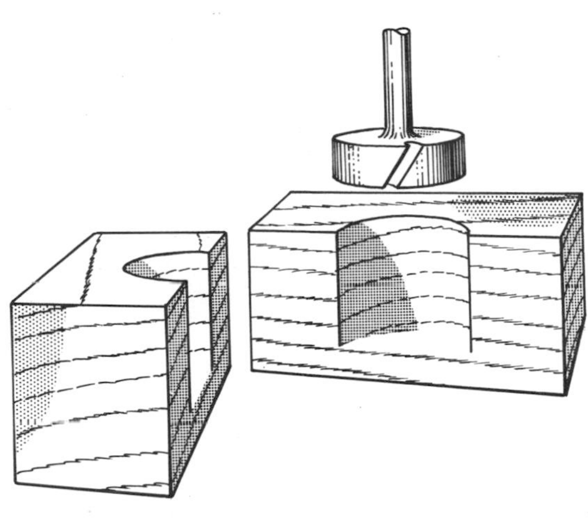

23–18. Boring a hole that has a flat bottom.

BORING WITH AN EXPANSION BIT

Choose a cutter of the correct size and slip it in the bit. Adjust the cutter until the distance from the spur to feed screw equals the radius of the hole. Figure 23–16. Fasten the bit in a brace. Then make sure the work is held tightly. It's a good idea to put a piece of scrap stock behind the work. As you rotate the tool, use just enough pressure to make a cut. Figure 23–17. After the feed screw shows through, reverse the stock and cut from the other side.

BORING WITH A FOERSTNER BIT

Foerstner bits are numbered the same as auger bits. The sizes range from ¼ inch to 2 inches. Locate the center of the hole. Draw a circle with a dividers the same size as the hole. Clamp the stock securely. Carefully guide the bit over the circle to start the boring. Figure 23–18.

CAN YOU ANSWER THESE QUESTIONS ON BORING HOLES?

1. What is an auger bit?
2. How is the size marked on the auger bit?
3. What is an expansion bit and how is it used?
4. The Foerstner bit has what primary use?
5. Name the parts of a brace.
6. Why do some braces have a ratchet attachment?
7. To bore holes in a vertical position, how can the tool be kept square with the work?
8. Should you bore the hole completely through the stock from one side? Explain.
9. Describe how the brace should be held when boring in a vertical position.
10. Describe a depth gauge and tell how it is used.
11. How is a depth gauge made?
12. Tell how to do angle boring.
13. How do you adjust an expansion bit to cut a 2½-inch hole?

Section VI

UNIT 24. DRILLING HOLES

Holes 1/4 inch or smaller must be drilled to assemble projects with nails and screws, to start an inside cut and for many other purposes.

DRILLS AND DRILLING DEVICES

A small set of *twist drills* ranging in size from 1/16 inch to 1/2 inch in intervals of 1/64 inch are used for drilling both metal and wood. Figure 24–1.

24–1. A straight shank twist drill can be used for drilling holes in both wood and metal. The size of the drill is stamped on the shank.

24–2. The bit-stock drill can be used in a brace.

If the drills are used only for wood, they can be made of carbon steel and the point ground at an angle of 80 degrees. The *bit stock* drill can be used in a brace. Figure 24–2. An *automatic drill* with drill points is handy to have when many small holes must be drilled. Figure 24–3. The drill points are numbered from one to eight. Number 1 is 1/16 inch, 2 is 5/64 inch, 3 is 3/32 inch, 4 is 7/64 inch, 5 is 1/8 inch, 6 is 9/64 inch, 7 is 5/32 inch, and 8 is 11/64 inch. Insert the drill in the chuck. Tighten the chuck. Place the drill point where the hole is needed. Then simply push down a few times, allowing the handle to spring back after each stroke. This will give you a good, clean hole. Figure 24–4.

The *hand drill* is used to hold the twist drill for drilling holes. It has three jaws in the chuck for holding round shanks. Figure 24–5. A *breast drill* is very similar but larger and is made to hold drills up to 1/2 inch in diameter. Figure 24–6.

USING A HAND DRILL

Select a twist drill of the correct size. Hold the shell of the chuck in your left hand. Pull the crank backward until the jaws are open slightly wider than the shank. Place the shank in the chuck and tighten the chuck by pushing the crank forward. Make sure the drill is in the chuck straight. Locate the position of the hole and mark it with a scratch awl. Hold the handle in your left hand and turn the

24–3. The automatic drill is very efficient for drilling many small holes, such as in boat construction or for installing hardware.

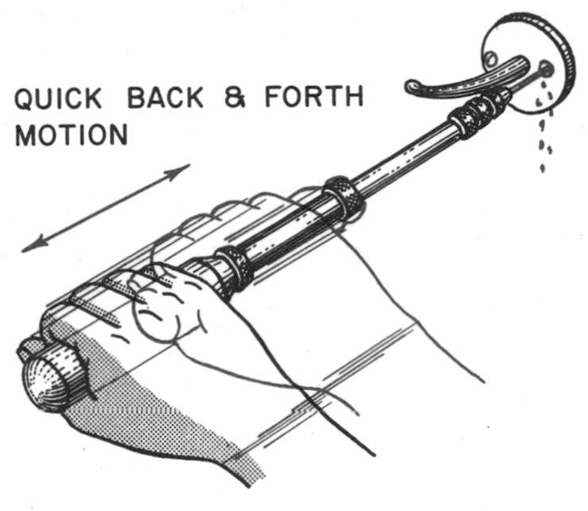

24–4. Using an automatic drill to install a coat hanger.

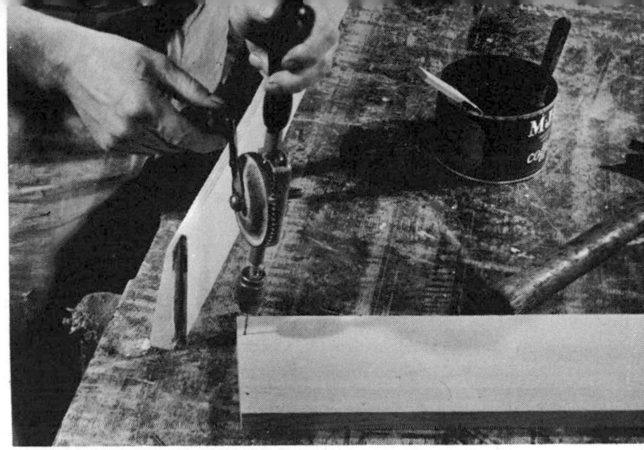

24–7. Vertical drilling with a hand drill. The handle is grasped in one hand and the crank turned with the other. Be sure to hold the drill square with the work.

crank with your right hand. Make sure the drill is square with the work. Figure 24–7. Never bend the hand drill to one side or the other. Small drills would break. Continue to turn the handle until the hole is drilled. If holes of a certain depth are needed, make a depth gauge from a piece of scrap wood or dowel rod. Figure 24–8.

24–5. Hand drill. **24–6. Breast drill.**

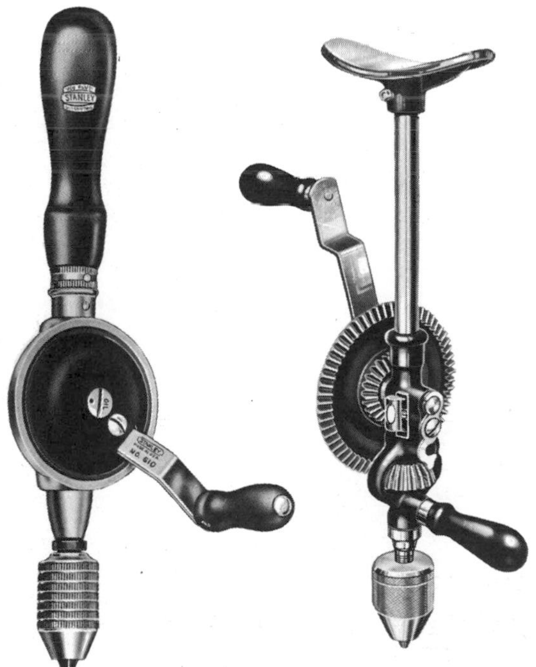

USING THE ELECTRIC HAND DRILL

The electric hand drill is an excellent all-around tool for drilling and boring holes. Drill size is shown by the largest twist drill it will hold. The most common sizes are ¼, ⅜, and ½ inch. Figure 24–9. Horsepower is also important. Light-duty, ¼-inch electric drills may develop as little as ⅛ horsepower. A good ½-inch electric drill should develop at least ⅔ horsepower.

Use the chuck wrench to open the jaws until the twist drill will slip in. Then tighten the drill firmly. Always remove the chuck wrench. Make sure

24–8. A depth gauge made from a piece of dowel rod which covers a part of the drill. Cut the piece until the drill extends the correct amount.

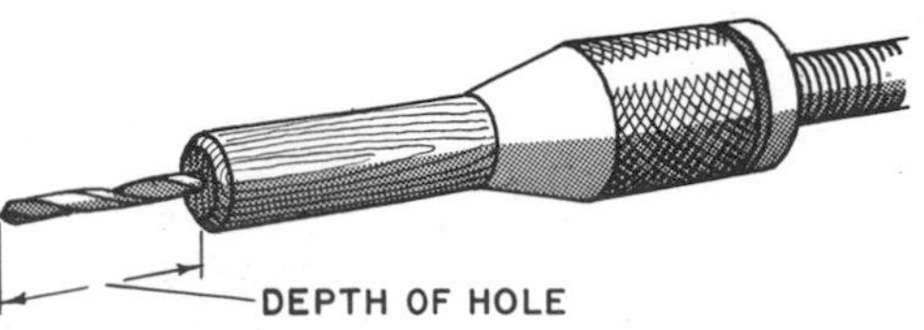

24–9. An electric hand drill.

that thin work is backed up with a piece of scrap stock. Grasp the control handle firmly and point the drill as you would a pistol. Use your left hand to control the feed as necessary. Make sure that the tool is straight. Always start with the power off. Place the point on the stock. Figure 24–10. Turn on the switch and guide the tool into the work.

CAN YOU ANSWER THESE QUESTIONS ON DRILLING HOLES?

1. Name the kind of cutting tool used for drilling holes in wood.
2. Describe a hand drill.
3. How can a breast drill be faster than a hand drill?
4. How is the hand drill held for doing horizontal drilling?
5. How is the size of an electric hand drill indicated?
6. What kind of bit should be used for boring larger holes?

24–10. Using an electric hand drill for drilling screw holes.

Section VII
Making Joints

The seventh 6 steps in hand woodworking—what you must know and be able to do.

25. The dowel joint and its variations, such as the edge dowel joint, corner dowel joint, and leg and rail dowel joints: what they are and how to make them, including layout, cut, fit, assembly, and fastening.

26. The rabbet joint and the steps in making this joint, including its assembly.

27. Constructing and assembling the dado joint and its variations, such as the rabbet and dado joint and blind dado joint.

28. Kinds of lap joints. Laying out, cutting, and assembling a cross-lap joint and what it is used for.

29. Using a miter box, either commercial or homemade, for cutting a miter joint, assembling the miter joint, and applications of this joint.

30. Kinds of mortise-and-tenon joints. Layout, construction, and assembly of the mortise and the tenon.

Would it surprise you to know that there are over a hundred different types of woodworking joints? Many are similar, of course, but each is used to join wood pieces together in a special way. All joints in woodworking are laid out, cut, fitted, and assembled. To do these things well, you must know how to use all of the common hand tools. You will not use more than one or two kinds of joints on any one project, but these ought to be chosen wisely, for each has a special purpose.

When you make larger articles such as desks and tables, you will have the added problems of joinery in making drawers and doors. See the "box" above. Further woodworking steps are on pp. 15, 43, 60, 94, 108, 132, 170, 219, 244.

Section VII

UNIT 25. DOWEL JOINT

A dowel joint on a leg and rail is sometimes used instead of a mortise-and-tenon joint. Dowels are also used to strengthen an edge, butt, or miter joint. Figure 25–1.

DOWEL TOOLS AND MATERIALS

Dowel rod is usually made of birch in diameters from 1/8 to 1 inch in 3-foot lengths. Small dowel pins are made with a spiral groove and pointed ends. A *dowel sharpener* points the ends of the dowels. *Dowel centers* are small metal pins used for spotting the location of holes on two parts of a joint. Figure 25–2.

25–1. The corners of this Early American sewing cabinet are fastened with dowels.

MAKING AN EDGE DOWEL JOINT

To make this joint, clamp the two pieces to be joined with the edges flush and face surfaces out. With a try square, mark across the edges of both pieces at the several points where the dowels will be. Next, set a marking gauge to half the thickness of the stock and mark the center locations of the dowel joints. Figure 25–3. Make sure that you mark these from the face side.

Decide on the size dowel you want to use and the depth to which the dowel will go. The diameter of the dowel should never be more than half the thickness of the stock. Usually the dowel should be no longer than 3 inches; therefore, the holes will be drilled about 1 5/8 inch deep. This provides about 1/8 inch clearance at the bottom on each side.

After the points have been located, make a small dent with a scratch awl. Select an auger bit the same size as the dowel rod. Carefully bore the hole to the proper depth, making sure that you are working square with the

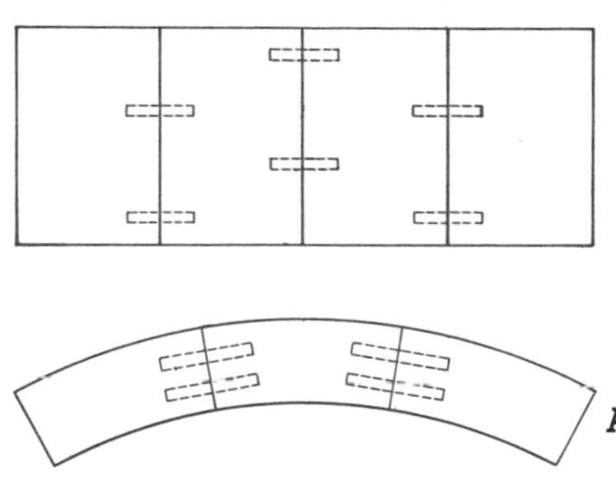

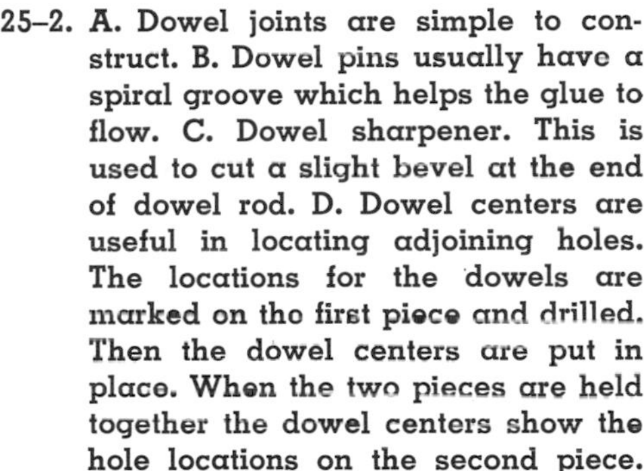

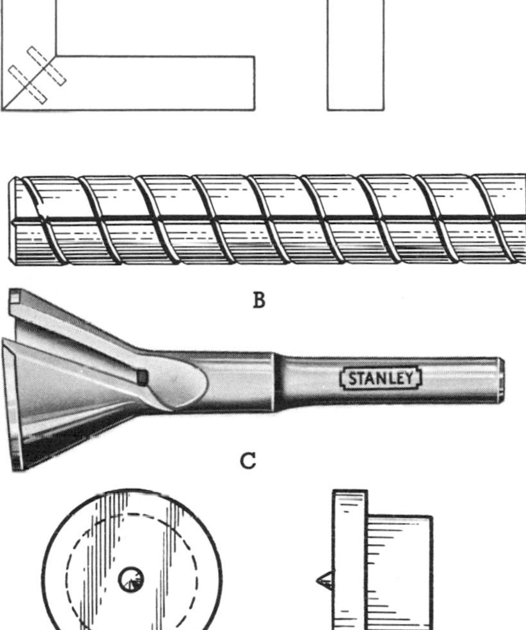

25–2. A. Dowel joints are simple to construct. B. Dowel pins usually have a spiral groove which helps the glue to flow. C. Dowel sharpener. This is used to cut a slight bevel at the end of dowel rod. D. Dowel centers are useful in locating adjoining holes. The locations for the dowels are marked on the first piece and drilled. Then the dowel centers are put in place. When the two pieces are held together the dowel centers show the hole locations on the second piece.

edge of the stock. Use a depth gauge as a guide. A doweling jig should be used if one is available. Figures 25–4a and 25–4b. With this tool you will always be able to bore the holes square and in the right place. Figure 25–5.

25–3. Marking the position for an edge dowel joint. The pieces are fastened in a vise with the face surfaces outward. Then a marking gauge is set to half the thickness of the stock and the center location is marked. The location for the three dowels has already been marked with a try square and pencil.

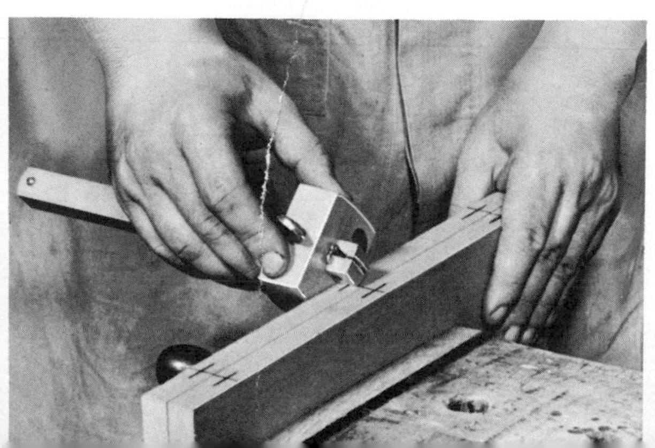

25–4A. A doweling jig that will help locate the position of holes and guide the auger bit for boring. This jig comes with several metal guides in sizes of $\frac{3}{16}$, $\frac{1}{4}$, $\frac{5}{16}$, $\frac{3}{8}$, $\frac{7}{16}$, and $\frac{1}{2}$ inch.

25–4B. A self-centering dowel drill guide. This holds the material like a vise. When the workpiece is clamped in the tool, the guide holes for the drill are automatically centered over the work. The jaws will clamp on work up to 2 inches in thickness. The guide accommodates five sizes of bits.

After the holes are bored, saw off the dowel. Cut a slight bevel at either end to make the dowel pieces slip into the holes easily. When gluing, dip the dowels about halfway in glue and drive them into the holes on one edge. Figure 25–6. Then coat the other half and other edges and assemble. Figure 25–7.

25–6. Gluing an edge dowel joint. The dowels have already been dipped in the glue and driven halfway into one edge. Glue is being applied to the two edges and to the other half of the dowels.

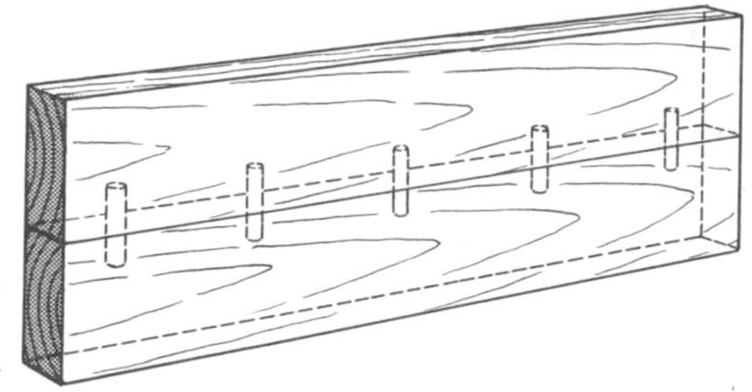

25–7. Edge dowel joint with the dowels installed.

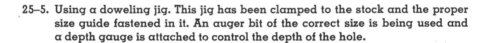

25–5. Using a doweling jig. This jig has been clamped to the stock and the proper size guide fastened in it. An auger bit of the correct size is being used and a depth gauge is attached to control the depth of the hole.

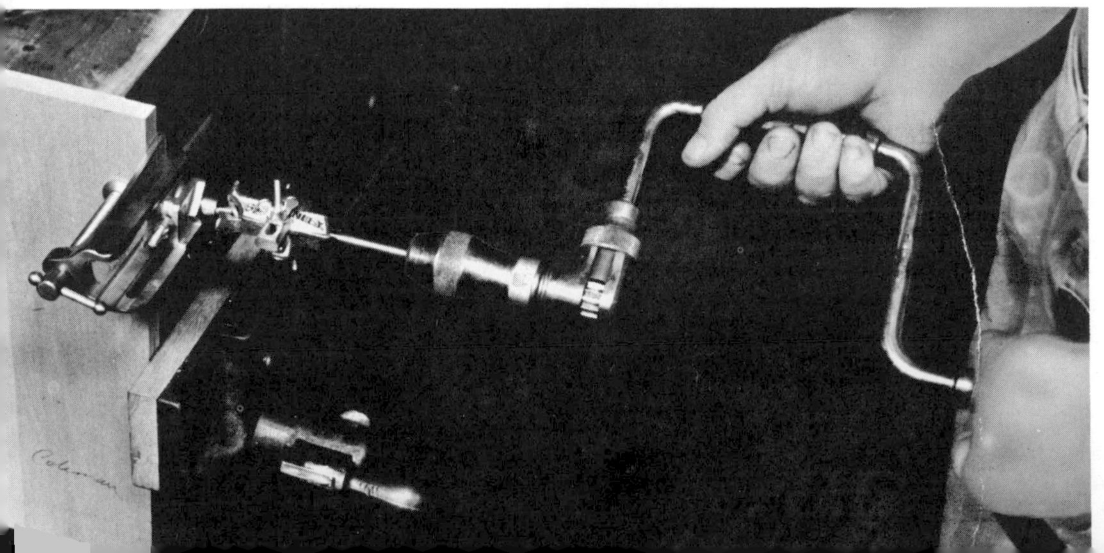

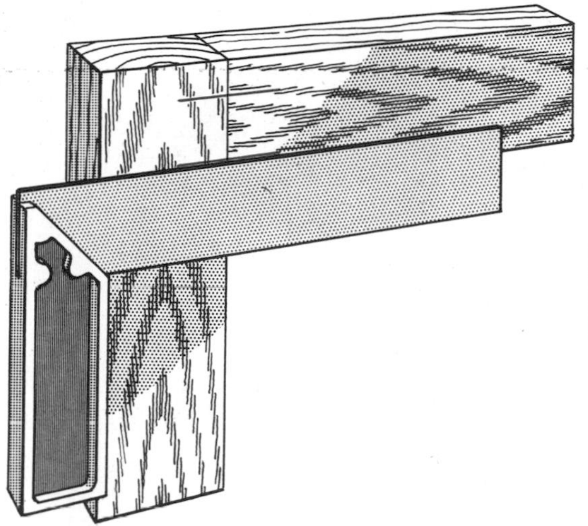

25–8. Using a try square to mark the locations of the dowels on the face surfaces.

MAKING A DOWEL JOINT ON A FRAME

One way to strengthen a butt joint on a simple frame is to install two or more dowels at each corner. Do this in the following manner:

1. Square up pieces of stock that are to go into the frame and carefully saw and sand the ends.
2. Lay out the frame and mark the corners with corresponding numbers.
3. Indicate on the face surfaces the location and number of dowels. Figure 25–8.
4. In a vise, place the two pieces that are to form one of the corners. Have the butting end and the butting edge sticking out a little, with the face surfaces of the two pieces out and the end and edge flush.
5. Hold a try square against one of the face surfaces and mark lines across to show the location of the dowel rods. Figure 25–9.
6. Set a marking gauge to half the thickness of the stock. Hold it against the surface of each piece and mark the exact location. Mark these points with a scratch awl and bore the holes as described above. Figure 25–10.

MAKING A DOWEL JOINT ON A LEG AND RAIL

For its ease and speed a dowel joint is often made on a leg and rail instead

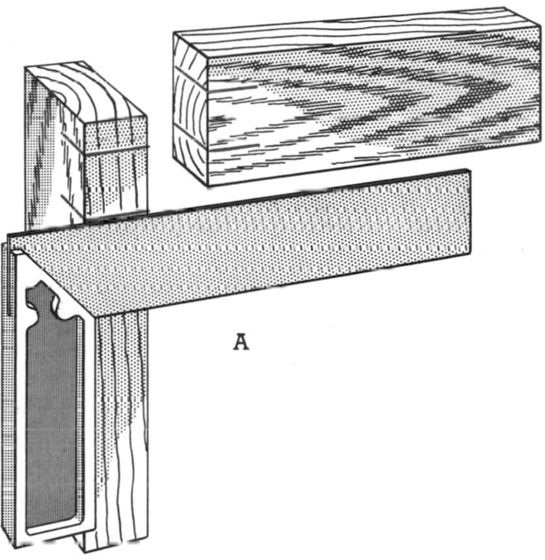

A

25–9. A. Squaring a line across the edge and end of both pieces. B. Here the butting edge and end are held in a vise while a try square is being used to lay out the position of the two dowels.

B

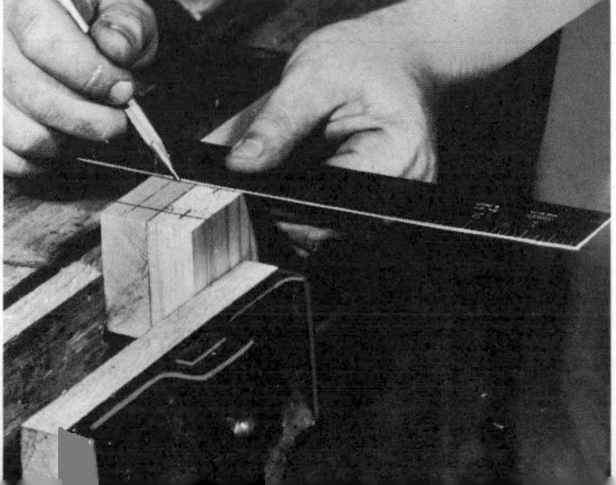

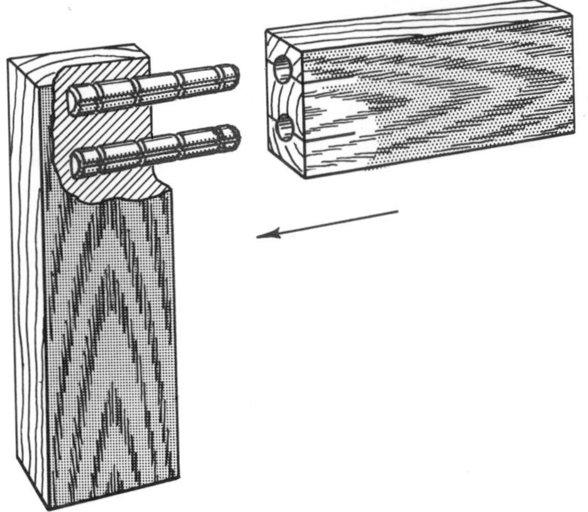

25–10. Installing dowels in a frame.

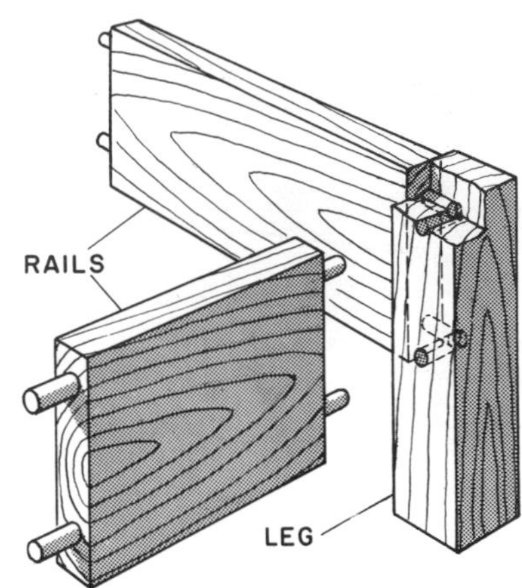

25–11. Notice that the rails are thinner than the legs. The dowels are centered on the ends of the rails and on the legs. If the rails must be flush with the surface of the legs, then the dowel holes on the legs must be closer to the outside surface.

of a mortise-and-tenon joint. Figure 25–11.

Square up the leg and rail as for any joint, making sure that the end of the rail is square. Next clamp the leg and rail in a vise with the butting end and the butting edge sticking out and the face surface of each turned out. Hold a try square against the face surface of the rail and mark the location of the dowels on the end of the rail and the edge of the leg. Next set a marking gauge to half the thickness of the rail. From the face surface of the rail, mark the crossline that will show the location of the dowel joints. Then decide how far you want the rail to set back from the face surface of the leg. Add this amount to the setting you already have on the marking gauge. From the face surface of the leg, mark the crossline that will show the exact location of the dowel. Bore the holes, cut the dowels, glue, and assemble as before.

CAN YOU ANSWER THESE QUESTIONS ON A DOWEL JOINT?

1. From what kinds of wood is dowel rod usually made?
2. Dowel joints are sometimes used as a substitute for another kind of joint. What is this joint and why is the dowel joint substituted?
3. Why are dowels used in making an edge joint?
4. State the rule for choosing the correct dowel diameter.
5. Should there be clearance at the bottom of a dowel hole? Why?
6. What is a doweling jig? Explain how it is used.
7. List the steps in making a dowel joint on a frame.
8. Why is it necessary to lay out a dowel joint very accurately?
9. What would happen if the dowel holes of two joint pieces were not aligned perfectly?
10. How do you think a dowel joint on a leg or rail will compare with a mortise-and-tenon joint?

Section VII

UNIT 26. RABBET JOINT

One of the simplest joints to make is the rabbet joint. Figure 26–1. A slot is cut at the end or edge of the first piece into which the end or edge of the second piece fits. Figure 26–2. It is made with the end grain hidden from the front. This joint is commonly found in drawer construction, boxes, and cabinet frames. It is also popular for modern furniture since it provides great simplicity in both construction and appearance.

LAYING OUT A RABBET JOINT

Make sure that the end on which the joint is to be made has been squared properly. Place the first board on the bench with the face surface down. Hold the second piece directly over the first, with the face surface of the second piece flush with the end grain of the first. Figure 26–3. This is called superimposing. You will frequently use this method in laying out many different kinds of joints.

With a sharp pencil or knife, mark the width of rabbet to be cut. Then remove the second piece. With a try square held on the joint edge, square a line across the surface of the first piece. Then mark a line down each edge. From the face surface, mark the depth of the rabbet on the sides and end with a marking gauge. In this type of joint the depth of the rabbet is cut half to two thirds the thickness of the stock. Figure 26–4.

26–1. These decorator shelves illustrate the use of the rabbet joint.

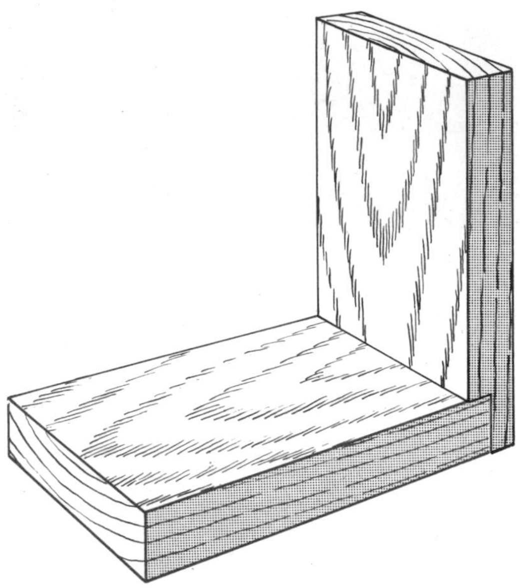

26–2. **A rabbet joint is a simple type of construction found in much modern furniture.**

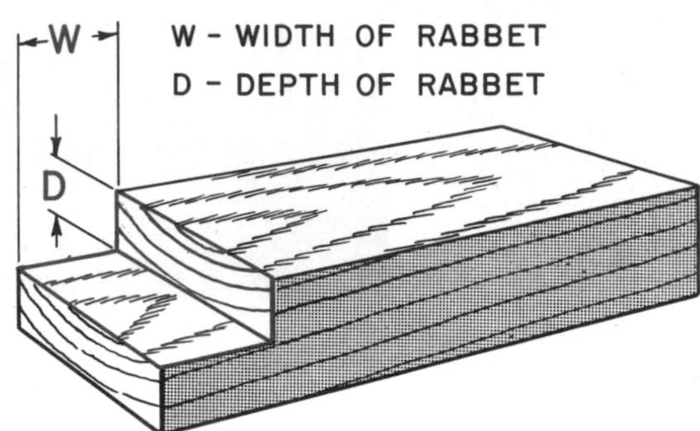

26–4. **The width of the rabbet must be equal to the thickness of the stock. The depth of the rabbet is usually ½ to ⅔ the thickness.**

CUTTING THE RABBET

In cutting the rabbet joint, the piece should be held firmly against a bench hook. For the beginner, it is better to clamp the stock directly to the bench top. Use a backsaw to make the cut. Make sure that the saw kerf is in the waste stock or inside the layout line. The beginner should clamp a square piece of scrap stock directly over the layout line. Then the backsaw can be held against this edge to make the saw cut. Figure 26–5. Cut the joint to the proper depth as indicated by the layout line.

The excess stock from the joint can either be sawed out or pared out with a chisel. If you decide to saw it out, lock the stock in a vise with the joint showing. With a backsaw, carefully saw out the excess stock. If you use a chisel, leave the stock clamped to the top of the bench. Pare out the

26–3. **Marking the width of the rabbet.**

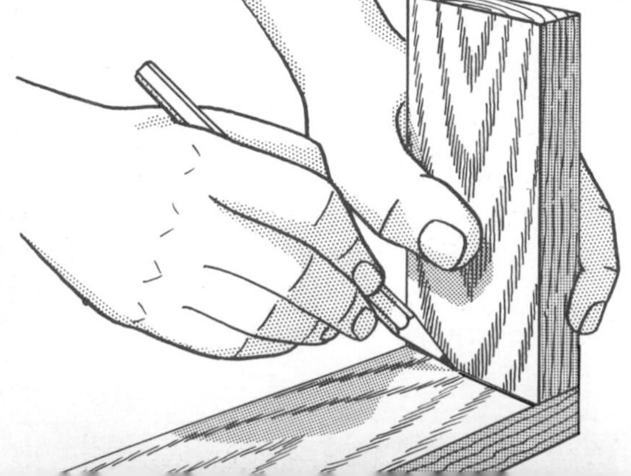

26–5. **Making a shoulder cut on a rabbet joint. Notice that a piece of scrap stock is clamped over the layout line with hand screws; then the backsaw is held against the edge of the scrap stock. This prevents the saw from jumping out of the kerf and damaging the wood.**

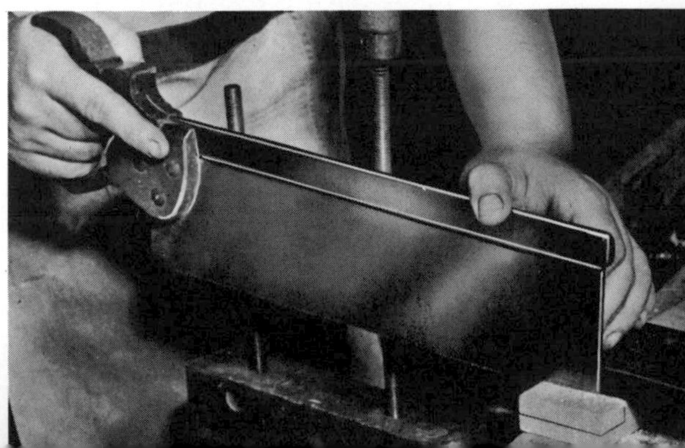

26–6. After the rabbet has been cut, it should be trimmed with a chisel. The blade of the chisel is being held between thumb and forefinger to trim the excess stock.

excess stock as you have learned from the unit on cutting with a chisel. Regardless of which method you follow, you will need to use the chisel for trimming the joint and making it fit properly. Figure 26–6.

It is a good idea to mark this joint on both edges with corresponding numbers. If there are several to be made, they can be easily identified when the project is ready for assembly.

ASSEMBLING THE JOINT

This type of joint is usually assembled with glue or with both glue and nails (or screws). Figure 26–7. If the joint is nailed, drive the nails in at a slight angle to help them fasten the joint more tightly. Figure 26–8. Screws should be long and thin, as they will have to go into end grain.

26–7. Nailing a rabbet joint, so that the front has no visible joint. Since the nails must be fastened in end grain, it is a good idea to drive them at a slight angle to give them more holding power.

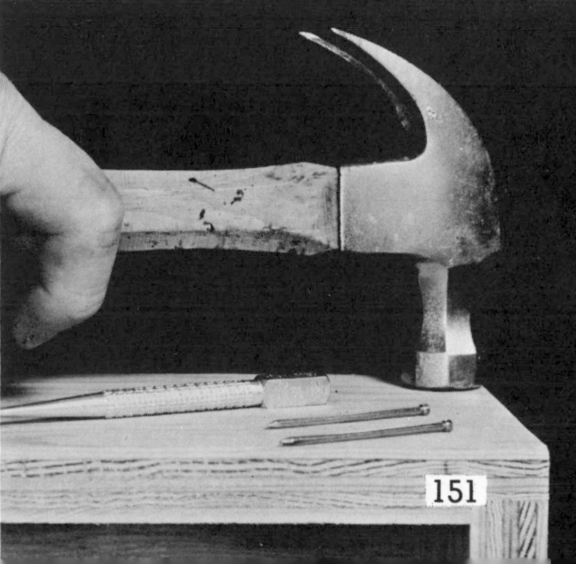

26–8. Rabbet joints are neat, strong, and easy to make. You'll find them the ideal choice for drawers, chests, and cupboards.

CAN YOU ANSWER THESE QUESTIONS ON A RABBET JOINT?

1. What is a rabbet?
2. How is the rabbet used?
3. Explain superimposing.
4. What tools should be used to mark a rabbet?
5. How can the pieces of several different rabbet joints be kept in order?
6. What kind of saw should be selected for cutting a rabbet?
7. When can a chisel be chosen for making a rabbet joint?
8. If you decide to assemble a rabbet joint with nails, how would you proceed to insert them?

Section VII

UNIT 27. DADO JOINT

A dado is a groove cut across the grain of wood. Figure 27–1. This joint is commonly found in bookracks, drawers, cabinet shelves, and such things as ladders and steps. Figure 27–2.

LAYING OUT A DADO JOINT

From the end of the board, measure in the correct distance to one side of the dado. Then square off a line across the surface of the piece at this point. Superimpose the other piece with one arris (edge) directly over the line. With a sharp knife or pencil, mark the correct width of the dado.

Remove the second piece and square off a line across the surface to show the proper width. Continue both lines down both edges. Figure 27–3. Then, with a marking gauge, lay out the correct depth of the joint.

CUTTING A DADO

Using a backsaw, follow the directions for cutting out a rabbet joint. Cut the dado to the proper depth at

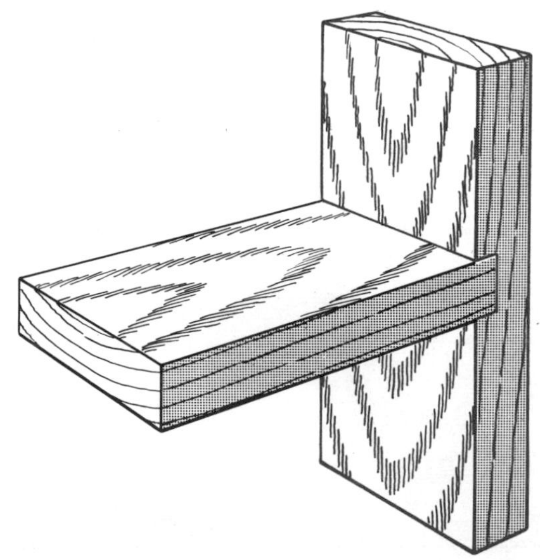

27–1. A dado joint is commonly used if the crosspieces must support considerable weight, such as for shelves, stairsteps, or ladders.

27–2. This attractive wall shelf makes use of the dado joint.

both layout lines. Make sure that the saw kerfs are in the waste stock and not outside the layout line. Figure 27–4.

With a chisel, cut and trim the dado to the proper depth. A router plane may be used to trim out the waste stock. Figures 27–5 and 27–6.

If the dado is very wide, you may need to make several saw cuts to

27–3. Making the layout for a dado joint. One line is laid out on the face surface and then, by superimposing, the width of the dado is marked. Finally the lines are drawn across the surface and down the edge of the stock.

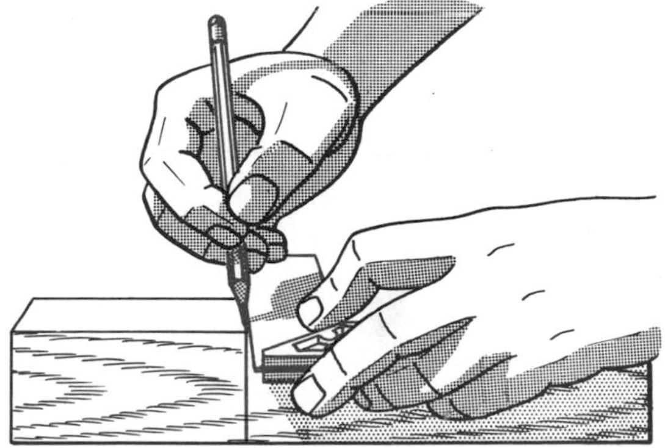

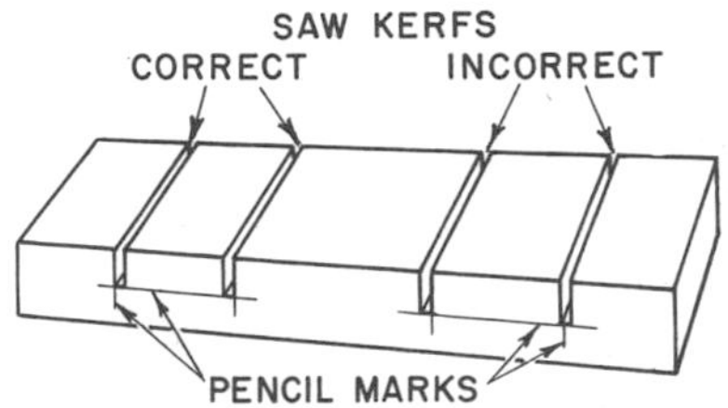

27–4. Make sure that the saw kerfs in the dado joint are inside the waste stock.

27–5. A router plane is equipped with blades of different widths. It is used for surfacing the bottom of a groove or other depression.

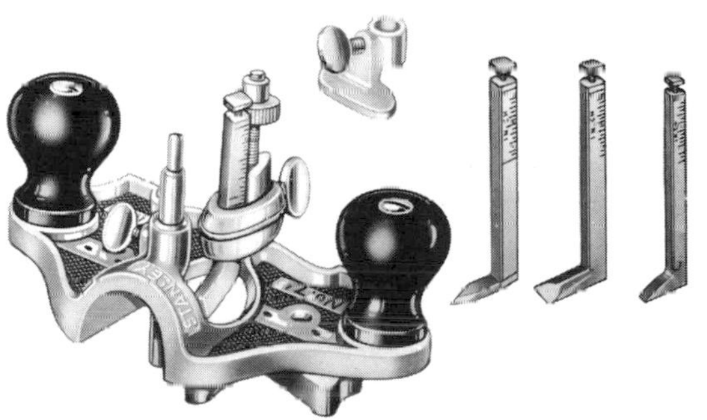

27–6. Using the router plane to trim out the bottom of a dado joint. A cutter that is the same width or slightly narrower than the width of the dado should be selected. The thumb screw is adjusted to the proper depth, and the cut is taken by holding the router plane firmly on the surface of the work and applying pressure with both hands. Don't attempt to cut the total depth with one setting.

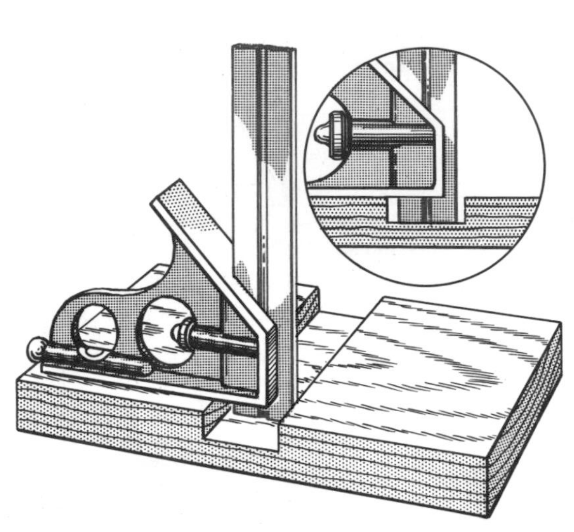

27–7. The depth of a dado joint can be checked by setting the blade of a combination square to correct depth.

depth so that the waste stock can be easily trimmed out. With a combination square, check the dado to make sure that it is the same depth throughout. Figure 27–7. Check the dado joint by inserting the piece in the joint. Figure 27–8.

27–8. Checking a dado joint. The second piece is inserted in the dado. If it is necessary to fit the joint, it is simpler to remove a little stock from the second piece rather than to cut the dado wider.

27–9. Assembling a shelf with dado joints.

You may have to trim the joint to make it a little wider. Or it may be easier to plane the side of the second piece slightly to make it fit into the joint.

ASSEMBLING THE JOINT

The dado joint is usually assembled either with glue alone or with glue and nails or screws in the same way as a rabbet joint. Figure 27–9.

MAKING A RABBET-AND-DADO JOINT

A rabbet-and-dado joint (Figure 27–10) is frequently used when additional strength and rigidity (stiffness) are needed. This joint is popular for drawer construction. The joint consists of a rabbet with a tongue. The tongue fits into the dado. To make this kind of joint, lay out and cut the rabbet first. Then lay out the position of the dado joint by superimposing the tongue of the rabbet. Mark the width of the dado. Make the dado as described earlier and fit the tongue of the rabbet into it.

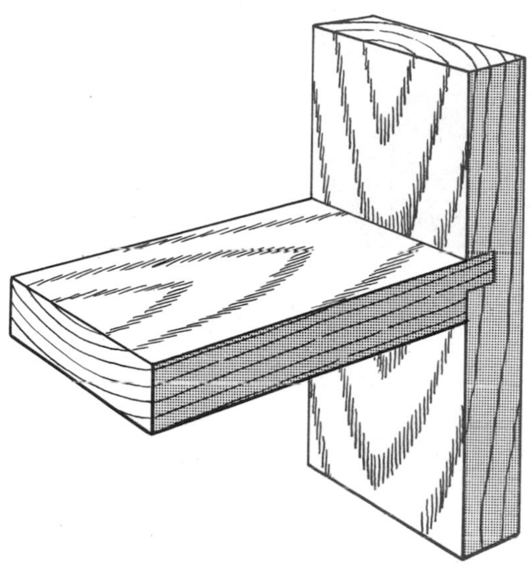

27–10. A rabbet-and-dado joint gives added strength and rigidity. It is commonly used for the back corner of drawers.

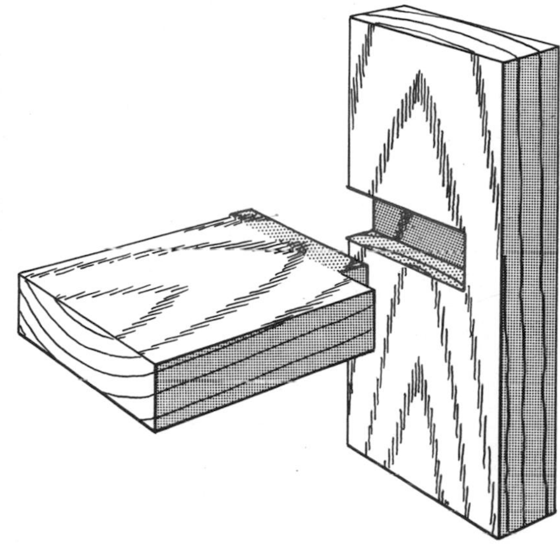

27–11. A blind dado joint has the same strength advantage as the dado joint and, in addition, does not show the joint. It is built into bookcases and other projects of this type on which a neat appearance at the front of the shelves is desirable.

MAKING A BLIND DADO JOINT

In a blind dado joint the dado is cut only partway across the board. Figure 27–11. The piece that fits into the dado is notched so that the joint doesn't show from the front. Lay out the width of the dado as described before. Mark the depth of the dado on the back edge only. Also lay out the length of the dado from the back edge to within ½ to ¾ inch of the front edge. The dado can be cut by boring a series of holes in the waste stock and then trimming out with a chisel.

CAN YOU ANSWER THESE QUESTIONS ON A DADO JOINT?

1. What is a dado?
2. Point out the difference between a dado and a rabbet.
3. When cutting a dado, where should the saw kerf be formed?
4. Explain a router plane. What is it used for?
5. How could you make a depth gauge to check a dado?
6. In fitting a dado joint, is it better to plane the side of the second piece or to cut a wider dado?
7. What advantage does a rabbet-and-dado joint have? Where is it frequently found?
8. Sketch a blind dado joint.
9. Why would a blind dado joint be found in more expensive furniture?

Section VII

UNIT 28. LAP JOINT

There are many different types of lap joints. Figure 28–1. The end lap is found in screen doors, chair seats, or any type of corner construction in which the surfaces of the two pieces must be flush. The middle lap is also found in screen-door construction, in

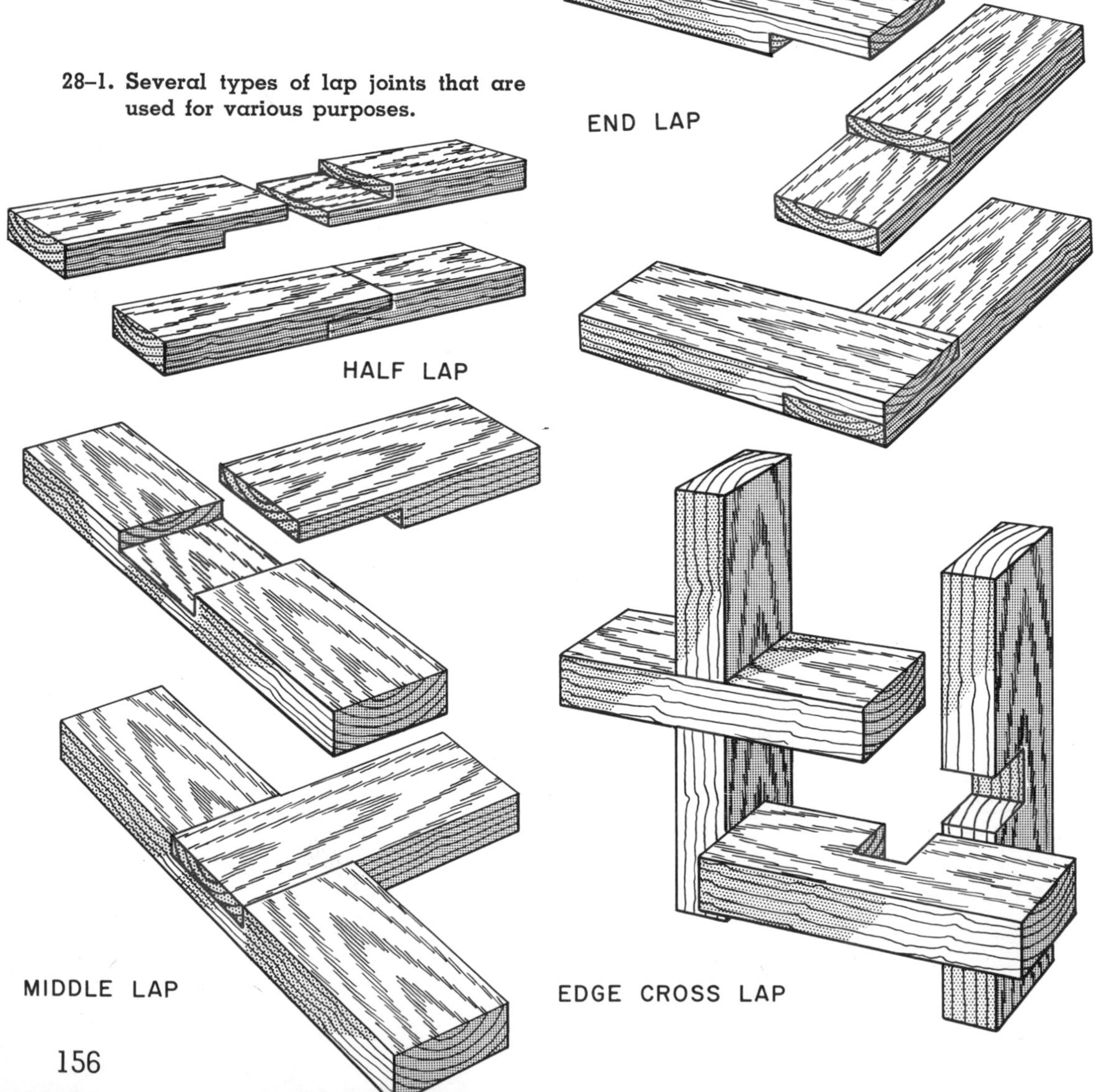

28–1. Several types of lap joints that are used for various purposes.

28–2. This attractive serving tray is made by joining many pieces of stock with edge cross-lap joints. When this many joints must be cut, it is almost a necessity to use a circular saw.

making cabinets, and in framing a house. The cross lap is widely used in furniture building whenever two pieces must cross and still be flush on the surface. A good example is this serving tray. Figure 28-2. The cross lap is by far the most common. To make any of the other types, follow the same general directions as for the cross lap.

LAYING OUT THE CROSS-LAP JOINT

The cross-lap joint is usually made in the exact center of the two pieces that cross at a 90-degree angle. However, a cross-lap joint can be made at any angle. The two pieces must be exactly the same thickness and width. Lay the two pieces on the bench side by side, with the face surface of one (piece A) and the opposite surface of the other (piece B) upward. Divide the length of each into two equal parts and lay out a center line across the two pieces. Measure the width of the stock and divide this measurement in half. Lay out a line this distance on either side of the center line. Figure 28–3.

Now check this measurement by superimposing piece B over piece A at right angles. Be sure to place it in the position that the joint will be when assembled. Figure 28–4. The layout line should just barely show beyond the edge of each piece.

Now continue the lines showing the width of the joint down the edge of each piece. Next, set a marking gauge to half the thickness of the

28–3. Correct layout for a lap joint. Both pieces should be marked at the same time.

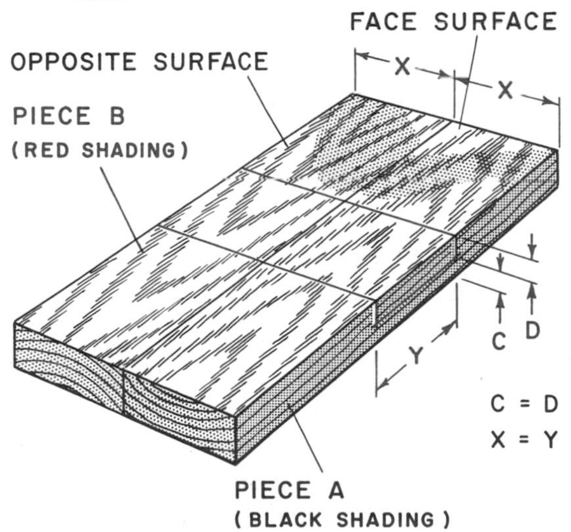

28–4. **The layout has been made and the lap joint is being checked. A try square keeps the pieces at right angles. The lines on the lower piece, which indicate the width of the lap joint, should be just visible.**

stock. From the face surface of each piece, mark along the edge on each side to show the depth of the joint. If you make this measurement from the face surface, the two pieces will be flush when the joint is made. This is because you will be cutting the joint from the face surface of one piece and the opposite surface of the other.

CUTTING THE LAP JOINT

Hold the piece in a bench hook or clamp it to the top of the bench. Cut with a backsaw to the depth of the joint just inside each of the layout lines, as you did to make a dado joint. If the joint is wide, you should make several cuts in the waste stock. This helps to remove the waste and also acts as a guide when you chisel it out.

Next, use a chisel to remove the waste stock. Work from both sides of each piece, tapering up toward the center. If you try to chisel out across the stock from only one side, you may chip the opposite side.

After you have brought the joint down to the layout line on either edge, continue to pare (cut) the high point in the center of the joint. (See the unit on shaping stock with a chisel.)

Complete this on both pieces; then try to fit them together. Figure 28–5. The pieces should fit snugly. They should not be so loose that they fall apart or so tight that they must be forced together. If the fit is too tight, it is better to plane a little from the edge of one piece rather than to try to trim the shoulder.

ASSEMBLING THE JOINT

When assembled, the surfaces of both pieces should fit flush with one another. Both glue and nails or screws are used. If the nails or screws are installed from the underside, they will not show and the joint will be very neat.

28–5. **Fitting a lap joint. The lap joints should fit together with a moderate amount of pressure. It is simpler to trim off a little from the edges of the stock than it is to make the joint wider!**

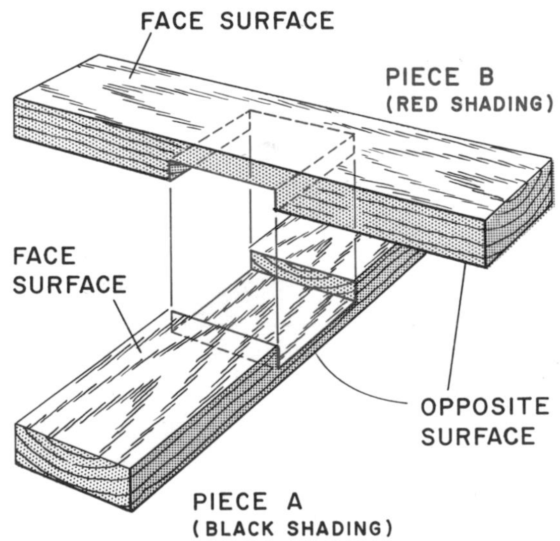

CAN YOU ANSWER THESE QUESTIONS ON A LAP JOINT?

1. Name several lap joints. What are the common uses of each?
2. Which type of lap joint is most common?
3. At what angle do the pieces of a lap joint usually cross?
4. How can you make sure that the two pieces will be flush when the joint is assembled?
5. Cutting a lap joint is similar to what other joint?
6. At what point in the fitting can you say that the two pieces fit together properly?

Section VII

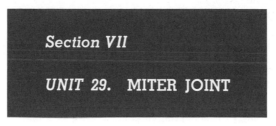

UNIT 29. MITER JOINT

A miter joint is used when the end grain should not show on the finished project. Figure 29–1. It is not a very strong joint and, therefore, is used mostly to make picture frames, casings, and decorative edges for furni-

29–1. The miter joint is weak by itself. It can be strengthened by adding dowels, a spine, or a key.

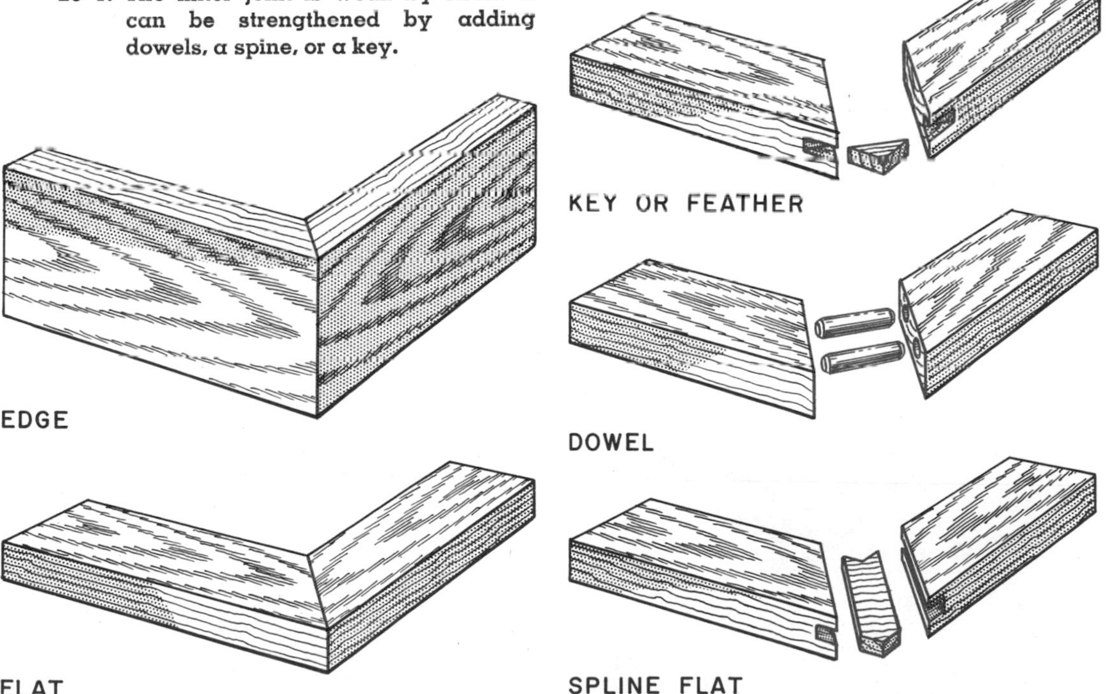

29–2. This attractive serving tray is joined at the corners with miter joints.

ture. Figure 29–2. It can be strengthened by adding dowels, a spline, or a key across the corner. Figure 29–3.

MITER BOXES

The metal miter box and saw has a metal box in which a saw can be adjusted to any angle from 30 to 90 degrees. Figure 29–4. If one is not available, it is quite simple to make one of your own. This can be done by fastening two pieces of stock to a base. Then, with a sliding T bevel, lay out a 45-degree angle in both directions. Usually this and a 90-degree angle cut are all that is ever needed. Figure 29–5. Cutting a picture frame is the most common use for the miter joint, so this will be described.

29–3. The miter joint is used for frames, contemporary furniture, and in places where end grain should not show. The corner can be strengthened by adding a spline as shown here.

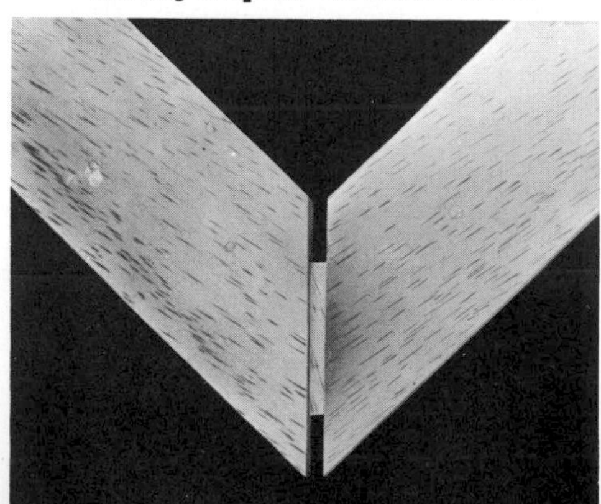

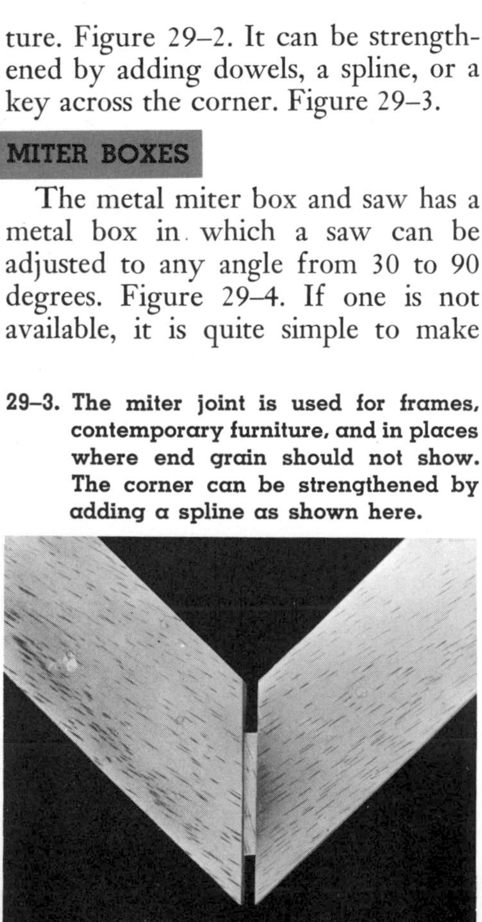

CUTTING A PICTURE FRAME

If a metal miter box is available, swing the saw to the left and set it at 45 degrees. If a wood box is used, use the cut that is to the left as you face it. Place the edge of the frame in the box with the rabbet edge down and toward you. Hold the stock firmly with the thumb of one hand against the side of the box. Figure 29–6. Then carefully bring the miter saw (or backsaw or fine crosscut saw if the box is homemade) down on the stock and cut the angle. Be especially

29–4. A metal miter box. This box consists of a frame and a saw which can be adjusted to various angles.

29–5. Cutting a miter joint with a home-made miter box and backsaw. Be certain that the line to be cut is directly under the saw teeth. Hold the work tightly against the back of the box; start the cut with a careful back-stroke.

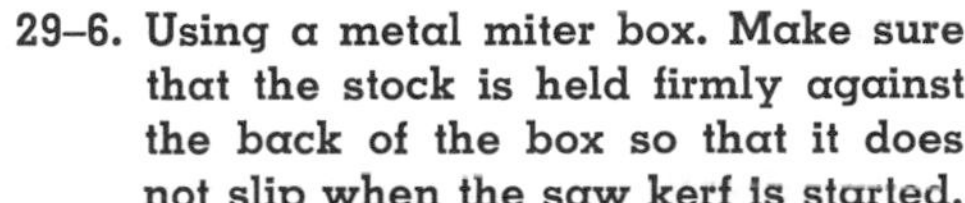

29–6. Using a metal miter box. Make sure that the stock is held firmly against the back of the box so that it does not slip when the saw kerf is started.

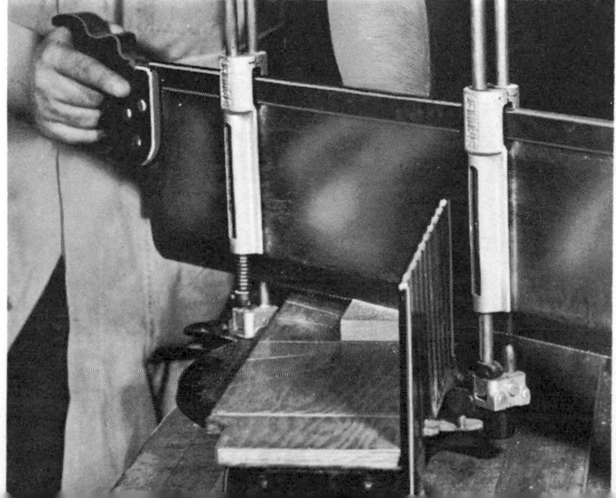

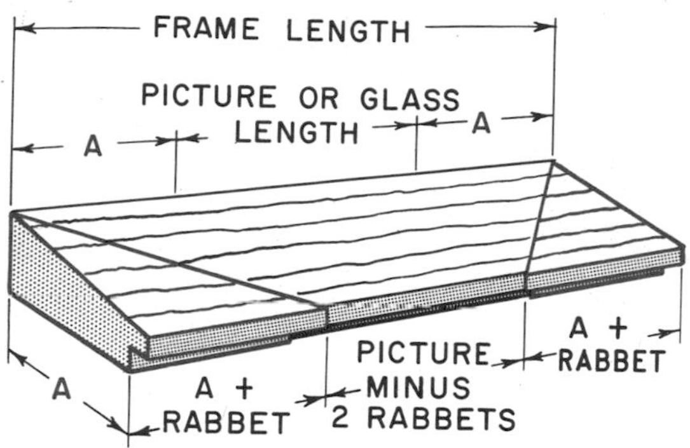

29–7. Laying out the proper measurement for cutting miter joints on a picture frame. The length as marked on the outside of the frame is equal to the length of the glass plus twice the width of the stock measured from the rabbet to the outside edge.

careful not to let the stock slip when starting the cut. This could ruin the surface of the frame.

Next, determine the length of the glass or the picture. Add to this length twice the width of the frame, measured from the rabbet edge to the outside edge. Lay out this measurement along the outside edge of the stock. Figure 29–7. Then swing the miter-box saw to the right and set it at 45 degrees. Hold the stock firmly with one hand and cut the stock to length, using your other hand to operate the saw. If you find this awkward, clamp the stock to the box with a hand screw and then operate the saw with your favored hand. Repeat this for the second side and the ends.

ASSEMBLING THE MITER JOINT

Check the joint to make sure the corners fit properly. Figure 29–8. The miter joint is usually put together by gluing and nailing. Dowels, a spline, or

29–8. Checking a miter joint to make sure that it fits properly.

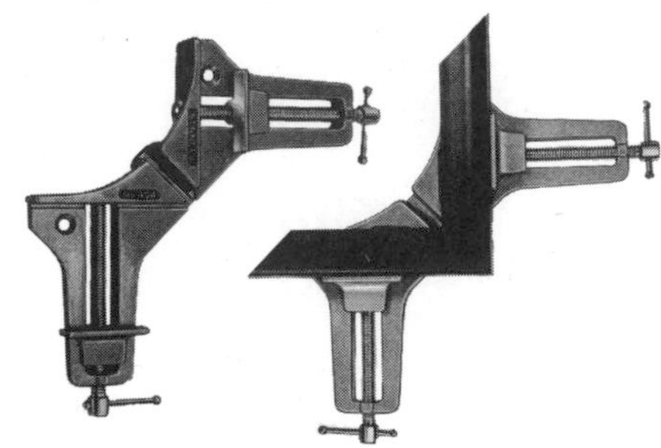

29–10. This miter-and-corner clamp holds the corners together as they are fastened.

a key may be added to strengthen the joint. To nail a miter joint, drive the nail partway into one piece. Lock the other piece in a vise in a vertical position. Hold the first piece over the vertical piece with its corner extending somewhat outside the edge of the vertical piece. Figure 29–9. As you nail the corners together, the top piece will tend to slip down until it fits squarely.

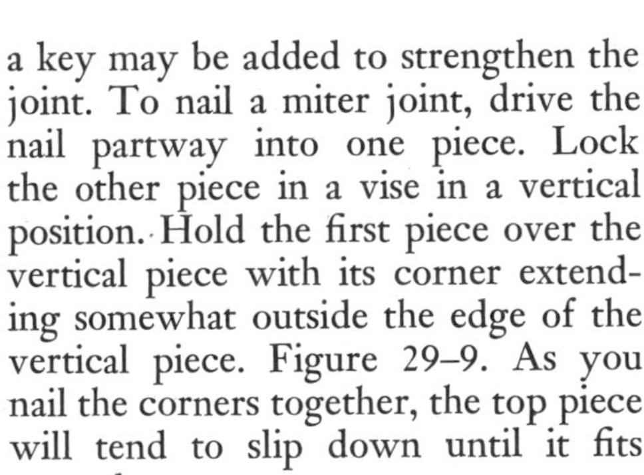

29–9. Nailing a miter joint. One piece is locked in a vise and the second piece held over it, with the corner extending slightly.

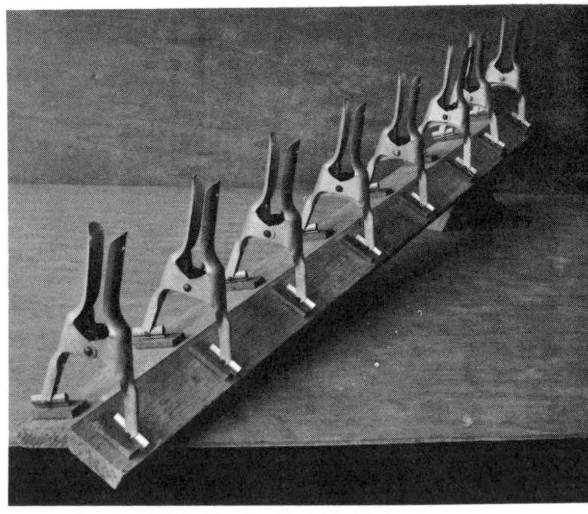

29–11. This spring clamp with special grooved teeth will hold a miter joint together after fastening.

A miter and corner clamp is the ideal clamp for assembling frames. This clamp allows you to fasten the corners with the two pieces held firmly in place. Figure 29–10. There are also special spring clamps that will hold a miter corner together. Figure 29–11. Another method is to use a little-known trick. With paper sandwiched between to permit easy removal, glue triangular blocks to the

29–12. This miter joint is held together by first gluing scrap stock to the exterior of each piece.

ends of each mitered piece. Let the glue set. Apply glue to the joint and pull together with C clamps. Remove the clamps after the glue has set and pry blocks away. Then sand the surface. Figure 29–12.

CAN YOU ANSWER THESE QUESTIONS ON A MITER JOINT?

1. What is the advantage of a miter joint? Disadvantage?
2. Name the common uses.
3. Describe a miter box.
4. Could you construct a miter box?
5. At what angle is a miter joint made?
6. What kind of saw is best for cutting a miter joint?
7. Are there any precautions that should be observed in starting a miter cut?
8. In what two ways can a miter joint be strengthened?
9. What implements would you choose for holding a miter joint after it is glued?

Section VII

UNIT 30. MORTISE-AND-TENON JOINT

The mortise-and-tenon joint is found in better furniture construction. Figure 30–1. There are many kinds of mortise-and-tenon joints. A few are shown in Figure 30–2. By far the most common is the blind mortise-and-tenon joint. As you will see, this is a rectangular projection on the end of a rail that fits into a rectangular hole in a second piece, usually a leg. Making

30–1. This attractive coffee table is joined together at the legs and nails with mortise-and-tenon joints.

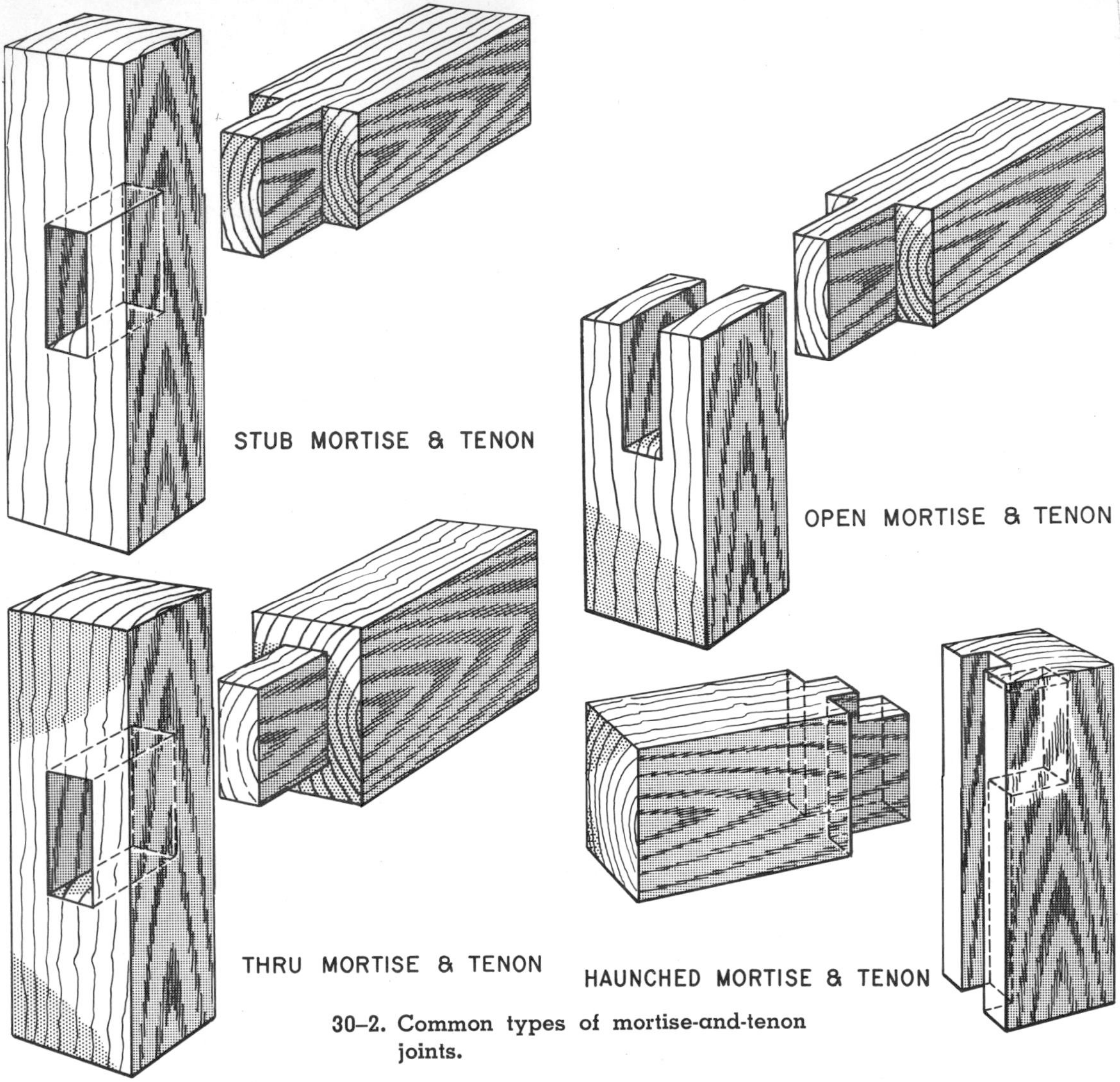

STUB MORTISE & TENON

OPEN MORTISE & TENON

THRU MORTISE & TENON

HAUNCHED MORTISE & TENON

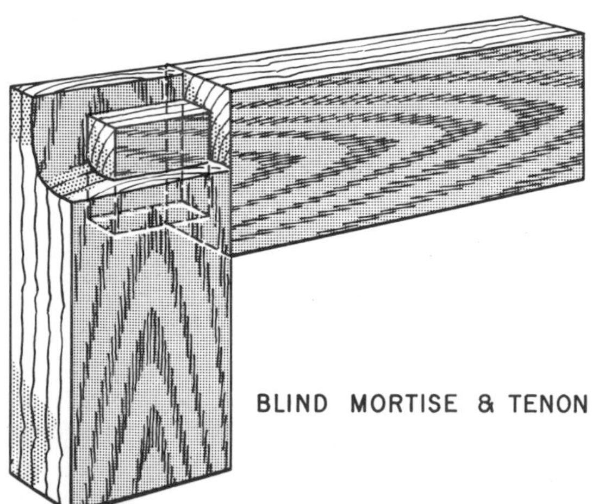

30–2. Common types of mortise-and-tenon joints.

a mortise-and-tenon joint by hand takes skill and should not be attempted if another type of joint will be just as satisfactory. Before beginning, note the names and measurements given in Figure 30–3. After the layout is complete, the joint can be cut with machines.

MAKING THE PRELIMINARY LAYOUT

For most projects it will be necessary to make several mortise-and-tenon joints. For example, a simple table with four rails and legs takes eight. Before laying out the joints, hold the several pieces to be assembled in the position they will be when the project is finished. Place the face surface of the rails and the face surface and joint edge of the legs outward. Begin at one corner to mark No. 1 on the leg and No. 1 on the adjoining rail, No. 2 on the next, etc. Do this until you have marked with matching numbers the pieces that make up each mortise-and-tenon joint. In this way, you will be sure the pieces will fit together in the proper order when you are ready to assemble them.

30–3. Study the parts of the mortise-and-tenon joint, as these will be referred to in its layout and construction.

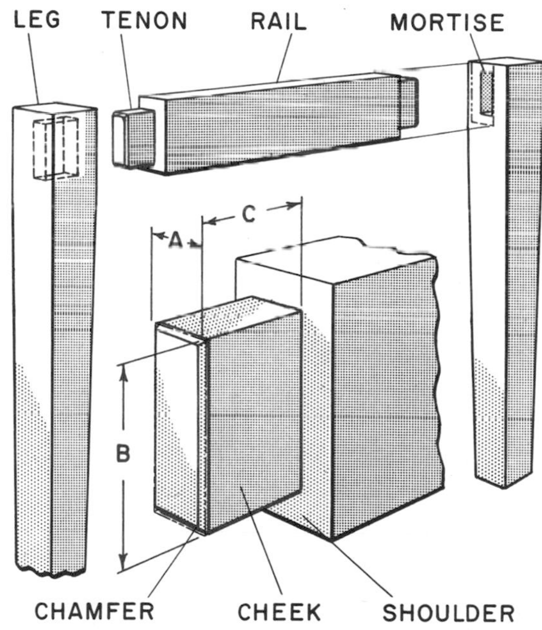

A - THICKNESS OF TENON
B - WIDTH OF TENON
C - LENGTH OF TENON

LAYING OUT THE TENONS

The size of the mortise-and-tenon joint is usually given on the drawing. These measurements should be followed carefully. However, if they are not given, the tenon is made half as wide as the total thickness of the piece and about ½ to ¾ inch narrower than the total width.

From the ends, mark out the length of the tenon and square a line completely around the end of each piece. Do this on all pieces and then check to see that all of the rails are the same length from shoulder to shoulder. Next, set the marking gauge to half the thickness of the stock to be removed and, working from the face side, mark a line across the end and down either edge.

Next, add to this measurement the thickness of the tenon and check the gauge. Again mark a line across the end and down the sides. Subtract the width of the tenon from the total width of the stock. Divide this amount in half and set this measurement on a marking gauge.

From the joint edge of the rail, mark a line across the end and down the side. Next, add to this measurement the width of the tenon and set the gauge again. Repeat the mark across the end and down the side.

Now you have all of the necessary measurements on the tenon. Figure 30–4. If several tenons are to be marked, make sure that you do them at the same time to keep from making a mistake.

LAYING OUT A MORTISE

With a pencil point on your marking gauge, make all lines on all four

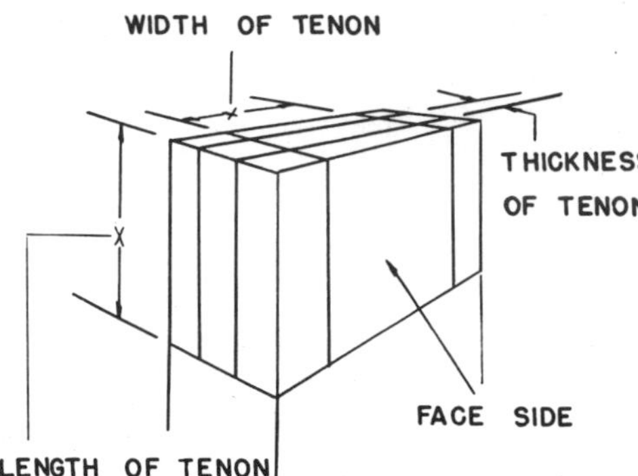

30–4. Proper layout for a tenon. These lines should be accurately made so the tenon will be the correct size and shape.

legs at the same time. From the top end of each leg, lay out two lines on the inside surfaces (opposite the face side and joint edge) that indicate the total width of the rail.

Next, lay out two more lines on these surfaces to show the width of the tenon. Decide how far back the rail is to be set from the outside edge of the leg. Add to this measurement the thickness of the stock removed from one side of the tenon. Set the marking gauge to this measurement. Now hold the marking gauge against the face side and joint edge and mark a line between the lines that indicate the width of the tenon. Add to this measurement an amount equal to the thickness of the tenon. Mark another line to complete the outline. This will be exactly the same as the thickness and width of the tenon. Figure 30–5. If an auger bit is to be used to remove the waste stock from the mortise, lay out a line down the center of the outline.

CUTTING THE TENON

Lock the stock in a vise with the marked tenon showing. Use a backsaw or fine crosscut saw to make four saw cuts in the waste stock that will shape the thickness and width of the tenon. Figure 30–6.

Next, remove the stock from the vise and clamp it on the top of the bench. Make the shoulder cuts to remove the waste stock which forms the thickness and the width of the tenon. *Be especially careful,* as it is essential that these saw marks be accurate for a tight-fitting tenon. The cutting of a tenon can be simplified by using a circular saw. See Unit 53. The tenon must then be trimmed with a chisel. Figure 30–7.

Cut a small chamfer around the end

30–5. The proper layout of a mortise. Only the part indicated by the shading is absolutely essential to the layout.

X - DISTANCE FROM EDGE OF LEG TO FACE SIDE OF RAIL

Y - THICKNESS OF RAIL

Z - WIDTH OF RAIL

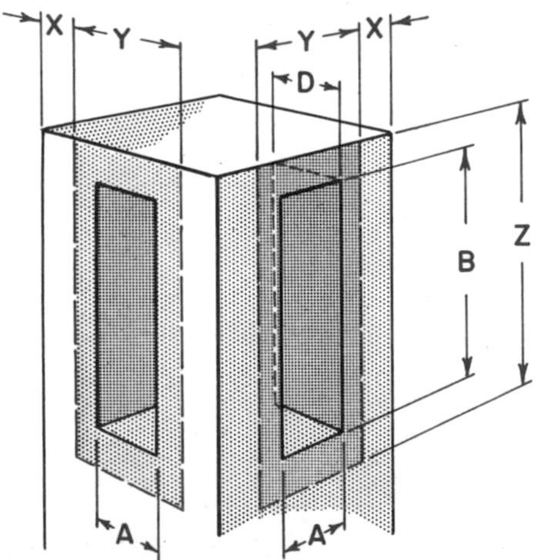

A - WIDTH OF MORTISE (TENON THICKNESS)

B - LENGTH OF MORTISE (TENON WIDTH)

C - LENGTH OF TENON

D - MORTISE DEPTH = C + $\frac{1}{8}$

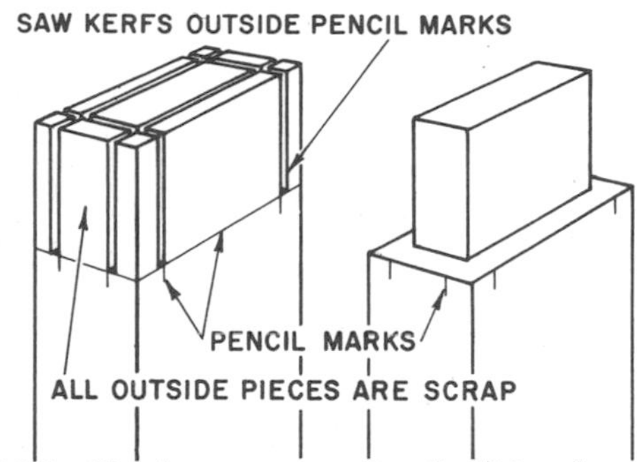

30–6. Cheek cuts completed. This shows the four cuts that will shape the thickness and width of the tenon. *Make the cuts in waste stock.*

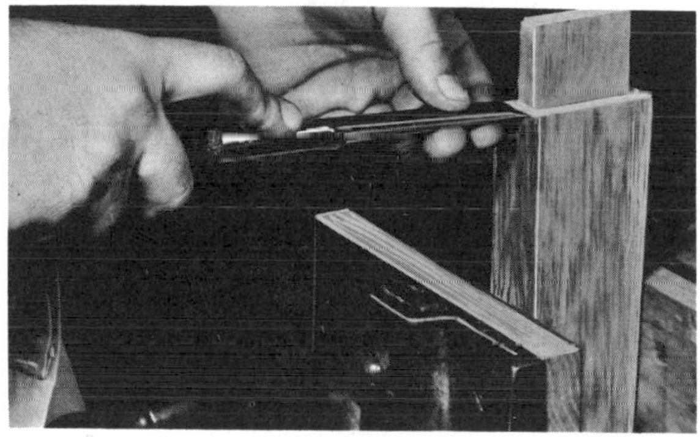

30–7. After the shoulder cuts are made, the tenon is trimmed with a chisel to make it fit accurately into the mortise.

of the tenon to help it slip easily into the mortise opening. This must be very slight.

CUTTING THE MORTISE

The most common way to remove most of the stock from the mortise opening is with an auger bit and brace. The auger bit should be the same diameter or slightly smaller than the width of the opening. Bore a series of holes to remove most of the stock from the mortise opening. Figure 30–8. Use a depth gauge set to make the holes slightly deeper than the length of the tenon.

With a chisel, pare out the sides and ends of the opening to the layout line. Figure 30–9. To finish the ends, use a narrow chisel. Some woodworkers prefer to remove all of the stock with a chisel. For this, use a heavy, thick mortise chisel that can stand quite a bit of pounding. The width of the blade should be exactly the width of the opening. Begin to cut at the center of the mortise. Hold the chisel in a vertical position with the bevel side toward the end of the mortise. Cut out a V-shaped notch to the

30–8. Boring out a mortise. Note that the bit selected has the same diameter as the thickness of the tenon or the width of the mortise. A depth gauge controls the amount of stock removed.

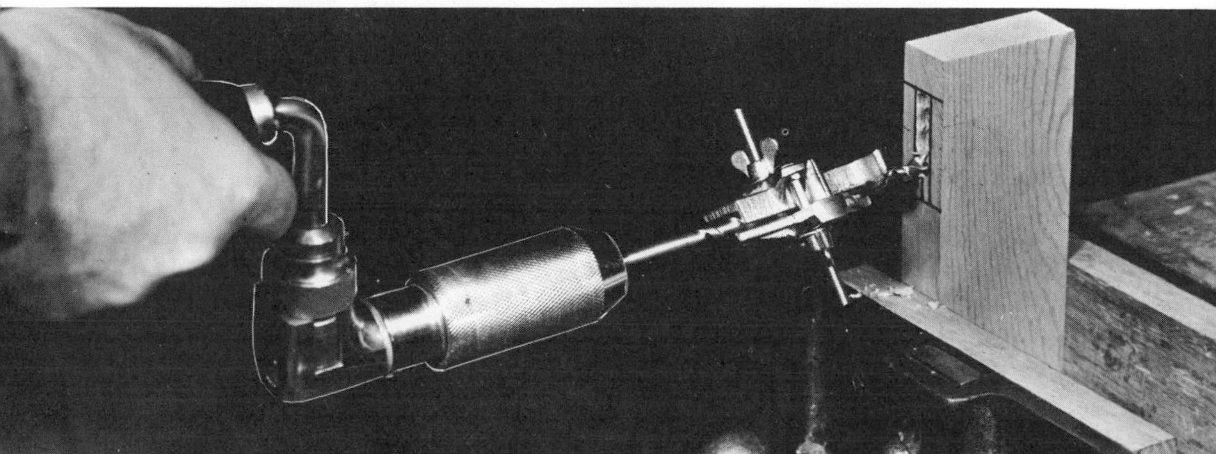

depth required. Then continue to remove the stock by driving the chisel down with a mallet. Draw down on the handle to remove the chips. Figure 30–10. Stop when you are within about ⅛ inch of the end of the opening. Turn the chisel around with the flat side toward the end of the mortise and cut out the remainder of the stock. Figure 30–11.

The mortise can also be cut on the drill press using a mortising attachment. See Unit 59.

ASSEMBLING THE MORTISE AND TENON

After the mortise-and-tenon joint has been cut, it will be necessary to do some fitting before the tenon will

30–9. Trimming out a mortise with a chisel. After the holes are drilled, it is necessary to trim out the sides and end of the mortise. To do this, hold the chisel with the flat side against the side of the mortise and take a shearing cut. It will be necessary to use a narrow chisel to trim out the ends.

30–10. Cutting a mortise with a heavy chisel that will take considerable pounding. The chisel selected must be the same width as the mortise.

30–11. Proper method of cutting a mortise with a mortising chisel. The center cuts are taken with the chisel held with the bevel toward the outside. Other cuts are taken with the bevel turned in.

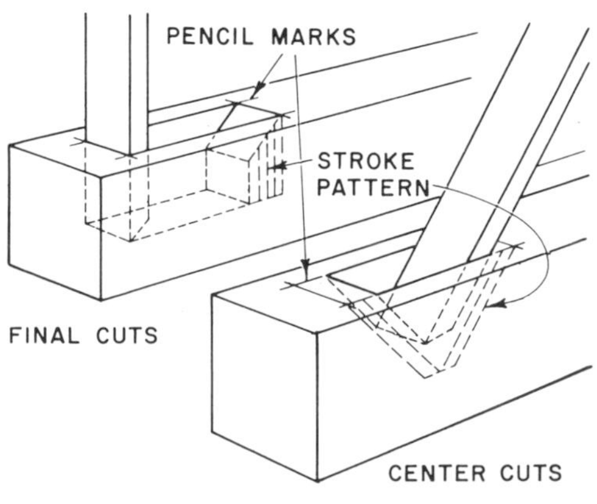

fit into the mortise properly. Use a chisel to pare off stock from the thickness and width of the tenon until you can force the tenon into the mortise with a moderate amount of pressure. Make sure that the shoulder of the tenon fits squarely against the face of the mortise.

This joint is usually glued. Gluing is discussed at length in another part of the book.

CAN YOU ANSWER THESE QUESTIONS ON A MORTISE-AND-TENON JOINT?

1. Is a mortise-and-tenon joint found on better-quality furniture? Why?
2. Which part is the mortise? The tenon?
3. Make a sketch showing the cheek. The shoulder.
4. Name several types of mortise-and-tenon joints.
5. How many mortise-and-tenon joints could be found on a simple table?
6. What is the rule for the thickness of the tenon? What should the length of the tenon be?
7. Tell how to lay out a tenon.
8. Could a marking gauge be used to lay out a mortise? Explain.
9. How do the width of the mortise and the thickness of the tenon compare?
10. Should the shoulder cuts be made first? Why?
11. Which of the two methods of cutting a mortise is the most common? What are these two methods?
12. How are mortise-and-tenon joints usually fastened for permanency?

Section VIII
Assembling

The eighth 11 steps in hand woodworking—what you must know and be able to do.

31. How to make a table or desk which has fitted drawers which make necessary special work in fastening down the table or desk top, building the drawers and their guides, and fitting the drawers in place.

32. The paneled door or frame: its parts and how to build and fit it.

33. Assembling a project with nails, kinds of nails, choosing the right nail and how to drive it correctly in both softwood and hardwood; how to remove a nail.

34. Driving a screw with a screw driver in assembling an article, kind of screw to select, how to set the screw, drilling clearance holes, plugging screw holes, making the surface flat by countersinking the wood for a flathead screw.

35. Securing a fine surface with a hand scraper; how to hold the scraper and using it on burly wood.

36. Getting the project ready for assembly by sanding it; kinds of sandpaper and how to achieve the smoothness you want on any kind of surface.

37. The trial assembly, with a final check of all parts of the project, equipment needed and steps to follow for the actual assembly, and correct gluing procedure.

38. Getting the project ready for finishing, removing excess glue, filling the cracks and holes, scraping, and sanding.

39. Pieces of cabinet hardware are first carefully fitted and then removed; how to fit and install such hardware as hinges, knobs, locks, and drawer pulls.

40. Applying plastic laminates; kinds of materials, correct tools to use, proper adhesive, method of applying.

41. Adding beauty and utility to wood products with mosaic tile; kinds of tile, tools and materials, methods of installing.

There are three common methods of permanently fastening pieces together: with nails, screws, or glue. Before assembly, be sure that each part of the project is scraped and sanded.

Before finishing,you must go over the project to remove excess glue, fill in dents, and scrape and resand the surface. Hardware should be fitted, then removed. See the "box" above. Further steps in woodworking are on pp. 15, 43, 60, 94, 108, 132, 143, 219, 244.

Section VIII

UNIT 31. BUILDING TABLES, DESKS, AND CABINETS

To build a table, desk, or cabinet you will do several new steps in addition to those already covered in this book.

STRENGTHENING CORNERS

Most tables, chairs, and simple desks are made with four legs joined by rails. The rail and leg are fastened together with dowel construction or mortise-and-tenon joints. To add strength to the adjoining parts, a corner block is cut and fastened in each corner. Figure 31–1. The block helps to hold the table square and gives added support at its weakest point. *Glue blocks* are small triangular blocks of wood placed along the edges of two adjoining pieces to strengthen them.

31–1. A block used to strengthen corners of a table.

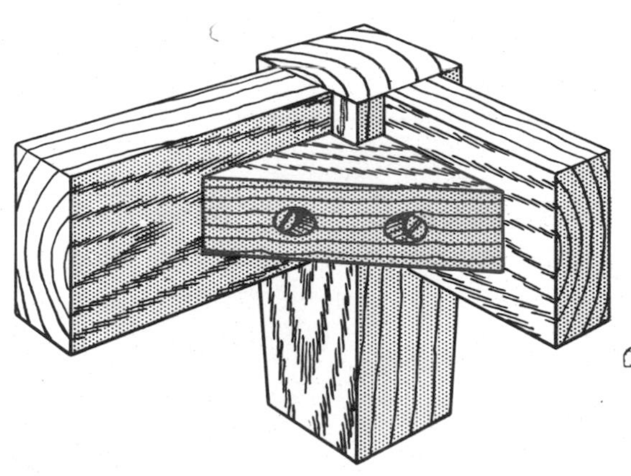

FASTENING TABLE TOPS

Figure 31–2 shows three common ways of attaching a table top to the rails.

DRAWER CONSTRUCTION

There are three steps in installing a drawer in a table: cutting the rail to receive the drawer, making a drawer guide, and making the drawer. In desk and chest construction only the last two steps need to be done.

1. Cutting the rail. To cut the rail to receive the drawer, first decide on the exact size of the drawer. Then cut an opening that is $1/16$ inch wider and $1/8$ inch longer than the drawer front.

2. Making the drawer.

a. The drawer may be made to fit flush with the opening, or it may be a lip drawer (fit over the frame). To make a lip drawer, a $3/8$-inch rabbet is cut around the inside edge of the

31–2. Several ways of attaching a table top to the rails. A. Square cleat. B. Square cleat with rabbet and groove. C. Metal tabletop fastener.

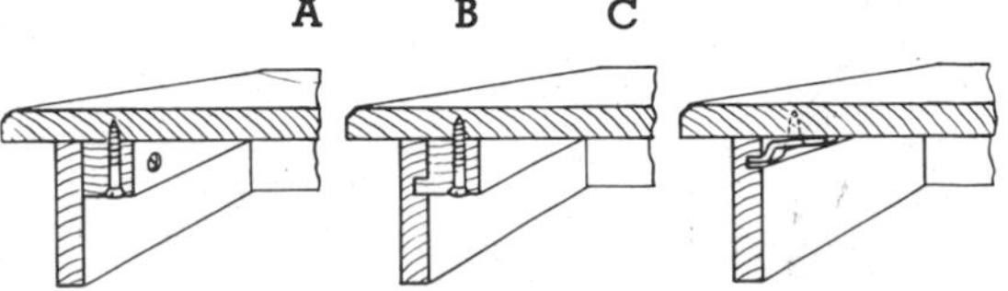

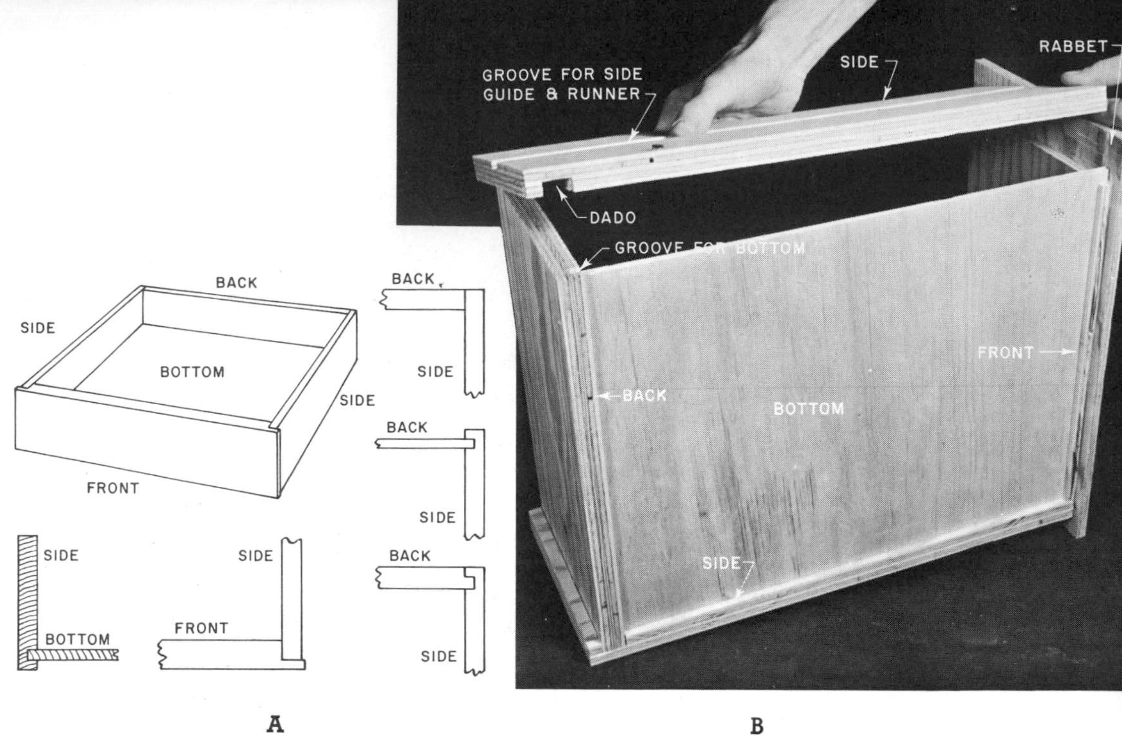

31–3. A. Simple ways of fastening the sides to the front and to the back in drawer construction. B. Parts of a drawer.

drawer front. Then the lip drawer overlaps the frame.

b. The front is usually made of 3/4-inch material. The grain and color usually match the material used in the project. The sides and back are made of 1/2-inch stock such as pine, birch, or maple. The bottom is usually made of 1/4-inch fir plywood or hardboard. Figure 31–3.

c. A common way of joining the front to the sides is with a rabbet joint. The rabbet is cut to a width of two thirds the thickness of the sides. This will allow some clearance for the drawer. Other kinds of drawer joints can also be used.

d. The back is joined to the sides with a butt or dado joint. The back should be cut so that the drawer is slightly narrower at the back than at the front.

e. Cut a groove (1/4 inch by 1/4 inch) about 1/2 inch above the bottom on the inside front and sides. Sometimes a groove is also cut across the back.

f. Cut the drawer bottom slightly smaller (about 1/16 inch) than the width between the grooves. This will allow for shrinkage and swelling.

g. Assemble the drawer. Glue and nail the sides to the front. Never put glue into the grooves for the bottom. Slip the bottom in place and then glue or nail the sides to the back.

3. Making drawer guides. The three most common drawer guides are the slide-block guide and runner (simple drawer guide), the center guide, and the side guide. Figure 31–4. Drawer guides support the drawer and keep it from slipping from one side to the other.

a. To make a slide-block guide

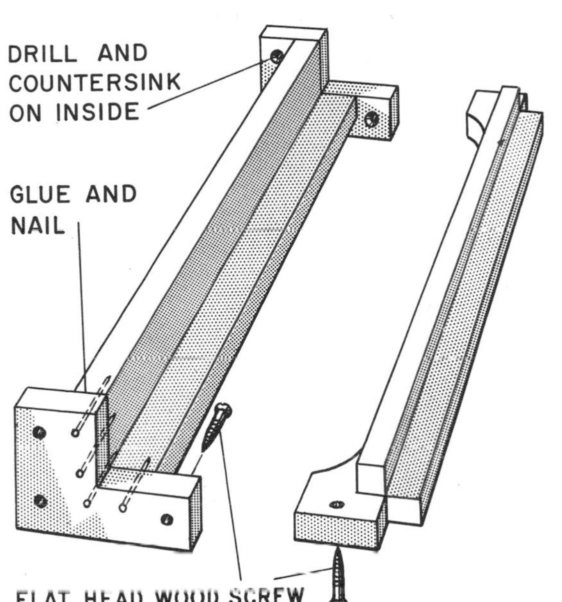

31–4. A simple drawer guide. This type can be easily made and will work well when fitting a drawer between rails.

and runner for a table drawer, cut a rabbet in a piece of wood. This piece will fit between the rails at the lower corner of the drawer.

b. Figure 31–5 shows a side guide with a groove in the side of the drawer and with the runner attached to the project itself. Another method is to attach a runner to the side of the drawer and then cut a groove in either side of the project.

c. The center guide is made by

31–5a. This beautifully crafted foot stool has a small drawer installed in the rail.

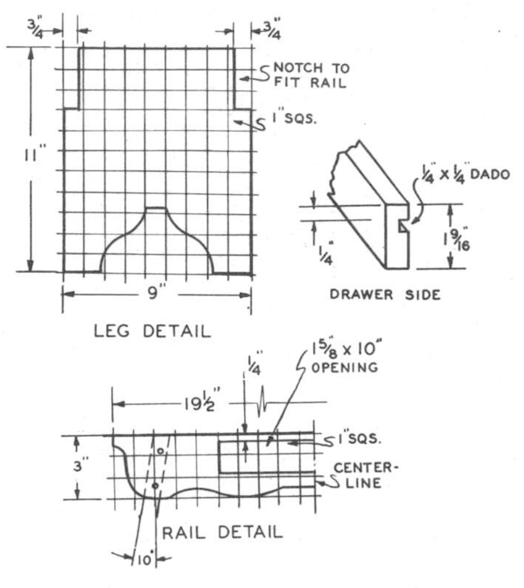

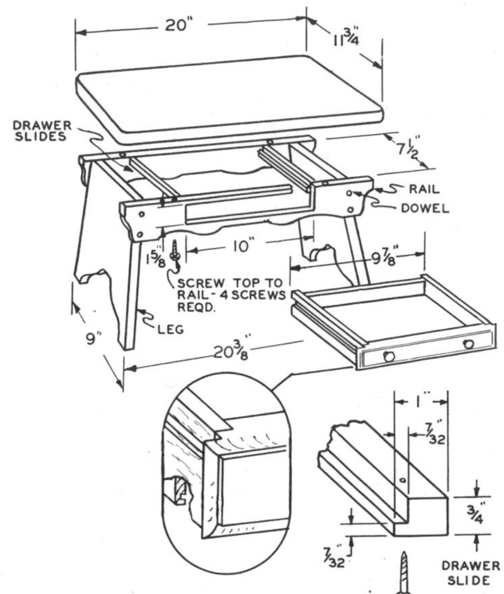

31–5b. A side guide and runner are used for a drawer fitted between the rails of the foot stool.

31–6. This distinguished bookcase is an example of case construction. The shelves are adjustable.

attaching a runner to the project. Then two extra pieces are attached to the bottom of the drawer to act as the guide. Or a groove can be cut in an extra piece that is fastened to the bottom as a guide.

For heavy drawers such as those for letter files, special ball-bearing guides should be fastened to either side of the drawer. If a drawer sticks, rub a little paraffin at the tight points. In best quality furniture, the dovetail joint is made to fasten the sides to the front and a rabbet-and-dado joint joins the back and sides. When there are several drawers, a dust panel is usually placed between drawers.

CASE CONSTRUCTION

Any case, such as a bookcase or hi-fi cabinet, is a box turned on its side. Figure 31–6. The corners are joined with a rabbet, miter, or similar joint. A rabbet is usually cut around the back edge so that the back will fit into it. The back is usually made of plywood or hardboard. If the case has fixed shelves, these are usually installed with a dado joint. The most common way to provide for movable shelves is to use adjustable shelf brackets with snap-on clips. Figure 31–7.

31–7. Movable shelves installed with adjustable shelf brackets.

31–8. This free-design coffee table shows the use of commercial legs.

These can be obtained in any lengths. Two are needed for either side. The best way to use them is to cut a groove into which the shelf bracket fits. Then cut the shelves to the correct length.

USING COMMERCIAL LEGS

There are many kinds of commercial legs that can be purchased for use on all types of furniture projects. Figure 31–8. They come in many lengths, shapes, and kinds of materials. Legs are made of metal, wood, and plastic. They may be round tapered, round straight, square tapered, or square straight. The common lengths are 7, 13, 17, 22, and 29 inches. The shorter lengths are used for cabinets and chests. The longer lengths are used on tables and desks.

Some types of commercial legs are made as a one-piece unit that is fastened directly to the wood. Other types come with metal attaching brackets. These are made so that the legs can be fastened either in a straight up-and-down position or at a slight angle.

CAN YOU ANSWER THESE QUESTIONS ON BUILDING TABLES, DESKS, AND CABINETS?

1. How can the corners of a table be strengthened?
2. What are three ways of fastening a table top to the base?
3. Describe a drawer guide. What purpose does it have?
4. Relate the three steps in installing a drawer in a table.
5. What is the best type of drawer guide?
6. What things should you think about when choosing the wood for the front of the drawer?
7. How can a simple drawer guide be constructed?
8. What joints are found in a drawer?
9. Explain why the sides of the drawer are not parallel.
10. What is case construction?
11. Tell how to use commercial legs for a table.

Section VIII

UNIT 32. PANELED DOOR OR FRAME

Panel construction is found in such things as chests, desks, and other pieces of cabinet furniture. Figure 32–1. It consists of a frame into which is fitted a piece or panel of plywood. It has the advantage over solid construction of less warpage since only the frame can change in size, while the panel inside is free to expand or contract. The construction is the same whether the panels are made for parts of furniture or for doors.

PARTS OF A DOOR

The upright parts of a door are called stiles and the cross parts are called rails. Figure 32–2. Door construction is similar to other panel construction in which the frame fits together with a haunched mortise-and-tenon joint. Window construction is also very similar, except that the open mortise-and-tenon joint is used.

MAKING A PANELED DOOR

Lay out and cut the stock for the frame. Allow extra length to provide for making the joint. Square up the stock. Select the panel to be used to fill the frame. Check this thickness and then cut a groove along the joint edges of each piece into which the panel will fit. This groove should be as deep as it is wide. The simplest way of cutting it is to use the circular saw, although it can be done with a hand combination plane.

The mortise should be far enough away from the ends of the stiles to keep it from breaking out under pressure. The mortise should be made the

32–1. **The top of this coffee table illustrates panel construction. The outside top panels are fitted with leather inserts. The center panel is fitted with a piece of glass.**

same width as the width of the groove, and the length should be about two thirds the width of the rail. The tenon should be cut as thick as the width of the groove. The length of the tenon should equal the depth of the mortise plus the depth of the groove.

Cut a notch out of the tenon. The long part of the tenon should fit into the mortise opening and the short part should fit into the groove of the stile. Figure 32–3. Sometimes, in making a panel frame, no mortise is cut and only a stub tenon is made which fits into the groove in the stiles.

Fit the panel temporarily into the frame to check it. Take the frame apart and cover the edge of the panel with soap or wax to keep any glue from getting into the groove or edge of the panel. Apply glue and clamp the frame together.

FITTING A PANEL DOOR

Check the opening for the door. Plane the edge of the stile which will fit against the frame and have the hinges straight and true. After the edge

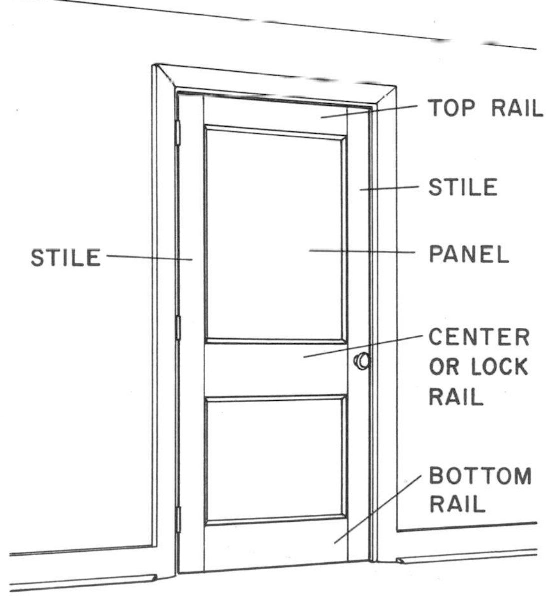

32–2. Parts of a door.

32–3. Methods of joining the corners for panel construction.

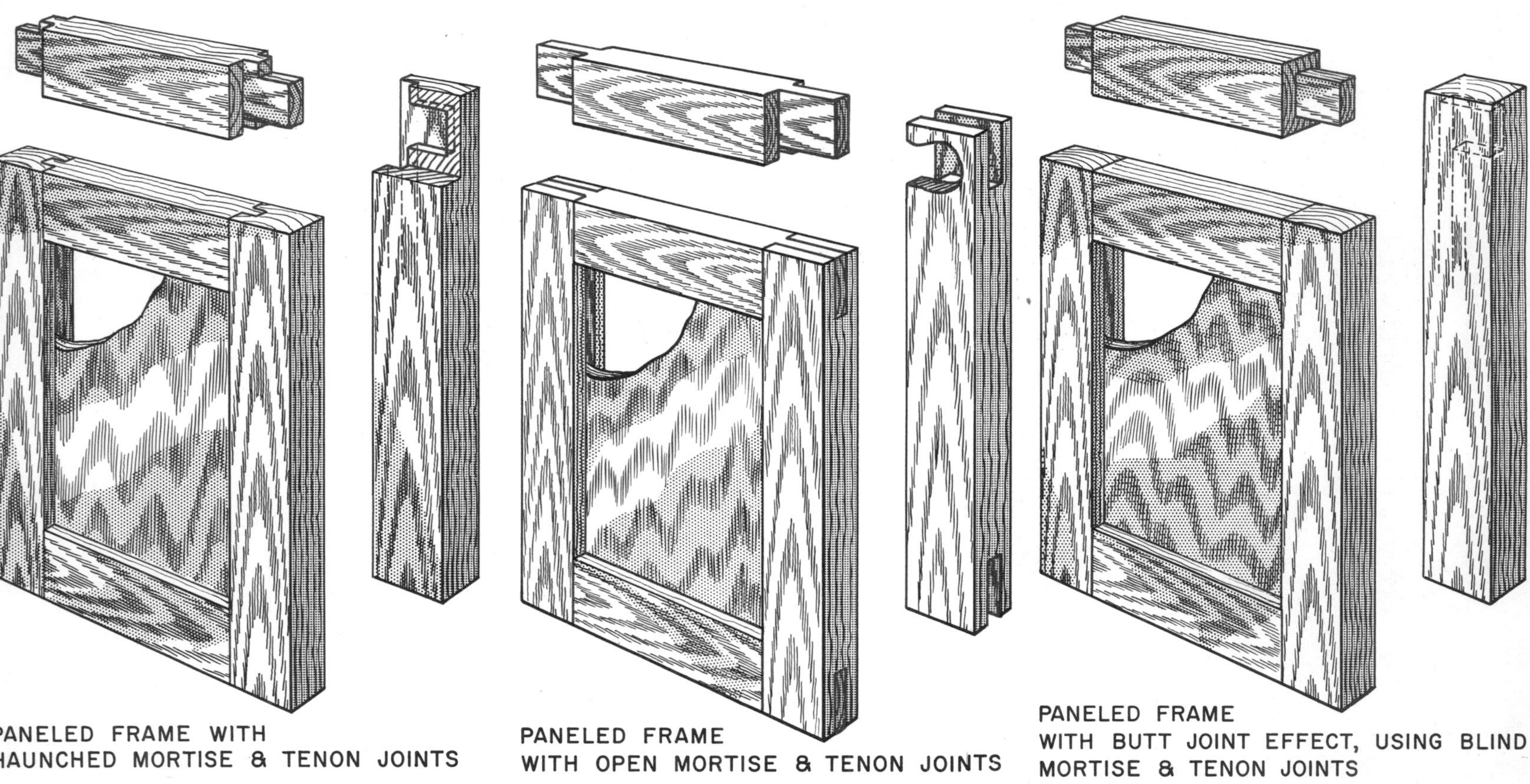

has been planed true, hold the door against the opening as close as possible to get a rough check on how well it fits. Make sure that each stile will be about the same width when the door is fitted. Use a framing square to check the frame. If the frame is square, then square off a line on the upper rail. Cut and plane this end square with the edge that has been fitted. Continue to check and plane until the door fits properly, since the frame sometimes is a little "out of square." Measure the height of the opening, and lay out and cut the bottom rail. If the frame is square, plane this end square with the first edge. Measure the width of the opening at the top and at the bottom. Sometimes the frame opening will not be exactly parallel from top to bottom. Lay out these measurements on the top and bottom rail and join these lines, using a straightedge, along the stile. Cut and plane the edge until the door fits properly. The door must not be too snug since, after the hinges are installed, it must have some "play" to swing open. This edge should be planed at a slight bevel toward the back of the door. This gives the stile proper clearance when the door is opened and closed.

CAN YOU ANSWER THESE QUESTIONS ON A PANELED DOOR OR FRAME?

1. Why are doors and frames made of panel construction?
2. Make a sketch of a door naming its parts.
3. What kind of joint is found most frequently in panel construction?
4. Should the panel be glued to the frame? Explain your answer.
5. List all of the steps in fitting a door in an opening.

Section VIII

UNIT 33. ASSEMBLING STOCK WITH NAILS

The simplest and easiest way to join two pieces of wood is with nails. You have probably done quite a bit of nailing. Yet, while it seems simple, much skill is needed to do it properly.

TOOLS FOR NAILING

The most common tool is the *claw hammer*. Figure 33–1. The face of the hammer head should be slightly rounded. Figure 33-2. This lets you drive the nail flush with the wood surface without damaging the wood itself. Be sure the hammer face is free from dirt, glue, etc., so it won't slip and mar the wood or bend the nail.

A *nail set* is a short metal punch with a cup-shaped head used to drive

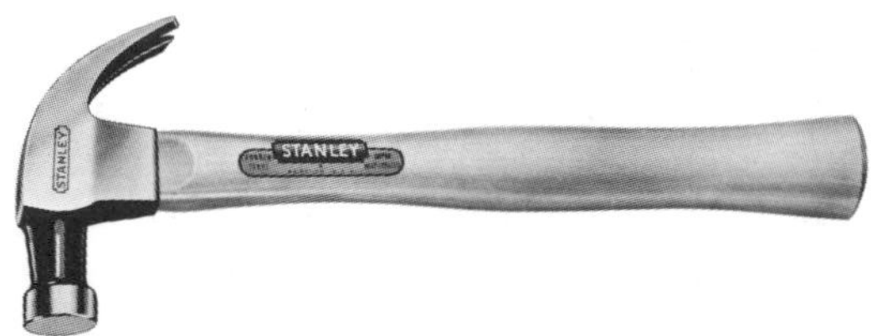

33–1. Claw hammers are available in many sizes with heads that weigh from 5 ounces to 20 ounces. A 13-ounce hammer is good for average work.

the head of the nail below the surface of the wood. Figure 33–3.

KINDS OF NAILS

There are so many kinds of nails, brads, and tacks that it would be impossible to list them here. Nails are made of mild steel, copper, brass, and aluminum.

Mild steel nails are sometimes galvanized (coated) to protect them from rusting. There are four kinds that you will use the most: common, box, casing, and finishing. Figure 33–4.

The system of nail marking with "penny" or "d" is rather old fashioned. This term comes from one of two sources: either it was considered to be the weight per thousand or the cost per thousand. Regardless of its origin, it is still used.

Nails range in size from 2d, the smallest, to 60d, the largest. Figure 33–5. You will find that a 2d common nail has a larger diameter than a 2d finishing nail. The larger sizes are called *spikes. Box nails* are mostly for construction of packing cases and other similar carpentry work. The *casing nail* has a small head. It is a rather heavy nail for more finished carpentry or for the assembly of projects on which the nail heads are to be recessed (below the surface). The *finishing nail*, the finest of all nails, is used for all fine cabinet and construction work. *Brads* are similar to finishing nails, but are marked a little

33–2. The head of the hammer is domed slightly to help keep the nail from bending if you don't strike it exactly square and to concentrate force at the contact point.

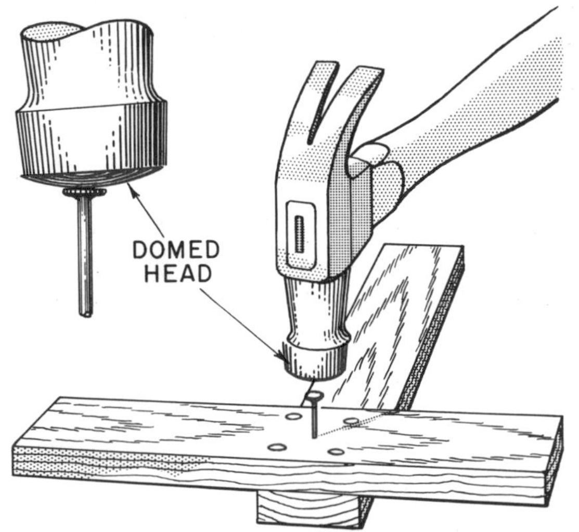

33–3. The nail set is used to drive the nail head below the surface of the wood. This hole is then filled with putty or similar material before the project is finished.

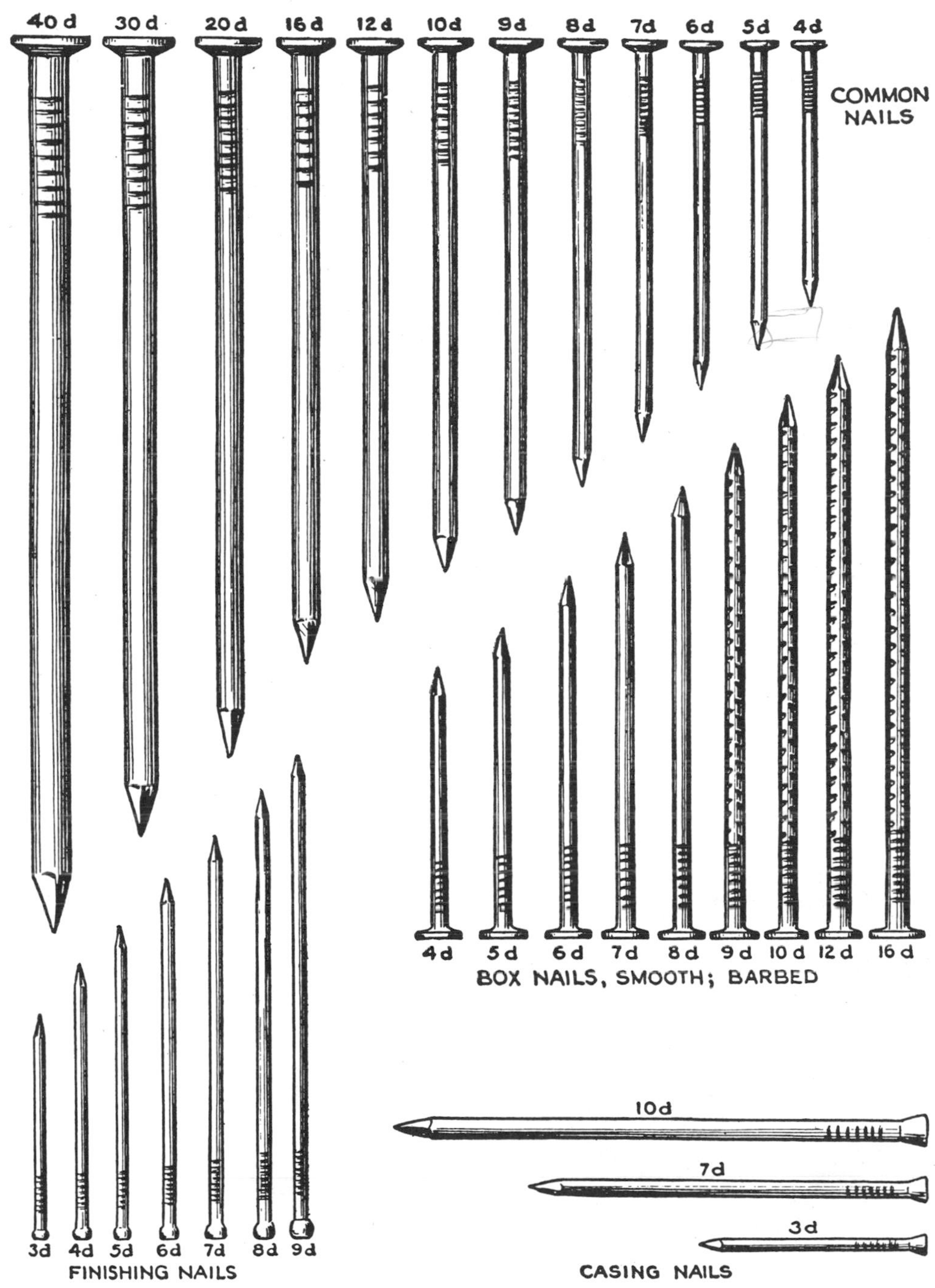

33–4. Common types of nails with which you should be acquainted.

NAIL CHART

Size	Length in Inches	American Steel Wire Gauge Number		
		Common	Box and Casing	Finishing
2d	1	15*	15½	16½
3d	1¼	14	14½	15½
4d	1½	12½	14	15
5d	1¾	12½	14	15
6d	2	11½	12½	13
7d	2¼	11½	12½	13
8d	2½	10¼	11½	12½
9d	2¾	10¼	11½	12½
10d	3	9	10½	11½
12d	3¼	9	10½	11½
16d	3½	8	10	11
20d	4	6	9	10
30d	4½	5	9	
40d	5	4	8	

*Note: The decimal equivalent of common gauge numbers is:

15 = .072	12 = .106	9 = .148	6 = .192
14 = .080	11 = .121	8 = .162	5 = .207
13 = .092	10 = .135	7 = .177	4 = .225

33–5. A chart showing the comparative sizes of nails. Note, for example, that a 2d common nail is larger in diameter than a 2d finishing nail.

33–6. Corrugated fasteners or "wiggle" nails are used in place of standard nails—for repair work and box-and-frame construction.

differently. They are indicated by the length in inches (¼ inch to 3 inches) and a gauge number from 11 to 20. The higher the gauge number, the smaller the diameter. They are sold in pound boxes. *Escutcheon nails* or pins are small brass nails with round heads. They are used to assemble small projects, especially if a decorative head is desirable. They come in lengths from ¼ inch to 1¼ inches and gauge numbers of 20 to 16. Corrugated fasteners, shown in Figure 33–6, are used for holding joints and are particularly good for repair work.

SELECTING NAILS

The first thing to consider is the proper kind and size of nail. You will learn that smaller diameters should be chosen for thinner stock and larger diameters for heavier. Nails can be driven either straight into the wood

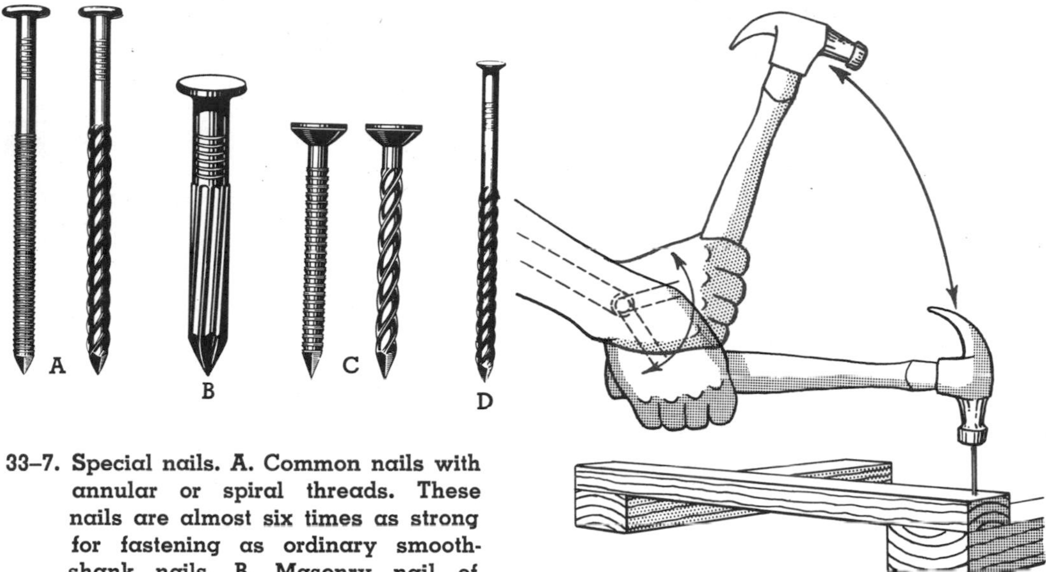

33–7. Special nails. A. Common nails with annular or spiral threads. These nails are almost six times as strong for fastening as ordinary smooth-shank nails. B. Masonry nail of hardened steel which can be driven into concrete. C. Roofing nails. D. Flooring nail.

33–9. Use wrist movement for driving smaller nails, and elbow movement as well for driving larger nails.

33–8. Starting a nail. The nail is held between the thumb and forefinger and the hammer grasped close to the head. Courtesy the Jam Handy Organization.

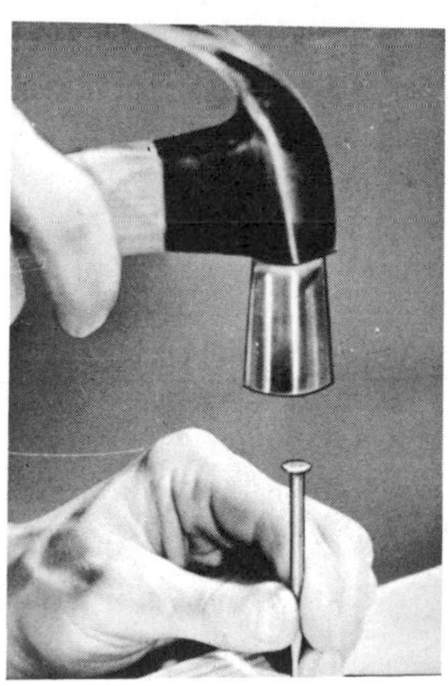

or, for a tighter joint, they may be driven at a slight angle. If two pieces are to be nailed together, as the corner of a box, first drive one or two nails through the first piece. Then hold this piece over the other piece to drive the nails in place.

DRIVING NAILS

Hold the nail in one hand between thumb and forefinger and close to the point. To start the nail, grasp the hammer with the other hand near the hammer head. Figure 33–8. To hammer, hold the handle near its end. Use wrist as well as elbow and arm movement, depending on the size of the nail being driven. Tap the head of the nail with the hammer to get it started. Figure 33–9. Then remove your fingers from the nail as you continue to

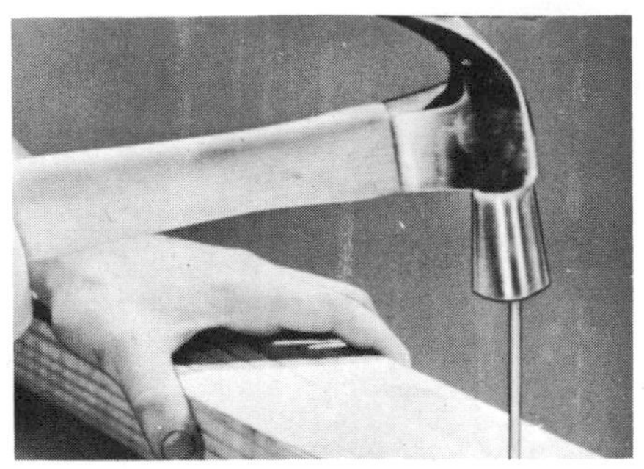

33–10. Hold the hammer handle at the end so that you can strike the hammer with firm, even blows. A few firm, well placed blows are better than many light taps. Courtesy the Jam Handy Organization.

33–12. Clinching a nail. It is better to clinch a nail with the grain than across. The nail will sink into the wood more easily since it does not have to break the fibers. Courtesy the Jam Handy Organization.

strike it with firm blows. Figure 33–10.

Watch the head of the nail and not the hammer. Try to drive the nail with a few well placed blows rather than with many quick taps. If a nail begins to bend, it is better to remove it and start over with a new one.

When nailing two pieces together, choose the location for the nails wisely. Do not put several nails along the same grain as this would split the wood. A few well placed nails will do a better job of holding than a larger number placed carelessly.

If you are using casing or finishing nails, do not drive the heads completely down to the surface. Complete the driving with a nail set. Hold the nail set in your left hand with the middle finger against the surface of the work and the side of the nail. Then drive the nail in until it is about 1/16 inch below the surface. Figure 33–11.

If you are nailing *hardwood*, special steps must be taken. In the wood, drive holes that are slightly smaller than the diameter of the nail. Apply a little wax to the surface of the nail and drive it in.

Sometimes you will need to use nails that are longer than the total thickness of both pieces being nailed together. In this case, the points of the nails should be driven completely through the pieces and then bent or clinched. Bend the nails over *with the grain* so they can be flattened easily. Figure 33–12.

Sometimes it will be necessary to

33–11. Using a nail set. The nail set is held between the thumb and forefinger and guided by the other fingers. This helps keep it from slipping off the nail head and marring the wood surface.

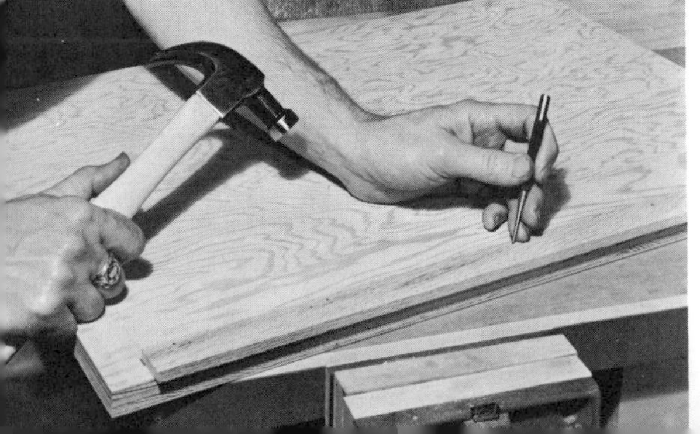

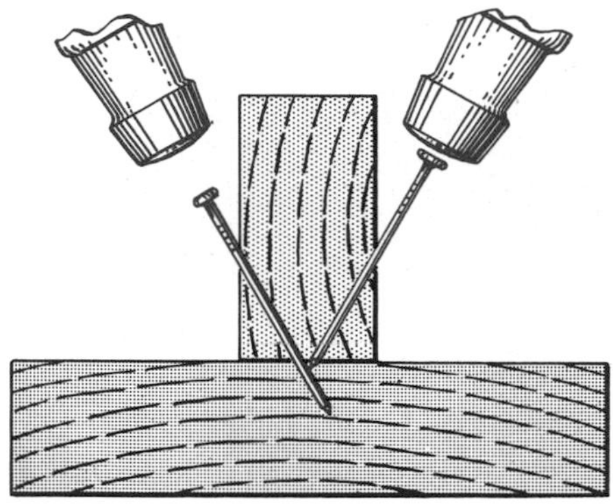

33–13. Toenailing. When it is necessary to nail the end of one piece to the side of another piece, the pieces should be toenailed together by driving the nails in at an angle on either side.

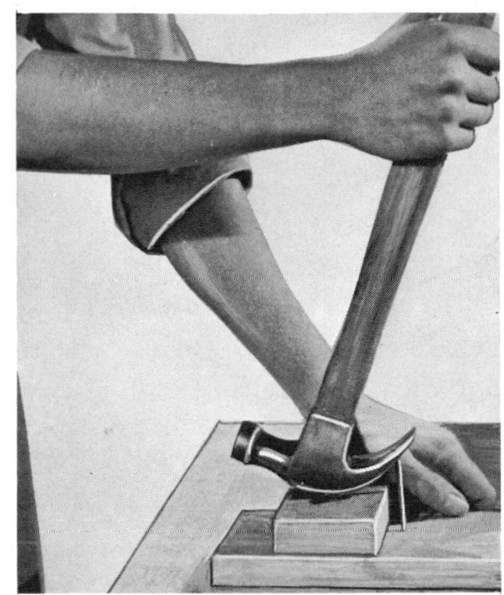

33–14. Removing a nail. A piece of scrap wood is placed under the hammer head to provide leverage for drawing it out and to save the surface. Courtesy the Jam Handy Organization.

nail the end of one piece of wood to the side of another. The nails are then driven into the wood at an angle from both sides. This is called "toenailing." Figure 33–13.

REMOVING NAILS

Force the claw of the hammer under the head of the nail and pull on the handle. When the nail is drawn partway out, slip a piece of scrap wood under the hammer head before continuing to draw out the nail. Figure 33–14. This is a good way to protect the wood.

CAN YOU ANSWER THESE QUESTIONS ON ASSEMBLING STOCK WITH NAILS?

1. Name the parts of a claw hammer.
2. Explain how to use a nail set.
3. Can you name and describe the four most common kinds of nails?
4. What does the word "penny" mean?
5. How large is a 7d finishing nail?
6. What are the larger sizes of common nails called?
7. How is a brad different from a finishing nail?
8. Tell how you would start a nail.
9. When you use a hammer, would you watch the head of the hammer or the nail?
10. How are finishing and casing nails set?
11. Hardwood is very difficult to nail. What would you do to overcome the difficulty?
12. Tell how to clinch a nail. Is this done with or across the grain?
13. Explain what toenailing is.
14. When it is necessary to remove a nail, how can you keep from marring the surface of the wood?

Section VIII

UNIT 34. ASSEMBLING WITH SCREWS

Screws take more time to assemble but they make a stronger bond. Also, the project can be taken apart. If screws are installed correctly, a few will do the work of several nails yet will hold much better.

THE SCREW DRIVER

There are three common types of screw drivers. The *plain screw driver* is used to install slotted-head screws. The size depends on the length and diameter of the blades. Figure 34–1. Make sure that the tip of the screw driver is about the same width as the diameter of the screw head. If it is wider, it may mar the surface of the wood as it is set in place. Figure 34–2. The *Phillips-head screw driver* is made for driving screws with recessed heads. Figure 34–3. The *spiral type screw driver* is usually sold in a set with three sizes of screw-driver bits and a No. 2 Phillips screw-driver bit. Figure 34–4.

Notice in Figure 51–15 the proper

34–1. Plain screw driver. Screw drivers are available with blades in lengths from 1½ inches to 12 inches and in diameters from 7/32 to 3/8 inch.

34–2. Selecting the proper size of screw driver. Note the following: A. The screw driver is too narrow with the result that it causes a burr on the head. B. The screw driver is the correct width. C. The screw driver is too wide. It would mar the wood surface. Courtesy the Jam Handy Organization.

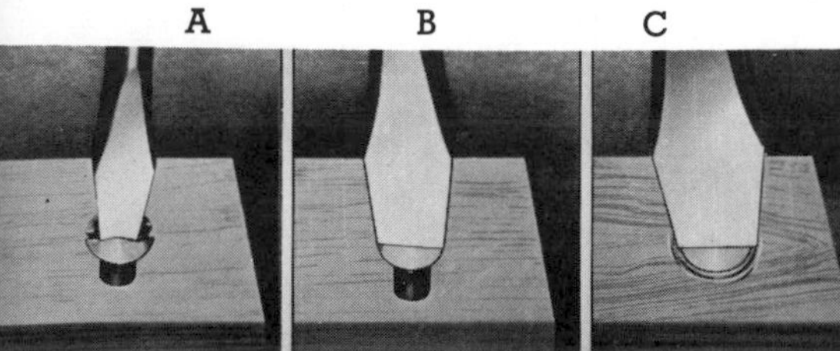

34–3. Phillips head screw driver. This is available in sizes from 1 to 4. Size number 1 is used for screws number 4 or smaller, number 2 for screws from 5 to 9 inclusive, number 3 for screws from 10 to 16 inclusive, and number 4 for screws number 18 or larger.

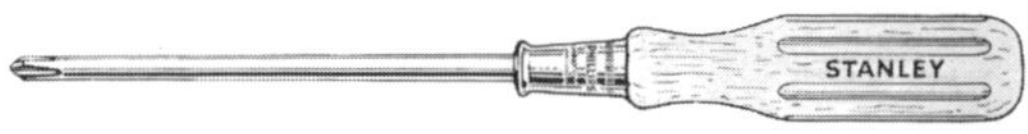

34–4. The spiral ratchet screw driver is excellent for quick installation of screws.

method of grinding a screw driver. This is very important. If a screw driver is ground to a sharp edge, it tends to slip out of the slot. This would mar the surface of the wood or injure the head of the screw. A screw that has been set with a poor screw driver usually has a ragged slot.

SCREWS

There are several things you should know about the size and kind of screw to use. These are: the kind of head, the diameter or gauge size, the length, the kind of metal, and the finish. As you see in Figure 34–5, screws are roundhead, flathead, oval head, and drive screw. Of course they come with either a slotted head or a Phillips head, and are almost any length from ¼ inch to 6 inches. Figure 34–6a. Most screws are made of mild steel, although it is possible to buy them in brass or aluminum. These last two are used primarily for boat construction or wherever moisture would rust the other kind. Most flathead screws have a bright finish. Roundhead screws are usually finished in a dull blue. Sheet-metal screws are ideal for fastening thin metal to wood such as attaching metal legs to a plywood top. The sheet-metal screw has excellent holding power because, unlike wood screws, the threaded shank is the same diameter through its length. Figure 34–6b.

34–5. The four kinds of screws. The portion of each style screw included in the length measurement is shown in the diagram. A. Flathead. B. Roundhead. C. Ovalhead. D. Drive screw.

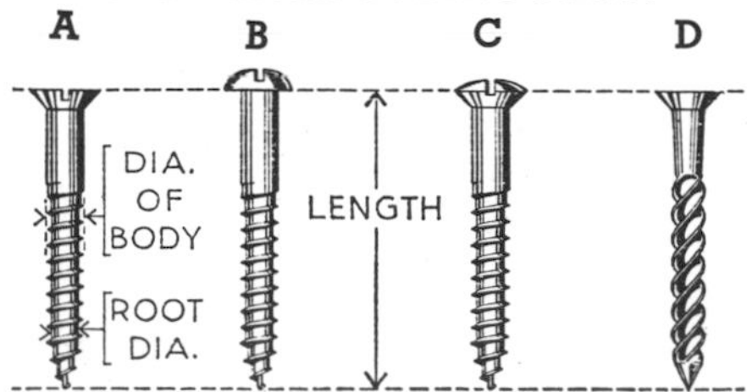

34–6a. The difference between slotted head and recessed Phillips-head screws.

34–6b. Installing a flathead sheet-metal screw. A. Drilling the clearance hole. B. Drilling the pilot or anchor hole. C. Countersinking. D. Screw installed. E. Hole for roundhead sheet-metal screw. F. Screw installed.

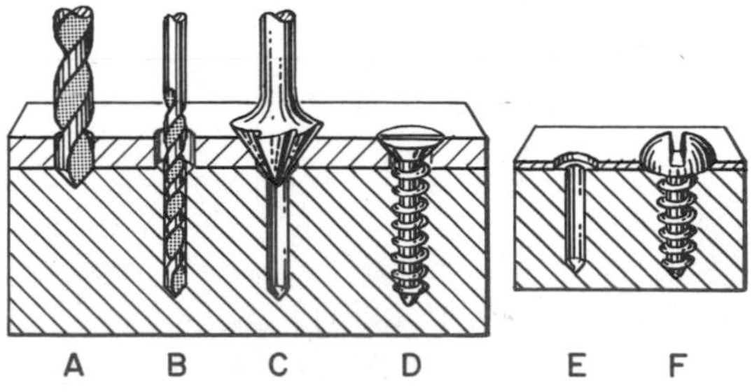

No. of Screw	For Shank Clearance Holes	For Pilot Holes*		No. of Auger Bit to Counterbore for Sinking Head (by 16ths)
		Hardwoods	Softwoods	
0	1/16	1/32	1/64	
1	5/64	1/32	1/32	
2	3/32	3/64	1/32	3
3	7/64	1/16	3/64	4
4	7/64	1/16	3/64	4
5	1/8	5/64	1/16	4
6	9/64	5/64	1/16	5
7	5/32	3/32	1/16	5
8	11/64	3/32	5/64	6
9	3/16	7/64	5/64	6
10	3/16	7/64	3/32	6
11	13/64	1/8	3/32	7
12	7/32	1/8	7/64	7
14	1/4	9/64	7/64	8
16	17/64	5/32	9/64	9
18	19/64	3/16	9/64	10
20	21/64	13/64	11/64	11
24	3/8	7/32	3/16	12

* Sometimes called "anchor holes."

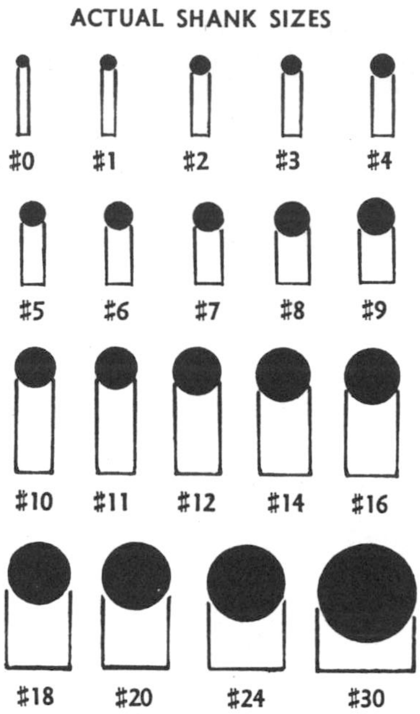

ACTUAL SHANK SIZES

#0 #1 #2 #3 #4

#5 #6 #7 #8 #9

#10 #11 #12 #14 #16

#18 #20 #24 #30

To determine Sizes of Screws, lay screws flat within parallel lines shown in border.

34–7. Table showing the proper size bit or drill needed for the shank hole and the pilot hole for assembling stock with screws.

Wood screw sizes are indicated by the American Screw Wire Gauge with numbers from 0 to 24. The smallest number is 0, which has a diameter of .060. The diameter of each succeeding number is .013 larger. For example, a number 5 screw is .125 (.060 + .013 × 5), or 1/8 inch in diameter. A number 11 screw would be .203, or 13/64 inch in diameter. You will notice that the shank clearance hole is always about this diameter. See Figure 34–7. Two screws can be the same length but have a different gauge size (Figure 34–8). This means that they have different diameters. In most cases, the size of the screw is shown on the drawing. For example, No. 8 R. H. 1½ means that the screw is No. 8 gauge size, roundhead, and 1½ inches long. If the size isn't shown, you should choose a screw

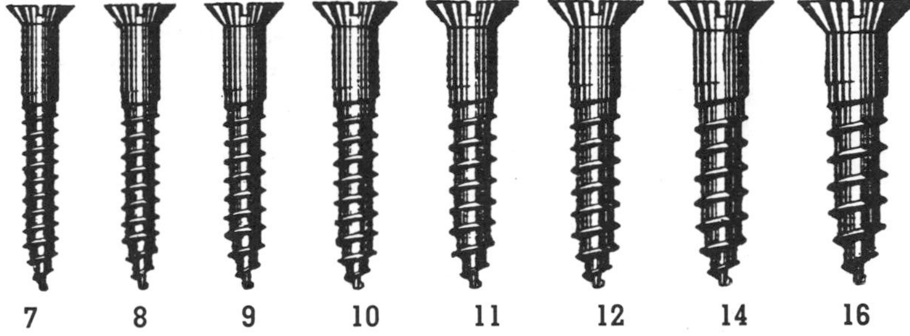

34–8. **Different gauge sizes of 1¼-inch screws. Wood screws range in length from ¼ to 6 inches and in gauge sizes from 0 to 24. Of course, each length is not made in all gauges, as shown by the 1¼-inch screw.**

that will go at least two-thirds of its length into the second piece. If the second piece is end grain, the screw should be even longer, since end grain does not hold well. Other screw devices are shown in Figure 34–9.

34–9. **Cup hooks (usually of brass) come in sizes from ½ to 1½ inches. *Screw hooks* are made in lengths from 1¼ to 2½ inches. "*L*" (square bent) *screw hooks* come in lengths from 1 to 2¼ inches. *Screw eyes* are made with either small or medium eyes in many sizes.**

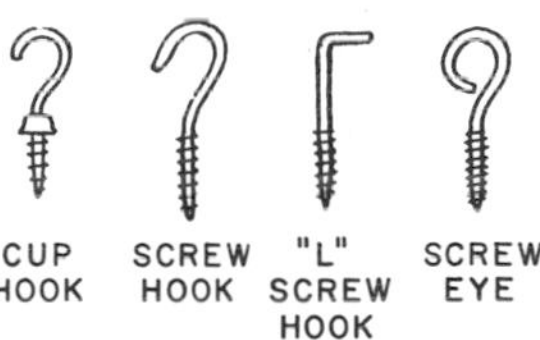

DRILLING CLEARANCE HOLES

Select the kind and size of screw needed. Note in Figure 34–7 the two drill sizes required. The first one is for the shank clearance hole, drilled in the first piece. The second one is for the pilot hole, drilled in the second piece. Figure 34–10. The shank clearance hole should be the same size or slightly smaller than the shank of the screw. In this way the screw can be inserted in the first piece without forcing.

Drill the shank clearance hole in the first piece of stock. Then hold this piece over the second and mark the location for the pilot hole with a scratch awl. If you are assembling softwood pieces, drill the pilot hole only about half the depth to which the screw will go. If you are drilling hardwood, make sure that it is drilled to the total depth of the screw.

34–10. **Here the shank hole and pilot hole are properly drilled and the screw is installed.** Courtesy the Jam Handy Organization.

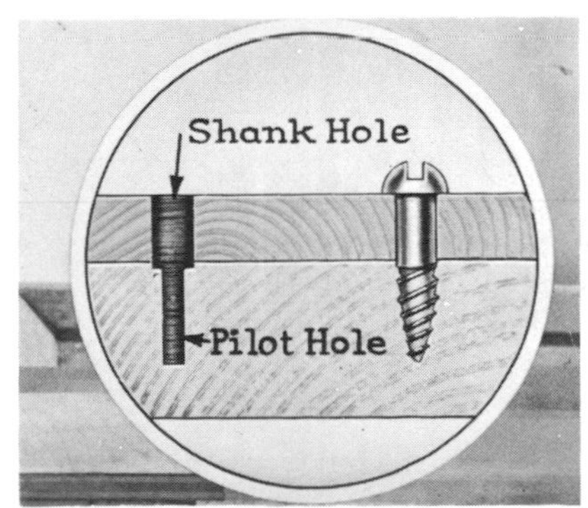

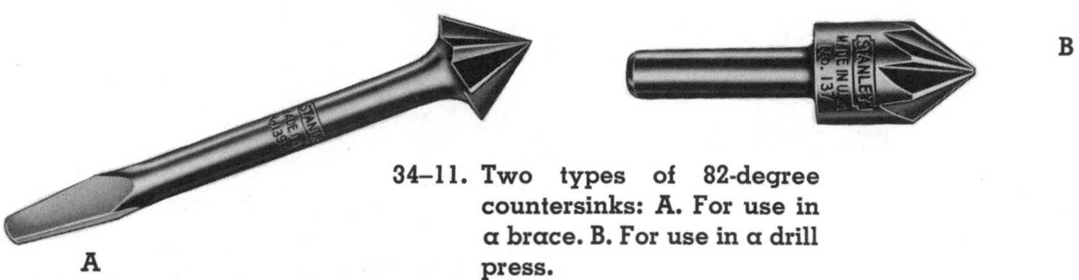

34–11. Two types of 82-degree countersinks: A. For use in a brace. B. For use in a drill press.

COUNTERSINKING FOR FLATHEAD SCREWS

Countersinking is a way of enlarging the top portion of a hole to a cone shape so that the head of a flathead screw will be flush with the surface of the wood. If flathead screws are being installed, countersink the upper surface of the first piece to allow the head of the screw to be flush with the surface. Figure 34–11. Check the depth of the countersunk hole by turning the screw upside down and fitting it in the hole. Figure 34–12. A *screw-mate drill* and *countersink* can be used with flathead screws. Figure 34–13. A counterbore will do all the operations performed by the screw mate, plus drilling plug holes for wooden plugs. Figure 34–14.

34–12. Steps in installing a flathead screw. A. Drill the shank hole. B. Drill the pilot or anchor hole. C. Countersink. D. Check the amount of countersink with the screw head. E. Install the flathead screw.

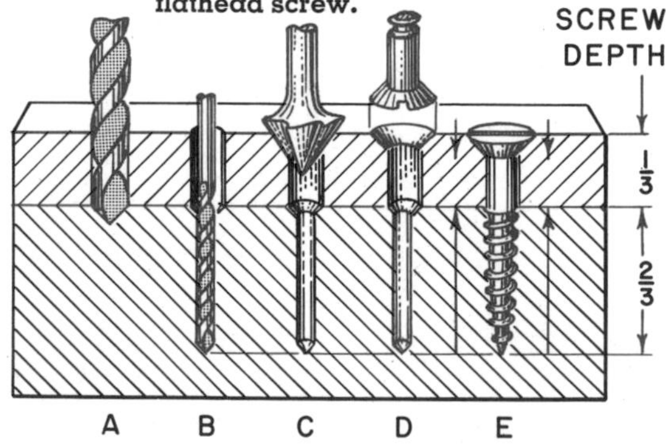

34–13. This tool will do four things: (1) drill to the correct depth, (2) do the countersinking, (3) make the correct shank clearance, and (4) drill the correct pilot hole.

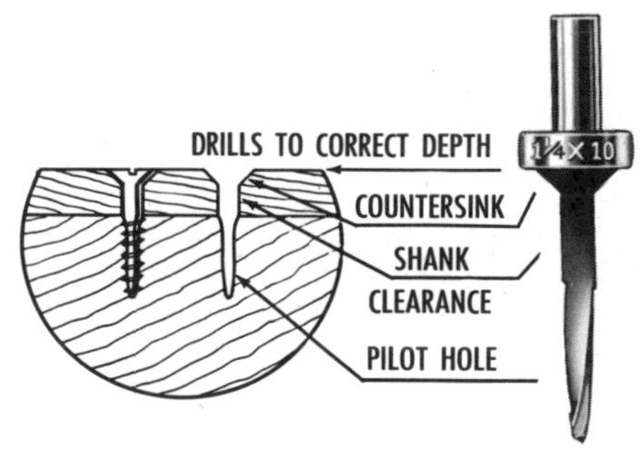

34–14. A screw-mate counterbore does five things at once. A wood plug can be used to cover the screw head.

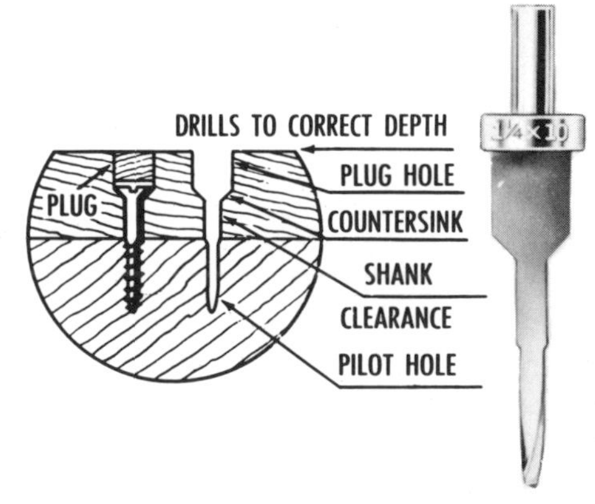

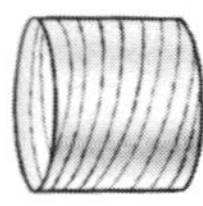

34–15. A plug cutter. Available in different sizes for cutting wood plugs.

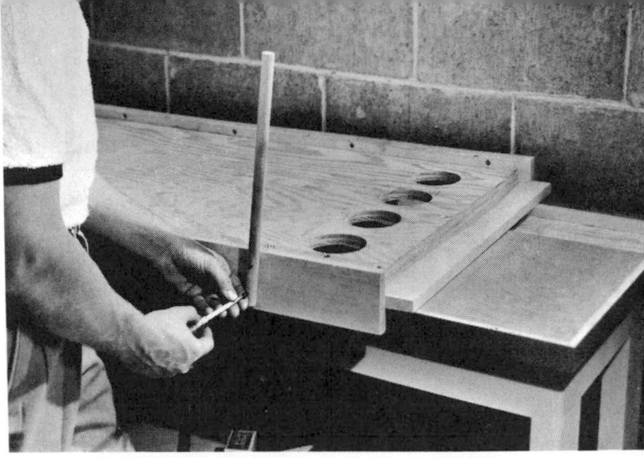

34–18. Starting a screw. Hold the screw and the tip of the screw driver as shown.

34–16. Using a plug cutter. The plug should be cut from the same kind of wood that is used in the project.

34–17. Three methods of covering the heads of screws: (a) with plastic wood, (b) with a plain wood plug, and (c) with fancy wood plugs.

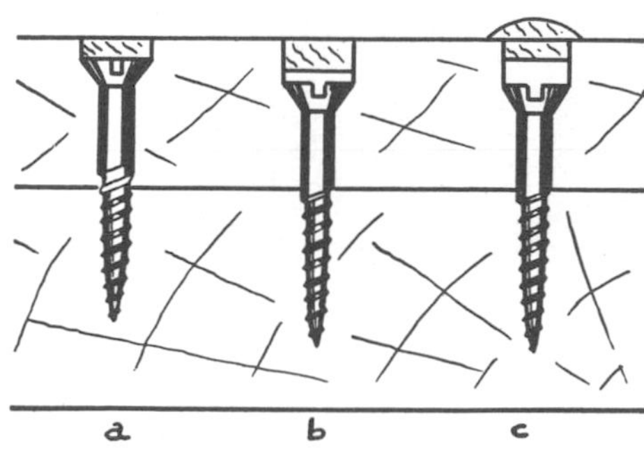

PLUGGING SCREW HOLES

In most furniture construction screws are not supposed to show. Choose a drill or auger bit the same size as the head of the screw. Counterbore a hole in the first surface about 3/8 inch deep. The screw will then be below the surface of the wood. After the parts are assembled, this hole can be filled with plastic wood. Or you can make a little screw plug with the tool shown in Figures 34–15 and 34–16. Furniture supply companies can supply fancy, decorated plugs. Figure 34–17.

DRIVING THE SCREW

To install a screw, hold the body between your thumb and forefinger. Figure 34–18. Grasp the handle of the screw driver in the palm of your hand. Let your thumb and forefinger point toward the shank. Start the screw and then move your left hand up just back of the point of the screw driver. This will guide the tool and keep it from slipping off the head as the screw is set in place. Continue to turn the screw until it is firmly set, but don't strip the threads or shear off the screw from the wood. Be especially careful if the screws are

A

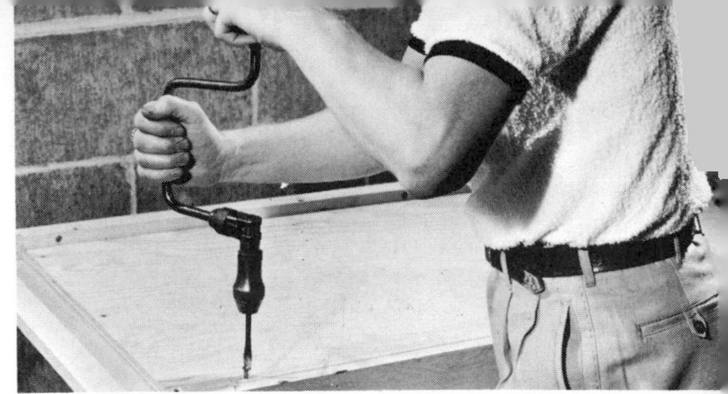

B

small or made of brass. A screw-driver bit can be used in a brace for setting screws. Figure 34–19.

34–19. A. A screw-driver bit to use in a brace. B. Installing a wood screw with a bit and brace.

CAN YOU ANSWER THESE QUESTIONS ON ASSEMBLING STOCK WITH SCREWS?

1. A screw has several advantages over a nail. Name them.
2. How do you know what size screw driver to choose?
3. Describe the proper way of grinding a screw driver.
4. What information must you have in order to secure the proper kind and size of screw for your work?
5. As the gauge number increases, how is the diameter of the screw affected?
6. What is the general rule for selecting screw lengths?
7. Name two types of screws.
8. What is the shank clearance hole and what purpose does it serve?
9. Why must a pilot hole be drilled?
10. Is the pilot hole drilled in softwood in the same way it is drilled in hardwood?
11. When is it necessary to countersink the hole?
12. How can you check the depth of the countersink hole?
13. What is the purpose of screw plugs?
14. Describe the proper method of holding a screw driver when starting a screw.
15. Why is it important to set the screw with the correct size screw driver?

Section VIII

UNIT 35. SCRAPING A SURFACE

For a really fine surface on open-grain wood such as oak, mahogany, and walnut, the wood can be scraped after the planing is done by using a hand or cabinet scraper. Figure 35-1. Scraping removes the small bumps left by the plane iron. Some woods, such as curly maple and cedar that can't be

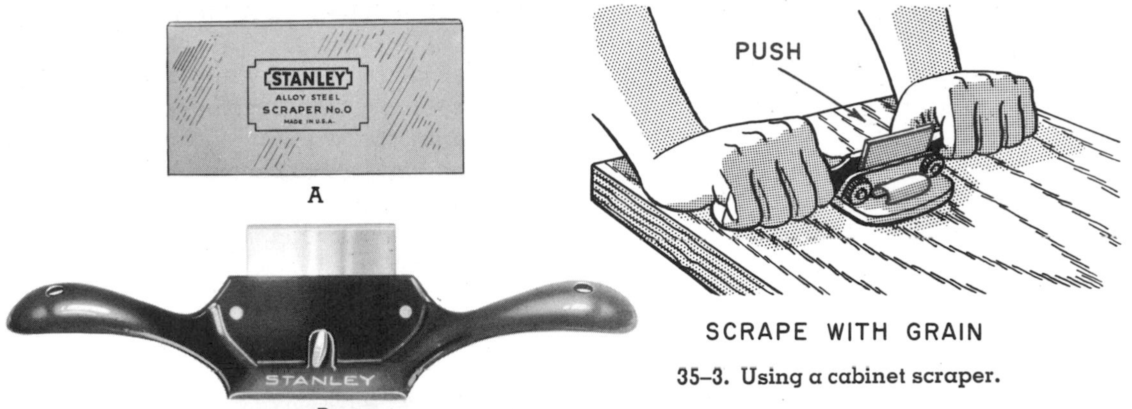

35–1. A. Hand scraper. B. Cabinet scraper.

35–3. Using a cabinet scraper.

planed very well, can be scraped for a very smooth surface. It is very important that the hand scraper be sharp. See Unit 51. It is always necessary to sharpen the scraper before each use—and frequently during its use.

SCRAPING PROCEDURE

Clamp the stock firmly in a visc or on top of the bench. Hold the hand scraper with both hands between the thumbs and forefingers, with the cutting edge toward the surface of the wood. Figure 35–2. Turn the blade at an angle of about 50 to 60 degrees to the wood surface. Apply firm pressure to the scraper blade and push or draw it across the surface. Be careful to keep the cutting edge flat against the wood so that the corners do not dig in or mar it. Always scrape with the grain. Sometimes the scraper is turned a little and a shearing cut made across the surface. Experience will help you decide. If you are working on curly maple or other burly-type wood, keep changing the direction of the scraping action to match the grain direction.

35–2. Scraping a surface with a hand scraper. Note that the scraper is held in both hands and tipped at an angle to the wood surface.

USING A CABINET SCRAPER

The cabinet scraper is simpler to use than the hand scraper. To adjust it, first loosen the adjusting thumb screw and the clamp thumb screws. Insert the blade from the bottom, with the bevel side towards the adjusting screw. Make sure the edge of the blade is even with the bottom. This can be done by standing the tool on a wood surface and pressing the blade lightly against the wood. Tighten the clamp thumb screws. Bow the blade slightly by tightening the adjusting thumb screw. Apply equal pressure with both hands as you push the scraper along the wood. Figure 35–3.

CAN YOU ANSWER THESE QUESTIONS ON SCRAPING A SURFACE?

1. On what kinds of wood is scraping necessary to produce a smooth surface?
2. At what times should a scraper be sharpened?
3. The scraper is held at what angle to the surface of the wood?
4. How can you prevent the corners of the scraper from marring or digging into the wood?
5. Tell how the scraper should be used on burly woods.
6. Explain how to adjust a cabinet scraper.

Section VIII

UNIT 36. SANDING A SURFACE

Sanding is one of the last steps both before and after a project is assembled. Figure 36–1. All planing, cutting, and forming should be completed before beginning to use sandpaper. Sanding is done to finish the surface of wood, not to form or shape it. Sandpaper should not be used in place of cutting tools.

36–1. Sanding is an important step in completing any project.

KINDS OF SANDPAPER

There is really no such thing as "sand" paper, though the name is given to several types of abrasives. Abrasives are made in a wide range of grades from very coarse to very fine. They are produced by bonding (gluing) graded sizes of abrasive material to paper or cloth backing. The common types are the natural abrasives such as flint and garnet and the manufactured or man-made abrasives such as aluminum oxide and silicon carbide. Further identification follows:

1. Flint or quartz, which has a yellowish cast, is an inexpensive abrasive that is commonly used for the hand sanding of woods.

2. Garnet, reddish-brown in color, is harder, sharper, and better for most woods, especially harder woods. It is long-lasting and fast-cutting.

3. Aluminum oxide is a man-made abrasive that is either reddish-brown

or white in color. It is used for both hand and machine sanding.

4. Silicon carbide is shiny black in color, almost diamond hard, and very sharp. It is used for sanding lacquers, shellac, and varnishes. It is also used for sanding between finishes and is made in wet or dry types.

Abrasive materials come in chunk form which must first be crushed into fine particles and sorted. These abrasive grains pass through screens of different sizes. For example, one screen may have 36 openings per inch while the next screen may have 40 openings per inch. The grains that pass through the screen with 36 openings and not through the next are numbered 36. The higher the number, the smaller the grain and, therefore, the finer the sandpaper. Abrasive papers are sold in many forms including sheets, discs, and belts. Figure 36–2. The common material used in the wood shop is garnet paper in 9- by 11-inch sheets. The paper ranges from 2½, which is very coarse, to 8/0, which is very fine. This is the old grit-size number system. The new system uses the mesh (symbol) number. For example, 30 is the same as 2½. Figure 36–3.

36–2. Grades and types of sandpaper. Nine by 10-inch sheets of flint, or 9- by 11-inch sheets of garnet paper are often used for hand sanding. For the belt sander, narrow-roll abrasive or cloth or prepared belts can be selected. On disc sanders wide-roll abrasive cloth or paper is needed. For machine sanding, No. 1 abrasive paper or cloth is generally used. No. 0 abrasive paper and No. 3/0 abrasive cloth are used for smoothing woods.

HOW COMMON ABRASIVES ARE GRADED

Coarseness	Flint (Common Sandpaper)	Garnet (Old Grit Numbers)	Garnet, Silicon Carbide and Aluminum Oxide (New Symbol Numbers)
Very Fine	Extra Fine	8/0 7/0 6/0	280 240 220
Fine	Fine	5/0 4/0 3/0	180 150 120
Medium	Medium	2/0 0 ½ 1	100 80 50
Coarse	Coarse	1½ 2	40 36
Very Coarse	Extra Coarse	2½	30

36–3. How common abrasives are graded.

TEARING SANDPAPER

To make the sheet of sandpaper softer, draw it over the edge of the bench. A 9- by 11-inch sheet is usually divided into four or six pieces. This depends on the work to be sanded and the size of the sanding block. To

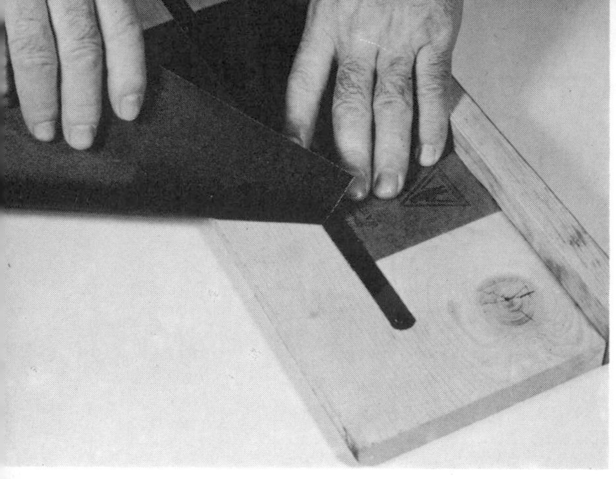

36–4. Cutting standard 9 by 11 inch sandpaper into smaller sizes can be done by tearing along a hacksaw blade nailed to a wood jig.

tear the sheet, fold it lengthwise with the abrasive surface toward the inside. Then hold one half of the sheet over the bench and tear the paper along the folded line. You can also tear the piece by holding a straightedge or the cutting edge of a hack saw blade over the folded line. Figure 36-4.

A sandpaper block is a good backing for most sanding. If the sheets are torn into six pieces, the block should be 1½ inches thick, 3 inches wide, and 5 inches long.

A piece of foam rubber or felt can be glued to the base to give a better surface.

SANDING A FLAT SURFACE

Fasten the piece between the vise dog and bench stop or hold it firmly against the surface of the bench. If the piece is held in the vise, grip the sanding block as shown in Figure 36-5. Apply even pressure to the block and sand the surface *with the grain* of the wood. Move the block back and forth and work slowly from one side to the other to get an even surface. Take special care to keep from sanding the edges too much.

After coarser paper has been used, substitute finer and finer grades. If the piece is held against the top of the bench, you can use the block with one hand. Figure 36–6.

SANDING AN EDGE

Lock the work in a vise with the edge showing. Grasp the sanding block in both hands. Place your fore-

36–5. Two kinds of sanding blocks. On the left is a commercial block with a foam-rubber base. The one on the right is homemade. It has a piece of leather tacked in place under the sandpaper.

36–6. Sanding a surface. The sanding block, held firmly against the surface, is moved back and forth.

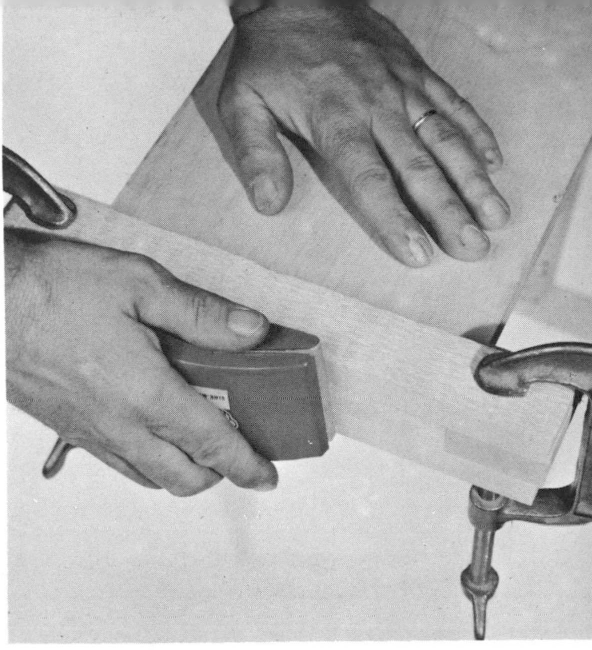

36–8. Sanding end grain. Sand in *one direction.* Notice the guide boards clamped over the end to keep the sanding square with the face surface.

fingers on either side of the edge to keep it square with the sides. Figure 36 7. It is just as important to sand an edge square as it is to plane it square. After the edge has been sanded, the arris (the sharp edge) should be rounded slightly by drawing the sandpaper over the edge.

36–7. Sanding an edge. The sanding block is grasped in both hands with the thumbs on top and the fingers curled underneath. This will keep the block square with the surface. If this is not done, there is danger of rounding the edge.

SANDING AN END

To sand an end, the same procedure as for sanding an edge is followed. However, the surface is sanded in only one direction rather than back and forth. This produces a smoother finish. Figure 36–8.

SANDING CONVEX SURFACES

Convex surfaces can usually be sanded with a block in the same way as an edge is sanded. A convex surface such as a rounded end can be sanded more satisfactorily by holding the paper in your fingers or the palm of your hand. Figure 36–9.

SANDING CONCAVE OR OTHER INSIDE SURFACES

These surfaces are most easily sanded by wrapping the paper around

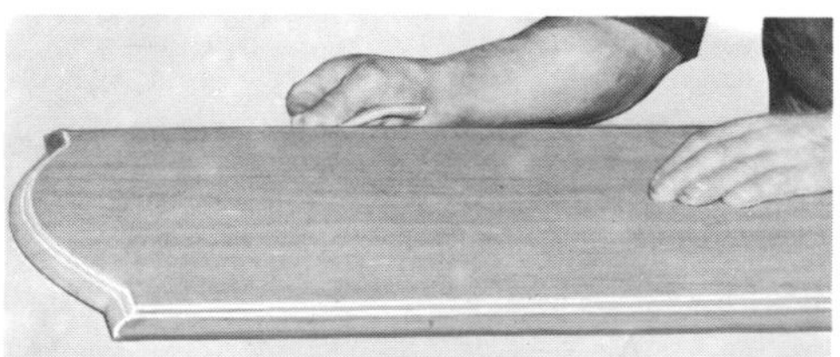

36–9. When sanding a molding by hand, the sandpaper is held in the fingers and guided along the edge.

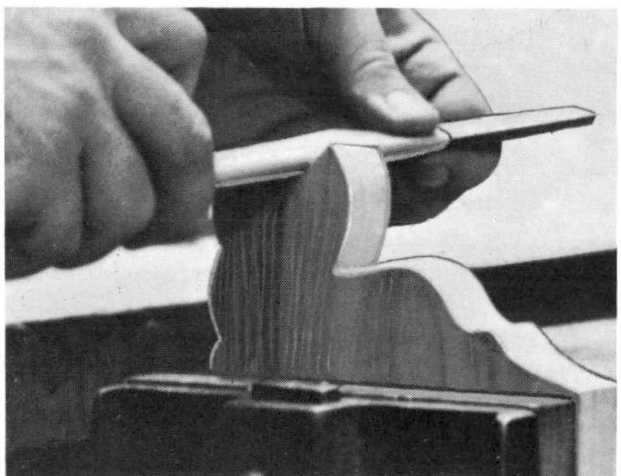

36–10. Sanding a concave surface. Here the sandpaper is wrapped around a half-round file so that it will conform to the general curve of the surface.

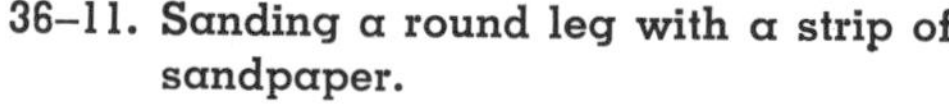

36–11. Sanding a round leg with a strip of sandpaper.

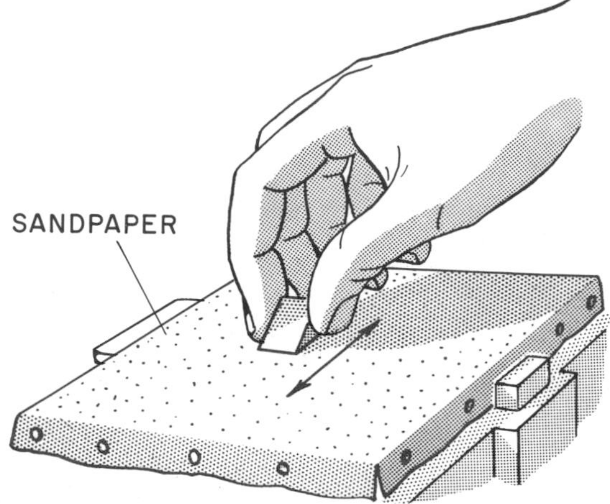

36–12. Sanding small pieces of a project.

a stick such as part of a broomstick or the handle of a tool. The half-round surface of a file also makes a good backing. Figure 36–10.

SANDING CURVED SURFACES

Certain round pieces such as turned parts will require cross-grained sanding. It is usually best to use a fine abrasive material for this kind of work. One method of sanding is to pull the material back and forth in a "shoeshine fashion." Figure 36–11. Straight turned parts can be sanded with the grain.

SANDING SMALL PIECES

The best method of sanding small pieces of wood is first to fasten a full sheet of abrasive paper to a jig board. This can then be clamped to the top of the bench. Then hold the small pieces on the abrasive paper and move them back and forth. Figure 36–12.

CAN YOU ANSWER THESE QUESTIONS ON SANDING A SURFACE?

1. Is sanding done for the purpose of forming or shaping wood?
2. At what point in building the project should the sanding be done?
3. Is there any sand on sandpaper? What are the abrasives used in sandpaper?
4. Which sandpaper is best for hardwood? For softwood?
5. How is sandpaper usually sold?
6. What number would you ask for when buying very coarse sandpaper? Very fine sandpaper?
7. What grades of sandpaper are commonly found in use in school shops?
8. How would you soften a sheet of sandpaper before using it? How would you tear it into smaller pieces?
9. How is a sanding block useful?
10. Is it correct to sand across grain? Why?
11. There is a very common error often made in sanding a flat surface. What is it?
12. How can you keep the edge square when sanding?
13. Describe how you would sand a convex surface.
14. How would you sand a concave surface?
15. When is the "shoeshine" method used?
16. How is a jig board used? For what kind of pieces?

Section VIII

UNIT 37. FITTING, ASSEMBLING, AND GLUING UP THE PARTS

You are now ready to assemble your project. How difficult this is, of course, depends on the kind of project and its size. For a three-piece project such as a footstool, the problem of assembly is fairly simple. For an end table, bookcase, or a desk with drawers, assembly is much more complicated. However, certain things must be done regardless of the size of the project.

COLLECTING THE PARTS

Get together all the parts that are to go into the finished project. If you were careful when you made them, your identification marks will still show. You will know how each part, joint, and piece fits to the next. This is very important. You will find yourself in a very unhappy position if, when you begin to glue, the joints don't fit or the parts don't match!

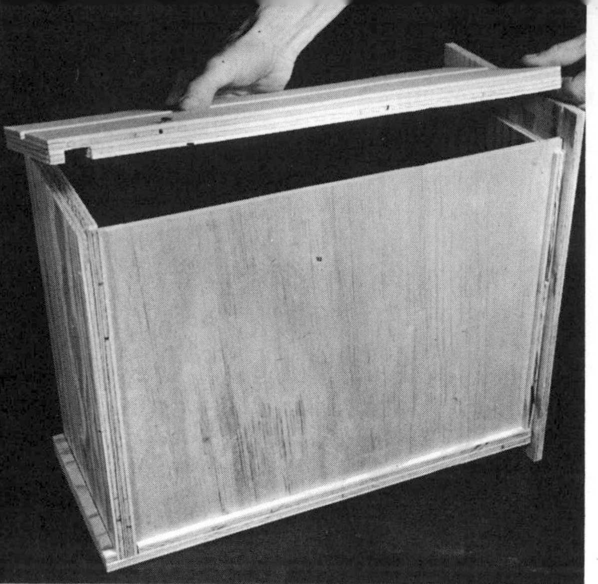

37–1. **Checking the joints of this drawer construction to make sure that everything fits properly before gluing.**

This can easily happen, unless you are careful.

CHECKING ALL THE PARTS TO SEE THAT THEY ARE FINISHED

To be considered completed, the parts should be scraped and sanded. If there are duplicate parts, rails, or legs, check each one of them to make sure that they are all exactly the same in size and shape. If the project has joints, try each joint to see that it fits properly. Figure 37–1. Check whether it is clearly marked in a place that can be seen after glue is applied and after the joint is assembled. This checking is especially important. You will usually find some small correction to make before you can go ahead with the assembling. Parts that have been stored for some time may have swelled slightly; therefore the joints may not fit just right.

Your plan of procedure or the drawing shows whether the project is to be assembled with glue, screws, or nails. If screws or nails are used, carefully check to see that you have the correct type and number to complete your job. You should have a couple of extra screws or several more nails than necessary as you may spoil a few. If glue is to be used, decide whether it is to be animal glue, casein, or plastic resin glue. Be sure that you have enough glue ready to apply.

MAKING PROTECTIVE PIECES

Before attempting to clamp the pieces together, cut some softwood pieces to place between the clamps and the project. Figure 37–2. It is a good idea to plane the surface of the pieces. These protective pieces are not needed if you use hand screws. It may be necessary to cut special shapes if the project is not square—for example, if you are clamping a table with legs that taper outward. Of course, you will know when this is necessary.

ASSEMBLING THE PROJECT TEMPORARILY

Now use cabinet clamps and hand screws to clamp all parts together

37–2. **Using scrap pieces of wood to protect the surface during gluing.**

37–3. Checking the project for squareness.

temporarily. This will give you an idea of how your pieces fit together and also you can see if any small corrections need to be made. Your problem is simple if you are assembling a project such as a bookcase or a hanging wall shelf made with parallel sides and crosspieces with dado or rabbet joints. All you need are flat pieces of scrap stock, cabinet clamps that fit across the project both on the front and back, and a pair of clamps for each shelf. Such projects as end tables, stools, and small desks usually have legs and rails with corners made with mortise-and-tenon joints or dowel joints. In either case, you will need clamps to go across the ends and cabinet clamps to go across the sides.

After the project is assembled with clamps, check with a square to make sure that the project is squared up. Figure 37–3. Also use a steel tape or rule to take measurements across the corners and up and down to see that the sides and ends are parallel and that the project is the same height throughout. Figure 37–4. By shifting a clamp or tapping a side or leg with a mallet, you can bring it into place.

This trial assembly will give you a chance to adjust all clamps to the correct width and get you ready for the final assembly.

ASSEMBLING WITH NAILS AND SCREWS

Follow the directions given in the unit on assembling stock with nails and screws. Figure 37–5.

ASSEMBLING WITH GLUE

It is helpful if a special glue bench or gluing room is available. If not, place wrapping paper over the bench or floor where the gluing is to be done. If the project is to be glued, carefully remove the clamps from top to bottom. Lay the clamps on the bench in definite order so that you can pick them up easily. Place the

37–4. Checking the project for levelness.

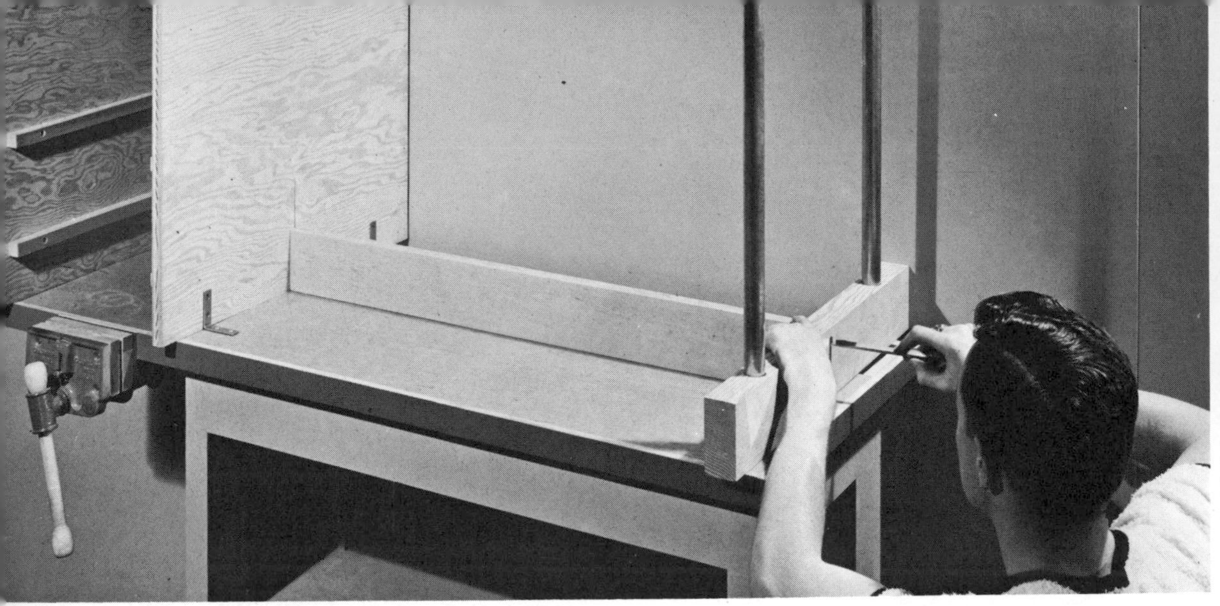

37–5. Assembling a desk with wood screws.

scrap pieces of wood next to the clamps so that everything will be on hand as you are ready for it.

If the project can be assembled all at one time, such as a book shelf or hanging shelf, go ahead and do it that way. If the project is a desk, table, or stool, you may assemble and glue the end section one day and then assemble the rest later.

In addition to your project parts, clamps, scrap pieces, and glue, have a *rubber mallet* ready, a *rule* or tape measure, and a *square*. If *hot animal glue* is used, heat the wood parts before assembling. Work very rapidly, as the glue sets quickly. If *cold liquid glue* is used, you do not need to work quite so fast.

37–6. Applying glue to a project before clamping it.

With a brush or stick, carefully apply the glue to both parts of the joint. Figure 37–6. Do not use too much glue, since any excess is just a problem to remove later. Animal glue, especially, tends to dribble. As quickly as possible, fasten the joints.

Place the scrap pieces over the proper places and lightly screw up the clamps. Do this until all the clamps are in place. Then turn up all clamps, each a little at a time. Check often to see that the project is squared and that it measures the same distance wherever there are parallels. You may need to use the rubber mallet to tap a joint in place or to change the position of a clamp.

As soon as the project is all clamped together, remove any excess glue with an old chisel or glue scraper. *Be careful not to mar the surface of the project.* Then put the project in a safe place where no one will bump it. Allow to dry from twelve to twenty-four hours. Carefully remove each of the clamps and the scrap pieces.

CAN YOU ANSWER THESE QUESTIONS ON FITTING, ASSEMBLING, AND GLUING UP THE PARTS?

1. Why should identification marks be kept on all pieces before they are assembled?
2. What things must be completed before a part of a project can be considered ready for assembly?
3. Should joints be checked again just before assembly? Why?
4. What should be a guide for determining how a project should be assembled?
5. Name the three things commonly used for fastening parts together permanently.
6. Why are protective wood pieces unnecessary when hand screws are chosen for assembly?
7. Think of several projects which require special shaped protective pieces.
8. Why is it necessary first to make a trial assembly?
9. Would you always assemble a project completely in one operation?
10. Describe the checks that should be made when the project is temporarily assembled.
11. How much glue would you apply?
12. How would you tap the parts into place and what kind of mallet should be used? How should excess glue be removed?
13. How long should a project be allowed to dry?

Section VIII

UNIT 38. PREPARING THE PROJECT FOR FINISHING

After the project is assembled, it is very important to go over it carefully to get it ready for finishing. This is an important step and one that is frequently neglected. As a result, a poor finish is attained.

REMOVING EXCESS GLUE

First of all, remove all excess glue from around the joints and anywhere else you see it. Use a good, sharp chisel. On flat areas, the glue may be removed with a hand scraper. Be especially careful not to gouge the wood or cut off a sliver of stock. This can easily happen when removing glue around a mortise-and-tenon joint, for example. Carefully separate the glue from the wood surface. Figure 38–1. Make sure that every fleck of glue has been completely removed, as glue will not take stain.

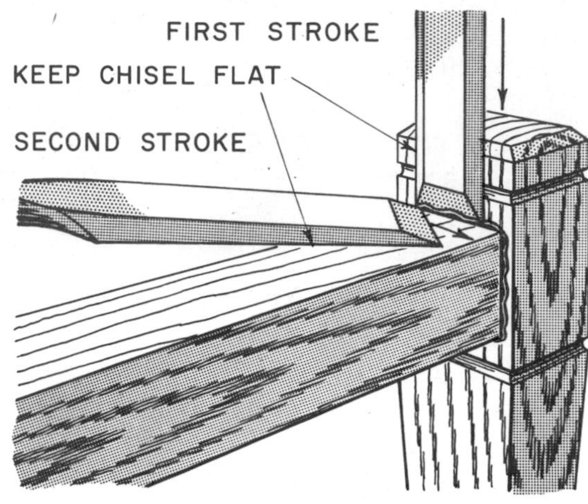

38–1. Removing glue around a joint with a sharp chisel. As much glue as possible should be wiped away when it is still wet. Hardened glue around the joints is difficult to remove.

If casein glue has been used, it may be necessary to apply a bleach to all glue spots. One bad thing about certain kinds of casein glue is that they darken the wood, especially open, porous types. There is one type of casein glue on the market that will not do this. However, if you think it necessary, bleach out these glue spots before staining. This can be done by mixing oxalic acid crystals in very hot water; then brush the solution on the areas and let them dry. These spots can then be sanded out. Commercial bleaching solutions are also very good.

CHECKING HOLES AND CRACKS

Go over the entire project carefully to see if there are any holes, cracks, or dents that need filling. There are several types of fillers that can be chosen. Plastic wood comes in neutral color, or in mahogany, walnut, oak, or other colors. Figure 38–2. You can also purchase stick shellac in various colors. Figure 38–3. If necessary, you can make your own filler by mixing equal parts of wood sanding dust and powdered glue. Add water to make a paste. Wood dough, a synthetic wood, can also be used for filling holes and cracks. Knots should be filled, sanded, and then covered with knot sealer such as white shellac.

38–2. Filling a crack with plastic wood. A natural shade can be tinted with colors in oil. Remember that plastic wood shrinks when it dries, so fill the hole above the level of the wood.

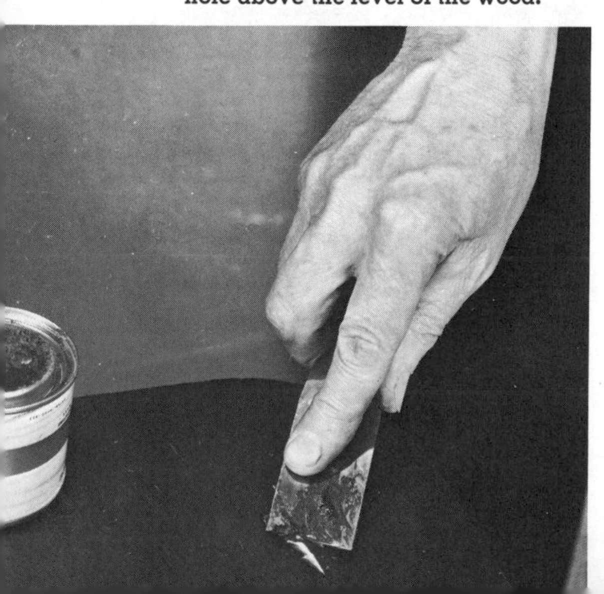

38–3. Filling a crack with stick shellac, using a warm putty knife.

38–4a. Drive all visible nails about 1/8″ below the surface and fill. The filler should be applied so that it is slightly higher than the wood, then sanded level when dry. Another method of covering nails is with pegs. Pegs can be made by using small 1/32-inch stock of the same material as the project. Point the end in a pencil sharpener. Apply glue to the point and insert in the hole. Then cut off and sand smooth.

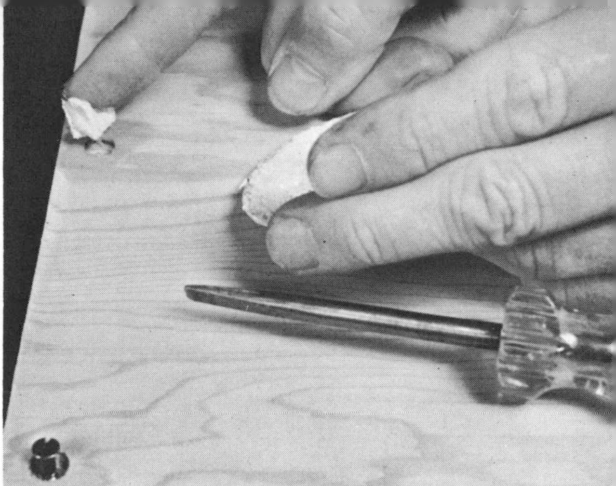

38–4b. Filling the tops of screw holes with putty. This can be used if the surface of the wood is to be painted.

If the project is to be painted, filling can be done with putty. Figures 38–4a and 38–4b. A shallow dent in the wood can sometimes be raised by applying a moist cloth and then covering it with a warm iron. Figure 38–5. Make sure that the iron is not so hot that it burns the surface. Also keep the iron moving so that the wood isn't scorched.

SCRAPING AND SANDING THE PROJECT

After all irregularities and holes have been filled, go carefully over the entire project, scraping and sanding where necessary. When you sand, change to finer and finer paper ending with No. 3/0 to 6/0 garnet paper. Figure 38–6. Before the final sanding, moisten the project slightly, allow it to dry, and then use a very fine sandpaper as a final finish. Wipe off any dust with a clean cloth. Now the project will be ready for the finish.

BLEACHING

Bleaching is done whenever a very light finish is to be applied to the wood surface, by using chemicals that remove some of the wood color. For simple bleaching, a solution of oxalic acid crystals mixed in hot water can be applied to the surface with a rope brush or sponge. This should remain

38–5. Swelling a dent in wood with a damp cloth and a hot iron. Remember that too much wetting is not good, especially if you are working with plywood.

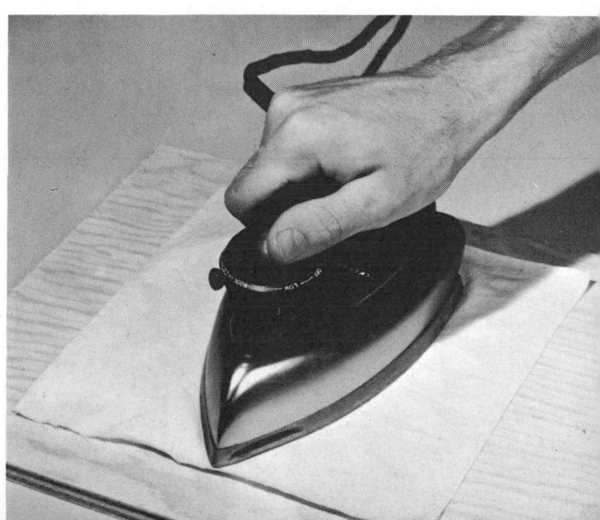

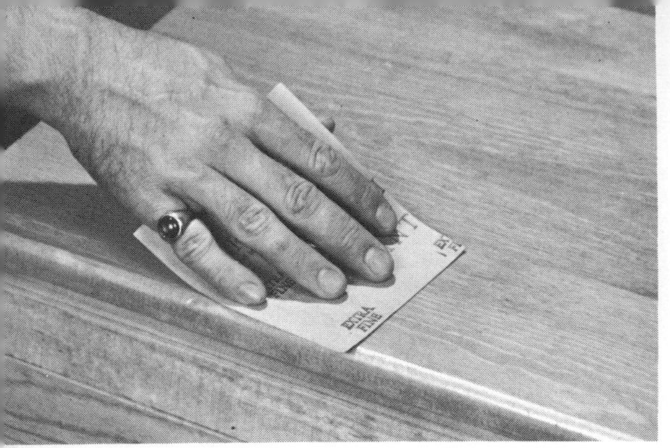

38–6. Give the project a final sanding with a fine abrasive paper. The corners should be *slightly* rounded.

38–8. Applying a commercial bleach with a synthetic rubber sponge. Caution: Remember always to wear rubber gloves to protect your hands when working with bleaches. When bleach is dry, sponge off lightly with water.

on the surface for ten or fifteen minutes. Then apply a solution made from 3 ounces of sodium hyposulphate to 1 quart of water. In a few minutes apply a mild solution of borax mixed in water to neutralize the acid. NOTE: For most large projects, it is better to use a commercial bleach and always follow the directions very carefully. Figure 38–7. All bleaches remove the color from the wood by a process of oxidation. Figure 38–8 and 38–9.

CAN YOU ANSWER THESE QUESTIONS ON PREPARING THE ARTICLE FOR FINISHING?

1. Why is it necessary to remove every bit of glue from the article after it is dry? How would you do this?
2. When is it necessary to bleach glued surfaces? Name a simple bleach.
3. List four materials that can be used for filling holes, cracks, and irregularities.
4. How can shallow dents in wood be raised?
5. A project is moistened before the final sanding. Why is this done?
6. Explain the purpose of bleaching.

38–7. There are several kinds of bleaches. Some require the application of two liquids—a bleach followed by a neutralizer. Others consist of two liquids that are mixed in equal parts at the time of use and applied as a single material. Use a glass or porcelain jar for mixing.

38–9. Bleaches are used to lighten the natural color of woods. Here you see one half of a table top bleached.

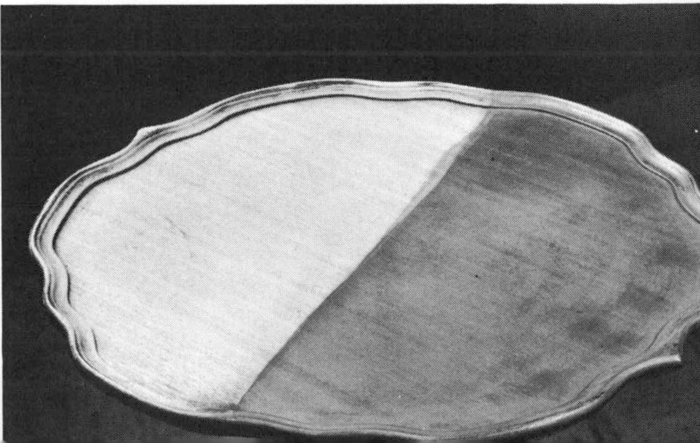

Section VIII

UNIT 39. INSTALLING CABINET HARDWARE

Hardware is installed on many large projects such as chests, cabinets, and desks. This is usually in the form of hinges, locks, pulls, or knobs. A hacksaw with 32 teeth per inch should be used to cut metal bolts, screws, and hardware. Figure 39–1.

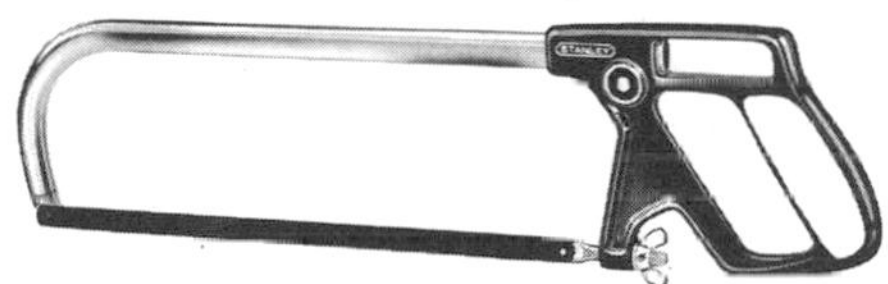

39–1. A hacksaw is necessary when hand-cutting any metal parts in the wood-shop.

KINDS OF CABINET HARDWARE

There are many different types of cabinet hinges. Figure 39–2. The butt hinge requires that a recess or gain be cut. In most cases, a gain is cut both in the door and in the frame on which the door is fastened. Sometimes a deeper gain is cut either in the frame or in the door so that the hinge is recessed in only one part of the two surfaces.

Figure 39–3 illustrates different types of drawer pulls and knobs suited to different furniture styles. The most common catches are friction, magnetic, elbow, and ball. Figure 39–4. The elbow catch holds one side of a double door closed when the other side is opened. Figure 39–5.

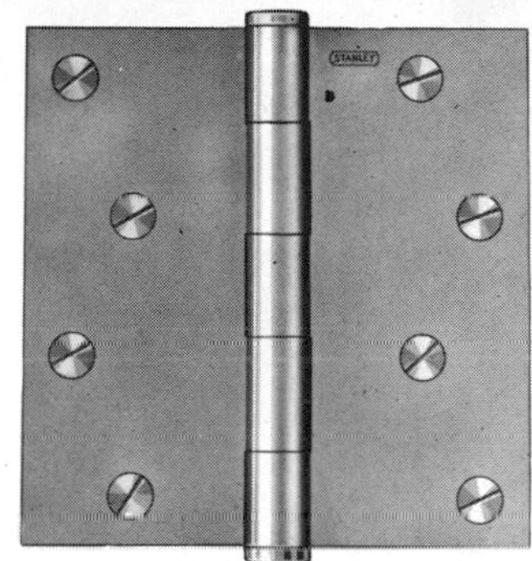

A

B

39–2. Kinds of hinges: A. Butt, B. Pivot. C. Semi-concealed.

C

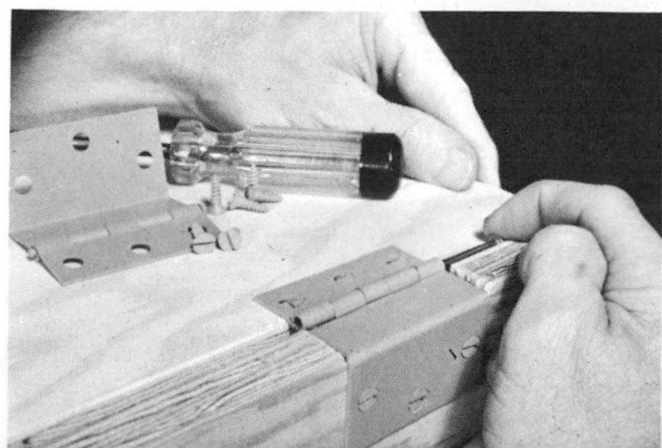

39–3. Various types of knobs and pulls. It is very important to select the one that fits the design of your article.

INSTALLING A BUTT HINGE

Select the proper size and kind of hinge for the door. The hinge size is indicated by its length. A 1-inch hinge is for a cabinet door for a desk, while a 3½-inch hinge is needed for a house door.

Fit the door into the opening. Place a thin piece of wood under the door, on the side away from the hinges, to hold the door in place. Measure from the top of the door to the upper location of the top hinge and from the bottom to the lower point of the bottom hinge. The hinges should be located just inside the upper and lower rail. A mark is made on both the door and the frame.

Remove the door and place it on the floor or bench with the hinge edge upward. Hold the hinge over the edge of the door with one end flush with the mark. Draw another line to show the length of the hinge. Mark this length on the door frame also. Then, with a try square held against the face side of the door, square off these lines across the edge. Repeat on the door frame. Determine the distance the hinge will set in from the face of the door. Set a marking gauge to this measurement. Hold the marking gauge against the face side of the door and mark a line between the two lines to show the position of the hinge. Repeat on the door frame. Then set a marking gauge to the thickness of one leaf of the hinge. From the edge, mark a line indicating the depth to which the stock must be removed both on the door and on

39–4. Four types of catches: A. Friction. B. Magnetic. C. Elbow. D. Ball.

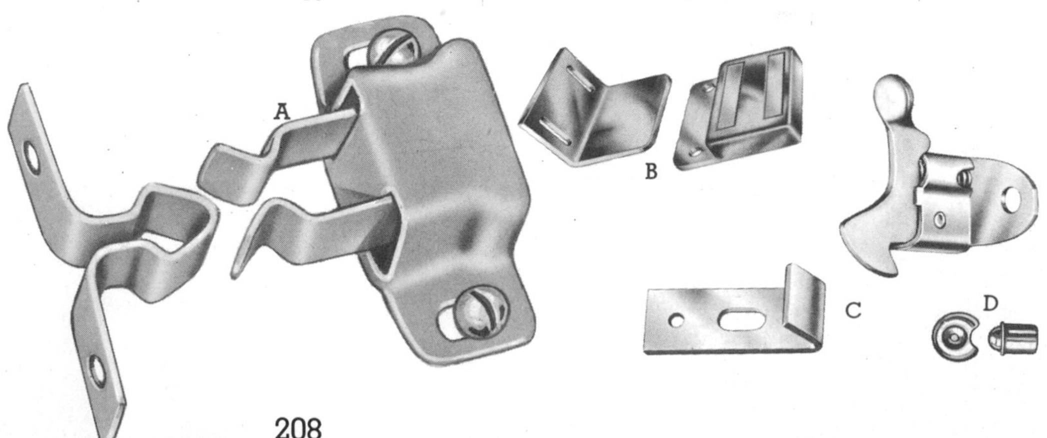

39–5. Installing a touch type catch. This allows the door to open by pushing lightly on the exterior.

the frame. This cut in the wood is called a gain.

With a chisel, outline the gain on the door as shown in Figure 39–6. Then make several V cuts in the stock to be removed. Figure 39–7. Pare out the stock to the depth of the gain. Try the hinge in the recess to see whether it fits flush with the edge of the door.

Mark the location of the screw holes and drill the pilot holes as needed. Fasten half the hinge to the door section.

Cut out the gains in the frame of the door. Locate the position of the holes, drill, and insert one screw. Put the door in position and place the pins in the hinges. Try the door to see how it operates. It may be necessary to shift slightly the position of half the hinge. Sometimes it is necessary to cut the gain a little deeper or to raise it by putting a piece of paper under it. After any needed correction has been made, drill the other pilot holes and fasten the other half of the hinges securely.

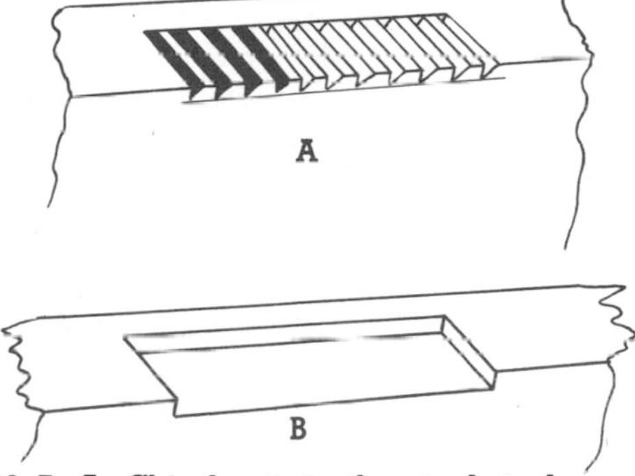

39–7. A. Chisel cuts in the stock to be removed to form the gain. B. The gain is cut and ready to have the hinge installed.

39–6. Here the gain has been laid out on the edge of the door and is being outlined with a chisel.

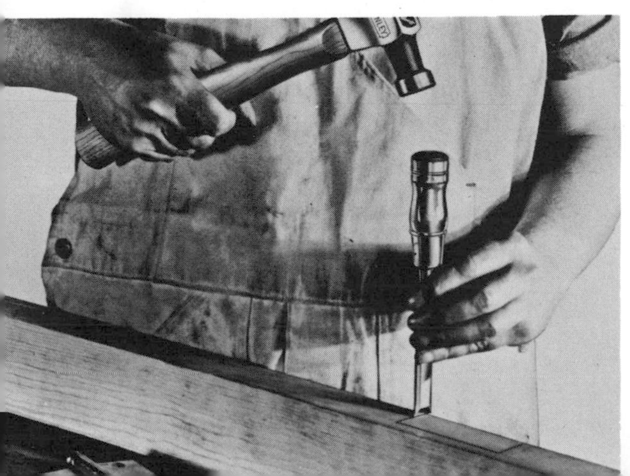

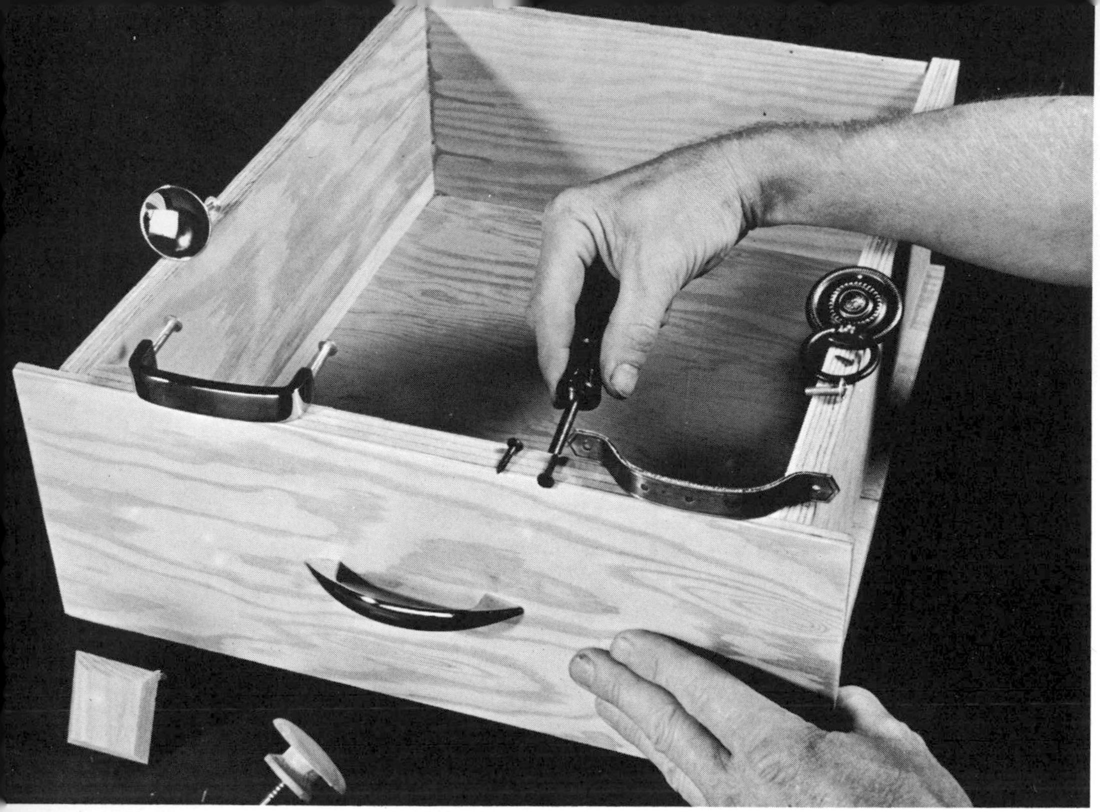

39–8. Attaching a handle to a drawer.

INSTALLING DRAWER KNOBS AND PULLS

Draw two parallel lines horizontally across the face of the door to locate the upper and lower edge of the knob. Then measure in from either end to the outside of the knob. Draw two vertical lines to complete the outline of the knob. Measure inward from this outline to locate the positions of the holes. Drill a hole the same size as the machine screws used to fasten the knob. Insert the machine screws from the back side of the drawer front and tighten the knob. Figure 39–8.

Pulls are installed in a similar way.

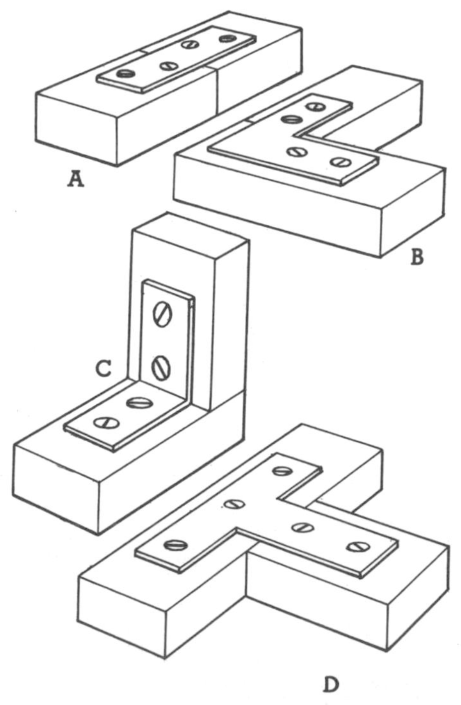

39–9. Four types of repair plates: A. Mending. B. Flat corner. C. Bent corner. D. T plate.

39–10. Removing the drawer knobs.

USING REPAIR PLATES

Repair and mending plates come in many sizes and shapes. Figure 39–9. Mending plates are used to strengthen a butt or lap joint. The *flat corner iron* is used to strengthen corners of frames such as a screen door or window. The *bent-corner iron* can be applied to shelves and the inside corners of tables, chairs, and cabinets. It can also be used to hang cabinets and shelves. *T plates* are used to strengthen the center rail of a frame.

REMOVING HARDWARE FOR FINISHING

Before applying a wood finish, remove any items such as knobs, hinges, locks, and catches that do not require the finish. Figure 39–10. You may also want to paint or enamel the metal hardware so that everything matches. Figure 39–11.

39–11. This hardware for a traditional piece of furniture has all been painted the same color.

CAN YOU ANSWER THESE QUESTIONS ON INSTALLING CABINET HARDWARE?

1. Name some of the common types of hinges.
2. Define a gain.
3. What indicates the size of a hinge?
4. Sketch the position of hinges on a panel door.
5. Describe the method of laying out a gain.
6. A gain is trimmed out with what tool?
7. How can you test a hinge to make certain that it has been installed correctly?
8. What should you think about before selecting drawer knobs or pulls?
9. What is the best practice to follow when installing locks?
10. Why are hardware pieces removed for finishing?

Section VIII

UNIT 40. PLASTIC LAMINATES

Furniture manufacturers cover the tops of tables, cabinets, and chests in many cases with an extremely hard material called plastic laminate. Most new homes feature this covering for the tops of kitchen cabinets and built-ins. For some furniture, plastic laminates imitate the wood grain appearance, matching natural wood. Plastic laminates are also made with patterns of almost any description such as the world map on the top of the coffee table in Figure 40–1.

You know this material by one of its trade names: Panelyte, Formica, or Texolite. Plastic laminate is what its name implies: a layer of materials, primarily kraft paper that has been impregnated with resin and a rayon surface paper covered with another kind of resin. The laminates are placed under high heat and pressure to produce a 1/16″ sheet of material that is very hard, but brittle. Such things as tea, coffee, ink, iodine, alcohol, and crayon wax have no effect on this surface. Soap and water can be used to clean it.

WORKING WITH PLASTIC LAMINATES

Although plastic laminates are very hard, they are brittle and must be well supported for doing any kind of cutting. Since a sheet is only 1/16″ thick, it cracks very easily. Plastic laminates are usually applied to plywood, solid wood, or hardboard. They can be cut with any of the standard woodworking tools. However, the carpenter or cabinetmaker usually prefers carbide-tipped tools, which are very hard and remain sharp longer than ordinary tools.

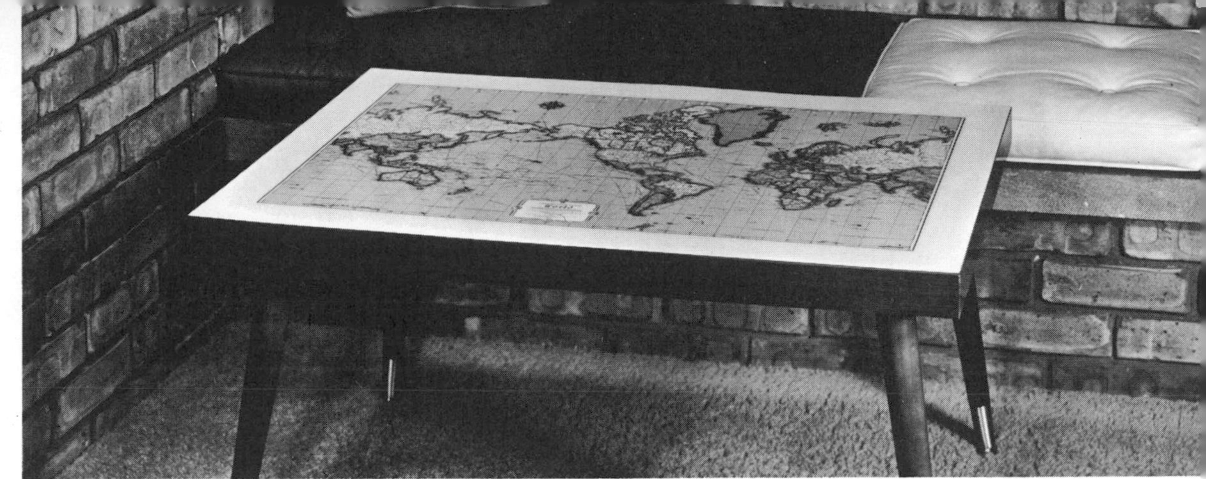

40–1. **This attractive coffee table has a plastic laminate top.**

The following is an example of the use of this material in replacing the top of a dresser table.

1. Lay the plastic laminate on a bench with the good side up. With a grease pencil, trace the size of plastic laminate needed by placing the table top over it. Figure 40–2. Allow about 1/8 to 1/4 inch oversize, as the material may chip slightly at the edges when sawed. This extra material is removed after the piece is fastened to the table top.

40–2. Tracing the shape of the table top with a grease pencil. With a larger table or kitchen counter, the top can be removed.

2. Cut out the laminate with a compass saw and a hacksaw. Always cut with the good side up. Make sure that it is firmly supported to keep it from cracking. Figures 40–3 and 40–4.

3. The best adhesive for attaching the plastic laminate to the wood top is contact cement. It can be applied with a brush or metal spreader that has a serrated edge. Figure 40–5. Make sure that the surfaces to be bonded are clean, dry, sound, and level. On an old surface, remove any varnish and sandpaper the surface smooth. Apply a coat of contact cement to both the table top and the back of the plastic laminate. Use the special applicator whenever possible on horizontal sur-

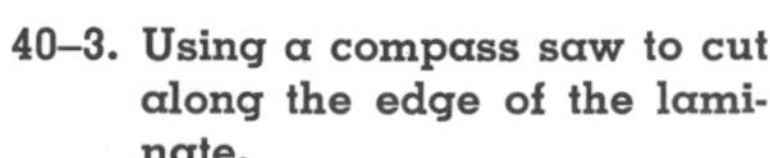

40–3. Using a compass saw to cut along the edge of the laminate.

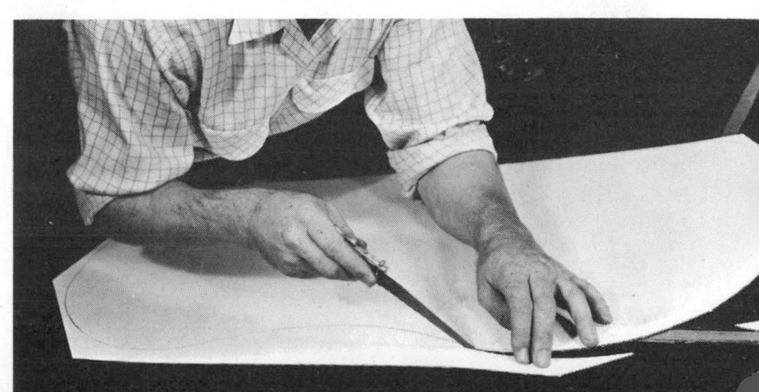

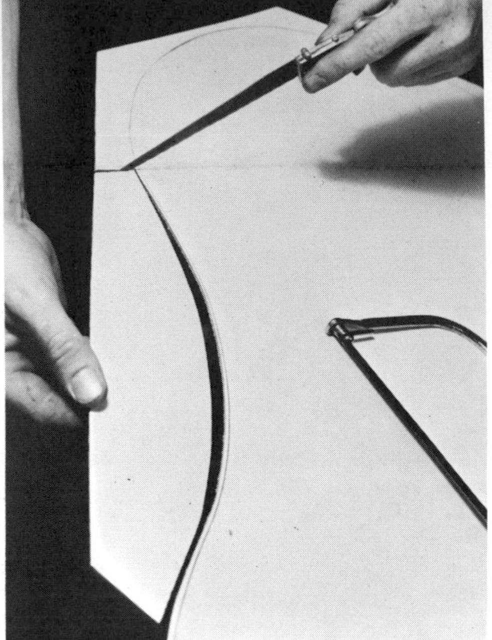

40–4. Cutting away a section of the waste material.

faces. Figure 40–6. Make sure that every square inch of both surfaces is completely and evenly covered with the cement. An adequately coated surface will have a glossy film when dry. Any dull spots after drying indicate that too little cement was used. These spots must have a second coat. Allow both surfaces to dry at least 30 to 40 minutes. You can test for drying by applying a small piece of wrapping paper lightly against the cemented surface. If no cement sticks to the paper, the cement is dry and ready for bonding.

4. The cemented surfaces can be bonded any time within 3 hours after the contact cement is applied, so don't rush. It is better to wait a little longer and be sure. Remember, there is a complete bond immediately when the two surfaces come in contact! Therefore no adjustment can be made. To avoid any mistake, use the following technique:

Place a piece of heavy wrapping paper lightly over the entire base surface. Figure 40–7. Now place the plastic laminate in position over the wrapping paper and align it carefully. Raise one side of the laminate slightly, and draw the paper away 2 or 3 inches. Now check to see that the parts are still aligned and press down where the paper has been withdrawn. Then remove the paper completely.

5. Roll the entire surface with a rolling pin or other hand roller. Figure 40–8. Now trim the edge with a block plane and/or file. Figures 40–9 and 40–10. Hold the tool at an angle of about 20 to 25 degrees for bevel finishing.

6. The edge of the table top can be covered with a metal or plastic laminate edge. Edge-banding material to

40–5. Applying contact cement to the top of the table.

40–6. Applying contact cement to the back of the laminate.

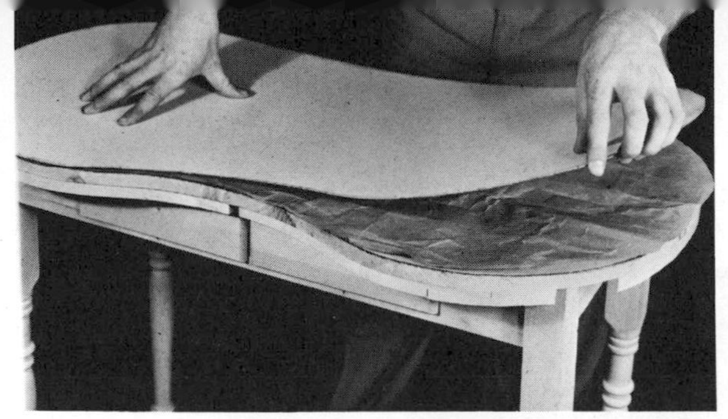

40–7. Fastening the plastic laminate to the table top. Do not press down! Notice the wrapping paper that is placed between. This must be removed slowly after the material is positioned properly.

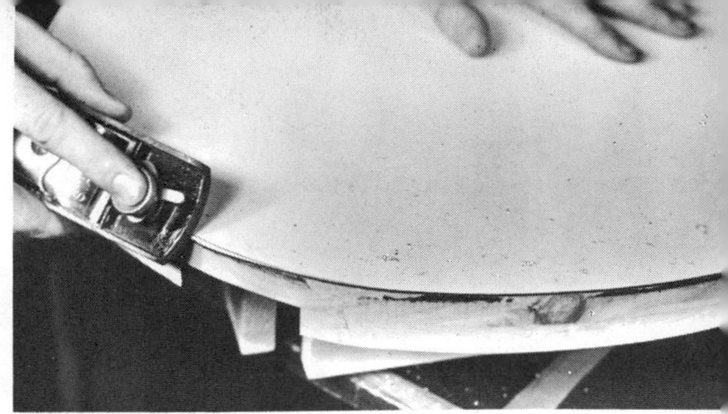

40–9. Trimming off the excess material with a block plane.

match the plastic laminate is available. It can be easily bent around a curved surface. A more pleasing appearance can be obtained on the edge of a table top by adding a strip of wood to the underside for added thickness.

CAN YOU ANSWER THESE QUESTIONS ON PLASTIC LAMINATES?

1. What is a plastic laminate?
2. Why is this material so popular for kitchen cabinet tops?
3. What is the best adhesive for gluing the material to the project?
4. How can you tell when the cement is ready for bonding?
5. Can you move the plastic laminate a little if you don't have it in the right place the first time? Explain why or why not.
6. Tell how to trim the edge of the plastic laminate after it is in place.

40–8. Using a rolling pin to flatten the surface.

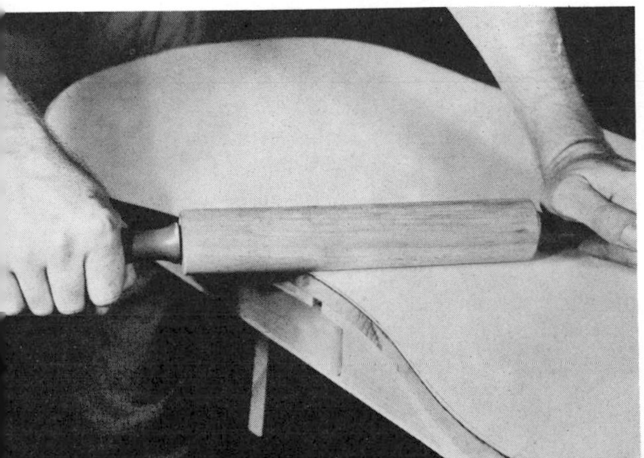

40–10. Beveling the edge of the plastic laminate with a file. Use light, regular strokes to keep the bevel even.

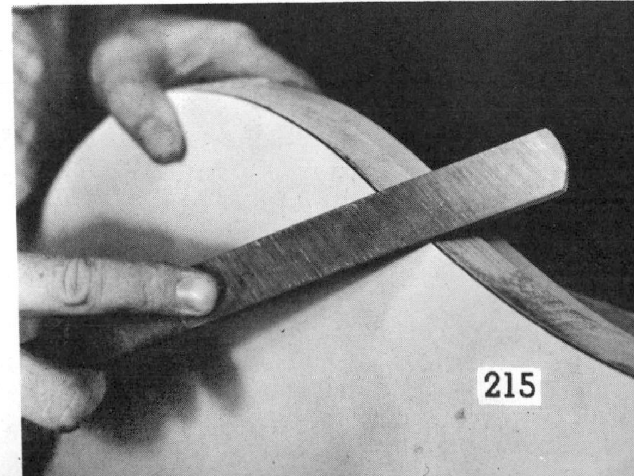

Section VIII

UNIT 41. MOSAIC TILES

Mosaic tiles are excellent for adding color and interest to cutting boards, hot pads, tops of tables, and similar projects. Unit 41–1. Three types of tiles can be used, namely, glass, ceramic, or vinyl plastic. Ceramic tile is best for small projects. The tiles can be applied over any kind of wood.

TOOLS AND MATERIALS

Tiles of solid glass, ceramics, or plastic can be purchased in a wide range of colors. The common size is 3/16″ thick and 3/4″ square. Tiles can also be purchased 3/16″ thick and 3/8″ square. They come either loose or fastened to a sheet of paper. The latter must be separated by soaking the sheets in warm water for fifteen minutes. Then allow the tiles to dry thoroughly before using.

41–1. Mosaic tiles are excellent for adding beauty and utility to the top of a wood table.

A cutter is needed to cut tiles into smaller or irregular shaped pieces. Figure 41–2. The cutter has curved edges that help prevent the tile from shattering. A palette knife—a flexible artist's tool with a narrow, thin blade—is used to spread the adhesive on small areas and to apply it to the individual tiles. The most common adhesive is white resin glue. It dries in a colorless state and is easy to apply from a squeeze bottle.

Grout is a cement paste that fills the spaces between the tiles. *Spackling cement*, available at paint or wallpaper stores, can also be used.

Silicon polish is applied to the finished tile surface to make it waterproof and to seal all joints. It also adds a protective luster to the tile surface.

PROCEDURE FOR APPLYING TILE

Design and build the project. Or a commercial kit can be purchased. When making a rectangular opening or form into which the tiles fit, remember tile size. Each tile is about 3/4″ square. About 1/16″ to 1/8″ between the tiles should be allowed for the grout.

The mosaic design can be a geometric pattern made from full-size tiles.

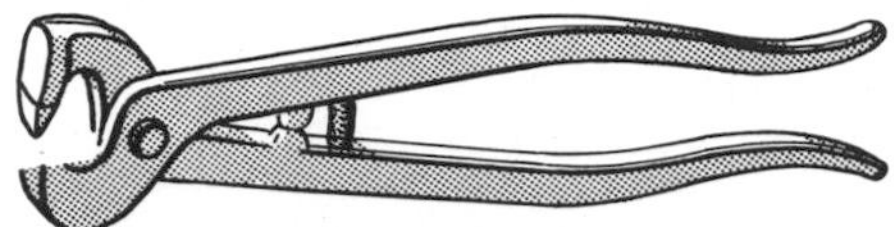

41–2. The cutter is used to divide the tile into smaller pieces. If the cutter blades are carbide-tipped and curved, the tile can be cut by holding it in the fingers, placing the entire cutting surface on the tile exactly where it should be broken. Then a quick squeeze on the handle cuts the material.

Figure 41–3. You can also make a design of irregular shape and cut tiles to fill in the spaces. If the design is geometric and the tiles full size, lay the tiles on the project and arrange them to suit your own taste.

Cutting tiles: Mark the tile where it needs to be cut. Holding it in your fingers, place the entire curved surface of the blade directly over the line. Then squeeze the handles quickly. This will give a precise, full-length cut. If a circle or curve is needed, make several tiny cuts until you have the curved shape you want.

Attaching tile: After you have worked out the design, start on the outside edge and work toward the center. Figure 41–3. On a round design, start by forming an outer rim. Remember that the tiles should be about 1/16 to 1/8 inch apart. Use white resin glue. Place a little on the back of each tile with a palette knife and attach to the surface. Press the tiles firmly in position and allow them to dry for twenty-four hours. Mix the grout or spackling cement with cold water (usually half and half) until it is a thick, creamy solution. Then, with a rubber scraper or your hands, rub the grout over a small area at a time, going both lengthwise and crosswise, until the paste is firmly forced into all of the cracks. Figure 41–4. Carefully wipe the extra grout from the surface without digging in between the tiles. Use a damp cloth for this. Wait about fifteen minutes or until a dusty film appears, then wipe the surface with a dry cloth.

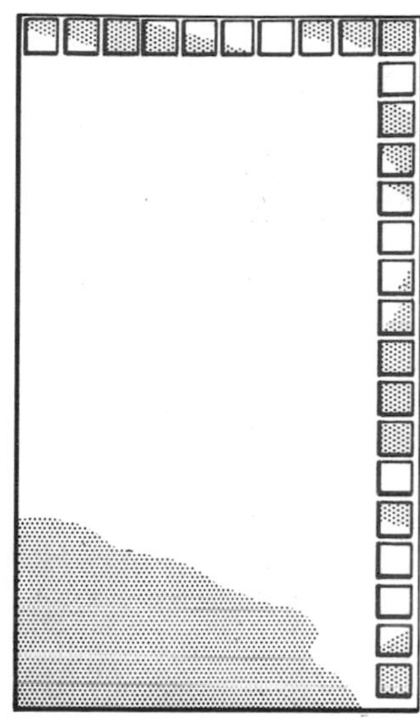

41–3. Spread the glue on the work and then start to arrange the outside edge. Set adjacent edges first to establish the spacing of the tiles.

41–4. Rub the grout between the tiles.

Allow the grout to dry overnight. If it is not flush with the tiles, you can apply a second coat as necessary. After the grout is completely dry, apply a silicon polish to make the tiles shiny.

CAN YOU ANSWER THESE QUESTIONS ABOUT MOSAIC TILES?

1. Name several kinds of materials used for tiles.
2. What kind of tool is needed to cut the tiles?
3. What is the best adhesive to use for attaching tile to a wood surface?
4. Describe the use of grout.
5. How much space should be allowed between tiles for the grout?

Section IX
Finishing Projects

The ninth 9 steps in hand woodworking—what you must know and be able to do.

42. Wood finishing and finishing supplies: basic steps in finishing, where supplies come from and how to use and keep them in good working condition; and materials used in applying finishes.

43. The kinds of stains which are applied to beautify or to imitate, what they are, and how to apply them to get the best results.

44. Using wood fillers of different kinds on open- and closed-grain woods.

45. The technique of applying shellac, what shellac is, and what makes it good for finishing.

46. Varnish finishes require a special technique, more time and better physical setup; method of application and steps in producing a varnish finish.

47. Penetrating and wipe-on finishes; what they are and how to apply them.

48. How a clear or colored lacquer finish differs from other finishes and how to apply lacquer.

49. How enamel differs from paint in its composition and application.

50. Painting a surface: mixing the paint and how to apply it with a brush.

A good start deserves a good "finish"! If you apply a good finish, your work will carry the mark of the fine craftsman. Don't ruin your project by applying the wrong finish or by putting on the right finish carelessly. Also remember that, while it is convenient to have a separate finishing room, you don't need one to do a good job. You do, however, need to do your part in taking care of the finishing area and supplies. Never, for example, use the shellac brush and then let it dry out; or open a can of varnish and not reseal it properly.

Before you begin to apply the finish, visit a furniture store to look at some pieces of fine furniture. Notice the rich finish which accounts greatly for its quality. You, too, will be proud of your work if you finish it well. For materials and methods, see the "box" above. Further steps in woodworking are on pp. 15, 43, 60, 94, 108, 132, 143, 170, 244.

Section IX

UNIT 42. WOOD FINISHING AND FINISHING SUPPLIES

Wood finishing is one of the most important steps in the completion of attractive projects. Figure 42–1. Thanks to the chemist and the magic of finishing materials, you can add a variety of color and finishes to the things you make. Modern paint chemistry makes it possible to give wood furniture new color, new beauty, and new style. An important part of a good finish in woodworking is having the proper finishing supplies in good condition.

BASIC STEPS IN ACHIEVING A FINE FINISH

Although the finishing materials may vary, all finishing is done in about the same way. The following are the basic steps necessary to a fine finish. They are not all necessary for the finishing of every piece of wood. You need to follow only the steps needed for the type of finish you want.

1. Bleaching. Bleaching is done to lighten or to even out the color of unfinished wood. Very light, natural wood finishes are popular for contemporary furniture. For natural and darker finishes, bleaching, of course, is not necessary.
2. Staining. Staining is done to enhance the grain and to achieve the color you want.
3. Sealing is done to seal the stain to prevent bleeding (running of the stain). A wash coat (one part shellac to seven parts alcohol) is good for most stains. If lacquer is used, a lacquer sealer can be applied.
4. Filling. Filling is required for porous and semiporous woods. Lumber from some broad-leaf trees such as oak, mahogany, and walnut contain large cells and, therefore, are very porous. When the lumber is cut and planed, the cells are ruptured, leaving what amounts to tiny troughs running lengthwise. These must be filled in order to obtain a smooth finish. Some woods such as birch, maple, and gum have smaller cells and these require a thinner filler or no filler at all. Nonporous woods such as pine, cedar, and redwood do not require a paste filler.
5. Sealing. A sealer should again be

42–1. Preparing a piece of furniture for finishing.

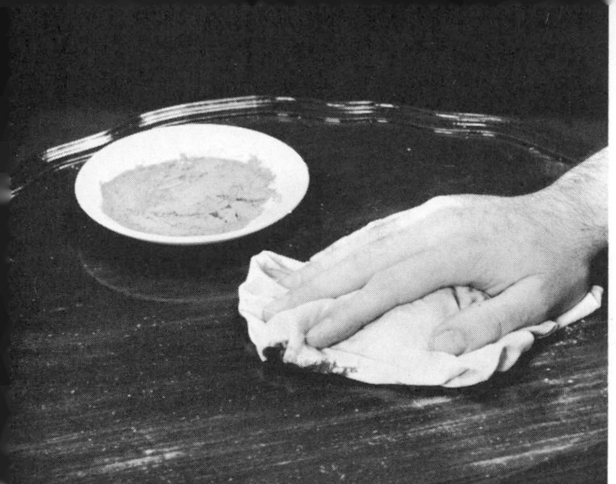

42–2. Rubbing a surface using a cloth and rottenstone.

42–3. Rubbing a surface using soapy water and wet-or-dry abrasive paper.

applied over a filler. It can be a commercial lacquer sealer or a wash coat of shellac.

6. Applying the standard finish. A shellac, varnish, lacquer, or synthetic finish is applied after sealing. Usually two or more coats are needed. Always sand the surface with 5/0 (180) sandpaper after each coat is dry. The final coat may be gloss or satin—a duller gloss.

7. Rubbing, buffing, and waxing. To get a hand-rubbed finish, the normal gloss is removed and reduced by using an abrasive material. The surface to be rubbed should have at least three or four coats of the final finish in order to withstand the rubbing. The common method of rubbing is to use a felt pad and pumice. Several layers of felt should be tacked to a piece of wood. Then mix the pumice in water to a paste consistency. Wet the surface. Dab the pad in water, then in pumice paste, and rub the surface with the grain. Use long strokes with moderate pressure. For an even finer polished surface, rub with a felt pad or cloth, using powdered rottenstone and water or rottenstone and rubbing oil. Figure 42–2. Another method of rubbing the surface is to use wet-or-dry sandpaper. Lubricate the surface with soapy water. Then rub with the grain, using long strokes. Use very fine wet-or-dry sandpaper, grades 360 to 380. Figure 42–3. When uniformly dull, polish with a clean, soft felt pad or cloth. A simpler method of getting a rubbed surface is to rub with 4/0 steel wool until the surface is uniformly dull. Figure 42–4. The final step is to apply a good coat of paste wax and rub vigorously with a soft cloth. Figure 42–5.

BRUSHES

There should be a variety of sizes for all different types of finishes. Most brushes for painting, varnishing, and enameling have Chinese, Russian boar, or nylon bristles set in rubber. The

42–4. Rubbing a surface using a steel wool pad.

brushes you need will vary in size from 1 to 4 inches. You should have a different brush with its own container for each different type of finishing material. A poor finish usually results when you use a shellac brush for varnish, as an example.

GOOD USE OF BRUSHES

The following are some general suggestions for using brushes:

1. Revolve a new brush rapidly by the handle to dislodge loose bristles. Remember that all new brushes have them. Figure 42–6.
2. Dip the brush into the finishing material about ⅓ the bristle length. Tap the excess against the side of the can. Figure 42–7. Never scrape against the rim of the can.
3. When using a brush, always hold it at a slight angle to the work surface.
4. Never paint with the side of the brush. This is one of the main causes of "fingering."
5. Never use a wide brush to paint small round surfaces such as dowel rods. Your brush will "fishtail."
6. Never let the brush stand on its bristle end. Its own weight bends and curls the bristle. Figure 42–8. This would make painting difficult.

When not in use, brushes should be put into a solvent suited to the material used on the brush. The proper solvents for finishing materials are:

42–5. Applying a coat of paste wax.

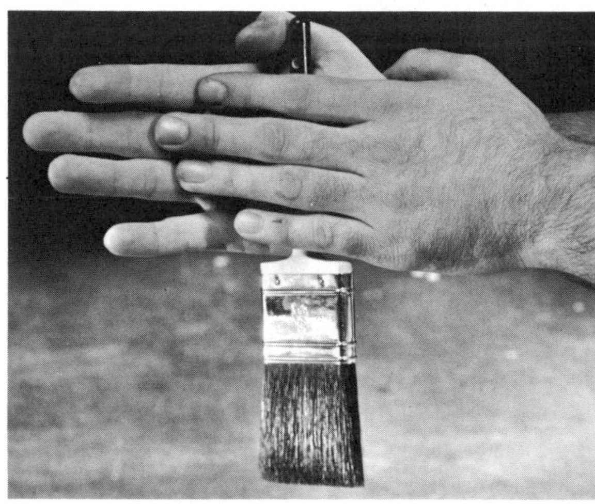

42–6. Twirling a brush to get rid of the loose bristles.

CLEANING BRUSHES

It pays to take care of brushes immediately after they have been used. The same solvents used to thin down finishes are generally recommended for cleaning brushes. There are also special

Solvent	Finishing Material
Turpentine	Oil stain Filler for varnish and shellac finish Varnish Enamel
Turpentine and linseed oil	Paint
Alcohol	Shellacs
Lacquer thinner	Filler for lacquer finish Lacquer

42–7. Tapping a brush on the side of a can. Never rub the bristles on the edge of the can. A larger mouthed container is better. Why?

brush and roller cleaners that can be used. Figure 42–9. Work the cleaner thoroughly into the heel of the brush and, with your fingers, open the hairs to clean out the waste material. Wipe the brush dry. If the brush is to be stored longer than just overnight, wash it in good commercial cleaning solvent mixed in water or a good grade of detergent. Figure 42–10. Wash the brush thoroughly. Comb the bristles

42–8. One method of suspending brushes to make sure that the bristles don't become bent.

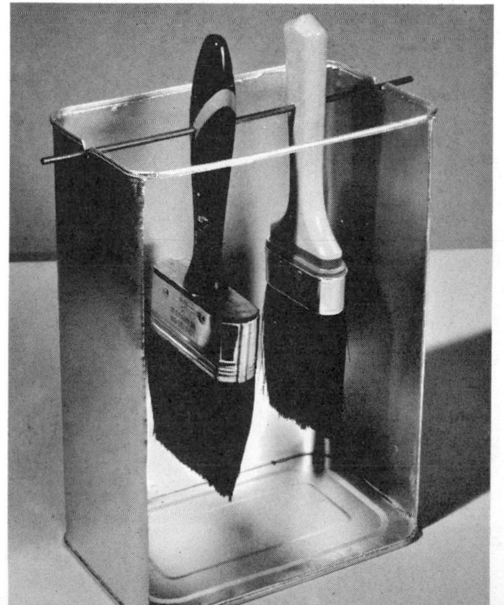

with a metal comb. Rinse well, shake out the excess water, and allow to dry. Then wrap the brush in heavy wax paper.

FINISHING SUPPLIES

Turpentine is made from the resin drippings of pine trees. These drippings are distilled by boiling in large copper vats and then running the solution through a condensing coil to a collection barrel. Turpentine rises to the surface and is drained off.

Linseed oil is made from flaxseed. The oil is obtained by compressing the seed under high pressure to squeeze out the oil. The oil is used either in its raw state or is boiled to improve its drying qualities as a paint ingredient. Linseed oil is used by itself to finish certain types of furniture. The oil is applied with a rag and then rubbed into the surface. Several coats are applied in this manner. After the oil is dry, a paste wax is applied and rubbed to a high polish.

The best *alcohol* for mixing shellac is made from wood drippings or chem-

42–9. Using a commercial brush cleaner.

42–10. Rinsing a brush. First use a commercial cleaning solvent or a good grade of detergent.

icals, if available. The Government has established a standard alcohol mix that is called Formula Special No. 1 denatured alcohol, which contains ethyl alcohol and wood alcohol.

Benzene, used as a solvent and a cleaning fluid, is made from coal tar.

Mineral spirits is a pure distillation of petroleum that will do everything that turpentine will do. It can be used as a thinner or solvent.

Waxes can be either liquid or paste. Both are made from a base of beeswax, paraffin, carnauba wax, and turpentine. Wax provides a good water-resistant surface that can be renewed often.

42–11. Wiping the surface of the project with a tack rag before applying a finish.

Steel wool is made of thin metal shavings. It comes in pads or rolls and can be purchased in grades from 000, very fine, to 3, coarse.

Pumice is a white-colored powder made from lava. It is available in several grades. The most common for woodworking finishing are FF and FFF. It is combined with water or oil to rub down the finish.

Rottenstone is a reddish-brown or grayish-black iron oxide vehicle that comes from shale. It is much finer than pumice. It is used with water or oil to produce a smoother finish after the surface has been rubbed with pumice.

Rubbing oil should be either petroleum or paraffin oil. If oil refined from petroleum is used, be sure it is a thin grade.

Abrasive papers needed are garnet or aluminum oxide finishing papers in grade No. 4/0 (150) and No. 6/0 (220). No. 4/0 (150) is used for sanding after staining, after applying the first coat of shellac, and before applying the filler coat. No. 6/0 (220) is used for final smoothing after shellac coats or other finish. These grades may be used dry or with oil.

Waterproof (wet-or-dry) abrasive papers in grades from 240 to 400 grit are used with water for hand sanding between lacquer coats or for rubbing enamel or lacquer.

A *tack rag* is a piece of cheesecloth or cotton rag moistened with thinned varnish. It is used to pick up tiny particles of dust from the wood surface before applying any finish. Figure 42–11.

1a. The planks for this Philippine mahogany wall have been rough-sawed and then finished in a reddish tone. The wood is easy to work and very durable. The mahogany shown here is called dark red. Other species are much lighter.

1b. Here is a wall of redwood which shows the distinct difference between heartwood and sapwood. The reddish-purple color is more typical of redwood as we know it than is the lighter sapwood. Redwood is excellent for both interior and exterior construction.

2. Good color ideas in a small space are illustrated by this sideboard arrangment. By repeating the vivid red of the rug, the screen becomes a strong accent. The abstract painting "catches" this same red and adds an eye-filling burst of other tints and tones. The buffet is walnut with a black plastic laminate top. Notice the effective use of burl veneer on the two vertical sliding doors.

3. This kitchen combines bright, contrasting color with an imaginative use of some of the newer materials of woodworking. The walls and ceilings are a bright blue with the cabinets a darker blue. Notice the perforated hardboard which holds many of the kitchen accessories. The wood serving spoons are good illustrations of carving. The tops of the kitchen cabinets are white plastic laminate. The cheese tray is a clever combination of wood and mosaic tile. How many ideas can you find in this kitchen for good projects you might like to build.

4. This bedroom illustrates the effective use of the warm colors of yellow, gold, orange, and red. The basic colors are harmonious with accents of blue. Even though this fine furniture was built of mahogany, most of it was finished in antique white with gold-leaf trim.

42–12. **Removing the finish by using a commercial paint remover.**

42–13. **Wiping the surface with a damp rag.**

REFINISHING

The first step in refinishing a project is to remove the old finish. A simple, inexpensive way to do this is to apply a paint and varnish remover. Flow on a liberal coat of remover on an area about 2′ x 2′ in size. Don't work too large an area at one time. Allow it to stand about 10 to 30 minutes until the old finish is soft. Figure 42–12. When the old finish is well softened, remove most of it with a wide scraper or putty knife. Then apply a second coat of the remover and quickly clean up the surface, wiping away the remaining paint with water and a cloth. Figure 42–13. A little detergent added to the water will help. After the old finish has been removed, sand the surface with fine sandpaper until the old finish has been removed down to the bare wood. *Use steel wool for carvings,* instead of sandpaper.

CAN YOU ANSWER THESE QUESTIONS ON WOOD FINISHING AND FINISHING SUPPLIES?

1. Explain how to achieve a fine finish.
2. What are the best bristles for most finishing brushes?
3. Tell what turpentine is.
4. What is linseed oil? What is the difference between raw and boiled linseed oil?
5. From what is the best alcohol made?
6. What are waxes made from?
7. What is pumice? Rottenstone? Which is finer?
8. Tell how to refinish a project.

Section IX

UNIT 43. STAINS

Stain is transparent color (can be seen through). It is applied to wood to improve its appearance and add color, to bring out the grain, to preserve it, and sometimes to imitate the more expensive woods. There are many kinds of stains, but only oil and water stains are used commonly by the beginner. It is a good idea to test the stain for color on a piece of scrap wood of the same kind as the project.

OIL STAIN

Oil stain is coloring that has been mixed in an oil base. You can mix your own oil stain by adding such pigments (colors) as raw and burnt umber, raw and burnt sienna, ochre, orange, light green, turquoise, dark green, blue, red oxide, Venetian red, black drop, and Vandyke brown to linseed oil and turpentine. However, it is much simpler and easier to buy ready-made oil stains. They are available in all ranges of colors: walnut, oak in light, medium and dark, various shades of mahogany, cherry, rosewood, and many others.

43–1. Applying stain. Dip the brush into the stain about one third of the bristle length and brush on a uniform wet coat, following the wood grain.

WATER STAIN

A water stain is made by mixing aniline dye in hot water. The dye usually comes in powdered form and you can mix it yourself. The strength of the stain can be changed by increasing or decreasing the amount of dye.

Water stains also come in ready-mixed form. Water stain has several advantages; it is cheaper than other stains, has a more even color, and is less likely to fade. However, it raises grain.

Stains are usually applied with a brush, sponge, or rag. Then the excess is wiped off with a clean cheesecloth or a pad of cotton waste. It is easiest to use a 1½- to 2-inch brush set in rubber, especially when applying water stains. Before applying the stain, a small scrap piece of the same kind of wood as the project should be stained first. In this way you can get a very good idea of the stain. If you are closely matching the color of another piece of furniture, the entire finishing process on the scrap piece has to be done to make sure you have the finish you want.

43–2. After the stain loses its wet appearance and looks flat, wipe lightly until the depth of color or desired effect is obtained. Use a clean, lint-free cloth formed into a pad and follow the grain of the wood.

APPLYING OIL STAIN

Choose the color stain you want and test it on a scrap piece. When you find the right color, mix up enough for the entire job. For example, it will take about 1 pint of stain to cover about 25 square feet of porous wood such as oak.

End grain of wood absorbs stain more than the surface grain and, therefore, looks darker. To prevent this, soak a rag in some linseed oil and rub the end grain before applying the stain. Now you are ready to apply the stain to the surface.

Pour out about one third cup into a porcelain, glass, or enamel container. Use a good brush. A rag or sponge can be used also, although not as easily.

If possible, apply the stain with the wood held in a horizontal position, to avoid streaking caused by gravity flow. Always stain the lower surfaces first, beginning at the corner and working out. To stain a large, flat surface, dip about one third of the brush into the liquid, wipe off the excess stain on the side of the jar, and begin at the center of the surface. Figure 43–1. With light strokes, work out toward the edges, brushing on the stain evenly. With each new brushful of stain, begin on the unfinished surface and stroke toward the stained surface. As you are near the edges and ends of the wood, brush carefully to keep from spattering the stain. Apply the stain to one small area at a time, wiping off the excess with a clean, dry cloth. Figure 43–2.

One reason oil stains are less satisfactory is that they are slow to dry. Make sure that you cover and wipe off the total surface evenly. Allow the work to dry from twelve to twenty-four hours before continuing with the finishing operation. Then apply a wash coat of shellac (6 parts of alcohol to 1 part shellac). When this is dry, resand lightly with 6/0 sandpaper.

APPLYING WATER STAIN

Before applying water stain, sponge the surface of the wood lightly with water. Figure 43–3. After the surface is dry, sand with No. 2/0 sandpaper. Figure 43–4. This will help the stain flow on evenly and give a clear, transparent color. Apply the water stain in

43–3. Dampening the wood surface with a sponge before water staining.

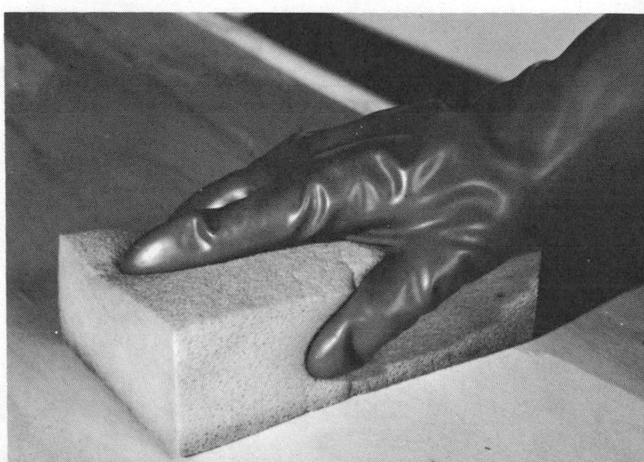

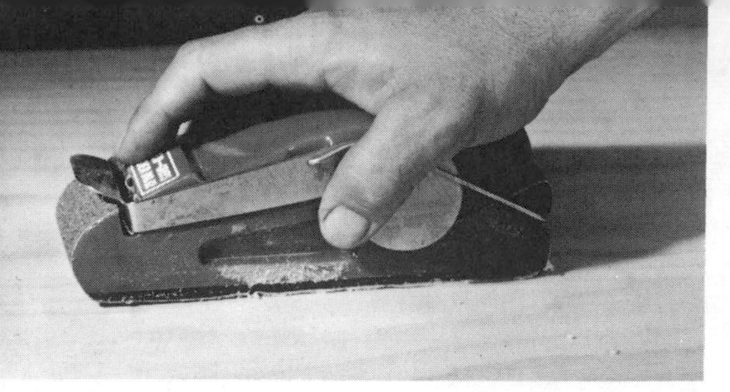

43–4. Sand the surface thoroughly with the grain before applying the water stain.

43–6. Applying a stain made by adding color to a sealer.

the same general way as the oil stain. Wipe off the excess with a cloth. Let it dry from twelve to twenty-four hours. Apply a wash coat of shellac. Then use a small piece of No. 6/0 sandpaper to sand the surface lightly, removing the high surfaces of the wood. Wipe clean of dust.

USING SYNTHETIC SEALERS AS STAINS

There are many commercial synthetic sealers that can be used for both the stain and the final finish. These materials give a "close-to-the-grain" appearance and are partly penetrating and partly surface finishes. The sealers are usually available in clear and satin type. The stain can be made by mixing a tube of tinting color (pigments) in the sealer. Figure 43–5. For example, ochre added to the sealer produces a pleasing, light walnut stain. The stain is brushed on and then wiped off with a cloth. Figure 43–6. Then, if necessary, a filler is added. Finally, the same sealer

43–5. Select the stain color you want and then add tinting color to get the desired effect.

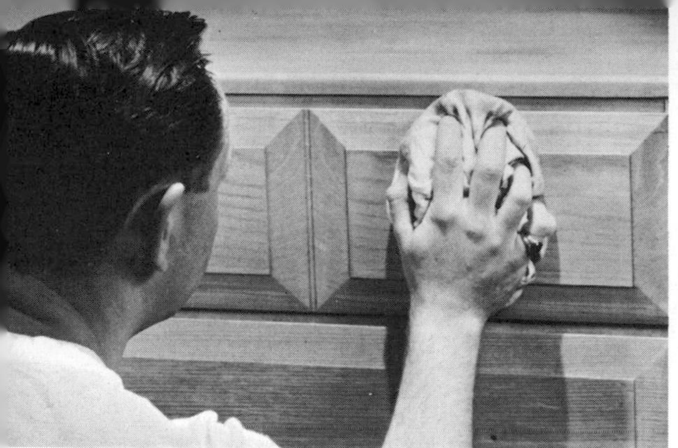

43–7. Wiping off the stain until it is uniform in color.

43–8. Using sealer for the finish coat.

without the coloring is used as the final finish. Figure 43–7. With this kind of material, avoid excessive brushing strokes. "Flow" it on the surface rather than brushing it on. Figure 43–8. Sand between coats and wipe the surface with a tack rag before applying the final coat.

CAN YOU ANSWER THESE QUESTIONS ON STAINS?

1. Name the two common types of stains.
2. What pigments are found in oil stain?
3. What is the advantage of buying commercially prepared oil stain?
4. How can the strength of water stain be varied?
5. What advantage has water stain? What disadvantage?
6. How can you judge the amount of oil stain needed?
7. Tell how stains are applied.
8. How can you prevent the end grain of wood from taking up too much stain?
9. Describe the brushing technique for staining.
10. How should the wood surface be prepared before water stain is applied?
11. Explain how to use a sealer finish as a stain.

Section IX

UNIT 44. APPLYING WOOD FILLER

Fillers are used to seal the pores of wood and to add beauty to the finish. Open-grained woods, such as oak, walnut, chestnut, hickory, ash, and mahogany, need a medium or heavy paste filler. For closed-grained woods like birch, fir, and pine, the best filler is a liquid type such as shellac.

Paste filler is made of ground silicon, linseed oil, turpentine, drier, and color-

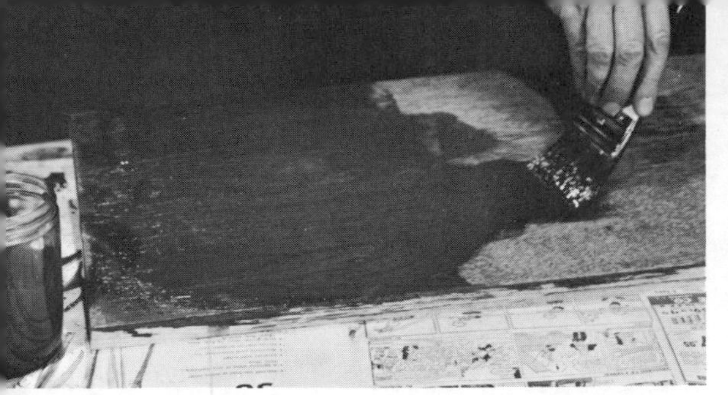

44–1. Applying a wood filler with a stiff brush. Brush both with and across the grain.

44–2. Rub across the grain with burlap or coarse cloth to remove the excess filler. Then wipe lightly with the grain using a fine cloth.

ing. You can buy it canned in natural color or in various colors to match wood stains. The paste usually is thinned a little with turpentine, but if applied under a lacquer finish the filler must be thinned with a lacquer thinner. On bleach finishes, white lead or pure zinc paste is sometimes the filler. Either of these can be colored by adding burnt umber, raw sienna, or other pigment. In preparing for use, add turpentine until the paste is like a thin cream. Remember the filler should be thicker for open-grained woods such as oak, elm, or chestnut, and it should be thinner for medium open-grained woods like cherry, red gum, soft maple, and redwood. If the filler is to be applied over a stained surface, a wash coat of shellac (1 part shellac to 6 or 7 parts of alcohol) should be applied on the stain. This prevents any bleeding of the finish. Then the surface should be sanded with No. 6/0 sandpaper before the filler is applied.

Apply paste filler with a stiff brush, thoroughly covering the surface. Brush first with the grain, then across it. Figure 44–1. Do not cover too large an area at one time as the filler dries very rapidly. Rub in the paste filler with the palm of your hand, going over the entire surface in a circular motion. Allow the filler to dry until the surface loses its shiny appearance. This will take up to twenty minutes. Then wipe across the grain with burlap or rough cloth to remove the excess filler. Figure 44–2. After most of the filler has been removed, you can use a thin, clean cloth (cheesecloth or cotton) to go over the surface lightly *with the grain* to remove the remainder of the surface filler. Do not press too hard, though, or you will rub some of the filler out of the pores. If necessary, you can add another coat of filler in the same way as the first one. After the filler has dried from six to eight hours, proceed with shellac, lacquer, or varnish finish.

CAN YOU ANSWER THESE QUESTIONS ON APPLYING WOOD FILLER?

1. Name the two kinds of wood filler.
2. What kind is applied to open-grained woods?
3. Filler is thinned with what solvent? Can this solvent be used for all types of finishes?
4. What filler is chosen for modern bleached finishes?
5. How can you make a wash coat of shellac?
6. How long should a filler remain on the surface before it is wiped off?
7. What is the purpose of filler?

Section IX

UNIT 45. SHELLAC FINISH

Shellac is a good finish for many projects because it is easy to apply, dries quickly, and produces a hard surface. It isn't a good choice, however, if the wood is to be exposed to moisture; shellac turns a cloudy color in dampness. Shellac is frequently used as a finish by itself. It is sometimes used as a sealer over a stain or filler coat before varnish is applied. It is also applied to knots before painting to seal in the pitch. Figure 45–1.

SHELLAC

The shellac itself is a resinous substance which is the product of the lac bug. Most of our supply comes from India and Siam, where these bugs feed on resinous material and deposit the lac on trees. This is removed twice yearly and heated, purified, and laid out in strips to dry. The lac is then ground and mixed in denatured alcohol. Standard shellac, called a 4-pound cut, is a mixture of 4 pounds to a gallon of alcohol. Natural shellac is orange in color and is a good, tough finish. However, on many of the lighter woods, this natural shellac gives the finish an unattractive, yellow-orange tint. Therefore it is used over dark woods or dark stains. Shellac is available in a bleached form, called white shellac. This is more satisfactory for general use, especially for lighter wood finishes.

APPLYING SHELLAC

The wood must first be clean and dry. The surface should be wiped clean with a lint-free cloth that has been dipped in alcohol. Pour a small amount of shellac into a glass or porcelain container and add an equal amount of alcohol to thin it.

It is far better to apply several thin coats than a few heavy coats. Thinned shellac sinks into the surface of the wood better, providing a smoother finish. Apply the shellac with a clean varnish brush about 1½ to 3 inches wide with bristles set in rubber. Dip about one third of the brush length into the shellac and wipe off the sides of the brush on the container. Begin at

45–1. Applying shellac over wood knots. This seals the knots and helps prevent resin in the wood from leaking out and discoloring the paint or enamel.

the center of a flat surface or near the top of a vertical surface and work out toward the edges. Work quickly and evenly, taking light, long strokes. Do not brush over the same surface several times as shellac dries very rapidly and becomes sticky.

A beginner tends to put shellac on too thick, producing a yellowish cast. On the edges of your project, be careful to keep the shellac from piling up and running. After the entire surface has been covered, soak the brush in pure alcohol. Allow the project to dry two to four hours.

APPLYING A SHELLAC FINISH

After the surface is dry, go over it with steel wool or 5/0 sandpaper. *Rub with the grain of the wood.* Steel wool has the advantage of following the wood better and covering both high and low spots. With sandpaper, do not use a sanding block, but hold the paper in your fingers.

Before applying the second coat, wipe the surface with a clean rag to remove all dust and dirt. This coat is applied the same way as the first coat, but may have only about 40 per cent alcohol. Again go over the surface with steel wool or sandpaper. Then apply a third coat with even less alcohol, perhaps 25 per cent. After the last coat, rub the surface lightly with fine sandpaper. To get a very even, smooth surface, mix some ground pumice in oil and rub down the surface with a felt pad. After this, a still smoother surface can be obtained by mixing rottenstone with oil and rubbing it in.

Clean off the surface with a clean cloth dipped in benzene. Allow it to dry about one-half hour. Apply a good coat of wax to the surface and let it dry thoroughly. For a good polish, rub briskly with a soft cloth.

The shellac brush should be cleaned immediately with alcohol.

CAN YOU ANSWER THESE QUESTIONS ON APPLYING SHELLAC?

1. What is the source of shellac? What countries supply it?
2. How is shellac made?
3. What is meant by a 4-pound cut?
4. Shellac is what color naturally?
5. What good rule should be followed in applying shellac?
6. Shellac is available bleached. Why?
7. Describe the special brushing technique for applying shellac.
8. What is the common error made by the beginner in applying shellac?
9. List the steps that must be followed in applying a shellac finish.

Section IX

UNIT 46. VARNISH FINISH

Varnish is an excellent finishing material which will produce a very fine, practical surface. However, it is difficult to get a good varnish finish anywhere but in a dust-free room. The objection to using varnish in the small shop is that it dries so slowly that the surface becomes marred with tiny dust particles.

VARNISHES

Varnish is a liquid that can be spread on a surface in a thin film, giving the wood an even, transparent coating. It protects the surface of the wood and brightens the color of the stain. Varnishes are made by mixing various gum resins with vegetable oils, plus necessary thinners and driers. Old-style natural varnish took from twenty-four to forty-eight hours to dry. Therefore, it had the disadvantage of giving dust more time to collect and mar the surface. Synthetic, quick-drying varnishes dry overnight and are dust free in two hours after applying. For most work, select a quick-drying high gloss or stain-finish varnish. It is easier to apply and makes it easier to get a satisfactory finish.

For outside finishes subject to moisture, the best type of varnish is spar varnish. Spar varnish is also excellent for the tops of tables, cabinets, and other pieces that will have hard wear. Spar varnish is made by adding China wood oil to regular varnish, making it water repellent and heat resistant.

For the small shop, varnish should be purchased in small cans. Once a can has been opened, a scum forms on the surface which is difficult to remove and interferes with a good finish. If necessary, the varnish can be strained through a silk or fine muslin cloth to remove the scum.

APPLYING VARNISH

Find a dust-free place. If no finishing room is available, wait to do your varnishing until no woodworking machines or tools have been used for some time. Then sprinkle the floor with water to settle the dust. Also, do not varnish anything on cold and damp or hot and humid days. Make sure that the temperature is between 70 and 80 degrees. Wipe the project completely with a tack rag to remove any dust particles.

Open a small can of quick drying (synthetic-resin) varnish and pour some into a porcelain or glass container. For a first coat, add about 25 per cent turpentine. Select a 2- to 3-inch brush with long bristles. Wipe the wood surface with a clean cloth dipped in benzene.

Dip the brush in the varnish to about one third the length of the brush. Do not overload it. *Do not wipe the brush on the side of the can*, or it will dry on

46–1. For a good varnish job, tap the side of the varnish brush against a wire stretched across the pail. Don't rub the varnish brush against the edge of the can.

the rim and on the inside. These dried particles fall into the varnish and mar the finish. Figure 46–1. Apply the varnish with long, easy strokes. Brush first with the grain and then across the grain. Figure 46–2 and 46–3. When the brush is "dry," brush out the varnish with the grain, using only the tip of the brush. You can do more brushing out with varnish than you can with shellac. Continue to work from the center toward the outside edges. As you near the edges, have very little varnish on the brush to keep it from running over the edges or from piling up along the arrises. Never put your brush down on a dusty surface.

After applying the first coat, soak the brush immediately in a can of turpentine. Also, cover the varnish left in the can to keep scum from forming. Allow the varnish coat to dry about twenty-four hours, or until all tackiness has gone. After it is dry, rub the surface with the grain, using No. 6/0 sandpaper.

APPLYING A VARNISH FINISH

Make sure that the varnish is perfectly dry before applying another coat. Most of the trouble that comes when applying a varnish finish is from being too quick to apply the second and third coats. When applying the second coat, use the varnish just as it comes from the can. Brush the same way as for the first coat. Allow it to dry and rub down the surface with No. 6/0 sandpaper. If you want a dull, rubbed appearance, you can either apply a dull finish (satin) varnish as a third coat or rub down the regular varnish with pumice and oil and rottenstone and oil. Figure 46–4. You can also rub the surface with 3/0 steel wool to get a dull finish.

After the varnish has dried thor-

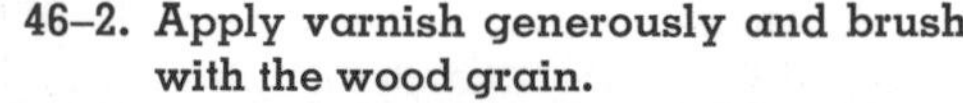

46–2. Apply varnish generously and brush with the wood grain.

46–3. Brush across the grain to level out the varnish.

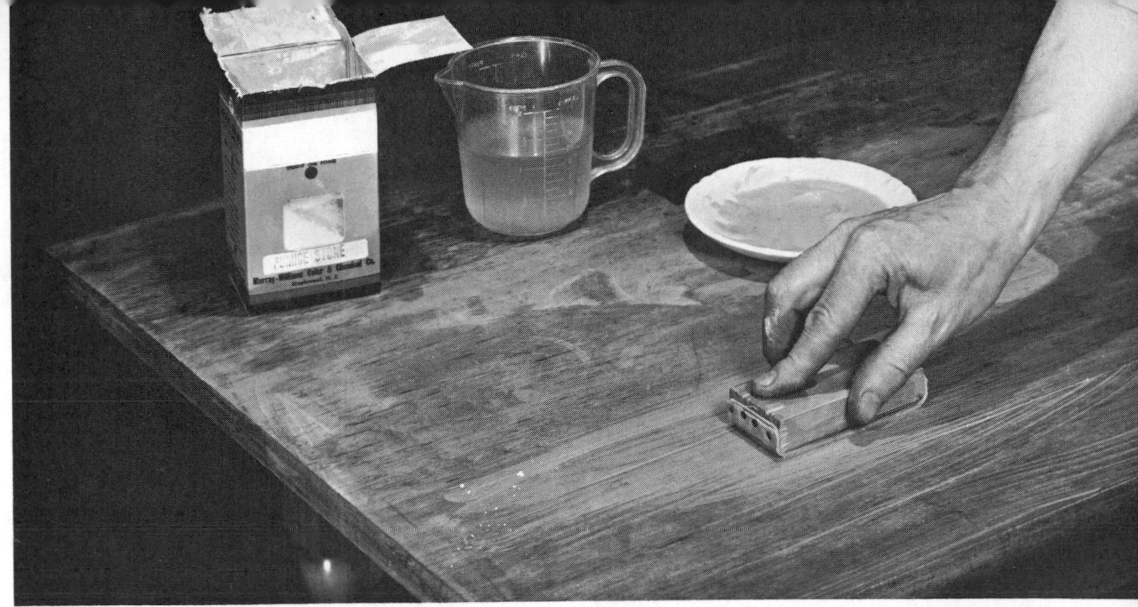

46–4. **Rubbing down a varnished surface with pumice and water, using a felt pad.**

oughly, apply a good paste wax. Polish with a clean piece of cheesecloth.

VARNISH STAINS

A simple finish for many projects is a varnish stain that will give the desired color and finish in one coat. Varnish stain finish is especially satisfactory for simple woodworking projects or when the time cannot be given to applying many coats of regular varnish. Varnish stains can be purchased in different colors. Apply the same as varnish; dry two to eight hours.

CAN YOU ANSWER THESE QUESTIONS ON APPLYING VARNISH?

1. Why is it difficult to obtain a good varnished surface?
2. Tell from what and how varnishes are made.
3. When buying varnish, what considerations should be taken into account?
4. How and why is varnish strained?
5. What conditions must prevail to obtain a good varnish surface?
6. Describe the technique for applying varnish. How does it differ from the technique for applying shellac?
7. Should the first varnish coat be applied full strength?
8. List the steps to be followed in applying a varnish finish.
9. Name the most common mistake made in varnishing.
10. How can a dull finish be obtained?
11. What is a varnish stain? Why is it commonly used by beginners?

Section IX

UNIT 47. APPLYING PENETRATING AND WIPE-ON FINISHES

There are many modern commercial finishes that can be used in the shop with a minimum of difficulty. These include finishes that sink into the wood. Figure 47–1. Most can be applied with a small cloth or pad, eliminating the need for spray equipment or brushes. These finishes also do away with the dust problem that is so bothersome when using varnish. Penetrating and wipe-on finishes are synthetic, chemical materials.

SEALACELL

This is a three-step process involving three different materials to complete the finish. Each can be applied with a rag or cloth. The materials include the following:

a. Sealacell is a moisture repellent, penetrating wood sealer that is applied over the raw wood. (Ground-in-oil pigments can be mixed with the Sealacell to serve as a stain). Stain and filler can be applied in one step by mixing paste filler in the Sealacell and then adding ground-in-oil pigment to get the wanted color. Apply very liberally with a cloth, as the depth of penetration depends upon the amount applied. Let dry overnight. Buff lightly with fine steel wool.

b. Varno wax is a blend of gums and waxes. To apply, make a small cloth pad about 1″ x 2″. Coat with wax and rub with a circular motion first and then wipe out with the grain. Buff lightly with 3/0 steel wool.

c. Royal finish is the final coat. It is applied in the same manner as the Varno wax. Two or more applications of Royal finish increase the depth and luster. A soft egg-shell finish can be obtained by buffing the finish with fine steel wool.

MINWAX WOOD

Minwax is a penetrating wood seal and wax that is applied directly to raw wood. Two coats will complete the job. The natural beauty of the wood is preserved because this finish penetrates and seals, leaving the finish in the wood with very little on the surface. Minwax is available in natural, light oak, pine, dark walnut, colonial maple, and red mahogany. It dries rapidly and more than one coat can be applied in one day. Although it isn't necessary to rub between each coat, it is a good idea to use 4/0 steel wool to obtain a very fine finish.

DEFT

Deft is a semi-gloss, clear, interior wood finish. It is easy to use, requires no thinning, will not show brush marks, and will not darken. This material seals, primes, finishes the wood, and dries in 30 minutes. Three coats are recommended. The first coat seals the wood. The second coat adds depth.

The third coat results in a mirror-smooth, fine furniture finish. The third coat can be sanded with 6/0 wet-dry sandpaper or rubbed mirror-smooth with pumice and rottenstone. All three coats can be applied in a few hours. Deft can also be applied from an aerosol spray can.

PENETRATING FLOOR FINISH AND WAX

There are many commercial penetrating floor finishes for projects. Apply one coat with a rag. Allow to dry as specified on the container. Buff the surface with a pad of 3/0 steel wool. Apply a second coat and buff with 6/0 steel wool. Then apply a good coat of paste wax and wipe with a soft cloth.

OIL ("FRENCH" STYLE) FINISH

Woods like walnut, mahogany, and cherry can be finished by applying many coats of linseed oil mixed with turpentine. The common mixtures are either two-thirds boiled linseed oil and one-third turpentine or one-half raw linseed oil and one-half turpentine heated quite hot. To apply the finish, soak a soft, lint-free cloth with the mixture and rub vigorously over the entire surface. Allow to dry for about 15 minutes and then wipe thoroughly with a clean cloth. Each coat must dry about twenty-four hours. Then rub the surface hard for about 15 minutes. Dry at least a week this time. Then apply a minimum of three additional coats in the same manner. This should be repeated over several weeks until a very lustrous finish appears. To prevent warping, oil the underside of the wood.

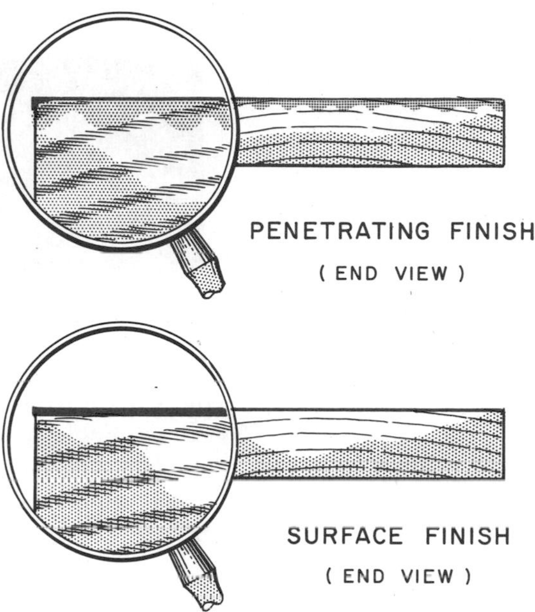

47–1. Here you see the difference between a penetrating finish and a surface finish.

CAN YOU ANSWER THESE QUESTIONS ABOUT APPLYING PENETRATING AND WIPE-ON FINISHES?

1. What does "penetrating" mean? How does it differ from a surface finish?
2. Describe the way to apply a Sealacell finish.
3. Tell how to apply an oil finish.
4. Why is Minwax a simple finish to apply?
5. How many coats of Deft should be used?
6. On what woods is an oil finish often applied?

Section IX

UNIT 48. LACQUER

Lacquer is a chemical composition of nitrocellulose, resins, and solvents. Lacquers have come into common use in both clear and colored forms for wood surfaces. They dry quickly and produce a hard finish. Most commercial lacquer finishes are applied by spraying, but the brush finish is usually done in most small shops. Because lacquer contains substances that are similar to paint and varnish remover, it cannot be applied directly over paint or varnish. Always use a lacquer thinner for thinning the materials and for cleaning the brushes.

APPLYING A CLEAR BRUSH LACQUER FINISH

Apply the stain and filler coats the same as for shellac and varnish finishes. It is better to use a water stain than an oil stain in a lacquer finish, since this does not "bleed" so much. Apply a thin coat of shellac as a sealer before applying the lacquer.

Open a can of clear brushing lacquer and stir it well. Lacquer usually does not have to be thinned but, if it does, use a commercial lacquer thinner. Select a brush with soft bristles such as a camel's-hair brush. Dip the brush about one third of the way into the lacquer but do not wipe any off on the side of the container. Load the brush heavily. Flow on the lacquer with long, rapid strokes. Lap the sides of each stroke. Do not attempt to brush it in as you would paint or varnish. Remember, lacquer dries very quickly and gives a smooth, tough surface. Allow the lacquer to dry about two hours. Then go over the surface lightly with No. 6/0 sandpaper.

Apply second and third coats in the same way. After the third coat is dry, the surface is rubbed with rottenstone and oil and pumice stone and oil. Lacquer brushes should be cleaned with commercial lacquer thinner.

APPLYING COLORED LACQUER FINISH

Sand the wood surface with No. 2/0 sandpaper. Then apply a thin coat of shellac to the wood as a base for the lacquer. Apply two or three coats of the colored lacquer the same as for clear lacquer. To finish the surface, rub it down with rottenstone and oil after the lacquer is dry.

APPLYING LACQUER FROM AN AEROSOL CAN

For small projects and for repair work, one of the best methods of

48–1. Applying lacquer from an aerosol can.

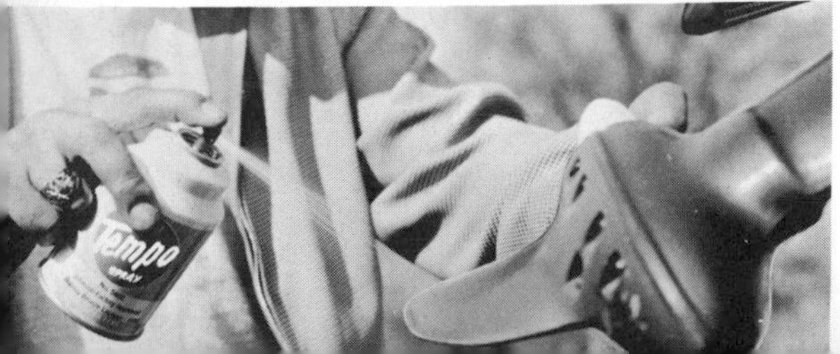

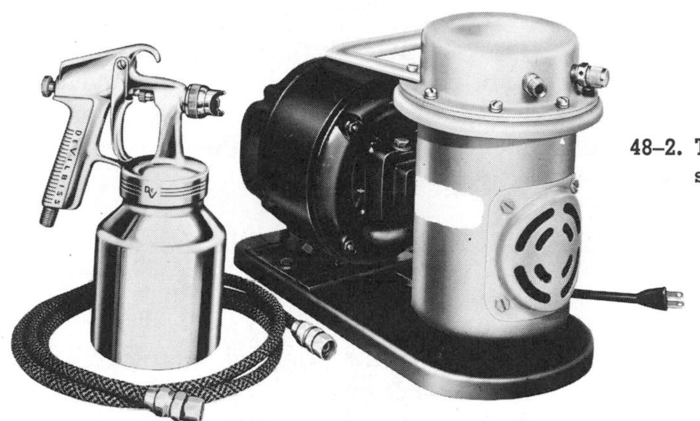

48–2. This type of spraying unit is satisfactory for small projects.

applying clear or colored lacquer is from a self-spraying (aerosol) can. The aerosol can contains about half lacquer (or paint) and half liquid gas. In using a spray can, hold so the valve is about 12 to 15 inches from the surface. Figure 48–1. Move the can back and forth, keeping it an equal distance from the surface. If sags or runs develop, you are trying to cover too fast. Remember that the hiding power of lacquers varies with the color. If you are spraying light-colored lacquer, apply a series of several light coats. If you are spraying on bare metal, apply a lacquer primer before the finish coat.

APPLYING A SPRAY LACQUER FINISH

Spraying is the most common method in industry of applying a lacquer finish. A spray booth should be available. Spraying can be done out of doors on a calm day; however, a mask must be worn. There are many kinds of spraying equipment. For simple work, a small spray gun and compressor are all you will need. Figure 48–2.

SPRAYING A PROJECT

1. Clean the surface first with a tack rag.

2. Check the gun to make sure that it is clean.

3. Fill the spray container about half full of lacquer and one fourth full of lacquer thinner.

4. Try the spray gun on a piece of scrap stock. It should spray with a fine even mist. Hold the gun about 6 to 8 inches from the work and move back and forth with straight, uniform strokes. Figure 48–3. Always keep the gun perpendicular to the surface at all times. Start the stroke off the work and pull the trigger when the gun is just opposite the edge. Release the trigger

48–3. Spraying a cedar chest in a ventilated spray booth.

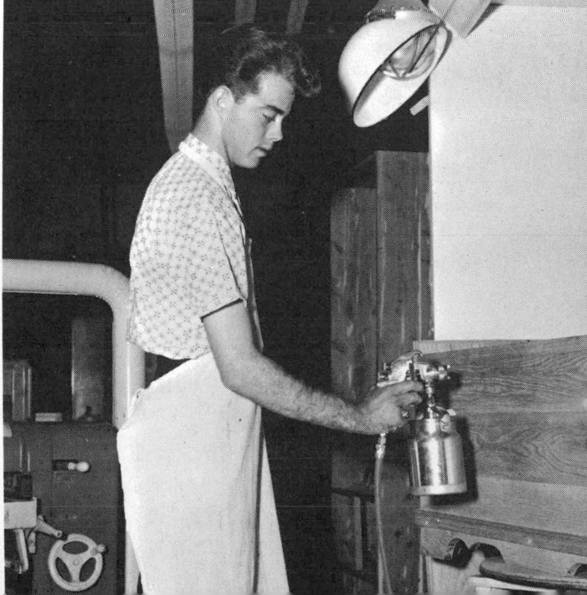

at the other end. After a lacquer (sanding) sealer has been applied and sanded, then spray on four or five coats of thin lacquer. Usually the first two coats are gloss or bright and then the last two coats are made dull or semi-gloss by rubbing. After you have finished spraying, clean all the equipment with lacquer thinner.

CAN YOU ANSWER THESE QUESTIONS ON LACQUER?

1. What is lacquer? Can it be applied over a painted or varnished surface?
2. How is lacquer most often applied commercially?
3. Describe the correct brushing technique for applying lacquer.
4. How many coats of lacquer are usually needed to obtain a good finish?
5. What is the principal advantage of a lacquer finish?
6. Describe the correct method of using spraying equipment.

Section IX

UNIT 49. ENAMEL

Enamel is composed largely of colored varnish. It differs from paint in that it contains varnish resins. Enamel is also only semiopaque (partly transparent). Therefore the primer coat must be opaque (can't be seen through) to be suitable. Enamels dry with either a high gloss or semigloss, depending on the amount of resins. Enamels are extremely satisfactory for small projects on which a colored finish is desired. Figure 49–1.

APPLYING ENAMEL FINISH

Sand the wood surface with No. 2/0 sandpaper. Cover all knots and sap

49–1. This decorator lamp was made from inexpensive wood and then finished by applying several coats of colored enamel.

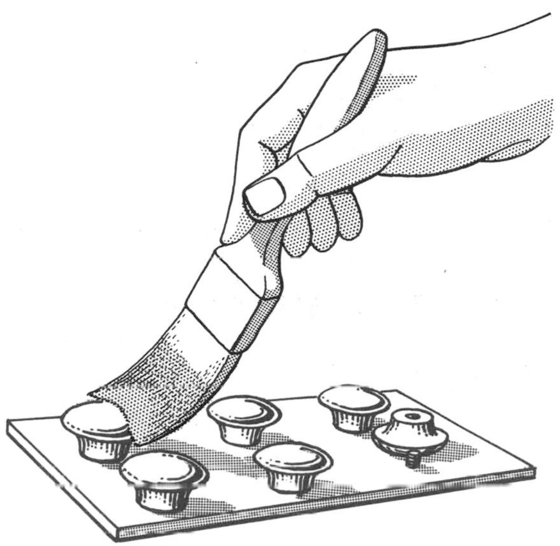

49–2. Paint knobs like this.

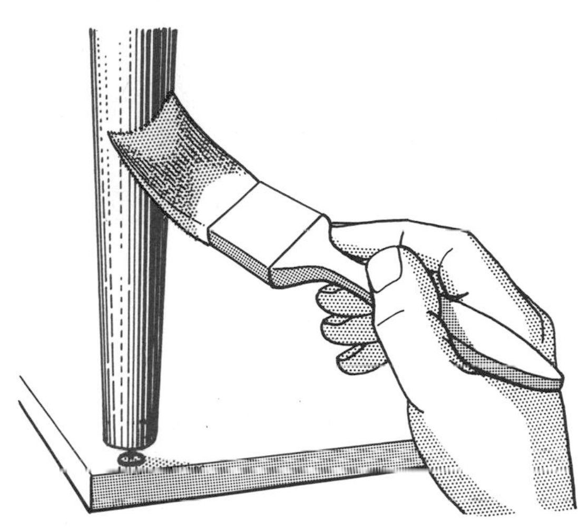

49–3. Note the correct technique for painting round tapered legs.

streaks with a coat of thin shellac. Select a can of enamel paint undercoat and mix it thoroughly. Use a 2- or 3-inch brush and apply the undercoat the same as varnish. In applying enamel, flow the finish on with short, light strokes. Work in small areas about two feet wide. When the brush is as dry as possible, go back over the surface, stroking the same direction. To paint knobs, first attach the knobs to a piece of cardboard and then paint with a small brush. Figure 49–2. To paint legs, first insert a large tack partway into the bottom of each table leg to raise the table slightly off the floor. Figure 49–3. Then apply the enamel from top to bottom with long, smooth brush strokes.

After the surface has thoroughly dried, sand lightly with No. 2/0 sandpaper. Then apply a second undercoat. Select quick-drying finish enamel of the desired color. Apply one or two coats the same way as the undercoat. If you want a dull finish use satin varnish or allow the final gloss coat to dry for a day or two and then rub down the surface with pumice stone and water.

CAN YOU ANSWER THESE QUESTIONS ON ENAMEL?

1. In what ways does enamel differ from paint?
2. Why is a primer coat put on first?
3. Why is enamel a desirable finish for small projects?
4. What things should be done before the first coat of enamel is applied?
5. How does the brushing technique differ from that for applying paint?
6. How can you get a dull finish?

Section IX

UNIT 50. PAINT

Painting is a good way to finish less expensive pieces of furniture and cabinetwork. Figure 50–1. Paints are made from many materials including white lead and zinc, linseed oil, turpentine, drier, and coloring. Many of the newer types of paint are made entirely from chemicals. The basic source of many paints is petroleum. Paints are available either as outside or inside types. In applying paint to a surface, usually three coats are given: primer, undercoat, and finishing.

50–1. Applying a primer coat to a cabinet made of fir plywood.

APPLYING A PAINT FINISH

Sand the wood surface with No. 1 or No. 0 sandpaper. Apply a light coat of shellac to wood that is porous or that contains knots and sap streaks. Open a can of the primer paint. Pour off the light liquid on the top into a second container. Thoroughly stir the primer and then gradually add the clear liquid until it is mixed. For the first coat, thin the paint with turpentine and/or linseed oil. Sometimes a small amount of yellow ochre is also added to the primer for better coverage. Use a good brush of the right size for the project and apply a thin coat of the primer.

To apply paint, put a small amount on the brush and brush it into the surface. Beginners usually apply paint too thick and do not brush it in thoroughly. Allow the paint to dry from twelve to twenty-four hours and then go over the surface with No. 1 sandpaper. Now apply the undercoat. This coat should be thinned somewhat with turpentine. Go over the surface thoroughly, covering all parts of the project. Apply the final coat just as it comes from the can, after a thorough mixing. Thoroughly brush the paint in, making sure that a smooth, even coat is applied. When painting two or more colors on the same project, it is a good idea to use masking tape for color separation. Figure 50–2.

50–2. Masking tape protects the edge of the top surface from accidental brush marks and smears. This eliminates the time-consuming job of clean-up. The tape is readily stripped off afterwards, assuring a neater finish than by any other method.

CAN YOU ANSWER THESE QUESTIONS ON PAINT?

1. From what are paints made?
2. How many coats are usually applied to obtain a good surface?
3. Describe the proper method of mixing a primer paint.
4. Should anything be added to the first coat? Explain.
5. Beginners usually encounter certain difficulties in learning to paint correctly. How can these difficulties be overcome?
6. What material can be added to the primer which will provide better coverage?
7. List the steps followed in painting a wood surface, beginning with the primer coat and continuing until the final coat is applied.

Section X
Tool Maintenance

The final step in hand woodworking—what you must know and be able to do.

51. Single-edge cutting tools: all steps in accomplishing a good, new cutting edge such as removing the old edge, grinding the angle, and whetting the edge; special problems in sharpening a hand scraper, grinding a screw driver and sharpening a handsaw.

In this book, only one unit is given to tool maintenance. However, this is a step ahead. In earlier woodworking experience, your teacher probably kept tools sharp for the class. Here is an opportunity to learn how to put a bad edge in condition by grinding to the correct angle and honing. The unit also includes sharpening an auger bit and maintaining a screw driver blade. See the "box" above. Further steps are on pp. 15, 43, 60, 94, 108, 132, 143, 170, 219.

Section X

UNIT 51. SHARPENING HAND TOOLS

If it would be possible to choose one rule which was more important than any other in woodworking, it might be this:

Successful woodwork depends upon good cutting edges.

For example, if you have used a plane that digs in, sticks, is hard to push, or leaves grooves in the work, you will understand why good cutting tools are so necessary. Time spent on tool sharpening is well rewarded in better and easier work.

Nothing is so important to good workmanship as well-conditioned tools. With tools that are correctly ground, woodworking can be interesting and pleasant. Dull, marred tools, on the other hand, cause accidents or bad temper and always result in poor workmanship.

SHARPENING SINGLE-EDGED TOOLS

Several single-edged tools, such as plane irons, chisels, and spokeshave blades, are sharpened in the same general way. A description of sharpening a plane iron will show how to sharpen all of these tools.

A plane iron needs to be reground if it is badly nicked or untrue, or if the bevel is rounded, too blunt, or too thin. Before regrinding the plane iron, decide what the shape of the cutting edge should be. For most general work the cutting edge should be straight with the corners slightly rounded to keep them from digging into the wood. For rough planing, the entire edge should be slightly rounded, with the center of the cutting edge about 1/32 inch higher than the corners.

REMOVE THE OLD EDGE

Leave the plane-iron cap fastened to the iron to act as a guide. Hold the plane iron at right angles to the grinding wheel. Move it back and forth to grind off the old cutting edge until all nicks are removed and the edge is square with the sides. (This last reshaping needs to be done only when the plane iron is in very poor condition.) Check the edge for squareness with a try square. Hold the handle against the side of the plane iron. After the edge is square, remove the cap.

GRIND THE PLANE IRON

The plane iron, chisel, and other single-edge tools usually are ground with a bevel that is 2 or 2½ times longer than the thickness of the blade. Figure 51–1. The smaller angle, about 20 degrees, is used on softwoods and the more blunt angle, about 25 to 30 degrees, on hardwoods. Before grinding the bevel, the wheel should be checked to make sure that it is true and that the face is square. Also, the wheel

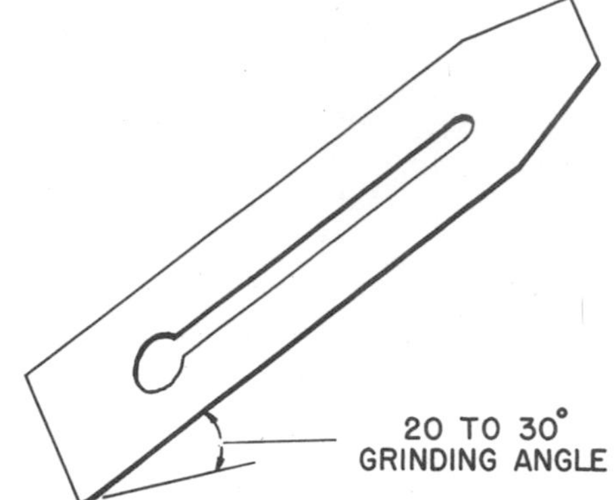

51–1. A plane-iron blade should be ground at an angle of 20 to 30 degrees. The length of the bevel should be about 2 to 2½ times the thickness of the blade.

must be turning towards the cutting edge.

If a grinding attachment is available, use it to hold the plane iron. This will assure you that the correct bevel will be ground. Figure 51–2. If one is not available, hold the plane iron in both hands as in Figure 51–3. Carefully move the plane iron back and forth across the grinding wheel. Figure 51–4. Do not apply too much pressure, as this would overheat the edge. Frequently remove the blade and dip it in water to cool it and to prevent the temper from being drawn from the steel. If you are grinding freehand, move the tool slowly back to the wheel to get the "feel" of the angle. Be sure that you continue grinding at the same angle as before. As the cutting edge is formed, a slight burr may appear. This will be removed later. As the final grinding is done, make sure that you have a single surface on the bevel and that the bevel is at the correct angle. This can be checked with a sliding T bevel or the protractor head of a combination set.

WHETTING OR HONING THE EDGE

Select an oilstone with a flat, true surface. There are two classes of oilstone for this purpose. The natural stones, such as the Arkansas and Washita, are white in color; the artificial oilstones are made either of aluminum

51–2. Grinding a plane-iron blade held in an attachment. This is the simplest method since, once the angle has been set, it is easy to keep the bevel even. However, care must be taken not to burn the cutting edge, especially when using a dry grinder as shown here. Courtesy the Jam Handy Organization.

51–3. Grinding a plane-iron blade without the use of a guide. In using this method, the plane iron should be moved from right to left constantly and should be cooled frequently in water. It takes considerable skill to keep the bevel even when grinding in this manner. Courtesy the Jam Handy Organization.

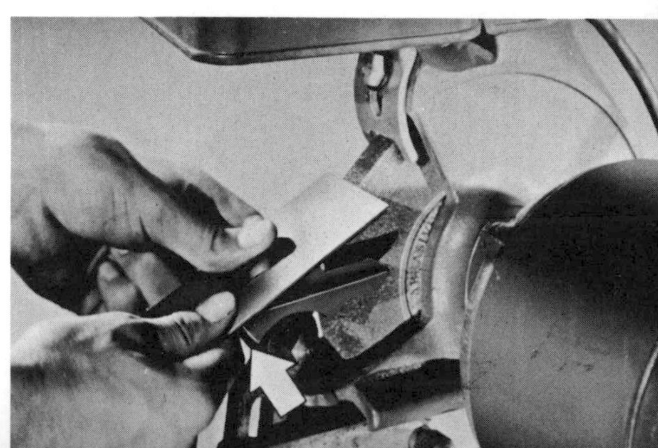

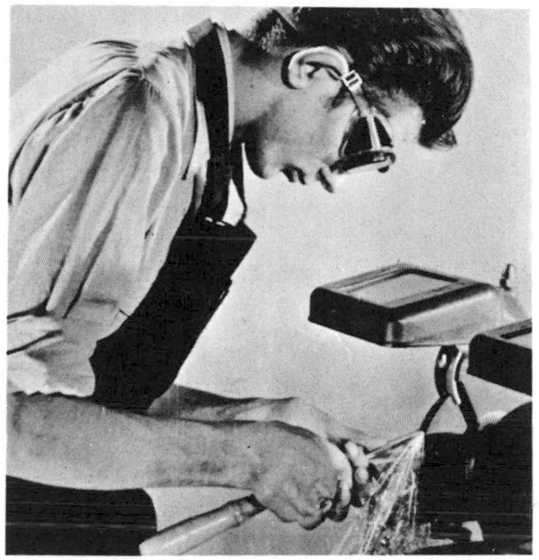

51–4. Grinding a chisel. Notice especially that safety glasses are being worn and that the eye shield is in place. Courtesy the Jam Handy Organization.

oxide, which is brownish in color, or silicon carbide, which is grayish in color. A combination artificial oilstone is best; one surface is coarse and the other surface is fine. Figure 51–5.

Wipe off the stone and then apply a mixture of half kerosene and half machine oil to the surface. Hold the plane iron on the oilstone with the bevel side down. First apply pressure on the heel of the bevel, then slowly raise the plane iron until the bevel is in contact with the oilstone surface. Figure 51–6.

51–5. Fine and coarse oilstones.

The whetting angle should be between 30 and 35 degrees. Move the tool back and forth on the face of the oilstone or in a circular motion to form a figure 8. A wire or feather edge will form on the cutting edge. To remove this, turn the plane iron around with the side opposite the bevel flat against the oilstone. Move it back and forth a few times. *Make sure that you hold the tool flat.* Figure 51–7. The slightest bevel on this side would prevent the plane-iron cap from fitting properly. Then chips would get between the cap and the iron.

If the wire edge is not completely removed, the cutting edge should be pushed across the corner of a piece of softwood. The finer side of the oilstone can be used to sharpen the plane iron to an even keener edge.

TEST THE PLANE IRON FOR SHARPNESS

One method is to hold the plane iron with the cutting edge down and allow

51–6. Whetting a plane iron. Hold the iron with the bevel side down at a slightly greater angle than that at which it is ground. Apply oil to the stone and move the plane iron back and forth or in a circle-8 movement.

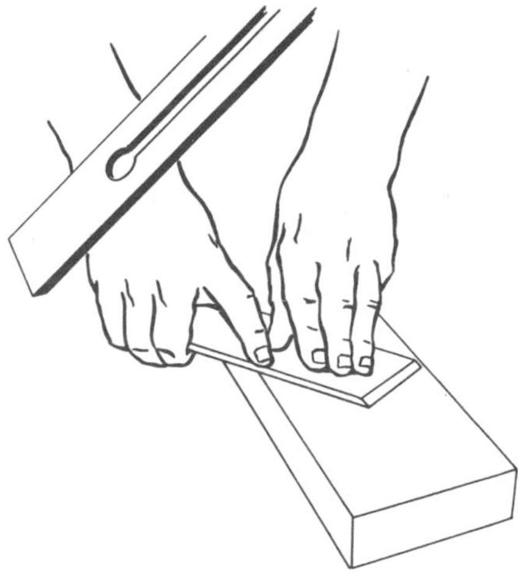

51–7. **Remove the burr from the cutting edge by holding the plane iron flat on the stone. The photograph above shows an enlargement of the cutting edge before and after the burr has been removed.**

the edge to rest lightly on the thumbnail. As the tool is moved, it tends to "bite" into the nail if it is sharp. It will slide across easily if it is dull. Another method is to look carefully at the edge. If it is sharp, the edge cannot be seen.

51–8. **Draw filing the hand scraper. Use a fine file in this manner until the edge is square with the sides of the scraper. To prevent surplus vibration, lower the scraper in the vise.**

If it is dull, a thin, white line can be seen.

Be careful when assembling the plane iron and cap and when inserting them into the plane so as not to nick the cutting edge.

SHARPENING A HAND SCRAPER

A hand scraper must be sharpened frequently. The good woodworker sharpens it every time he uses it. Place the tool in a vise with the cutting edge showing. To remove the old cutting edge, hold a file flat against the side of

51–9. **Whetting the edge of the scraper. Hold the scraper at right angles to the stone and move it back and forth.**

51–10. Hold the scraper flat against the stone on both sides to remove any burr.

the scraper and take a few strokes. Then use a fine file to drawfile the edge until it is square with the sides of the scraper. Figure 51–8.

Whet the cutting edge by moving it back and forth across an oilstone. Hold the blade at right angles to the surface. Figure 51–9. Then hold the sides of the blade flat against the stone, again working it back and forth, to remove the wire edge. Figure 51–10.

Place the scraper flat on the bench with the cutting edge extending slightly over the edge of the bench. Hold a burnisher flat on the side of the scraper and take a few, firm strokes toward you to draw the edge. Figure 51–11.

51–11. A burnisher.

51–12. Drawing out the edge. Use a burnishing tool. Hold the scraper on the bench top as you work.

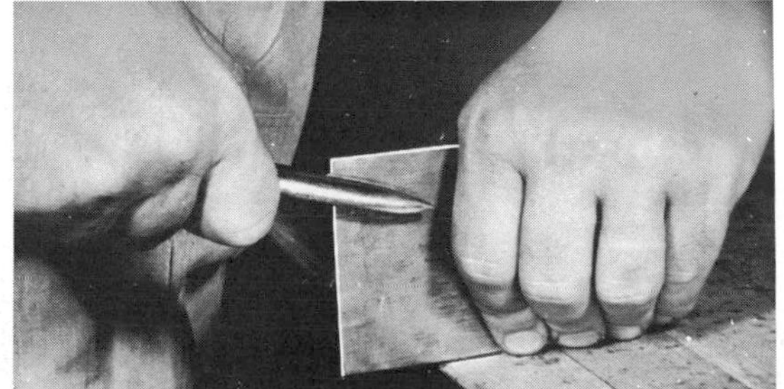

Then hold the scraper on edge as shown in Figure 51–12. Use the burnishing tool held at an angle of about 85 degrees to turn the edge of the scraper. Figure 51–13. This is done by drawing the burnisher up with a firm, brisk stroke. The edge is sharp when it will "catch" your thumb as it is drawn across it.

SHARPENING AN AUGER BIT

The auger bit must be kept sharp to obtain best results. Sharpening is done by filing the spur and the lip with a small half-round or three-cornered file. Figure 51–14. File the spur on the inside to keep the same general shape. Never file the outside. File the lip on the underside or the side toward the

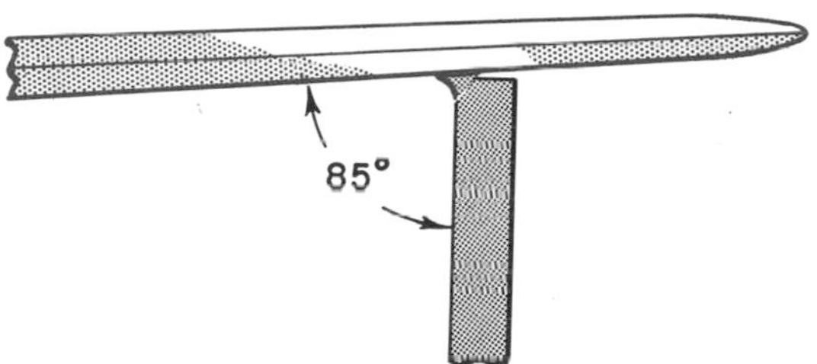

51–13. After the edge is drawn out, hold the burnishing tool at an angle of about 85 degrees to the side of the scraper and turn the edge.

51–14. Sharpening an auger bit.

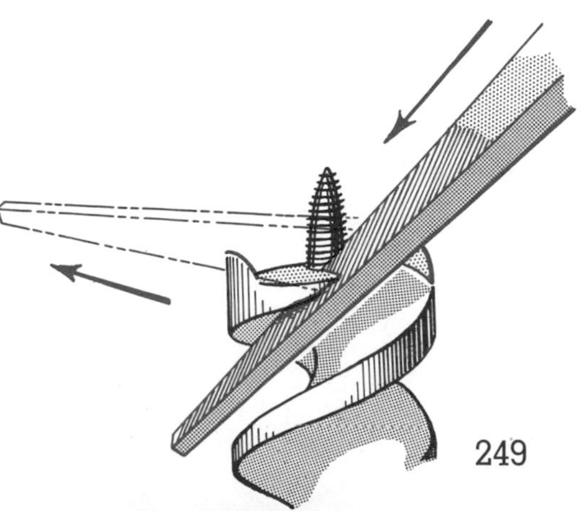

shank until it has a sharp cutting edge. Keep the bits in good condition by cleaning off the pitch with solvent. Use steel wool to polish the surface.

51–15. Good and bad tips: a damaged tip that needs regrinding, a worn tip that should be reground, and the correctly ground screw driver. Courtesy the Jam Handy Organization.

51–16. Sharpening the tip of the screw driver.

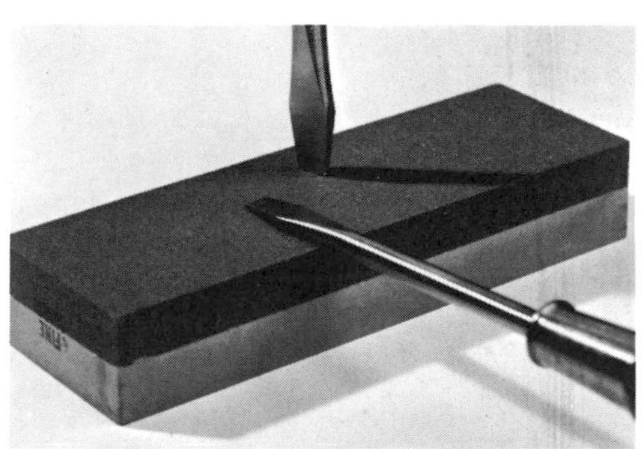

SHARPENING A DRAWKNIFE

The drawknife can be sharpened on the grinding wheel in the same general way as a plane iron. Hold the drawknife with one handle against the top of the bench and the other handle in your hand. Hold a small oilstone in the other hand and move it back and forth along the bevel to make a keen edge.

GRINDING A SCREW DRIVER

The screw driver is one of the most badly misused tools in the woodshop. Figure 51–15. Very often it is not ground properly, with the result that a burr forms when screws are set. These burrs in screws are both dangerous and unsightly. The screw driver should be ground with a slight taper on either side and the end flat, as shown in Figure 51–16.

SHARPENING A SAW

Sharpening and setting a handsaw takes much experience. It should not be attempted by anyone who does not perform the job frequently. All the teeth have to be filed until they are all the same height. Then they must be reshaped by filing. Finally the teeth have to be set by bending them alter-

51–17. Grinding angles for wood-turning tools.

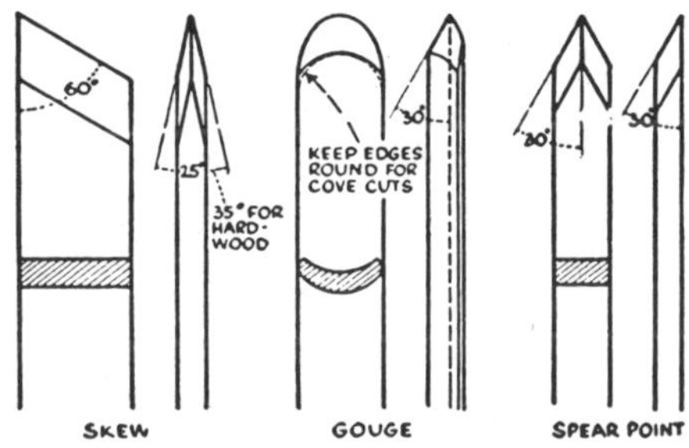

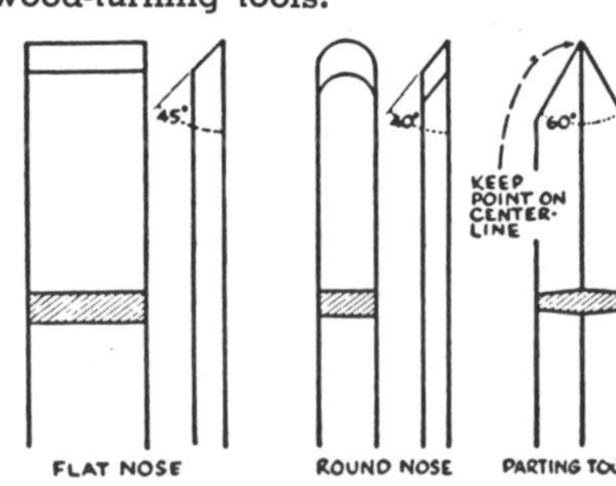

nately to left and right. In using a saw, therefore, one should appreciate how difficult resharpening is. The need for sharpening can be greatly cut down by proper use of the saw at all times.

SHARPENING TURNING TOOLS

Proper grinding angles for wood-turning tools are shown in Figure 51–17. Sharpening is done the same as for a chisel.

CAN YOU ANSWER THESE QUESTIONS ON SHARPENING HAND TOOLS?

1. Why is it important to keep the tools sharp?
2. What can be done to correct a badly nicked cutting edge?
3. At what angle should a plane iron be ground for softwood? For hardwood?
4. At what angle should a plane iron be whetted?
5. How is the edge of a hand scraper shaped? At what angle should the burnishing tool be held?
6. Tell how to test a plane iron for sharpness.
7. Describe the correct way to grind a screw driver.
8. Are saws commonly sharpened by beginners in woodworking? Explain your answer.

Section XI
Machine Woodworking

Industry makes use of power equipment to process lumber from raw material to the finished product. With machines, much of the hard work of using hand tools is eliminated. Machines also do a much more accurate job than can be done by most woodworkers with hand tools. However, machine tools require skill that is entirely different. Also, they can be dangerous, especially if used carelessly or by inexperienced persons. Make sure that you study the safety rules and regulations and learn the proper procedure before attempting to use machines. You should also obtain your instructor's permission. He will decide when you are ready to use power tools.

Making wood products with power tools is an interesting and satisfying experience. The work progresses very rapidly as well as with much less effort. Of course, it is very important to make sure that all power tools are in top working condition before attempting to use them.

GENERAL SAFETY RULES

1. Never use woodworking machinery until you have been given proper safety instruction. Always get your teacher's permission before using a machine.
2. Keep all safety guards in proper position. There are few operations on the circular saw for which it is necessary to remove the guard. Make sure that you use special setups and extreme care for these operations.
3. Always wear clothes properly. Roll up your sleeves, tuck in your tie, and put on a shop apron.
4. Always remove rings, wristwatches, pins, and other jewelry before operating a machine.
5. Plan your work before you start to use the machine.
6. Never start or stop a machine for another student.
7. Keep your fingers and hands away from moving parts of machines.
8. Keep the floor around the machine clear of lumber scraps, waste pieces, and oil.
9. Never force material into the machine faster than it will cut.
10. Never stand in line with a revolving blade or wheel.
11. Make sure that all clamps are

securely fastened before turning on the power.

12. Never remove or change a guard without getting your teacher's permission.

13. Inspect wood carefully for nails, screws, and knots before machining.

14. Keep the table of the machine and other work surfaces clear of excess materials and tools.

15. Never feed stock into a machine until it has reached full speed.

16. Never hurry when working on a machine.

17. Always make sure that the machine has come to a dead stop before oiling, cleaning, or adjusting.

18. Always clean sawdust and scraps of wood from the machine with a brush.

19. Turn off the power immediately if the machine does not sound right.

20. Never attempt to do cutting with a dull blade.

21. Never stand around a machine that is operated by other students.

22. Use hand tools and processes for very simple operations or for work on very small pieces of wood.

23. For special setups make sure that all clamps are securely fastened. It is a good idea to have the instructor check the setup before doing the machining.

24. Keep your mind on your work. Don't become distracted by other students in the class. Be careful not to bother other students who are operating a machine.

25. If a machine is not operating properly, always report it to your instructor.

26. Take your time when working with a machine. Most accidents happen by not following instructions or by trying to do things too fast.

27. Never try to stop a machine after the power is off by forcing a piece of wood into the blade or knives.

28. Always stay next to a machine until it has come to a dead stop.

29. When you are through using a machine, always remove any special setups, clean off the waste stock and place it in the scrap box, and leave the machine in its normal operating condition with the power shut off.

Section XI

UNIT 52. PLANER OR SURFACER

The thickness planer or *surfacer* is a simple machine to use. It is designed to do one job, namely, to surface boards to thickness. Figure 52–1. It will not straighten a board that is warped! The cutting head of the planer is mounted above the table so only the top of a board is surfaced. This machine is self feeding. After stock has been fed into it, it will continue through the machine by itself. The size of the planer is indicated by the maximum width and thickness that can be surfaced. For example, if the capacity is 18 by 6 inches, the largest pieces that can be surfaced are ones that are 18 inches wide and 6 inches thick.

PARTS OF THE PLANER

Major parts include a motor, cutter head, in-feed and out-feed rolls, chip breaker, pressure bar, table, and feed control wheel. The machine operates as follows: As the stock is fed in, the upper corrugated *in-feed roll* grips the stock and moves it toward the cutter head. Figure 52–2. The *chip breaker* presses firmly on the top of the wood to prevent the grain from tearing out. The *rotating cutter head* surfaces the board much like a jointer. Then the

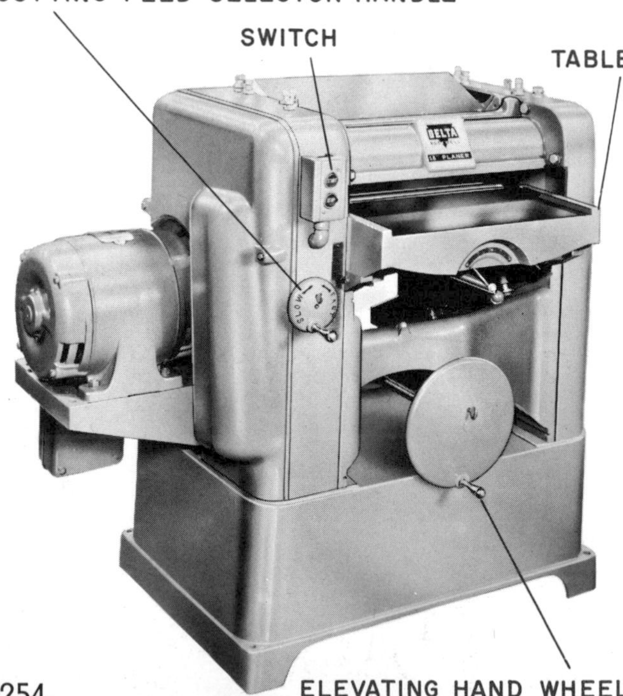

52–1. An 18-inch thickness planer or surfacer.

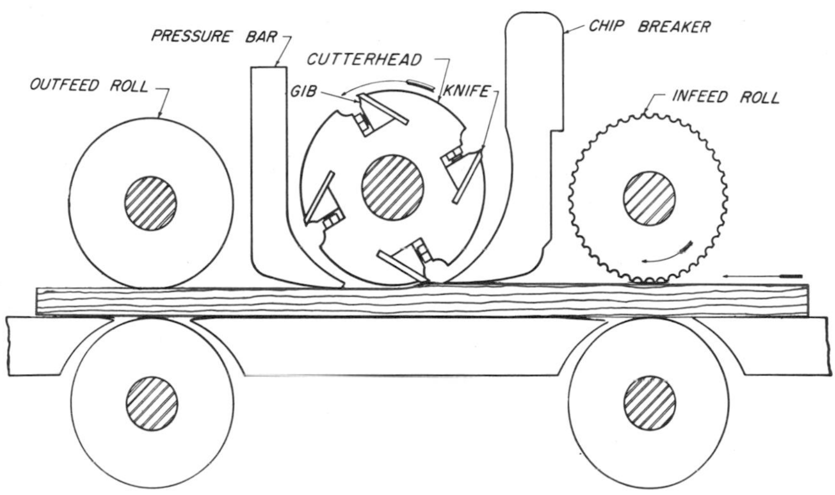

52–2. Cross section of a planer head.

pressure bar, back of the cutter head, holds the stock firmly against the table. The *out-feed roll* helps move the stock out the back of the machine.

On small machines the controls are relatively simple: (a) a switch to turn on the machine, (b) a hand wheel which elevates or lowers the table, (c) the pointer on the table that indicates thickness of the stock after it has been fed through the machine, (d) a feed control lever which operates the feed control, and (e) a control that regulates the rate of feed from slow to fast (some machines do not have this feature). Figure 52–3.

SAFETY

1. Check the board to be sure it is free of nails, loose knots, and other imperfections.
2. Always stand to one side when planing, never directly behind the board.
3. Never attempt to plane more than one thickness at a time. If several boards of different thicknesses are to be surfaced, always plane the thick one first until it is about the same thickness as the others.
4. Never look into the planer as the board is passing through. Loose chips may be thrown back with great force, causing an eye injury.
5. Plane a warped board only when one surface has been trued on a jointer.
6. Make sure that the board is at least two inches longer than the dis-

52–3. The variable speed cutting feed makes it possible to select any feed range from 15 to 36 feet per minute.

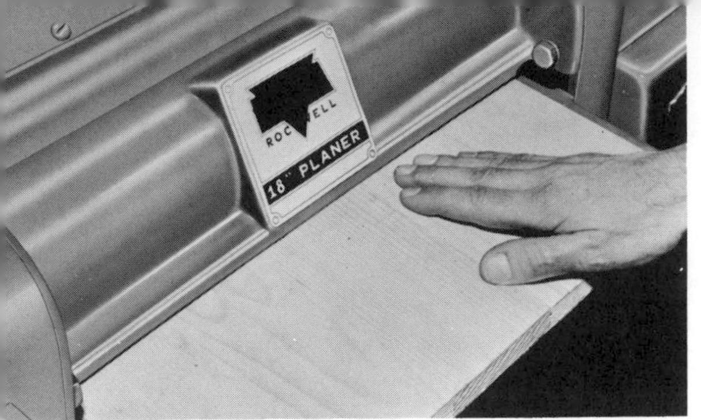

52–4. Feeding the stock through the planer.

tance between the feed rolls. For a small planer, this usually means a board should be at least 14 inches long.

7. When thin stock is to be planed, always place it on a thicker piece that has larger dimensions of width and length.

8. Keep your hands away from the board after it starts through the planer.

9. If a board should stick, lower the table and turn off the switch.

USING THE PLANER

1. Measure the thickness of the board at its thickest point. Then adjust the machine to about $\frac{1}{16}$ to $\frac{1}{8}$ inch less than this. Never try to remove more than $\frac{1}{8}$ inch in thickness for rough work and $\frac{1}{16}$ inch for finished work. Figure 52–4.

2. Adjust the machine for the correct thickness.

3. Turn on the power and pull in the feed control.

4. Place the working face of the stock on the table so that the stock will feed with the grain.

5. Start the stock into the surfacer. As soon as it takes hold, remove your hands. If it should get started at a slight angle, a quick shove may straighten it.

6. After at least half the board has passed through the machine, walk around to the back and hold the end up as it goes the rest of the way through. On long stock it is a good idea to ask a helper to guide the board as it comes off the table.

7. Check the stock and then reset for thickness if another cut is to be made. The last cut should remove not more than $\frac{1}{32}$ to $\frac{1}{16}$ inch of material.

CAN YOU ANSWER THESE QUESTIONS ON THE PLANER AND SURFACER?

1. What is the purpose of a planer?
2. Will it remove warp from a board?
3. List eight safety rules to follow when using the planer.
4. What is the maximum amount of stock that should be removed at one cut?
5. Tell what to do if the board sticks in the planer.

Section XI

UNIT 53. CIRCULAR SAW

The circular saw is used more than any other machine tool in the woodshop. It consists of a *frame*, an *arbor* to hold the saw blade, the *saw blade*, a *table*, a *ripping fence*, and a *crosscutting* or *mitering gauge*. In addition, the machine should be equipped with a *guard* and *slitter* to protect the operator from injury. Figure 53–1. The size of the circular saw is indicated by the largest diameter of saw blade that can be used on the machine. The most common sizes for small shops are the 8- and 10-inch *tilt arbor saws*.

The two adjusting levers used the most are the raising wheel and the tilting wheel. The *raising wheel* is usually located under the front of the table. It is used to raise and lower the saw blade. The *tilt wheel* is usually on the left side. It is used to tilt the arbor. There are three common types of saw blades: the ripsaw, the crosscut, and the combination. Figure 53–2. In the small shop in which many different operations must be done, one after another, it is a good idea to keep a combination saw blade in the machine. Then it can be used for ripping, crosscutting, beveling, rabbeting, and many other operations. Figure 53–3.

SAFETY

The circular saw is one of the most dangerous tools in the woodshop, especially in the hands of the beginner. Therefore it is suggested that the fol-

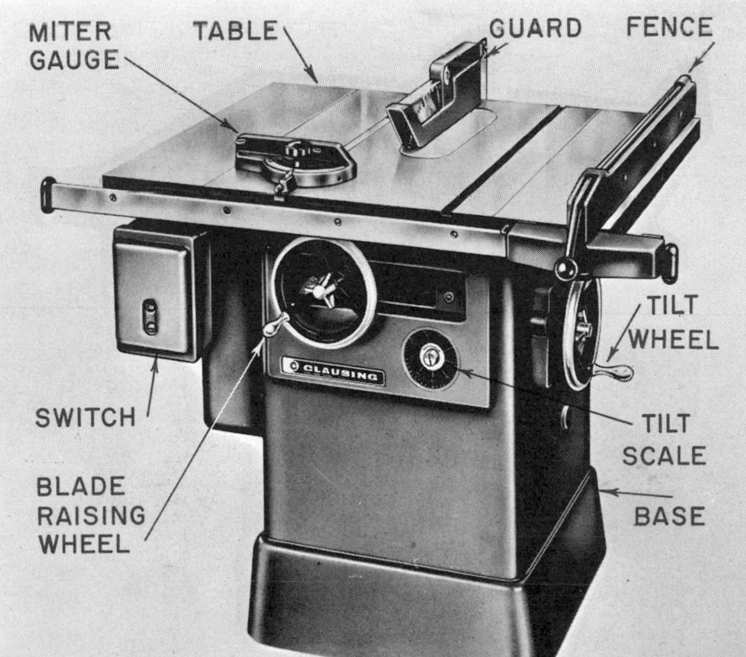

53–1. A ten-inch, floor-type circular saw of the kind most suited to school shops. Study the names of the parts. You should become familiar with them.

53–2. Three common types of saw blades, *crosscut* or *cutoff*, *rip*, and *combination*. The combination blade should be chosen when a variety of cutting operations must be done at one time.

lowing safety practices be followed when using a circular saw:

1. Make sure that the saw has a guard and slitter. The slitter holds the stock open after it has been cut so that it won't tend to bend or kick back. Figure 53–4.

2. Always stand to one side of the saw blade, never directly back of it. If a piece does kick back it won't strike you.

3. Make sure that the saw blade is sharpened properly. A dull saw is frequently the cause of kickback.

4. Always set the saw so that it is about ⅛ inch higher than the thickness of the stock to be cut.

5. Never reach over the saw with your hand.

6. When ripping stock to narrow widths, always use a push stick to complete the ripping. Never place your hand between the saw and the ripping fence.

7. Never saw freehand on a circular saw. Always use the guide intended for this purpose.

8. Pay attention to business when using the circular saw. One small lapse in your attention could cost you a finger or hand.

CHANGING A BLADE

Snap out the throat plate around the saw. Obtain a wrench that will fit the arbor nut. On most circular saws, the arbor has a lefthand thread and must be turned clockwise to loosen. Figure 53–5. However, some manufacturers use a righthand thread on the arbor. If so, you must turn it counterclockwise to remove. Always check the thread before loosening. If the nut doesn't come off easily, force a piece of scrap wood against the blade to keep the arbor from turning. Remove the nut, the collar, and the blade. Now mark the arbor with a slight file cut or prick-punch mark. Always turn the arbor so the mark is "up" before putting on a new blade. Place the trade mark on the blade at the top, in line with the mark on the arbor. Replace the collar and nut.

RIPPING

Before you rip stock to width on the circular saw, make sure that one edge of the stock is true. If it is not, plane one edge. Then, with the power off, adjust the saw blade to a height of ⅛ inch more than the thickness of the

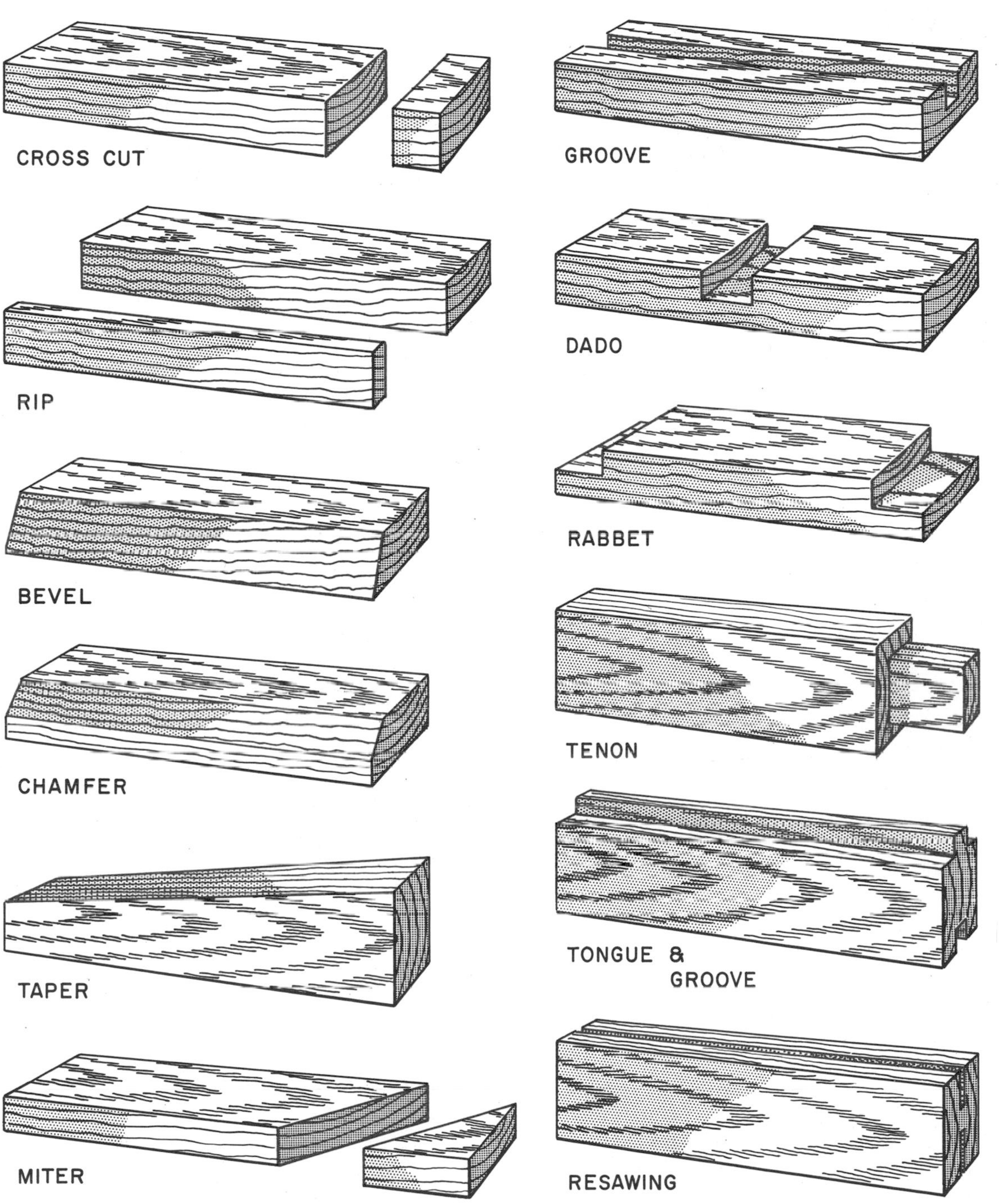

53–3. Common cuts that can be done on the circular saw.

53–4a. A standard basket-type saw guard with splitter and anti-kickback device.

stock. Adjust the ripping fence to the correct width by holding a rule or try square against the fence and measuring the distance to the saw blade. On many machines, the width for ripping is found directly on a scale mounted on the front edge of the saw table. Figure 53–6. Lock the ripping fence tight. Turn on the power. Place the stock on the table. Stand to one side, not directly back of the saw blade. To start the cut, apply forward pressure with one hand as you hold the stock with the other.

53–4b. The guard should be used for sawing operations whenever possible. With this double-basket guard, many more operations can be done than with a standard guard, including such cuts as rabbeting and dadoing. The *splitter* directly behind the saw blade is slightly thicker than the blade. It keeps the saw kerf open as the cutting is done.

Do not apply too much forward pressure on a small saw, as this will make the saw burn or stop altogether. Continue to feed the work into the saw easily.

If the stock is hardwood and quite thick, it may be necessary to begin with the saw set at less than the total thickness and run it through several times rather than to try to cut through the thickness in one operation.

When you are cutting to narrow widths, hold the push stick in your right hand. As the rear edge of the stock clears the table, apply forward pressure with the push stick until the cut is completed. Figure 53–7. Another method of sawing thin stock is shown in Figure 53–8.

CROSSCUTTING

The mitering or crosscutting gauge fits into either groove of the table but

53–5. Removing a blade. Hold a piece of wood against the blade to keep it from turning. Then turn the nut with a wrench of the proper size. On most saws the arbor has a lefthand thread and must be turned clockwise to loosen it. However, some arbors have a righthand thread. If so, you must turn it counterclockwise to remove it.

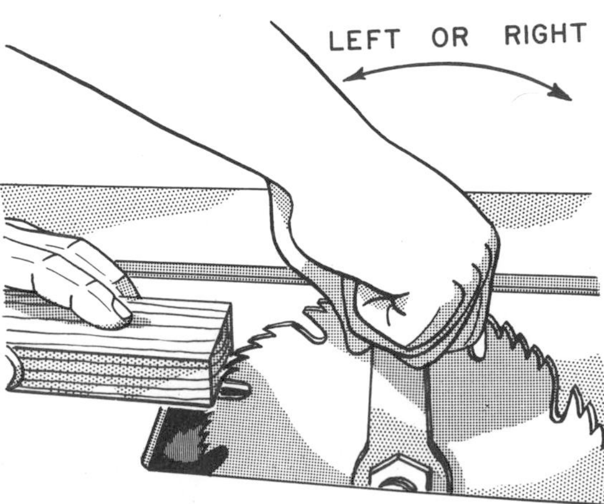

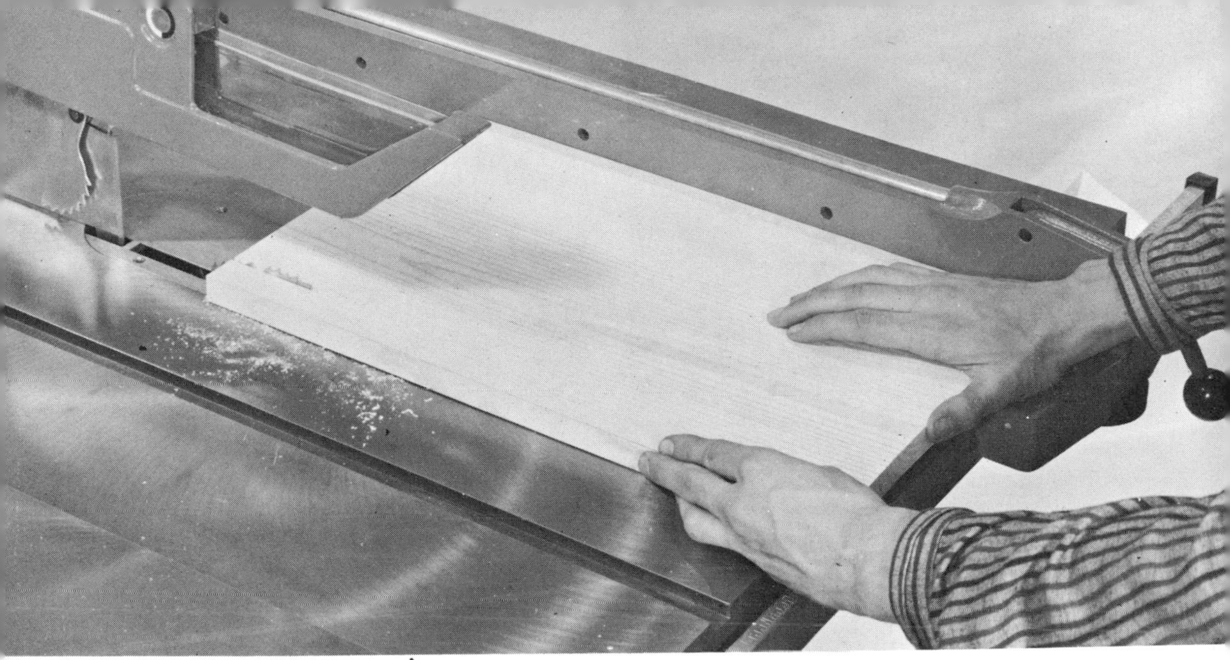

53–6. Ripping stock to width. ***The guard is raised to show the operation.***

is most often placed in the left groove. Some operators attach a squared piece of stock the same width as the miter gauge to its face. This provides better support for the work. To make a square cut, set the gauge at a 90-degree angle. This can be checked by holding a try square against the gauge and the saw blade. Carefully mark the location of the cut, making the mark very clear on the front edge or face of the stock. Set the blade to the correct height. Hold the stock firmly against the gauge and slide both the work and gauge

53–7. Cutting stock to narrow width. A push stick is used to apply the forward pressure. Never run your hand between the revolving blade and the fence if narrow widths are being ripped. ***The guard is removed to show the operation.***

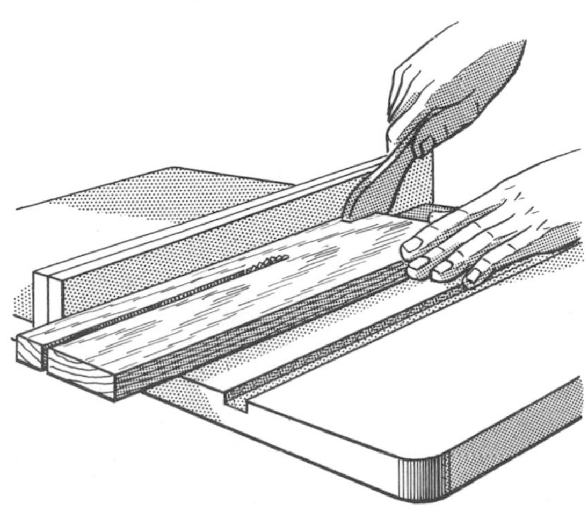

53–8. Another method of ripping narrow stock. Note that you saw halfway through and then remove the material. Turn the stock end for end to complete the cut.

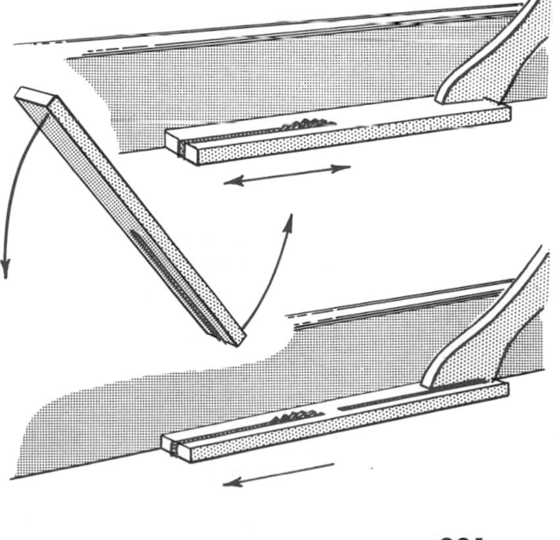

53–9. Crosscutting. The miter gauge is set at a right angle to the blade. An even forward pressure should be applied to the stock and gauge.

53–11. Cutting stock to length with a block attached to the ripping fence. This is one of the simplest methods of cutting many pieces of stock to the same length. Note that as the stock is cut off there is plenty of clearance between the saw blade and the fence. In this way there is never a danger of kickback. *The guard is removed to show the operation.*

along the table to complete the cut. Figure 53–9. If you must cut several pieces to the same length, one of the following methods can be followed:

1. Set the stop rod that is attached to the miter gauge to the correct length. Figure 53–10.

2. Clamp a small block of wood to the ripping fence just in front of the saw blade. The fence with block attached acts as a length guide. Figure 53–11. Never use the ripping fence as a length guide only. If you do, the piece will become lodged between the revolving saw and the ripping fence and may kick back with terrific force.

3. Fasten a wood extension to the miter gauge. Then clamp a stop block to it to control the length of cut. Figure 53–12.

MITERING

To make a miter cut, adjust the miter gauge to the correct angle and then proceed as in crosscutting. Make sure that you hold the stock firmly against the miter gauge, as it tends to creep toward the revolving saw as the cut is made. Figure 53–13. To make a compound miter cut, the gauge must be set to the correct angle and the blade tilted. Figure 53–14.

BEVELING AND CHAMFERING

To cut a bevel or chamfer when you are either ripping or crosscutting, you

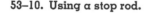

53–10. Using a stop rod.

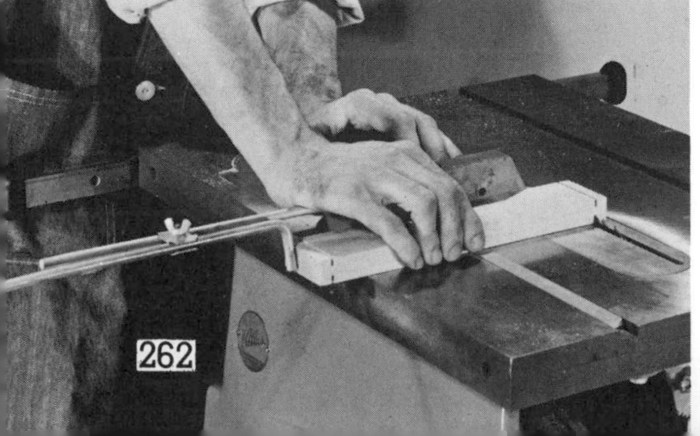

53–12. An auxiliary wood fence has been fastened to the miter gauge. Then a stop block is clamped to this fence.

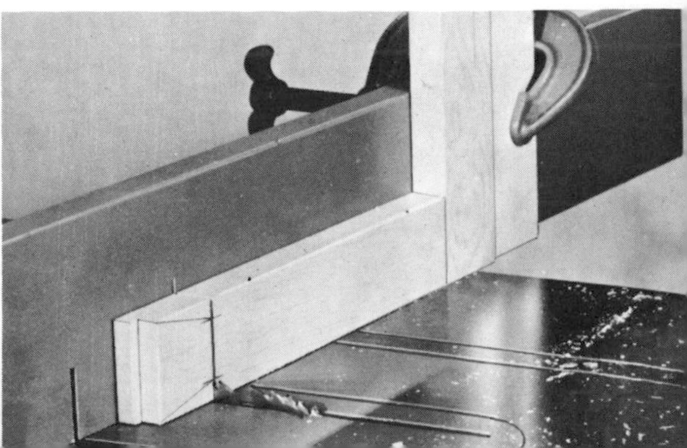

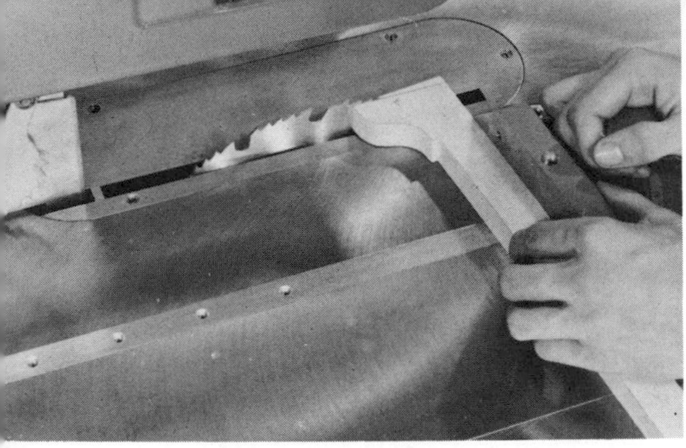

53–13. **Making a miter cut. Adjust the miter gauge to the correct angle. Hold the stock firmly against the gauge as the cut is made.** ***The guard is raised to show the action.***

must tilt the saw blade to the correct angle for the cut. The gauge which shows the angle of tilt of the saw blade is found on the front of the saw just below the table. After the adjustment is made, check the angle by holding a sliding T bevel against the table top and saw blade. After you have the correct angle, you can proceed as for ripping or crosscutting. Figure 53–15.

GROOVING

Cutting a groove on the circular saw will simplify the making of a spline joint. Figure 53–16. Lay out the groove on the edge of the stock. Set the circular saw to a height equal to the depth of the groove. Adjust the ripping fence to allow the cut to be made just inside the layout line. Hold one surface of the stock firmly against the fence and make a cut. Reverse the stock and make a second cut. If necessary, you can make several cuts in the waste stock of the groove. Clean out the groove with a sharp chisel. A groove can also be cut with a dado head.

RABBETING

A rabbet can easily be cut on the end or edge of stock with a circular

53–15. Cutting a bevel with the grain. The blade should be tilted to the correct angle and a fence fastened to control the width of the cut.

53–14. Making a compound miter cut. The miter gauge is set at an angle and the blade is tilted. The stop rod on the miter gauge is used to control the length of cut.

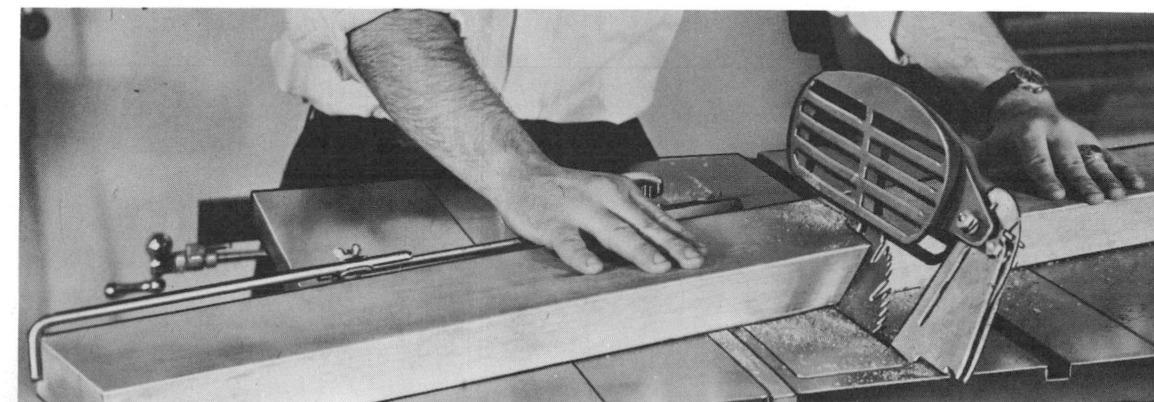

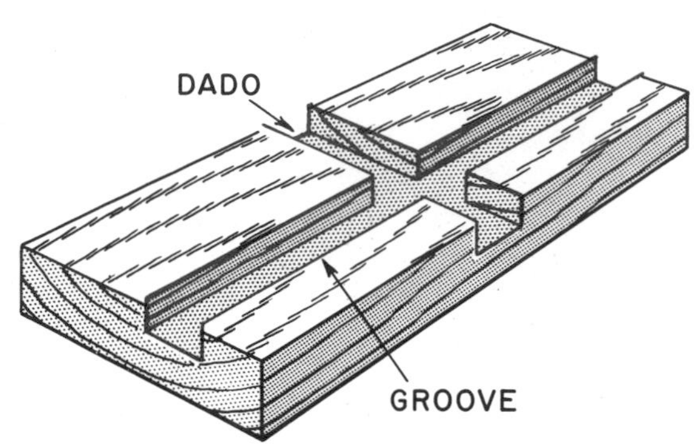

53–16. Here you see the difference between a groove and a dado.

53–17. Making the first cut of a rabbet.

53–18. A commercial tenoning jig is an excellent accessory for cutting tenons and grooves. This one will take stock up to 2¾ inches thick and any width within the capacity of the saw.

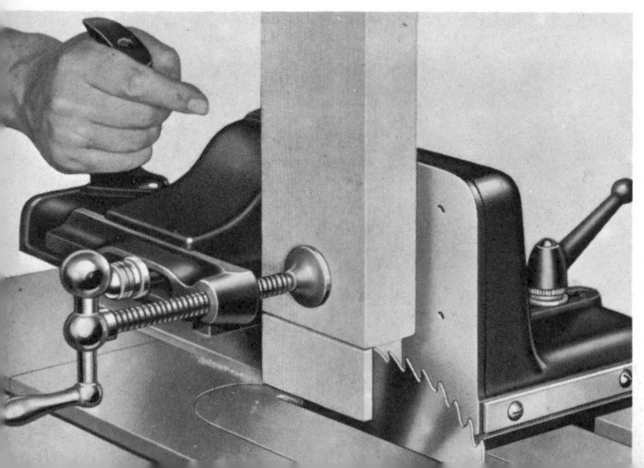

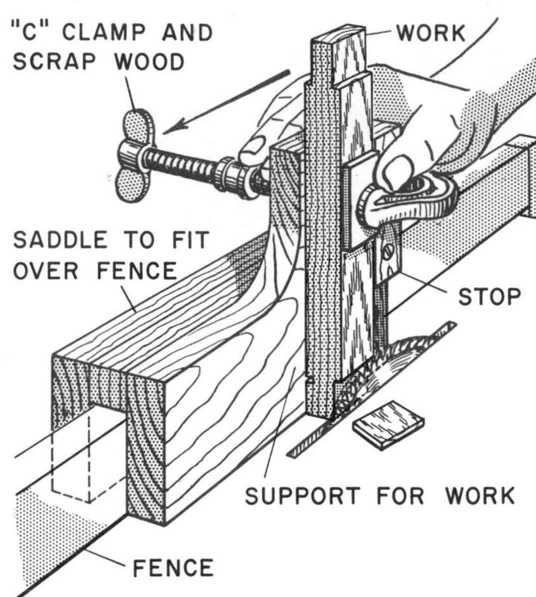

53–19. Making the cheek cut with a handmade tenoning jig.

saw. Lay out the rabbet joint (see the unit on making a rabbet joint). Set the saw blade to a height equal to the depth of the rabbet. If the rabbet is to be cut at the end of the board, hold the stock against a miter gauge and make the shoulder cut. Figure 53–17. Then set the saw blade to a height equal to the width of the rabbet. Set the ripping fence to a position that will permit the saw kerf to be just inside the layout line. Hold the stock on end with the surface opposite the rabbet firmly against the ripping fence. Make the second cut.

An edge rabbet is cut in the same way except that the ripping fence is used for making both cuts.

TENONING

Making mortise-and-tenon joints is quite simple when the tenon is cut on the circular saw. Lay out the tenon

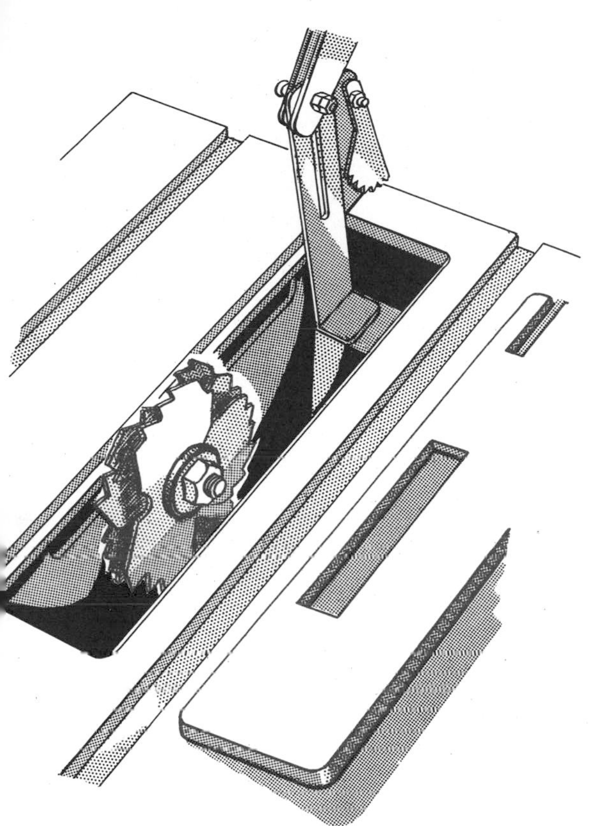

53–20. A dado head attached to the saw arbor in preparation for use. The plate that must be used over the head has a wider opening than that used with the regular saw blade.

(see the unit on making a mortise-and-tenon joint). Set the saw blade to a height equal to the thickness of stock to be removed from one side of the tenon. Hold the stock against the miter gauge and make the *shoulder* cuts. After this is done, set the saw blade to a height equal to the length of the tenon. Figure 53–18. Now select a homemade or commercial tenoning jig. The simplest method of cutting the cheek is to clamp the stock to the tenoning jig and position the jig and fence so as to cut out the cheek on the side away from the jig. Figure 53–19. Then turn the stock around and cut the other cheek without changing the location of the fence.

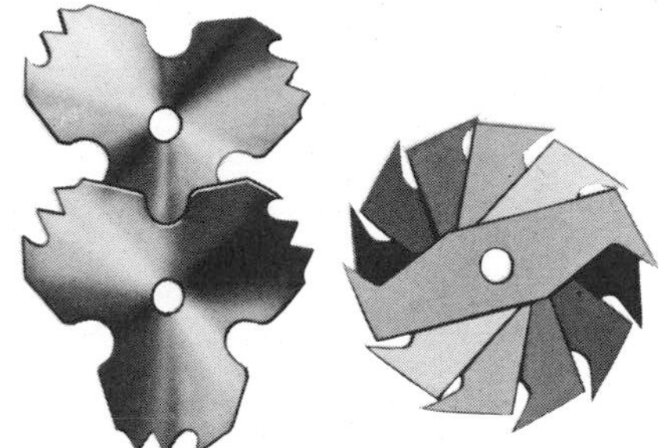

53–21. A typical dado head consists of two ⅛-inch outside blades and one 1/16-inch thick chipper blade, two ⅛-inch chipper blades and one ¼-inch-thick chipper blade. With this assortment you can cut grooves from ⅛ inch to 13/16 inch in intervals of 1/16 inch.

USING A DADO HEAD

A dado head (Figures 53 20 and 53–21) can be purchased that will cut grooves or dadoes from ⅛ to 2 inches in width and which is equally adapted to cutting with or across the grain. One dado blade will cut a groove ⅛

53–22. Cutting a groove with a dado head. Note how simple it is to cut a groove of any width and depth with this attachment. When the groove is cut across grain, it is called a dado, which is a common type of joint construction.

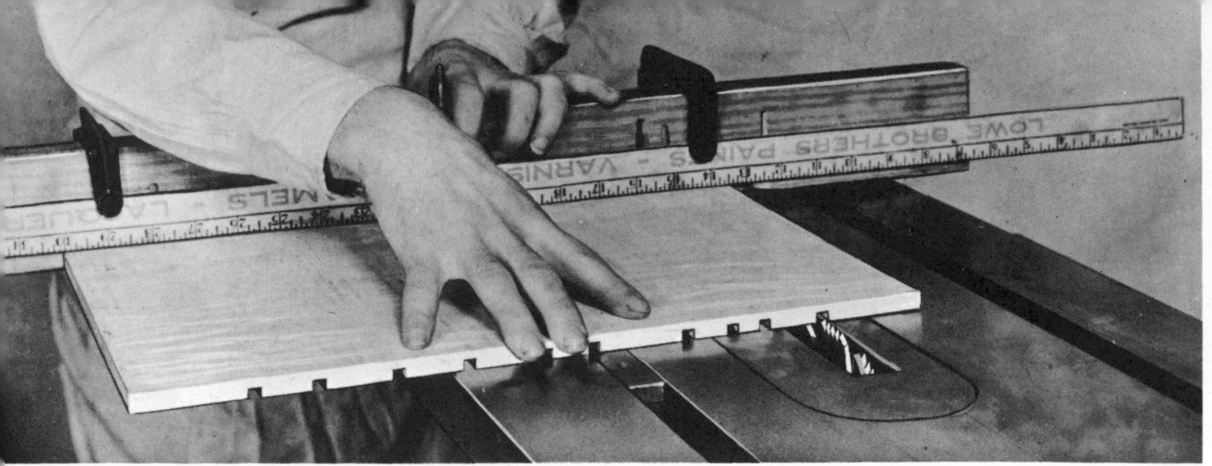

53–23. Cutting a series of dadoes.

inch thick and two will make a cut ¼ inch thick. Cutters of different widths can be put between these two dado cutters to cut a groove of any width. This attachment is especially useful for cutting grooves, Figure 53–22, tenons, dadoes (Figure 53–23), and lap joints.

CAN YOU ANSWER THESE QUESTIONS ON THE CIRCULAR SAW?

1. Sketch a circular saw and name the parts.
2. Name the two types of circular saws.
3. What are the three types of saw blades? Which is best for use in the average shop?
4. List the safety precautions to observe when using a circular saw.
5. At what height should the saw blade be set for ripping?
6. Tell how to make a cut on hardwood that is quite thick.
7. At what times should a push stick be used?
8. Name the gauge employed for doing crosscutting.
9. How can a compound miter cut be made?
10. Relate the three methods of cutting several pieces to the same length.
11. What is the difficulty frequently encountered when making a miter cut?
12. Point out the difference between a bevel and a chamfer.
13. How can a groove be cut?
14. What difference is there between cutting a rabbet on the end and on the edge of a piece of stock?
15. Tell how to make the cheek cut in tenoning.
16. What is a dado head? What is it used for?
17. What is the difference between a dado blade and cutter?

Section XI

UNIT 54. RADIAL-ARM SAW

The radial-arm saw is an ideal machine for many kinds of cutting operations. It is an upside-down saw on which you can see all the mechanisms for adjusting and cutting. For this reason, some people consider this saw more dangerous. The truth, however, is that if handled correctly it is as safe as any other type of circular saw. For all crosscutting operations, including straight cutting and cutting a miter, bevel, dado, or rabbet, the stock is held firmly on the table in a stationary position and the saw is moved to do the cutting. For all ripping operations, the saw is locked in a fixed position and the stock moved into the revolving blade just as in using a circular saw. There are several designs for the radial-arm saw. On one type the saw unit moves back and forth under the overarm. Figure 54–1. Another type has an extra track under the overarm on which the saw moves. Figure 54–2. The size of the machine is determined by the size of the blades. The common size for the school shop is 9- to 10-inch.

ADJUSTMENTS

The *overarm* or *track* can rotate in a complete circle. The *yoke* that holds the motor can be turned at a 360-degree circle, and the blade can be tilted to the right or left 90 degrees. The three principal adjustments can be made as follows: 1. The *depth of cut* is made by turning the elevator crank that is located either directly above the column or on the front of the machine. 2. The *angle of cut* is adjusted by turning the overarm or track to the correct angle. There is a *locking lever* at the column or the outer end of the overarm for making this adjustment. 3. *Bevel cuts* are made by tilting the motor to the right or left.

54–1. On this type of radial-arm saw, the saw moves back and forth under the overarm.

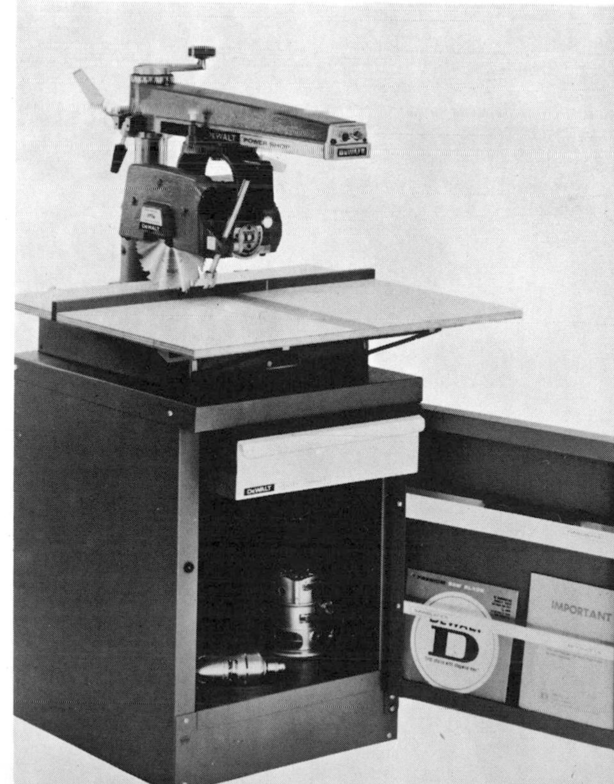

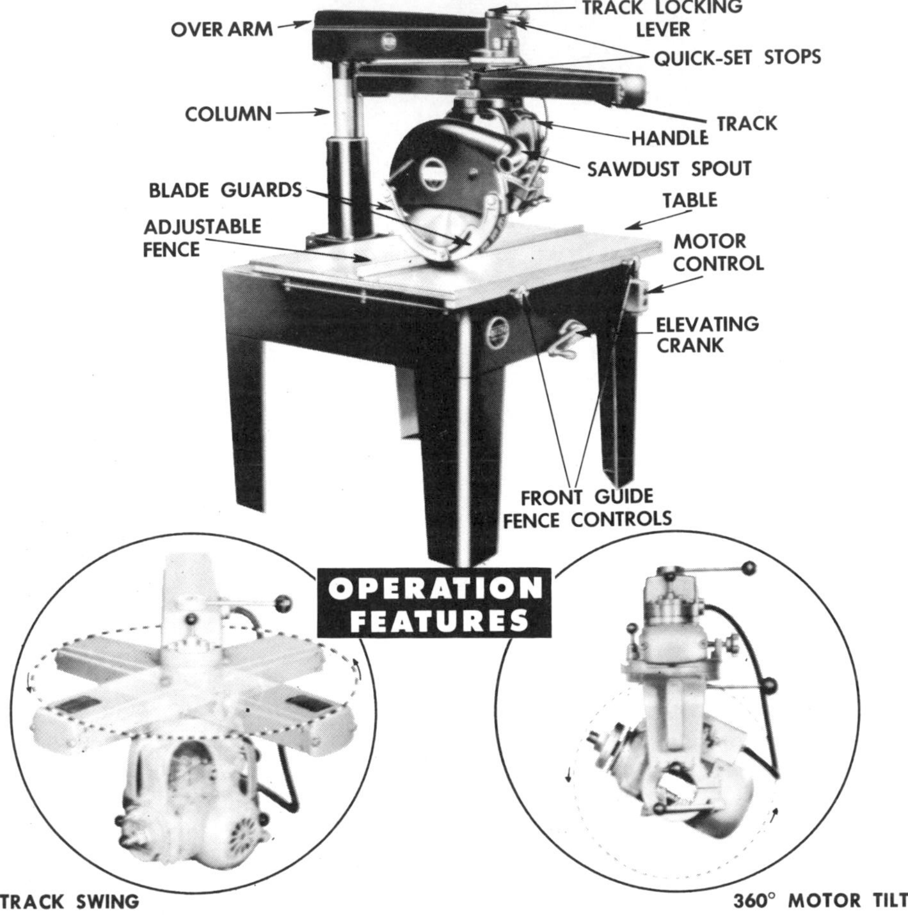

54–2. On this type, the saw moves back and forth under a track that is attached to the overarm.

SAFETY

1. Get personal instruction on the use of this machine before operating it.

2. Make sure a sharp blade of the correct kind is installed. The same kinds of blades are used on the radial-arm saw as on the circular saw.

3. Mount the blade on the arbor so that the cutting edges turn towards you.

4. Make sure the guard is always in place.

5. See to it that all clamps are tight before starting the motor.

6. Hold the stock firmly against the table for doing all kinds of crosscutting operations.

54–3. To do straight cutting, pull the saw smoothly through the stock.

7. Keep your hands away from the danger area—the path of the blade.

8. Don't try to stop the blade after turning off the machine by holding a stick or similar item against it.

9. Make all adjustments *with the motor at a dead stop.*

CROSSCUTTING OPERATIONS

To make a straight crosscut, make sure that the arm or track is at right angles to the guide fence. Adjust the depth of cut so that the teeth of the blade are about 1/16 inch below the surface of the wood table. Set the anti-kickback device about 1/8 inch above the work surface. This will act as a safety device to keep your fingers away from the rotating blade. Hold the stock firmly on the table with the cutoff line in line with the saw blade. Start the machine and allow it to come to full speed. Now pull the motor slowly so that the blade cuts into the stock. Figure 54–3. This will take very little effort, since the cutting action tends to feed the blade into the stock. After the cut is made, return the saw to its place behind the guide fence and turn off the machine. To make a miter cut, simply adjust the arm or track to the angle you want and do the cutting as you would for straight crosscutting. Figure 54–4. To cut a bevel, adjust the track or arm for straight crosscutting and then tilt the saw to the desired angle. Figure 54–5. The angle is 45 degrees for most bevel or end miter cuts. A compound miter is made by adjusting the arm or track to the correct angle and then tilting the saw. Figure 54–6. A rabbet or dado can easily be cut by installing a dado head on the arbor and using it as you would a saw blade.

RIPPING OPERATIONS

Set the track or overarm at right angles to the guide fence. Turn the saw so that the blade is parallel to the guide fence. Then move the saw in or out until the correct distance between the guide fence and blade is obtained. Lock it in position. Set the depth of

54–4. The arm adjusted to make a miter cut.

54–5. Making a bevel cut.

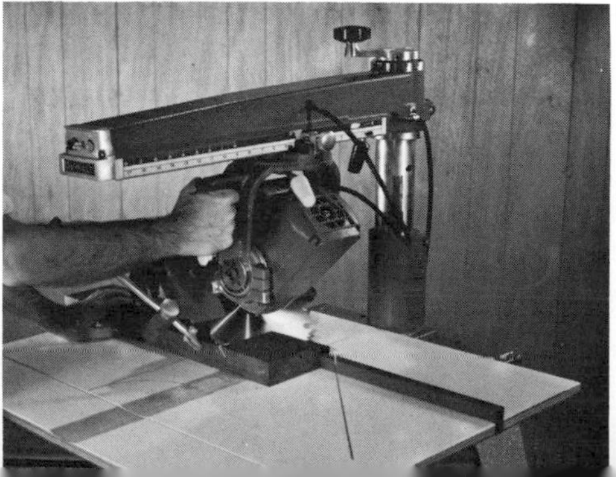

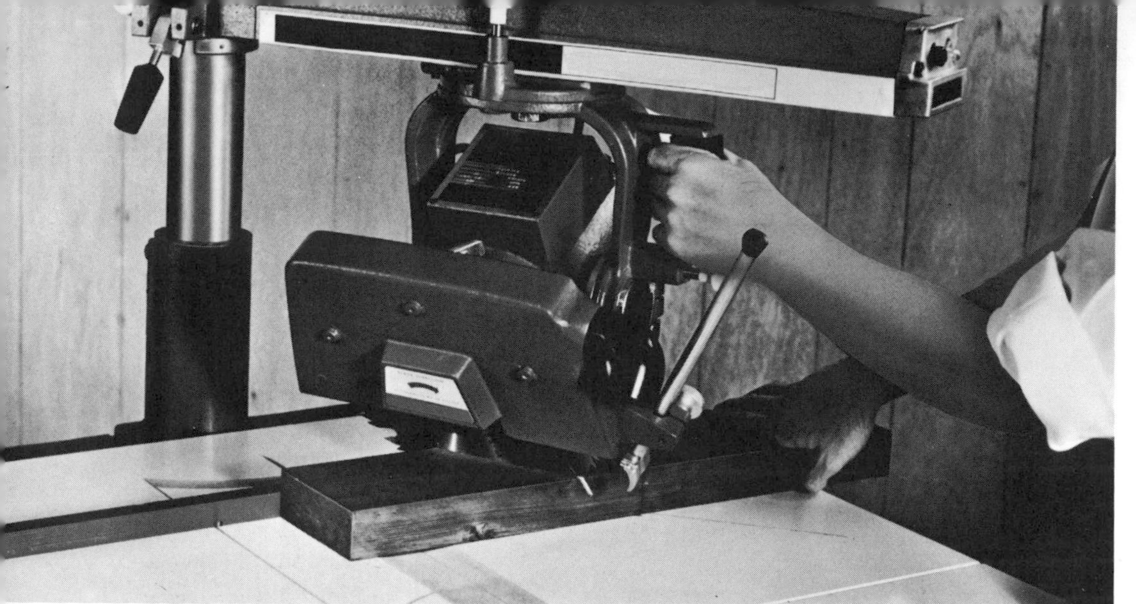

54–6. Making a compound miter or hopper cut.

cut. Adjust the guard so that it is close to the work. Set the anti-kickback device so that the fingers rest firmly on the wood surface and hold it against the table. Check to make sure that the saw is rotating up and toward you. Turn on the power and move the stock slowly into the blade. Figure 54–7.

CAN YOU ANSWER THESE QUESTIONS ON THE RADIAL-ARM SAW?

1. How does the radial-arm saw differ from the circular saw?
2. What advantage does the radial-arm saw have over the circular saw?
3. Tell how the size of the machine is indicated.
4. Describe the three principal adjustments that are made on a radial-arm saw.
5. List five safety precautions to follow when using this saw.
6. Tell how to adjust the saw for straight crosscutting.
7. Describe two other types of crosscutting operations.
8. Tell how to adjust the saw for ripping.

54–7. Ripping.

Section XI

UNIT 55. THE BAND SAW

A band saw has two wheels mounted on a *frame*, a *table*, *guides*, a *saw blade*, and *guards*. Figure 55–1. In addition, a *ripping fence* and *miter gauge* are sometimes used. The table can be tilted at various angles. The size of the band saw is indicated by the diameter of the wheels. The saw is used mostly for cutting curves, circles, and irregular designs. Figure 55–2. It can also be used for straight cross-cutting, ripping, and resawing. Figure 55–3.

To install a saw blade, remove the guards over the wheel, loosen the top wheel, and remove the throat plate.

55–1a. A 20-inch band saw.

55–1b. A small type, 14-inch band saw that can be mounted on a table or bench. It has all the features of a larger machine such as a tilting table, ball-bearing guides, and an adjustable upper wheel. It differs only in that it has a smaller capacity.

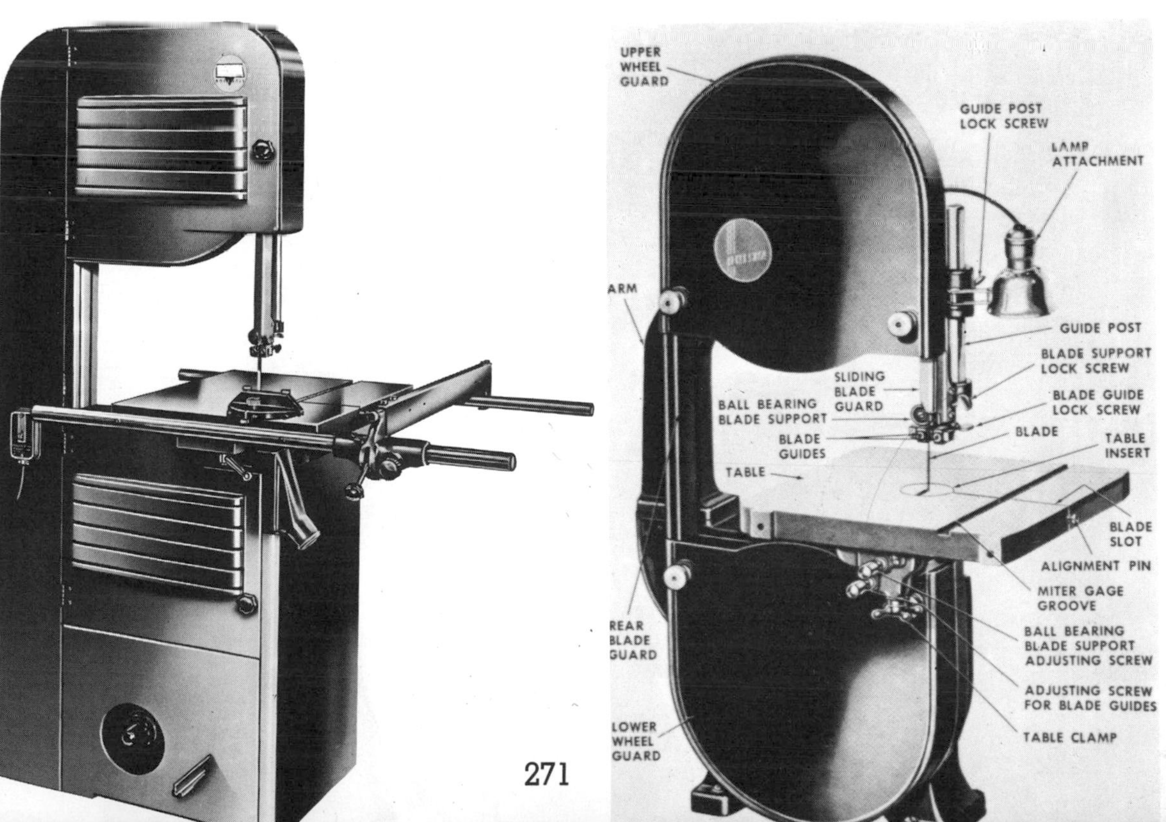

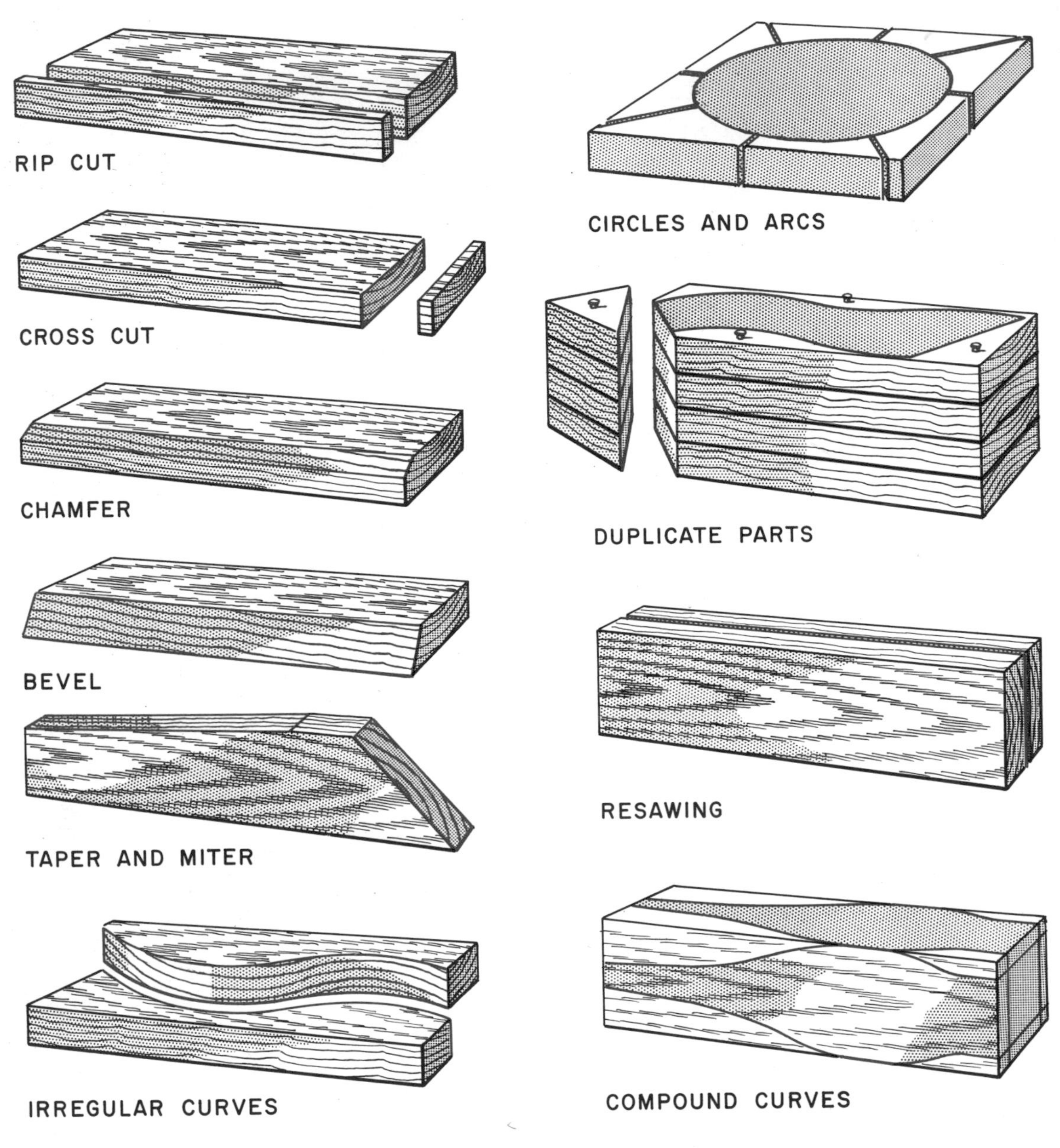

55–2. Common cuts that can be made on the band saw.

Grasping the blade in both hands, slip it through the slot in the table and then over the wheels. Figure 55–4. Then tighten the upper wheel to apply tension to the blade. This wheel can be tilted to move the blade forward or

55–3. Many parts of this corner gun rack can be cut out on a band saw.

backward. Replace the little throat plate around the blade and look to see if the blade is running in the guide properly. Turn the wheels over by hand once or twice to check the operation of the blade.

CUTTING WITH A BAND SAW

Adjust the upper saw guide just to clear the stock. Figure 55–5. Stand slightly to the left and in front of the table. Guide the stock with one hand and apply forward pressure with the other. Do not force the work into the saw. Follow these general suggestions:

1. *Watch the feed direction.* Before making the cut, think through the path that it must make. Some pieces will swing in such a way as to hit the upper arm if the plan is not correct. Figure 55–6.

2. *Make short cuts before long cuts.* It is much easier to backtrack out of a short cut than a long one. Figure 55–7.

55–4. Installing a band-saw blade. The guards have been removed and the upper wheel released to permit the new blade to be slipped over the two wheels. There are adjustments on the reverse side of the upper wheel for tension and for tilting the wheel back and forth. This will, of course, move the blade.

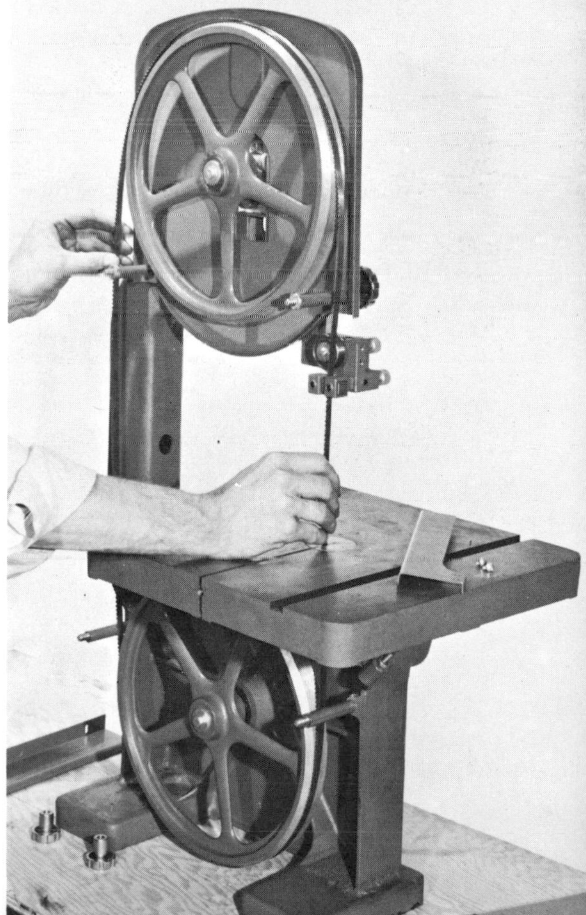

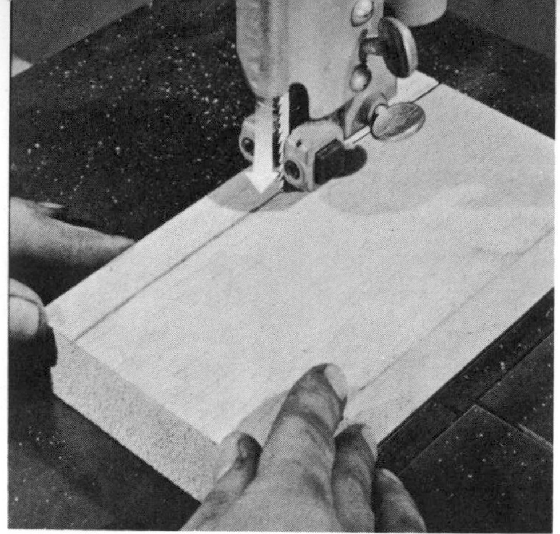

55–5. The band saw with the guide properly adjusted. The stock, which just clears the guide, is being held with the thumb and forefingers of both hands.

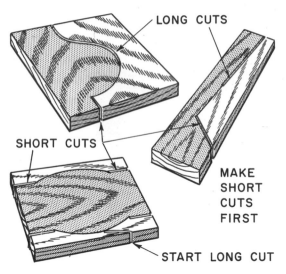

3. *Make use of turning holes.* Depending on the design, a round or square hole can first be cut in the waste stock before band-sawing.

4. *Break up complicated curves.* Look at each job to see if a combination cut can be completed by making several simpler cuts. Figure 55–9.

5. *Rough cut complex curves.* Make a simple cut through the waste stock to follow as much of the line as possible. Then cut to the layout line. Figure 55–10.

6. *Backtrack out of corners.* Narrow grooves are cut out by "nibbling" at the closed end. On larger rectangular openings, cut to one corner and

55–6. Checking the feed direction so that the work does not hit the saw arm.

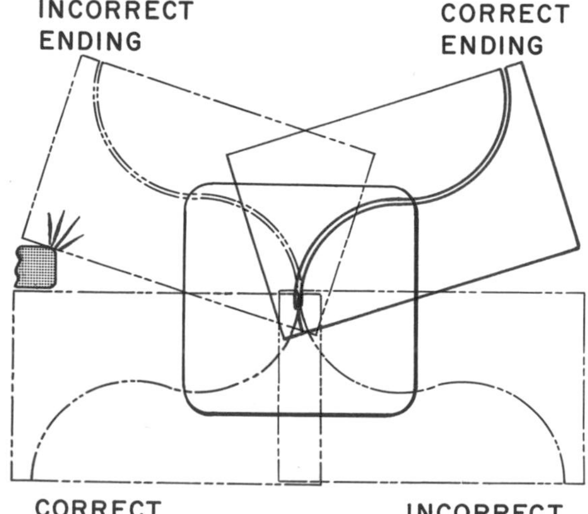

55–7. Make short cuts before long cuts.

55–8. Use the auger bit and mortising chisel to cut starting holes shown.

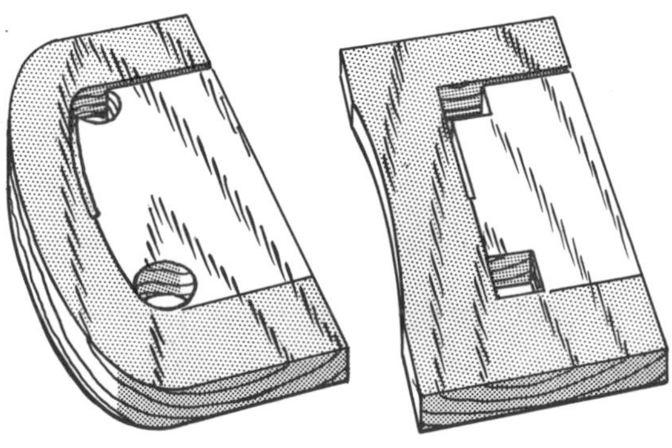

AN AUGER AND MORTISING CHISEL USED TO MAKE TURNING HOLES

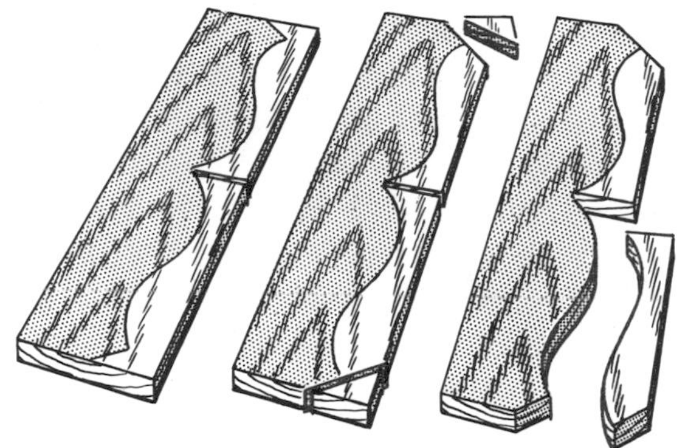

55–9. The correct sequence in cutting a combination curve.

then backtrack slightly before cutting to another corner. Figure 55–11.

CUTTING CURVES

Select a band-saw blade for cutting curves, following this general rule: A ⅛-inch blade will cut down to about a ½-inch circle, while a ⅜-inch blade will cut down to about a 2-inch circle. Figure 55–12. The width of blade depends on the thickness and kind of wood to be cut, and also on the sharpness of the curve.

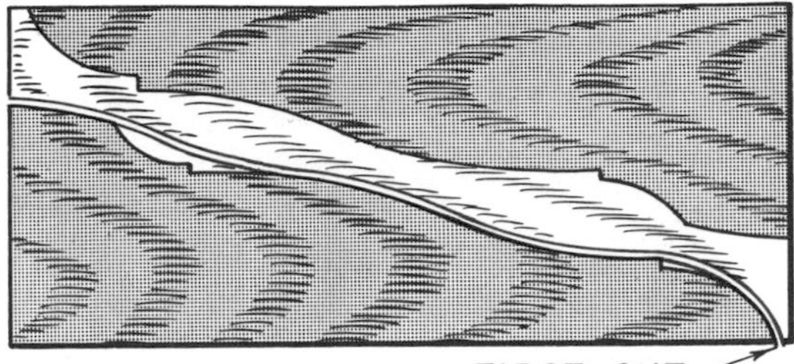

55–11. Rough-cut for a curve.

55–10. Sequence in cutting rectangular openings.

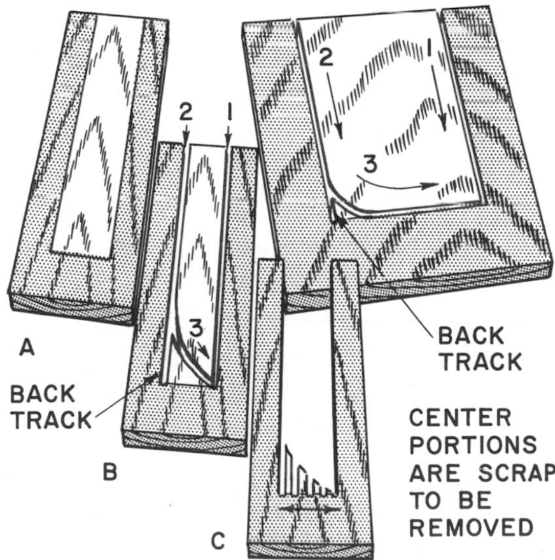

In cutting curves, apply even forward pressure. Carefully guide the work with your left hand to keep the cut just outside the layout line. Figure 55–13. If you are cutting sharp curves, you should make many relief cuts from the outside edge to within less than the thickness of the blade from the layout line. Figure 55–14. Then, as you cut along the layout line, the waste stock will fall away freely. Circles can be cut freehand or with a circle jig. Figures 55–15 and 55–16.

55–12. This chart shows how to select the right blade. For example, a ½-inch blade cannot cut a circle smaller than 2½ inches in diameter.

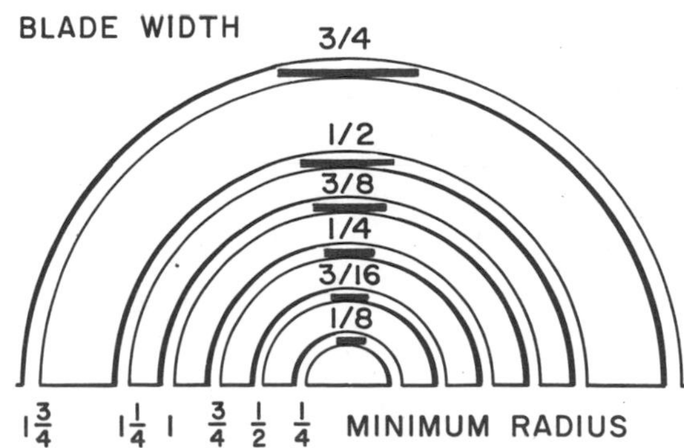

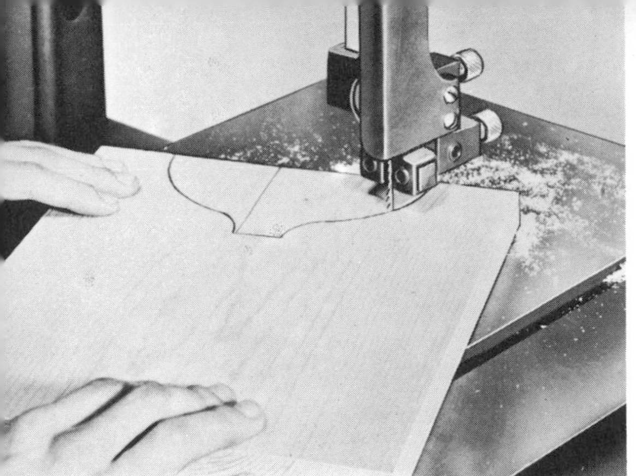

55–13. Cutting a curve on a band saw. The stock is carefully guided along the layout line.

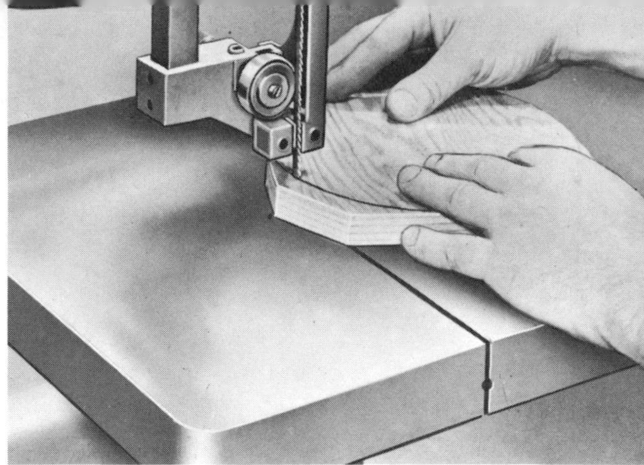

55–15. Cutting a circle freehand on the band saw.

RESAWING

When stock is much thicker than needed, it is resawed. This can be done on the band saw. The widest possible blade should be selected and a fence or pivot block attached to the table. A layout line across the end and edge of the board is helpful. Hold the stock against the fence or block and slowly feed the work against the blade. Figure 55–17.

RIPPING

If a circular saw is not available, stock can be ripped to width by fastening a fence or pivot block to the table and proceeding in the same way as with a circular saw. Figure 55–18.

CROSSCUTTING AND MITERING

The table of the band saw has a groove into which a miter gauge will fit. Stock can be held against this miter gauge to do accurate crosscutting or miter cutting on a band saw.

TILT-TABLE WORK

The table can be tilted to do many jobs such as beveling and chamfering on curves and irregular designs.

55–14. Cutting a sharp curve. When the blade on the band saw is a little too wide, a "closer" cut can be made with the aid of relief cuts.

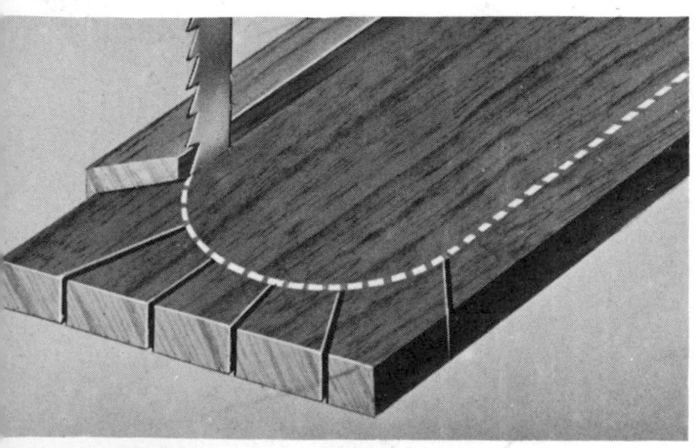

55–16. Using an extension guide bar type of circle jig for cutting a true circle.

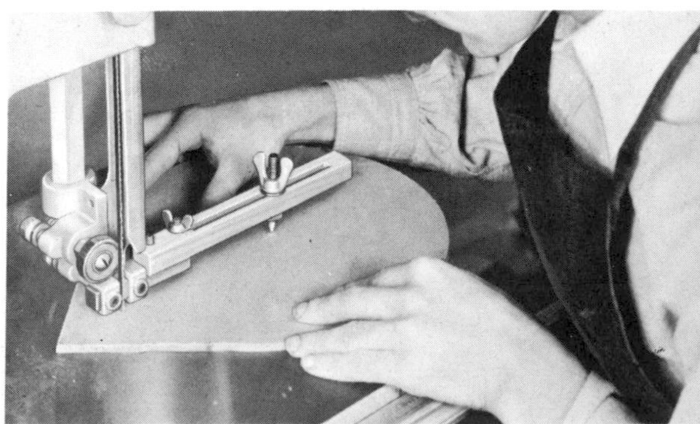

CAN YOU ANSWER THESE QUESTIONS ON THE BAND SAW?

1. Name the parts of the band saw.
2. How is the size of the band saw determined?
3. Describe the method followed for installing a saw blade.
4. Where should you stand when cutting with a band saw?
5. How can a sharp curve be cut?
6. There is a rule for selecting a band-saw blade for cutting curves. What is it?
7. What is resawing?
8. What is the advantage of resawing on a band saw over resawing on a circular saw?
9. How can ripping be done on the band saw?

55–17. Resawing stock. A pivot block is fastened to the table with a C clamp to control the thickness of the cut. A band saw is better for resawing than a circular saw because less stock is wasted with the thinner blade and because the exposed blade is longer. Notice the tension nut for tightening the upper wheel and the adjustment for tilting the wheel.

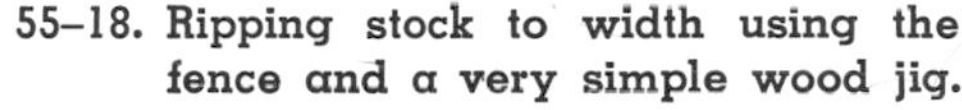

55–18. Ripping stock to width using the fence and a very simple wood jig.

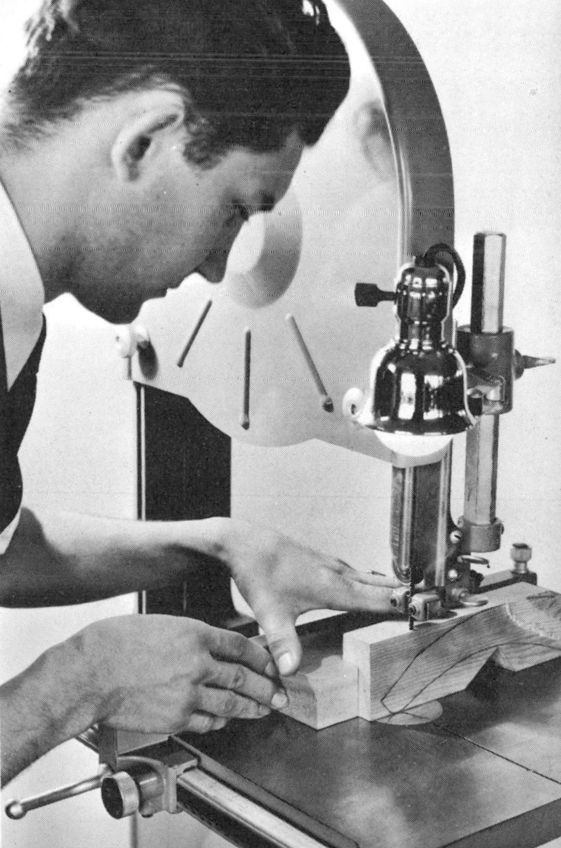

Section XI

UNIT 56. JIG OR SCROLL SAW

The jig or scroll saw is a mechanically operated cutting tool. Figure 56–1. The saw moves up and down to do the same type of cutting that can be done by hand with a coping or compass saw. It will cut curves or irregular designs both externally and internally. Figure 56–2. It differs from other curve-cutting machines because it can make cuts inside a pattern without cutting through the stock. The saw consists of a *frame* with *overarm* and *base*, a *driving mechanism* to convert rotating action into up-and-down action, *table*, *guide*, and *saw blade*. A tension sleeve is mounted in the end of the overarm, through which a plunger moves. The size of a jig saw is indicated by the distance between the blade and the overarm measured horizontally. The speed of the jig saw can be adjusted by shifting a belt to various positions. There are three types of blades. *Power jig-saw blades* are used for many kinds of cutting on wood. The *saber blade* is fastened only in the lower chuck. *Jeweler's piercing blades* are used to cut thin metal, while the saber blade is for heavier stock. Figure 56–3.

56–1. A jig or scroll saw with the names of the major parts.

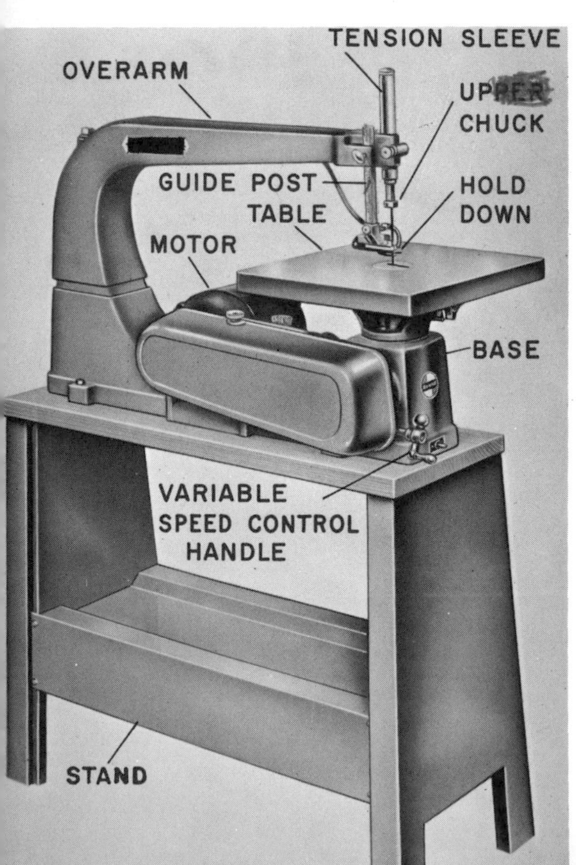

CUTTING WITH A JIG SAW

Install a blade in the machine. Figure 56–4 and 56–5. Cutting with the jig saw requires the same care and attention as cutting with a coping saw. Adjust the guide so that the small spring tension holds the stock firmly against the table. Figure 56–6. Hold it with thumb and forefinger of both hands. Apply even, forward pressure. Figure 56–7. Do not force the stock into the work. Turn the stock slowly when cutting a curve. If it is turned too sharply it will break the blade. If

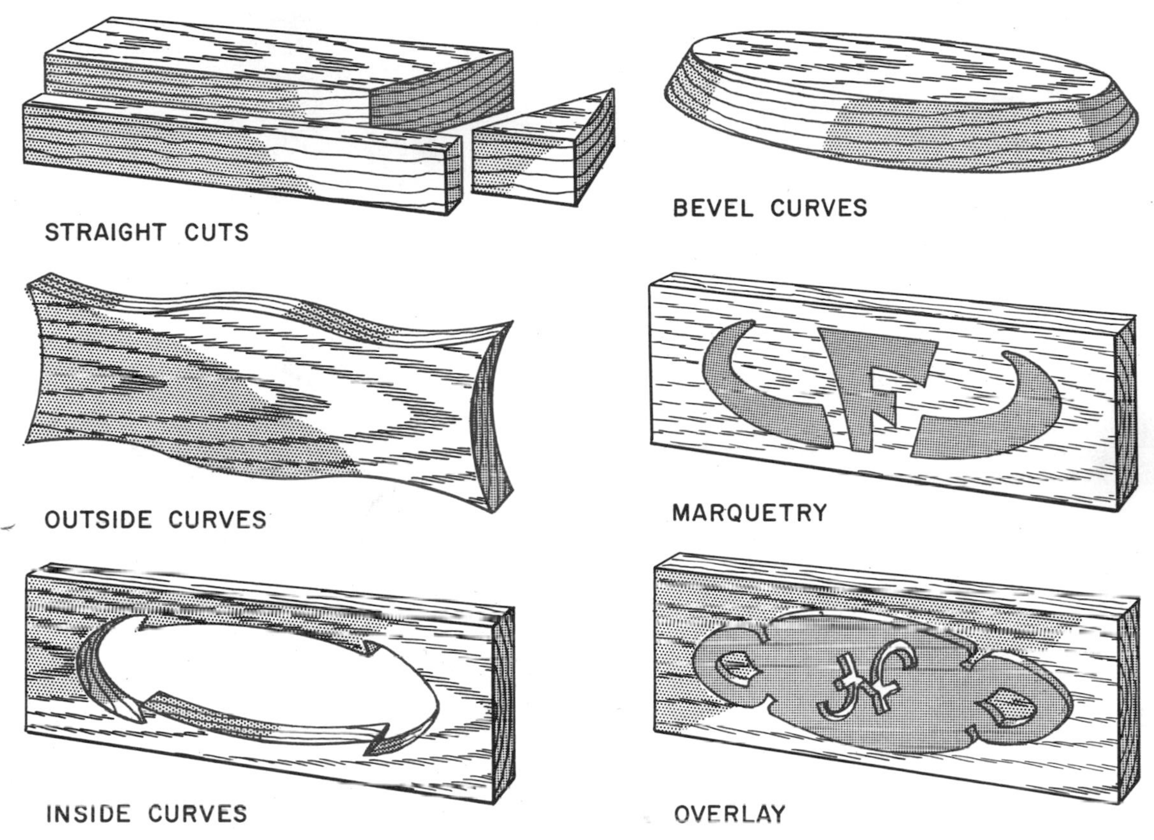

56–2. Common cuts that can be made on the jig saw.

56–3. Blade selection chart.

Material Cut	Thick In.	Width In.	Teeth Per Inch	Blade Full Size
Wood Veneer Plus Plastics Celluloid • Hard Rubber Bakelite • Ivory Extremely Thin Materials	.000	.035	20	
Plastics • Celluloid Hard Rubber Bakelite • Ivory Wood	.019	.050	15	
	.019	.055	12	
	.020	.070	7	
	.020	.110	7	
Wall Board • Pressed Wood Wood • Lead Bone • Felt • Paper Copper • Ivory • Aluminum	.020	.110	15	
Hard and Soft Wood	.020	.110	10	
	.028	.187	10	
	.028	.250	7	
Pearl • Pewter Mica Pressed Wood Sea Shells Jewelry • Metals Hard Leather	.016	.054	30	
	.016	.054	20	
	.020	.070	15	
	.020	.085	12	

rather complicated cuts must be made, plan the cutting carefully before you proceed. Figure 56–8.

CUTTING INTERNAL CURVES AND DESIGNS

Drill a relief hole in the center of the waste stock. Figure 56–9. If a jeweler's blade is to be used, remove the throat plate. After the blade is fastened in the lower chuck, put the stock over the blade. Fasten the other end of the blade to the plunger chuck, and then replace the throat plate. Adjust the guide to correct height. Then make a

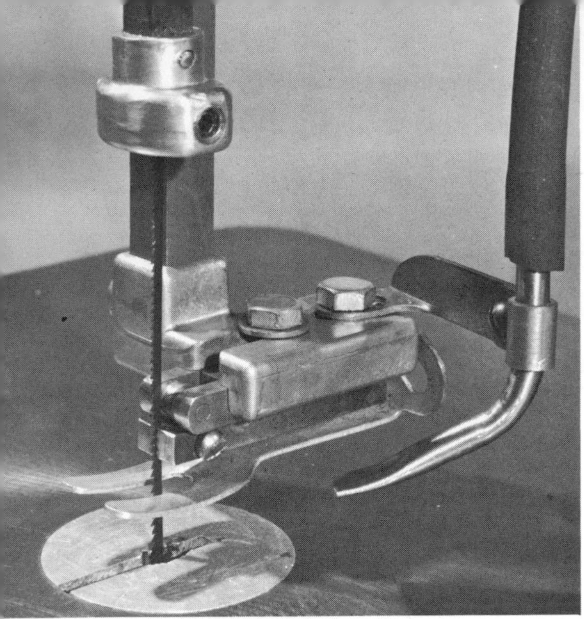

56–4. Proper method of fastening a jeweler's blade in the upper and lower chucks of a jig saw.

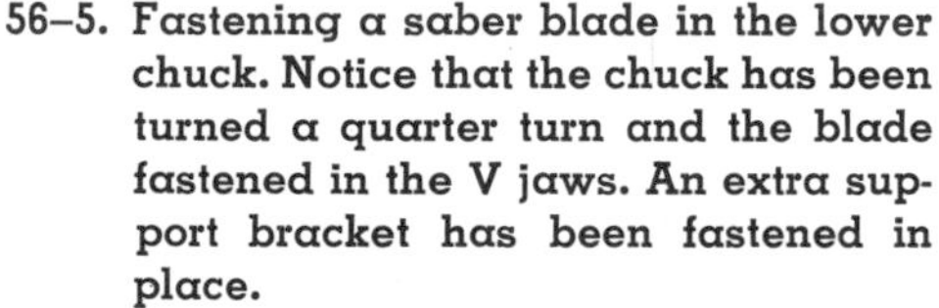

56–5. Fastening a saber blade in the lower chuck. Notice that the chuck has been turned a quarter turn and the blade fastened in the V jaws. An extra support bracket has been fastened in place.

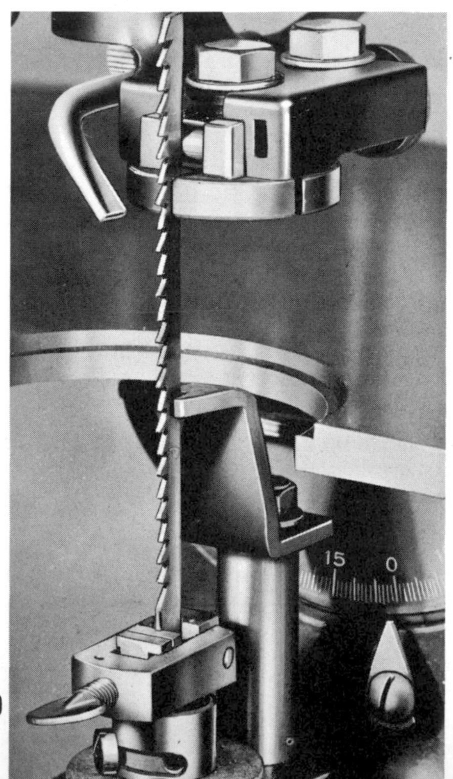

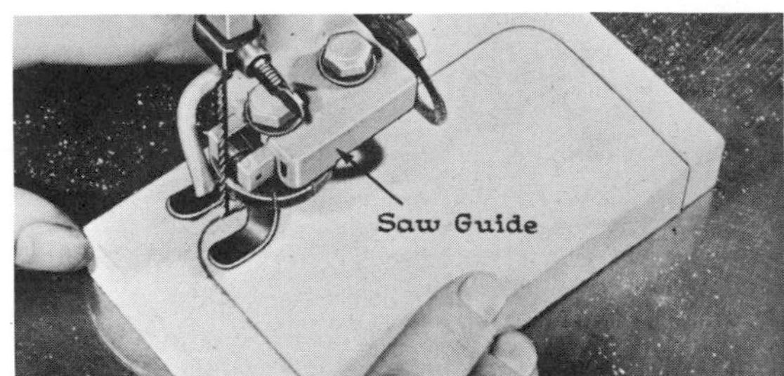

56–6. The saw guide properly adjusted. The small spring tension in the bottom of the saw guide holds the stock firmly against the table of the saw.

56–7. Guiding the work with the fingers as forward pressure is applied with the thumbs.

56–8. Proper method of making complicated cuts on the jig saw. In cutting out this design, a straight cut is made first. Then the stock is backed off the saw and a curved cut is made until it joins the straight cut. This eliminates the necessity of trying to cut a sharp corner.

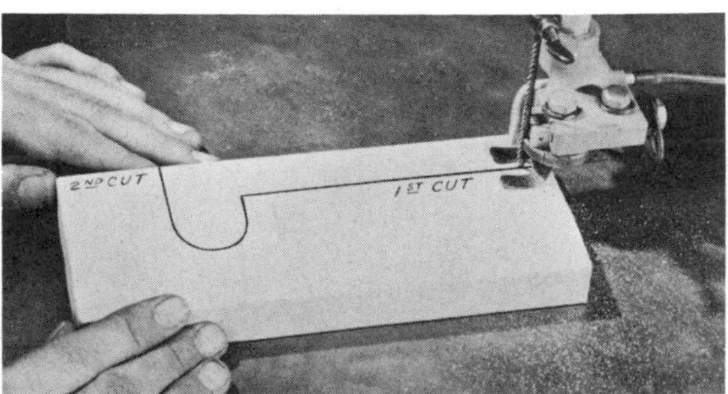

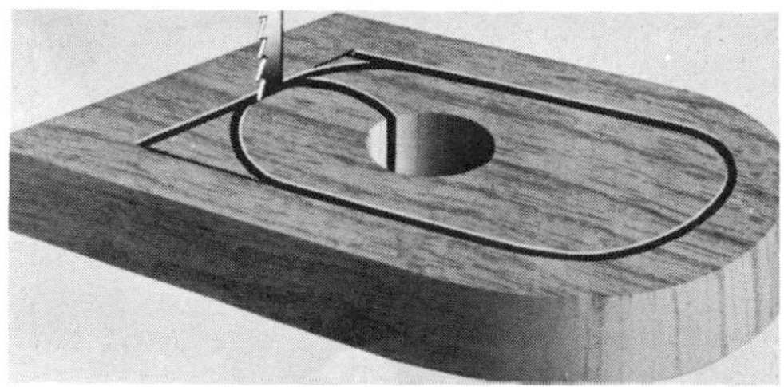

56–9. Making an internal cut on the jig saw. The relief hole has been drilled in the center of the waste stock and the cut is made to the layout line.

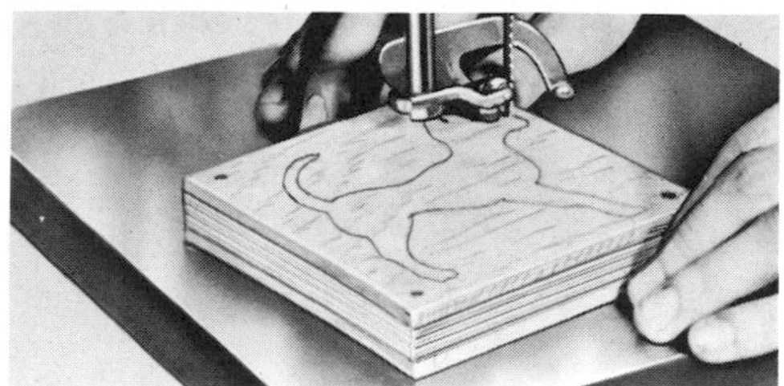

56–11. A pad of material has been nailed together in the corner as the design is cut out.

circular cut from the relief hole to the layout line. Figure 56–10.

TILT-TABLE WORK

The table of the jig saw can be tilted to cut a bevel on a straight, circular or irregular design.

MAKING AN INLAY OR SIMPLE MARQUETRY

Inlaying (or marquetry) is a way of forming a design by using two or more different kinds of wood. To make a simple inlay, first fasten two pieces of wood together in a pad and nail them together with small brads at each corner. Drill a small hole at an inside corner of the design to start the blade. Now tilt the table of the saw 1 or 2 degrees. Make all necessary cuts with the work always on the same side of the blade. Figure 56–11. Take the pad apart and assemble the design. When pieces with a beveled edge are fitted together, there will be no space caused by a saw kerf. Figure 56–12.

56–10. Doing internal cutting on the jig saw.

56–12. Steps in making a simple inlay.

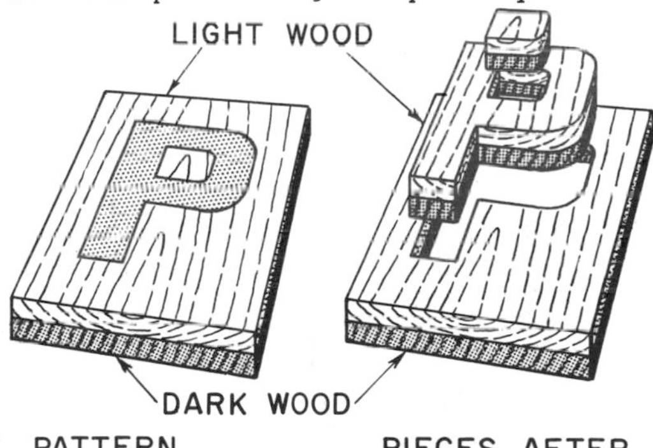

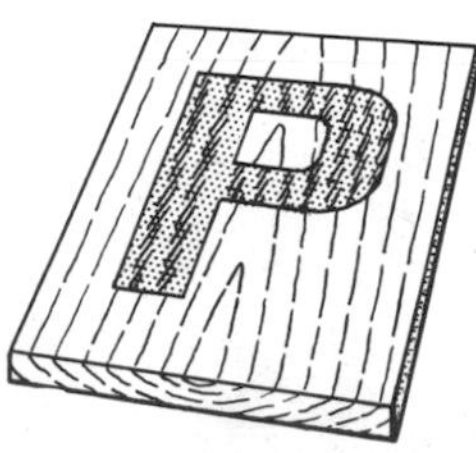

DARK WOOD INLAID ON LIGHT WOOD

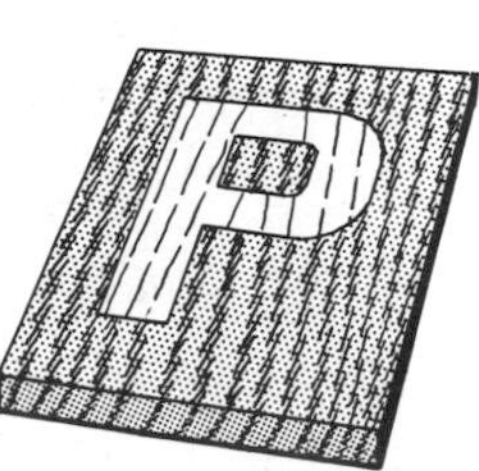

LIGHT WOOD INLAID ON DARK WOOD

CAN YOU ANSWER THESE QUESTIONS ON THE JIG OR SCROLL SAW?

1. Sketch a jig saw and locate its parts.
2. How is the size of the jig saw indicated?
3. Name the two types of blades.
4. What is the most common cause of blade breakage?
5. How can internal cutting be done?
6. Explain how to make an inlay.

Section XI

UNIT 57. PORTABLE SAWS

The portable electric saw is a versatile tool that can cut materials ranging from thin plastics to thick lumber. Figure 57–1. With the correct change of blades, it can also be used for cutting metal, cement, and ceramics. The cut-off (power hand or circular) saw is designed primarily for straight cutting of heavier lumber and plywood. It is used by the carpenter for presizing lumber or for trimming off uneven ends of boards that are already nailed in place. Figure 57–2. In this way, the cut-off saw eliminates much measuring and fitting. The *hand jig* (saber or bayonet) saw is the best choice for making curved and internal cuts. Some of these saws are designed to cut right up to a vertical wall. This is especially convenient when cutting openings for electrical outlets. Figure 57–3.

57–1. A cut-off or hand power saw.

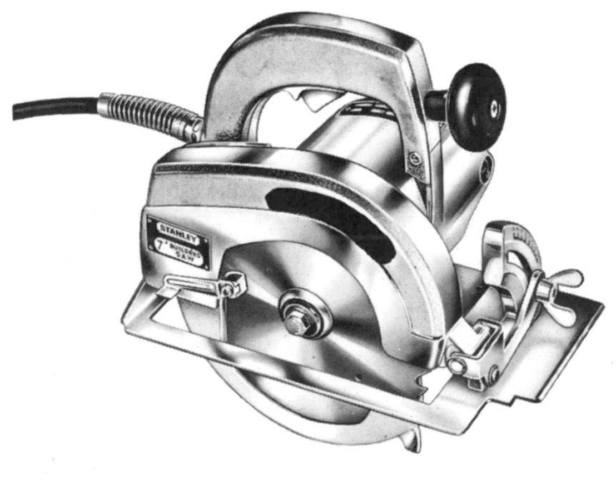

57–2. The cut-off saw is popular with carpenters, since wood can be cut after it is fastened in place.

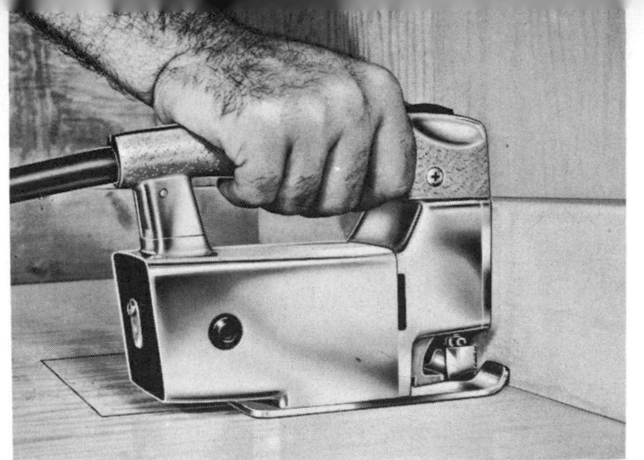

57–3. This type of hand jig saw will cut right up to a vertical wall.

57–5. The saw should be used with the good face of plywood down.

THE CUT-OFF OR POWER SAW

The power hand saw consists of a *motor*, *handle*, *base plate* or *shoe*, a *fixed* and a *movable guard*, a *blade* and a *switch*. The saw is rated principally by the size of the blade, which determines the maximum depth of cut. A good size for most work is a 6- or 8-inch blade size with at least a ¾ horsepower motor. Before connecting your saw, make sure that it is grounded to protect you from possible shock. If an extension cord must be used, make sure that it is 12 gauge or larger—up to 100 feet—and 10 gauge or larger—up to 150 feet. Unlike the regular circular saw, the portable saw cuts with the thrust upward. Figure 57–4. Because

57–4. The cutting action of the cut-off saw is exactly opposite that of the regular circular saw.

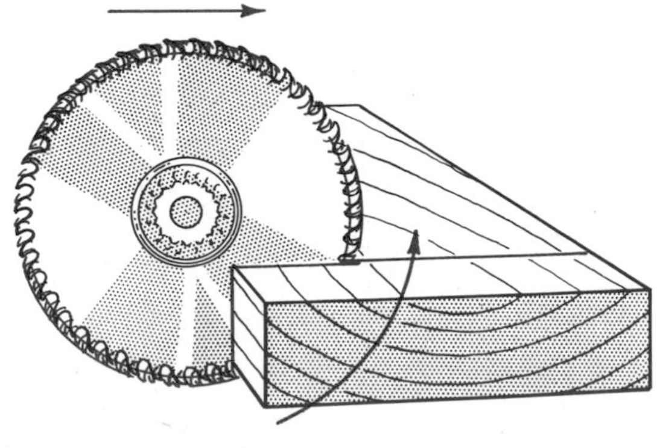

of this, the good side of plywood and other materials should be placed face down for doing the cutting.

Crosscutting and ripping. Place the work to be cut over two or more saw horses with a scrap piece of wood under each horse. Adjust the saw to a depth so that it will be slightly lower than the thicknesss of the saw. Figure 57–5. Rest the front of the base plate on the work and in line with the layout line. A combination blade is usually installed so that both crosscutting and ripping can be done. Hold the tool firmly against the work. Squeeze the switch and allow the blade to come to full speed before starting the cut. There is a line or guide edge on the front of the base plate which is exactly in line with the saw blade. Use this as a guide. Move the saw slowly along the line. If the blade slows down, back it out and re-start. If the motor should stall, always back out the blade and let it run free. *Don't turn off the machine.*

Ripping can be done freehand, but it is better to use some kind of guide. A guide can be attached to the saw, which makes ripping simpler. Figure 57–6. When making a long cut that is beyond your arms' reach, either walk with the saw or stop the saw and pull it back a few inches; then take a new

57–6. Ripping with a fence. Note the ruled guide to assist in setting the width of cut.

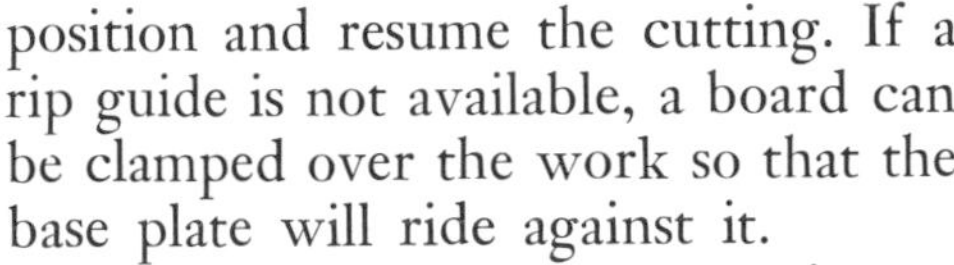

position and resume the cutting. If a rip guide is not available, a board can be clamped over the work so that the base plate will ride against it.

For more accurate crosscutting, a simple T board can be held against the edge of the stock and used as a guide for the saw. Bevels can be cut by adjusting the base plate to the correct angle. A miter can be cut freehand or by using a miter gauge. Figure 57–7.

Pocket cutting. To make a pocket cut, swing the guard out of the way. Figure 57–8. Then place the front edge of the base plate on the work. Start the saw and slowly lower the blade into the stock. When the cut is made, clean out the corners of the saw.

57–7. Making a compound miter cut with the saw.

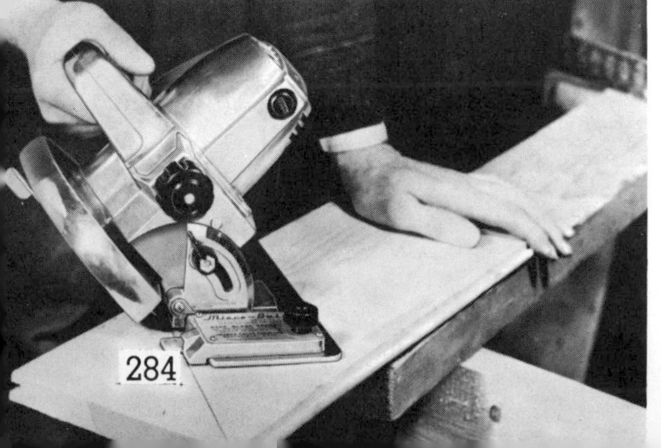

57–8. Starting a pocket cut.

HAND JIG OR SABER SAW

The hand jig (saber or bayonet) saw is used for straight or irregular cutting. It will do the same kind of work as the floor type jig saw. The machine consists of a *motor*, a *switch*, a *blade*, and a *base plate* or *shoe*. On some machines the base plate or shoe can be adjusted for making bevel cuts. The saw blades are designed to do many different kinds of cutting. Figure 57–9. Select a blade that will have at

57–9. Chart for selecting the correct blade of a hand jig saw.

Heavy cuts 2″ x 4″ at 45°	6 teeth per inch
General cutting	7, 10
Smooth cuts	12
Plywood	12
Hardboard	12
Cardboard	Knife
Leather	Knife

57–10. Using a fence for ripping.

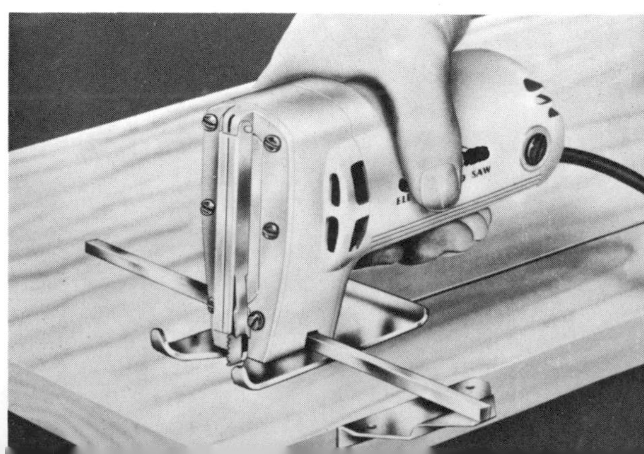

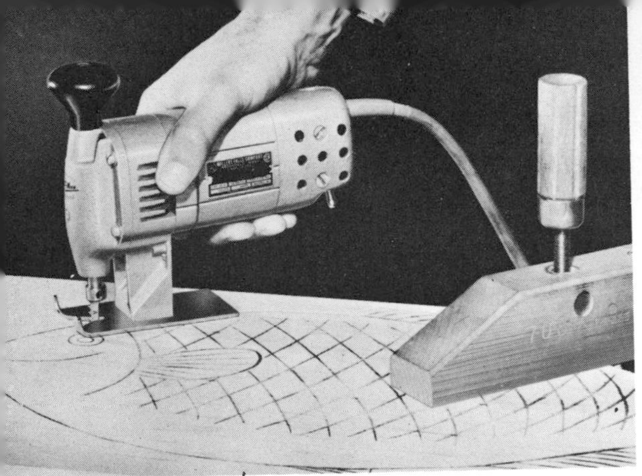

57–11. Cutting a curve. Note that the work has been firmly clamped to the top of the bench.

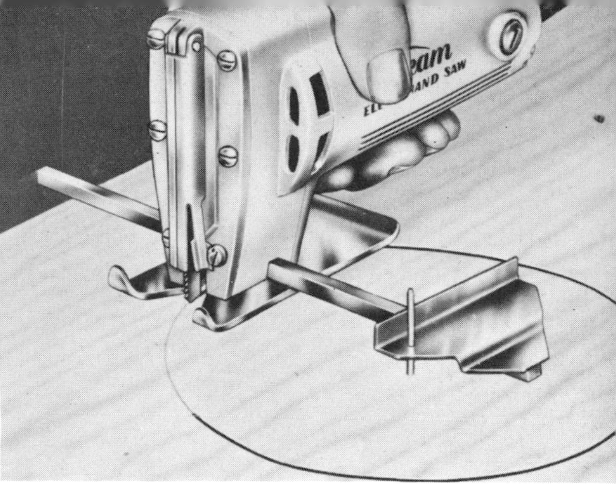

57–12. Using the ripping guide to cut a true circle.

least two teeth in contact with the work at all times. To install the blade, loosen the set screws or clamp and slip the blade in the slot. In using this saw, *always turn on the power* before bringing it in contact with the wood. Another most important thing to remember is that the base shoe must be held firmly against the material. If not, it will vibrate and break the blade.

Straight cutting. Straight cutting can be done freehand. However, it is always best to use a guide. Some machines come equipped with a rip guide that makes the job much simpler. Figure 57–10. If a standard guide is not available, clamp a piece of extra material over the stock as a guide. For crosscutting, a simple T board is best.

Curves. Regular and irregular curves both can be cut. Remember that the smallest radius to be sawed should be at least three times the width of the blade. Fasten the work firmly to a bench, allow the saw to come to full speed, and then carefully guide it along the layout line. Figure 57–11. Circles can be cut by using the rip guide as a jig. Figure 57–12.

Cutting internal openings. The simplest method of cutting openings is to drill a clearance hole in the scrap stock. However, the cut can be made without first drilling the hole. This is called *plunge cutting*. Mark the opening to be cut. Then hold the tool at an angle with the shoe resting on the surface. Turn on the power. Slowly lower the saw blade into the work until the blade cuts through the material. Then cut the opening. Figure 57–13.

57–13. Starting an internal cut. Whenever possible it is better practice to drill a small hole in the waste stock.

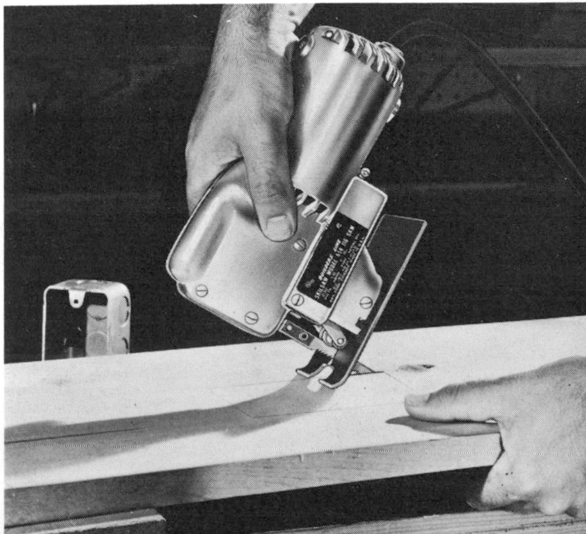

CAN YOU ANSWER THESE QUESTIONS ABOUT PORTABLE SAWS?

1. Name the two kinds of portable hand saws.
2. Why should plywood be cut with the good face down when using portable saws?
3. What is pocket cutting?
4. Describe the methods of guiding portable saws for ripping.
5. Tell what plunge cutting is and how to do it.

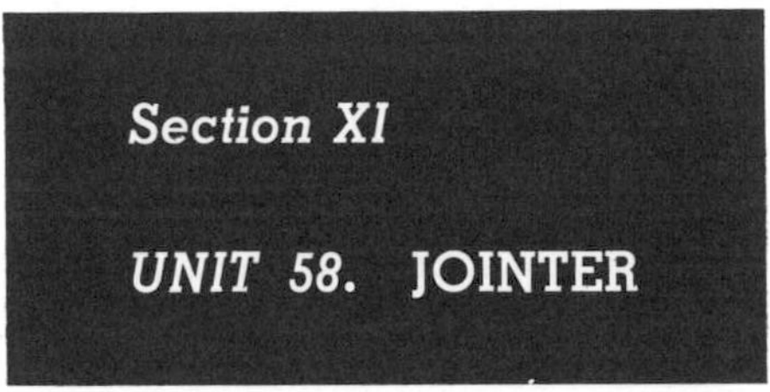

Section XI

UNIT 58. JOINTER

The jointer is used for surfacing or face-planing, jointing an edge or end, beveling, chamfering, tapering, and rabbeting. Figure 58–1. It consists of a *base*, two *tables* (the front or in-feed table and the rear or out-feed table), a *cutter head*, a *fence* and a *guard*. Figure 58–2a.

The circular cutter head usually holds three knives firmly mounted with wedges and set screws. The size of the jointer is determined by the

58–1. Common processes that can be done on the jointer.

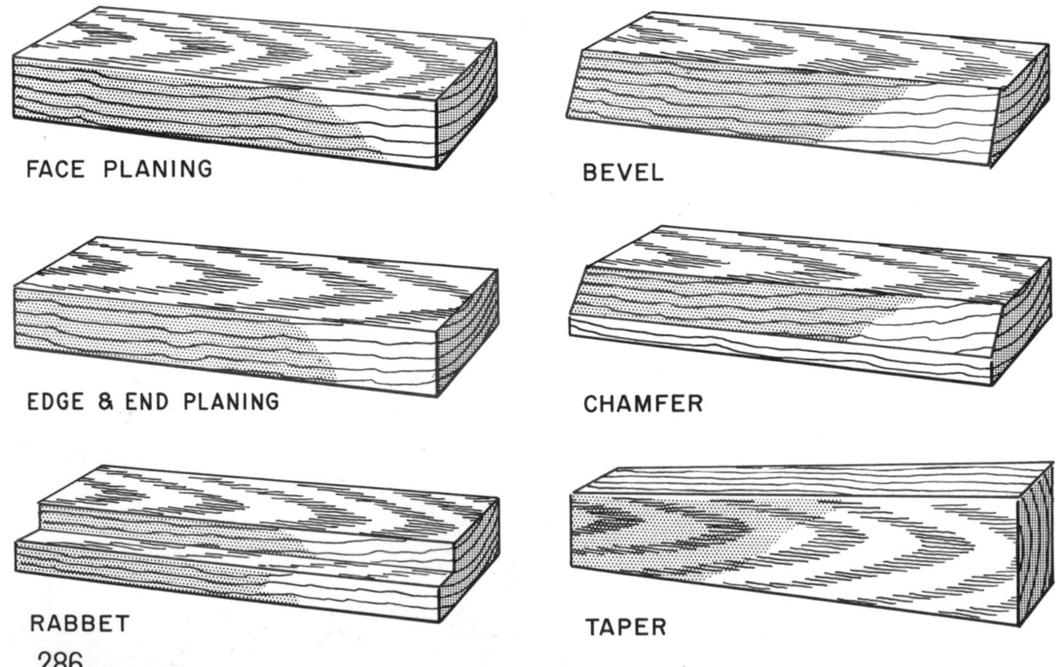

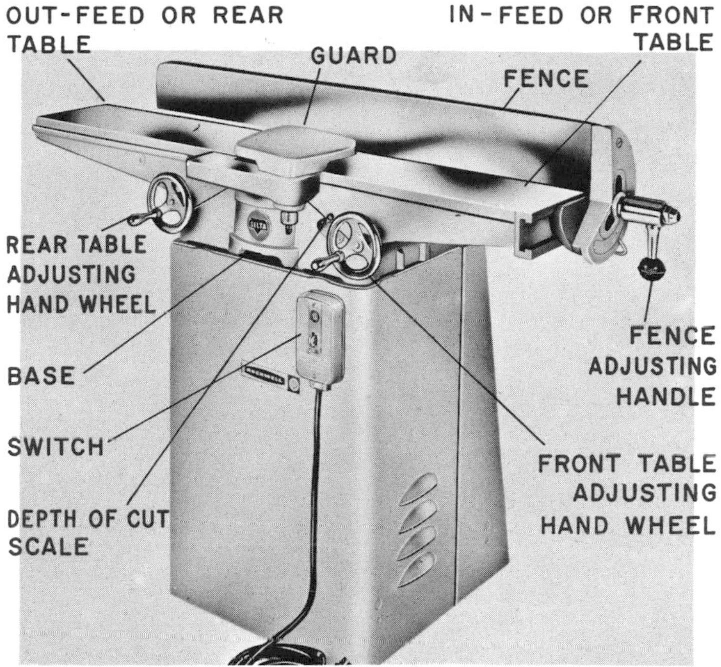

58–2a. A jointer with fence and guard. The parts include a base, the cutter head, the in-feed or front table, and the out-feed or rear table. This is a 6-inch jointer.

length of these knives. The most common size for the small shop is the 6- or 8-inch machine.

The in-feed and out-feed tables are mounted on sliding ways so that they may be raised and lowered to make adjustments. The out-feed table supports the work after it has been cut and therefore should be the same height as the cutting knives at their highest point. Figure 58–2b. The in-feed table supports the work before it is cut. Therefore the height of this table determines the thickness of the cut to be taken. Once the out-feed table has been adjusted to proper height, it can be locked in position and does not need to be changed. Only the in-feed table should be moved up or down to change the thickness of the cut. The fence of a jointer is usually set at right angles to the table but it can be adjusted at any angle when you want to plane a bevel or chamfer.

SAFETY

The jointer is not dangerous if used correctly. It can be a hazard, however,

58–2b. Using a straightedge to check the position of the out-feed table so that it is level with the knives.

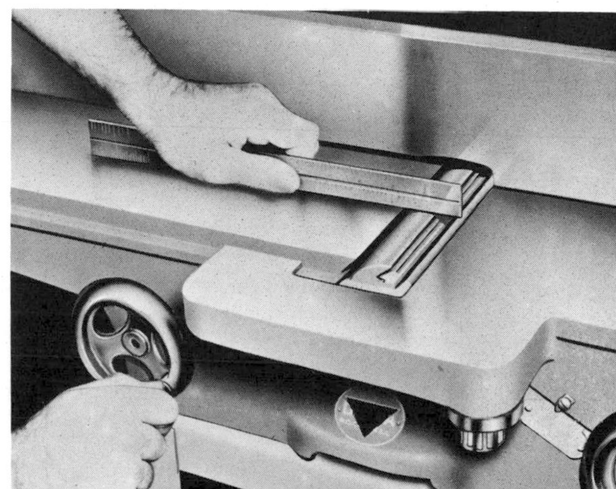

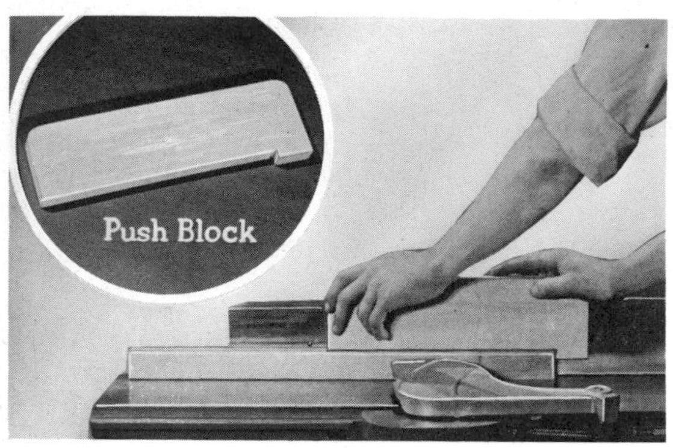

58–3. Using a push block. Never attempt to surface thin stock or to joint the edge of narrow pieces without using a push block to keep your fingers away from the revolving cutter.

if the following rules are not observed:

1. Always make sure that the guard is over the cutter head.
2. Use a push block when surfacing thin stock. Figure 58–3.
3. Feed the stock with the grain. Figure 58–4.
4. Keep your hands clear of the danger zone. Figure 58–5.
5. Never attempt to surface stock that is less than 10 inches in length.
6. Stand to the left of the jointer, never directly in back of it.
7. Do not attempt to take too heavy a cut.

FACE PLANING OR SURFACING

Face planing or surfacing means planing the surfaces of stock true. Only stock that is less in width than the blades of the jointer should be face planed. *Generally speaking, the jointer is not used for face planing.* If it is used, set the in-feed table to take a very thin cut. Hold the stock firmly against the table. With one hand push the stock with a push block as the other hand holds the front of the stock down. Slowly push the board through the cutters. As in hand planing, most pressure should be applied to the front of the board as the cutting is started. Then equal pressure is applied to both front and back as the board passes across the cutter. Finally more pressure is applied to the rear of the board as the

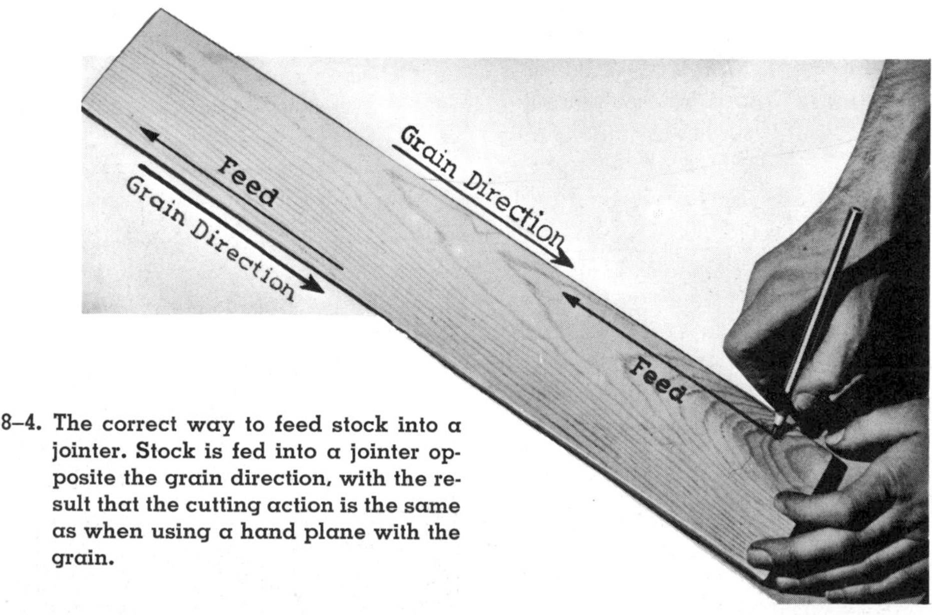

58–4. The correct way to feed stock into a jointer. Stock is fed into a jointer opposite the grain direction, with the result that the cutting action is the same as when using a hand plane with the grain.

major portion of it has passed the out-feed table. Figure 58–6.

JOINTING AN EDGE

The most common use of the jointer is to square an edge true with the face surface. To do this, make sure that the fence is at right angles to the table. Check this with a try square. Hold the stock on the in-feed table with the face surface against the fence. Use one hand to guide the stock and the other hand to apply forward pressure. Figure 58–7. Do not push the stock through the jointer too fast, as this will cause little ripples to be formed by the revolving cutter.

BEVELING AND CHAMFERING

To cut a bevel or chamfer on an edge with a jointer, set the fence at the

58–6. Surfacing or face planing. A push block should be used after the surfacing has started.

proper angle to the table. The fence may be tilted in or out. Figure 58–8. Check this angle with a sliding T bevel; then proceed as in jointing an edge.

58–5. The *danger zone* of a jointer is the area directly over the revolving cutter. This is the area you must guard against.

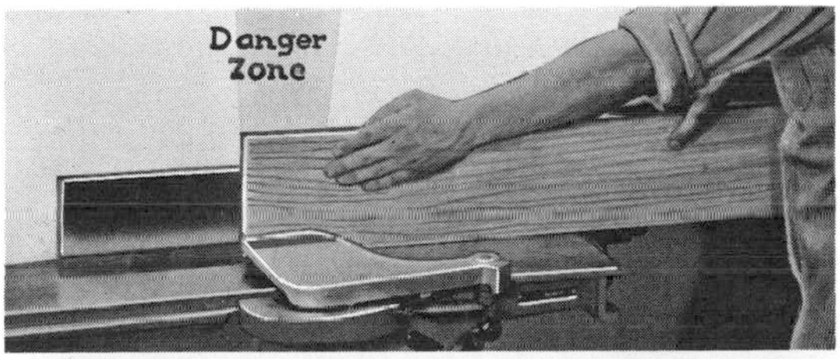

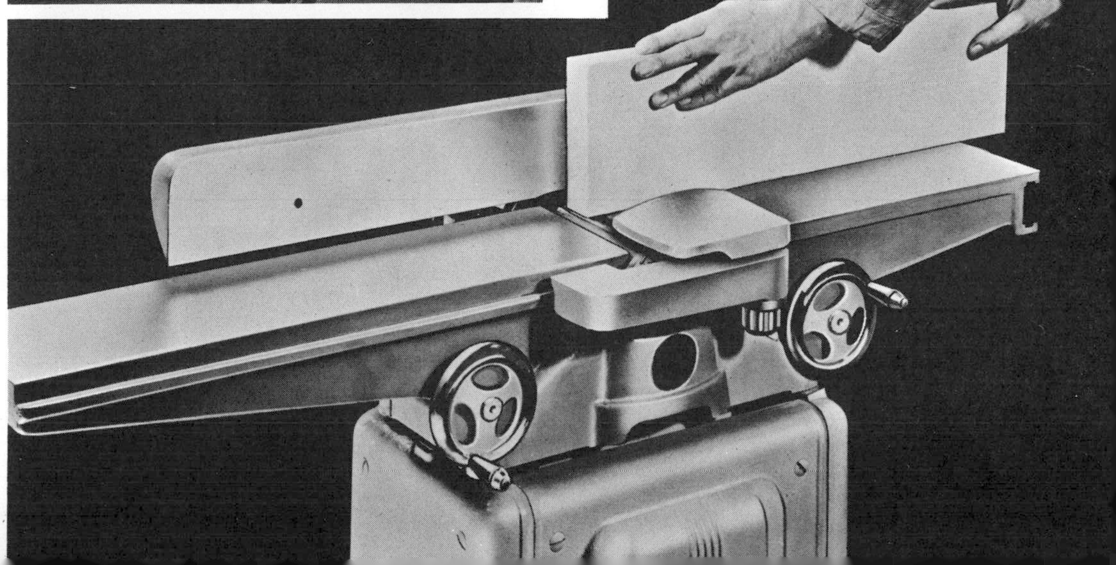

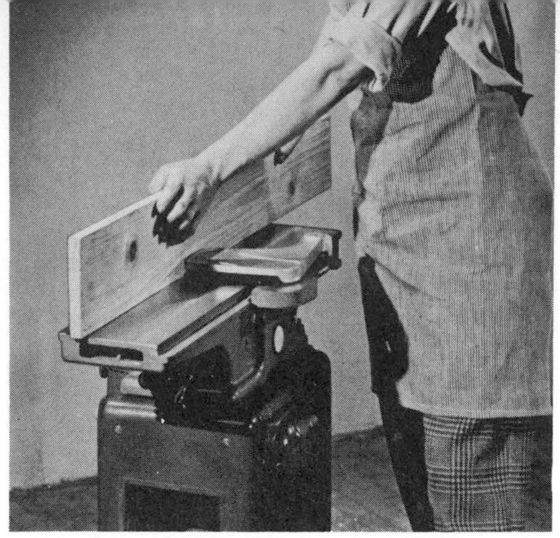

58–7. **Jointing an edge. The stock is held firmly against the in-feed table at the beginning of the cut; then even pressure is applied. Finally, pressure is applied on the out-feed table.**

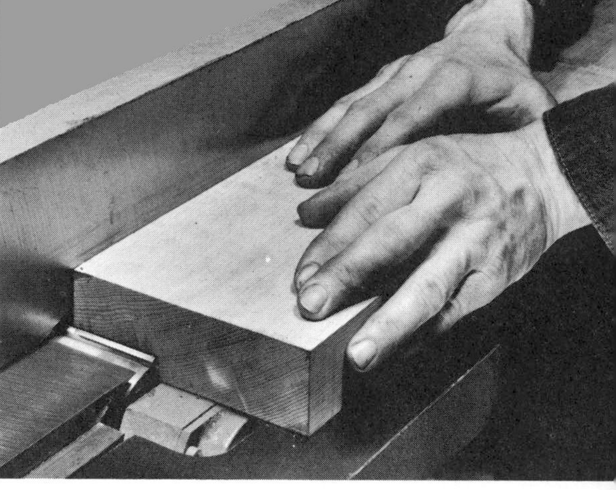

58–9. **Cutting a rabbet on the jointer.**

RABBETING

A rabbet can be cut with the grain by first adjusting the fence to an amount equal to the width of the rabbet. Then the in-feed table is adjusted to an amount equal to the depth of the rabbet. If the rabbet is quite deep, it may be necessary to cut it in two passes. CAUTION: The guard must be removed for this process, so be especially careful. Figure 58–9.

CAN YOU ANSWER THESE QUESTIONS ON THE JOINTER?

1. Name the parts of a jointer.
2. How can you tell what size it is?
3. Name the two common sizes of jointers used in school shops.
4. How is the depth of cut controlled?
5. List the safety precautions to be observed in operating the jointer.
6. Is the jointer commonly used for face planing? Explain.
7. How can the fence of the jointer be checked for squareness?

58–8. **Cutting a bevel or chamfer. The fence of the jointer can be tilted for the operation.**

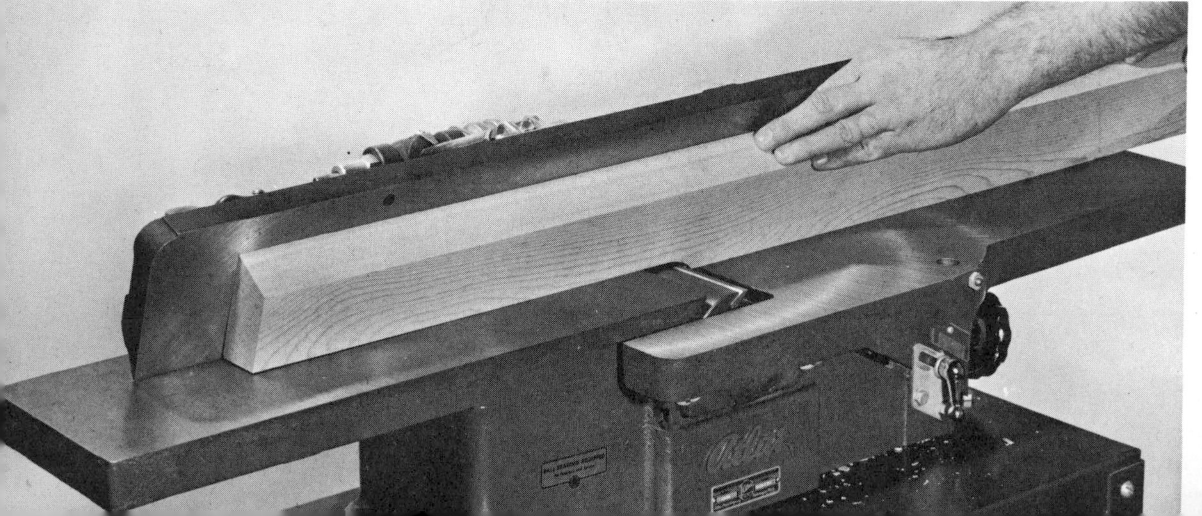

8. What causes ripples to be formed on a board when it is run through the jointer?
9. How can you check the fence for cutting a bevel or chamfer?
10. Explain how to cut a rabbet.

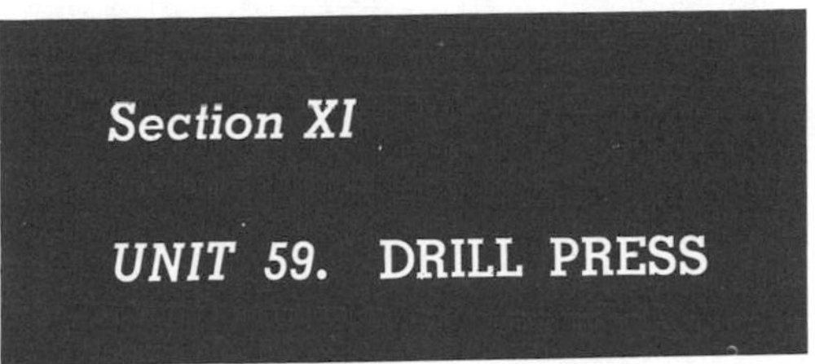

Section XI

UNIT 59. DRILL PRESS

The drill press, although used less than the circular saw, is one of the most valuable tools to have in a small shop. Figure 59–1. It can be used not only for drilling, boring, and countersinking, but for such common operations as shaping, routing, carving, sanding, and mortising. Figure 59–2. Because of this and because the drill press is fairly inexpensive, it should be one of the first additions to a small shop. To do all types of work the drill press should have variable-speed pulleys for varying spindle speed, from a low speed of 450 to 500 r.p.m. for such work as drilling and mortising, to a high speed of 5,000 r.p.m. for shaping and routing. Figure 59–3.

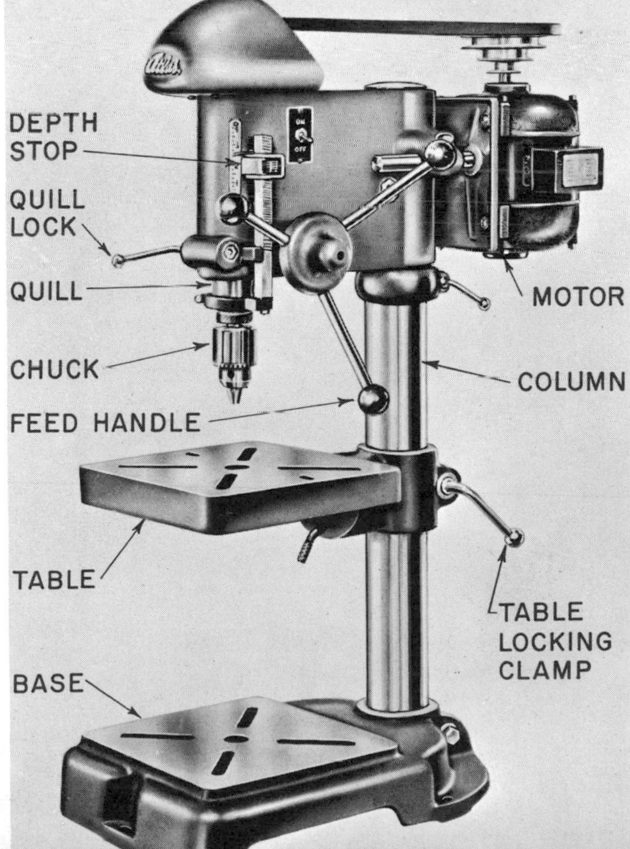

59–1. A bench-type drill press showing the major parts. Size is indicated by the largest diameter of stock through which a hole can be drilled.

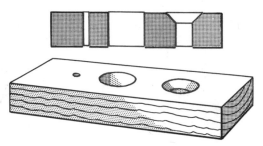

DRILLING, BORING, & COUNTERSINKING

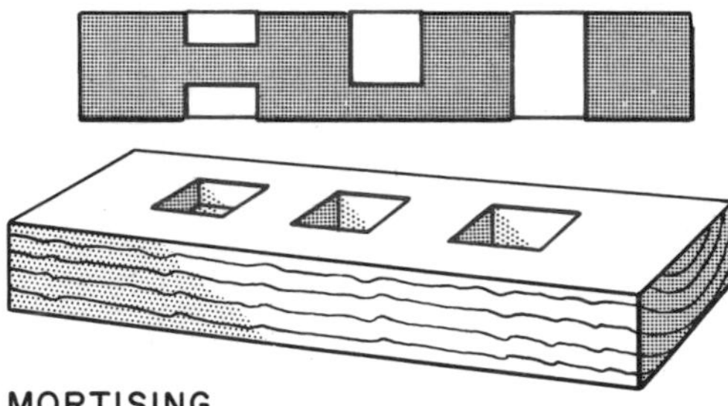

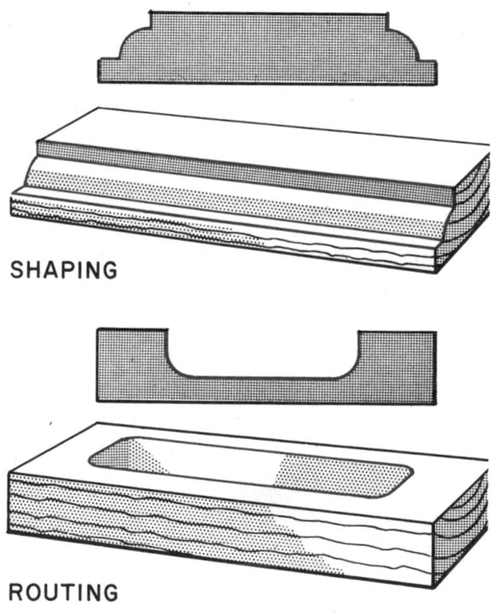

59–2. Common operations that can be performed on the drill press.

DRILLING, BORING, AND COUNTERSINKING

Drill presses are usually equipped with a Jacob's chuck to hold drills, auger bits, and other cutting tools. To drill or bore holes, locate and punch

59–3. Drill press with variable speed pulleys. The range of speed is from 450 r.p.m. to 5,000 r.p.m. The speed is changed by moving the dial lever while the drill press is running. Never try to change the speed when the machine is off. This is the ideal machine for doing a wide variety of drill-press operations.

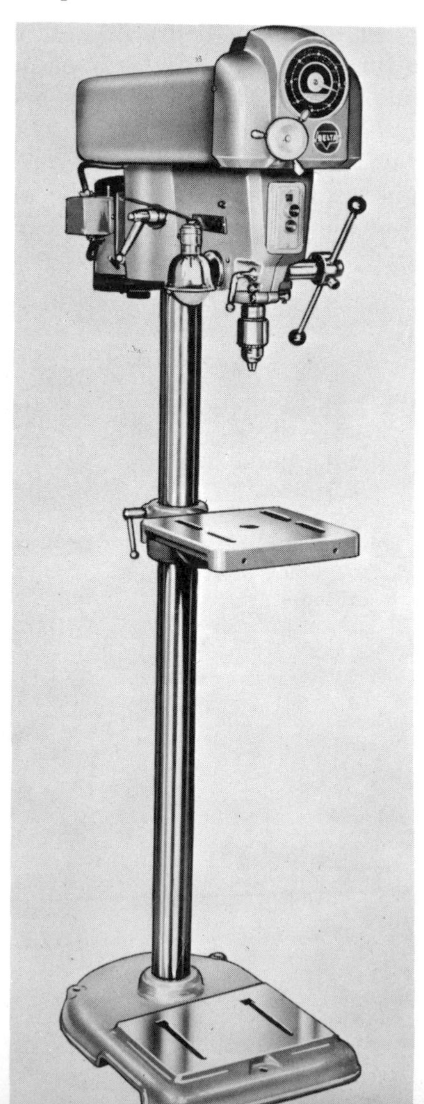

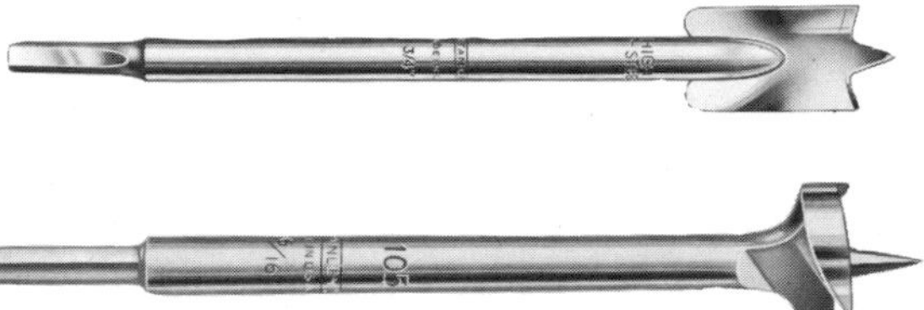

59–4. Speed or machine bits that can be used in the drill press.

the center of the hole. Select a drill or auger bit of the correct size and fasten it in the chuck. An auger bit must have a straight shank and brad point. There are several kinds of machine bits that can be used. Figure 59–4. Adjust the spindle speed to a slower speed for larger drills and auger bits and a faster speed for smaller ones. Adjust the table to correct height. Make sure that the hole in the table is directly under the drill, or place a piece of scrap stock on the table under the piece to be drilled or bored. Hold the piece securely and apply even pressure as you feed the drill slowly into the wood. Figure

59–5. Drilling wood with a twist drill. Make sure that the stock is held firmly against the table of the drill press while the drilling is done.

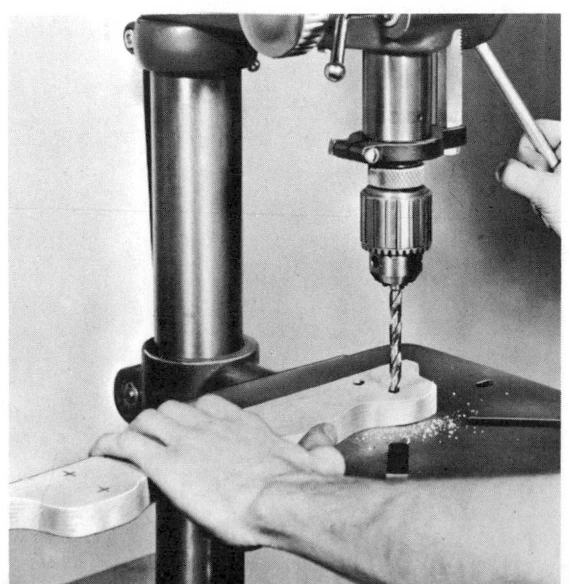

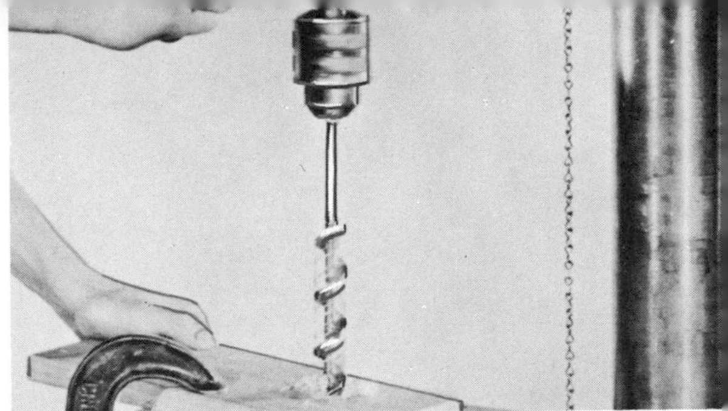

59–6. Boring a hole with an auger bit. Stock is clamped to the bed with a C clamp. The auger bit must have a straight shank in order to be used in a three-jaw chuck.

59–5, 59–6, and 59–7. Never force a drill or auger bit into the wood. Drilling or boring holes in round stock can be done by holding the work in a V block. Figure 59–8. Countersinking is necessary when installing flat head screws. Figure 59–9.

MORTISING

If much furniture construction is being done, a mortising attachment should be available. This greatly simplifies cutting a mortise-and-tenon joint. A mortising attachment consists of a hollow, square mortising chisel in

59–7. Using a power Foerstner bit with the work securely clamped to the table.

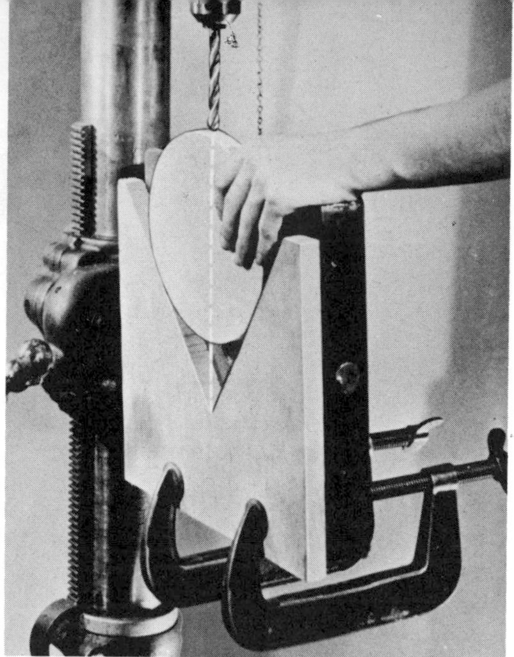

59–8. **Drilling holes in a cylindrical piece of stock, using a V block. The table has been turned at a 90-degree angle to its original position and a V block clamped to the table with two C clamps.**

which an auger bit revolves. The chisel itself is ground to a sharp point at each corner. These points enter the wood just after the revolving bit and cut the square opening after the bit has removed most of the stock. On most mortising attachments, the chisel is fastened to the quill of the drill press and a straight-shank auger bit fastened in the chuck. Of course, the chisel should be the same width as the width of the mortise to be cut. A fence should be attached to the table to guide the stock. Figure 59–10.

59–9. **Countersinking holes on the drill press.**

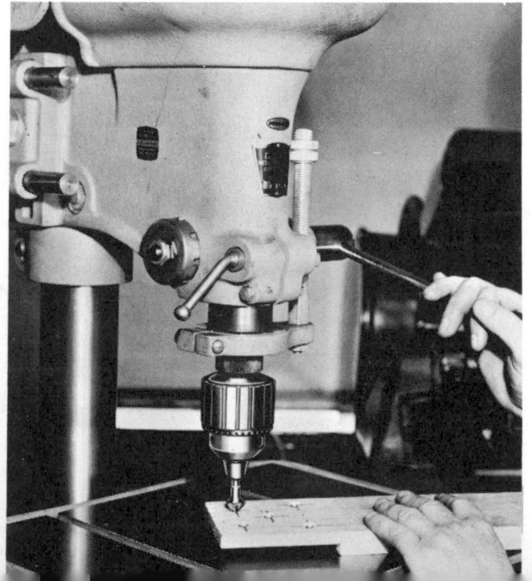

SHAPING

For shaping, it is necessary to have a spindle speed of 5,000 r.p.m. This speed can be attained by using the variable-speed pulley or a high-speed motor. It is also necessary to have a special adapter that will hold the shaper cutter. Figure 59–11. This adapter can be attached to the spindle of the drill press. Then an inexpensive set of shaper cutters will enable you to construct setups that will cut a variety of shapes. Never use a shaper cutter in a chuck. Select the shaper cutters for the particular shape you want to make. Figure 59–12.

59–10. **Using a mortising attachment. The part for holding the chisel is locked to the quill of the drill press, and the auger bit is fastened in the chuck. A fence is locked to the table and clamps are attached to hold the stock in place.**

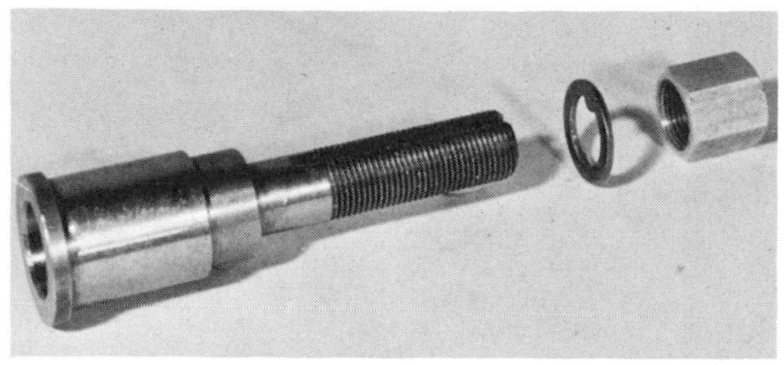

59–11. An adapter for holding shaper cutters. This one is fastened to the spindle of the drill press so that side pressure can be exerted on the shaper cutters. Never attempt to hold shaper or router cutters in a drill-press chuck unless you are sure that the chuck is a part of the spindle assembly as a unit.

59–12. Shaper cutters. Various shapes are needed to make the designs in shaper operations.

The depth of the cut can be controlled by placing a collar of the correct diameter just above or below the cutter or by using a fence. Fasten the cutter and collar to the special adapter. Raise the table to the correct position and lock it in place. Make a trial cut in a piece of scrap stock of the same thickness as the finished piece. In using a shaper attachment, force the wood into the cutter very slowly. Sometimes it is a good idea to cut the design to partial depth and then to go over it again. If the design is cut on three or four edges, finish the ends first and then the sides. If the trial cut is satisfactory, cut the edge. Figure 59–13.

ROUTING

A routing tool is fastened in a special router attachment. The spindle speed must be about 5,000 r.p.m. Various types of routing such as grooves, slots, and irregular openings can be done on the drill press. Figure 59–14.

59–13. Using the drill press as a shaper. When doing shaping operations, a high spindle speed is required.

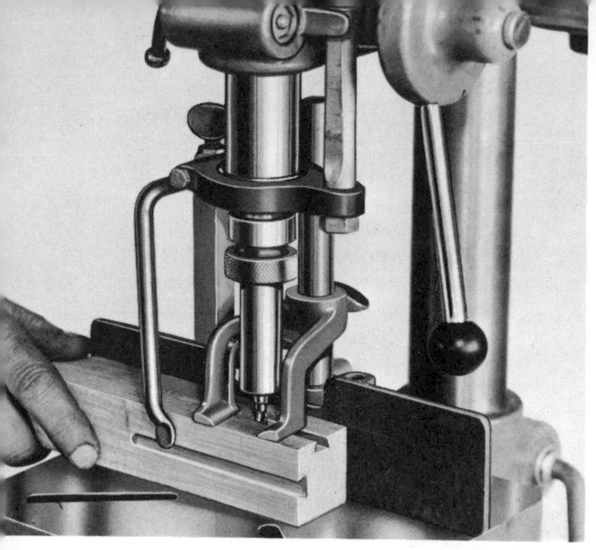

59–14. Doing router work on a drill press. Router cutters are fastened in a special adapter. Make sure that the stock is firmly held against the table and a fence when doing the routing. Notice the guides that have been clamped to the machine to hold the stock in place.

CAN YOU ANSWER THESE QUESTIONS ON THE DRILL PRESS?

1. Drilling is not the only operation performed on the drill press. Name several others.
2. About what speed is necessary for shaping and routing?
3. What kind of auger bits can be fastened in the drill press?
4. Name the parts of a mortising attachment and describe how it is used.
5. What two machines are most commonly used for making mortise-and-tenon joints?
6. What is meant by shaping an edge?
7. How do you control the depth of cut for shaping?

Section XI

UNIT 60. SANDERS

With the correct power sander you can save much tedious work yet give the project a smooth finish. All sanders make use of an abrasive paper or cloth in the form of a sheet, disc, or belt.

BELT AND DISC SANDER

The combination bench or floor belt and disc sander is used when the workpiece can be brought to the sander. Figure 60–1. It is especially good for sanding individual parts. The *belt sander* consists of two drums over which an endless abrasive belt moves. One drum has two adjustments on it, one for belt tension and the other for centering the belt on the drums. The machine also comes equipped with a table against which the work can be held. Figure 60–2. Before using the machine, make sure that the belt is not too tight and that the guards are in

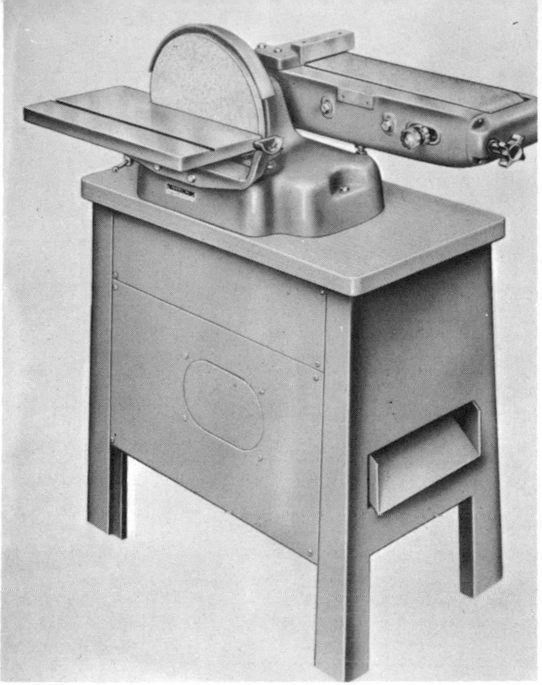

60–1. **A combination disc and belt sander. While these can be separate machines, the combined sander works very well.**

Section XI. Unit 60. Sanders

The *disc sander* is really a motor with a flat disc on one end to which an abrasive cloth is cemented. It has rather violent action, so is good for fast, rough work. When using, always work on the side that revolves into the table. Remember that the outside of the disc cuts faster than the inside.

This machine is very good for sanding the edge of irregular-shaped pieces.

PORTABLE BELT SANDER

A portable belt sander operates in a manner similar to the floor machine except that the revolving belt is placed

60–3. **Sanding the edge of an irregular-shaped piece on a disc sander.**

over the work instead of the work against the belt. As this machine is used, the belt tends to carry it away from the operator. Therefore always grip the sander firmly with both hands. Figure 60–3. Then move it evenly in a straight line with the wood grain. Never apply pressure to this machine since it will cut very rapidly. Move the machine evenly in a straight line with the grain. Also be careful that you do not round the edges. Remember never

place. When sanding work, hold it square with the abrasive belt. CAUTION: Never attempt to hold a very small piece in your hand since the belt will tend to pull it out of your fingers. Always use a push block when sanding thin pieces.

60–2. **Using a belt sander to sand end grain.**

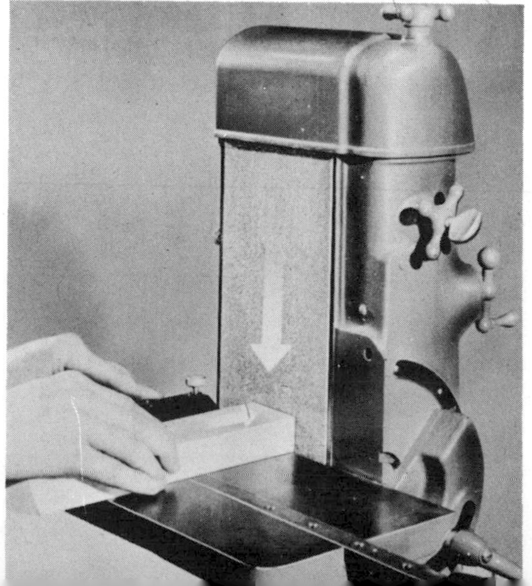

60–4. Portable belt sander. This machine will sand large surfaces such as a table top.

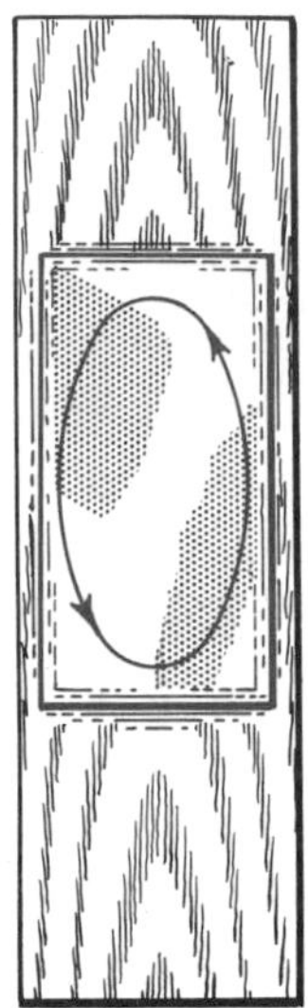

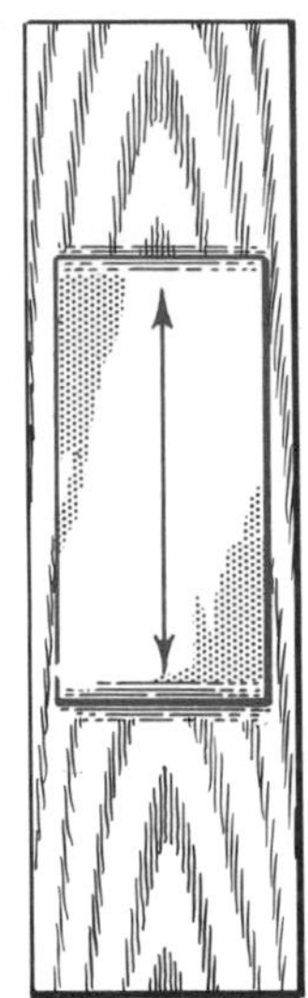

60–5. Sanding action of finishing sanders. On some machines two types of action can be obtained by moving a switch.

to turn on the motor while the machine is resting on the wood to be sanded.

FINISHING SANDER

There are several kinds of finishing sanders, all of which operate on one of three basic principles: rotary, orbital, or straight-line action. Figure 60–4. Straight-line action leaves the least amount of cross-grain scratches. Finishing sanders are used primarily for fine sanding after the project is completed. Figure 60–5.

CAN YOU ANSWER THESE QUESTIONS ON SANDERS?

1. Name four sanders commonly found in the shop.
2. What determines the quality of smoothness or roughness of the wood surface after sanding?
3. What is the best sander to use for a light finishing sanding after the project is assembled?
4. Describe the way to use a portable continuous-belt sander.

60–6. Using the finishing or pad sander. This is the best machine to use after the project is assembled.

Section XI

UNIT 61. PORTABLE ROUTER

The portable router can do many cutting and shaping jobs. Figure 61–1a-b. It consists of a powerful motor mounted in an adjustable base. There is a collet chuck at the end of the motor shaft that can hold many different kinds of cutting tools. Some of the common router bits and cutters are shown in Figure 61–2a-b. To install the cutter bit, loosen the nut on the chuck and slip the bit in place. Then tighten the nut or nuts. Figure 61–3.

61–1a. A portable router. This model is open on one side and has a light under the motor, to make it easy to see the working section.

61–1b. Common cuts made with a router.

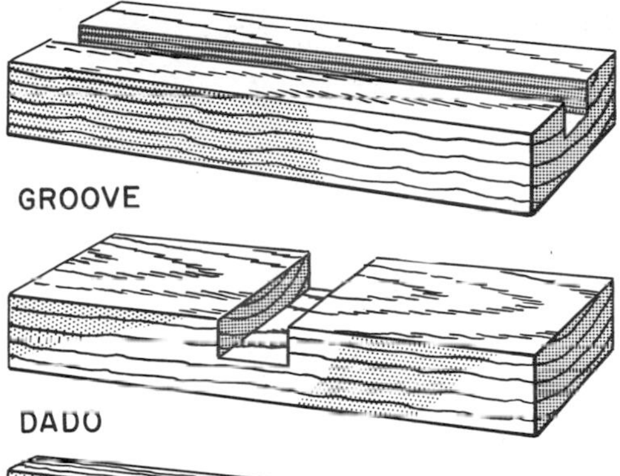

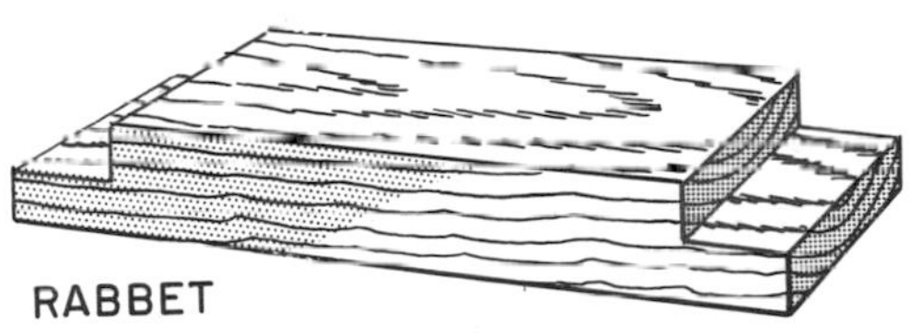

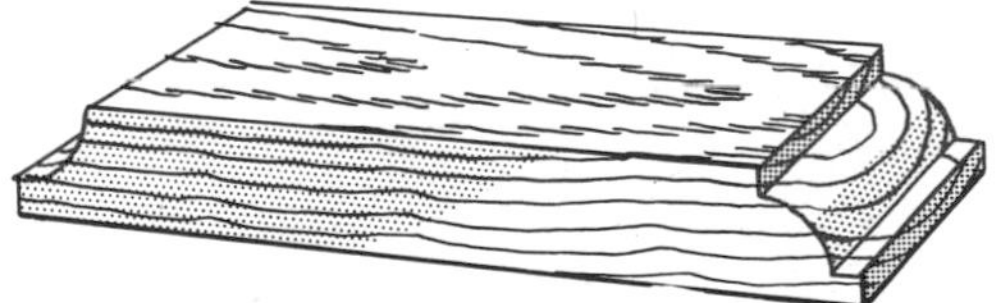

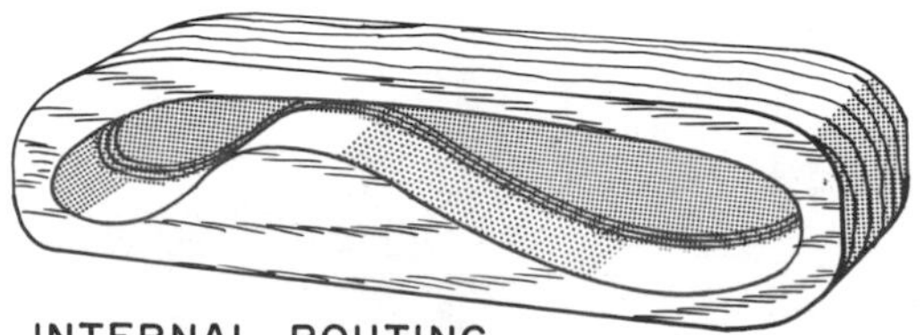

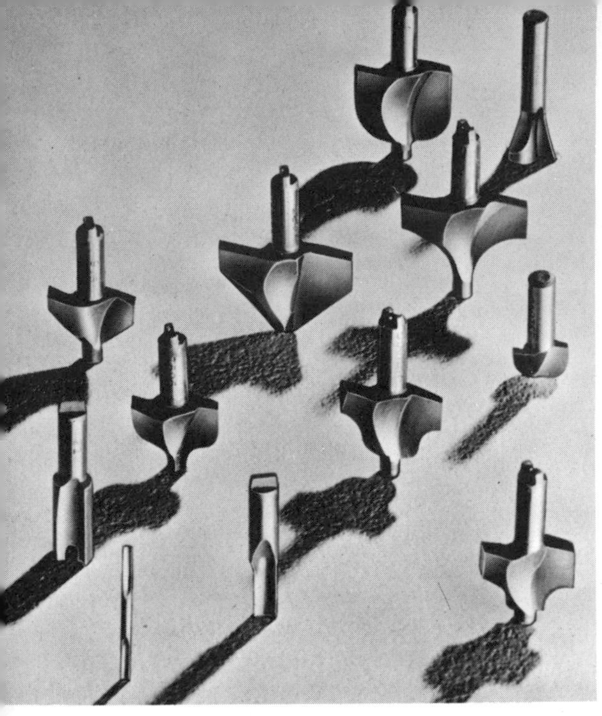

61–2a. Some standard sizes and shapes of router bits.

To adjust for depth of cut, the base is raised or lowered. In some routers the base screws onto the motor housing.

61–2b. A few of the common router bits. a. Straight bit. b. Rounding-over bit. c. Beading bit. d. Cove bit. e. Rabbeting bit. f. V-grooving bit.

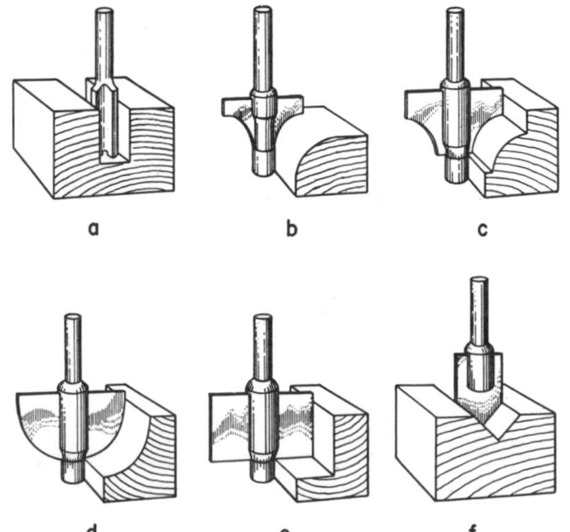

61–3. Select the proper bit and insert it all the way into the collet chuck. With the safety switch in a locked position, the shaft is held firmly. The chuck can be tightened readily, using only one wrench.

In others it slides up and down. The bit revolves clockwise. Therefore, when cutting straight edges, move the router from left to right. When making circular cuts move the router in a counterclockwise direction. Figure 61–4. Common uses are:

1. Freehand routing. Routing is called freehand when the operator does the routing without guides. Figure 61–5. A good example of this would be routing out a name plate or numbers of

61–4. Use the correct direction of feed in cutting with a router.

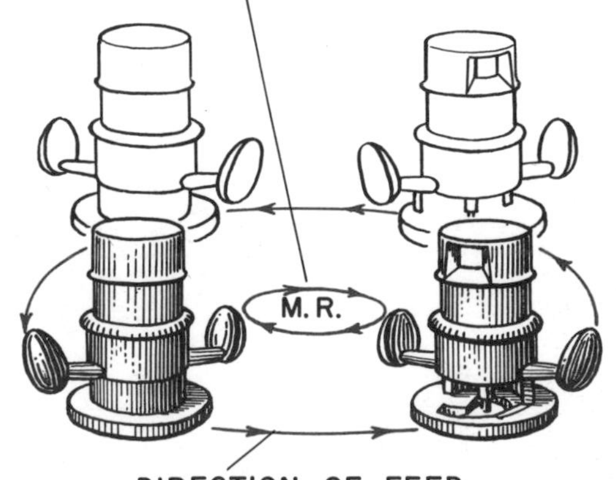

61–5. Freehand routing. The router is moved and controlled by the operator.

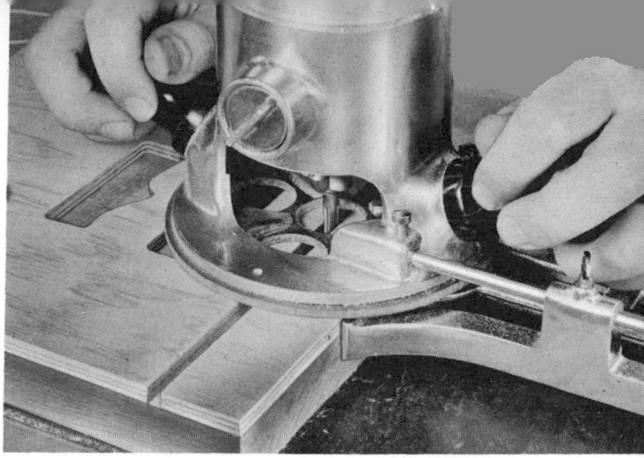

61–7. Using a guide attachment for cutting a dado.

an address. Sometimes the letters or numbers are formed by the cutter bit. In other cases, the background around the letters and numbers is routed so the numbers stand out.

2. Shaping an edge or making a molding. By using a bit with a pilot on the end, the edge of a table top or molding for a picture frame can be made. Figure 61–6. The pilot edge can be shaped without a guide. Select the right bit shape and fasten it in the chuck. Move the base up and down until the bit is out the correct distance. Select a piece of scrap wood of the same thickness as the finished article. Try the bit on the scrap stock.

3. Routing with a guide. For making such cuts as a groove or a dado, a guide is attached. Figure 61–7. The width of the cut is determined by the bit. Of course, a wider cut can be made with a narrower bit by making two or more passes. The depth of cut can be changed by adjusting the base to the motor housing.

INLAYING

An interesting surface decoration for wood is the addition of a strip or block of inlay for contrast. To add this strip, first cut a groove the desired distance from the edge using a lefthand spiral bit. Use a gauge of some sort to guide the router. Set the bit for the correct depth, which should be equal to the thickness of the inlaying material. Carefully cut a groove around the edge of the material. Figure 61–8. The corners will be rounded and must be trimmed out with a chisel. The groove must be cut the exact width of the inlay strip. Then cut the strip of inlay material with a miter corner. Fit each piece in to check the final design. Then apply glue to the back of the inlay and fasten it in the groove. Place a piece of wood over the inlay and

61–6. The pilot on the end of the cutter controls the amount of cut. It rides on the edge and does no cutting.

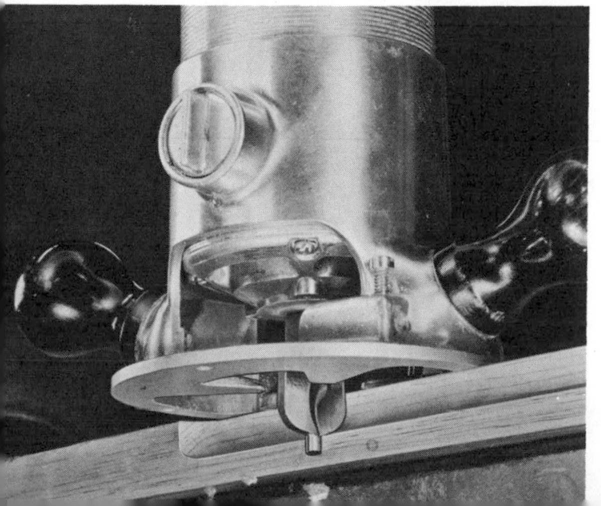

61–8. A router can be used to cut the groove for inlaying.

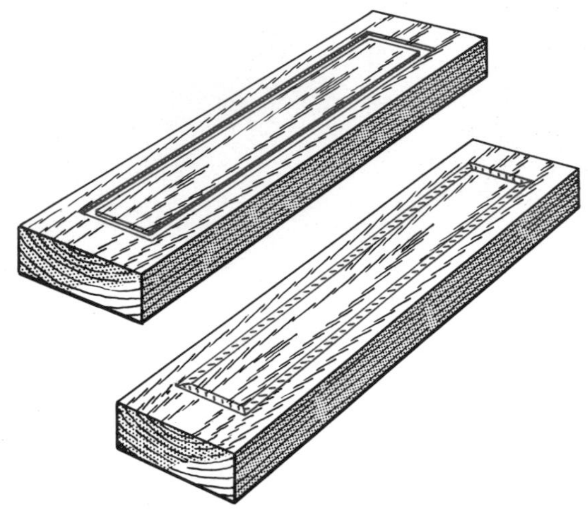

clamp it until the glue is dry. Interesting block inlays can be purchased for mounting in the tops of tables and other projects. Place the piece of inlay material over the location and trace the outline with a sharp pencil. Then mark it with a sharp knife. Set a bit to the correct depth and rout out the area in which the block inlay is to be placed. The sharp corners must be cleaned out with a knife. Then glue the inlay in place.

CAN YOU ANSWER THESE QUESTIONS ON THE ROUTER?

1. Name the major parts of the router.
2. What is freehand routing?
3. Is a guide necessary in shaping an edge?
4. Name some of the common router bits.
5. Explain how to do inlaying.

Section XI

UNIT 62. WOOD LATHE

The wood lathe performs many basic operations that cannot be done by hand. It has important industrial uses. You will find a variety of uses for it in making turned parts for your projects. Figure 62–1a and 62–1b. The machine consists of a *bed*, the *headstock assembly* that is permanently fastened to the bed, a *tailstock* that slides along and can be locked in any position on the bed, and a *tool rest.* Figure 62–2. The *headstock spindle* has a hollow-ground *taper* into which is fastened the *spur* or *live center*. The outside of the spindle is threaded to receive the faceplate. The speed of the lathe is controlled by changing the belts to the various positions. Figure 62–3. The tailstock is also taper-ground and a dead or cup center is inserted in the spindle.

The common cutting tools include a

62–1a. Parts of this cherry tier table were expertly turned on a wood lathe.

1-inch gouge, a *½-inch gouge*, a *1-inch skew*, a *½-inch skew*, a *round-nose*, a *spear* and a *parting tool*. Figure 62–4. In addition, the operator must have a good *bench rule*, a pair of inside and outside *calipers*, Figure 62–5, a *pencil*, *dividers*, and *hermaphrodite caliper*.

METHODS OF TURNING

There are two basic methods of turning wood, namely cutting and scraping. In *cutting*, the tool is held so that the cutting edge actually digs into the revolving stock to peel off the shaving. Figure 62–6. This is a faster method, but it requires much skill. It produces a smooth surface that requires very little sanding. In *scraping*, the tool is held at right angles to the surface and fine particles are worn away instead of shavings. Figure 62–7.

62–1b. Common cuts that can be made on the wood lathe.

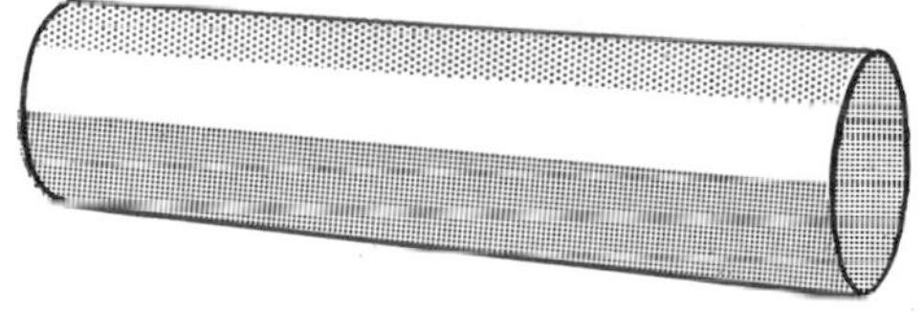

CYLINDER

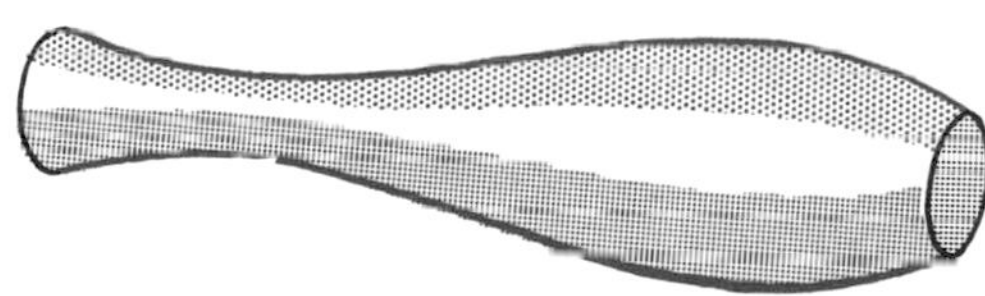

CONCAVE & CONVEX

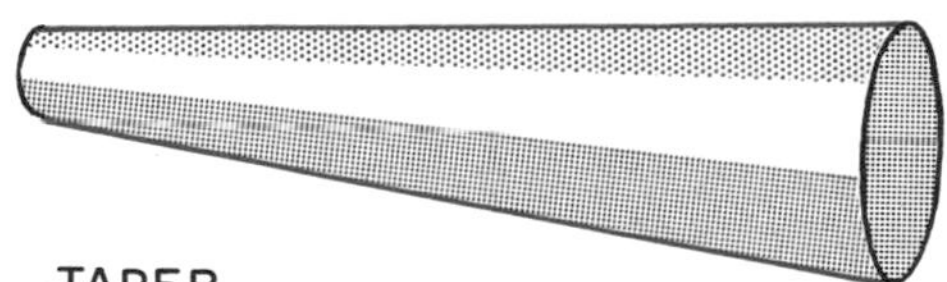

TAPER

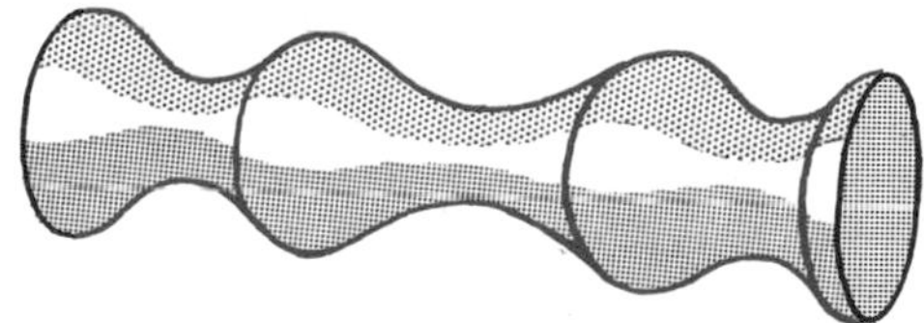

BEADS & COVES

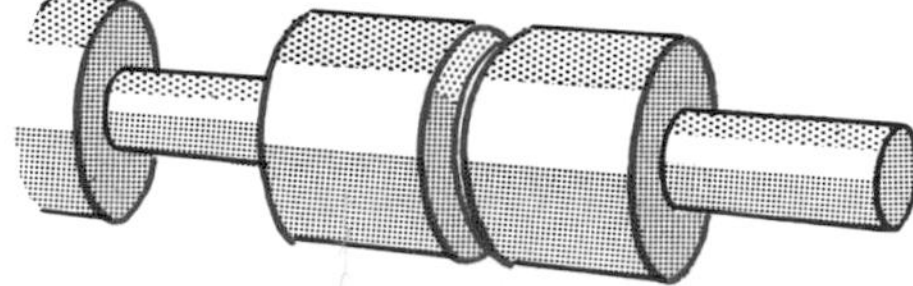

SHOULDERS & V'S

EXTERIOR & INTERIOR FACE PLATE TURNING

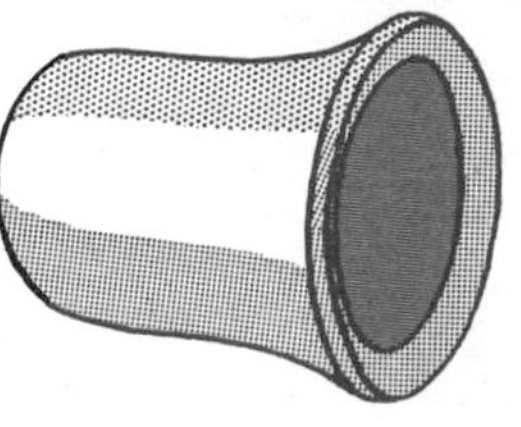

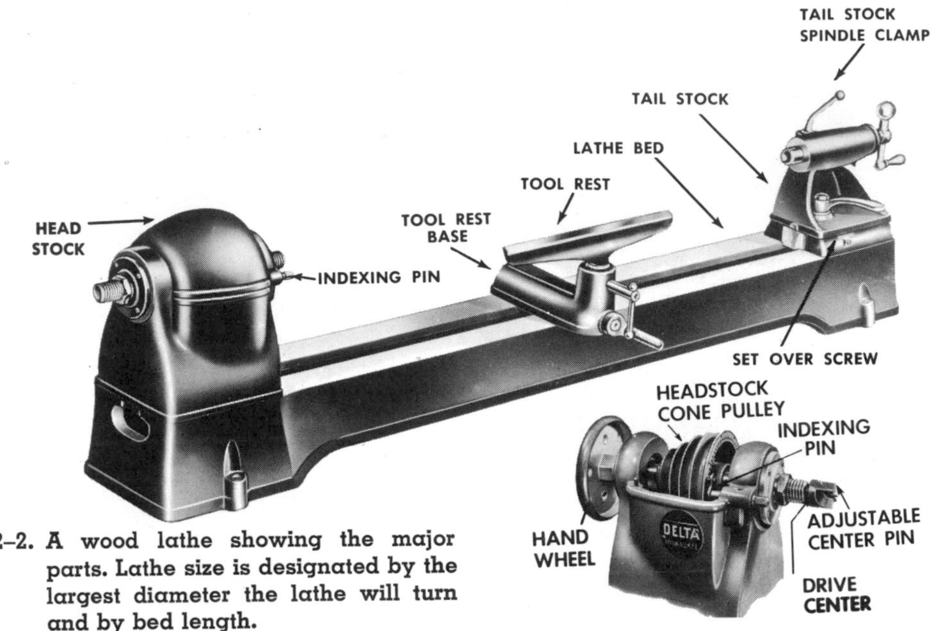

62–2. A wood lathe showing the major parts. Lathe size is designated by the largest diameter the lathe will turn and by bed length.

62–3. The headstock assembly, illustrating the threaded headstock spindle. The inner end has a right-hand thread and the outer end has a left-hand thread. Note the V pulley and also the indexing mechanism. The assembly is used for dividing faceplate work and for doing such jobs as fluting and reeding.

Scraping is easier to do and is accurate, but the surface is rougher and requires more sanding. All faceplate turning is done by the scraping method.

PREPARING STOCK TO BE TURNED

Choose a piece of wood with a rectangular measurement larger than the diameter to be turned. It should be about 1 inch longer than the finished piece will be. Mark a line across the corners of either end or locate the center of the stock. Figure 62–8. Place the live center over the stock and tap it with a wooden mallet to force the spur into the wood. Figure 62–9. With hardwood, it may be necessary to make two saw kerfs across the corners so that the wood will hold. If the stock is over 3 inches thick, the corners should be trimmed off to form an octagon shape before inserting the wood in the lathe. Hold the wood against the live center and bring the tailstock to within about 1½ inches of the end of the

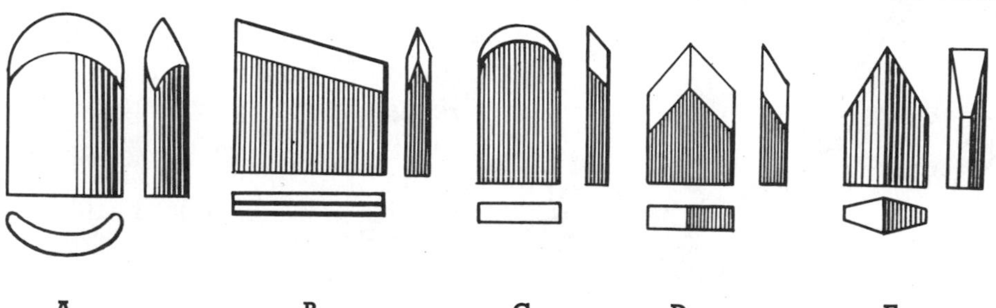

62–4. The common turning tools include: A. A large gouge for roughing cuts and a smaller gouge for smaller concave cuts. B. A large skew for smoothing and a smaller skew for squaring ends, cutting shoulders, V-grooves, and beads. C. A roundnose for cutting out concave curves. D. A spear point for finishing V-grooves and beads. E. A parting tool for cutting off, and for cutting to specific diameters.

62–5. Tools needed for measuring.

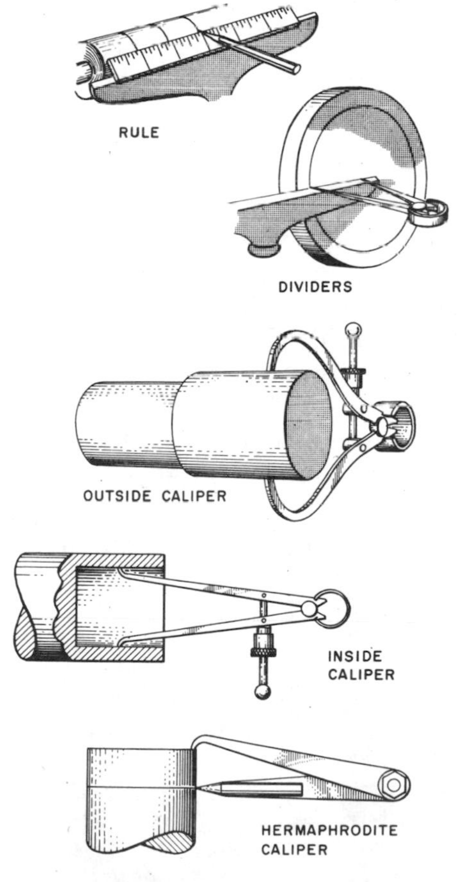

RULE

DIVIDERS

OUTSIDE CALIPER

INSIDE CALIPER

HERMAPHRODITE CALIPER

62–6. How the chisel cuts away the chips.

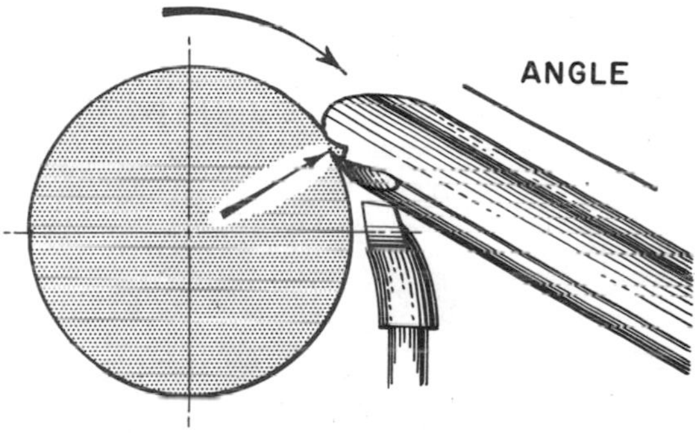

ANGLE

62–7. Action of the chisel scraping fine particles instead of shavings.

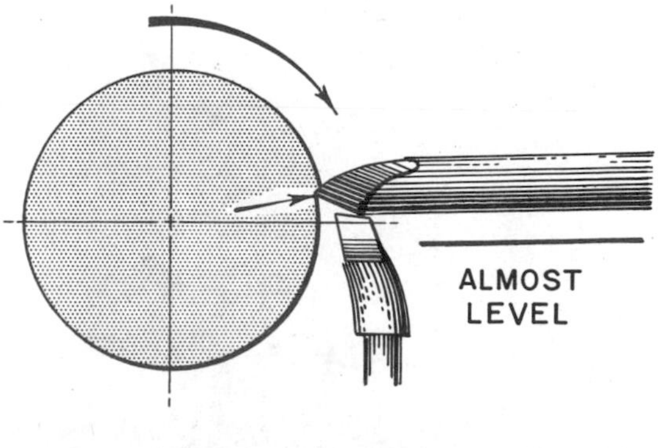

ALMOST LEVEL

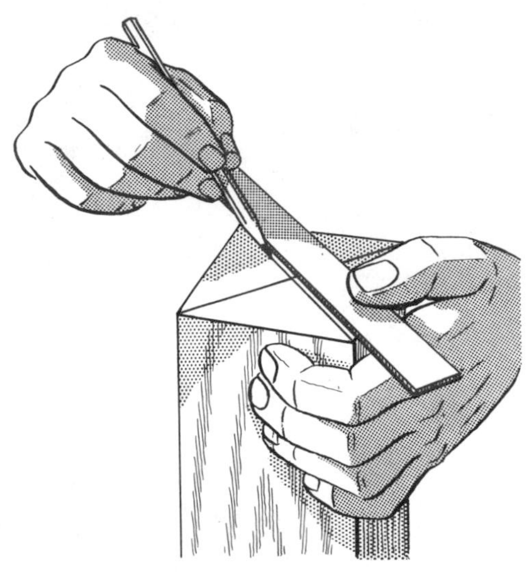

62–8. Here a line is being drawn across the corners to locate the center of the stock.

62–9a. One method of setting a spur or live center is to drive it into the wood with a mallet.

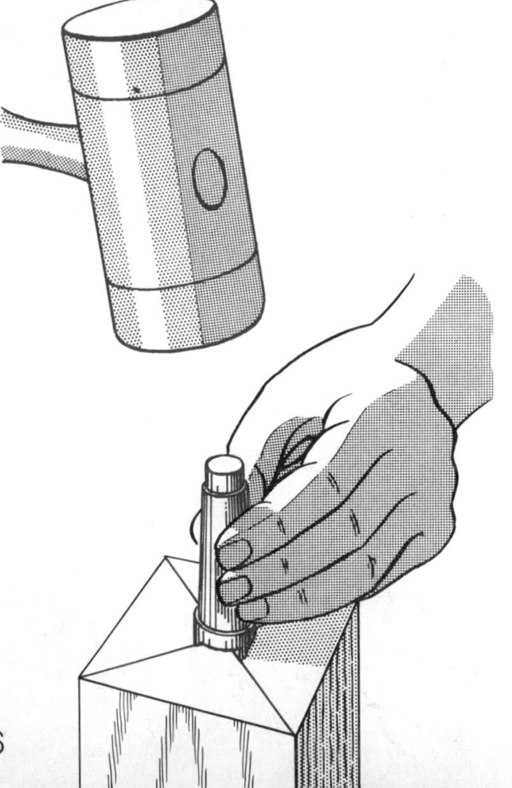

stock. Lock the tailstock to the bed and then turn up the tailstock handle, forcing the cup center into the wood about 1/32 inch. Back off the cup center and rub a little oil or wax on the end of the stock to lubricate it. Then tighten up the tailstock handle and lock it in position. Adjust the tool rest to clear the stock by about 1/8 inch and about 1/8 inch above center. If the stock is rather large in diameter, adjust the lathe to its lowest speed; if medium diameter, at medium speed; and if small diameter, at the highest speed.

Rotate the stock by hand to see if it has enough clearance.

ROUGH TURNING USING A GOUGE

The blade of a large gouge can be held in two ways. It can be grasped close to the cutting point with the hand underneath and the thumb over it. The forefinger then serves as a stop against the tool rest as shown in Figure 62–10. Another way is to place your hand over the tool with the wrist bent at an angle to form the stop, as shown in Figure 62–11. Grasp the handle of the gouge in the other hand, tilting it

62–9b. On hardwoods it is a good idea to cut a saw kerf across the corners.

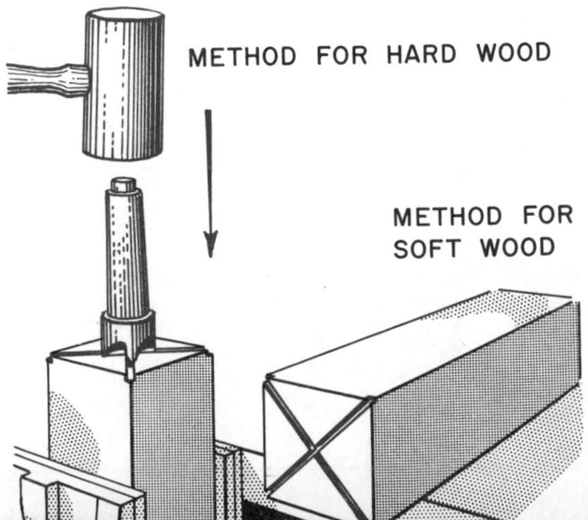

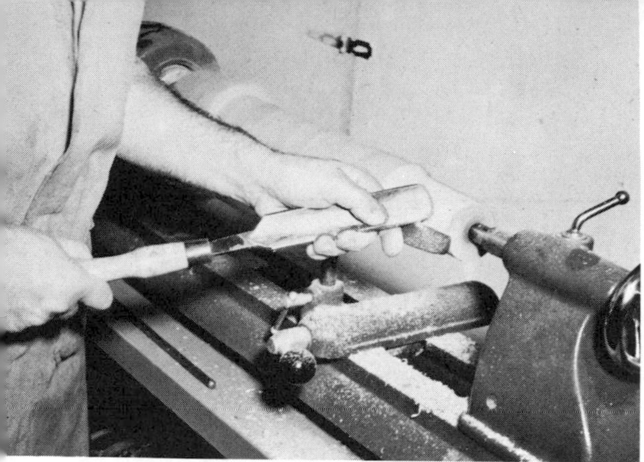

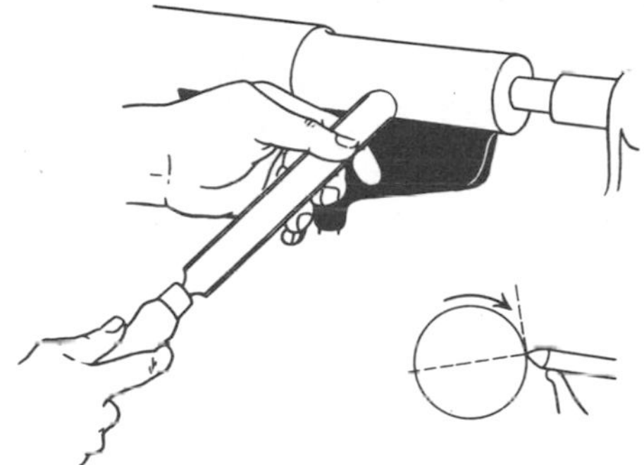

62–10. The first method of holding a gouge. The thumb is placed over the tool and the other fingers under it; the forefinger is used as a guide against the rest.

down and away from the direction in which the cut is to be made. Be sure to hold the tool tightly against the tool rest. Begin about one third of the way in from the tailstock. Twist the gouge to the right so that a shearing cut will be taken. Then move the cutting edge toward the dead center. Make certain that you grasp the tool firmly during this operation, since the revolving corners tend to throw the tool out of your hand. After each cut, begin about 2 inches closer to the live center.

To finish the rough turning, tip the cutting edge to the left and work toward the live center. Turn off the lathe and check the diameter of the stock with an outside caliper. Continue to use the large gouge to rough-turn until the stock is about 1/8 inch over finished size. The beginner can hold the point of the gouge at right angles to the work to produce a scraping action. The tool rest position is less important than it is in cutting. When scraping with the gouge, it is important to remove the tool occasionally so that it doesn't become overheated.

FINISH TURNING WITH A SKEW

The skew is more difficult to handle. The cutting edge is tapered. The uppermost point is called the toe and the lower point the heel. Grasp the tool, holding it firmly against the tool rest with the cutting edge well above and beyond the work. Then slowly draw the skew back, turning it at a slight angle until the center of the cutting edge comes in contact with the wood. Figure 62–12. Lift the handle slightly and force the cutting edge into the wood. Work from the center toward the live and dead centers, taking a shearing cut. CAUTION: Never attempt to start at the ends of the stock to do the cutting. Make sure that the toe does not catch in the revolving stock, since this could easily throw the tool out of your hands. A little practice will tell you when you are getting a

62–11. The second method of holding a gouge. Here the hand is placed over the tool—with the wrist bent—and against the tool rest.

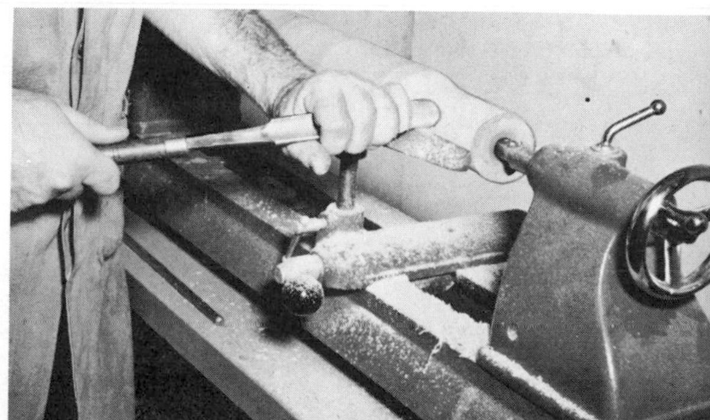

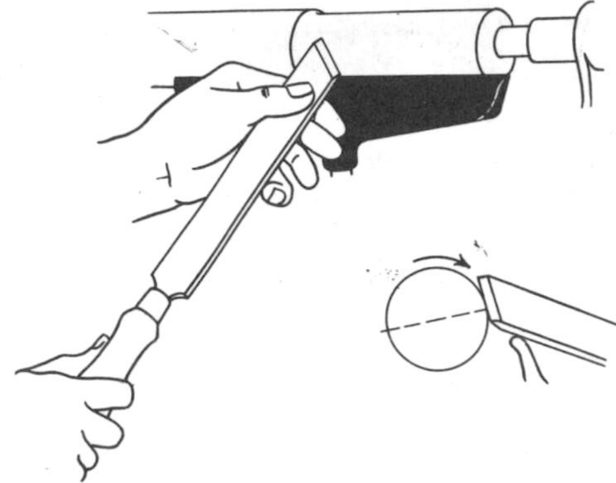

62–12. Using the skew as a cutting tool.

good cut. If the skew is properly sharpened, the surface will be so smooth and true that it needs no sanding.

To scrape stock to finish the sides, use a square-nosed tool or a large skew. Adjust the lathe for high speed. Hold the cutting edge parallel to the cylinder and force it into the stock until the scraping begins. Figure 62–13. Then move it from one side to the other.

62–13. Using the skew as a scraping tool. This is the simplest method of using turning tools, but is satisfactory only for making a straight cut.

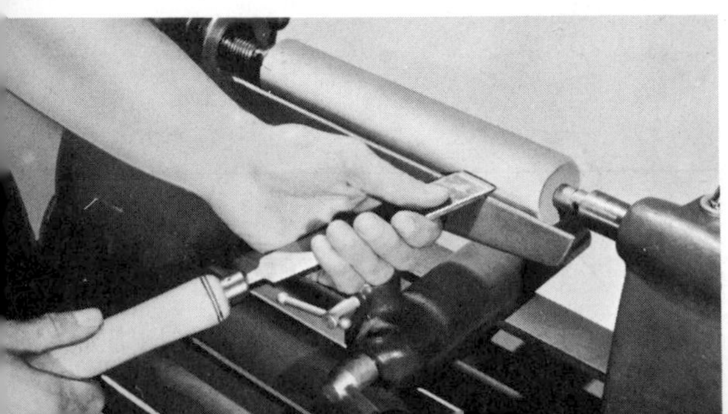

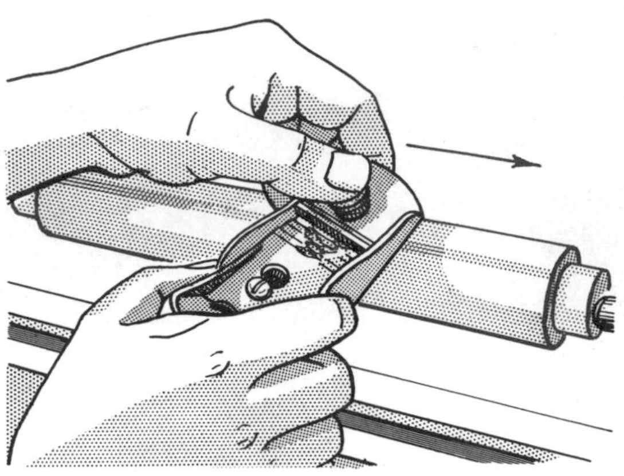

62–14. Using the block plane to smooth a cylinder.

Always start the scraping some distance in from the ends to prevent the tool from catching and splitting the wood. On long cylinders or tapers, work can be smoothed down accurately with a small block plane. The plane is held at an angle of approximately 45 degrees with the axis of the work. Figure 62–14. Make sure that the tool is adjusted for a very light cut so that there will be a clean, continuous shaving and a smooth surface. The plane can be supported on the tool rest.

SQUARING OFF THE ENDS

When the stock is turned to the correct diameter, use a pencil and rule to lay out the length needed. Force a parting tool into the revolving wood about 1/8 inch from the measured length. Figure 62–15. Make the groove slightly wider than the width of the tool so that the cutting edge will not burn as it is forced into the wood. Reduce the stock at this point to a diameter of about 3/8 inch. Use a small skew to finish off the end. Hold it with the toe edge against the tool rest. Turn

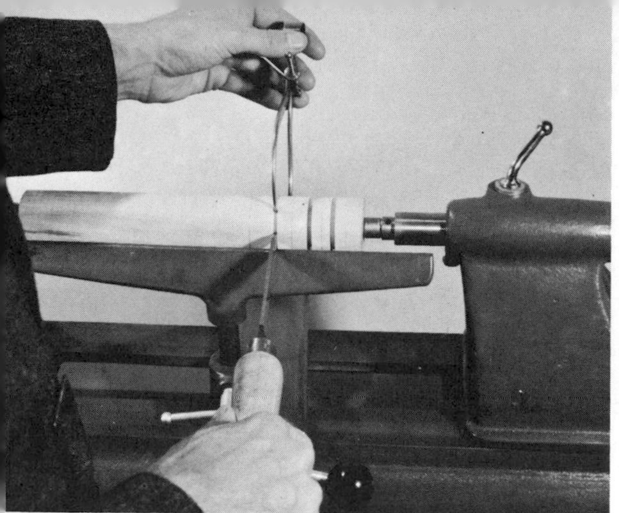

62–15. Using a parting tool. It is held with the narrow edge against the rest and is being forced into the wood. At the same time, the diameter is being checked with an outside caliper. In using the caliper on revolving stock, be careful not to apply any pressure, as this will cause it to spring over the stock.

the handle until the bevel or ground edge of the tool is parallel with the surface to be cut. Figure 62–16. Use the toe of the tool to do the cutting and remove about 1/32 inch with each cut. As the cut becomes deeper, it will be necessary to provide clearance for the tool. This can be done by turning the handle away from the cuts being made

62–16. Using a small skew to square off the end of the stock. The toe of the skew is doing the cutting, with the bevel or ground edge parallel to the end of the stock. This is accomplished by tipping the handle to the right.

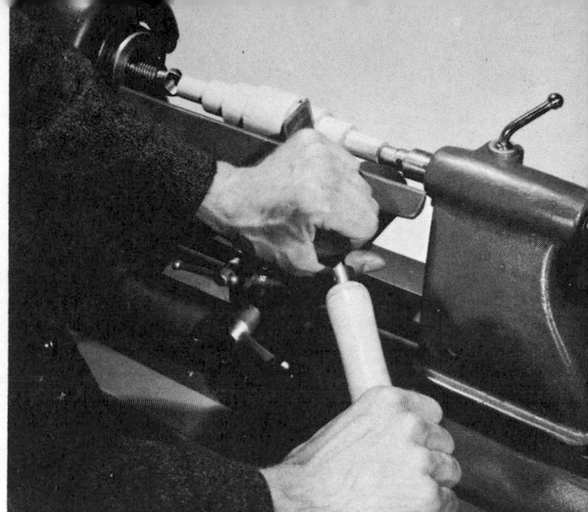

62–17. Using the skew to make a horizontal cut of a shoulder. The heel of the skew is doing most of the cutting.

and then making some tapered cuts to form a half V.

CUTTING A SHOULDER

The procedure for cutting a shoulder is similar to that for squaring off the end. First use a parting tool to cut a groove, cutting down the diameter at this point to slightly more than the smaller size. Then, with a small gouge, remove most of the stock from the smaller diameter. Cut the vertical part of the shoulder, using the toe of the skew. Cut the horizontal part of the shoulder with the heel of the skew in a manner similar to finish turning. Figure 62–17. It is also possible to form a

62–18. Forming a shoulder by the scraping method.

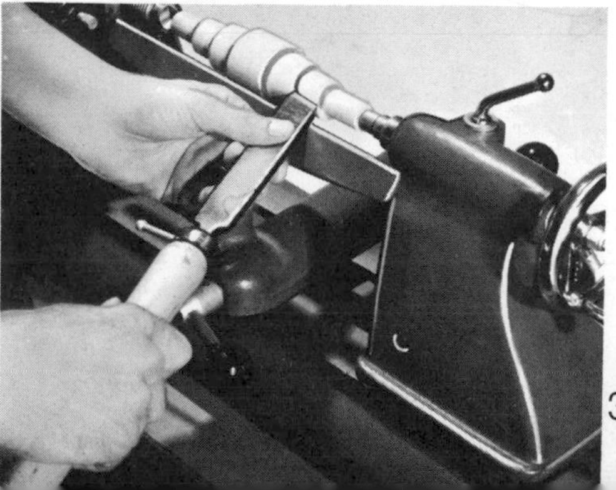

62–19. Using the skew to cut a taper.

62–21a. Cutting beads. Here again the skew is being used. The cut is started with the tool held fairly high, and as the bead is formed the tool is drawn back and turned at the same time.

shoulder or square an end by the scraping method. Figure 62–18.

CUTTING A TAPERED SURFACE

Turn the stock to the largest diameter. Then use a parting tool to mark the smallest diameter. Make several grooves each of lesser depth as guides for the turning. Rough out the taper with a gouge. Then finish-turn the taper with a skew, using the heel to do most of the cutting. Figure 62–19.

62–20. Cutting V's with the heel of the skew. The tool is forced into the stock at the angle of the V.

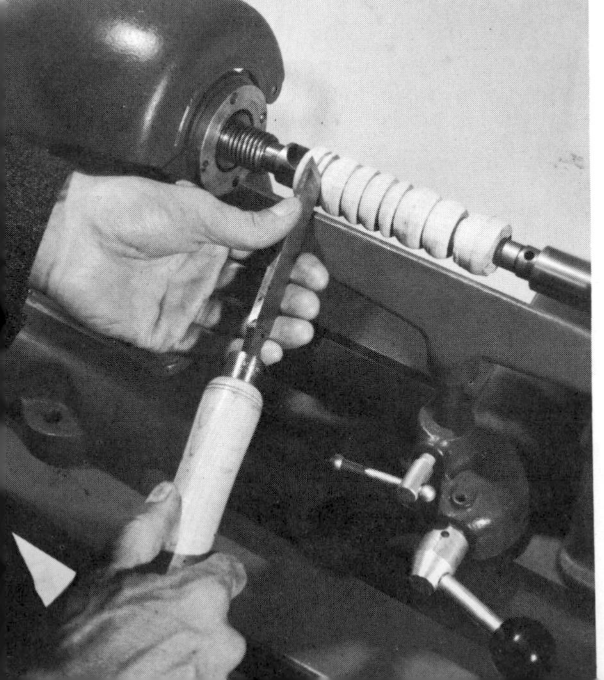

CUTTING V'S

Use a small skew to do the cutting. Force the heel into the stock a small amount and then work in at an angle, as shown in Figure 62–20, to cut one side of the V. Continue to correct depth and then turn the skew in the opposite direction to finish the V on the other side.

CUTTING BEADS

Cutting accurate beads is rather difficult. With the toe of a small skew, mark the point at which the beads are to join. Continue to cut a V shape in the stock with the toe of the skew. Now turn the skew around and use the heel to cut the bead. Hold the tool high on the stock to start the bead. Then slowly draw the handle back, at the same time turning the cutting edge to form the arc. Figure 62–21. Repeat in the opposite way to form the other half of the bead.

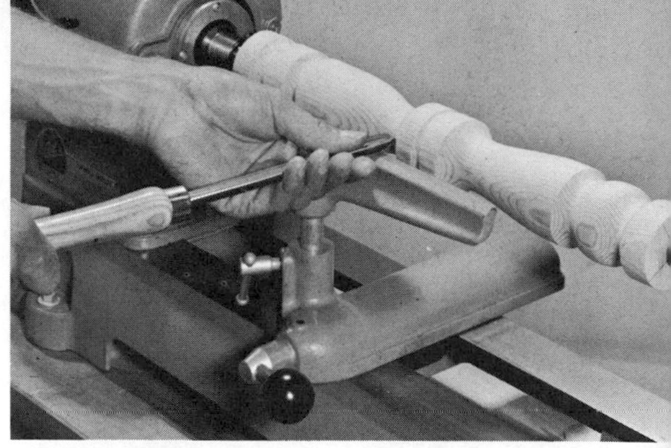

TURNING CONCAVE SURFACES

Concave surfaces can be turned either by scraping with a roundnosed tool or by cutting with a small gouge. The simplest way is to force a roundnosed tool into the wood and work the handle back and forth to form the concave surface. If a small gouge is used, tip it on edge and begin the concave cut by rolling the gouge as pressure is applied. Continue to take shearing cuts, first from one side and then the other, until the concave surface is formed. Figure 62–22.

TURNING CONVEX DESIGNS

Most turned pieces are a combination of straight turning, beads, V's, and long concave or convex surfaces.

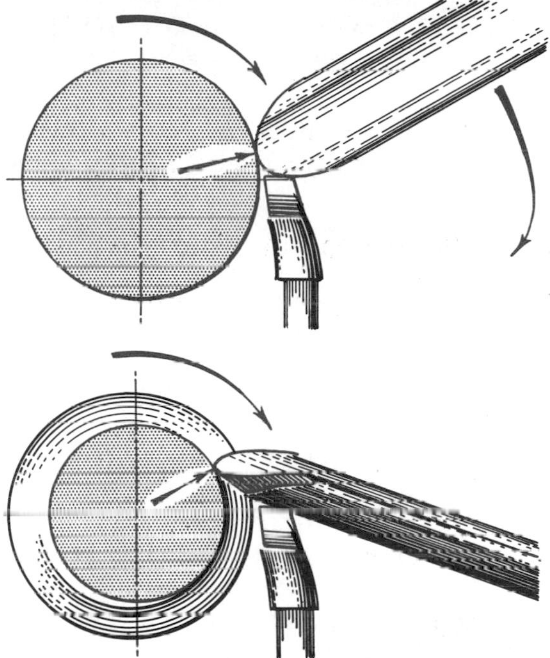

62–22. Using a small gouge to turn a concave surface. The tool should be rolled to form the curve.

62–21b. Correct steps in cutting beads.

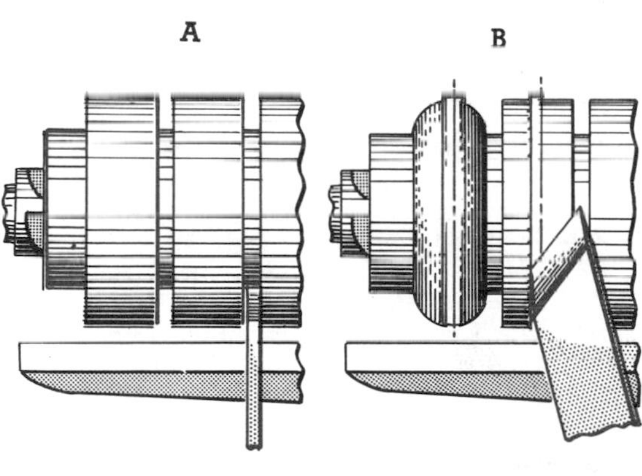

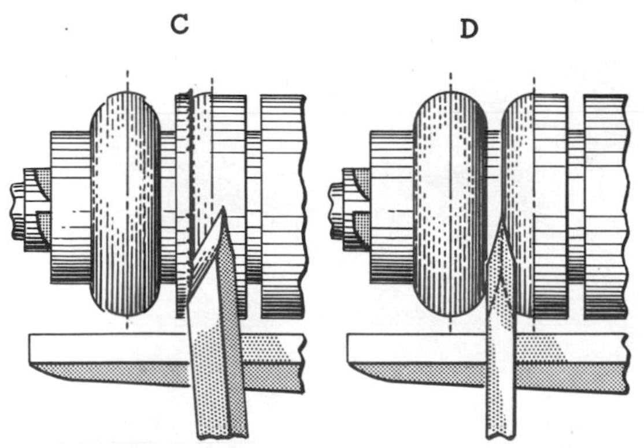

For convex work, the usual procedure is to turn the piece to the largest diameter to be finished and then, with a parting tool, mark points along the stock where extra material is to be removed. In many cases the parting tool is used at several points to show where stock is to be removed and to what depth. Then the gouge, skew, and roundnosed tool are used to form

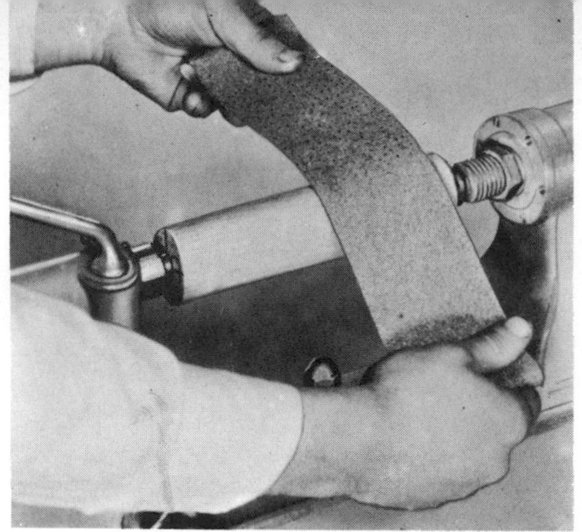

62–23. Smoothing the surface with abrasive paper.

the design. If necessary, a file and sandpaper may be used to smooth the surface. Figure 62–23.

TURNING ON THE FACEPLATE

To turn many small articles such as bowls, the stock is fastened to a faceplate and then all of the cutting is done by the scraping method. Figure 62–24. Two common types of faceplates are the *screw center* for small work and the *standard faceplate* with screw holes for larger work. Figure 62–25. The cutting tools most commonly used for faceplate turning include the *roundnose*, *spear*, and *gouge*. To make a small bowl, first cut out stock of correct thickness on a band or scroll saw to a circle slightly larger than the project itself. See Unit 20 for treatment of wood to prevent splits, checks, or warping. If the back of the stock will be damaged greatly by screws, protect it with a piece of scrap stock. Cut a piece of scrap stock at least an inch in thickness and about the same size as the base of the bowl. Glue the two pieces together with a piece of wrapping paper between them so that they will separate easily later. Figure 62–26. Fasten the material to the faceplate with about ¾-inch screws. Make sure that

62–24. These interesting salad bowls are typical of projects that can be turned on a faceplate.

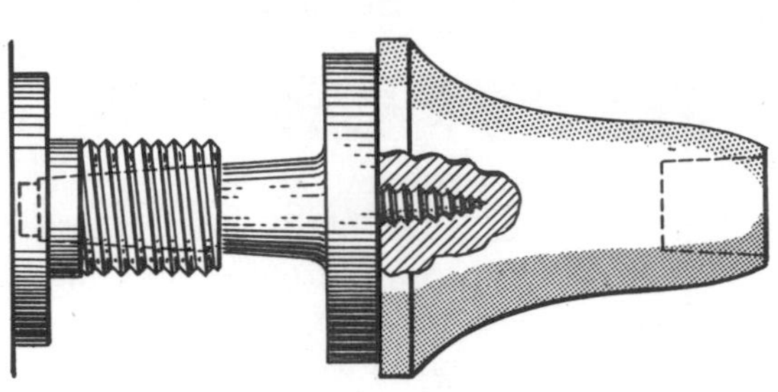

62–25a. Screw center for holding small work.

62–25b. Fastening stock to the headstock spindle. The work has been fastened to the faceplate with short wood screws. The faceplate is being attached to the headstock spindle.

SCRAP STOCK PAPER JOINT

62–26. How a piece may be glued to waste stock to do the turning.

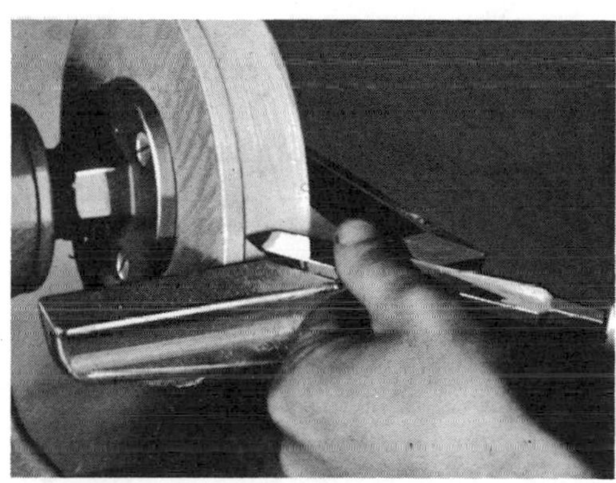

62–27. Truing the outside of stock fastened to the faceplate.

62–28. Using a roundnosed tool to shape stock on the faceplate.

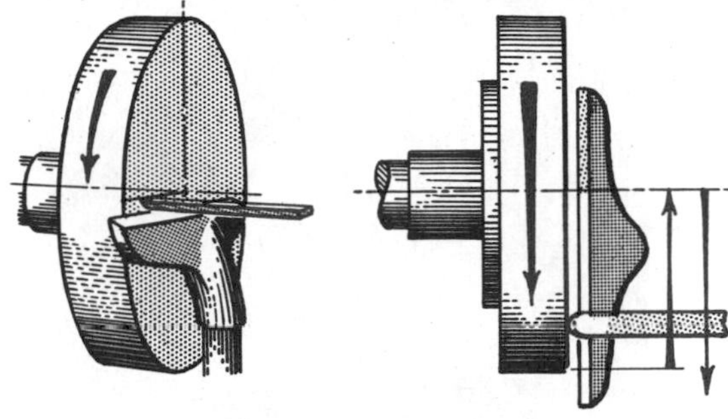

62–29. Keep the cutting tool on the side nearest you. Never try to cut across the entire diameter.

they are not so long that they will mar the bottom of your bowl. Remove the live center and fasten the faceplate on the headstock spindle. Adjust the rest parallel to the outside of the round stock about ¼ inch away. Set the lathe to a slow speed and dress the outside edge of the stock. Figure 62–27. Once the circle is trued, the speed can be increased. Now make a cardboard templet that will match the interior and exterior shape of the bowl. Turn the tool rest parallel to the face of the bowl and begin to shape the inside. Figure 62–28. Use a gouge or a roundnose tool and always work from the outside edge nearest you to the center. Figures 62–29 and 62–30. Never try to cut across the entire diameter, since once you pass the center the tool will move up and away from a tool holder. After the inside is shaped, sand it with 2/0 or 1/0 sandpaper. Now move the tool rest around and shape the exterior of the bowl. Then sand this surface. Apply a finish to the bowl.

After turning is complete, the scrap stock can be cut or split away from the finished product with a sharp chisel. Figure 62–31. To do turning in which the base must be formed, a wood chuck

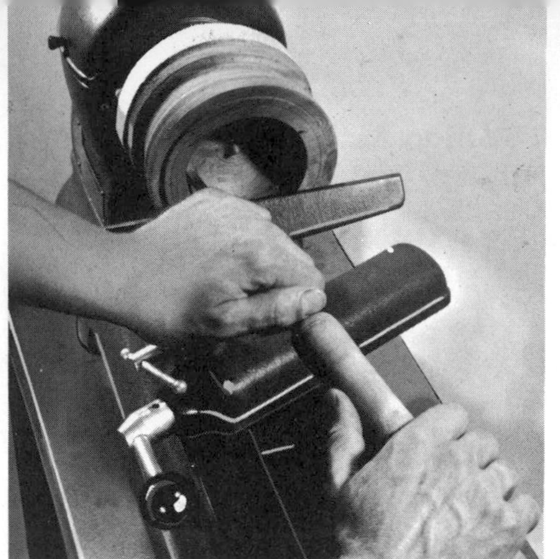

62–30. Turning a trinket box with a small gouge doing the internal work. The box has been glued to a piece of scrap stock and that piece then fastened to the faceplate with short screws.

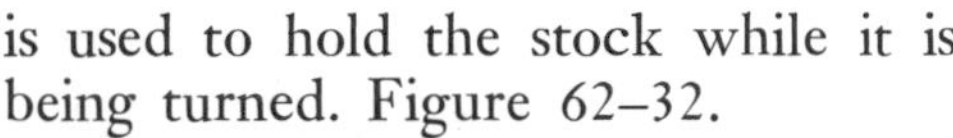

is used to hold the stock while it is being turned. Figure 62–32.

FINISHING ON THE LATHE

There are several ways to apply a finish as the piece revolves in the lathe. A simple method is to apply paste wax to a folded cloth and hold it on the revolving stock. You should repeat

62–31. Using a parting tool to cut off the project after it has been turned.

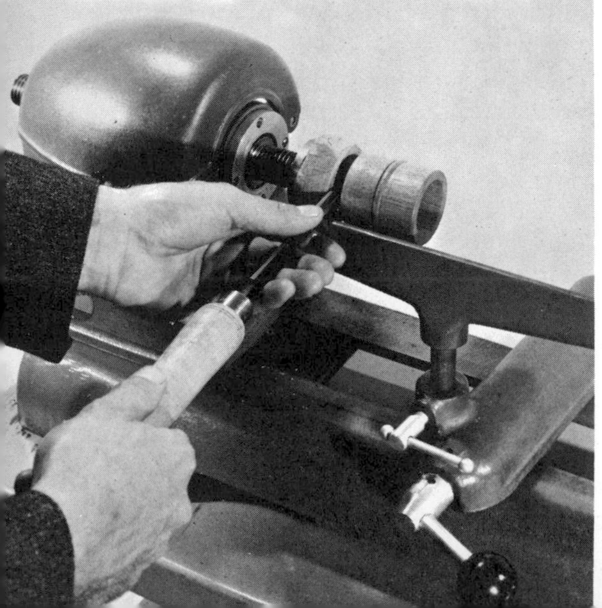

62–32a. This shows a bowl that has been fastened in a wood chuck to turn the back.

this application about a dozen times. To apply a French-type oil polish, fold a piece of fine cotton or linen cloth into a pad. Apply about one teaspoon of white shellac to the pad and then add several drops of linseed or mineral oil. Hold the pad over the

62–32b. Turning a shallow tray with the piece held in a wood chuck. Whenever it is necessary to turn both the front and back of a piece, make a chuck to hold the stock for turning the second side.

spinning work, moving it back and forth. As the pad gets dry, apply more shellac and oil to keep it moist until you get a mirrorlike finish. You can also add a good wax coating to the surface after it is dry. Still another method of finishing a bowl is to apply several coats of clear lacquer before the bowl is removed from the faceplate. Then return the piece to the lathe. Apply a little rubbing oil and rottenstone to the cloth and polish the surface.

CAN YOU ANSWER THESE QUESTIONS ON THE WOOD LATHE?

1. Describe a wood lathe and name its parts.
2. What are the tools needed for wood turning?
3. Describe the two methods of turning.
4. What are the two methods of fastening a live center to the stock?
5. What is the largest size stock that can be turned from a square without first trimming the corners?
6. Cup centers need what lubricants?
7. What is the relation between the diameter of the stock and the speed of the lathe?
8. What tool is selected for rough turning?
9. Holding a gouge can be done in two ways. What are these?
10. How can the cutting action of a gouge be controlled?
11. What makes the skew a difficult tool to use?
12. What is the major danger involved in using the skew?
13. Tell how you can square off the ends of stock in the lathe.
14. What tools are used for cutting a shoulder?
15. When a tapered surface is to be produced, what part of the skew should do most of the cutting?
16. Cutting V's is done with what tool?
17. What kinds of work are turned on a faceplate?
18. Is it good practice to use a file and sandpaper on the lathe? Explain.
19. Tell how to apply a finish.

Section XII Upholstery

By becoming acquainted with simple upholstery, you learn valuable methods and gain in understanding of design and materials. Furniture and automobile upholstery is important to our way of life. It represents a tremendous industrial investment and fine opportunities for careers. As a consumer, you will probably choose at least three sets of upholstered furniture in your lifetime. You will select from many choices of automobile upholstery fabrics. Personal experience with the subject today will bring real returns tomorrow.

Section XII

UNIT 63. SIMPLE UPHOLSTERY

While upholstery can be complicated, there are several simple procedures that the beginner can follow. Of the four basic types of upholstery work, the first three are done by older methods. (1) The simplest is a *pad seat* (made without springs) that fits into or on the completed chair. Dining-room chairs may have pad seats. Figure 63–1. (2) The next type is the *tight spring seat* found mostly in living-room chairs. A webbing foundation supports the springs. Figure 63–2. (3) Next is the *overstuffed seat and back* used in large chairs and sofas. In this type there are springs in both the seat and back. Figure 63–3. (4) The last type is the most modern: *no-sag springs with foam rubber* or rubberized hair.

MATERIALS

Some upholstery materials must be ordered from a special supply house. Others can be found in hardware and department stores. Before starting a project, it is well to see if needed materials are easy to find in your community.

Upholstery tacks are flathead tacks used for holding materials in place. The larger sizes (12 or 14 ounce, about ¾ inch long) are needed for tacking webbing; the smaller (6 or 8 ounce, about ½ inch long) are used for fastening the coverings. The *gimp tack* is a small roundhead used wherever the head is meant to show.

Webbing is made from jute fiber; it is used as the foundation. The 3½-inch width is usually specified.

Burlap is used as a covering over webbing, springs, and stuffing. An 8- to 10-ounce (per square foot) weight in 40-inch widths is best.

Stuffing means a variety of materials used for filling. Among the most common are *curled animal hair*, *Spanish moss*, a plant fiber, *tow* made from the

63–1. The pad seat is the simplest form of upholstery. The base can be of plywood, hardboard, or a frame covered with webbing.

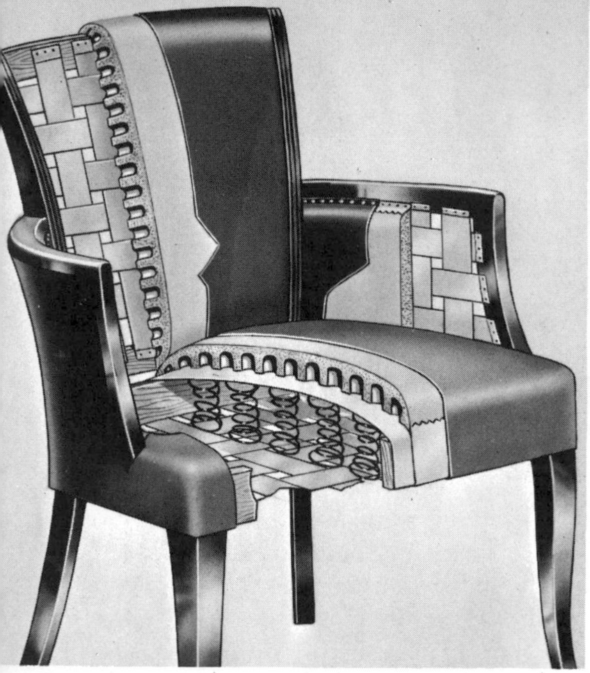

63–2. **This cutaway shows the construction of a tight spring seat. Note that the base is webbing to which the springs are tied. Over these is a piece of burlap. Over this is a fibrous padding or foam rubber. Finally, the cover is applied.**

stalks of flax plants, and *shredded foam rubber*.

Rubberized hair is a light, elastic material made from curled hair and rubber. It comes in pads of standard thickness from ¾ inch to 2½ inches.

Foam rubber (padding) is made from liquid latex. *Slab stock* comes in thicknesses of ½, ¾, 1 inch, etc. It is possible to buy *cored utility stock* that has molded cylindrical openings in it. You can also buy fully *molded cushions* in many different sizes and shapes. Figure 63–4. *Rubber cement* is used to fasten tacking tape to foam rubber.

Tacking tape is a muslin cloth tape used to fasten the foam rubber to the base.

Cotton comes in batts that are 27 inches wide and about ½ inch thick. It is purchased in a roll to use over stuffing. *Muslin* of the unbleached type is 36 to 40 inches wide. *Fancy furniture nails* come in a wide variety of head styles for places where the nails will show.

Final covers can be of fabric, plastic material, or leather.

Other materials include coil springs and sewing twine, for more extensive work.

COMMON TOOLS

1. An *upholsterer's hammer* for extensive work in upholstery. One head should be magnetized for holding tacks. For simple jobs, a small claw hammer is satisfactory. Figure 63–5.

2. The *spring-driven stapler or tacker* is an ideal machine for stapling on burlap, muslin or the finished cover. Figure 63–6.

63–3. **This lounge chair is an example of frame construction with springs in both seat and back. The loose cushion can contain either fibrous padding or foam rubber.**

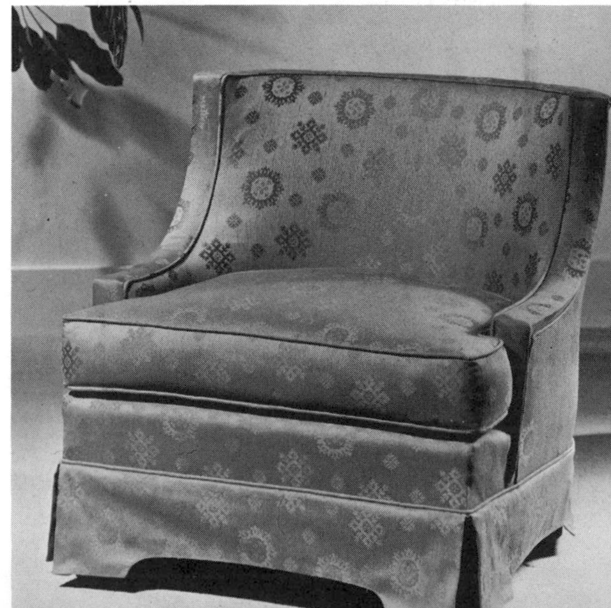

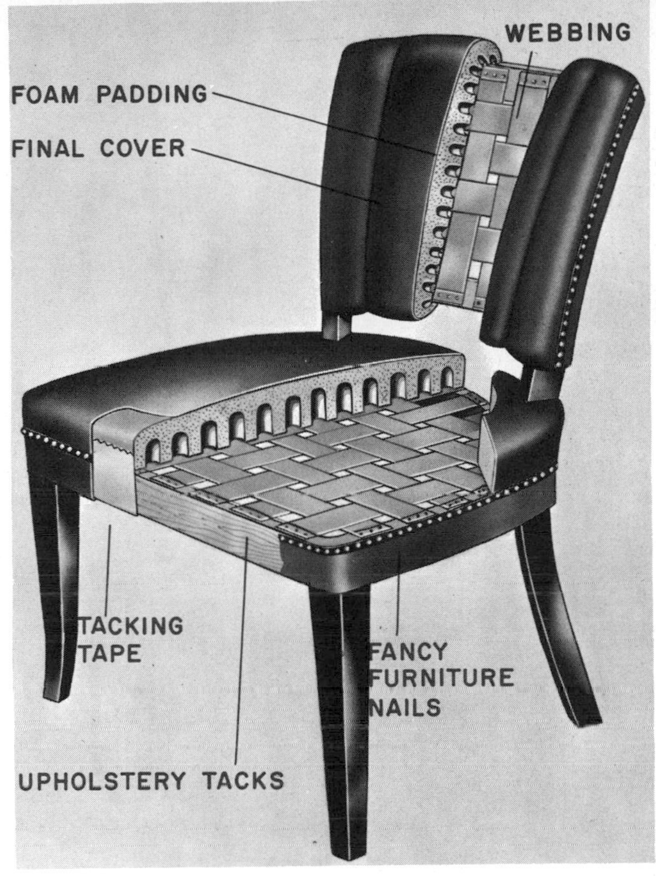

63–4. This cutaway of a pad seat illustrates some of the basic materials used in upholstery.

3. A *webbing stretcher* (about 6 inches long) for stretching the webbing before tacking it down. Figure 63–7.

4. *Trimmer's shears* for cutting foam rubber, rubberized hair, and fabrics.

5. A *stuffing regulator*—a 10-inch metal pin with one sharp and one blunt end. It is used to even out irregularities under temporary coverings. An *ice pick* makes a good substitute.

MAKING A PAD SEAT

Some of the more common ways of making a pad seat are as follows:

MAKING A PAD SEAT WITH A SOLID BASE AND FOAM RUBBER. Figure 63–8.

1. Cut a piece of ¼- to ½-inch fir plywood to the required shape for the base. Drill several small holes distributed over the wood for air venting.

2. Select a piece of foam rubber about 1-inch thick.

3. Decide on the kind of edging you want on the seat.

a. *For a cushioned edge.* Cut the foam rubber to shape with shears, al-

63–5. Upholstery hammer.

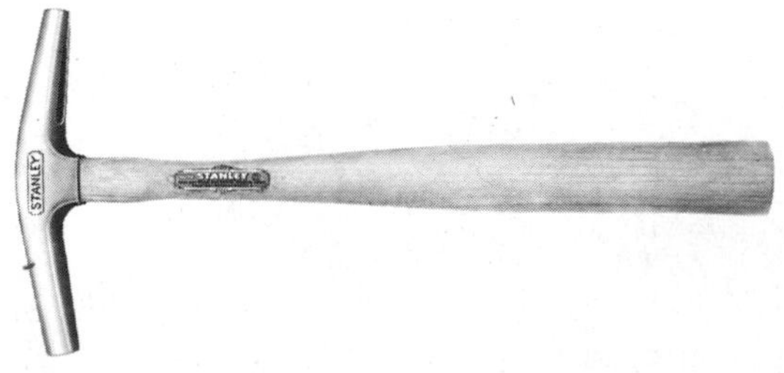

63–6. A spring-driven stapler is much quicker than tacks and a hammer. A heavy-duty shears is needed to cut the material. When cutting foam rubber, it helps to dip the shears in water to "lubricate" it. Do not use too much water. The foam rubber can also be cut on a band saw with a ¼-inch blade.

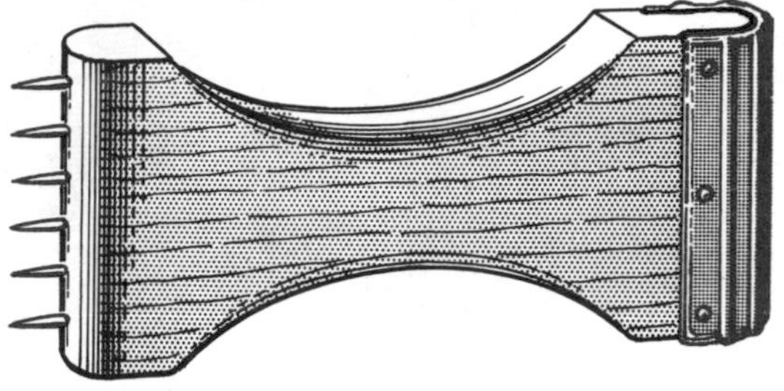

63–7. Webbing stretcher.

63–8a. This contemporary chair has a pad seat and back.

63–8b. Bill of materials for the chair.

BILL OF MATERIALS

Important: All dimensions listed below are FINISHED size.

No. of Pieces	Part Name	Thickness	Width	Length	Material
2	Back Posts	1″	3″	30″	White Oak
2	Front Legs	1¾″ dia.		16⅛″	White Oak
2	Side Rails	¾″	1⅝″	14″	White Oak
2	Back Rungs	¾″ dia.		12¾″	White Oak
2	Side Rungs	¾″ dia.		16¾″	White Oak
1	Front Rung	¾″ dia.		13¾″	White Oak
2	Cross Rails	1″	1¾″	12¾″	Hardwood
1	Seat	½″	15½″	17½″	Fir Plywood
1	Back	½″	8″	16″	Fir Plywood
8	Dowels	⅜″ dia.		1½″	Hardwood
6	No. 10 x 1½″ F.H. Wood Screws				
2	No. 12 x 1½″ Oval Head Nickle Plated Wood Screws				
2	No. 12 x 2″ Oval Head Nickle Plated Wood Screws				
	Foam Rubber Padding				
	Upholstery Material				
	⅝″ Carpet Tacks				

lowing about ¼ inch extra all around, plus an extra ½ inch on the cushion edge or edges. Apply rubber cement to about half the width of the tacking tape and 1 inch along the upper edge of the foam rubber. Figure 63–9. Cement the tape to the smooth top of the stock, about 1 inch from the edge. Tuck the bottom edge of the cushion under so that its thickness is held flat against the base. Figure 63–10. Keep the tape taut to avoid wrinkling. Tack the tape on the underside with upholstery tacks.

b. *For a feathered edge.* Cut the stock about ¼ inch oversize all around. Cement the tacking tape to the smooth top side about 1 inch from the edge. Bevel the lower edge as shown in Figure 63–11. Draw the tape down so that the beveled edge is held flat against the base; tack it in place.

c. *For a square edge.* Cut the rubber, allowing the usual ¼-inch addition all around. Cement the tape flat against the edge of the material and tack the overhang to the base. Figure 63–12.

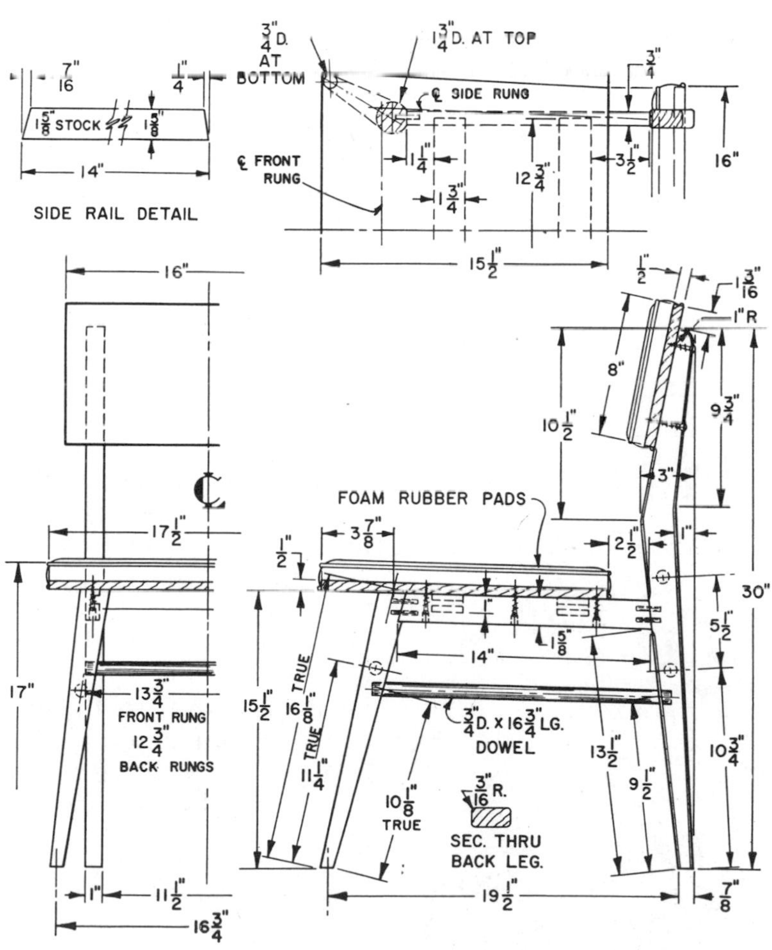

63–8c. Drawing for the chair.

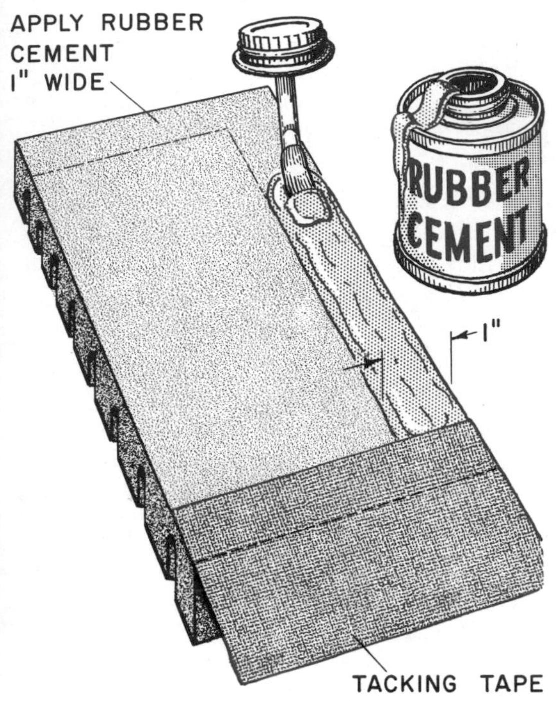

63–9. Apply rubber cement along the upper edge of the foam rubber and then fasten the tacking tape in place.

63–10. Cushioned edge.

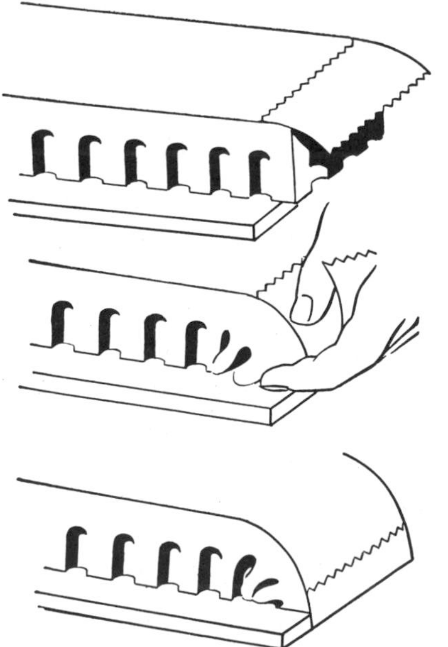

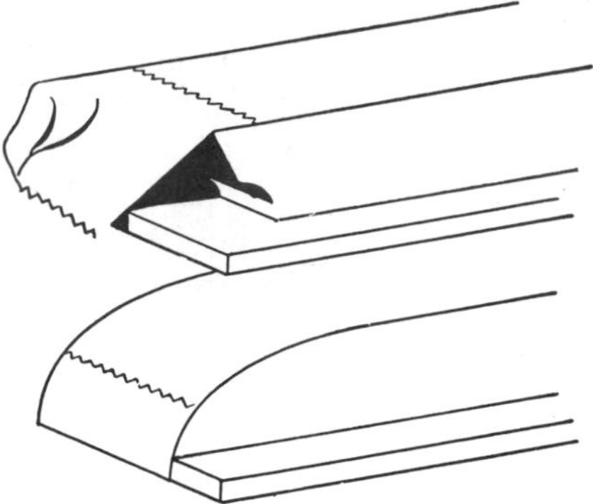

63–11. Feathered edge.

4. Cover the foam rubber with a final cover.

MAKING A SLIP PAD SEAT WITH WEBBED BASE AND UPHOLSTERY COTTON

1. Make an open frame of four pieces of ¾-inch stock that will fit into the main frame of the chair or bench. The corner can be made with dowel joints (Figure 25–2), end-lap joints (Figure 28–1), or open mortise-and-tenon joints (Figure 30–1). Round the upper edge so it won't cut the upholstery fabric.

2. Fold the end of the webbing under about 1¼ inch and tack about ½ inch from the outside of the frame. Figure 63–13. The tacks are staggered to keep the wood from splintering. Stretch the webbing tightly over the frame as shown in Figure 63–14, and tack it on the other side of the frame. Cut the webbing about 1¼ inch beyond the frame, fold over and tack down again. Figure 63–15. Place the next piece of webbing about 1½ to 2 inches away. Space the webbing so the piece will cover the opening. Then weave the other pieces through in the other direction.

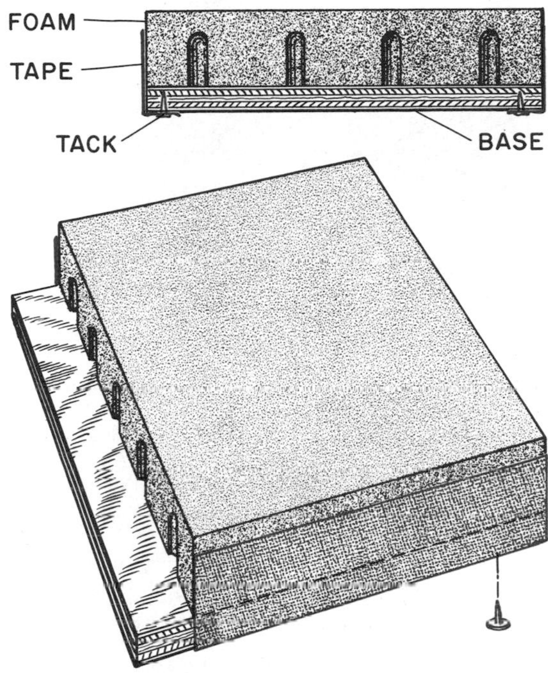

63–12. Square edge. Note that the tacking tape has been glued to the edge of the foam rubber and then tacked to the base. Note also the holes in the foam rubber for air ventilation.

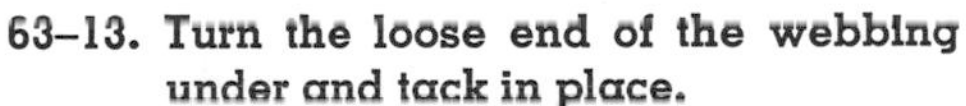

63–13. Turn the loose end of the webbing under and tack in place.

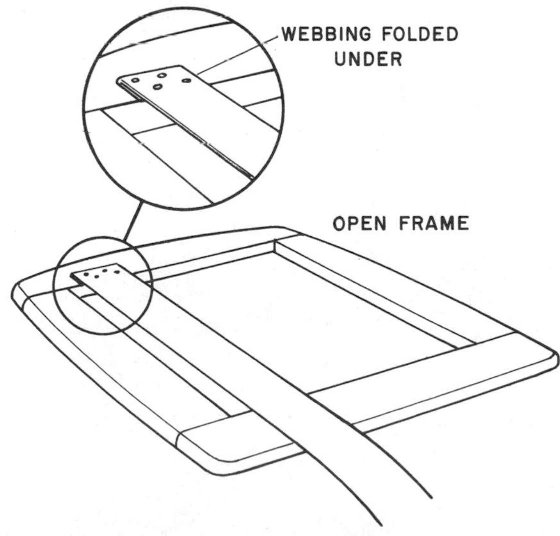

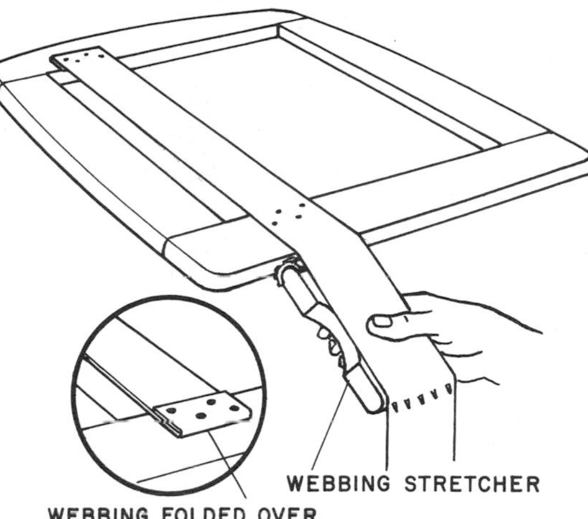

63–14. Stretch the webbing and tack to the other side.

3. Tack a piece of burlap over the webbing, making sure that it is not drawn tightly. If tacked too tightly, the cloth will tear when in use.

4. Cut a piece of upholstery cotton about 2 inches smaller in all directions than the frame. Center this over the burlap.

5. Cut another piece of cotton about ½ inch larger in all directions than the frame. Center this over the first piece.

6. Cut a piece of final covering that is about 2 inches larger in all directions than the frame. Place the cover material with the good side down on the

63–15. Webbing completed. Burlap must be fastened over the webbing.

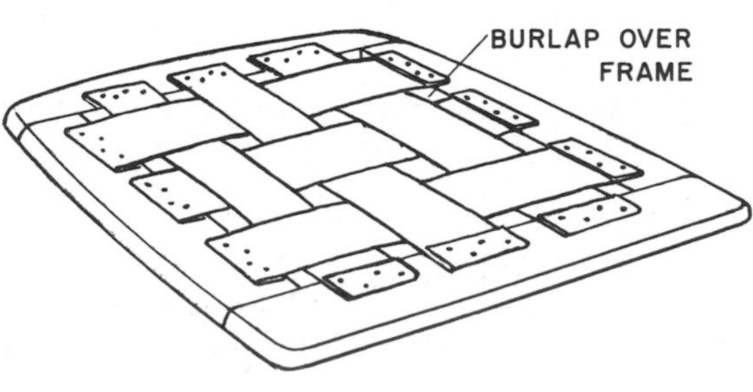

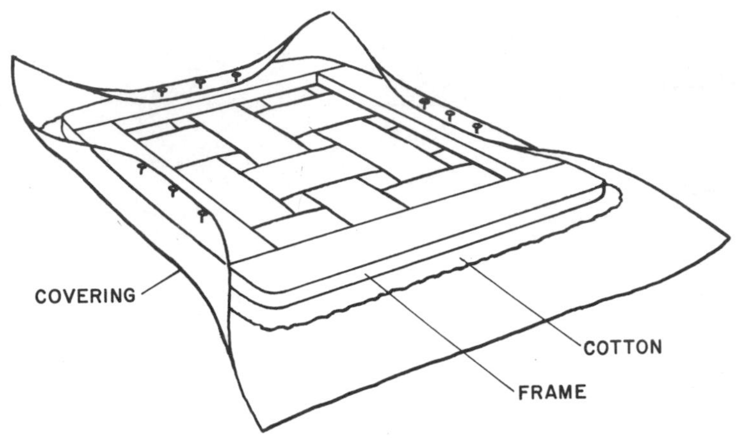

63–16. Two layers of cotton are in place and the cover is then tacked on.

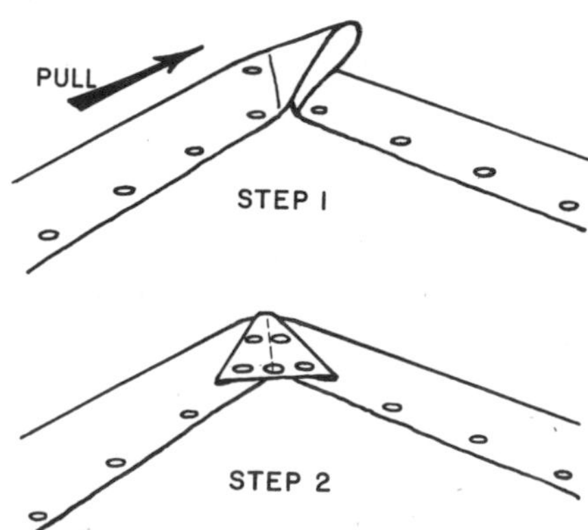

63–17. Tack the sharp corners carefully.

bench. Lay the seat face down and start tacking at the center of each side. Figure 63–16. Work toward the corners. Tack the corners as shown in Figure 63–17.

MAKING A SLIP PAD SEAT WITH A WEBBED BASE AND STUFFING

1. Make an open frame and cover with webbing and burlap.

2. Place stuffing of hair or moss over the burlap. Make sure the material is well separated and free of foreign matter such as sticks. Distribute handfuls of the stuffing over the base, working it together with your fingers. Cover to a depth of about 2 inches. (A rubberized hair pad 1-inch thick, cut to size, can be used instead of the stuffing.)

63–18. A chair frame with a foundation of no-sag springs.

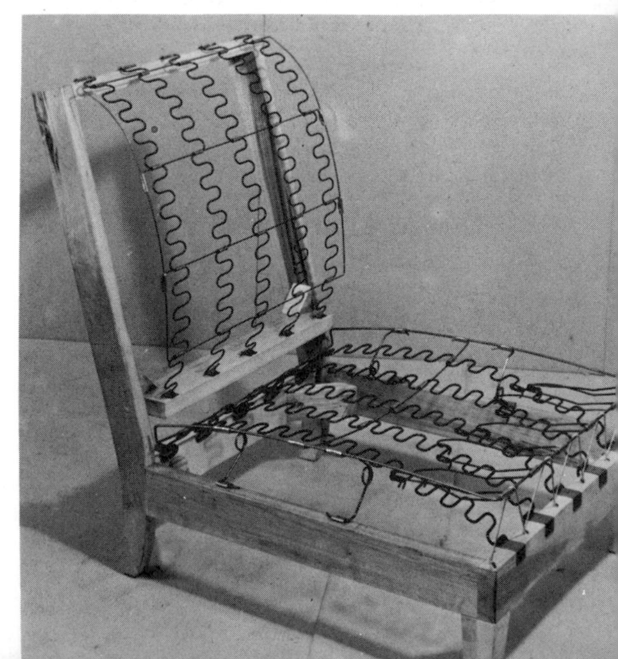

3. Cut a piece of burlap or muslin about 2 inches larger in all directions than the frame. Lay the cloth over the stuffing and hold it in place as you turn the entire unit over.

4. Start tacking at the center of each side and work toward the corners. Drive the tacks only a little way into the wood so you can remove them if necessary to tighten the cover. Check to see that the stuffing is distributed evenly. If not, poke a *regulator* through the cloth to move some of the stuffing around.

5. Place a layer of cotton over the cloth and then apply final cover material.

MAKING A SPRING SEAT WITH NO-SAG SPRINGS AND FOAM RUBBER

An excellent upholstered spring seat or back can be made quite easily with no-sag springs. Figure 63–18. Complete directions for ordering and installing these springs are available from the manufacturer, along with complete kits.*

* No-Sag Spring Company, Detroit, Michigan.

CAN YOU ANSWER THESE QUESTIONS ON SIMPLE UPHOLSTERY?

1. Name the three traditional methods of upholstery.
2. What kinds of materials are used for stuffing?
3. From what is foam rubber made?
4. Name some of the common tools needed for upholstery.
5. What are the three kinds of edges that can be used on a foam-rubber pad seat?
6. Describe how to make a pad seat with a webbed base and cotton upholstery.

Section XIII
Materials and Opportunities in Woodworking

We all admire a rich wood finish. To appreciate quality, however, we must go back to the sources of our fine woods. We must recognize the talents and methods of men who work with woods. We must analyze what goes into designing and creating wood objects that please us and give maximum service. Previously called "related information," these subjects are really as much a part of valuable woodworking experience as is the making of a product in the shop. Your study of wood materials and design, covered in this section, will help open the way to job opportunities, as well as to advantages in the selection and use of wood structures—from a home on down to a small piece of furniture.

Section XIII

UNIT 64. TREES AND LUMBER

Since woods are the raw material of woodworking, it is well to learn about their structure, names of their parts, classification, and identification. *Wood* is, of course, the basic substance under the bark of trees and shrubs.

HOW A TREE GROWS

The tree is one of the most interesting of Nature's plant life. As you will see in Figure 64–1, the basic structure consists of long, narrow tubes or cells. These narrow tubes or cells, which are about as fine as human hairs, are lined with still finer, spiral-wound strands of *cellulose*. The cells themselves are held together with a substance called *lignin*. These cells or tubes provide the passageways into the tree for water and other growth-giving materials from the earth. During the spring and early summer (springwood) when there is much moisture, the tree grows rapidly, while in the summer and fall (summerwood) the tree develops much slower. When you look at the cross-section of a tree, you see the dark or summer wood, called annular growth rings. Figure 64–2. Some idea of the age of the tree can be obtained by counting these rings.

PARTS OF A TREE

Figure 64–3 shows the cross-section of a tree trunk. Beginning at the center is a porous material called the *pith*.

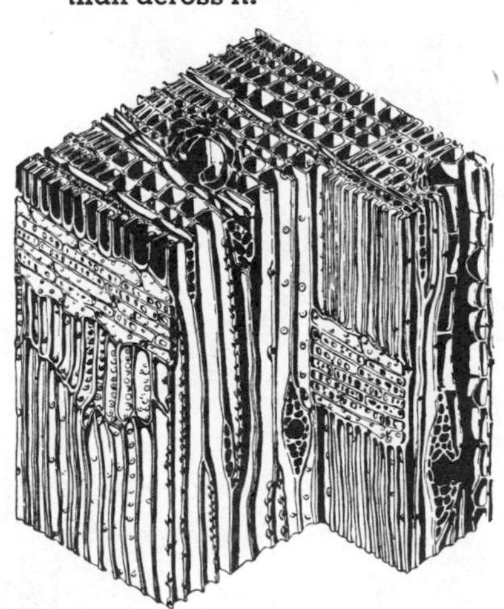

64–1. An enlarged view of wood, showing the tube structure. Here you can see why it is easier to cut with the grain than across it.

64–2. A section of a log showing the annular rings.

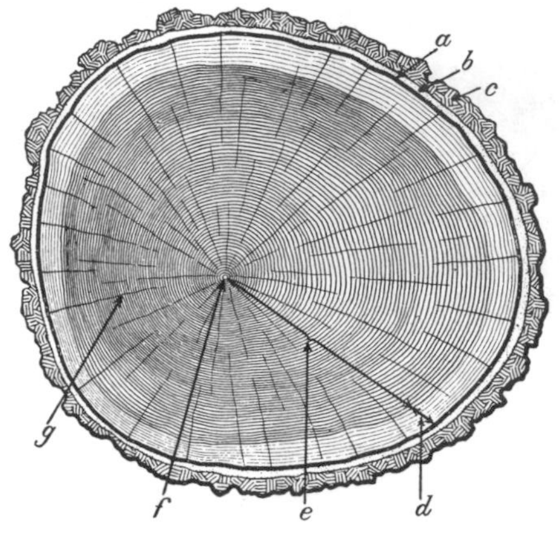

64–3. Cross-section of a tree trunk showing: a. Cambium. b. Phloem. c. Bark. d. Sapwood. e. Hardwood. f. Pith. g. Medullary ray.

64–4b. Twigs and leaves of white ash.

This sometimes becomes rotten, leaving a hollow center in the tree. Around the pith is the mature wood, the *heartwood*. This is generally darker in color because of the presence of resin and other materials during the many years of growth. Beyond the outside of the heartwood is the newer growth of *sapwood* which is usually lighter in color. Between the sapwood and the

64–4a. A stand of mixed hardwood, including white ash.

64 4c. A map showing where white ash grows.

inner bark is a pitchlike material called *cambium* in which the cell formation takes place to form more sapwood. Radiating out from the pith center of the tree are ray cells or *medullary rays.* These cell-like structures form passageways for food in feeding the tree for growth and development. The *outer bark* (protecting the tree) is the dead, corky covering that varies in thickness with the kind of tree. The *inner bark* (bast or phloem) carries the food made in the leaves down to the branches, trunk, and roots.

HARD AND SOFT WOODS

There are several ways of classifying woods into hard and soft. One of the most common is to divide all trees into two classes: those that shed their leaves annually and those which are "ever" green or produce cones. Those which shed their leaves—including such trees as oak, walnut, maple, ash, basswood, birch, cherry, and gumwood—are called *hardwoods.* Figure 64–4. Those that are evergreen or produce cones (conifers)—including such trees as fir, pine, cedar, spruce, and redwood—are called *softwoods.* Figure 64–5. However, in this method of classification, many of the so-called softwoods are harder than some of the hardwoods!

For purposes of use, woods are classified according to their *actual hardness* or *ability to resist wear*. In this method, which is most practical for the woodworker to follow, we have the following classifications:

HARD	MEDIUM HARD	SOFT
Ash	Fir, Douglas	Basswood
Beech	Gum	Pine, Ponderosa
Birch	Mahogany, true	Pine, Sugar
Cherry	Mahogany, Philippine	Poplar
Maple	Walnut	Redwood
Oak, red		Willow
Oak, white		

64–5a. **Trees like these big Douglas firs grow very slowly and may deteriorate and die when they become old. In commercial forests big trees are "clear cut" in blocks, leaving others standing to grow and reseed logged-off tracts.**

64–5b. Douglas fir branch with cones.

Another important method of classification is based on whether the wood has open or closed grain. The wood finisher, especially, is concerned with this problem because the open-grained woods offer greater opportunity for finishes and contrasting filler colors.

OPEN GRAIN	CLOSED GRAIN
Ash	Basswood
Mahogany, true	Beech
Mahogany, Philippine	Birch
Oak, red	Cherry
Oak, white	Gum
Walnut	Maple
Willow	Poplar
	Fir, Douglas
	Pine, Ponderosa
	Pine, Sugar
	Redwood

METHODS OF CUTTING LOGS

Boards are cut from logs in two major ways. The cheapest and most economical is called *plain-sawed*

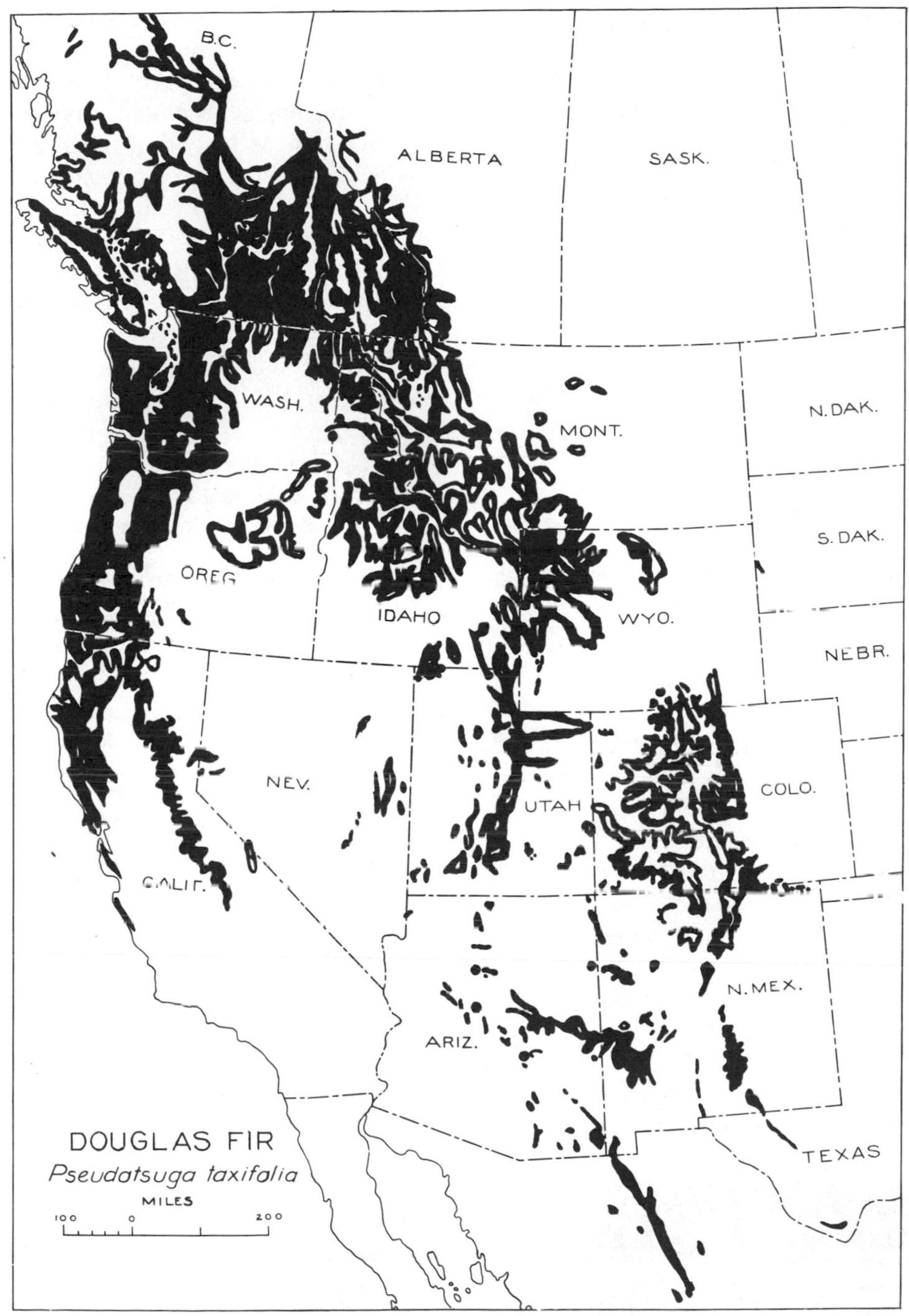

64–5c. A map showing where Douglas fir grows.

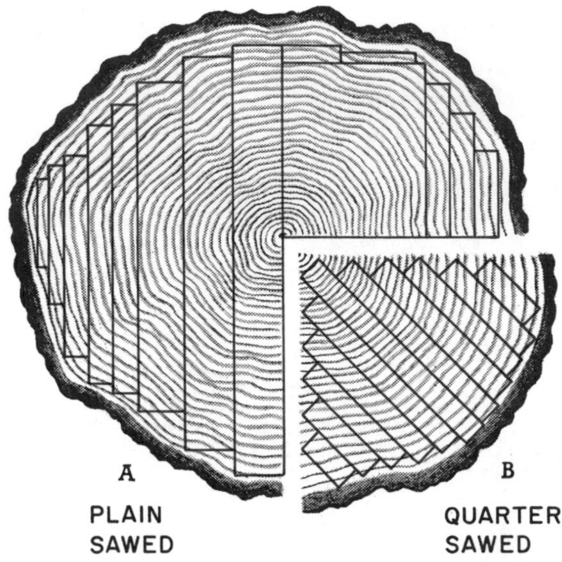

64–6. Two common methods of cutting lumber. A. Plain-sawed lumber (flat-grained). B. Quarter-sawed lumber (edge-grained).

(when it is a hardwood tree) or *flat-grained* (when it is a softwood tree). The log is squared and sawed lengthwise from one side to the other. *Quarter-sawed* (for hardwood) or *edge-grained* (for softwood) is a more expensive method of cutting. This shows a better grain pattern especially in oak and other hardwoods. In quarter-sawed lumber, the wood is cut as shown in Figure 64–6, or parallel to the medullary rays. Wood is quarter-sawed also to prevent warpage and to provide a better wearing surface.

MOISTURE CONTENT AND SEASONING

When a tree is cut down, it may contain between 30 and 300 per cent moisture. Before the wood can be used, a large part of this moisture must be removed. This is done by air and/or kiln drying. See Unit 65. Moisture in green wood exists both inside the cells and in the cell walls. In drying, the free water inside the cell cavities is removed first. When all of this is gone, it is said to be at the *fiber-saturation point*, and the wood will still contain about 23 to 30 per cent moisture. When the water in the cell walls begins to evaporate, the wood shrinks in size. When wood is dried to 15 per cent moisture, it will have attained about half its total shrinkage. Lumber for house framing construction is usually dried to about 19 per cent moisture. The way shrinkage affects lumber cut from different sections of a log

64–7. Here you see how lumber will warp when cut from different parts of the log.

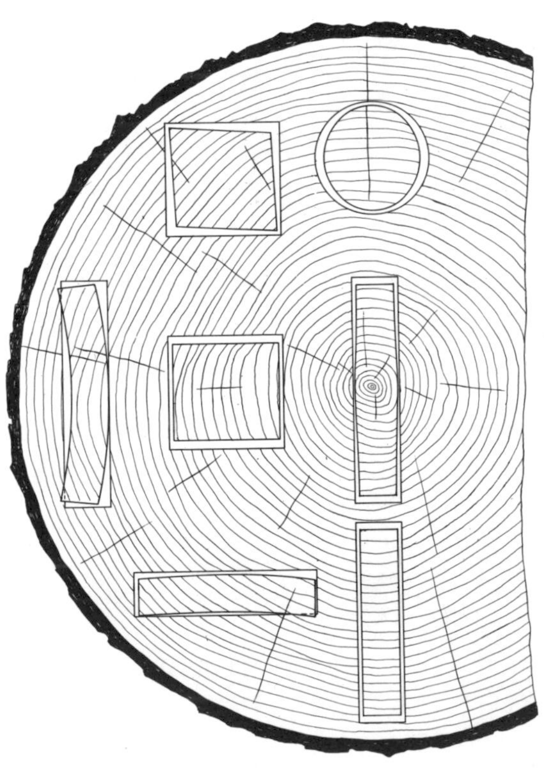

is shown in Figure 64–7. Lumber for furniture construction, however, should have only about 6 to 10 per cent moisture content. If wood has too much moisture when the project is built, the wood will continue to dry out in the shop and at home, causing warpage and cracked joints. Remember, wood will continue to dry out or take on moisture until the moisture in the wood equals the moisture in the air.

SHRINKAGE AND SWELLING

Wood shrinks as it dries and swells as it absorbs moisture. Most of the difficulties of shrinkage and swelling can be avoided by making sure the wood has been dried to the correct moisture content. Wood shrinks or swells very little lengthwise. Most of the change in size is across the grain. However, flat-grained or plain-sawed lumber will change almost twice as much in width as quarter-sawed or edge-grained stock. Can you see why?

FIGURE IN WOOD

A figure in wood is the pattern formed by the coloring matter, by the annular rings and the medullary rays, and by cross grain, wavy grain, knots, and other irregularities. As said, there is generally a difference in color between the heartwood, that is darker, and the sapwood, that is lighter. Some woods such as walnut and gumwood contain darker streaks that give the wood a distinctive figure. All woods have some figure, but in many cases it is so difficult to see that the wood is considered uninteresting. The woods that have a distinct figure are considered superior for fine furniture. You'll find that no two pieces of wood have the same figure. This difference adds interest and beauty to a well constructed piece of furniture.

CAN YOU ANSWER THESE QUESTIONS ON TREES AND LUMBER?

1. Name the substance that holds the tubes or cells of a tree together.
2. At what time does most of the growth take place in trees?
3. How can you determine the age of a tree?
4. Name the parts of a tree.
5. What are the three classifications of wood?
6. For *use*, which of the following woods are classified as hardwoods: oak, maple, white pine, fir, poplar, ash, hickory?
7. What is the advantage of quarter sawed lumber?
8. What is "fiber-saturation point"?
9. What forms the figure in wood?

Section XIII

UNIT 65. STORY OF LUMBERING

Lumbering has always been one of the most fascinating and romantic of occupations. It has been glorified in song and story in our history. However, while some lumbering practices have not changed in the last 100 years, most lumbering has become mechanized and modernized into a highly efficient process. The actual methods of lumbering vary with geographic location and the size of the company. Generally speaking, however, the procedure includes cutting the trees, taking them to the mill, cutting the logs into lumber, and seasoning the lumber.

CUTTING TREES

The first step is to locate and lay out the site for the logging camp. After this, the necessary roads and camps are built to provide working and living facilities for the men. The mature trees are marked for cutting. The first step

65–1. Putting in the undercut. Logger uses a power saw to put in the undercut in a big pine being felled. The undercut determines the direction of fall of the tree.

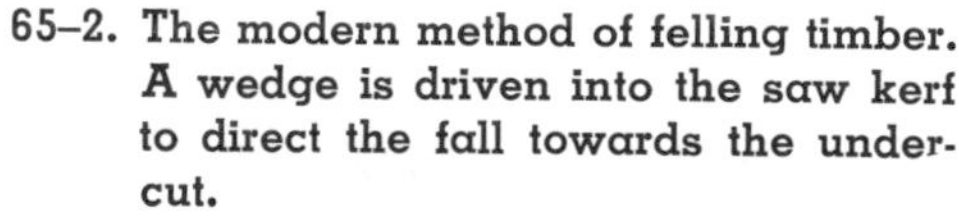

65–2. The modern method of felling timber. A wedge is driven into the saw kerf to direct the fall towards the undercut.

65–3. Hauling logs to a loading site. Here the logs are being dragged by a tractor to a truck or train landing where they will be loaded and hauled to the mill.

in cutting the trees is to cut a notch in the side of the tree toward which the tree is to fall. Figure 65–1. Then, with a hand crosscut saw or a power saw, the tree is cut from the opposite side of the notch. Figure 65–2. As the cut is made, a wedge is driven into the saw kerf to force the tree to fall in the proper direction. After the tree is felled, the small branches are trimmed off. The logs are then dragged or pushed to a loading site where they are stacked. Figure 65–3.

TRANSPORTING THE LOGS TO THE MILL

In years past, logs were moved to the nearest river or stream and allowed to collect there during the winter. In the spring, as the water rose, the logs were floated down the river to the mill. While this still continues in some places, it is not nearly so common. Today, most logs are loaded by crane onto trucks or railroad flatcars and taken directly to the mill. Figure 65–4. At the mill they are placed in a millpond to keep them from drying out before cutting. Figure 65–5.

LUMBER MANUFACTURE

From the millpond, the logs are taken to the mill on a bullchain. Figure 65–6. As they rise to the mill, they are sprayed with water to clean off the dirt. Inside the mill each log is loaded on a carriage which holds it as it is being cut. Here the sawyer takes over. He is one of the most important men in the mill since he knows lumber grades. He knows how to get the largest amount of high-quality lumber from each log. He does it by controlling the movement of the headrig (the carriage and the headsaw), where logs are cut into boards or timber. Smaller mills usually use a circular saw as a headsaw. In large mills, however, the headsaw is a band saw. As the carriage moves forward, the log is carried straight into the saw's sharp teeth. When the saw has passed through the log from one

65–4. This shows the way logs are loaded onto large trucks or railroad flat cars.

65–5. Unloading logs from trucks into a millpond. Logs are stored in water because it helps protect the wood from insect damage and decreases fire hazards.

65–6a. Bull chain lifts log into mill.

end to the other, the carriage shoots back and the position of the log is shifted for a second cut.

After the log is cut to size, it is carried by conveyors to other saws that trim the bark off the edges and cut it into standard sizes. All soft lumber is cut into standard dimensions in thickness, width, and length. Hardwoods are cut in standard thickness only, since they are much more expensive and too much waste would result otherwise. Also, the very nature of hardwood use does not require standard lengths.

Farther along the production line, an edger saws the boards into different widths, and trimmer saws cut the boards to proper lengths.

SEASONING THE LUMBER

The "green" chain, which is a conveyor belt or chain, moves the boards into a sorting shed. Here the lumber is sorted and graded as to its size and

65–6b. Log is mounted on carriage for sawing.

65–6c. Edger saw squares edges of boards.

65–6e. Green chain moves boards for grading and sorting.

quality. (The "green" refers to the sap-moisture of the freshly cut lumber, not its color.) Then it is stacked in piles with small blocks between each piece to permit air to circulate around the wood.

Wood that comes from the mill contains a great deal of moisture. It is necessary to dry it out or season it before it is fit for use. There are two common methods of doing this. As said in unit 64, in the first, called *air drying*, the stacks of lumber are left out in the open in sheds where the wood can dry naturally over a period of several months. Much of our soft lumber is air-dried. The second and more efficient way of controlling the moisture content of lumber is to dry the lumber artificially in a controlled moisture-temperature room called a kiln. Here, woods are allowed to dry for several months. Then they are placed in a building usually made of cement brick or hollow tile. The stacks are first sprayed with steam, then the steam is turned off and the building closed. Warm air is circulated through the lumber. This continues over a period of two to eight days until the moisture content of the lumber is down to 6 to 10 per cent. This lumber is called kiln dried. Kiln-dried lumber is the only satisfactory kind to use for furniture making and for all better construction.

PLANING

Larger sawmills usually have a planing mill section in which the rough lumber is finished by passing the boards through a set of rotating knives which give it a smooth surface. Boards are also made into flooring, siding, moldings, and other kinds of building "trim." There are also separate planing

65–6d. Trimmer saw cuts boards into various lengths.

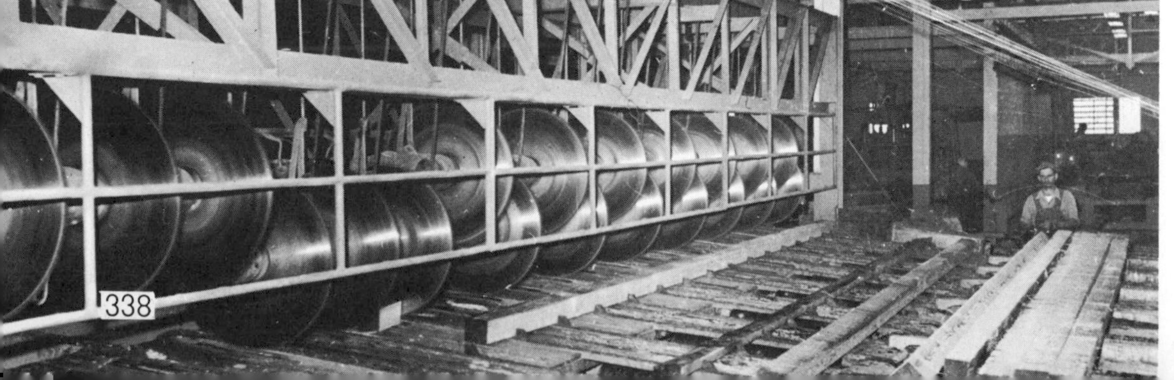

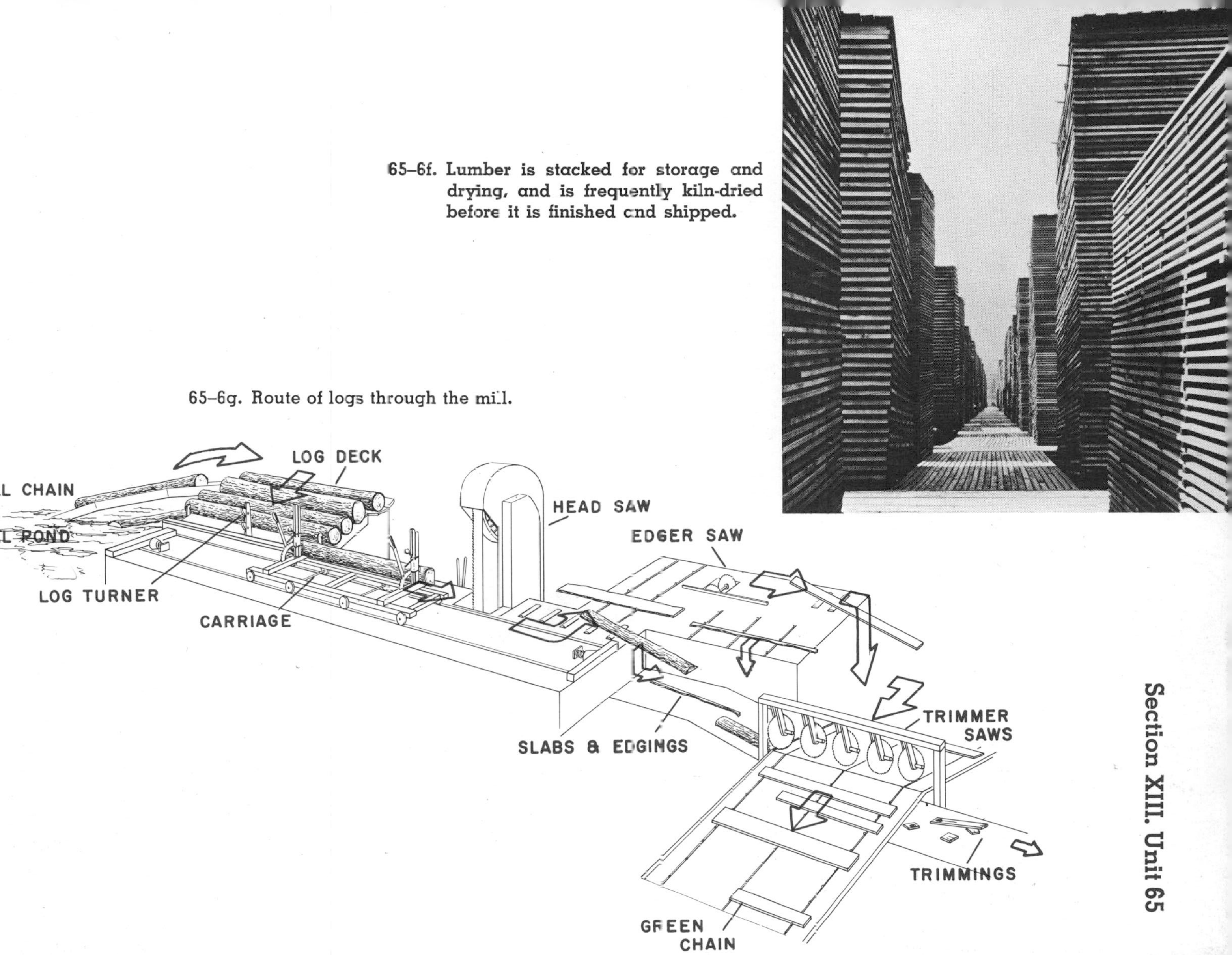

65–6f. Lumber is stacked for storage and drying, and is frequently kiln-dried before it is finished and shipped.

65–6g. Route of logs through the mill.

mills which buy rough lumber from small mills and sell the finished product, called "surface lumber." Finished lumber is again graded before it is shipped.

CAN YOU ANSWER THESE QUESTIONS ON THE STORY OF LUMBERING?

1. Name the many ways in which lumbering has become mechanized.
2. What is the first step in cutting trees?
3. Why is a notch cut in the tree on the side toward which it is to fall?
4. Are most logs moved to the mill by floating them downstream? How else?
5. Why are logs kept in a millpond for a time?
6. Describe the sawing of logs into planks, timbers, and boards.
7. Why is soft lumber cut into standard dimensions?
8. What are the two common methods of drying lumber? Which kind is better for furniture wood?
9. Explain the planing operation.

Section XIII

UNIT 66. PRODUCTS OF OUR AMERICAN FORESTS

Our forests are a storehouse of wealth for our use. Figure 66–1. Woods and lumbers and their by-products are such an important part of our life that we cannot list here all of their uses. Figure 66–2. There are at least 4,500 specific uses for wood and wood products: from the lowly toothpick to the thousands of telephone and telegraph poles; from the woods used in novelties and trinkets to the woods used in home and industrial construction; and from the by-products that make paper to those used for making rayon, plastics, and other chemical materials.

SAW LOGS

Each year, well over 37 billion board feet of lumber are needed for construction and industrial use, not to mention the uncounted amounts of unsawed wood and fuel wood. Enough lumber is cut each year to build 3,600,000 one-family homes. The main use of construction lumber is, of course, in the building of homes, public buildings, commercial buildings, and other large frame structures. Each year 3½ million poles are purchased by telephone and utility companies. Our railroads use about 50 million railroad ties a year and our farmers 400 to 600 million fence posts.

Most hardwoods go into industrial lumber which is used primarily for furniture making and vehicle construction such as boats and trucks, for machinery and equipment, and for such manufactured products as amusement

Forest Regions of the United States

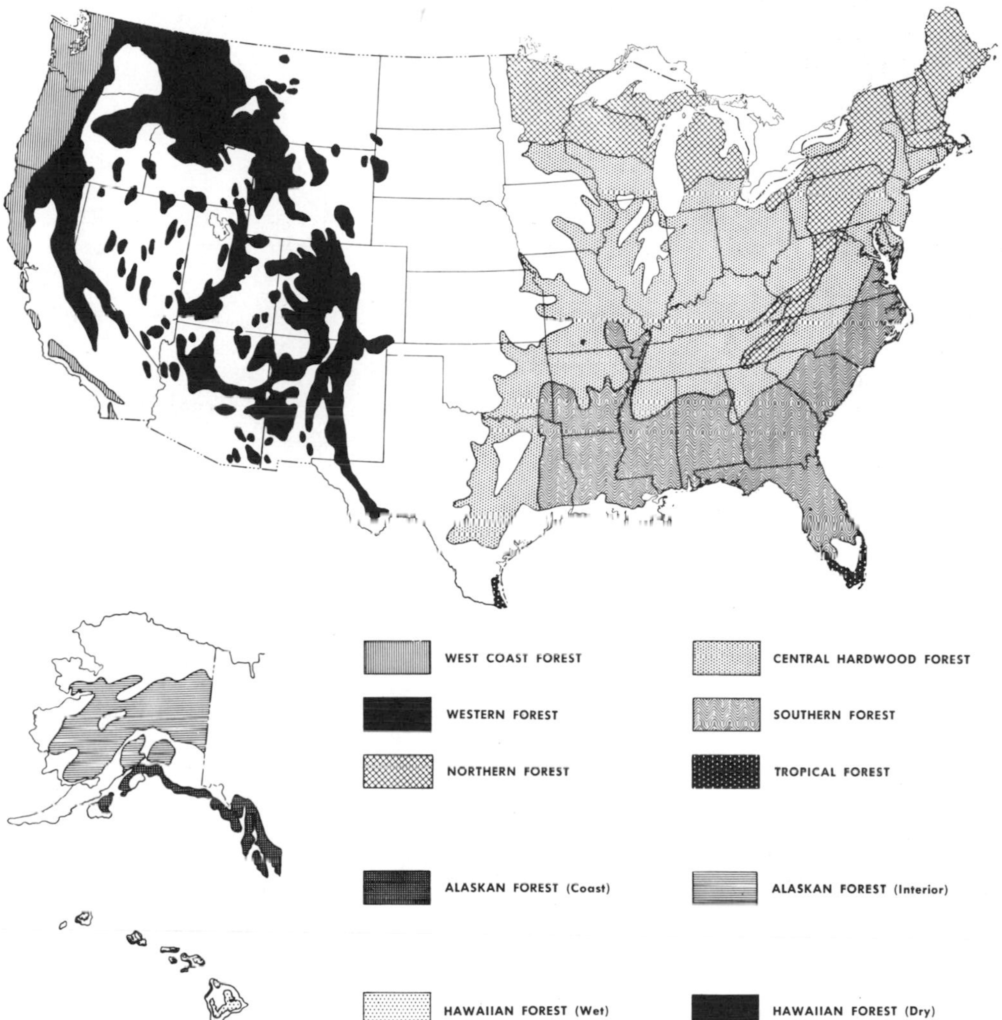

66–1. This map shows areas of renewable natural wealth. The West Coast or Pacific forests are primarily Douglas fir. However, they also have western red cedar, spruce, and hemlock. The western forests include much of our softwood timber, primarily pine, although there are some hardwoods. The northern forests have such trees as hemlock, red spruce, white pine, and several kinds of hardwoods. The central hardwood forests include oak, cherry, birch, and many other kinds of hardwoods. In the southern forests are such softwoods as pine and cypress and many kinds of hardwoods. The tropical forests have ebony and palm trees. The coast regions of Alaska have primarily western hemlock and spruce, while the interior forests are heavy with white spruce and white birch. The Hawaiian forests include many softwoods and some unusual types such as monkey pod and koa.

devices, athletic equipment, and children's toys.

VENEERS AND PLYWOOD

Veneer is a very thin sheet of wood that is sawed, peeled or sliced from a log. Several sheets of veneer may be glued (laminated) to lumber to make *lumber-core plywood*, or they may be bonded to other sheets of veneer to

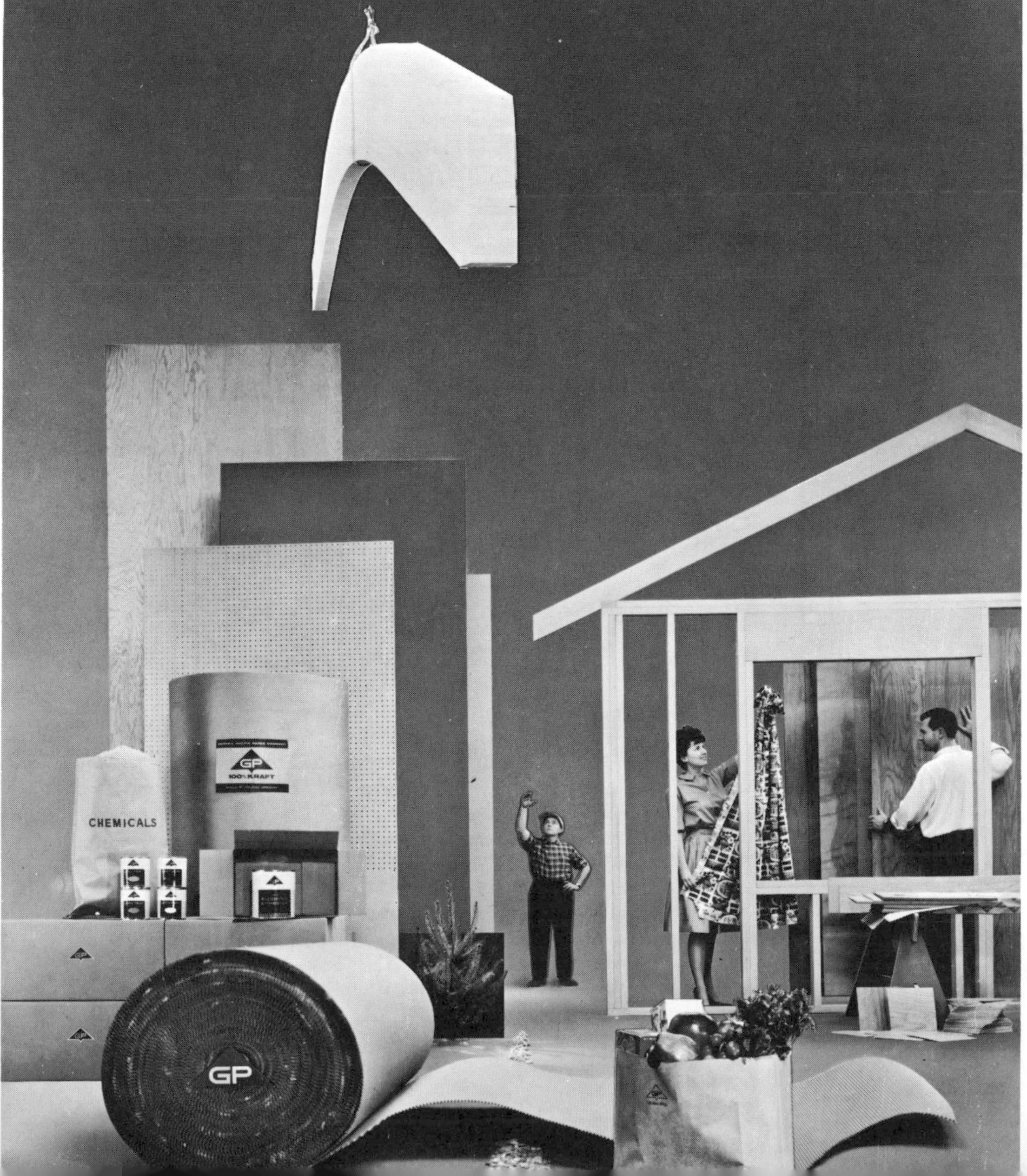

66–2. All of these materials are forest products. They include glue-laminated beam, hardwood plywood, hardboard, paper, chemicals, rayon and just plain lumber. It is hard to believe that so many different items are products of American forests.

make *veneer-core plywood.* Veneer plywood is built-up veneer sheets with the grain of adjacent sheets (or plies) running at right angles to the sheets above and below. This change in direction gives thin plywood great strength and rigidity. Veneer is cut on giant lathes or on slicers in three ways: *rotary cut*, *flat sliced*, or *quarter sliced.* Figure 66–3. Hardwood veneers are usually flat sliced or quarter sliced. Figure 66–4. Fir plywood is rotary cut. The veneer logs are cut into blocks 8, 10, or 12 feet long and then the bark is removed. Figure 66–5. These veneer logs are placed in gigantic lathes which turn them against a razor-sharp knife. The thin, continuous sheet of wood that is peeled off the log looks very much like thick wrapping paper being peeled off a roll. Figure 66–6. The veneer is cut to specific width, eliminating any defects. It is then sorted as to grade. Sheets of green veneer are put through driers that remove much of the moisture content. Figure 66–7. Glue is applied to the veneer and the sheets are stacked with the grain of each at right angles to the sheet above and below it. Figure 66–8. The glued sheets are placed in huge hydraulic presses in which the glue is set under heat and pressure. Figure 66–9. When dry, the panels are sanded to specified thickness and cut to certain lengths and widths. Figure 66–10.

Plywood is usually made in an odd number of plies (layers), such as 3-ply, 5-ply, or 7-ply. Figure 66–11. Plywood is held together with either moisture-resistant glue or moisture-proof glue. The former is used on

66–4. Flat-slicing hardwood veneer.

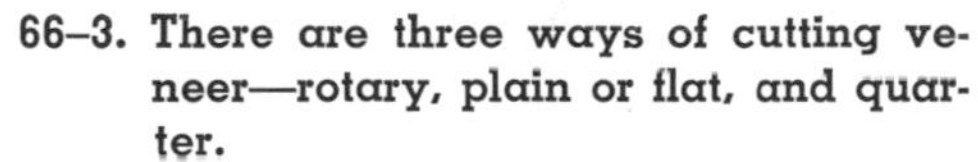

66–3. There are three ways of cutting veneer—rotary, plain or flat, and quarter.

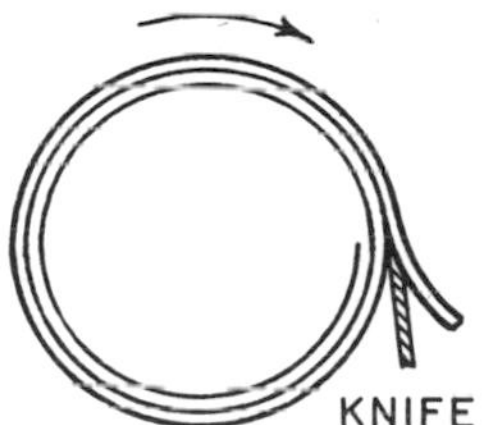

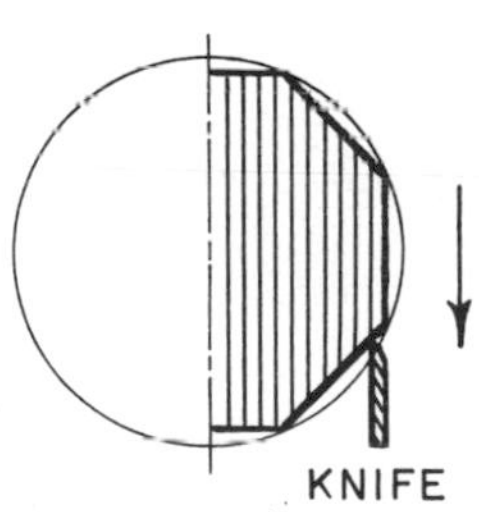

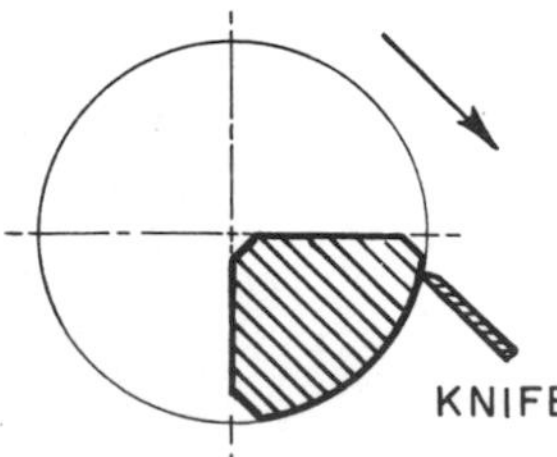

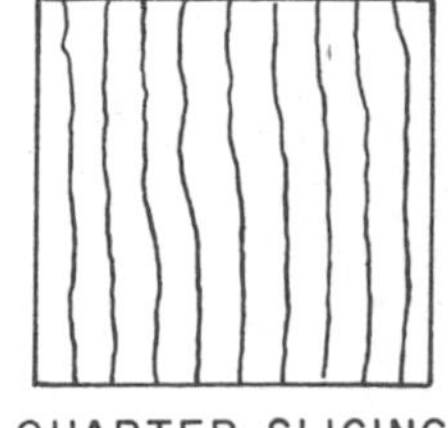

66–5. Removing the bark from the log before cutting the veneer.

interior plywoods; the latter is for exterior use. Plywood provides great strength and, at the same time, surprising lightness. In addition to the soft and hard plywoods, there are many specialty types. These include those with special or decorative surfaces. The face of plywood may have a

66–6. Rotary cutting of veneer.

66–7. Drying the veneer.

striated (lined) surface to give it a combed look. Figure 66–12. Another may have a brushed face to accent the grain, another a sandblasted surface. Plywoods are also available in many special grades for special purposes.

66–8. Applying adhesive to the veneer.

66–9. Gluing up plywood. The sheets of veneer have been coated with adhesive and arranged with the grain of each ply at right angles to the ones above and below. These layers are then placed in a hot press in which the combination of heat and pressure "welds" the plies together.

66–11. Plywood construction. A piece of 1 inch, 7-ply wood is cut away to show the direction in the grain of the alternate pieces. Plywood, pound for pound, is stronger than steel.

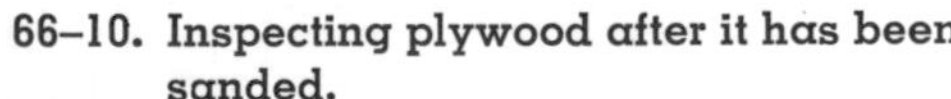

66–10. Inspecting plywood after it has been sanded.

WOOD CHEMISTRY

While the commercial uses of wood involving chemistry are not of direct concern to the woodworker, it is important to have an appreciation of woods in this respect. Figure 66–13. Much of the paper we make is a product of wood pulp. Each year about 15½ million cords of pulpwood are made into paper and paperboard. A more recent development in the use of pulpwood flour and sawdust is the making of cellulose products such as rayon cloth, plastics, dyes, paints, explosives, linoleum, turpentine, and resins. Wood is also a source of sugar, alcohol, and feed for cattle. With many new chemical developments, wood provides the raw material being developed into thousands of commercial products.

66–12. This plywood has a V-cut in the surface to give it a plank effect to help accentuate the nautical flavor of the room. Plywood is available in many different surface treatments.

MISCELLANEOUS USES

In addition to all of the previously discussed uses, many of the by-products of wood that once were considered waste materials are now valuable. Sawdust, for example, is used for insulation, for packing, and other commercial uses. Bark is made into flavorings, drugs, and chemicals. Roots are made into oils and tea, and are used for making smoking pipes and trinkets.

66–13. Some of the materials we get from trees.

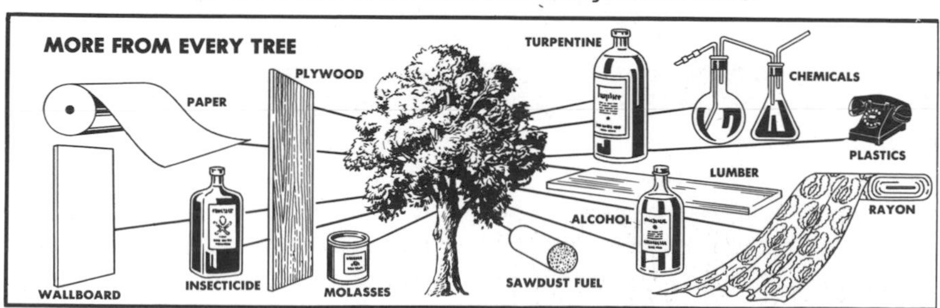

CAN YOU ANSWER THESE QUESTIONS ON PRODUCTS OF OUR AMERICAN FORESTS?

1. Make a list of the uses of wood and wood products. There are hundreds, of course, but name as many as you can, using your study of other subjects to help you.
2. How many board feet of lumber are needed annually for construction and industrial use?
3. Which needs the most lumber, the railroad or the telephone and utility companies?
4. What is veneer? Describe and tell how it is used.
5. What advantage has plywood over solid wood?
6. How is the grade of plywoods indicated?
7. Name the common sizes of plywood as to thickness, width, and length.
8. What kind of plywood has a grain-like surface?
9. Boat construction requires what kind of plywood?
10. From what is most of our newspaper "newsprint" made?
11. List some of the products of wood chemistry.
12. What by-products of wood are common today?

Section XIII

UNIT 67. OPPORTUNITIES IN WOODWORKING

Many products that once were made of wood are now being produced of metal, plastics, and other materials. Nevertheless, wood and wood products are still the source of employment for over one million people. Indirectly, over two million in the United States alone depend for a living on products of the American forests. There are over 20,000 concerns which produce lumber and lumber products to make up the fifth largest manufacturing industry. There are many and varied opportunities available to anyone who is interested in wood. These range from the professional, such as research worker or furniture designer who must have years of training, to routine factory workmen. Opportunities in woodworking closely follow the flow of lumber and lumber products as follows:

1. Many men work in and around sawmills where logs are converted into rough lumber.

2. Others are employed in the process of grading and seasoning lumber.

3. Still other thousands earn a living moving lumber from forest to mill and from mill to factory.

4. In factories, many machine operators use woodworking machines such as the planer, jointer, circular

saw, tenoner, dovetailer, and many others.

5. There are many jobs in assembling and finishing of products in furniture factories and manufacturing concerns, such as sash-and-door or box-making industries.

6. There are many others who do maintenance work on woodworking machines such as saw filing and other repair jobs.

7. A more select group earn a living at the craft level of woodworking. These will be discussed a little more completely. Your background in the woodworking shop can give you a good start in the craft occupations.

8. Of utmost importance are the thousands of people who earn a good living teaching woodworking in industrial arts programs, in vocational education apprentice training, and in other educational areas. Of the 35,000 and more industrial arts teachers alone, a large majority teach woodworking either fulltime or as a part of general shop. Industrial teaching as a career is not so competitive as some other types of teaching since it largely represents a man's world.

Those who teach in other areas of industrial arts and vocational education have urgent need for a thorough knowledge of woodworking. Some idea of the popularity of woodworking both as a school subject and as a later-years activity is shown by the fact that woodworking is the second most popular creative hobby in the United States. Most adults who enjoy this hobby learn the fundamentals in school shops from an industrial arts instructor.

9. Other professional occupations that require a knowledge of woods and woodworking include those of the architect, furniture designer, forester, and interior designer. The *architect* works with customers in designing and building homes and commercial buildings. Figure 67–1. The *furniture de-*

67–1. The architect must understand building materials and must also be a good draftsman.

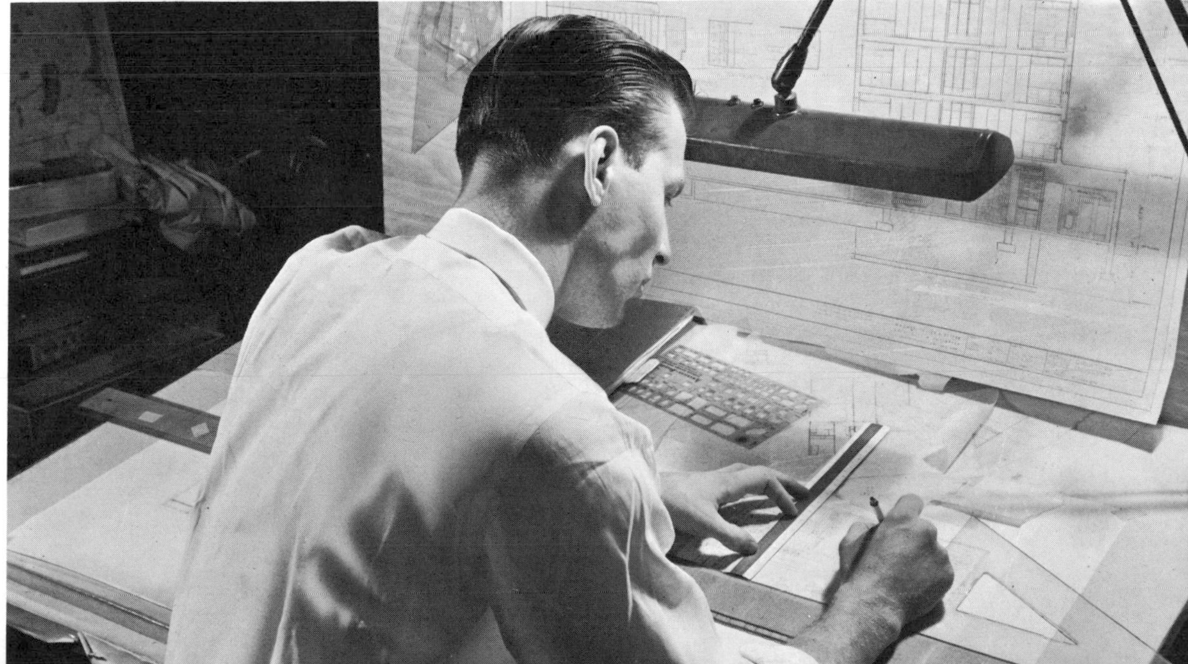

signer develops new models of furniture and other wood products. The *forester* supervises and manages forest lands and the cutting of trees. The *interior designer* plans the layout and furnishing for homes and offices. All of these occupations require from three to five years of college plus several years of on-the-job experience.

THE CRAFT OCCUPATIONS

If you have a real interest in woodworking, the careers in crafts can provide a real future. These include the cabinetmaker, carpenter, furniture finisher, patternmaker, wood carver, boat builder, and millman. Each requires trade school training and/or an apprenticeship. A person entering any of these must be a skilled operator of all hand tools and common woodworking machines. In addition, one must possess special talents for this particular kind of work.

67–2. A skilled cabinetmaker needs to know how to use all kinds of hand and machine tools.

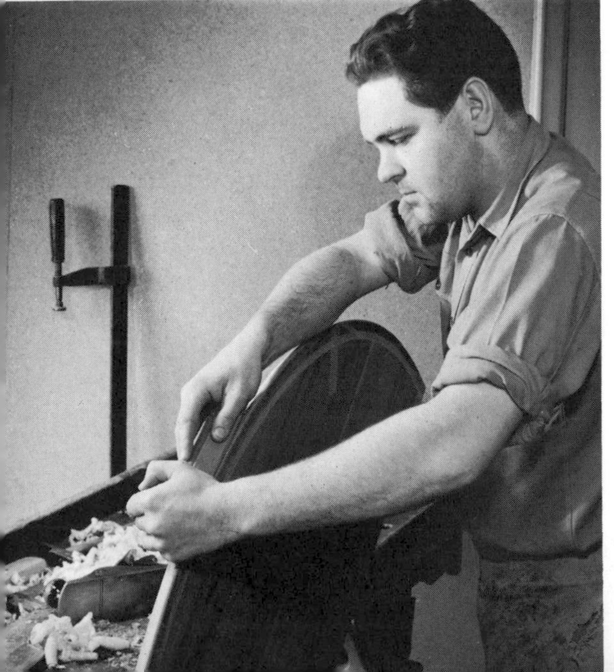

67–3. These carpenters are installing a new kind of roof.

The *cabinetmaker*, for example, must be qualified to make fine furniture and to do fine interior work. Figure 67–2. The *carpenter* must have a knowledge of commercial and home construction and be able to read architectural drawings. Figure 67–3. The *patternmaker* must know and understand foundry work and how castings are made, and be able to use special tools. Figure 67–4. The *wood carver* must have special talents in design and must be skilled in doing detailed hand work. The *boat builder* must understand the special problems of ship transportation and be able to use the different woods and methods of construction needed in the solution of these problems. Figure 67–5. The *millman* must have a thorough knowledge of the construction and operation of all woodworking machines and must be able to make machine setups.

In considering a job in woodworking, you need to realize a few facts. Many of these jobs require that you work in somewhat noisy and dusty surroundings or, at times, exposed to the elements. There is also some danger of accident to the hands and fingers. On the other hand, all of the craft jobs offer great satisfaction to the individual as well as an opportunity to construct and build. An expert in any of the craft occupations will not only earn a good living, but he will be doing a real man's job.

There is much opportunity for advancement in the woodworking field. The carpenter, for example, can work toward becoming a contractor or the patternmaker can become a foreman or supervisor.

Anyone interested in a particular woodworking occupation can send for a bulletin published by the United States Department of Labor, Washington, D. C., titled, "Job Descriptions for the Lumber and Lumber Products Industries." This gives details as to what training you will need, how you can get experience, what you will earn, and what promotions are in prospect.

67–5. Boat builders must know how to build, refinish, and repair a craft.

CAN YOU ANSWER THESE QUESTIONS ON OPPORTUNITIES IN WOODWORKING?

1. How many people indirectly earn a living from the products of American forests?
2. Name three professional occupations in which an understanding of woodworking is important.
3. What are four of the major craft occupations in woodworking?
4. How can you learn more about a particular woodworking occupation?

67–4. A patternmaker working on a wood pattern for an engine cylinder block.

Section XIII

UNIT 68. WOODS: KINDS, QUALITIES, AND USES

Here is a brief description of some of the woods in common use. Selection of the wood for each project should be made with care. Each kind of wood has its own peculiar color, working qualities, and properties. Figure 68–1. If you become particularly interested in one furniture wood, you can find many books and government bulletins devoted entirely to that one kind. There are also national associations which will supply all information concerning a particular wood. Some of these associations are: American Walnut Manufacturer's Association, Mahogany Association, Western Pine Association, and National Oak Flooring Manufacturer's Association.

The Forest Products Laboratory at Madison, Wisconsin, will send upon request technical and scientific information about wood and wood products.

HARDWOODS (Broad-leafed species)

ASH, WHITE

The three most common types of ash are white, green, and black. White

68–1. Common woods and their characteristics.

Kind	Color	Working Qualities	Weight	Strength	Lasting Qualities (Outside Use)
Hardwoods					
*Ash	Grayish brown	Hard	Heavy	Strong	Poor
Basswood	Lt. Cream	Easy	Light	Weak	Poor
Beech	Lt. Brown	Hard	Heavy	Medium	Medium
Birch	Lt. Brown	Hard	Heavy	Strong	Fair
Cherry	Dk. Red	Hard	Medium	Strong	Fair
Gum	Red-Brown	Medium	Medium	Medium	Medium
*Mahogany (true)	Gold-Brown	Easy	Medium	Medium	Good
*Mahogany (Philippine)	Med. Red	Easy	Medium	Medium	Good
Maple, sugar	Red-Cream	Hard	Heavy	Strong	Poor
*Oak, red	Flesh-Brown	Hard	Heavy	Strong	Fair
*Oak, white	Grey-Brown	Hard	Heavy	Strong	Fair
Poplar	Yellow	Easy	Medium	Weak	Fair
*Walnut	Dk. Brown	Medium	Heavy	Strong	Good
*Willow	Brown	Easy	Light	Low	Fair
Softwoods					
Fir, Douglas	Orange-Brown	Medium	Medium	Medium	Medium
Pine, Ponderosa	Orange to Red-Brown	Easy	Light	Weak	Poor
Pine, sugar	Creamy Brown	Easy	Light	Poor	Fair
Redwood	Dk. Red-Brown	Easy	Light	Medium	Good

Woods marked with (*) are open grain and require a paste filler.

ash is very popular for furniture construction; it is used widely for sports equipment such as skis, baseball bats, and toboggans. Figure 68–2. It is well suited to these things because of its strength and hardness but particularly because it holds its shape well after it has been formed.

BASSWOOD, AMERICAN

Softest of commercial hardwoods, basswood is white with a few black streaks. Figure 68–3. It is fuzzy because of its long fibers, is fairly strong for bending, is nonwarping, and has little or no grain marking. Basswood is the best wood for drawing boards, for small moldings, for burned designs, and for thin lumber for jigsaw work. It is not durable for outside uses. It makes a very strong glue joint and is easy to plane or sand. However, it does not scrape well because of its long fibers and yielding surface. It is usually painted but may be stained to imitate other woods.

BEECH, AMERICAN

Beech is one of the very best of the utility hardwoods. The wood is white or slightly reddish. Figure 68–4. It has no figure to make it ornamental and it is rarely used for the exterior of furniture, other than chairs. It is sometimes chosen as a substitute for more expensive birch or hard maple. Beech is high in strength and very durable. It is commonly used for medium-priced chairs.

BIRCH, YELLOW, AND CURLY

Birch is a hardwood of fine texture and close grain, coming primarily from the north-central states and Canada. Figure 68–5. Yellow birch is the most common. Curly birch is found only in occasional trees, the result of rare grain development. It has a delicate, wavy figure and is sought after for fine furniture and panels. It is difficult to work and must be finished by scraping. The heartwood is red in color and the sapwood is white. Therefore a single board may be either red or white, or red with white edges. It is a good wood for table tops, doors, rails, and any furniture parts that require extra strength. Birch will take practically any color of stain and is one of the finest woods for enamel finishes. It is sometimes finished to resemble mahogany, walnut, or maple.

CHERRY, BLACK

Black cherry is found generally in most parts of the United States. Figure 68–6. It is not abundant enough to be a common furniture wood, even though it is very desirable for that purpose. The heartwood is a reddish brown in color, while the sapwood is white. Cherry resembles unfinished mahogany. It is a very durable wood, does not dent easily, and warps very little. There are many heirlooms of genuine cherry, indicating that it was more common many years ago. Cherry darkens with age. It is best finished with shellac or lacquer. Because of this it has a natural suitability to contemporary as well as period furniture.

SWEETGUM OR RED GUM

Gumwood is a native of river deltas throughout the south. Figure 68–7. Because of its tendency to warp in seasoning, gumwood was not commonly used for many years. Only recently has it become popular. Previously, when used at all, it was finished

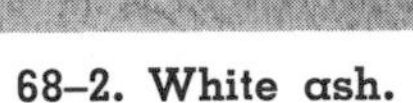

68–2. White ash.

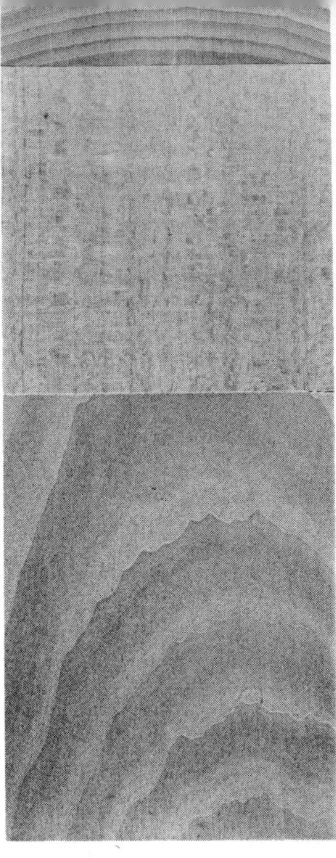

68–3. American basswood.

68–4. American beech.

From top to bottom you see the end surface, a quarter-sawed surface, and a plain-sawed surface.

68–5. Yellow birch.

68–6. Black cherry.

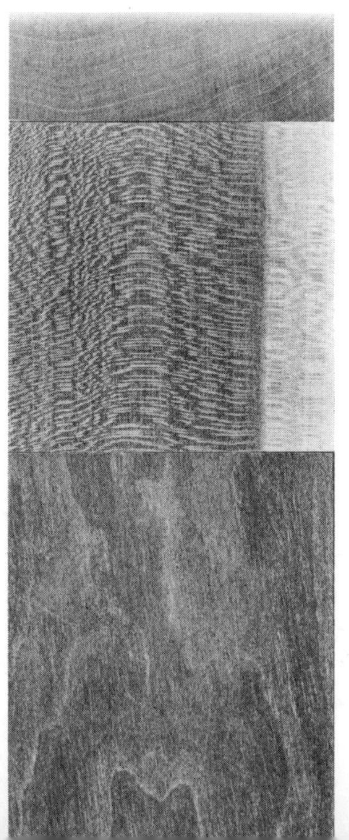

68–7. Sweetgum.

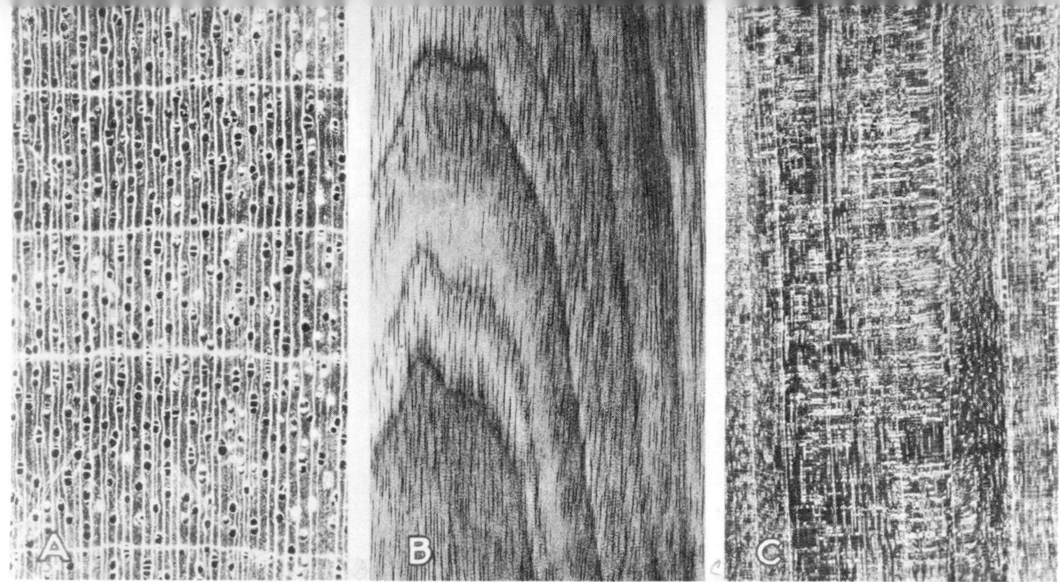

68–8. True or genuine mahogany. A. End surface (magnified 7½ diameters). B. Plain-sawed surface (natural size). C. Quarter-sawed surface (natural size).

to imitate some other wood. Now it is recognized as a wood of great beauty with a wide range of usefulness. The heartwood, called red gum, ranges from light to deep reddish brown. The sapwood is light colored and is referred to as sap gum. While gumwood is considered a hardwood by its producers, it really is a medium hardwood, not so hard as maple and harder than many pines.

Fine furniture and trim are made from gumwood. It is one of our most decorative woods. One of its unusual features is that no two long boards produce the same figure in the wood. The wood is closed-grained and has a very fine texture. Gumwood is plain-sawed, quarter-sawed, or veneered. Selected gumwood finishes very well in the natural color, but best results come when it is given a light brown stain. Light streaks often appear next to the dark. When this happens it is good practice to give the light wood a thin preparatory coat, wipe it off, and then treat the entire surface.

Water stains should always be chosen for gumwood even though these raise the grain. A light sanding is required before the finishing can be completed. The beauty of gumwood is better preserved by a dull treatment than by a gloss or polished finish. Dull lacquer, dull varnish, or hand-rubbed varnish produce the best effect on either interior trim or furniture. Because of its coarse grain, gumwood is excellent for enameled finishes.

MAHOGANY, TRUE OR GENUINE

The two kinds of genuine mahogany most commonly used for furniture are the Honduras and the African. Figure 68–8. True mahogany is considered the ideal cabinet wood. The heartwood of mahogany varies in color from pale to a deep reddish brown, becoming darker on exposure to light. It is tough, strong, easy to work, and polishes well. Mahogany is prized for its distinctive, fine grain figure, uniform texture, and natural color. It can be finished either dark, for traditional

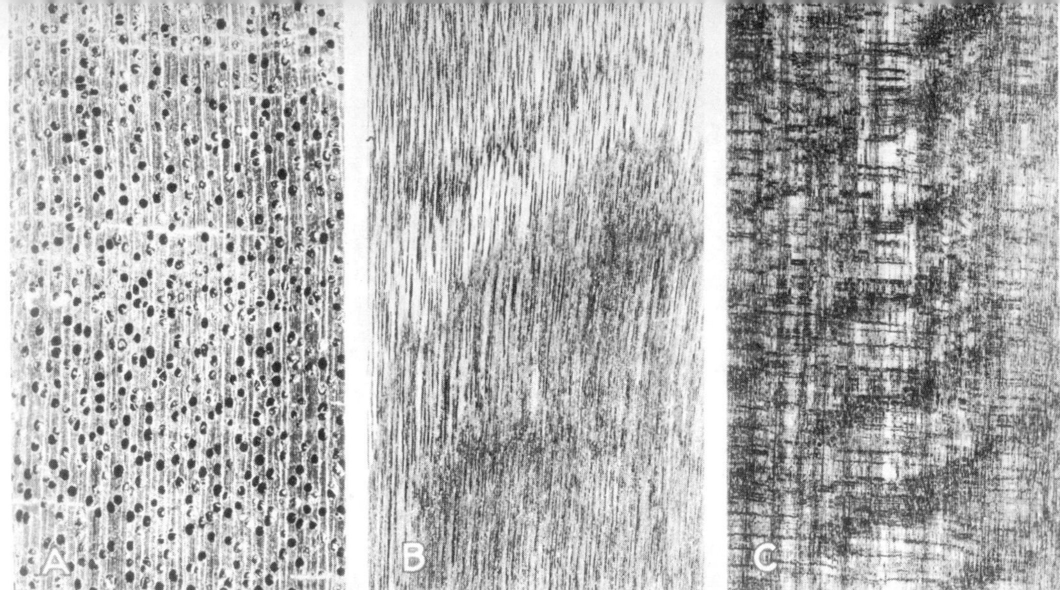

68–9. Philippine mahogany. A. End surface (magnified 7½ diameters). B. Plain-sawed surface. C. Quarter-sawed surface.

furniture, or bleached or natural for contemporary designs.

MAHOGANY, PHILIPPINE

Philippine mahogany is the name given to a group of woods known as lauans that come from the Philippine Islands. Figure 68–9. While they resemble genuine mahogany, these woods are coarser in texture and general appearance. They are usually classified as light red or dark red Philippine mahoganies. The dark red looks most like true mahogany. This wood is free from knots, checking, and shrinking. It is very easy to work with hand tools. Many different kinds of finishes can be used. It is an excellent, inexpensive wood to use for furniture, cabinet work, trim, and boats.

MAPLE, SUGAR

Maple is a hard, tough, strong wood that wears very well and has good resistance to shock. Figure 68–10. The grain is usually straight and fine in texture. The heartwood is light reddish-brown and the sapwood is white. Because of its wear-resisting qualities, maple is ideal for fine flooring. It is used extensively for both Colonial and contemporary furniture. A white, clear grade of maple, which comes from the sapwood, is especially light. It is the white wood which can be made into furniture and finer floors on which natural finish is to be used. The brown heartwood makes a good base for a brown, mahogany, or dark stain. Curly maple is the result of twisted growth and the manner in which the lumber is sawed. Bird's-eye maple is cut from sugar-maple trees and the texture is probably the result of thwarted bud growth.

OAK, RED

There are nearly 300 kinds of oak in the United States but, from the woodworker's standpoint, there are only two main kinds, namely red and white oak. Red oak is one of the most widely distributed trees in the United States.

Figure 68–11. Because of its slightly reddish tinge and its coarseness in grain, it is used very successfully to get certain decorative effects. Red oak is used largely for furniture, flooring, interior finish, and for construction. It is hard, heavy, and strong. Red oak is quite difficult to work.

OAK, WHITE

White oak is preferred for furniture and other items that are to be given a natural finish. Figure 68–12. They are usually free of the reddish tinge. White oak is one of the most valuable trees in the United States. It has better color, finer texture, and more prominent figure than the red oak. White oak has always been one of the most popular cabinet woods. Now and then one or more other woods come in vogue for a few years, but there is always a sure demand for oak. White oak is fairly difficult to work. The finished product, however, is beautiful and durable.

POPLAR, YELLOW

Poplar is a durable, soft, medium-strong hardwood. Figure 68–13. It is one of the largest native trees supplying lumber. The sapwood, which is frequently several inches thick, is white while the heartwood is yellowish brown with a green tinge. The wood is moderately light in weight, straight-grained, uniform in texture, and easy to nail because it does not split readily. It is easy to glue, stays in place well, holds paint and enamels well, is easily worked, and finishes smoothly. Because of all these qualities, it is excellent for inexpensive furniture which is painted and enameled. It is a good wood for beginners.

WALNUT, BLACK

Walnut, a medium hardwood, is one of the most beautiful native woods. Figure 68–14. It is found in the eastern half of the United States. The heartwood is brown while the sapwood is nearly white. Walnut is a strong, durable, and stiff wood. It is used chiefly for cabinetwork, furniture, veneers, and gunstocks. The veneer is cut from the best grade of walnut and is made into panel stock and plywood. Walnut is excellent for cabinetwork because it works well, glues up very satisfactorily, and takes a good finish. Walnut is usually finished natural. It is open-grained and requires a filler. Usually the filler is very dark, but at times a lighter filler is applied for contrast. The wood can be finished with a high-gloss varnish and rubbed to a high polish. Hand-rubbed oil finishes are also very popular.

WILLOW, BLACK

Willow is a hardwood that is extremely light and soft-textured. It is easy to work, glue, and finish. Figure 68–15. It is frequently used as a substitute for walnut. Willow is pale reddish-brown in color. It is commonly used in furniture and for veneer cores. There is a wide color range in willow. Since it is easy to work with hand and machine tools and much less expensive than walnut, it is a good wood to use for beginning projects.

SOFTWOODS (Cone Bearing species)

DOUGLAS FIR

Douglas fir is used very extensively for lumber and plywood manufacture. Figure 68–16. The wood is moderately

68–10. Sugar maple.

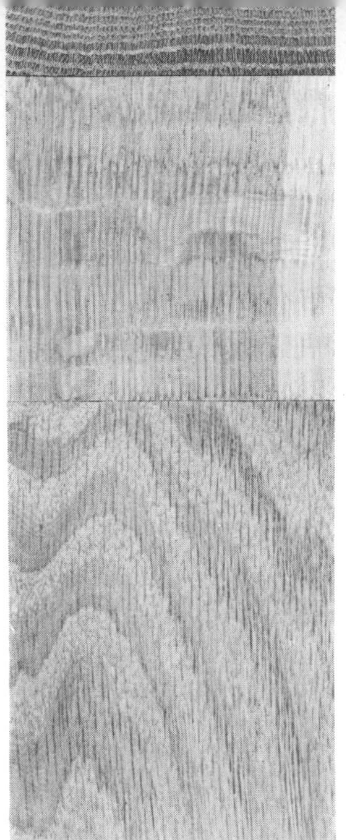

68–11. Red oak.

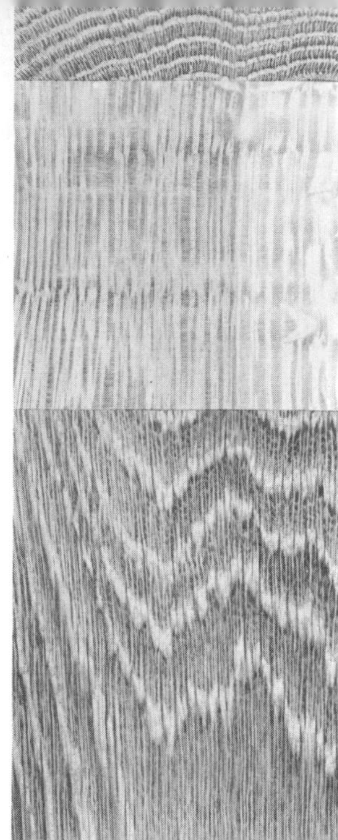

68–12. White oak.

Top view shows end surface. Middle view shows quarter-sawed surface. Bottom view shows plain-sawed surface.

68–13. Yellow poplar.

68–14. Black walnut.

68–15. Black willow.

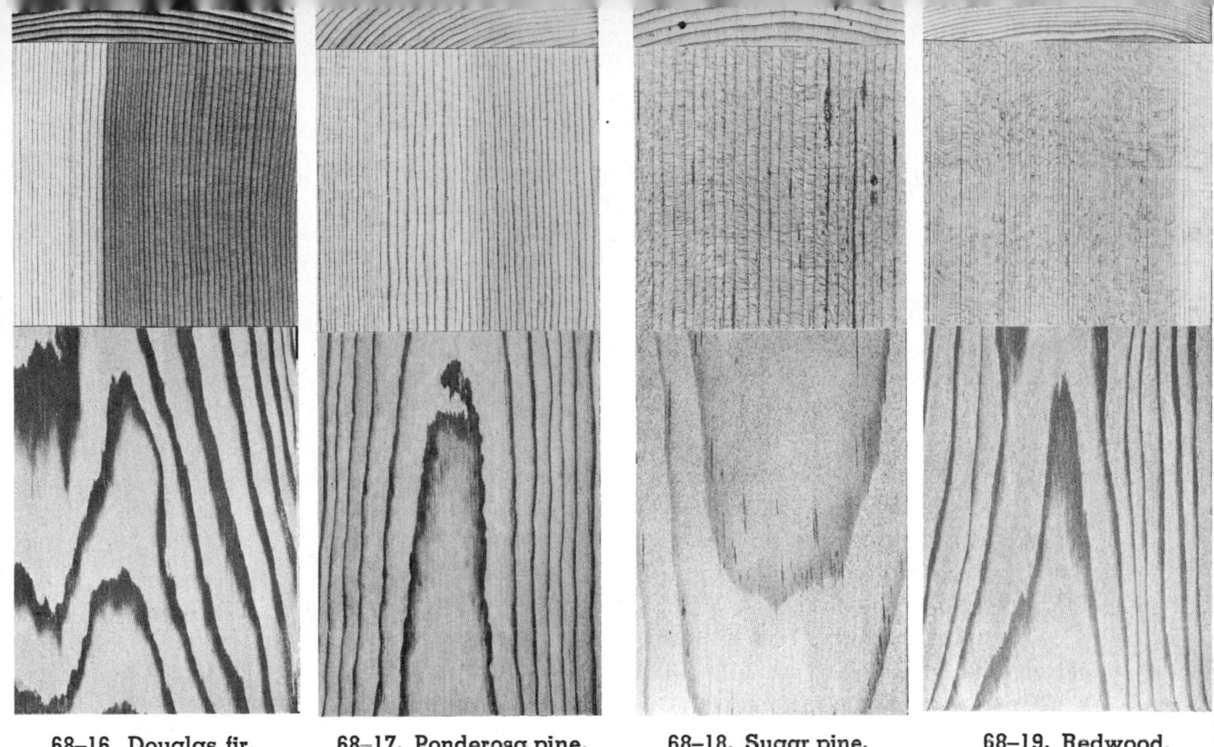

68–16. Douglas fir. 68–17. Ponderosa pine. 68–18. Sugar pine. 68–19. Redwood.

Top view shows end surface. Middle view shows edge-grained surface. Bottom view shows flat-grained surface.

hard, heavy and very stiff. It has a pronounced grain pattern, especially when made into plywood. The largest known fir tree in the world exists in Oregon. It measures more than 48 feet in circumference. The first limb is 104 feet up. The tree, 200 feet, 6 inches tall, is believed to be at least 1,000 years old. It contains enough lumber for 10 two-bedroom frame houses.

PINE, PONDEROSA

Ponderosa pine is used primarily for building lumber and to a lesser degree for post poles and veneers. Figure 68–17. The wood from this tree varies considerably in its properties. It is moderately light in weight, soft, and low in resistance. It is an excellent wood for home construction.

PINE, SUGAR

Sugar pine is used almost entirely for lumber for building boxes, foundry patterns, and mill work. Figure 68–18. The wood is light in color, soft, smooth, straight-grained, and easily worked. The wood has very small shrinkage and seasons very readily. An oil stain or shellac finish can be used very easily on sugar pine.

REDWOOD

Redwood is a widely used wood for home construction, fences, and outdoor furniture. Figure 68–19. It is light in weight, moderately hard, and strong. Redwood is very resistant to decay. This wood shrinks very little, is quite easy to season, and holds its shape well after seasoning.

CAN YOU ANSWER THESE QUESTIONS ON WOODS: KINDS, QUALITIES, AND USES?

1. Where can you obtain information of a technical and scientific nature about wood and wood products?
2. Name the three common types of ash. What are among the chief uses of ash?
3. Why is basswood a good choice for beginning projects?
4. What is the color range of birch? Why is birch chosen for making bed rails?
5. For what kind of wood is willow used as a substitute?
6. Cherry resembles what other kind of wood?
7. Is cherry as common today as it was many years ago? Why or why not?
8. Has gumwood increased or decreased in popularity in recent years? Why?
9. What kind of stain should be put on gumwood?
10. What are the characteristics of true mahogany that make it a desirable furniture wood?
11. Would you consider true mahogany a rather common wood? What are the chief sources of this wood?
12. Why is maple considered a very desirable material for flooring?
13. What style of furniture is usually made from maple?
14. What is bird's-eye maple?
15. How many kinds of oak are there? Why is oak consistently popular as a cabinet wood?
16. Name the two large classifications of oak. Why is oak quarter-sawed?
17. Is sugar pine usually finished by staining? Explain in detail.
18. Yellow poplar is a very good selection for beginning woodworking projects. What are the reasons for this?
19. Give the color range for yellow poplar.
20. Name the chief uses for walnut. Why is walnut so often chosen for gunstocks and other articles that must be formed?
21. Describe the grain of walnut.
22. Is Douglas fir used for furniture? What are its uses?
23. Describe the characteristics of redwood. Compare with ponderosa pine.

Section XIV
Project Design and Development

Section XIV

UNIT 69. DESIGN

Every day you see and use things that have been designed. Your home, the furniture in it, cars and parts of cars, appliances, and even lead pencils and bars of soap have been developed from a design on paper. Some of these things are pleasing in design, some are not. Figure 69–1.

A design is the outline, shape, or plan of something. There is no one who will agree completely with everyone else as to what is good or bad design. Everyone looks at things in a slightly different way and sees in them things he likes or dislikes. Here, for example, are designs of some modern chairs. Figure 69–2. Not everyone will agree that they are *attractive*. They are, however, *well designed*. The three keys to good design are function, appearance, and solid construction. Function answers the question: "What is the purpose of the product?" A lamp, for example, should give the kind of light that is correct for a specific purpose. A lamp for reading would be much different from a night light. A reading lamp might be made of metal or wood, with a shade that is straight or tapered, and in any four of the main furniture styles. Sound construction means that the product is well built of the correct material so that it will last a long time with a minimum of maintenance. The purpose or function of an archery bow, for example, is to shoot an arrow straight and true with great force. The bow is poor, of course, if it breaks after being used a few times. Design defects may be due to the

69–1a. and 69–1b. Do you think this tray is well designed? How about the salt and pepper shakers? Study each.

SALT AND PEPPER SHAKERS

Bill of Materials

STOCK: Birch, Mahogany, or Maple
Important: All dimensions listed below are FINISHED size.

No. of Pieces	Part Name	Thickness	Width	Length	Material
2	Shakers	2″	2″	3½″	Birch, Mahogany, or Maple
1	Plug	1″	1″	4″	Hardwood
2	Corks	¾″ D.			

69–1c.

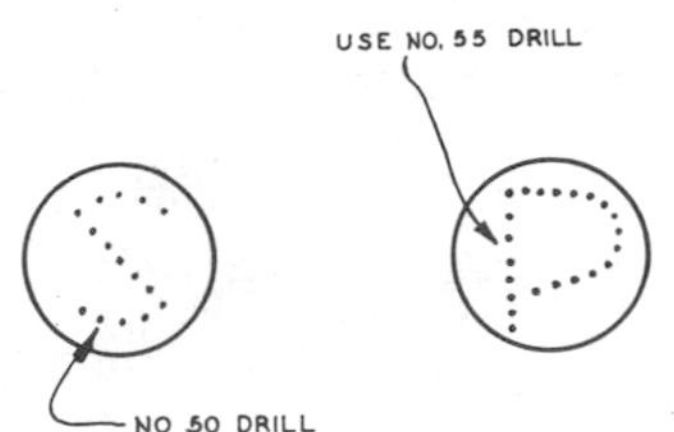

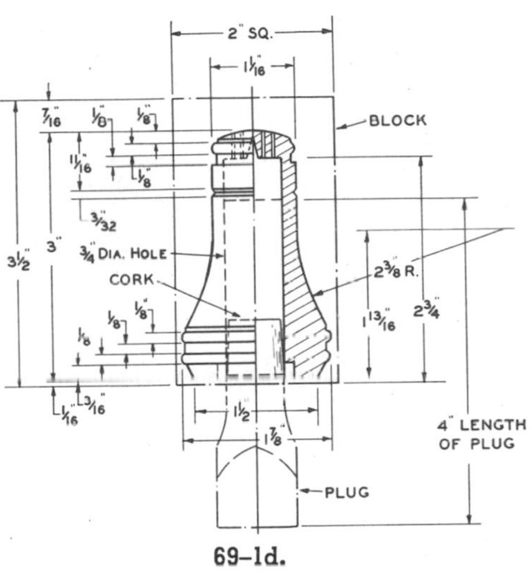

69–1d.

wrong kind of wood or to poor construction.

The things that are made in woodworking can be divided, as far as design goes, into three groups:

1. *Trinkets or gadgets which are made to satisfy your own interests and desires.* You may make a "dachshund-dog" tie rack or a "bowling-pin" pin-up lamp. You like it because you made it for yourself or for someone in your

69–2. These chairs look a good deal different from those most of us are used to seeing but are very comfortable. If you could try them, you'd know why they are well designed.

69–3a. How many and what kinds of lines can you see in this cabinet?

family. You may have used your own idea completely in designing it. Oftentimes it will be something you may like for a few years and then discard or redesign and make over. It was fun to design and make this project even though the design might not have been the best. You can learn and improve each time you make something.

2. *Practical objects that must be some standard size if they are to be any good at all.* For instance, a basketball backboard must be 4 x 6 feet. A high hurdle must be a certain size also. These things might not always be ornamental to look at but they are well designed because they serve a certain purpose. *If you were to make these things a different size,* they would be poorly designed!

3. *Artistically designed objects* include furniture, accessories for the home, and the home itself. In furniture there are many different designs and styles. You should become well acquainted with the best designs of today. *One of the great mistakes made in the home and school workshop in building furniture is the making of something with no design or style.* You shouldn't waste your time building furniture that is out-of-date, like the "moderne" of 1930, or the plain, "production-line" kind of furniture often seen in public buildings. You might say, "Yes, but I see some of these things in furniture stores." It is true that a certain percentage of the furniture made today is what we call "commercial" or "unstyled" furniture. This is the cheapest and poorest kind. You might as well buy it already made.

WHAT GOES TO MAKE UP DESIGN

1. First of all, an object is made up of *lines: straight, wavy, curved,* and *circular* lines. Figure 69–3. You can see examples of this in many furniture pieces.

69–3b. Common kinds of lines.

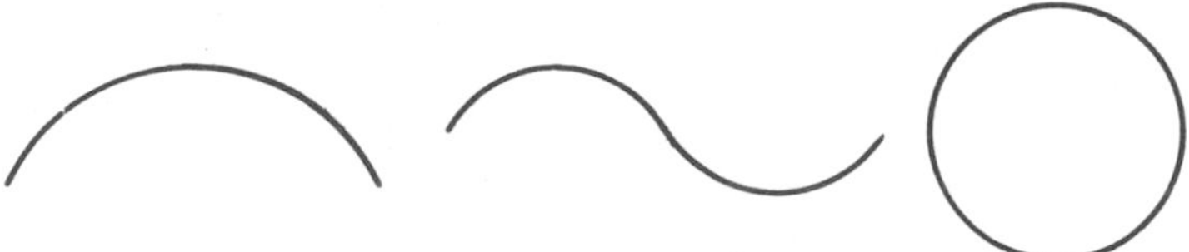

69–4a. Most of the common shapes are shown here. Point them out.

69–4b. Common shapes.

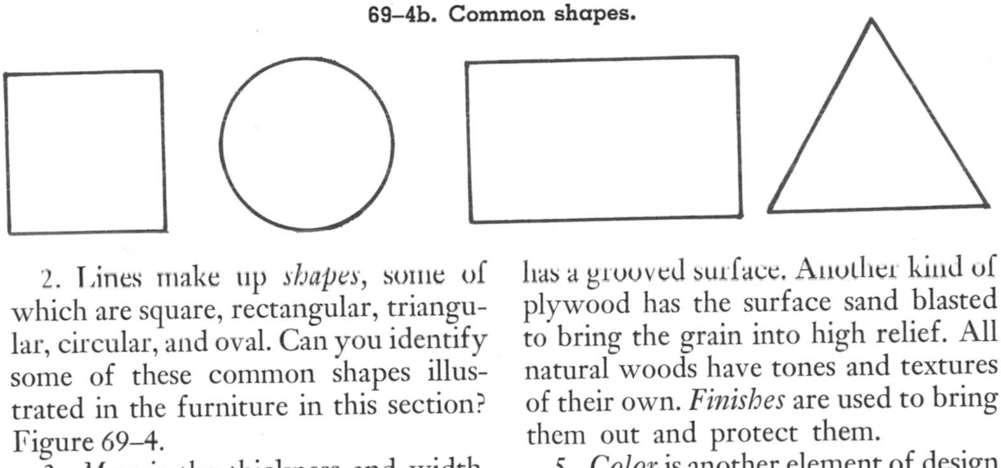

2. Lines make up *shapes*, some of which are square, rectangular, triangular, circular, and oval. Can you identify some of these common shapes illustrated in the furniture in this section? Figure 69–4.

3. *Mass* is the thickness and width, or bulk, of design. (Shapes make up cubes, boxes, spheres, cones, and rods, all of which are part of the mass).

4. *Tone and texture* add to the surface design. In woodworking each different kind of wood has a texture. Wood is given additional texture by many processes. For example, the plywood used in the lamp, Figure 69–5, has a grooved surface. Another kind of plywood has the surface sand blasted to bring the grain into high relief. All natural woods have tones and textures of their own. *Finishes* are used to bring them out and protect them.

5. *Color* is another element of design used to add interest. We can add color to any woodworking project by selected woods and using stains, paints and enamels. Figure 69–6, page 368.

WHY DOES A THING LOOK ATTRACTIVE?

In designing anything there are certain principles that should be followed.

69–5a. Part of this lamp is made with a special striated plywood. Notice the texture.

This is especially true in good furniture design. Some of these principles include:

1. *Balance.* Exactly what it sounds like. It makes things look stable. People are balanced. They have an arm on either side, two eyes in balance, etc. We don't like to look at lopsided or unstable things.

There are two kinds of balance, formal and informal. Formal balance is present when both sides of an object are exactly equal. People are examples of formal balance. The lamps in Figure 69–7, page 368, show *formal* balance. *Informal balance* gives the impression of things being stable and balanced by the "grouping" of the parts. For instance, two *small* boys on one side of the teeter totter and one *large* boy on the other makes an example of informal balance. Figure 69–8, page 368, illustrates informal balance by the clever placement of the lamp, flower arrangement, and picture.

2. *Proportion.* A well-proportioned piece is any object that looks well in relation to everything else in life. A dachshund dog doesn't look well proportioned because his legs are so short. We think a clown is funny if he has a great big nose and tremendous feet.

In designing many wood projects, we use a rectangular shape instead of a square one simply because it looks better proportioned to us. Figure 69–9, page 369. Proportion in design is achieved when the thing is not too fat, not too tall, not too thin, or not too square, but just right to our eyes, and for the use we have for it. That is why large chairs should not have spindly legs. Babe Ruth was often referred to

69–5b.

LAMP

Bill of Materials

Important: All dimensions listed below are FINISHED size.

No. of Pieces	Part Name	Thickness	Width	Length	Wood
1	Column Cap	1″	4⅛″	4⅛″	Oak
1	Column Base	1¼″	11″	11″	Oak
4	Column Sides	¼″	4″	11″	Weldtex Plywood
1	Corner Block	1″	4⅛″	4⅛″	Oak
4	Corner Glue Strips	⅜″	⅜″	10¼″	White Pine
1	No. 8 IES Shade				
1	2¼ inch Shade Holder				
1	3 way Switch				
1	3 way Bulb				
1	⅛ inch Pipe, 13⅝ inches long, and Nut				
1	Lamp Cord 6 ft. long				
1	14 inch Lamp Shade				

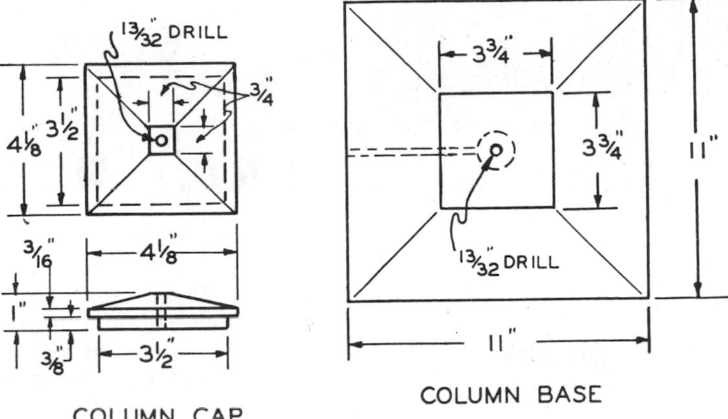
13/32" DRILL
3/4"
4 1/8"
3 1/2"
3/16"
4 1/8"
1"
3/8"
3 1/2"
COLUMN CAP
3 3/4"
3 3/4"
11"
13/32" DRILL
11"
COLUMN BASE

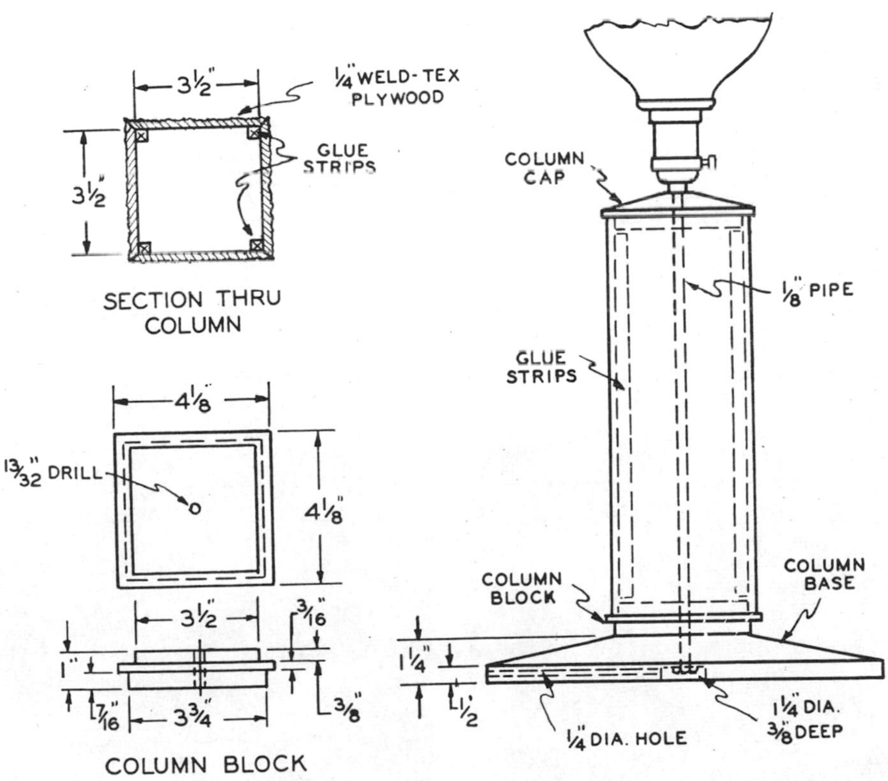
3 1/2"
1/4" WELD-TEX PLYWOOD
GLUE STRIPS
3 1/2"
SECTION THRU COLUMN
4 1/8"
13/32" DRILL
4 1/8"
3 1/2"
3/16"
1"
7/16
3 3/4"
3/8"
COLUMN BLOCK
COLUMN CAP
1/8" PIPE
GLUE STRIPS
COLUMN BLOCK
COLUMN BASE
1 1/4"
1/2
1/4" DIA. HOLE
1 1/4" DIA.
3/8" DEEP

69–5c.

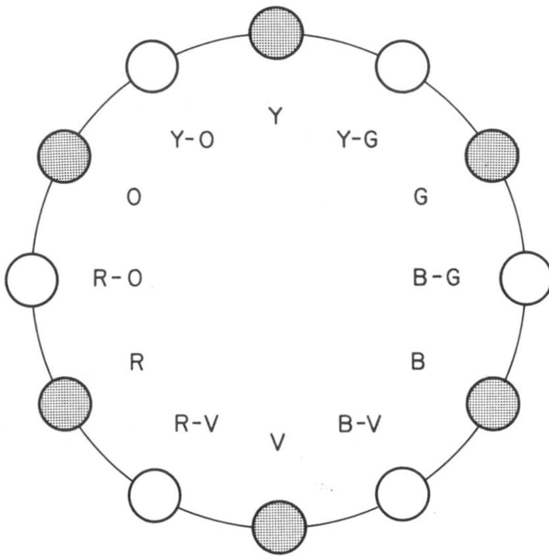

Y	YELLOW	V	VIOLET
Y-G	YELLOW-GREEN	R-V	RED-VIOLET
G	GREEN	R	RED
B-G	BLUE-GREEN	R-O	RED-ORANGE
B	BLUE	O	ORANGE
B-V	BLUE-VIOLET	Y-O	YELLOW-ORANGE

69–6. Color wheel.

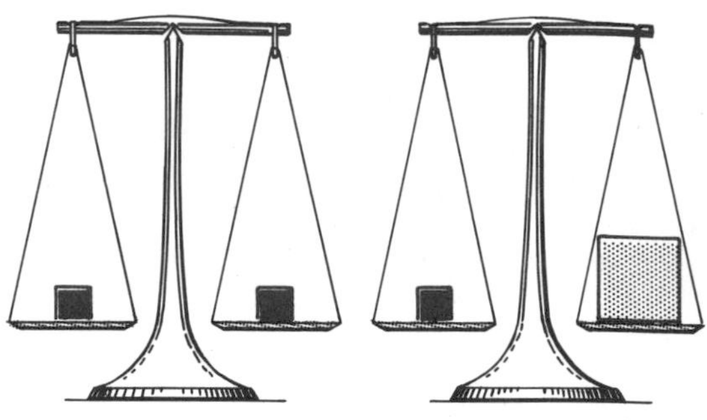

69–7b. These balance scales illustrate formal and informal balance. The one on the left has units of equal size and shape. The scale on the right is balanced by units of different size but of the same weight.

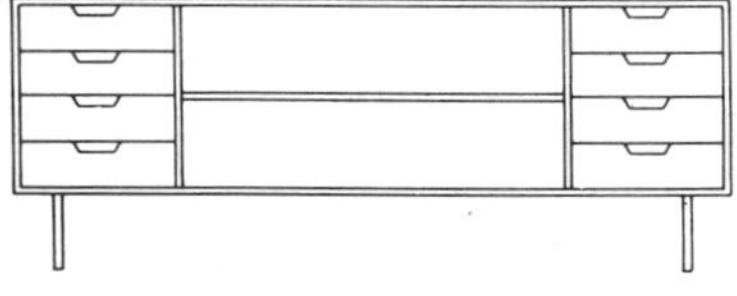

69–7c. A desk front that illustrates formal balance.

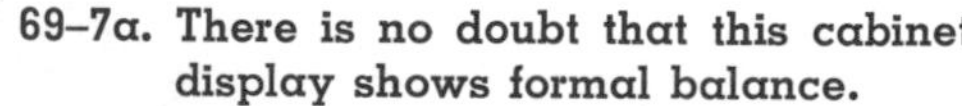

69–7a. There is no doubt that this cabinet display shows formal balance.

69–8a. Informal balance takes more thought and experience to create.

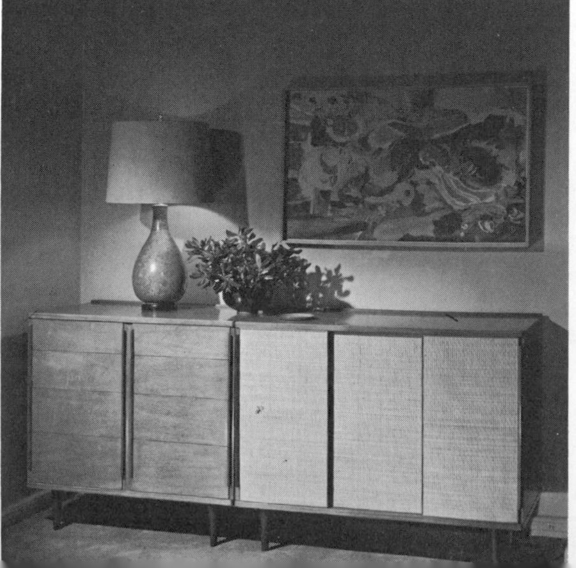

69–8b. A desk front that illustrates informal balance.

as "piano-legged" because his legs seemed too thin for his powerful body.

3. *Harmony or unity.* When the parts, colors, shapes, and textures of an object seem to get along well together, we say the object has harmony or unity. Figure 69–10. Today, *many different materials are used in furniture* but they are blended together to be pleasing. A good example of the *lack of harmony* is putting rough welded legs on a smooth, dainty table top. A piece of furniture with modern lines would not be used with Chippendale "ball-and-claw" legs.

4. *Emphasis.* An "accent" or special point of interest. Oftentimes in furniture this will be a beautiful piece of hardware on a cabinet or desk, the fine finish itself, or an interesting grain in the wood of a door or drawer.

In deciding whether something is well designed, you should ask yourself the following questions:

1. Does the piece serve the purpose for which it is intended?
2. Does it perform its job efficiently? For example, if it is a chair, is it comfortable to sit in?
3. Is it within your ability to construct and maintain?
4. Is it pleasing to the eye? Figure 69–11. (Here everyone won't agree.)
5. Does it satisfy you and other people that you want it to satisfy?

SERVING TRAY

Bill of Materials

Important: All dimensions listed below are FINISHED size.

No. of Pieces	Part Name	Thickness	Width	Length	Material
2	Sides	½″	1½″	22″	Maple or Birch
2	Ends	½″	2″	12″	Maple or Birch
1	Bottom	¼″	12″	21½″	Birch Plywood
16	No. 18 x ¾″ Wire Brads				

69–9b.

69–9a. This project illustrates the 5-to-8 unit relationship.

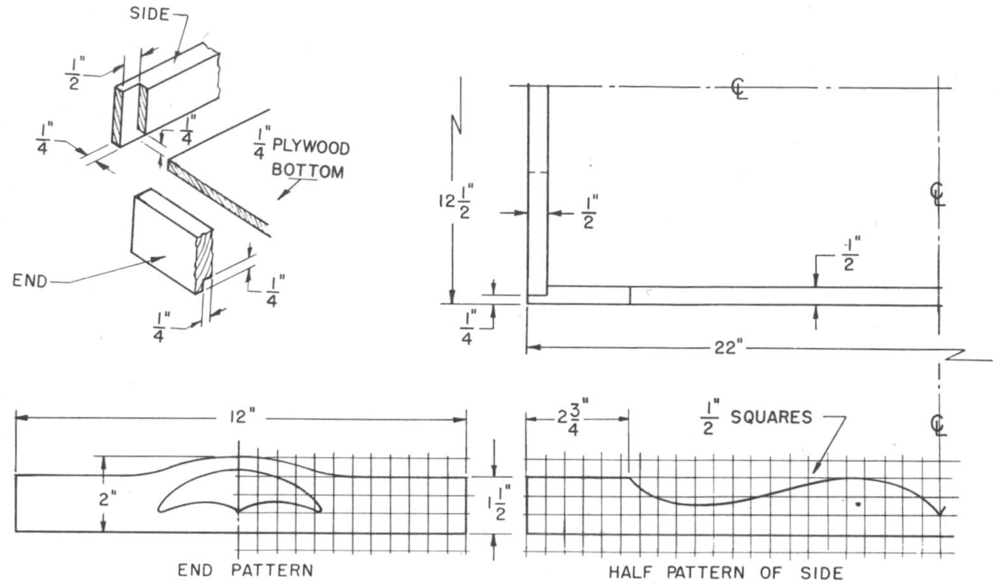

69–9c.

69–9d. A way of enlarging a 5 by 8 proportion to whatever size you want for a tray, pin-up board, or picture frame. Make AB eight units long and BC five units long. Then lay off along the line AX any length you want, for example, AE. The distance for width, then, would be EO.

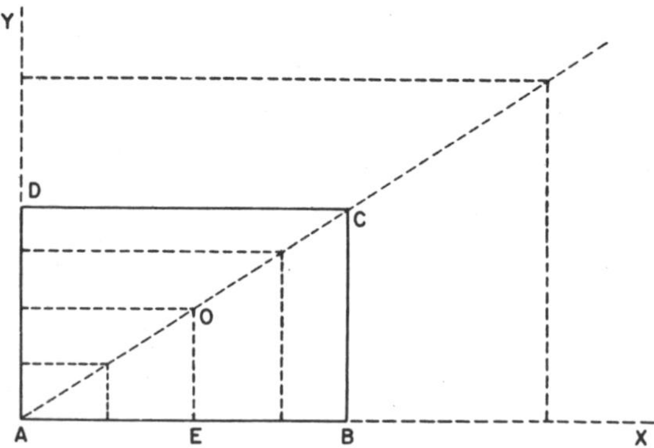

DESIGNING A WOODWORKING PROJECT

After you have had some experience and know what you can do with tools and machines, you may get a chance to

69–10. This modern table is made of metal, wood, and chemical composition. Don't they "get along" well together?

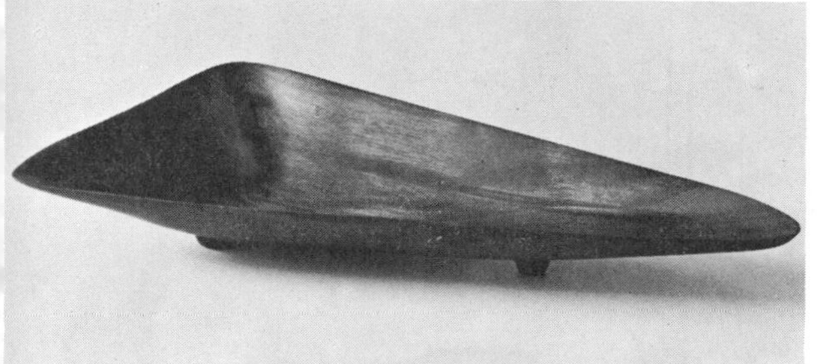

69–11. You can design and make a small snack container just as attractive as this.

design a project of your own. This is an interesting thing to do. It gives you an opportunity to be creative, which is not easy, but very fascinating.

To design and make a project in wood, follow these steps:

1. *Get the idea for the project you would like to build.* Maybe you have something in mind that you've always wanted to make. If not, popular magazines and books with projects in them are good sources of ideas. Another way to get ideas is to visit different stores selling furniture, hobby, or sporting goods. Some of the things you might like to build would include:

69–12. A model truck made of wood.

69–13a. There are standard openings for different birds. Here is a point to check in designing a project.

a. Toys, models, games, puzzles and other hobby equipment. Figure 69–12.

b. Shelters for birds and pets. Figure 69–13.

69–13b.

BLUEBIRD HOUSE

Bill of Materials

Important: All dimensions listed below are FINISHED size.

No. of Pieces	Part Name	Thickness	Width	Length	Wood
1	Top	¼″	7¼″	8½″	Redwood or Pine
2	Sides	¼″	5½″	8½″	Redwood or Pine
1	Front	¼″	5″	8″	Redwood or Pine
1	Back	¼″	5″	6⅜″	Redwood or Pine
1	Bottom	⅜″	5¼″	7″	Redwood or Pine
1	Perch	3/16″		1¾″	Hardwood Dowel
1	Asphalt Roofing		7½″	8¾″	
	No. 16 x ¾″ Wire Brads				
	No. 16 x ½″ Wire Brads				

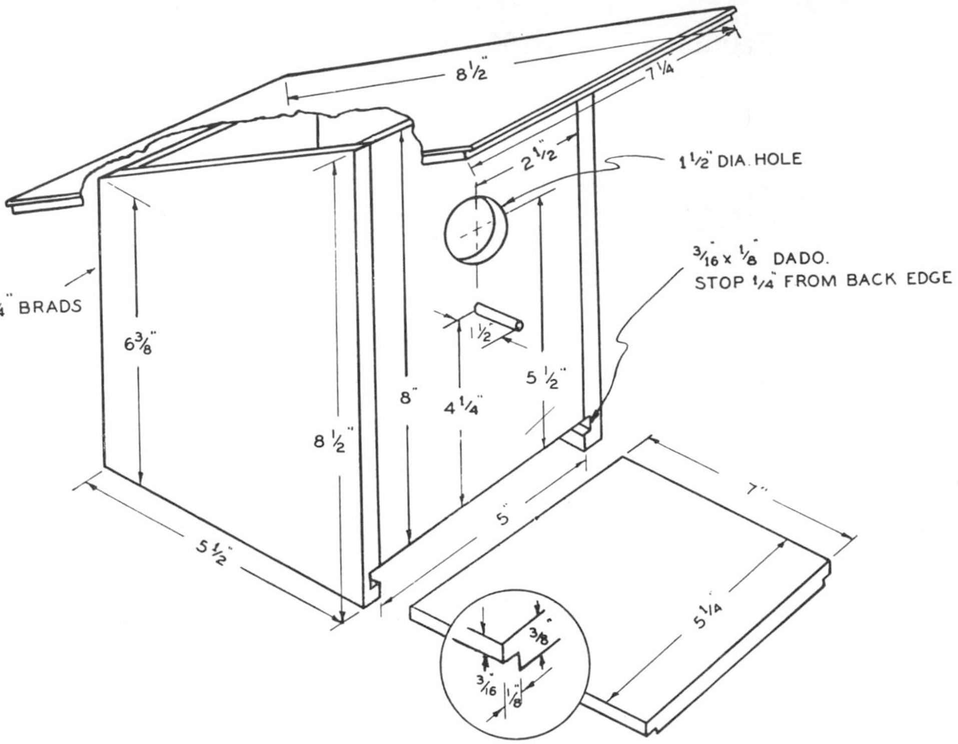

69–13c.

69–14a. A beautiful lamp you could turn on the wood lathe.

69–14b.

CONTEMPORARY TABLE LAMP

Bill of Materials

Important: STOCK: White Oak
All dimensions listed below are Cut-out size.

No. of Pieces	Part Name	Thickness	Width	Length
4	Column Stock	1¾″	5¼″	15″
4	Column Stock	¾″	2¾″	15″
1	Base	¾″	7¼″	7¼″
1	Cap	¾″	4½″	4½″
1	Harp Support	2″	2″	3½″
2	Plugs	¾″	2″	2″
1	⅛″ Std. Pipe			19″
1	⅛″ Pipe Hex Nut			
1	Push Thru Brass Socket			
1	9″ or 10″ Harp to suit shade			
1	Brass Finial			
1	Felt Pad 7″ dia.			
4	No. 8 x 1¼″ F. H. Wood Screws			
1	Lamp Cord of length to suit			
1	Lamp Shade to suit			
1	Male Plug			

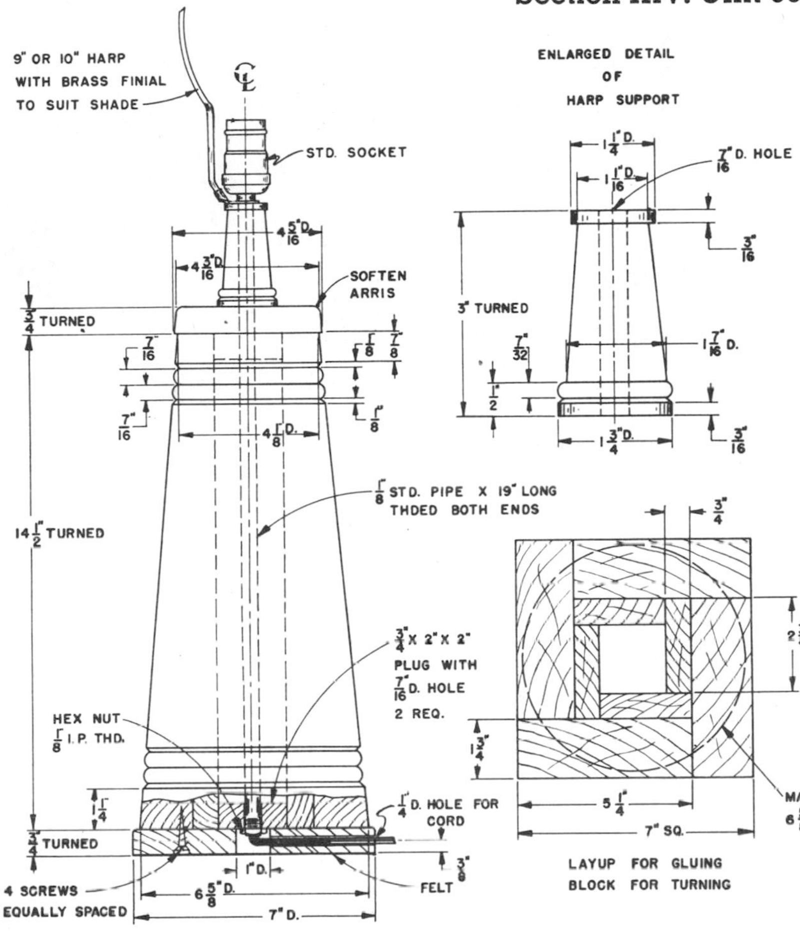

69–14c.

c. Things for your room or home such as lamps, bookends, shoe racks and tie racks. Figure 69–12.

d. Kitchen items such as cutting boards, salt and pepper shakers, shelves. Figure 69–15.

e. Sports equipment like boats and skis. Figure 69–16.

69–15a. A wooden salad set made by cutting and carving.

69–15b.

SALAD FORK & SPOON

Bill of Materials

1 piece light colored hardwood 3″ x 7/8″ x 24″
1 piece dark colored hardwood 4″ x 1/4″ x 4 1/2″
8″ of 3/8″ dowel.

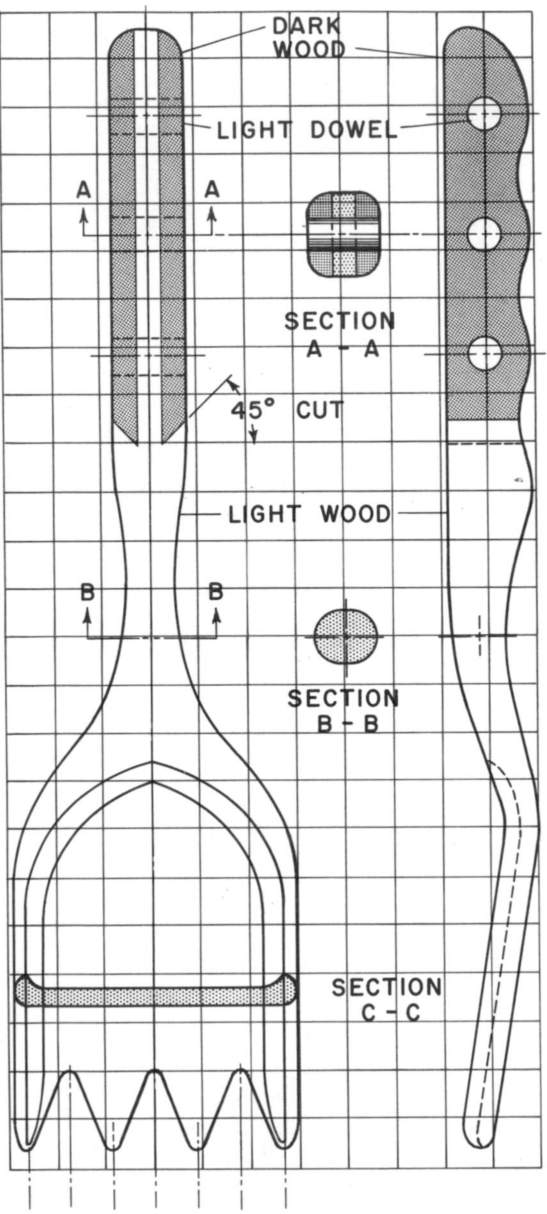

69–15c.

69–16a. A picnic table is a piece of sports equipment you could make.

CHILD'S PICNIC TABLE

Bill of Materials

STOCK: Pine, Redwood, Cypress, Spruce or Cedar

Important: All dimensions listed below are FINISHED size.

NO. OF PIECES	PART NAME	THICKNESS	WIDTH	LENGTH
*4	Legs	1⅝″	3″	25″
*3	Cross Ties	1⅝″	3″	26″
*2	Seat Ties	1⅝″	3″	47″
*2	Braces	1⅝″	3″	18″
5	Top Boards	¾″	5⅝″	46″
2	Bench Seats	¾″	9⅝″	46″
32	2¾″-14 F.H. Wood Screws	2¾″		
42	1¼″-14 F.H. Wood Screws	1¼″		

*May be ripped from standard 2 x 4's or other 2″ stock.

69–16b.

f. Furniture including chairs, tables, chests, desks. Figure 69–17.

2. After you've decided what to make, ask yourself, "What is the purpose of the object?" For example, if it's a book rack or book trough, it is supposed to hold books conveniently. How large are books? What must be the depth of the shelf? If there is to be more than one shelf, what should the distance between the shelves be? If the

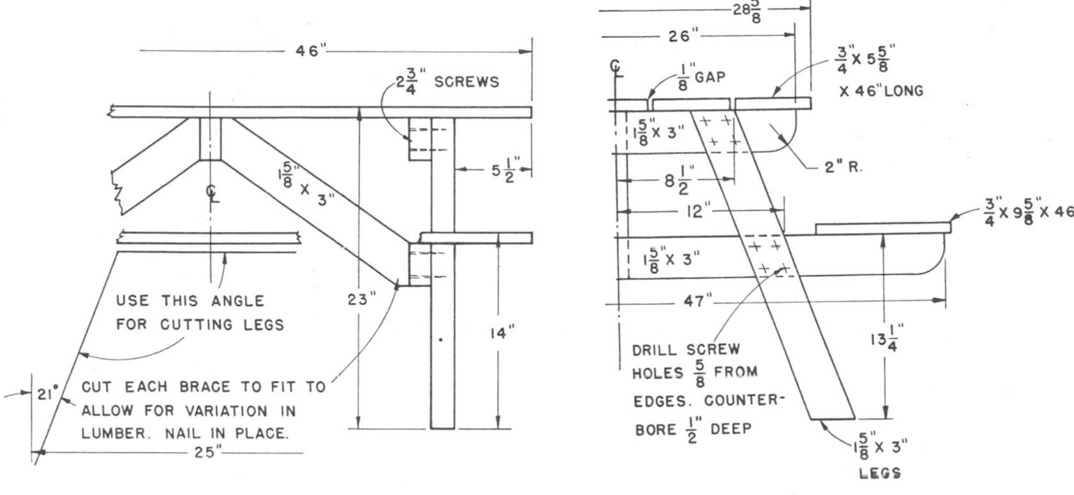

69–16c.

project is a shoe rack, it must be able to hold shoes efficiently. Figure 69–18. It is surprising to find many commercial objects that look nice but don't do the job properly. For instance, there is on the market a fancy shoe rack on which the distance from the wall to the rung that holds the heels of the shoes is too short. The shoes won't stay on it. If you design one, remember that it must be different for men's and women's shoes.

69–17. This table combines metal and wood.

69–18. Remember, the location of the dowel rod is an important design feature of this shoe rack.

If you are designing a piece of furniture, there are certain standards, especially of height, that must be observed. See the Standard Sizes of Furniture, Figure 69–19.

3. Decide on the style or design of furniture. It should blend with your room or home. If, for example, your room is furnished in Early American, then the lamp or wall shelf should follow this trend. Furniture designs have evolved over the years, and designers of one period have often borrowed ideas and designs from another period. The four most popular designs of furniture today are Traditional, Early American or Colonial, French Provincial, and Modern or Contemporary. The *Traditional* design came from the best features of the 18th Century designers of England. This period is also sometimes known as the Golden Age of English furniture. The big four of the 18th Century designers included Thomas Chippendale, Thomas Sheraton, George Hepplewhite, and the Adams brothers. Thomas Chippendale, the first and most famous of these designers, was a leading London cabinetmaker from 1750–1775. The Adams brothers, who were both designers and architects, were greatly influenced by the classic art of Italy. George Hepplewhite was a skilled designer and craftsman who developed furniture styles of delicate design. Figure 69–20. Thomas Sheraton, a very creative designer and cabinetmaker, produced furniture with a subtle gracefulness. While contempo-

69–19.

STANDARD SIZES OF FURNITURE

Item	Height	Item	Height
Tables		*Cabinets*	
Coffee	16″ to 18″	Sectional	30″
Card	29″	China Storage	54″ to 60″
Game	30″	Kitchen	30″ to 34″
Writing	30″		
Kitchen	32″	*Chests*	32″ to 54″
End	30″	*Bookcases*	32″ to 82″
Dining	32″	*Desks*	30″
Chairs			
Desk	16½″		
Dining	18″		

rary adaptations of these men's works are still popular, a more typical traditional piece is a combination of all of these designs. Figure 69–21. Duncan Phyfe was the most influential American designer of the traditional period. Many of the original designs of his work are still very popular. Figure 69–22. The *Early American* or *Colonial* style is a development of the kind of furniture used in this country just before and after the Revolutionary War. Figure 69–23. *French Provincial* is an adaptation of the furniture that was popular during the reign of Louis XV and XVI. Figure 69–24. Modern design is best characterized by clean, beautifully contoured work with emphasis on simplicity. *Modern* or *Con-*

69–21. A chair in the traditional style.

69–20. A beautiful Hepplewhite chairside table with a top fitted with genuine black leather.

69–22. The lyre-back chair illustrates one of the best known Duncan Phyfe designs.

69–23. **Many turned parts are found in Early American and Colonial designs.**

69–24. **A distinguishing feature of French Provincial is the graceful, curved legs.**

temporary furniture tends to be less ornate and omits unnecessary hardware. Much of its beauty lies in the clean lines and use of beautiful woods. Figure 69–25.

4. Now make a sketch of the thing you would like to build to see how it will look. Suppose you decide to make a wall rack for your mother. Here are several sketches of possible designs. Figure 69–26. Let's suppose you decide on sketch A.

69–25. **This modern dining room group is made of oil-rubbed teakwood.**

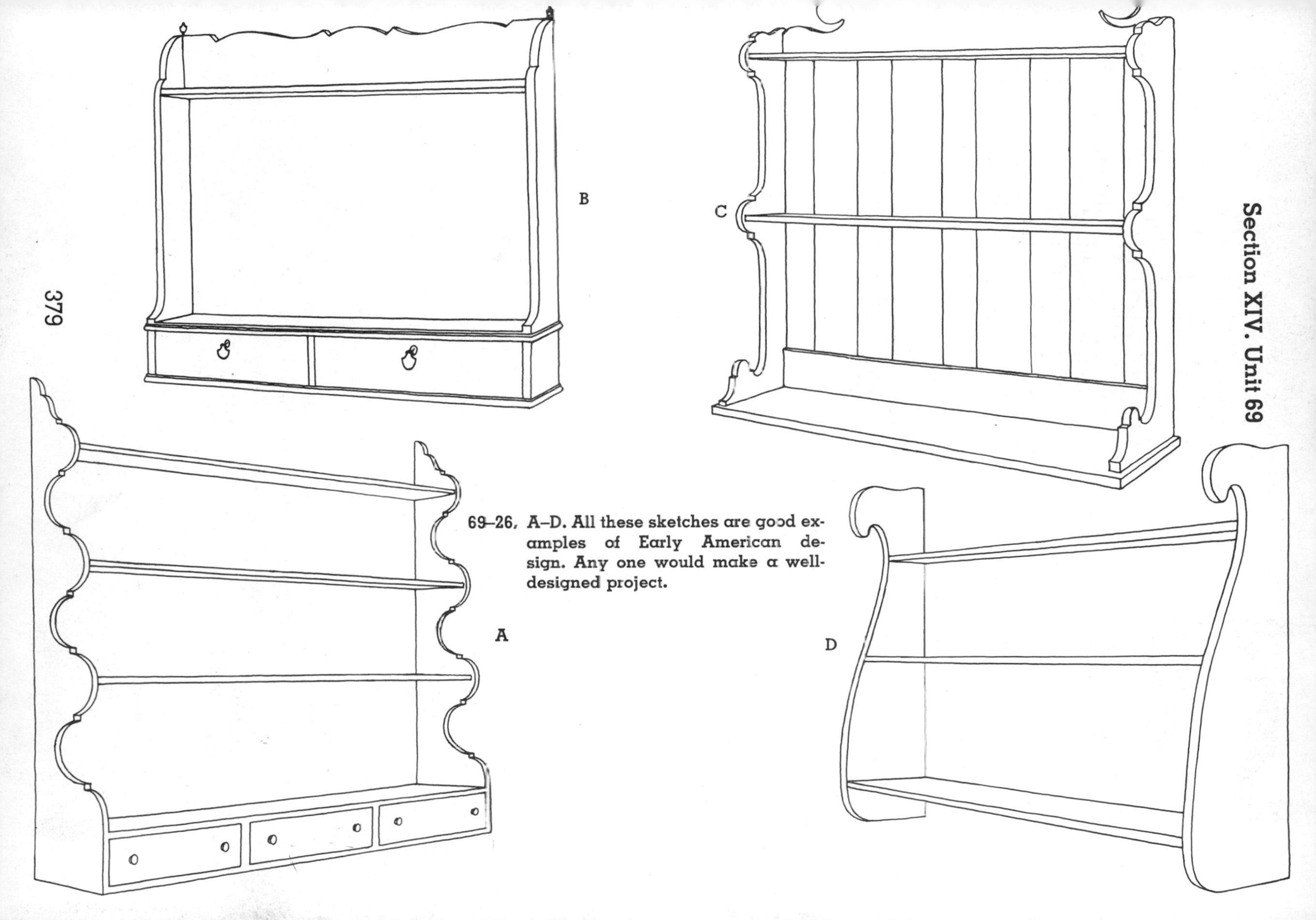

69–26, A–D. All these sketches are good examples of Early American design. Any one would make a well-designed project.

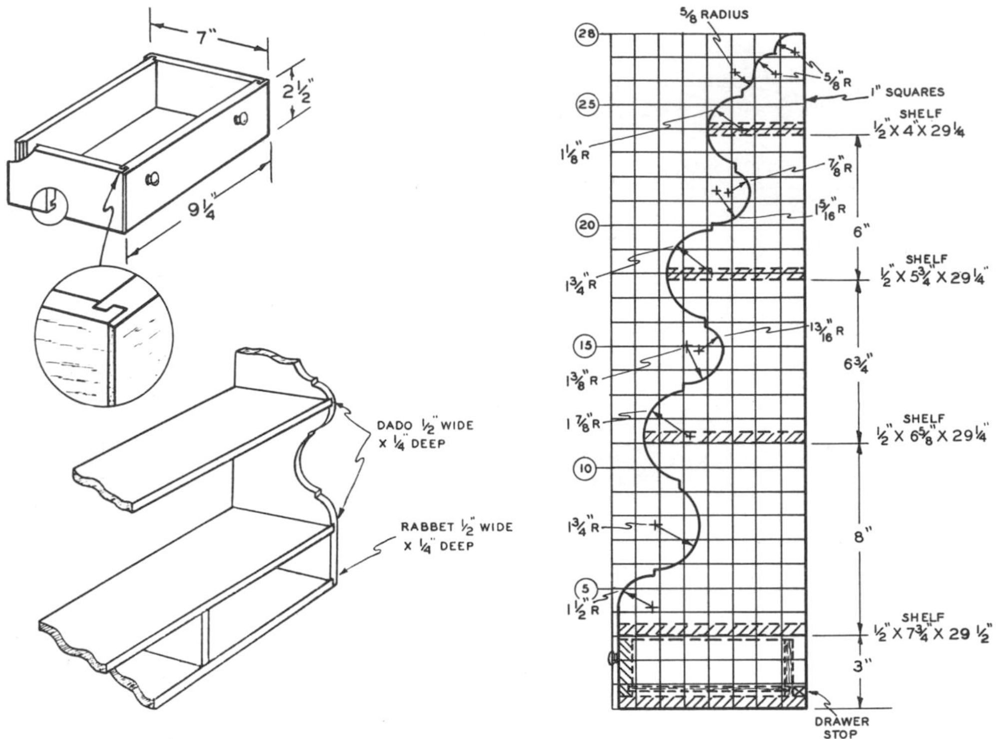

69–27. A working drawing of sketch A, page 379.

5. The next thing is to make a working drawing of the project. Figure 69–27. This will be necessary to determine exactly the size of each part and how it is to be made.

6. *Making a model*. It is sometimes difficult to imagine what the finished article will look like with only sketches and drawings. It is helpful to see the three-dimensional appearance of the item by making a small model. This can be made of balsa wood or some other light material that cuts easily with a knife. The model does not have all the small details but will give the general appearance.

7. Now make a bill of materials. Here you need to keep in mind the sizes and kinds of woods and plywoods and the kinds of fasteners to be used. Figure 69–28.

8. You are now ready for the plans for building the project. You will decide on what is to be done first, then second, etc. Figure 69–29A. Usually this will include *making a layout*, *cutting out the pieces and parts*, *shaping the parts*, *making the joints*, *fitting and assembling*, and *finishing*. You have already made a detailed plan of procedure when you planned your work for the first projects you made.

9. The next thing is to decide on what tools and machines you will need. Your experiences in woodworking will help you decide on how to use the

Bill of Materials

Important: All dimensions listed above, except for length of dowel, etc., FINISHED size.

No. of Pieces	Part Name	Thickness	Width	Length	Wood
2	Ends	½″	7¾″	28″	Knotty Pine
1	Shelf	½″	4″	29¼″	Knotty Pine
1	Shelf	½″	5¾″	29¼″	Knotty Pine
1	Shelf	½″	6⅝″	29¼″	Knotty Pine
2	Shelves	½″	7¾″	29¼″	Knotty Pine
2	Drawer Separators	½″	2½″	7¾″	Knotty Pine
3	Drawer Fronts	½″	2½″	9¼″	Knotty Pine
6	Drawer Sides	⅜″	2½″	7″	Clear Pine
3	Drawer Backs	⅜″	2½″	8⅞″	Clear Pine
3	Drawer Bottoms	¼″	6¼″	8¾″	Fir Plywood
6	Drawer Stops	½″	½″	1″	
1	Hardwood Dowel	¼″		36″	
6	Hardwood Knobs	¾″			

69–28. Bill of materials for the wall rack.

69–29a. Plan of procedure for the wall rack.

WORKING A PLAN

1. Lay out pattern of the ends on paper and trace on wood. Cut out on a jig saw.

2. Cut the dadoes for the shelves and the rabbet for the bottom board.

3. Saw the shelves and bottom board.

4. Dowel and glue the shelves and bottom in place. Before the glue sets be sure the entire structure is square.

5. Make drawer separators; install dowels and glue in place.

6. Cut the drawer fronts and fit into each opening. Then complete the drawers, using the joints suggested in the detailed drawing—or make a simple rabbet joint to fasten the sides and front, and a dado joint to fasten the sides and back. Glue drawer stops in place so the drawer fronts will be flush.

7. Sand edges to give a worn appearance.

8. Apply an antique pine finish, and add knobs.

equipment. For example, the jig saw is the ideal tool for cutting out the ends of the wall rack. Figure 69–29B.

10. Now the building can be done. Here's the time when you can display your craftsmanship by doing a fine job on each part.

11. The last step in designing is to judge the project in several ways. Figure 69–29C. You will decide if the job was done well enough so you could answer "yes" to all the questions found on page 384, "Rating" a project.

69–29c. The finished project. Isn't it a beauty?

PROJECT PLANS AND SUPPLIES

A. American Plywood Association Tacoma, Washington.

B. Woman's Day Workshop, 19 West 44th Street, New York 36, New York.

C. The George S. Thompson Corporation, 509 Mission St., South Pasadena, California.

D. Western Wood Manufacturing Company, Portland, Oregon, or regional dealer.

E. Masonite Corporation, 111 West Washington St., Chicago 2, Illinois.

F. Skil Corporation, Chicago 30, Illinois.

CAN YOU ANSWER THESE QUESTIONS ON DESIGN?

1. Describe the meaning of design.
2. Name three keys to good design.
3. How can products be grouped as far as design is concerned?
4. Name four kinds of lines.
5. What is mass?
6. How can color be added to wood products?
7. Name the two kinds of balance.
8. Is a square in good proportion? Explain your answer.
9. What is emphasis?
10. Describe some of the kinds of things that you can build.
11. What are the most popular furniture styles?
12. What is the value of making a model of the project you wish to build?
13. Tell what a bill of materials is.

69–29b. Cutting out an end on the jig saw.

Section XIV

UNIT 70. PROJECTS—THE FINISHED PRODUCT

SOME SUGGESTIONS BEFORE BEGINNING YOUR PROJECT

Your experiences in woodworking and the fun you get out of it depend largely on how much enthusiasm you have and the kind of projects that you decide to make. To make any project and to get the most out of it, you must carefully do four things:

1. Make a good selection.
2. Plan wisely.
3. Construct well.
4. Rate your work.

SELECTING

What should I make? That's the question you will be asking yourself as soon as you get started. Well, what can you use? Do you need a new lamp for your room at home or can your home use a new set of house numbers? Perhaps your dad will have a birthday soon and would be able to use a pipe rack or pants holder. How about a shoeshine box for yourself or for the entire family to use? These are cues to what to select.

Of course, you should start on something that you can complete and that isn't too difficult. It's usually a good idea to select the first project, at least, from a plan that has already been drawn. With this in mind, the projects that appear on the following pages have been grouped so that you can tell about how difficult they are to build. See list, page 384. If this is your first experience in the woodshop, you ought to select a project from Group 1 of the beginning projects and progress from there. Your instructor may also have some ideas for your first project.

Whatever you decide upon, you will find that there is a lot of fun in making such things as the fruit tray or the house numbers.

PLANNING

Ask anyone who builds things and he will tell you to plan well, for in so doing you will save time, eliminate errors, and do a better and more enjoyable job. It is a good idea for anyone in woodworking to make a written plan of procedure or planning sheet in which he tells what tools he is going to use, what materials he will need, and exactly how he is going to proceed to make the project. In addition, it is an excellent idea to make a picture sketch of the article and a working drawing, if one is not available.

The exact way in which you build the project will differ with its size and difficulty, but in general you will proceed about the same and in the approximate order described below.

BUILDING

If you have looked through the ten sections on hand woodworking in Part I of this book, you will note an order of arrangement. These are in approximately the order in which projects should be built. As you make out your plan of procedure, look over these sections and decide exactly what you must do to make your own project. In general, you will be doing the following:

1. Getting out the stock.
2. Planing the surfaces.
3. Making curved parts.
4. Shaping and forming parts.
5. Cutting holes.
6. Making joints.
7. Assembling with nails, screws, and glue.
8. Finishing.

The larger the project, the more steps there will be to carry out and the more pieces there will be to make. When you qualify to use the machines, many of the steps that you first did with hand tools can be accomplished faster and with greater efficiency. Remember, however, that you must know how to use hand tools before you can expect to go on to machine work.

RATING

When you have finished your project you should take a few minutes to rate your own work, because in doing this you will improve as you go along. Don't be one of those fellows who say, "I could have done it better, but I was in a hurry."

Some of the things you should ask yourself are:

1. Is the project as good as I expected it to be?
2. What could I have done better?
3. How could I have completed it sooner?
4. What have I learned how to do that I didn't know before?
5. Have I improved in any of the skills I learned before?
6. What have I learned about materials that I have used?
7. How have I become a better and more coöperative worker?
8. Have I applied anything I have learned in other subjects to the making of this project?

YOUR GUIDE FOR SELECTING THE PROJECT TO MAKE

BEGINNING PROJECTS

(All the work can be done by hand. Only the butt joint is used.)

Group 1

Candelabra
House Numbers
Mailing List Cover
Walnut Fruit Tray

Group 2

Pants Holder
My Shine Box
Pennsylvania Wall Box
Book Ends

Group 3

Storage Hassock
Plant Base
Wastepaper Basket
Pilgrim Footstool
Pilgrim Cradle
Spoonrack
Turtle Stool

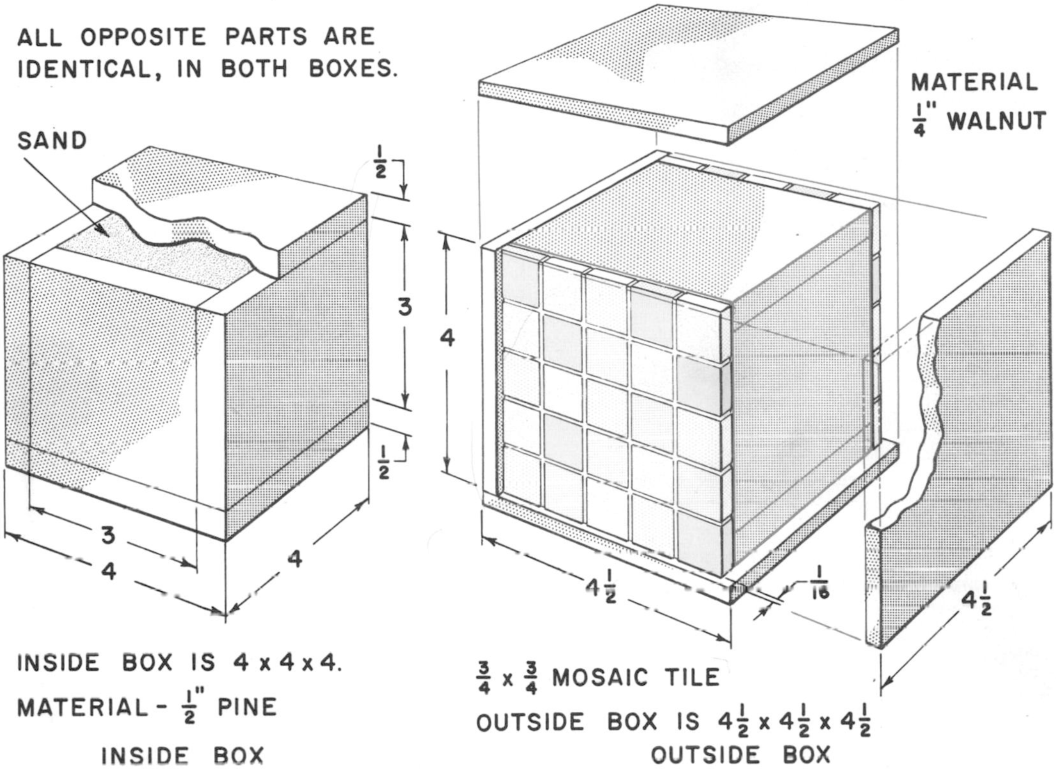

ALL OPPOSITE PARTS ARE IDENTICAL, IN BOTH BOXES.

SAND

$\frac{1}{2}$

3

$\frac{1}{2}$

3

4

4

4

INSIDE BOX IS 4 x 4 x 4.

MATERIAL - $\frac{1}{2}$" PINE

INSIDE BOX

MATERIAL $\frac{1}{4}$" WALNUT

4

$4\frac{1}{2}$

$\frac{1}{16}$

$4\frac{1}{2}$

$\frac{3}{4}$ x $\frac{3}{4}$ MOSAIC TILE

OUTSIDE BOX IS $4\frac{1}{2}$ x $4\frac{1}{2}$ x $4\frac{1}{2}$

OUTSIDE BOX

1. Book ends with the handsome modern touch of mosaic tile. Made of ¼ inch walnut, the book ends are 4½ inches square. They were filled with sand for more weight. (Reprinted by permission of Woman's Day Magazine.)

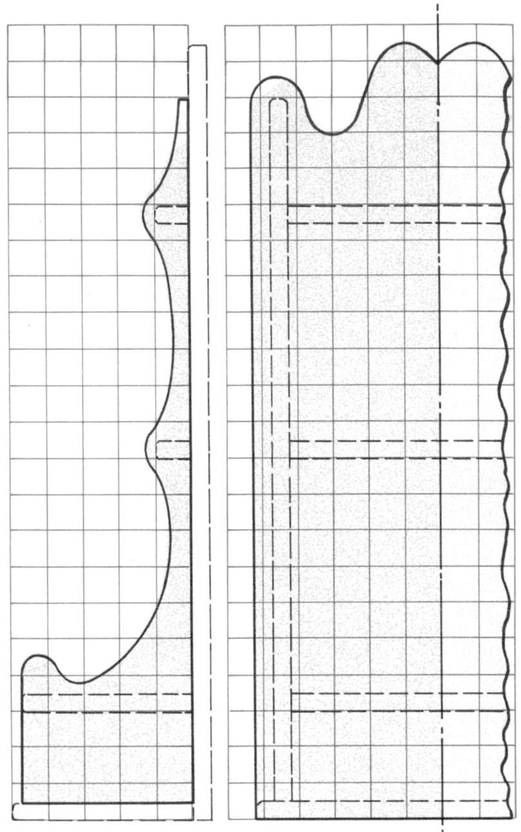

2. A spoonrack for your prize beauties. It's made from ½ inch pine with an antique pine finish and fitted with a small drawer and porcelain knob. (Reprinted by permission of Woman's Day Magazine.)

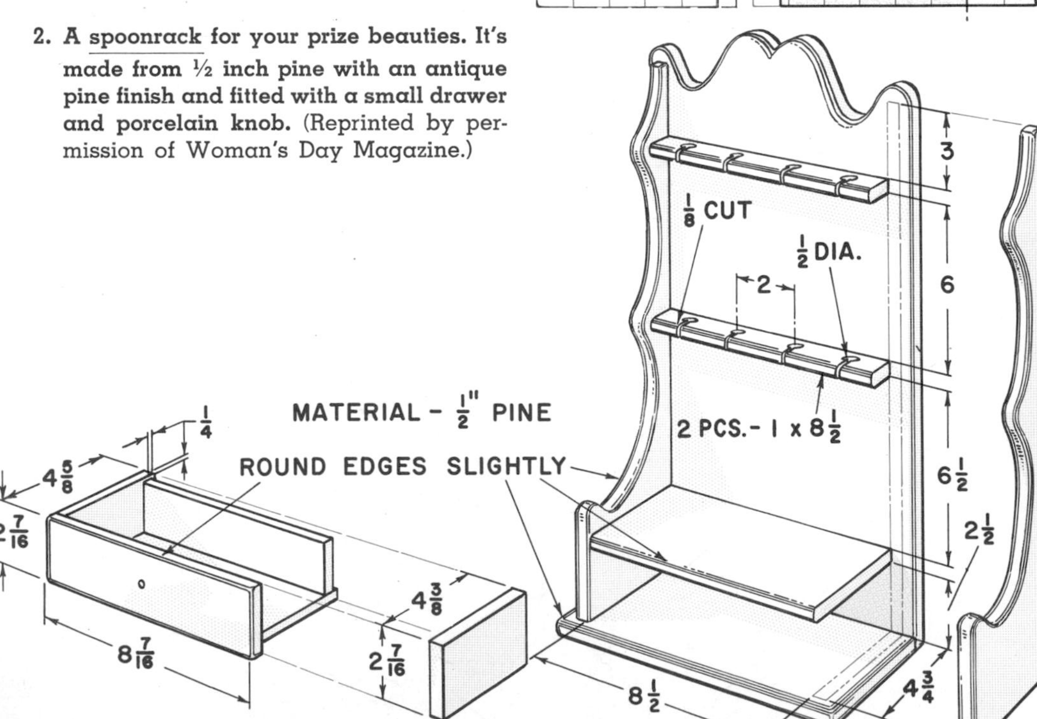

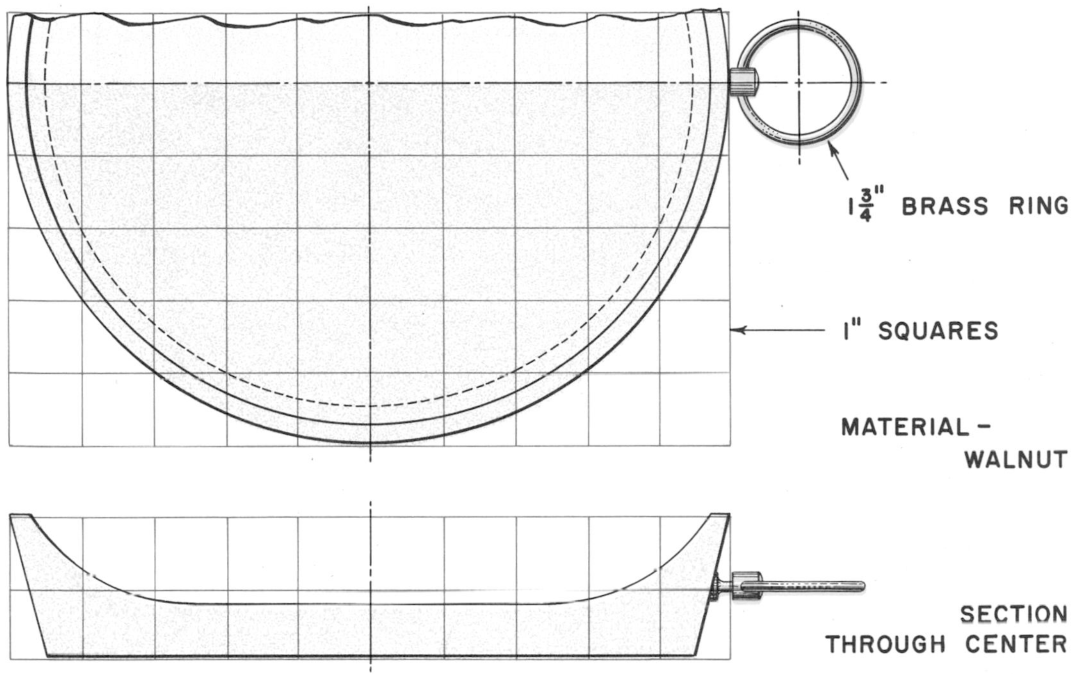

3. This fruit bowl when turned over can double as a cutting board. It hangs from a brass ring and measures 10 inches in diameter. The wood is 2-inch walnut with a vegetable-oil finish. (Reprinted by permission of Woman's Day Magazine.)

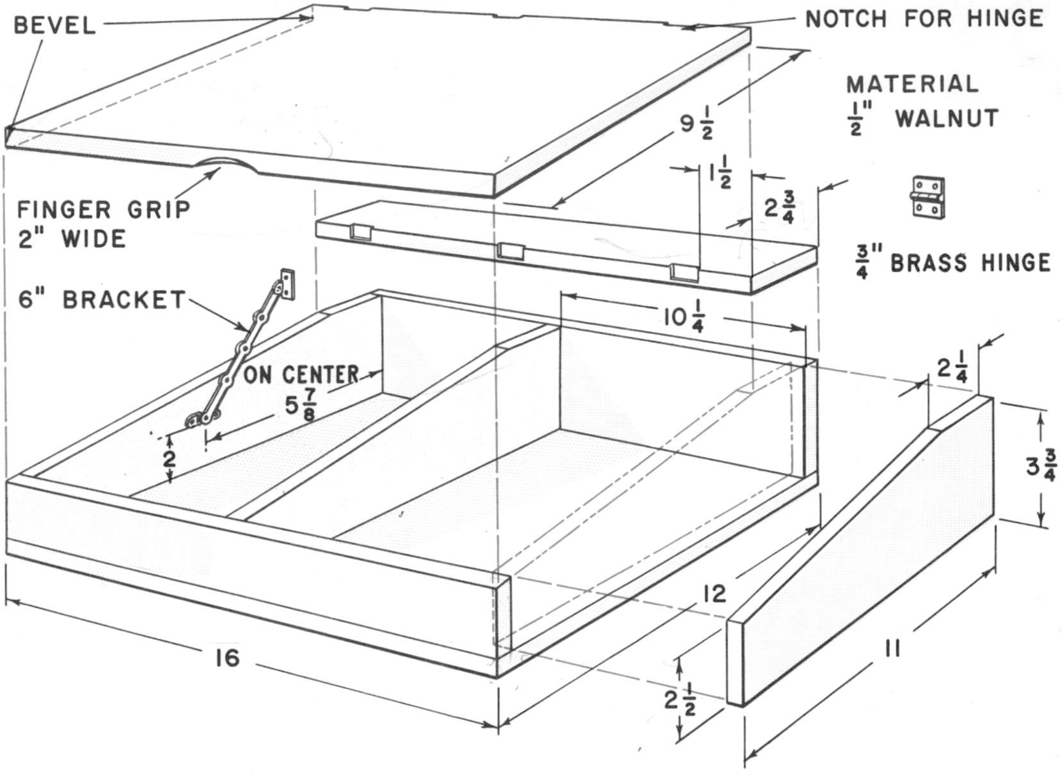

4. Writing box. A collector's piece measuring 12 inches x 19 inches, this was fashioned from ½-inch walnut with a varnish finish. A slanted hinged cover makes writing easy. Also a convenient lap desk. (Reprinted by permission of Woman's Day Magazine.)

5. Walnut fruit tray with a vegetable-oil finish. The actual tray is ¼-inch walnut, the bases are ½-inch walnut. A piece of many uses. (Reprinted by permission of Woman's Day Magazine.)

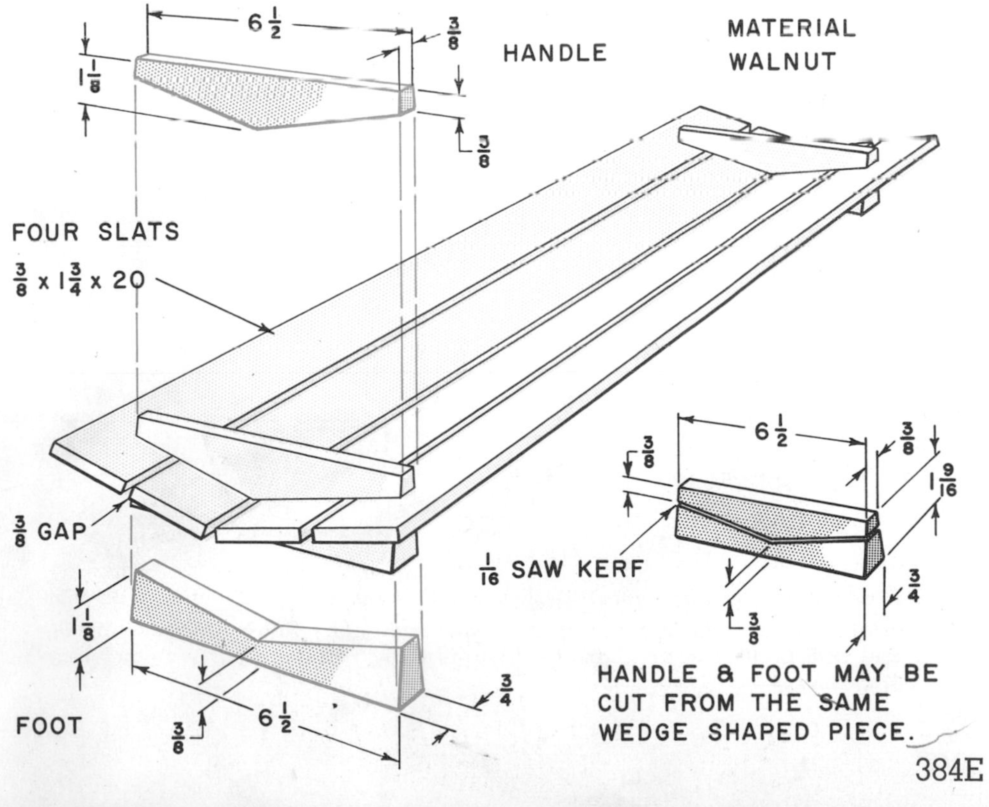

HANDLE

MATERIAL
WALNUT

FOUR SLATS
$\frac{3}{8} \times 1\frac{3}{4} \times 20$

$\frac{3}{8}$ GAP

$\frac{1}{16}$ SAW KERF

FOOT

HANDLE & FOOT MAY BE CUT FROM THE SAME WEDGE SHAPED PIECE.

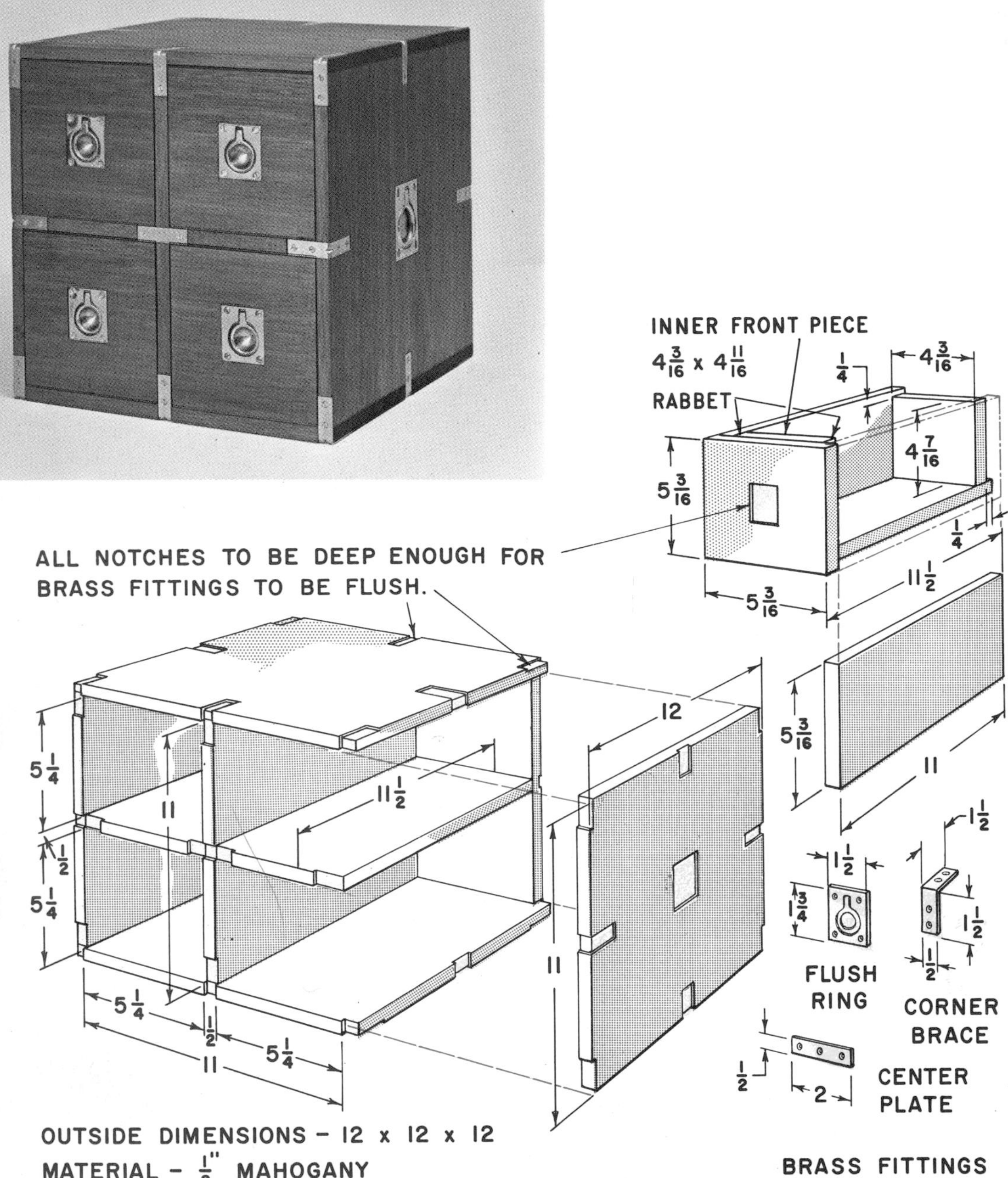

6. A miniature campaign chest, 12 inches, by 12 inches by 12 inches, with four drawer compartments. It is made of ½-inch mahogany with a linseed-oil finish, and with brass trim and handles. (Reprinted by permission of Woman's Day Magazine.)

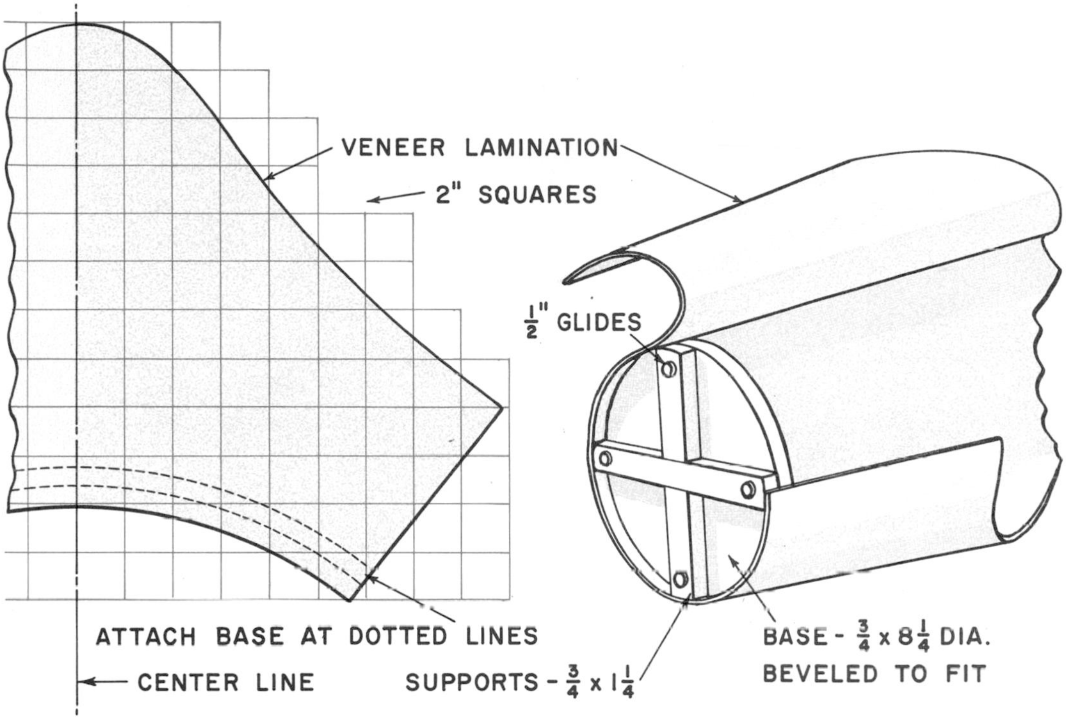

VENEER LAMINATION

2" SQUARES

$\frac{1}{2}$" GLIDES

ATTACH BASE AT DOTTED LINES

CENTER LINE

SUPPORTS - $\frac{3}{4}$ x $1\frac{1}{4}$

BASE - $\frac{3}{4}$ x $8\frac{1}{4}$ DIA. BEVELED TO FIT

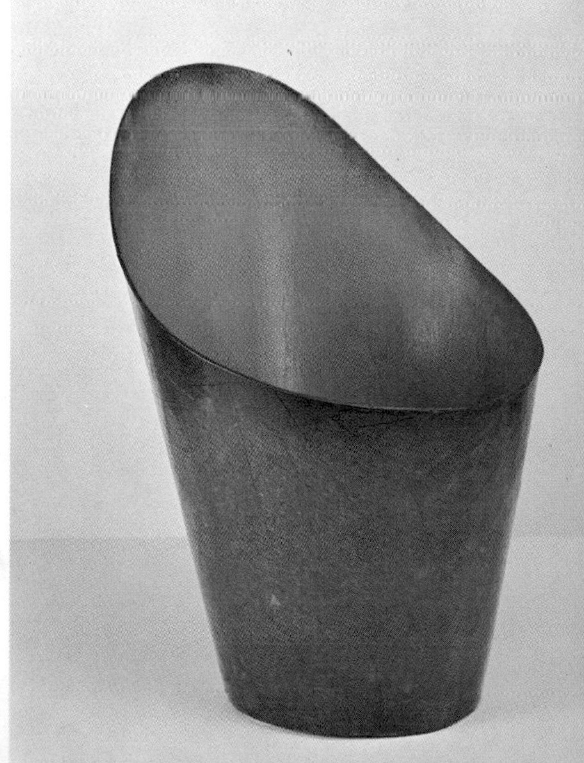

7. **Elegant wastebasket, 20 inches high, with 8-inch wooden bottom. Made from three layers of thin veneer, it is antique finished and shellacked.** (Reprinted by permission of Woman's Day Magazine.)

8. A turtle stool is bound to be a favorite. It's simple to make. Paint it in one of your favorite colors. After it is dry, paint an eye on either side of the head. A ready-made 16-inch round pillow just fits the top nicely. The walls of this playroom are knotty pine. Notice the interesting magazine rack built into the wall.

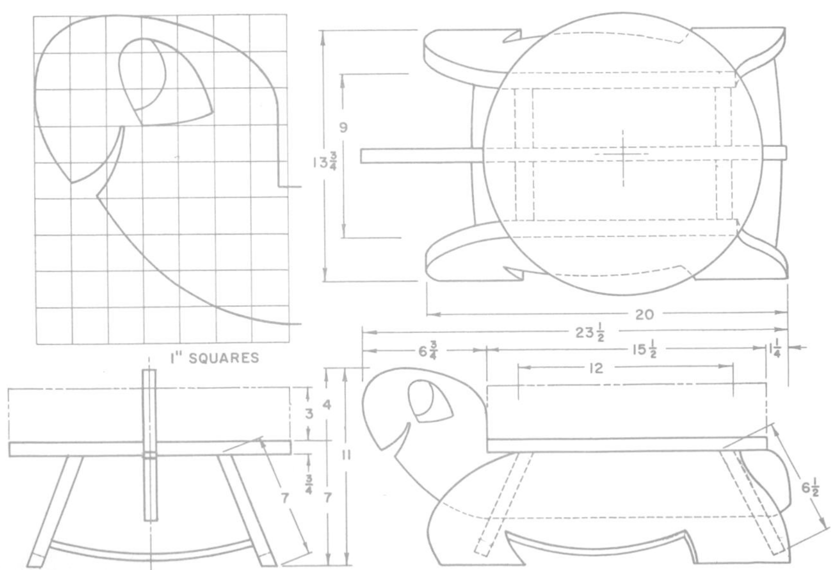

INTERMEDIATE PROJECTS

(First use of machines. Use of all types of joints.)

Group 1

Treasure Chest
Fruit Bowl
Campaign Chest
Writing Box
Knife Holder
Pine Pipe Box
Circular Tie Rack
Salt Shaker and Pepper Mill
Courting Mirror
Book Ends
Letter Rack
Cracker Tray

Group 2

Tile Hot-Dish Holder
Cribbage Board
Pin-Up Board
Weldtex Lamp
Weldtex Flower Holder
Knife Box
Pipe Rack
Elegant Wastebasket

Group 3

Shelf-All
Hanging Wall Shelf
Book Trough
Spice Cabinet
Planter Letter Rack

ADVANCED PROJECTS

(For those with experience in woodworking.)

Group 1

Jewel Box
Chip and Card Holder
Lawn Chair

Group 2

Desk
End Table
Skis
Telephone Stand
Early American Lamp
Portable Sewing Cabinet

1. *Knife Holder*. This knife holder has an excellent safety feature in that the cutting edges are all protected by glass. This is a good problem in box construction. Materials: back, 1/4″; sides, 1/2″; top and bottom, 3/8″.

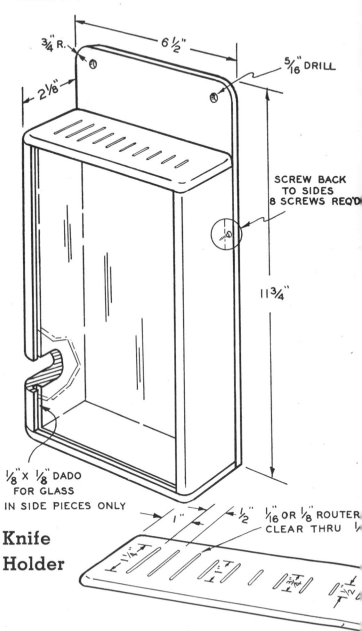

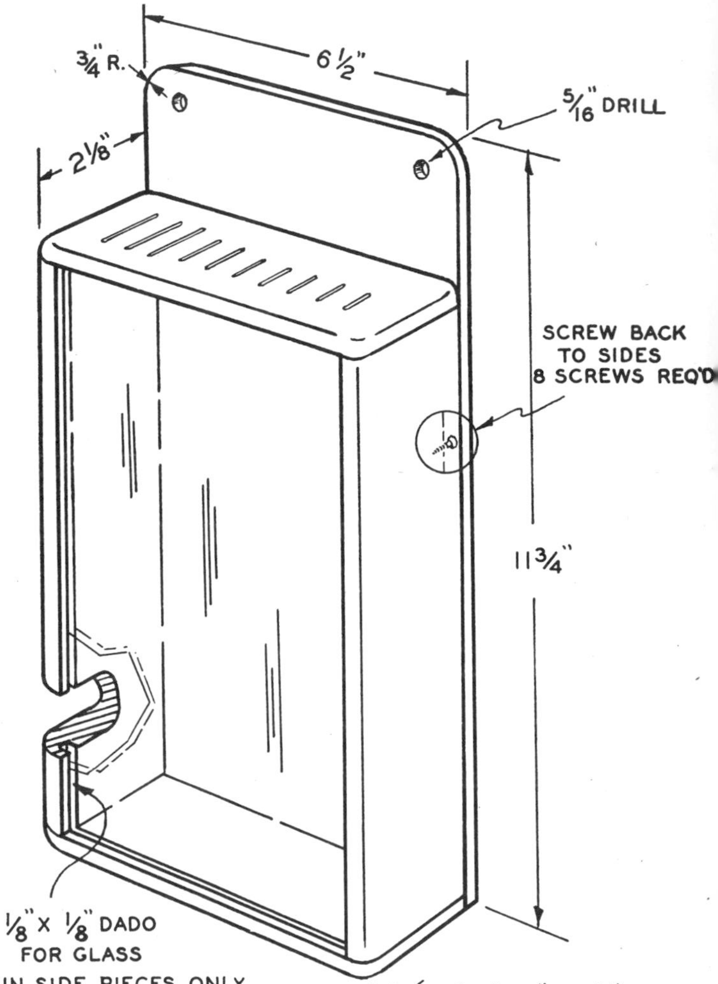

3/4" R.
6 1/2"
5/16" DRILL
2 1/8"
SCREW BACK TO SIDES 8 SCREWS REQ'D
11 3/4"
1/8" X 1/8" DADO FOR GLASS IN SIDE PIECES ONLY
1"
1/2"
1/16 OR 1/8 ROUTER CLEAR THRU
1 1/4"
1"
3/4"
1/2"

Knife Holder

2. *Pine Pipe Box*. This hanging wall box was originally used for holding clay pipes. It can be used as a planter box or simple wall decoration. All material is 3/8″ except sides, back, and bottom of drawer which are 1/4″.

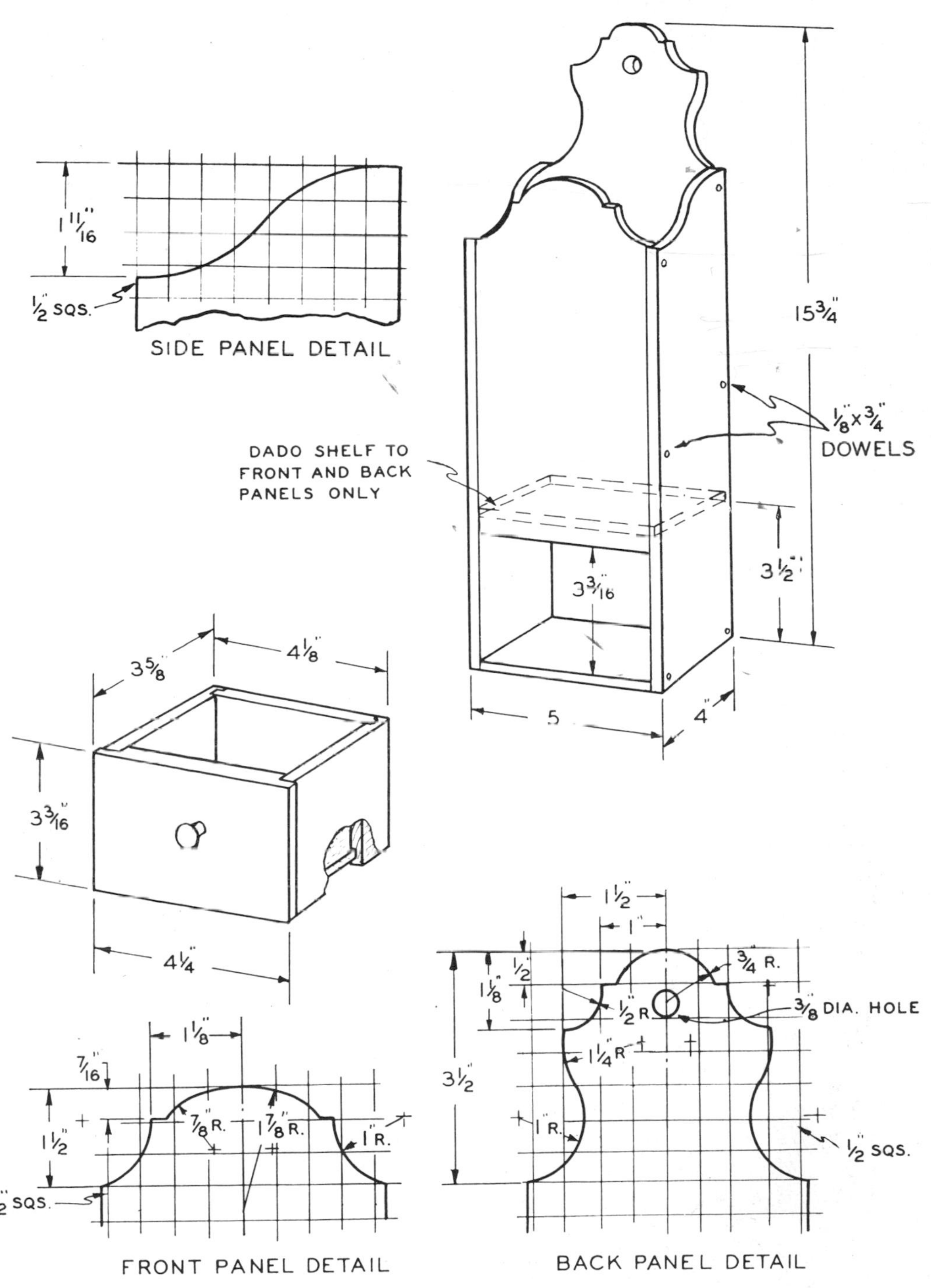

Pine Pipe Box

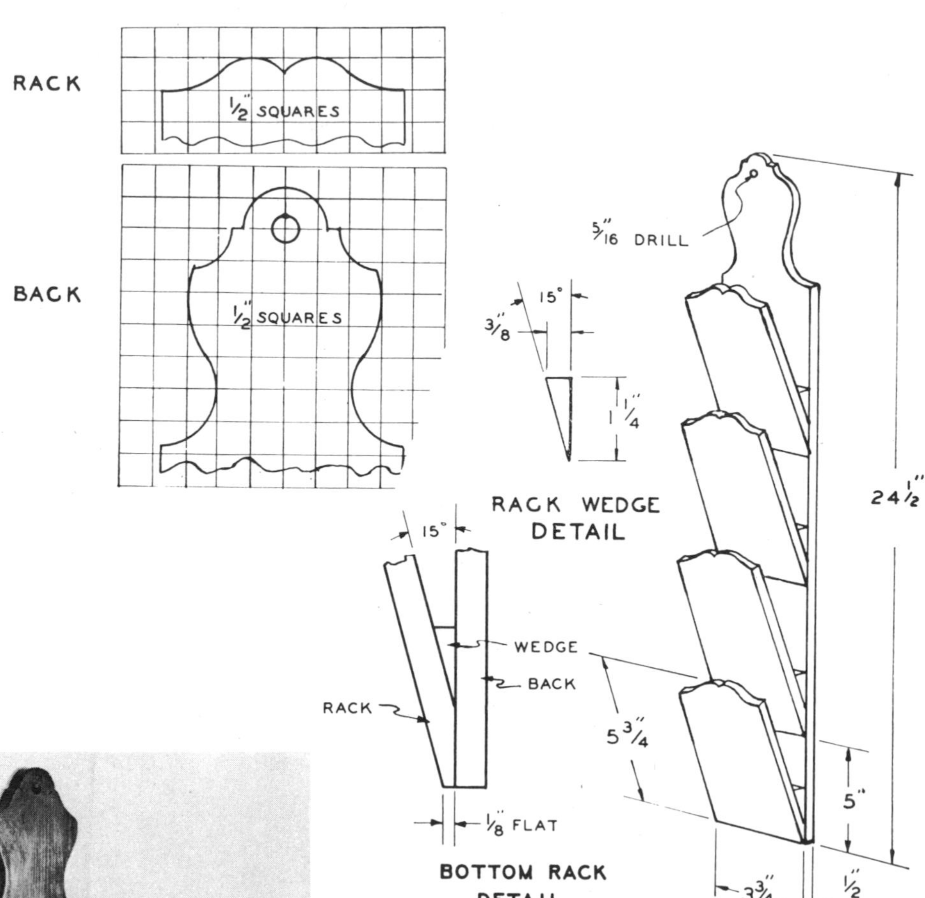

Letter Rack

3. *Letter Rack.* This is just right for sorting the family mail. Additional holders can be added for the larger family. Materials: back, 1/2"; racks and wedges, 3/8".

Section XIV. Unit 70

4. *Spice Cabinet.* Such a cabinet as this would be a welcome addition to an Early American kitchen. With some changes in the design this would make a useful cabinet for the storage of stamps, jewelry, or other small items.

Spice Cabinet

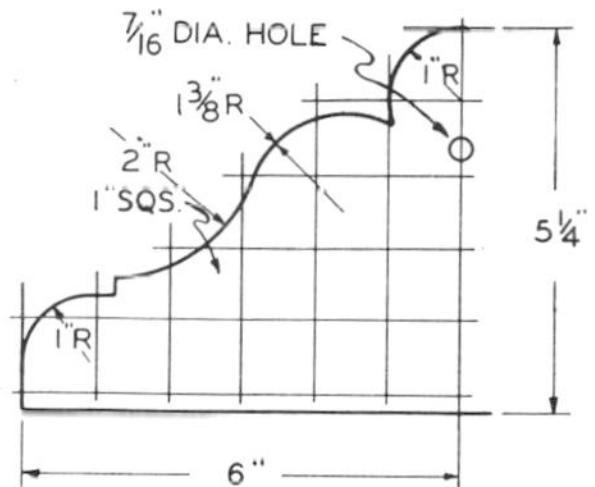

BACK RAIL DETAIL

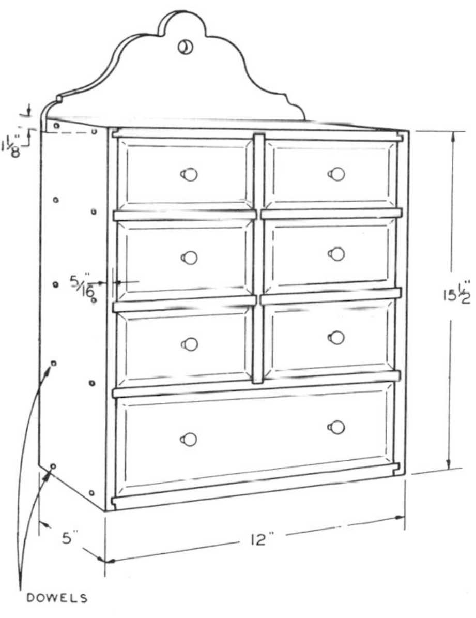

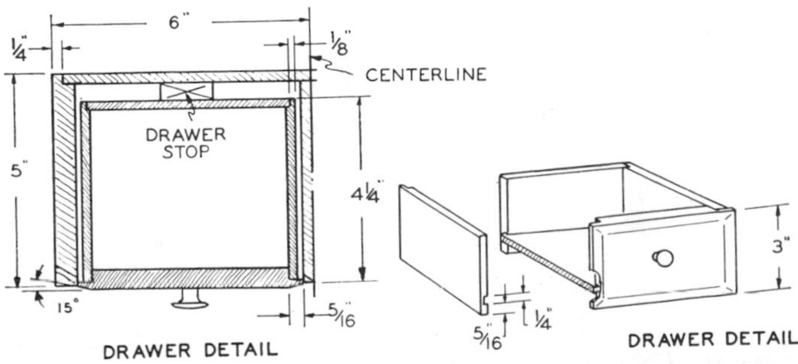

DRAWER DETAIL

DRAWER DETAIL

BILL OF MATERIALS

Important: All dimensions listed below, except for length of dowel, are *finished* size.

NO. OF PIECES	PART NAME	THICKNESS	WIDTH	LENGTH
2	Sides	1/2"	5"	15 1/2"
1	Top	1/2"	4 1/2"	11 3/8"
1	Bottom	1/2"	5"	11 3/8"
1	Back Rail	1/2"	5 1/4"	12"
4	Drawer Shelves	1/2"	4 3/4"	5 5/8"
1	Drawer Shelf	1/2"	4 3/4"	11 3/8"
1	Drawer Partition	1/2"	4 3/4"	11 3/8"
1	Back	1/4"	11 1/2"	14 3/8"
6	Drawer Fronts	1/2"	3"	5 1/4"
1	Drawer Front	1/2"	4"	11"
12	Drawer Sides	1/4"	3"	4 1/4"
2	Drawer Sides	1/4"	4"	4 1/4"
6	Drawer Backs	1/4"	3"	4 7/8"
1	Drawer Back	1/4"	4"	10 5/8"
6	Drawer Bottoms	1/4"	4"	4 7/8"
1	Drawer Bottom	1/4"	4"	10 5/8"
8	Drawer Stops	3/8"	3/8"	1 1/4"
1	Dowel	1/4"		3 feet
8	Brass Knobs			

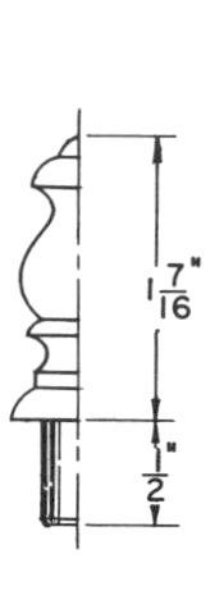

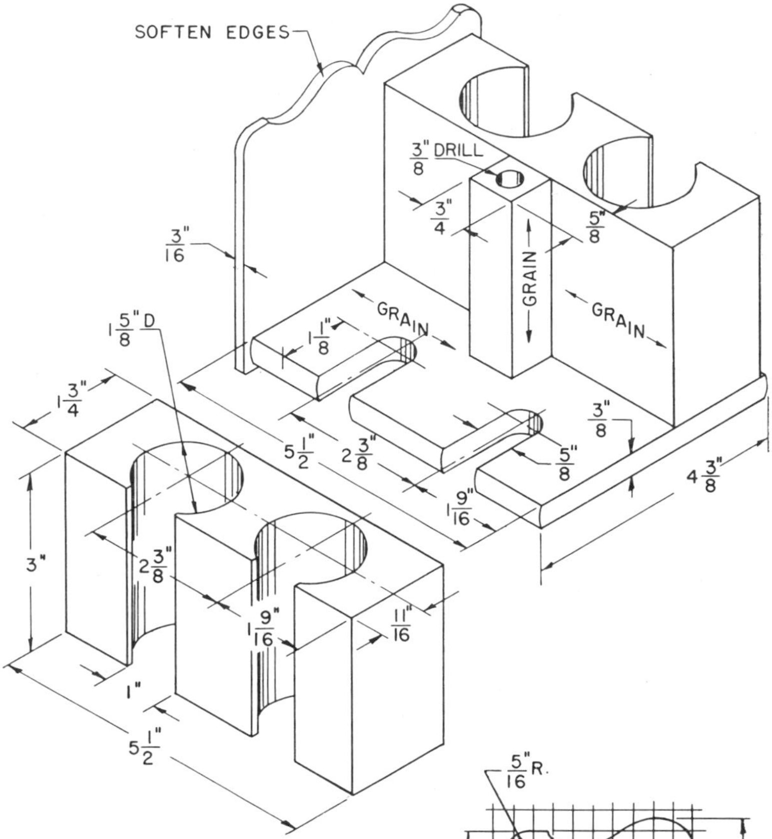

Chip and Card Holder

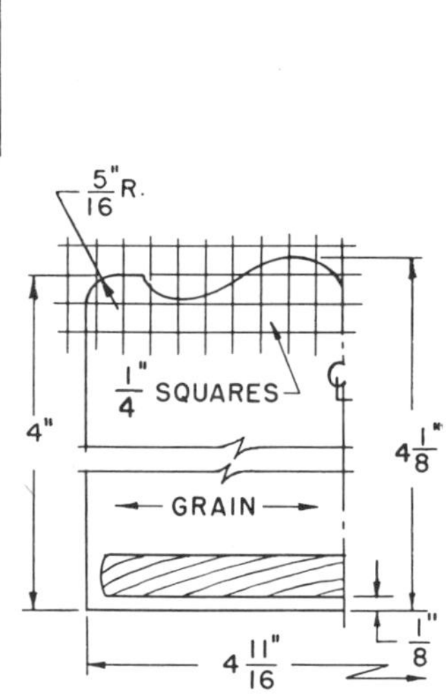

5. *Chip and Card Holder.* This is a handy accessory for any family that enjoys card games.

6. *Pipe Rack*. With this design the rack can hang on the wall or be used on a table.

Pipe Rack

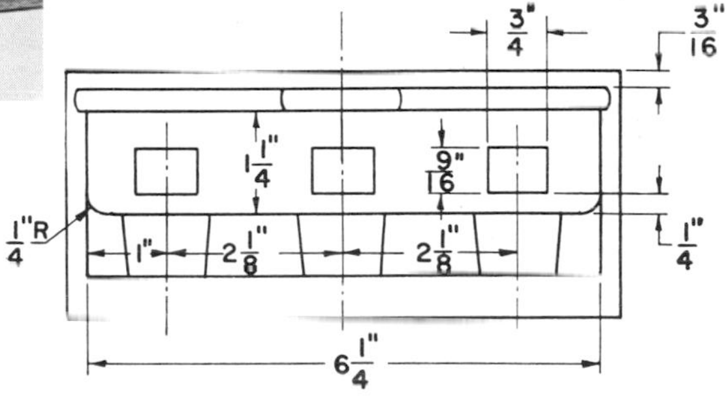

TOP VIEW

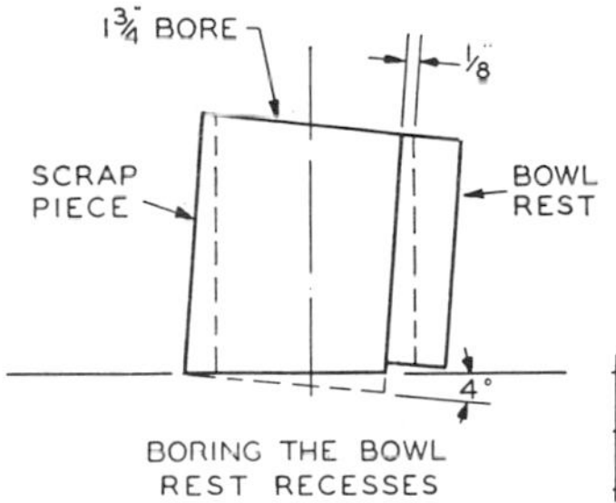

1¾" BORE
SCRAP PIECE
BOWL REST

BORING THE BOWL REST RECESSES

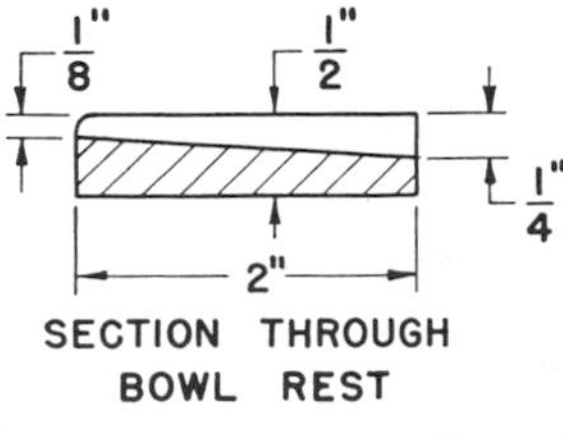

SECTION THROUGH BOWL REST

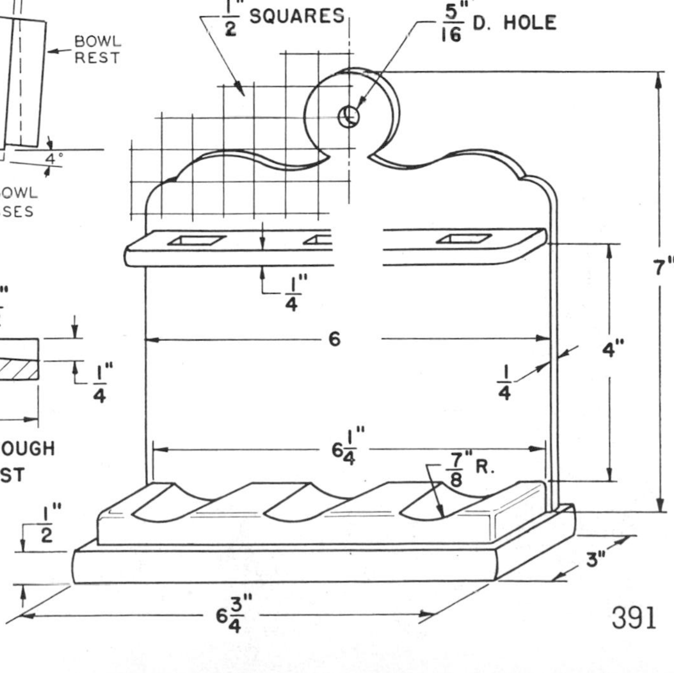

½" SQUARES

5/16" D. HOLE

7. *Telephone Stand.* This hand stand has a drawer for storing pencils and a date book. The opening will hold a telephone directory of any thickness. This would be a useful addition to any home.

8. *Early American Lamp.* Here is a real challenge to your wood-turning ability. The base has an interesting small drawer which is both a decorative and a functional feature.

9. *Hot Dish Holder.* Combines the best in wood and ceramics. The soft appearance of the oak frame makes a pleasing contrast to the bright tile pattern. Makes a good base for hot dishes, but four or six of them grouped on the wall over the mantel or bookcase would add a highly decorative note. Assemble by gluing the frame to the base and then inserting the tile. A square of felt has been glued to the base.

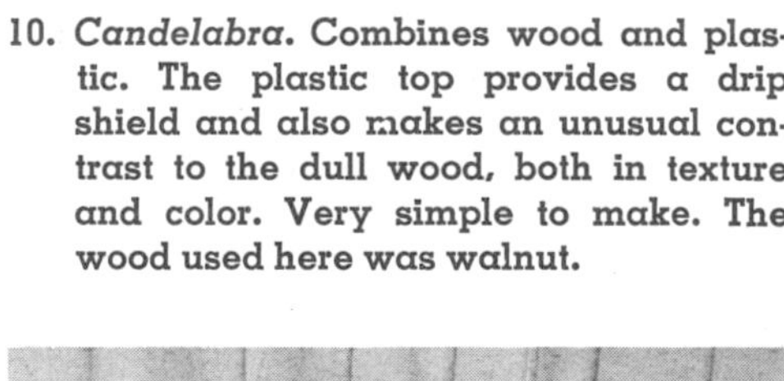

10. *Candelabra.* Combines wood and plastic. The plastic top provides a drip shield and also makes an unusual contrast to the dull wood, both in texture and color. Very simple to make. The wood used here was walnut.

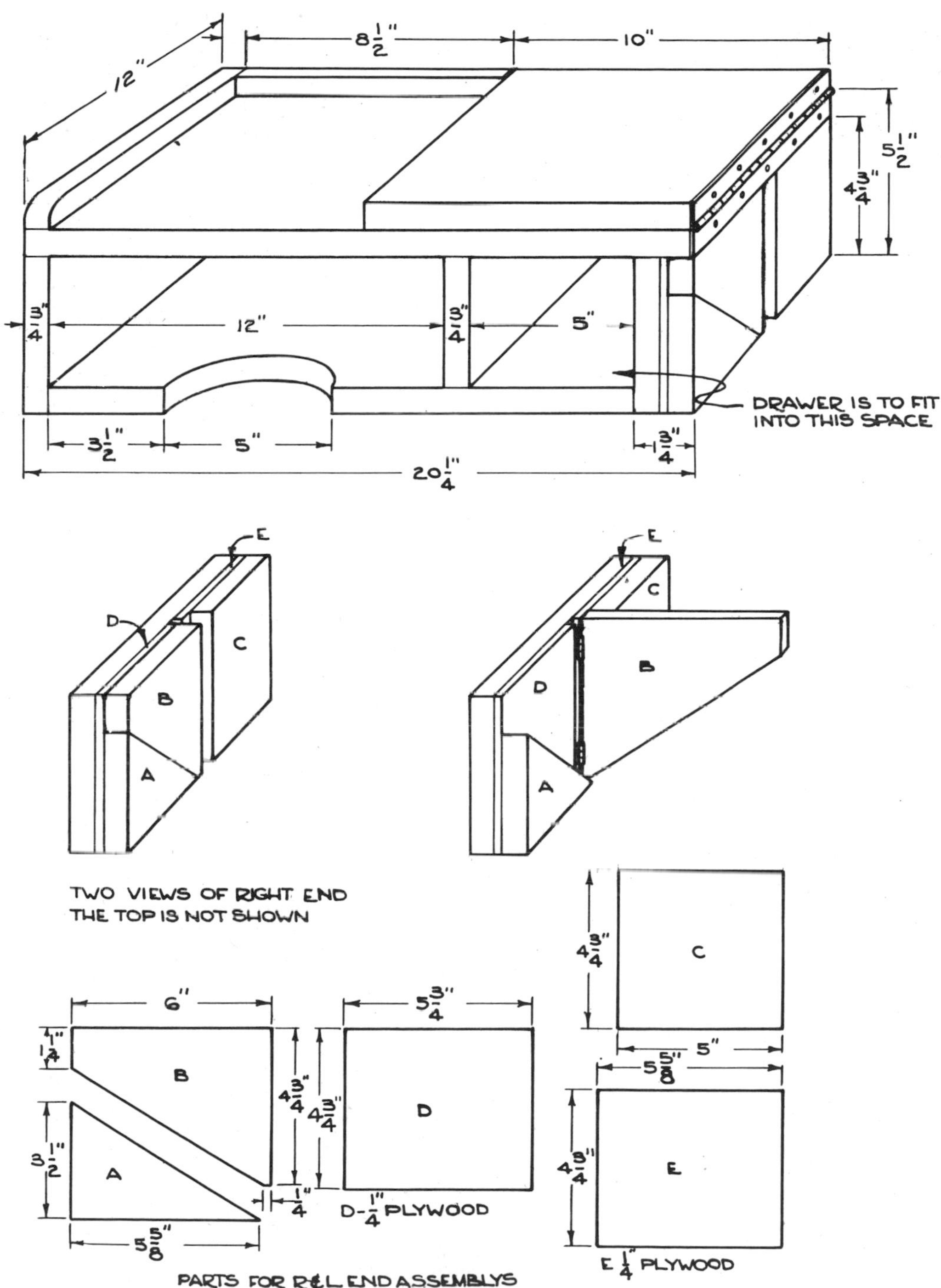

Telephone Stand

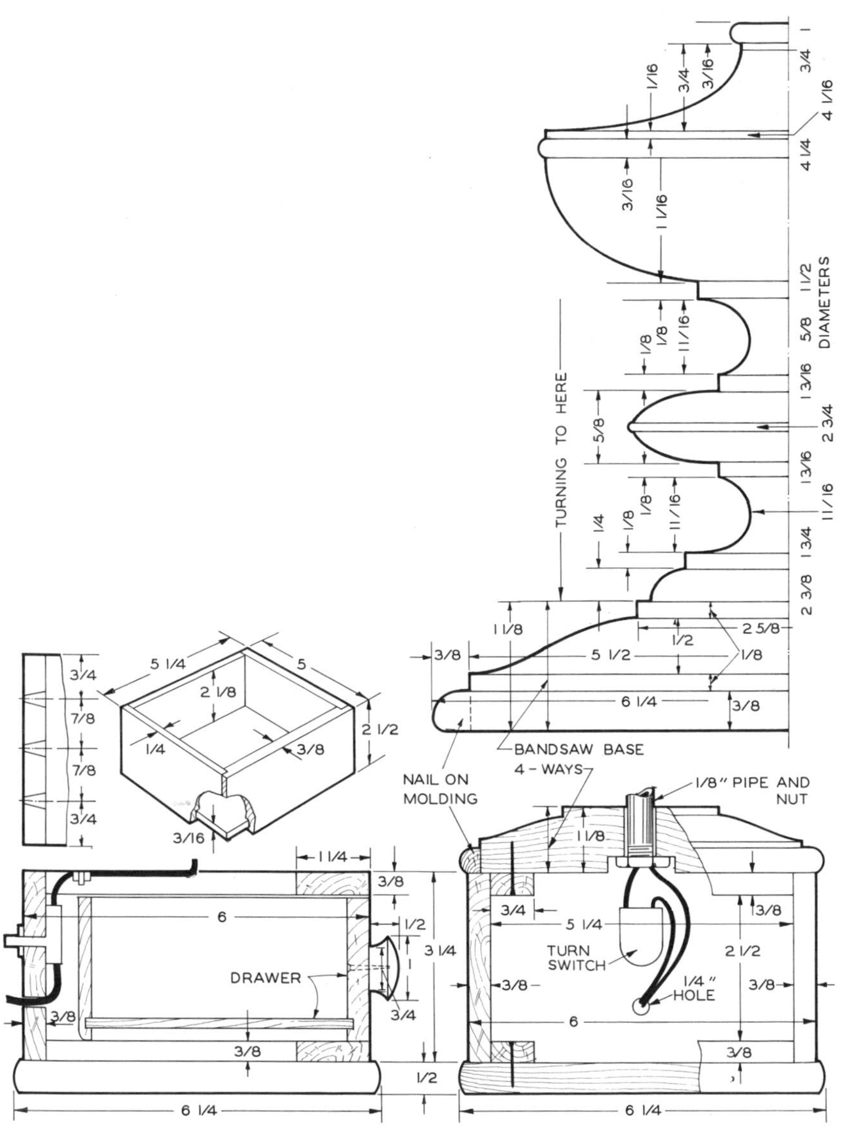

Early American Lamp

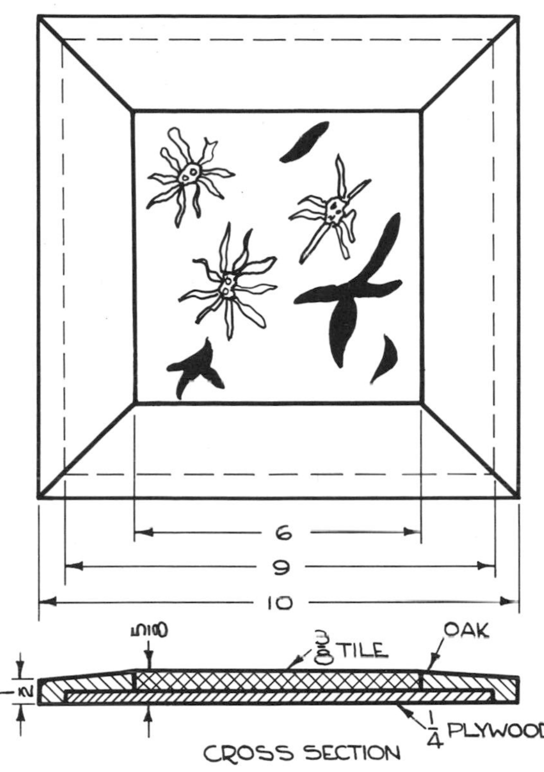

Tile Hot Dish Holder

Candelabra

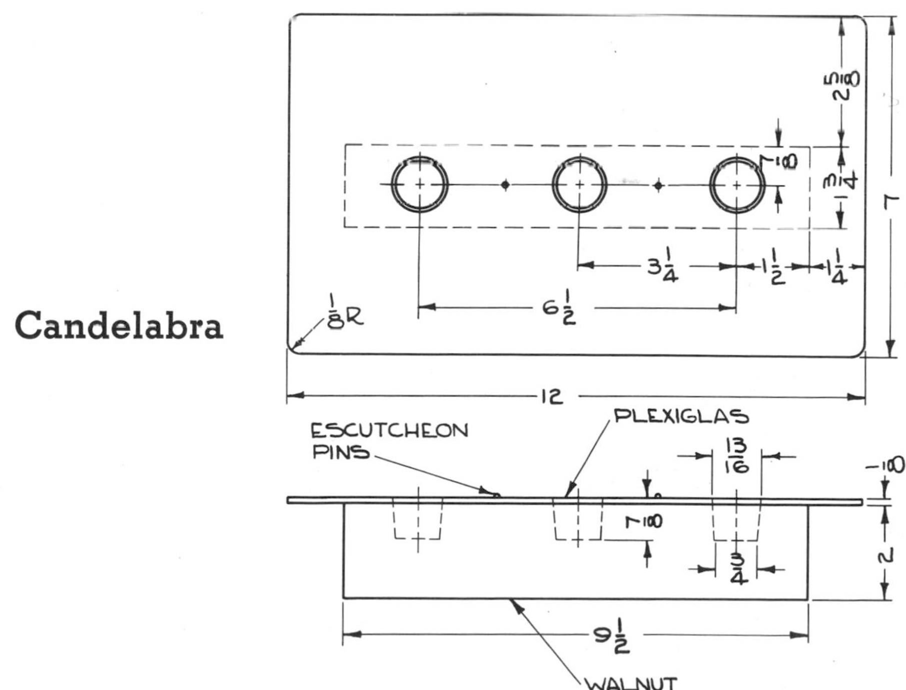

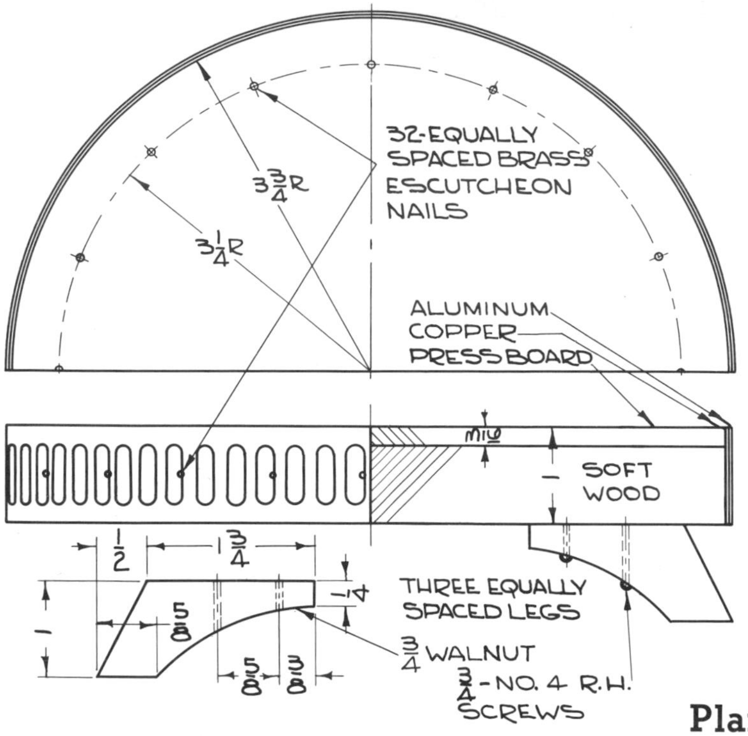

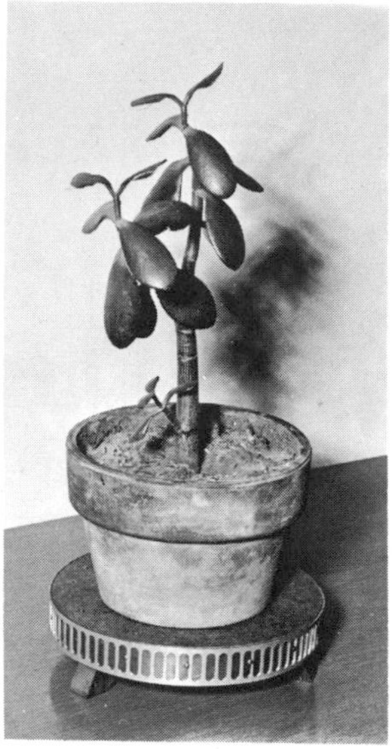

32-EQUALLY SPACED BRASS ESCUTCHEON NAILS
3 3/4 R
3 1/4 R
ALUMINUM
COPPER
PRESS BOARD
1/16
1
SOFT WOOD
1/2
1 3/4
1/4
5/8
1
THREE EQUALLY SPACED LEGS
3/4 WALNUT
5/8
3/8
3/4 - NO. 4 R.H. SCREWS

Plant Base

11. *Plant Base*. This three-legged plant base is made of walnut and two kinds of metal. Two circles are cut, one of wood and the other of a water-repellent material, and glued together. The legs are fastened to the wood with screws and the metal wrapped around the circle and held with escutcheon pins.

MY
SHINE
BOX

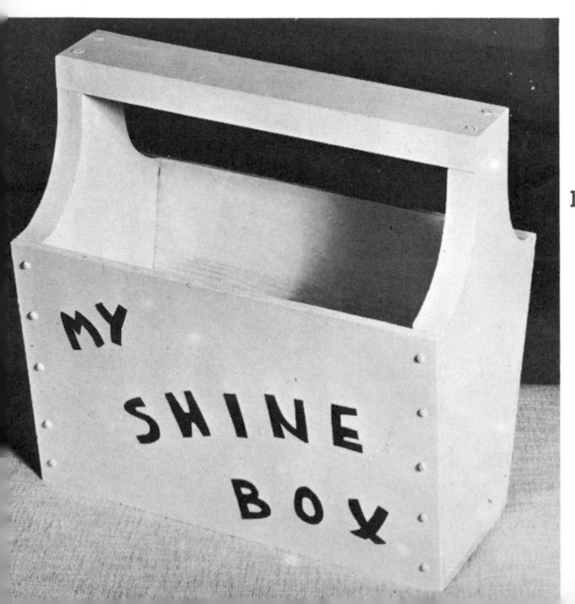

12. *My Shine Box*. Keeping shoeshining equipment together all in one place is always a problem unless you have a compact container for the purpose. Then, too, when you are actually shining your shoes, the handle becomes an excellent footrest. This one is built of poplar and 1/8-inch fir plywood. It is another good beginner's project. You and everyone else in the house will enjoy using it.

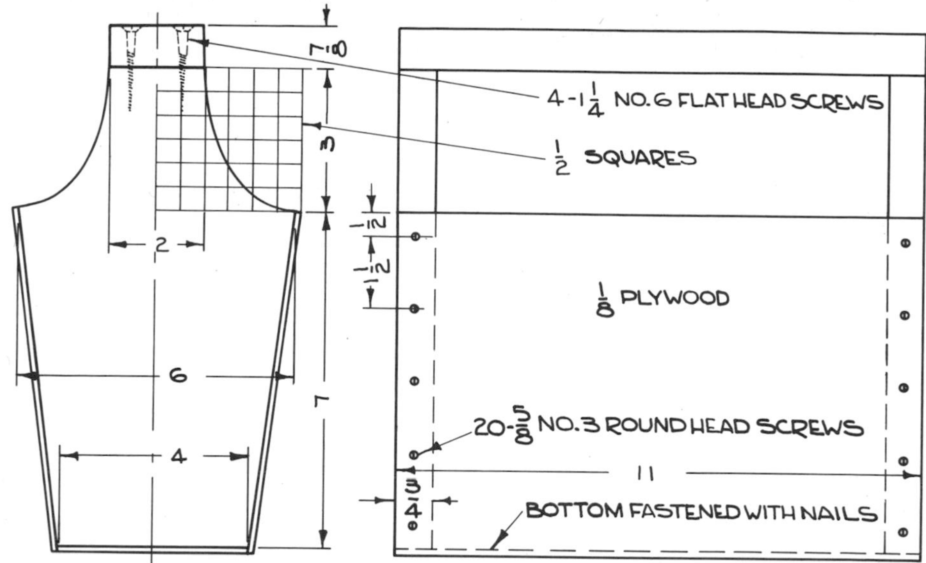

My Shine Box

13. *Treasure Chest.* A miniature version of the good old pirate chest! The pine surface is gouged and burned to give it the appearance of age, and the brass trim is patterned after the Captain's Sea Chest of old. This one, however, is just the right size for jewelry, trinkets, a boy's marbles, or small change.

Treasure Chest

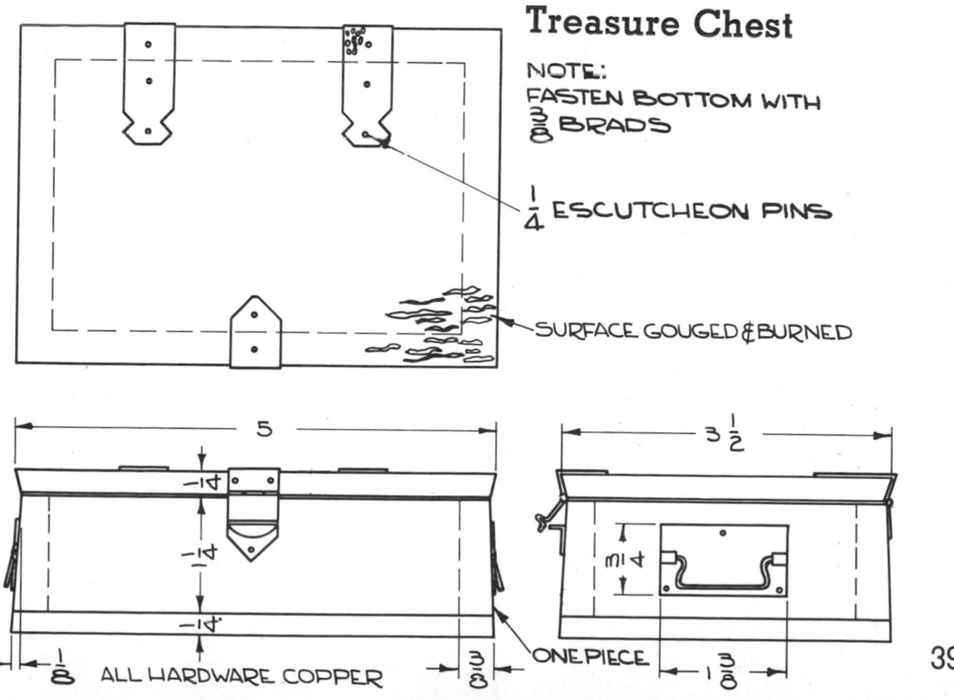

Circular Tie Rack

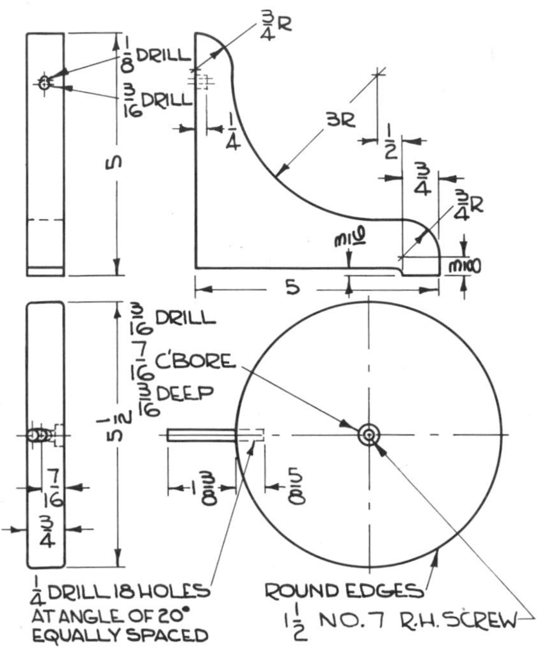

Pants Holder

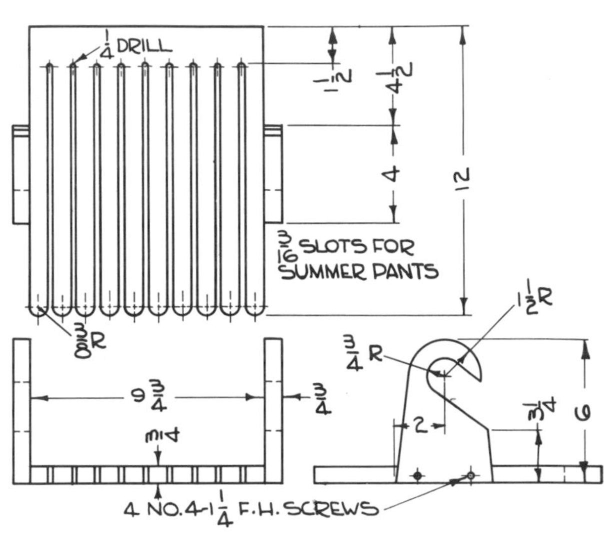

14. *Circular Tie Rack.* The rack can be flicked around with your finger to bring forward any tie for easy choice. The rack has plenty of room for all of your ties and none of them is hidden from view. Can be made of almost any kind of wood. While it is not quite so simple as some kinds of tie racks to build, it will provide a real challenge to the fledgling woodworker.

15. *Pants Holder.* This is a real convenience. No more wrinkles in your trousers when you use this holder. This one holds 9 pairs of trousers at one time, and each can be removed without disturbing the others. Another useful feature is that the holder hangs from the closet rod like a hanger, thus conserving closet space.

16. *House Numbers.* An idea that you can apply to many different projects. You might make a set of house numbers, room identification numbers, or you could design cut-out letters for a nameplate for a desk or for your room. By fastening these numbers or letters to a simple background, you will obtain squaring-up experience and still have an article that you will be proud to take home.

House Numbers

$\frac{3}{32}$ PLYWOOD

$\frac{1}{2}$ SQUARES

$\frac{1}{2}$ ESCUTCHEON PINS

Planter Letter Rack

17. *Planter Letter Rack.* **This project will reward you in many ways. It will give you experience in several woodworking operations, and in metalworking as well. Moreover, you will have a handsome product to show for your efforts.**

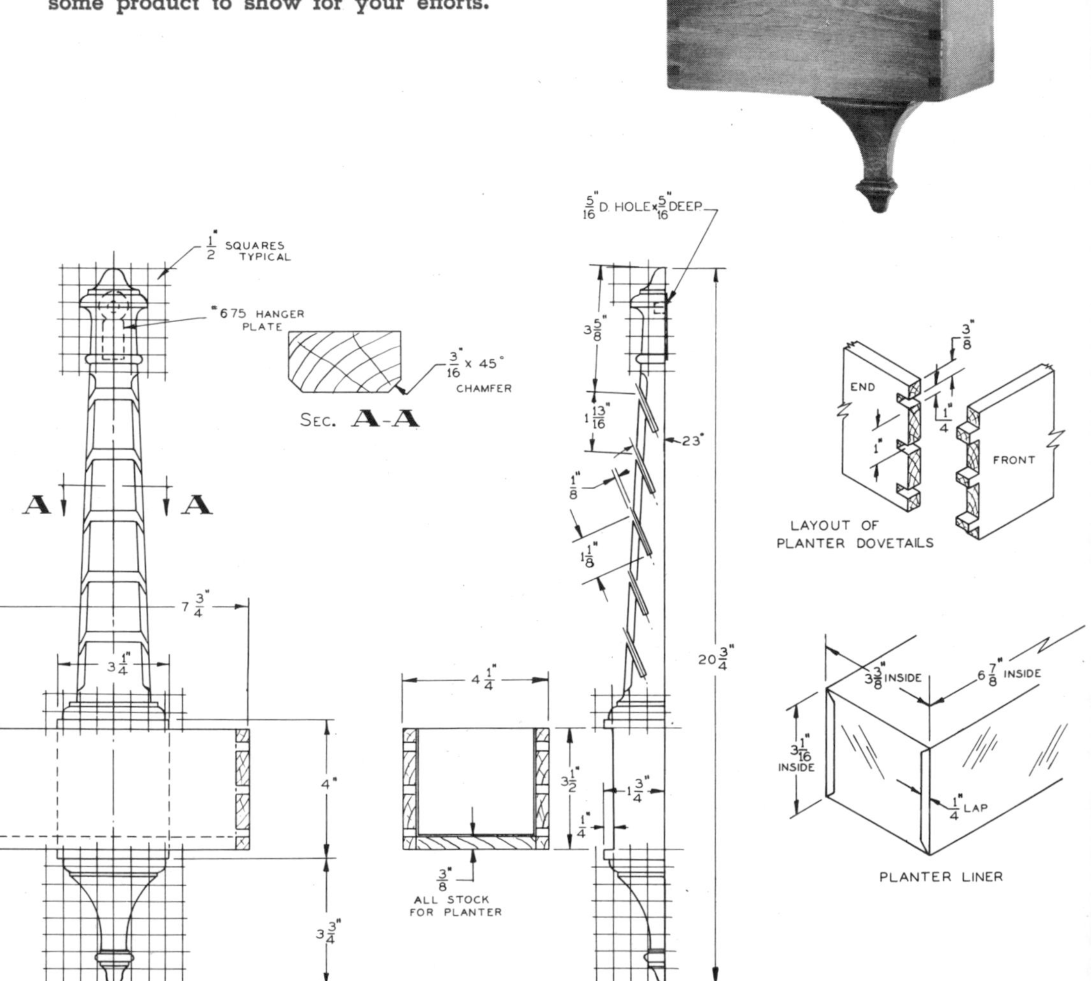

Cribbage Board

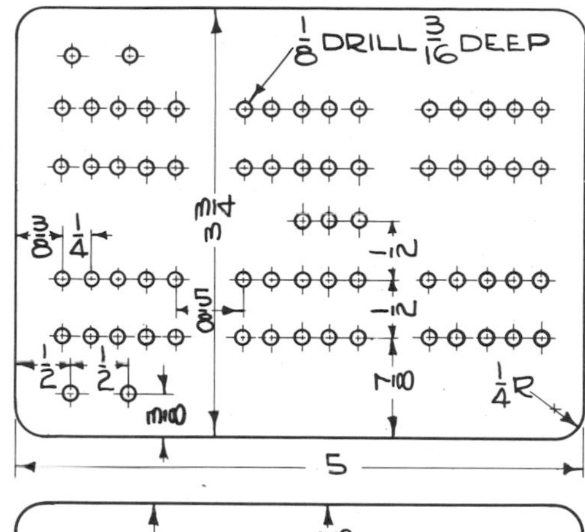

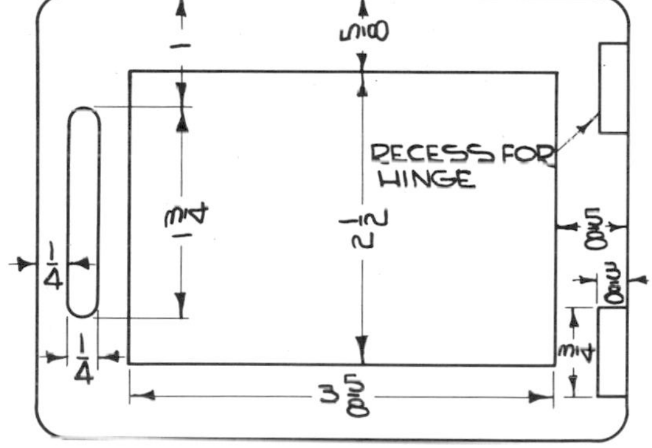

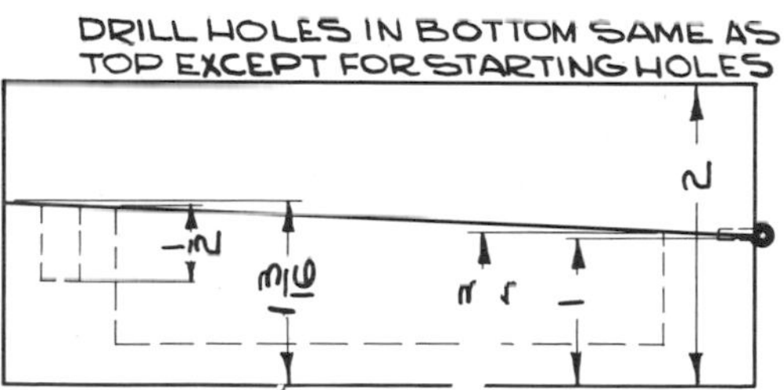

18. *Cribbage Board.* Anyone who plays cribbage or who would like to own a good board would certainly want to make one of these folding boards. It is ideal for traveling because it folds into a small, compact box shape. Inside are compartments for both the cards and pegs. Because it has to be formed, the ideal wood is walnut. When drilling the holes, it is a great help to use a little metal jig. Hinge sizes can vary.

Cracker Tray

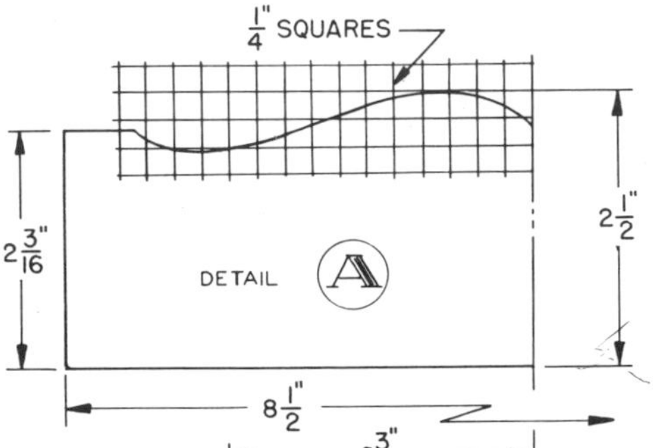

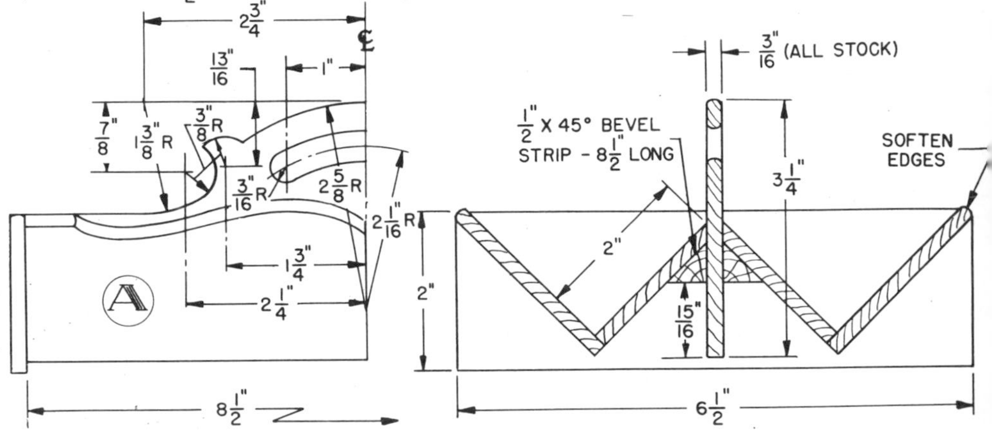

19. *Cracker Tray.* Your mother or sister will find this tray convenient for serving snacks. It is interesting to make, and not too difficult.

20. *Portable Sewing Cabinet.* Compact and pleasing to the eye, this cabinet provides storage for many of the items needed by the seamstress in your family. (Drawing on page 403.)

Portable Sewing Cabinet

(Photograph on page 402)

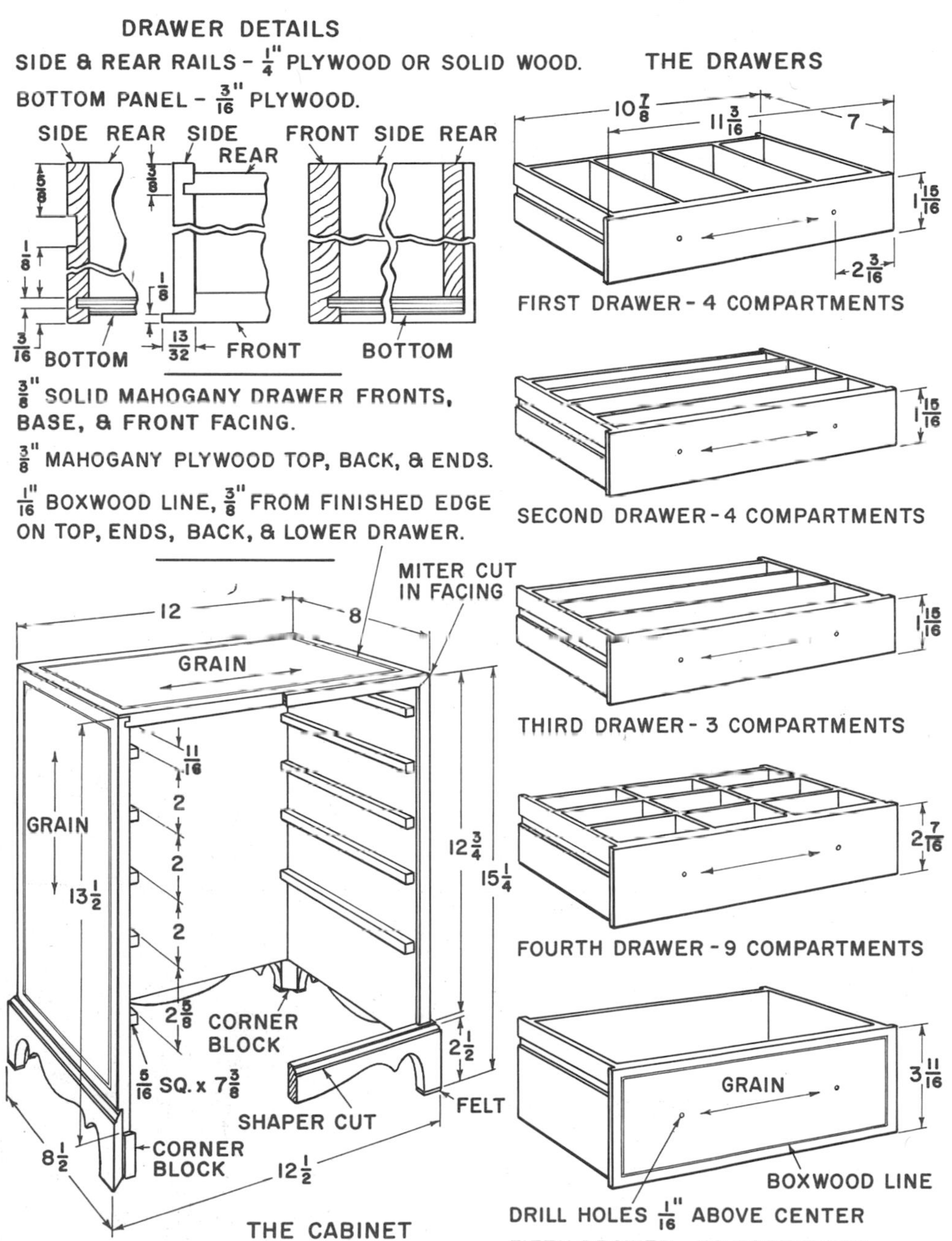

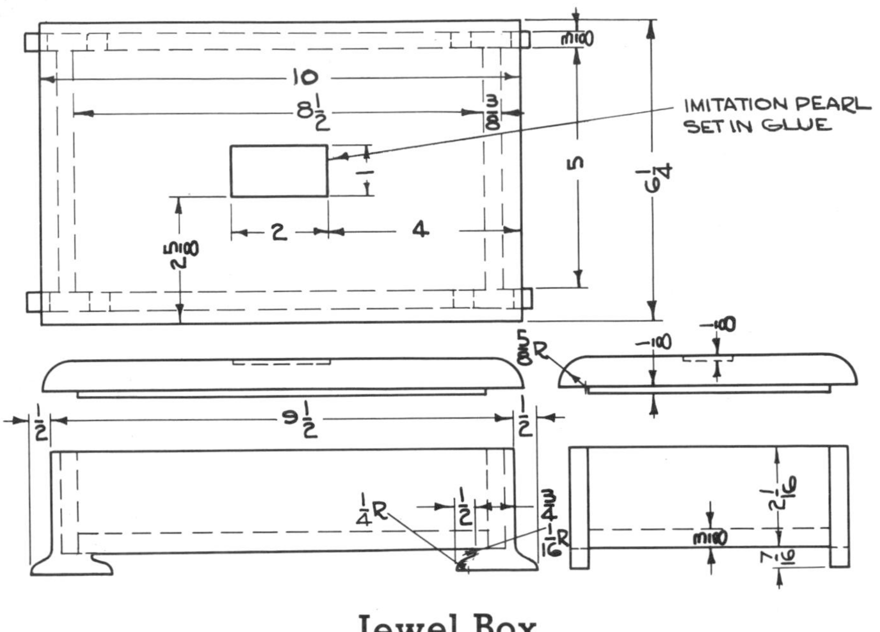

Jewel Box

21. *Jewel Box*. The beauty of this box is in its simple lines, the unusual grain, and the hand-rubbed finish. It is made of curly maple giving it fine grain formation. Assemble with dowels and glue. An imitation pearl piece is set in the top with glue.

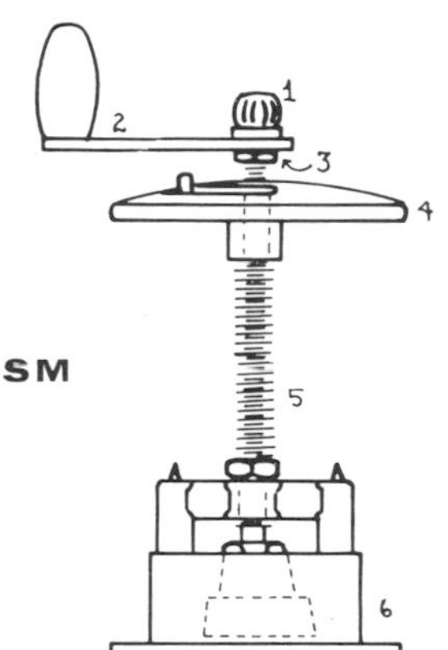

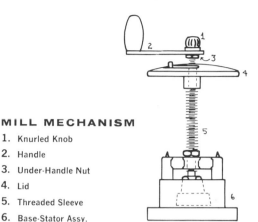

MILL MECHANISM

1. Knurled Knob
2. Handle
3. Under-Handle Nut
4. Lid
5. Threaded Sleeve
6. Base-Stator Assy.

22. *Salt Shaker and Pepper Mill.* The outside shape can be varied in many ways to express your own design ideas. Source C—Page 382

Salt Shaker and Pepper Mill

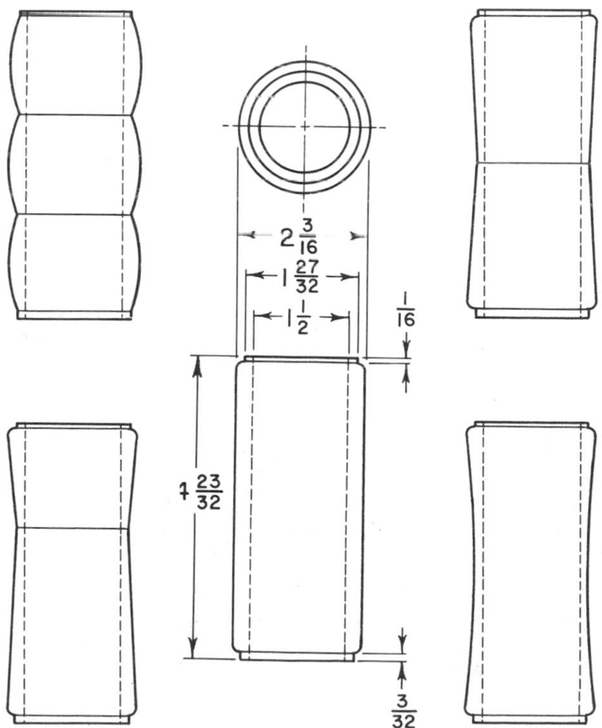

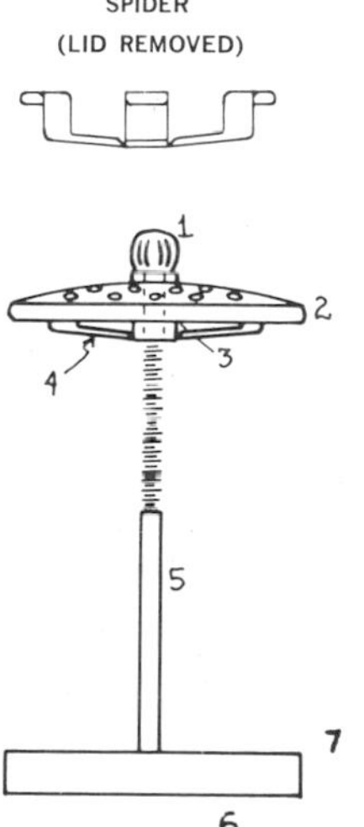

SALT HARDWARE

1. Knurled Knob
2. Lid
3. Spider Nut (Hidden)
4. Spider
5. Threaded Shaft
6. Base
7. Plastic Liner (Hidden)

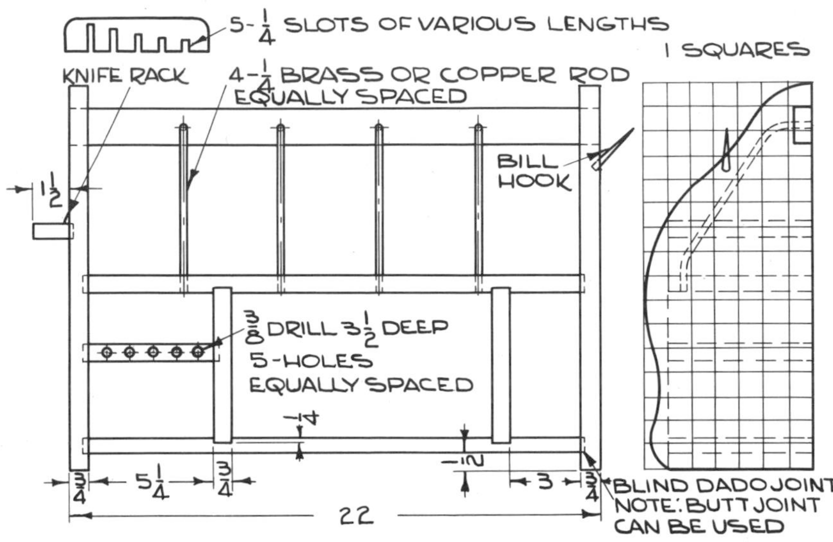

Shelf-All

23. *Shelf-All.* An all-purpose shelf for the kitchen. The top shelf is built for cookbooks and reference materials; the left part of the bottom shelf is just right for 3 × 5-inch cards and, with the places for pencils, it is immensely helpful for taking notes and making lists. The right opening is made for note pads. A hook for bills is on the right side. Joints are glued.

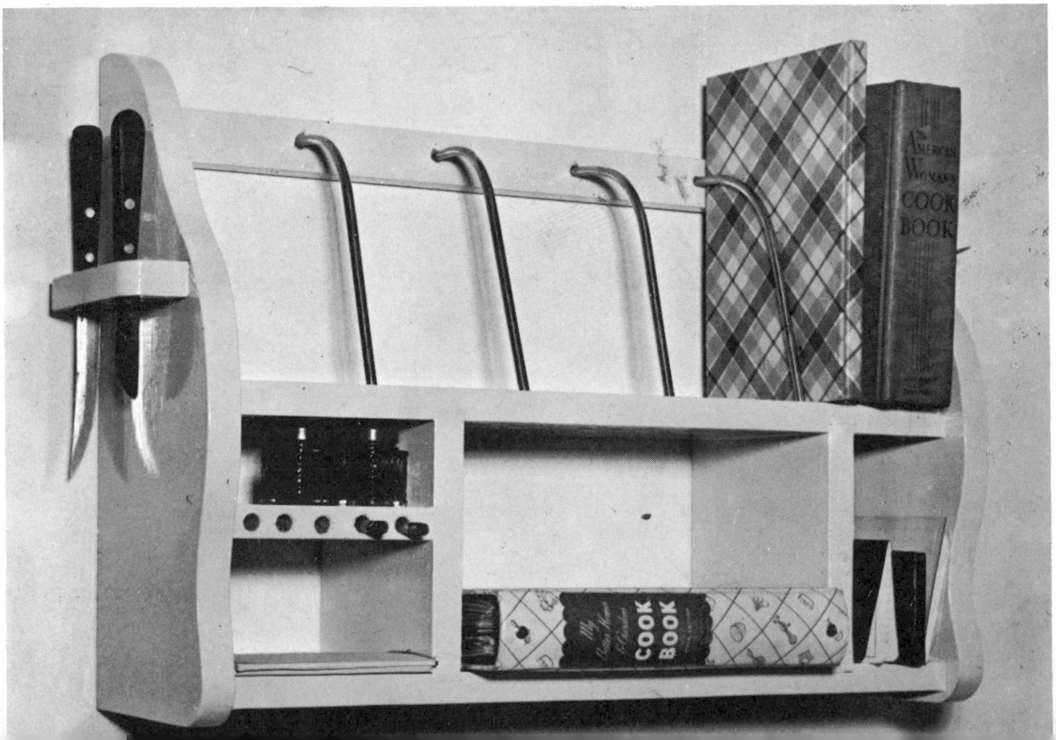

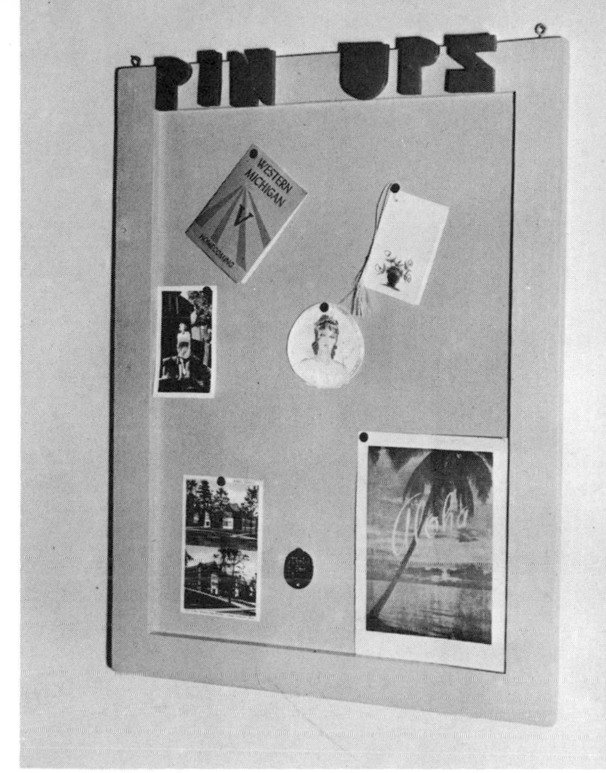

24. *Pin-Up Board.* Just the thing for a young boy's or girl's room is this board which will keep pin-ups, pictures, and clippings where they belong and also provide a convenient place to jot down important dates and appointments. It is an excellent example of the use of the miter joint.

Pin-up Board

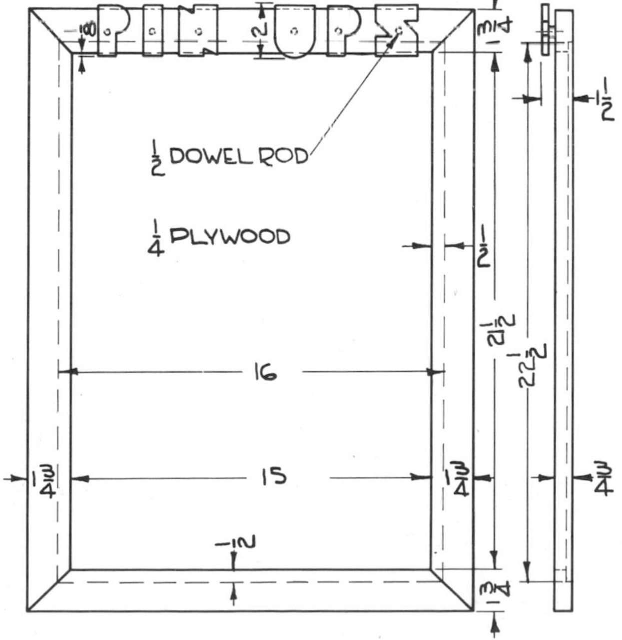

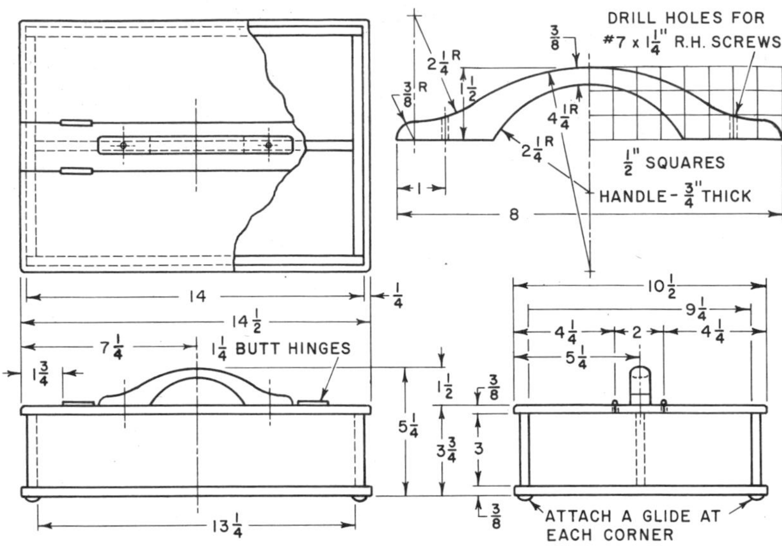

Knife-and-fork Box

25. *Knife-and-fork Box.* **An attractive Early American design that could be put to many different uses. It can be made of pine, cherry, or birch.** (Courtesy of Woman's Day)

26. *Mailing List Cover.* There is always a need for a convenient place to keep Christmas mailing lists, addresses, or other reminders. Here is one made with plywood covers, with the letters cut out of a darker colored ⅛″ plywood. The same idea would be good for a photograph album or scrapbook.

Mailing List Cover

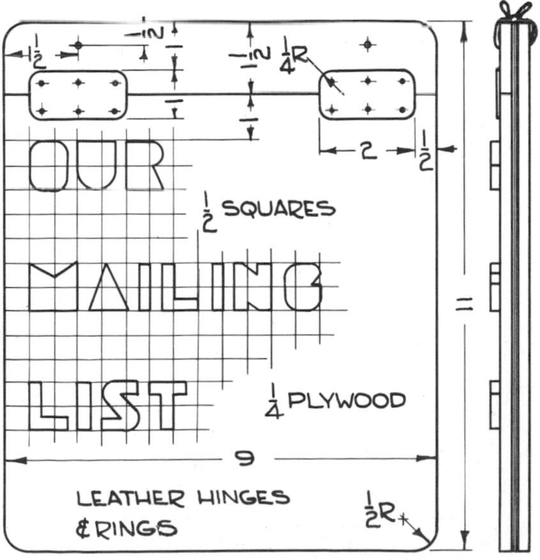

27. *Storage Hassock.* Here is an excellent beginning project which includes some simple upholstery. It is a handy seat as well as a storage unit.

28. *Student's Desk.* This is a simple, practical desk for your room which can be made in a short time of fir plywood. The whole desk can be cut from one 4- by 8-foot panel ¾-inch thick. There are roomy pigeon holes for small items and shelf space. Under the drop-leaf writing surface are two drawers. See Source A, page 382.

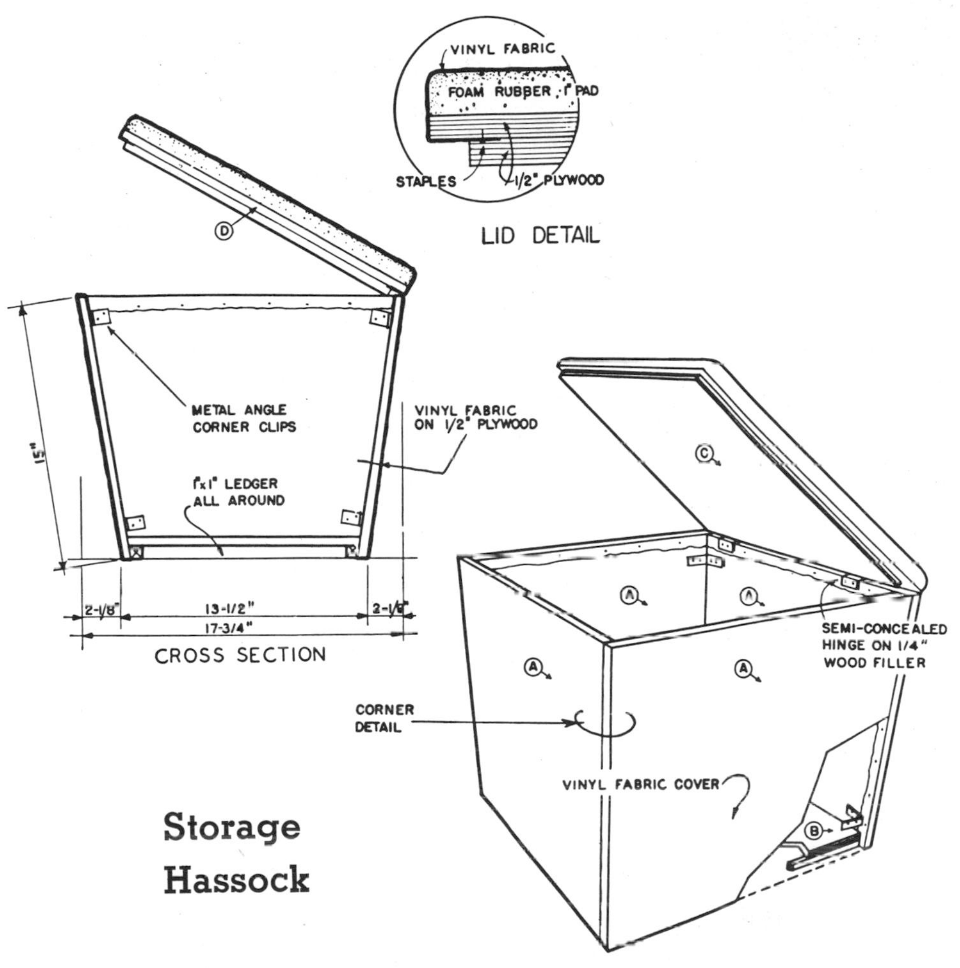

Storage Hassock

PARTS SCHEDULE FOR HASSOCK

CODE	NO. REQ'D	SIZE	PART IDENTIFICATION
A	4	15" x 17¼"	Sides
B	1	12½" x 12½"	Bottom
C	1	16¼" x 16¼"	Underside of Lid
D	1	17¾" x 17¾"	Lid
	1 Pc.	17¾" x 17¾"	1" Foam Rubber
	1 Pc.	3' x 5'	Vinyl Fabric
	5 Lin. Ft.	1" x 1"	Ledger Strip
	8 Ea.	—	Clip Angles
	1 Pr.	—	Semi-Concealed Hinges

Miscellaneous—4d Finish Nails, Staples and Glue

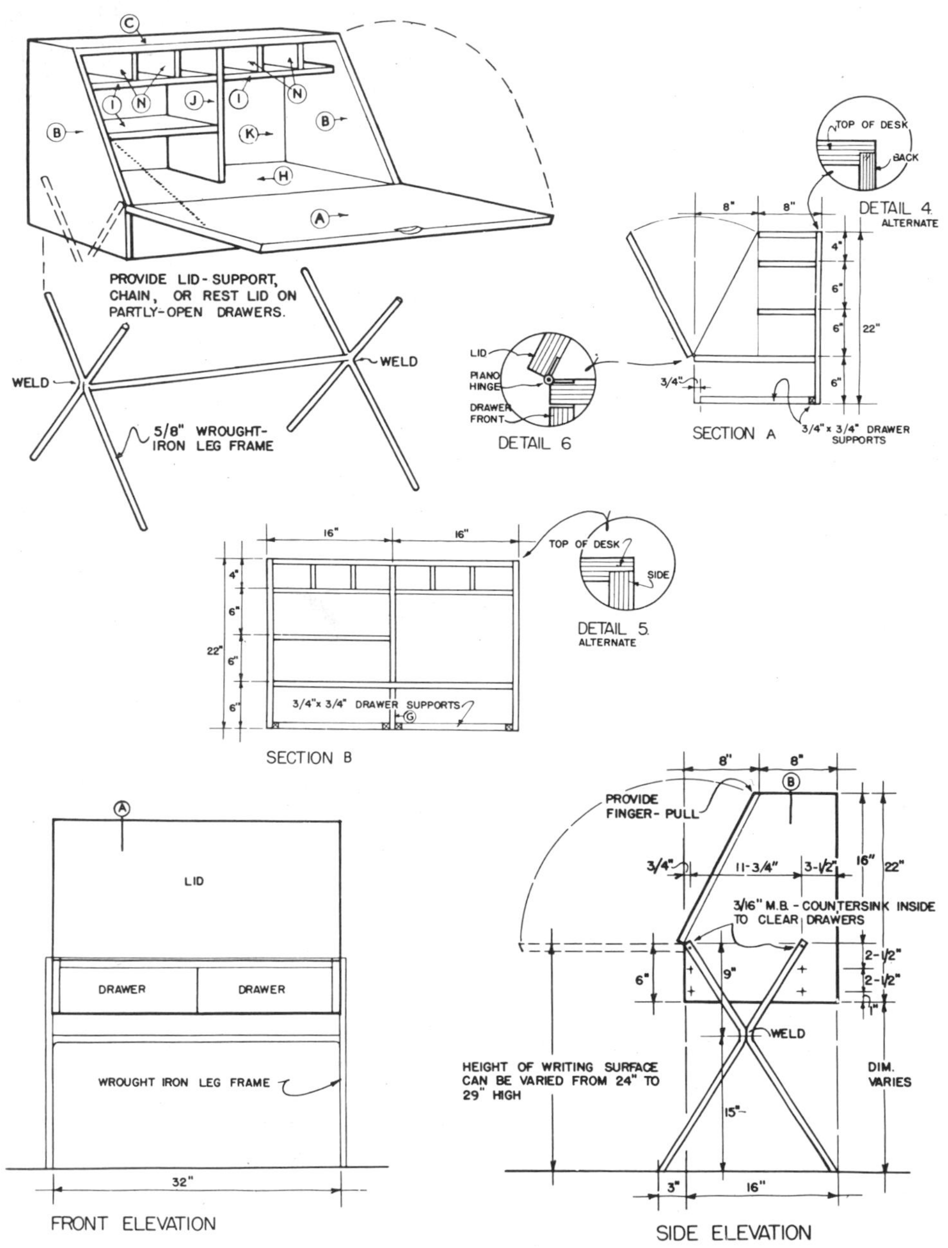
C
I
N
J
I
N
B
B
K
H
A
PROVIDE LID-SUPPORT, CHAIN, OR REST LID ON PARTLY-OPEN DRAWERS.
WELD
WELD
5/8" WROUGHT-IRON LEG FRAME
TOP OF DESK
BACK
DETAIL 4
ALTERNATE
8"
8"
4"
6"
6"
22"
6"
3/4"
LID
PIANO HINGE
DRAWER FRONT
DETAIL 6
SECTION A
3/4" x 3/4" DRAWER SUPPORTS
16"
16"
TOP OF DESK
SIDE
DETAIL 5
ALTERNATE
4"
6"
22"
6"
6"
3/4" x 3/4" DRAWER SUPPORTS
G
SECTION B
A
LID
DRAWER
DRAWER
WROUGHT IRON LEG FRAME
32"
FRONT ELEVATION
8"
8"
B
PROVIDE FINGER-PULL
3/4"
11-3/4"
3-1/2"
16"
22"
3/16" M.B. - COUNTERSINK INSIDE TO CLEAR DRAWERS
2-1/2"
2-1/2"
6"
9"
1"
WELD
HEIGHT OF WRITING SURFACE CAN BE VARIED FROM 24" TO 29" HIGH
DIM. VARIES
15"
3"
16"
SIDE ELEVATION

Student's Desk

29. *Book Trough.* Traditional in design, this book trough is made of cherry. Its construction is different from most of the other projects here in that a pinned mortise-and-tenon joint holds the parts together. The stock is shaped to simulate age.

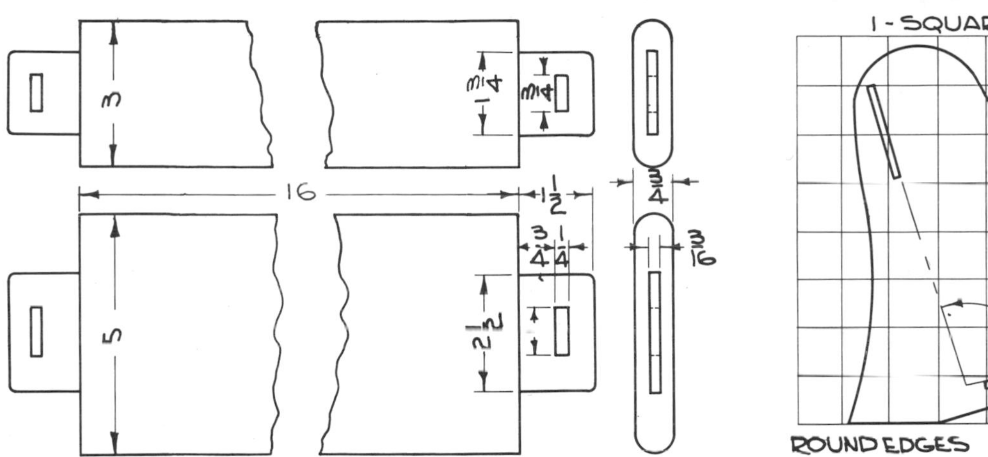

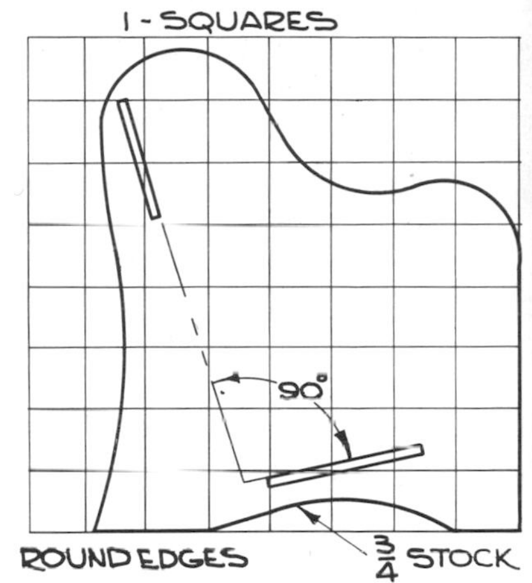

Book Trough

Student's Desk (cont'd.)

PARTS SCHEDULE FOR DESK

CODE	NO. REQ'D	SIZE	PART IDENTIFICATION
A	1	17¾″ x 32″	Desk Lid
B	2	16″ x 22″	Side
C	1	7½″ x 30½″	Top
D	2	5¼″ x 15¼″	Drawer Front
E	2	4⅜″ x 13¾″	Inside Drawer Front
F	2	4⅜″ x 13¾″	Drawer Back
G	1	5¼″ x 14¾″	Divider Between Drawers
H	1	15½″ x 30½″	Bottom Shelf
I	3	7½″ x 14⅞″	Shelf
J	1	7½″ x 15¼″	Vertical Divider
K	1	22″ x 30½″	Back of Unit
L	2	13¾″ x 13¾″	Drawer Bottom
M	4	4⅜″ x 15¼″	Drawer Side
N	4	3¼″ x 7¼″	Vertical Dividers
	9 Lin. Ft.	¾″ x ¾″	Drawer Supports
	1 Only	See Drawings	Wrought Iron Frame
	1 Pc.	32″ Long	Piano Hinge
	1 Only	As Required	Chain or Lid-Support

Miscellaneous—6d Finish Nails and Glue
3/16″ Machine Bolts as required

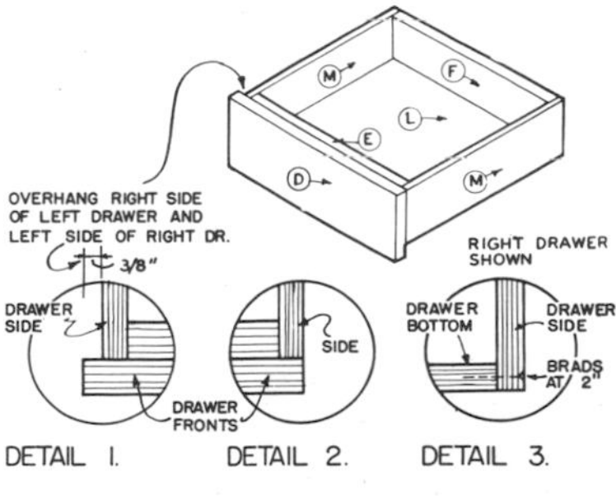

30. *Wastepaper Basket.* The wood part is plywood, good on one side; the metal is copper; and the stain is dark, followed by varnish. Gives lots of opportunity for designing to suit yourself. The sides of the basket are attached to the base with escutcheon nails, and the sides themselves are joined with copper bands or clips.

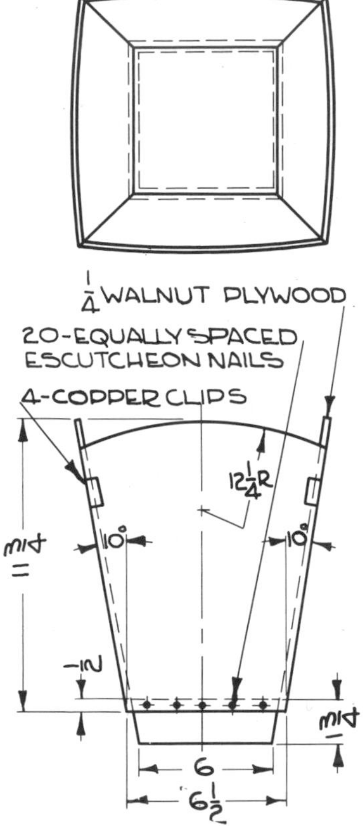

Wastepaper Basket

31. *Water Skis.* Here's an excellent sports-equipment project that doesn't take too long to make. The blanks are obtained pre-bent. All that remains is the shaping and finishing. Source D—Page 382.

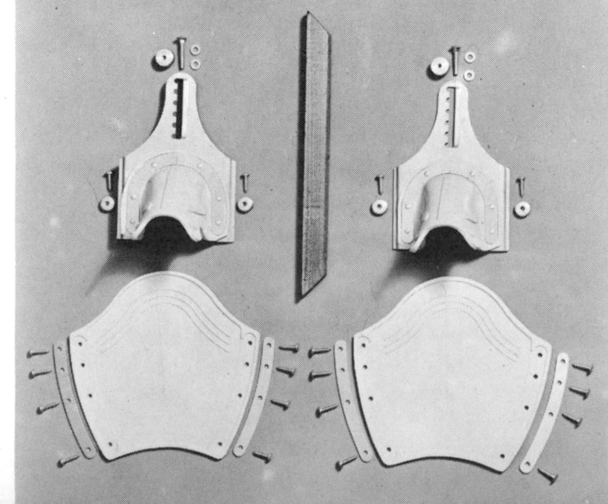

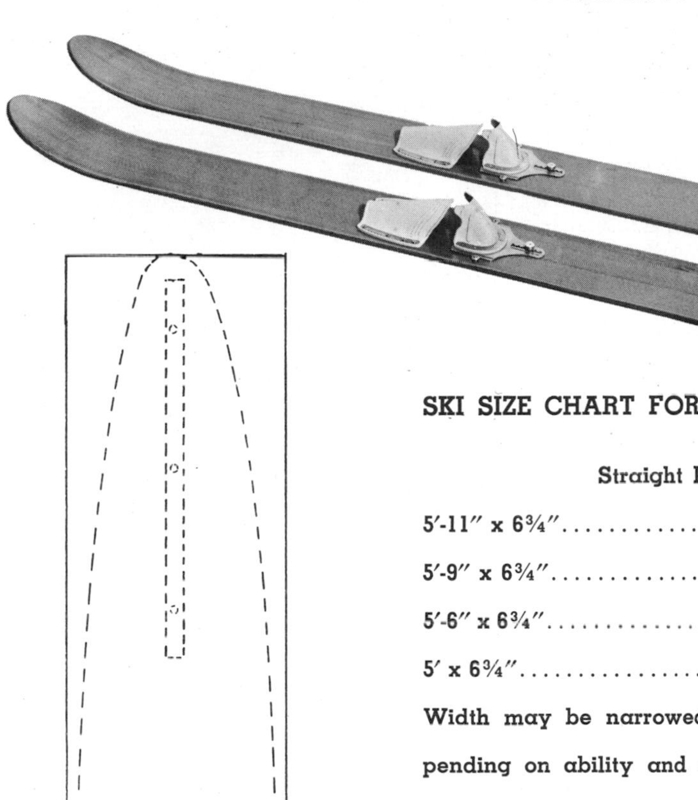

Assembling Ski-craft Water Skis

SKI SIZE CHART FOR SKIER WEIGHTS

Straight Pairs

5′-11″ x 6¾″ . . . . 175 pounds or over

5′-9″ x 6¾″ . . . . 130 to 175 pounds

5′-6″ x 6¾″ . . . . 100 to 130 pounds

5′ x 6¾″ . . . . 75 to 100 pounds

Width may be narrowed to 6½″ or 6″ depending on ability and experience of skier.

Banana Shape Pairs

5′-11″ x 6¾″ . . . . 130 pounds or over

5′-8″ x 6¾″ . . . . 75 to 130 pounds

LOCATION OF FITTINGS

Figure A shows the location of fittings for the 5′-11″ x 6¾″ blanks. For other length skis locate as follows, keeping in mind that relationship between toe and heel pieces remains same as shown in drawing at left:

5′-11″ length, screw hole "X" 34″ from heel

5′-9″ length, screw hole "X" 33″ from heel

5′-6″ length, screw hole "X" 31½″ from heel

5′ length, screw hole "X" 29″ from heel.

32. *Hanging Wall Shelf.* Simple to construct, hanging shelves are always a pleasant addition to a room and very useful as well. This one was made of inexpensive stock and painted. However, it could be greatly improved by making it of a better wood and finishing it with stain.

Hanging Wall Shelf

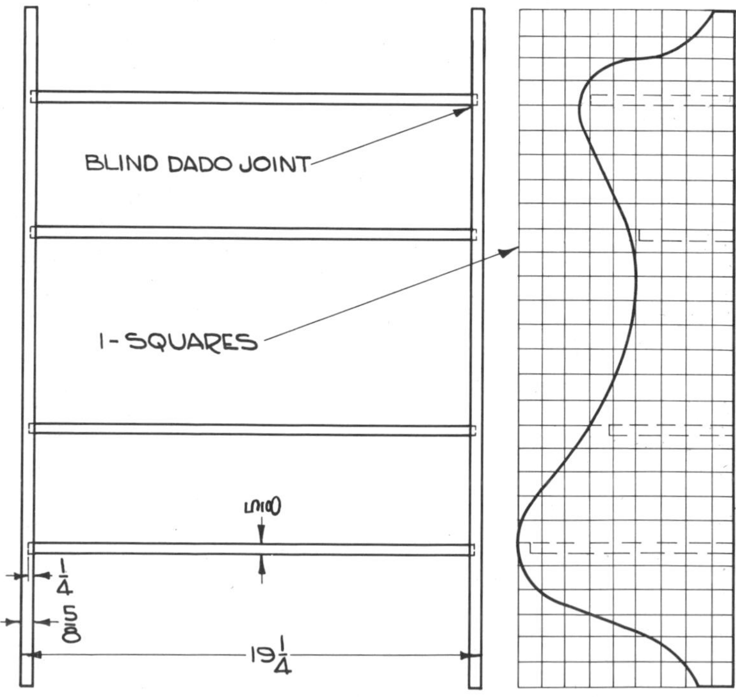

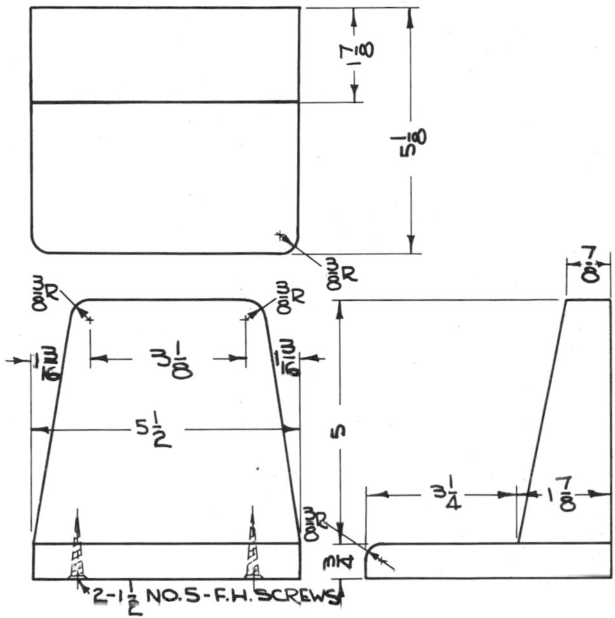

Book Ends

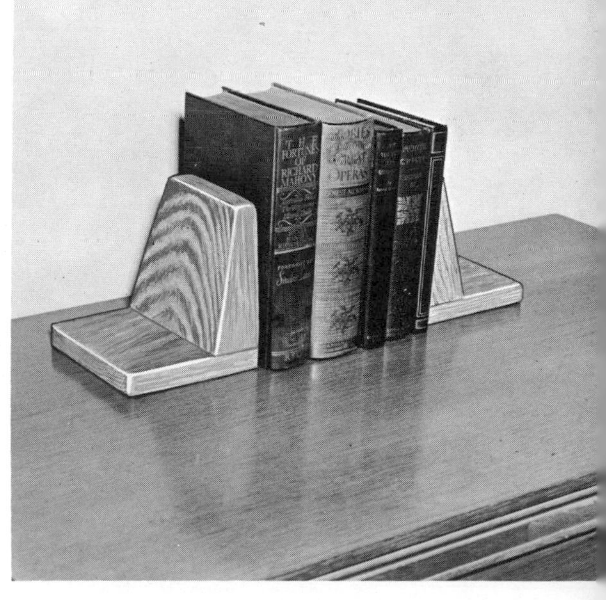

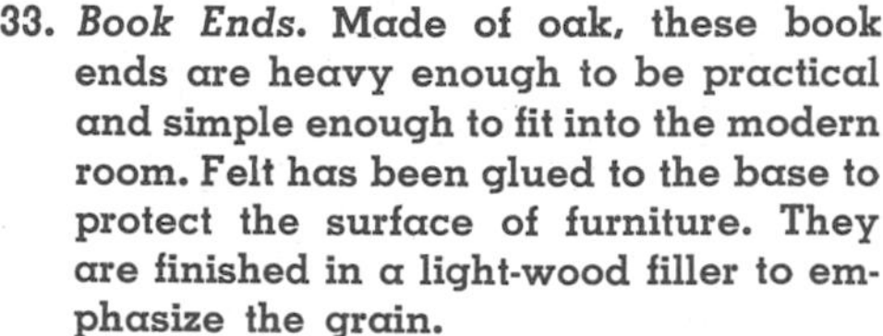

33. *Book Ends.* Made of oak, these book ends are heavy enough to be practical and simple enough to fit into the modern room. Felt has been glued to the base to protect the surface of furniture. They are finished in a light-wood filler to emphasize the grain.

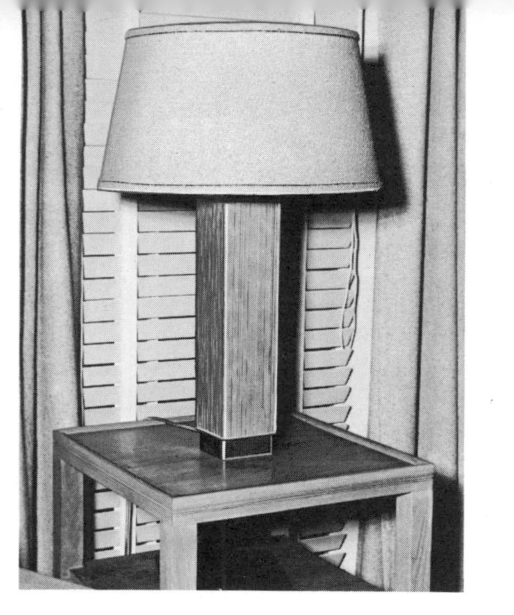

34. *"Weldtex" Lamp.* Plywood with a "weldtex" surface on one side forms the base of the lamp, and its dull texture is enhanced by the bands of bright brass above and below the column of the base. Since these lamps are rather tall, the core is hollow to keep them from being top heavy. The "weldtex" can be attached to the adjoining pieces with either glue or brads.

35. *"Weldtex" Flower Holder.* "Weldtex" plywood is the material in this flower holder, which was made as a companion piece to the "weldtex" lamp. The top edging, however, is made of oak, finished with a light stain and filler. A sheetmetal, waterproof container fits inside it to make it usable for cut flowers or plants. The metal around the bottom is brass, the same as on the lamp. Join same as lamp.

"Weldtex" Flower Holder

"Weldtex" Lamp

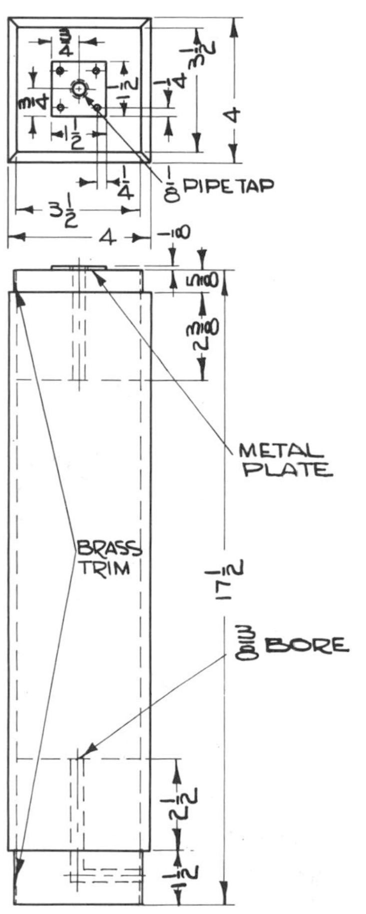

End Table

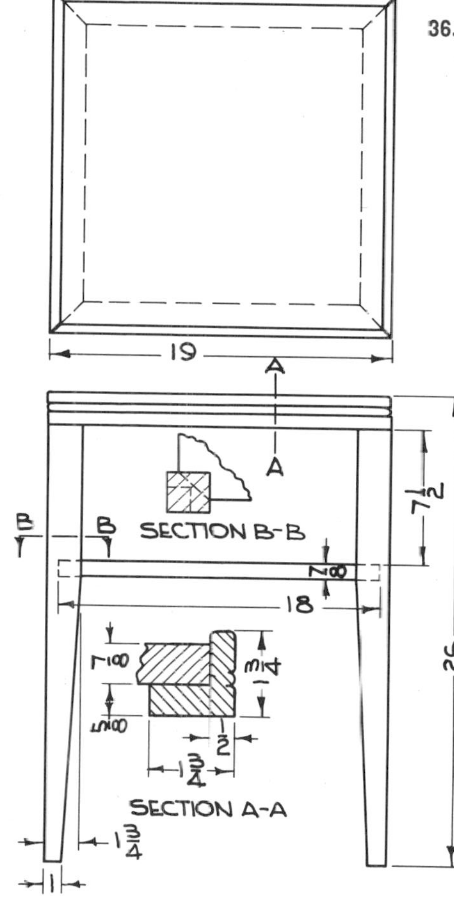

36. *End Table*. The construction of this table could be varied to suit your needs and tastes. This one is high enough to double as both lamp table and magazine storage. As a pair they would be especially effective. It is made of birch but would be equally suited to mahogany or maple.

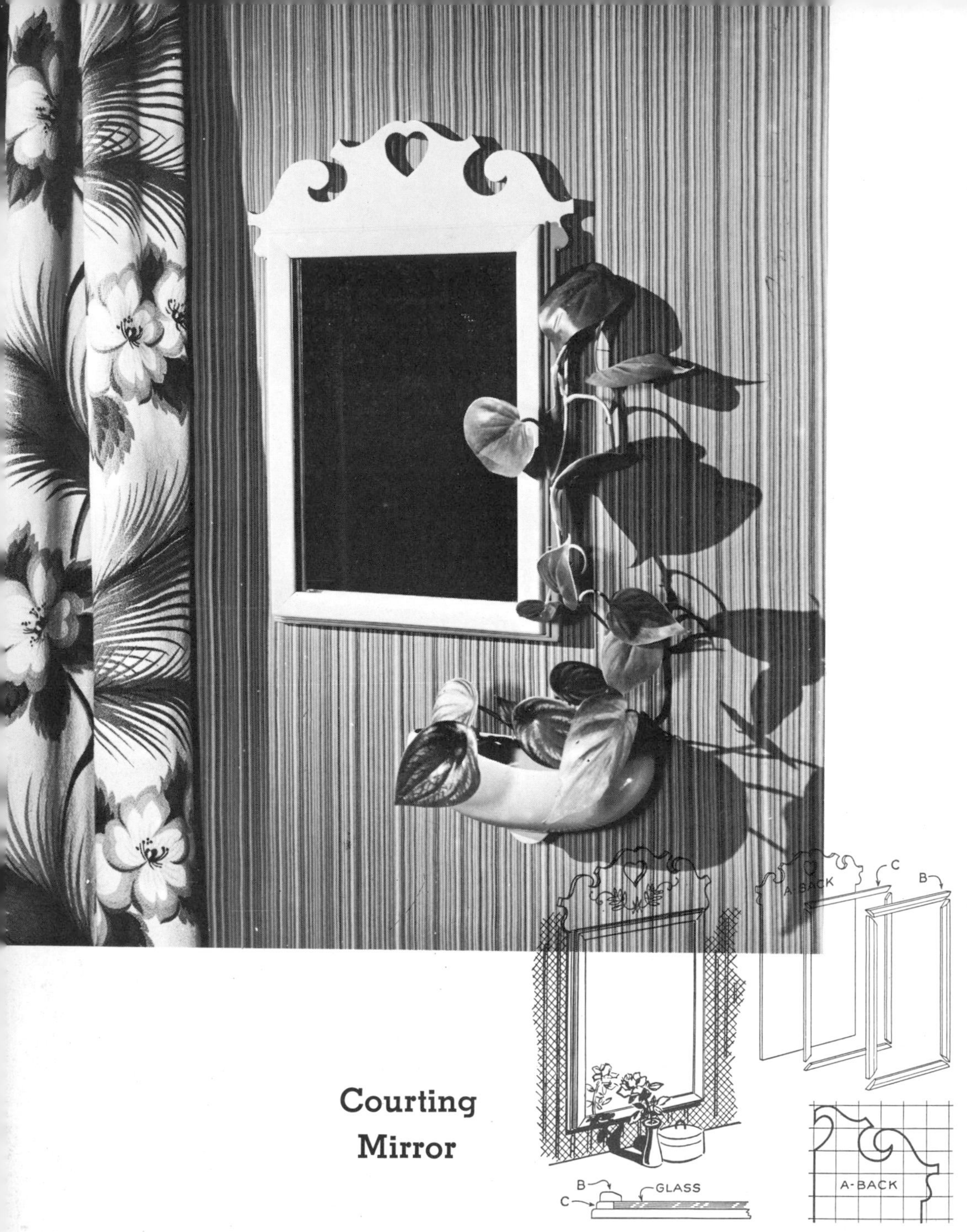

Courting Mirror

37. *Courting Mirror*. Here's a charming accessory that would fit nicely in a bedroom, living room, or study. Use one-inch squares to make an enlarged pattern of the back. The back is made of ¾-inch thick plywood, 12 inches by 16 inches. (B) is made of 4 feet of standard molding ¾ inch wide. (C) is made from a piece of stock ¼ inch by ½ inch by 4 feet. (Courtesy of American Plywood Association.)

38. *Pennsylvania Wall Box.* This is an authentic reproduction of an Early American Pennsylvania wall box. It was used for candles, spices, and other household items. Make a full-size pattern of the back and side by using one-inch squares. The other pieces you will need include: (C) 1 piece 5¼ inch by 10½ inch, bottom; (D) 1 piece 2⅞ inch by 9 inch, front, and (E) 1 piece 5 inch by 9 inch, lid. (Courtesy of American Plywood Association.)

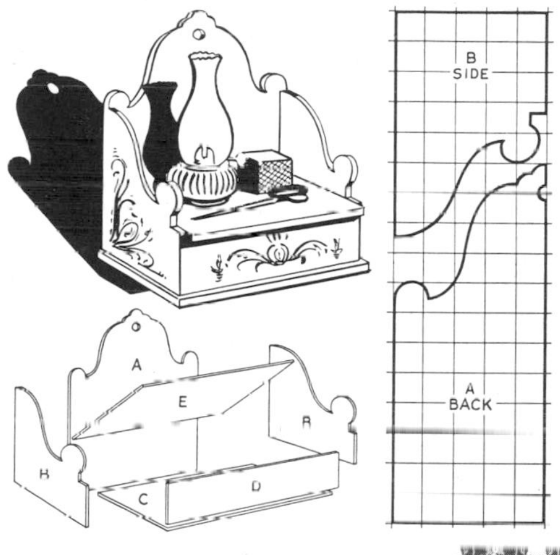

Pennsylvania Wall Box

Pilgrim Cradle

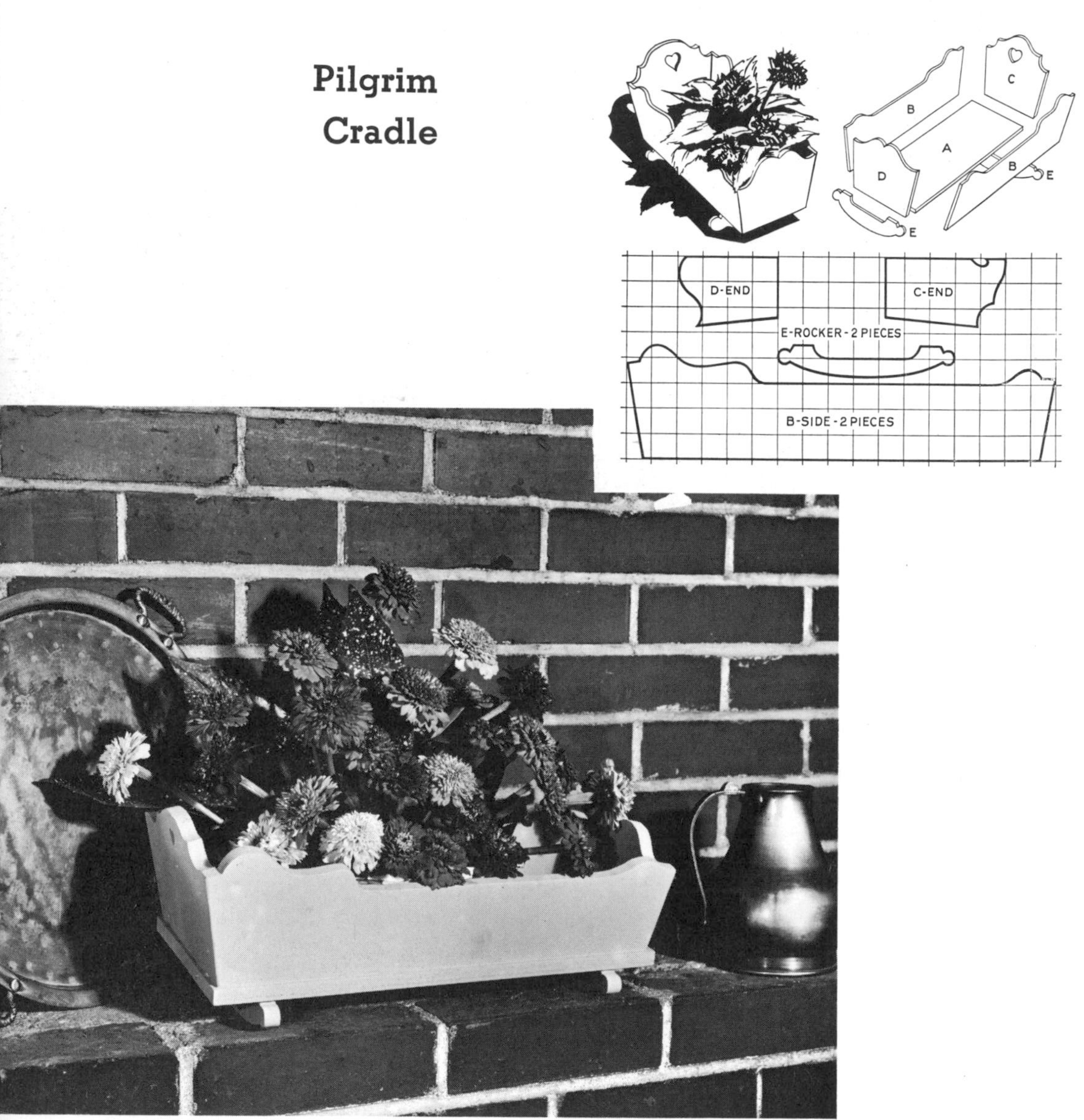

39. *Pilgrim Cradle*. **Here is a pattern for making a striking reproduction of an authentic Pilgrim cradle. It can be used as a toy or as a letter holder or planter. Part (A) is a piece 6 inches by 15¼ inches. All other parts are determined by making a full-size pattern using one-inch squares.** (Courtesy of American Plywood Association.)

40. *Pilgrim Footstool.* **This is a footstool just like the ones made by early craftsmen. You can make one for your own family or as a gift for a friend. Part (A) is a piece ¾ inch by 8 inches by 17 inches. The sides and ends are made by enlarging a pattern to full size using one-inch squares.** (Courtesy of American Plywood Association.)

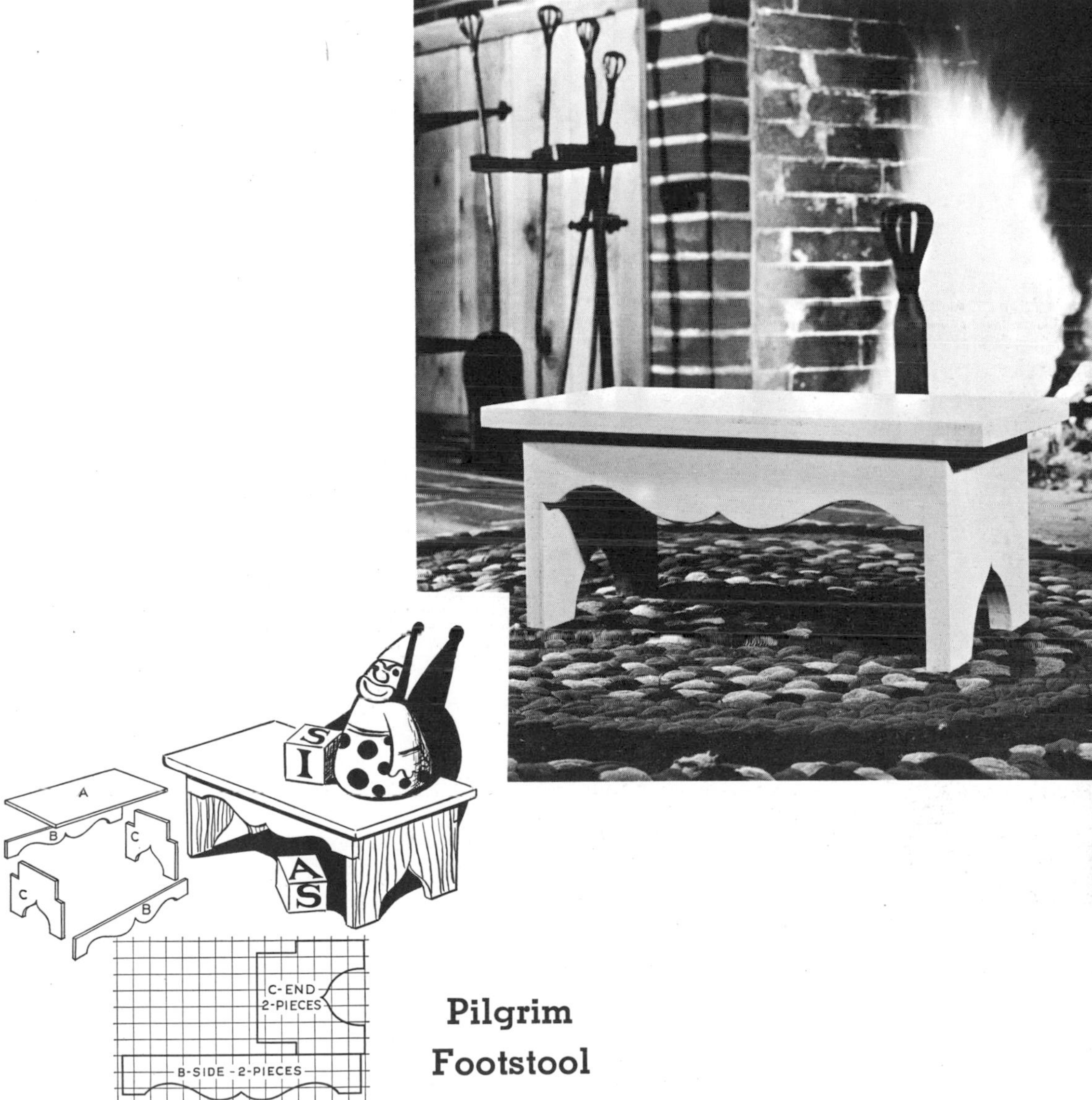

Pilgrim Footstool

Lawn Chair

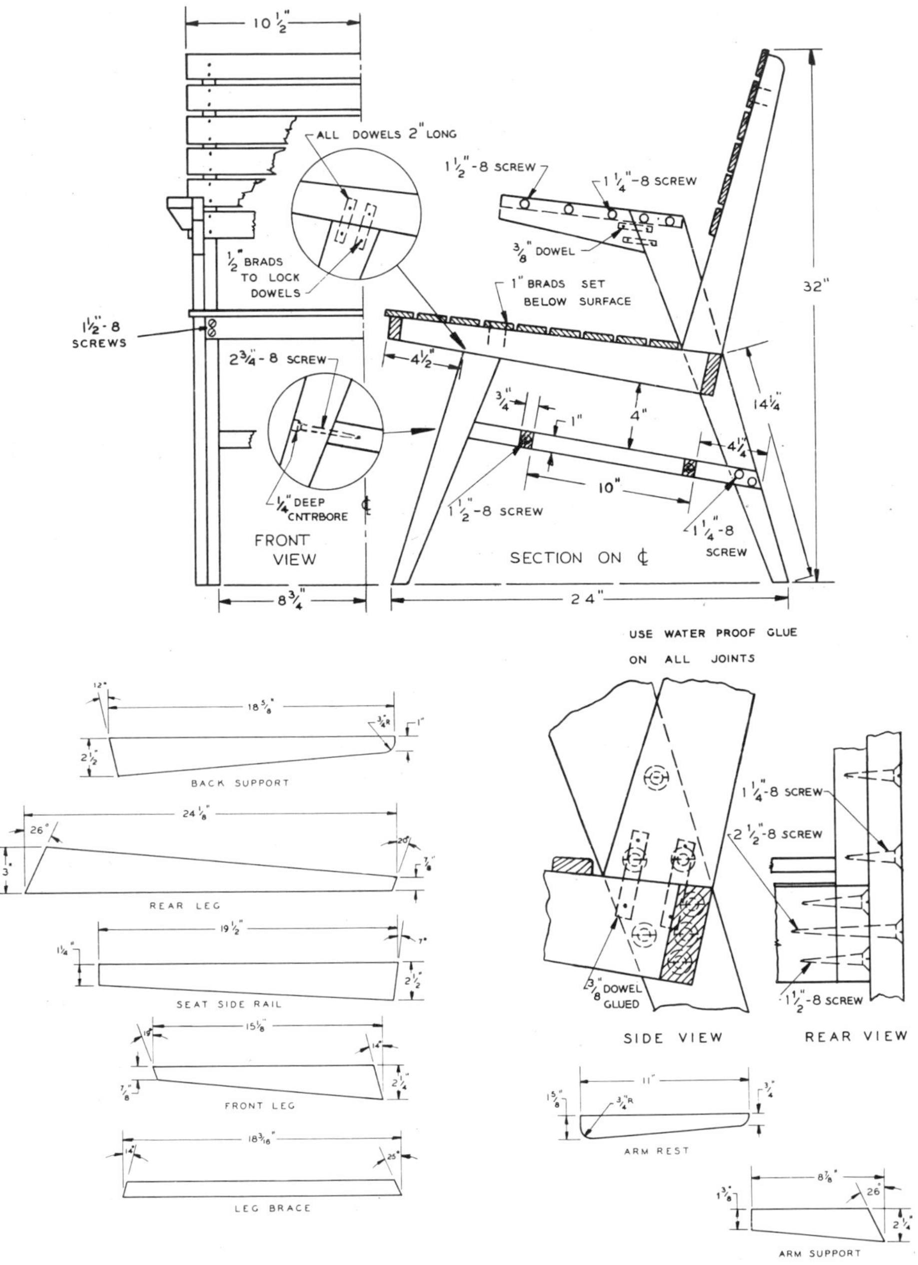

41. ***Lawn Chair.*** **With skillful use of the circular saw, drill press, and disc sander, you can construct this well-designed chair. A photograph of the finished product is on page 16.**

INDEX

Q

R

S

Z